2013-2014

EVANGELICAL SUNDAY SCHOOL LESSON COMMENTARY

SIXTY-SECOND ANNUAL VOLUME
Based on the
Pentecostal-Charismatic Bible Lesson Series

Editorial Staff
Lance Colkmire—Editor
Tammy Hatfield—Editorial Assistant
Terry Hart—General Director of Publications

Lesson Exposition Writers

Ayodeji Adewuya	Lee Roy Martin
Lance Colkmire	Homer G. Rhea
Dale Coulter	Joshua F. Rice
Rodney Hodge	Sabord Woods

Published by

PATHWAY PRESS Cleveland, Tennessee

*To place an order, call 1-800-553-8506.
*To contact the editor, call 423-478-7597 or
email at *Lance_Colkmire@pathwaypress.org.*

Lesson treatments in the *Evangelical Sunday School Lesson Commentary* for 2013-2014 are based on the outlines of the Pentecostal-Charismatic Bible Lesson Series prepared by the Pentecostal-Charismatic Curriculum Commission.

Copyright 2013

PATHWAY PRESS, Cleveland, Tennessee

ISBN: 978-1-59684-743-9 Hardbound
ISBN: 978-1-59684-744-6 Large Print

ISSN: 1555-5801

Printed in the United States of America

TABLE OF CONTENTS

SPRING QUARTER LESSONS

SUMMER QUARTER LESSONS

INTRODUCTION TO THE 2013-2014 COMMENTARY

The *Evangelical Sunday School Lesson Commentary* contains in a single volume a full study of the Sunday school lessons for the months beginning with September 2013 and running through August 2014. The twelve months of lessons draw from both the Old Testament and the New Testament in an effort to provide balance and establish relationship between these distinct but inspired writings. The lessons in this 2013-2014 volume are drawn from the first year of a seven-year series, which will be completed in August 2020. (The series is printed in full on page 15 of this volume.)

The lessons for the *Evangelical Commentary* are based on the Pentecostal-Charismatic Bible Lesson Series Outlines, prepared by the Pentecostal-Charismatic Curriculum Commission. (The Pentecostal-Charismatic Curriculum Commission is a member of the National Association of Evangelicals.) The lessons in this volume, taken together with the other annual volumes of lessons in the cycle, provide a valuable commentary on a wide range of biblical subjects. Each quarter is divided into two or more units of study.

The 2013-2014 commentary is the work of a team of Christian scholars and writers who have developed the volume under the supervision of Pathway Press. All the major writers represent a team of ministers committed to a strictly evangelical interpretation of the Scriptures. The guiding theological principles of this commentary are expressed in the following statement of faith:

1. WE BELIEVE the Bible to be the inspired, the only infallible, authoritative Word of God.

2. WE BELIEVE that there is one God, eternally existing in three persons: Father, Son, and Holy Spirit.

3. WE BELIEVE in the deity of our Lord Jesus Christ, in His virgin birth, in His sinless life, in His miracles, in His vicarious and atoning death through His shed blood, in His bodily resurrection, in His ascension to the right hand of the Father, and in His personal return in power and glory.

4. WE BELIEVE that for the salvation of lost and sinful men, personal reception of the Lord Jesus Christ and regeneration by the Holy Spirit are absolutely essential.

5. WE BELIEVE in the present ministry of the Holy Spirit by whose cleansing and indwelling the Christian is enabled to live a godly life.

6. WE BELIEVE in the personal return of the Lord Jesus Christ.

7. WE BELIEVE in the resurrection of both the saved and the lost—they that are saved, unto the resurrection of life; and they that are lost, unto the resurrection of damnation.

8. WE BELIEVE in the spiritual unity of believers in our Lord Jesus Christ.

USING THE 2013-2014 COMMENTARY

The *Evangelical Sunday School Lesson Commentary* for 2013-2014 is presented to the reader with the hope that it will become his or her weekly companion through the months ahead.

Quarterly unit themes for the 2013-2014 volume are as follows:
- Fall Quarter—Unit One: "Great Events in Genesis"; Unit Two: "Discourses in Matthew"
- Winter Quarter—Unit One: "Songs and Hymns in the New Testament"; Unit Two: "Wisdom From Ecclesiastes and Proverbs"
- Spring Quarter—Unit One: "Hope in the Book of Isaiah"; Unit Two: "Principles for Christian Living (1, 2, 3 John)"
- Summer Quarter—Unit One: "The Exodus"; Unit Two: "The Doctrine of Salvation"

The lesson sequence used in this volume is prepared by the Pentecostal-Charismatic Curriculum Commission. The specific material used in developing each lesson is written and edited under the guidance of the editorial staff of Pathway Press.

INTRODUCTION: The opening of each week's lesson features a one-page introduction. It provides background information that sets the stage for the lesson.

CONTEXT: A time and place is given for most lessons. Where there is a wide range of ideas regarding the exact time or place, we favor the majority opinion of conservative scholars.

PRINTED TEXT: The printed text is the body of Scripture designated each week for verse-by-verse study in the classroom. Drawing on the study text the teacher delves into this printed text, exploring its content with the students.

CENTRAL TRUTH and FOCUS: The central truth states the single unifying principle that the expositors attempted to clarify in each lesson. The focus describes the overall lesson goal.

EXPOSITION and LESSON OUTLINE: The heart of this commentary—and probably the heart of the teacher's instruction each week—is the exposition of the printed text. This exposition material is organized in outline form, which indicates how the material is to be divided for study.

QUOTATIONS and ILLUSTRATIONS: Each section of every lesson contains illustrations and sayings the teacher can use in connecting the lesson to daily living.

QUESTIONS are printed throughout the lesson to help students explore the Scripture text and how it speaks to believers today.

CONCLUSION: Each lesson ends with a brief conclusion that makes a summarizing statement.

The GOLDEN TEXT CHALLENGE for each week is a brief reflection on that single verse. The word *challenge* is used because its purpose is to help students apply this key verse to their life.

DAILY DEVOTIONS: Daily Bible readings are included for the teacher to use in his or her own devotions throughout the week, as well as to share with members of their class.

SCRIPTURE TEXTS USED IN LESSON EXPOSITION

Genesis

1:1-31	September 1
2:7	September 1
3:1-14	September 8
3:1-14	July 27
3:15	August 3
3:15-17	September 8
3:16-17	July 27
3:21	August 3
3:23	September 8
6:5-10, 13-14, 18	September 15
7:4, 11-12, 23-24	September 15
8:1, 18-19, 20-22	September 15
9:11	September 15
12:1-3, 5	September 22
15:1, 5-7, 18	September 22
17:1-7	September 22
18:16-26	September 29
19:24-29	September 29
21:1-3	September 22
21:1-7	October 6
22:1-19	October 6

Exodus

2:1-6, 10, 21-23	June 1
3:2-4, 10-14, 21-22	June 1
4:1-5, 10-17	June 1
5:1-9, 22-23	June 15
6:1-9	June 15
7:1-7	June 15
7:8-13, 20-23	June 22
8:5-7, 16-19, 24	June 22
9:6-7, 10, 24	June 22
10:13-15, 22-23	June 22
11:1-8	June 22
12:21-24, 28-31, 36-42	June 29
13:1-4, 6, 8-10	June 29
14:6-31	July 6
20:1-17	July 13
24:3-8	July 13
28:1-4, 26-30, 36-38	July 20
29:44-46	July 20

Numbers

11:24-29	June 8

Proverbs

1:10, 15-26, 32-33	February 9
6:1-2, 6-11	February 16
7:1-5, 21-27	February 9
11:16, 24	February 16
15:1-2, 4, 7	February 23
15:16-17	February 16
15:23, 28	February 23
16:23-24	February 23
18:21	February 23
20:25	February 23
22:1-2, 7, 9	February 16
26:13-16	February 16
26:17-22, 23-25, 28	February 23
27:1, 5, 21	February 23
28:19, 22	February 16

Ecclesiastes

3:1-15	January 19
3:16-17	January 26
4:1-12	January 26
5:10-17	February 2
8:1-5, 11-13	January 26
9:1-10	January 19
10:1-12	February 2
11:1-6	February 2

Isaiah

6:1-13	March 2
7:14-16	March 9
8:14-15	March 9
9:2-7	March 9
11:1-9	March 9
25:1-12	March 16
26:1-4	March 16
35:1-10	March 23
43:15-21	March 23
49:13-17	March 23
51:4-11	August 3
53:1-12	August 10
55:1-7	August 3
59:1-2, 8-13, 19-21	March 30
60:1-3, 18-22	March 30
61:1-9	April 6
62:10-12	March 23
64:1-9	April 6
65:17-19, 23-25	April 6

Jeremiah		Romans (cont.)	
31:31-34	August 3	5:8	September 8
		5:16	August 10
Ezekiel		5:18-19	September 8
16:49-50	September 29	5:18-21	August 10
		8:14-17	August 24
Matthew		10:5-13	August 17
1:18-23	December 22		
1:22-23	March 9	**1 Corinthians**	
1:24-25	December 22	15:50-58	August 31
2:1-12	December 22	15:53-58	January 5
5:1-14, 16, 20-24, 28,	October 13		
43-45, 48		**2 Corinthians**	
6:1-8, 16-34	October 20	1:21-22	August 24
7:1-16, 20-21, 24-27	October 27	3:5-6	June 8
10:1, 5-9, 13-16,	November 3	5:17-21	August 24
23-33, 37-39			
11:20, 23-24	September 29	**Galatians**	
13:18-25, 30-33, 44-50	November 10	2:16	August 17
18:1-6, 10-16, 19,	November 17	3:6-9, 16	September 22
21-22, 26-27, 32-35		3:21-26	August 17
24:3-13, 27, 30,	November 24	3:29	September 22
35-37, 41-51		5:22-25	June 8
Luke			
1:26-55	December 1	**Ephesians**	
1:57-80	December 8	1:11-14	August 24
2:1-20	December 15	2:1-3	July 27
2:21-40	December 29	2:4-7	August 3
24:13-18, 26-35	April 20	2:8-10	August 17
		5:8-14	January 5
John		5:18-21	June 8
1:12-13	August 24		
3:14-17, 36	August 10	**Philippians**	
14:6	August 10	2:5-11	January 5
20:1, 11-18	April 20	3:20-21	August 31
21:1-2, 15-19	April 20		
		1 Thessalonians	
Acts		4:13-18	August 31
2:1-4, 16-17	June 8		
2:36-41	August 17	**1 Timothy**	
2:41-47	June 8	3:16	January 5
4:12	August 10		
4:31-35	June 8	**2 Timothy**	
		2:11-13	January 5
Romans			
1:28-32	July 27	**Titus**	
3:18-20	July 27	3:3-7	August 3
4:4-8	August 24		

Hebrews		2 John	
10:8-10, 18	August 10	1-2	April 13
		4-6	May 18
1 Peter		7-11	May 11
1:3-9	August 31		
2:4-10	July 20	**3 John**	
2:9-10	August 24	5-11	April 13
		Revelation	
1 John		4:8-11	January 12
1:1-10	April 13	5:9-13	January 12
2:3-11, 15-29	April 27	7:9-12	January 12
3:1-18	May 4	11:15-18	January 12
3:19-24	May 11	15:3-4	January 5
4:1-6	May 11	19:1-7	January 12
4:7-21	May 18	19:1-9	August 31
5:1-21	May 25		

SCRIPTURE TEXTS USED IN GOLDEN TEXT CHALLENGE

Genesis		Isaiah	
1:31	September 1	6:8	March 2
		7:14	December 22
Exodus		26:4	March 16
3:20	June 22	43:19	March 23
5:1	June 15	60:1	March 30
12:13	June 29	65:17	April 6
14:29	July 6		
24:7	July 13	**Matthew**	
		1:23	March 9
		5:3	October 13
Psalms		6:33	October 20
29:2	December 15	7:24	October 27
34:1	December 8	10:7	November 3
34:3	December 1	18:14	November 17
98:2	December 29		
116:1	June 1	**Luke**	
146:2	January 12	16:11	February 16
Proverbs		**John**	
1:33	February 9	3:16	August 10
4:26-27	February 2	**Romans**	
15:4	February 23	3:23	July 27
		5:8	September 8
Ecclesiastes		10:9	January 5
3:14	January 19	10:9	August 17
7:19	January 26	14:17	November 10

2 Corinthians		**2 Peter**	
5:17	August 24	2:5	September 15
		3:9	September 29
Galatians			
3:29	September 22	**1 John**	
		1:7	April 13
Ephesians		2:3	April 27
2:4-5	August 3	3:18	May 4
5:18-19	June 8	4:1	May 11
		4:7	May 18
Philippians		5:5	May 25
1:21	November 24		
3:10	April 20	**Revelation**	
		19:7	August 31
Hebrews			
11:17	October 6		
1 Peter			
2:5	July 20		

ACKNOWLEDGMENTS

Many books, magazines, and Web sites have been used in the research that has gone into the 2013-2014 *Evangelical Commentary*. The major books that have been used are listed below.

Bibles
English Standard Version (ESV), Good News Publishers, Wheaton, Illinois
King James Version, Oxford University Press, Oxford, England
Life Application Study Bible, Zondervan Publishing House, Grand Rapids
New American Standard Bible (NASB), The Lockman Foundation, La Habra, California
New English Translation, bible.org
New International Version (NIV), Zondervan Publishing House, Grand Rapids
New King James Version (NKJV), Thomas Nelson Publishers, Nashville
New Living Translation (NLT), Tyndale House Publishers, Carol Stream, Illinois
New Spirit-Filled Life Bible, Thomas Nelson Publishers, Nashville
The Message (TM), NavPress, Colorado Springs
The Nelson Study Bible, Thomas Nelson Publishers, Nashville
Word in Life Study Bible, Thomas Nelson Publishers, Nashville

Commentaries
Adam Clarke's Commentary, Abingdon-Cokesbury, Nashville
Barnes' Notes, BibleSoft.com
Commentaries on the Old Testament (Keil & Delitzsch), Eerdmans Publishing Co., Grand Rapids
Ellicott's Bible Commentary, Zondervan Publishing House, Grand Rapids
Illustrating the Gospel of Matthew, Broadman Press, Nashville
Jamieson, Fausset and Brown Commentary, BibleSoft.com
Life Application Commentary, Tyndale House, Carol Stream, Illinois
Matthew Henry's Commentary, BibleSoft.com
The Bible Exposition Commentary: New Testament, Warren Wiersbe, Victor Books, Colorado Springs
The Bible Knowledge Commentary, David C. Cook, Colorado Springs
The Expositor's Bible Commentary, Zondervan Publishing House, Grand Rapids
The Message of Ecclesiastes, Derek Kinder, IVP Academic, Downers Grove, Illinois
The Pulpit Commentary, Eerdmans Publishing Co., Grand Rapids
The Wesleyan Commentary, Eerdmans Publishing Co., Grand Rapids
The Wycliffe Bible Commentary, Moody Press, Chicago
Tyndale Old Testament Commentaries, Nashville, Tyndale House
Zondervan NIV Bible Commentary, Zondervan Publishing House, Grand Rapids

Illustrations
Quotable Quotations, Scripture Press Publications, Wheaton, Illinois
The Encyclopedia of Religious Quotations, Fleming H. Revell Co., Old Tappan, New Jersey
The Face of God, The Hands of God, and *The Heart of God*, Woodrow Kroll, Elm Hill Books, Nashville
Who Said That?, George Sweeting, Moody Press, Chicago

Reference Books

Biblical Characters From the Old and New Testament, Alexander Whyte, Kregel Publications, Grand Rapids

Pronouncing Bible Names, Broadman & Holman Publishers, Nashville

The Complete Word Study Old Testament, AMG Publishers, Chattanooga, Tennessee

The Interpreter's Dictionary of the Bible, Abingdon Press, Nashville

The Moody Handbook of Theology, Paul Enns, Moody Press, Chicago

Vincent's Word Studies in the New Testament, W. E. Vincent, Hendrickson Publishers, Peabody, Massachusetts

Vine's Complete Expository Dictionary of Old and New Testament Words, W. E. Vine, Thomas Nelson, Nashville

Wuest's Word Studies From the Greek New Testament, Kenneth Wuest, Eerdman's Publishing Co., Grand Rapids

Pentecostal-Charismatic Bible Lesson Series (2013-2020)

Fall Quarter September, October, November	Winter Quarter December, January, February	Spring Quarter March, April, May	Summer Quarter June, July, August
Fall 2013 1 • Great Events in Genesis 2 • Discourses in Matthew	**Winter 2013-14** 1 • Songs and Hymns in the New Testament 2 • Wisdom From Ecclesiastes & Proverbs	**Spring 2014** 1 • Hope in the Book of Isaiah 2 • Principles for Christian Living (1, 2, 3 John)	**Summer 2014** 1 • The Exodus 2 • The Doctrine of Salvation
Fall 2014 1 • Great Stories of the Bible 2 • Parables of Jesus (Stories Jesus Told)	**Winter 2014-15** 1 • Law and Grace in the New Testament 2 • Universal Moral Law (Genesis–Deuteronomy)	**Spring 2015** 1 • Life of Samuel 2 • The Early Church (Acts, Part 1)	**Summer 2015** 1 • Different Types of Psalms 2 • Practical Christianity (James)
Fall 2015 1 • The Book of Joshua 2 • Mark (Jesus in Action)	**Winter 2015-16** 1 • Messianic Prophecies 2 • Normal Christian Living (Ephesians)	**Spring 2016** 1 • Jeremiah and Lamentations 2 • Lessons From 1 Corinthians	**Summer 2016** 1 • David & Solomon 2 • Life's Transitions (Adult Life Stages)
Fall 2016 1 • More Great Stories of the Bible 2 • 1 & 2 Peter, Jude	**Winter 2016-17** 1 • Minor Prophets (Part 1) 2 • Letter to the Romans	**Spring 2017** 1 • The Era of the Judges 2 • Paul's Journeys (Acts, Part 2)	**Summer 2017** 1 • Good Lessons From Bad Examples 2 • Good Lessons From Good Examples
Fall 2017 1 • Luke (The Compassion of Jesus) 2 • The Holy Trinity	**Winter 2017-18** 1 • Kings of Judah 2 • The Christian Family	**Spring 2018** 1 • Ezekiel 2 • 2 Corinthians	**Summer 2018** 1 • Ezra & Nehemiah 2 • Philippians & Colossians (Philemon)
Fall 2018 1 • Abraham, Isaac, & Jacob 2 • Pastoral Letters	**Winter 2018-19** 1 • Minor Prophets (Part 2) 2 • Miracles of Jesus	**Spring 2019** 1 • Women of Faith 2 • Fruits & Gifts of the Spirit	**Summer 2019** 1 • Best-Known Psalms 2 • Hebrews
Fall 2019 1 • Job: A Life of Integrity 2 • John (The Son of God)	**Winter 2019-20** 1 • Major Christian Beliefs 2 • 1 & 2 Thessalonians	**Spring 2020** 1 • Daniel 2 • Galatians	**Summer 2020** 1 • The Bible's Influence in Society 2 • Revelation

Introduction to Fall Quarter

"Great Events in Genesis" covers six biblical stories: the Creation, the Fall, the Great Flood, God's covenant with Abraham, judgment on Sodom and Gomorrah, and Abraham on Mount Moriah.

Dr. Sabord Woods, longtime professor of English at Lee University, who now lives in Jesup, Georgia, wrote the expositions. He holds B.A. and M.A. degrees from Georgia Southern College; M.A., Church of God Theological Seminary; Ph.D., University of Tennessee.

The second unit presents seven "Discourses in Matthew." It begins with three studies from Jesus' Sermon on the Mount, and continues with studies from four other discourses by Jesus.

Expositions were compiled by Lance Colkmire (B.A., M.A.), editor of the *Evangelical Commentary* and the *Church of God Evangel* for Pathway Press. He also serves the South Cleveland (TN) Church of God as pastor of Royal Family Kids and missions coordinator.

September 1, 2013 (Lesson 1)

The Creation

Genesis 1:1 through 2:7

Unit Theme:
Great Events in Genesis

Central Truth:
God is the Creator of all things.

Focus:
Acknowledge and worship God as the Creator of everything.

Context:
God creates the world at the beginning of time.

Golden Text:
"God saw every thing that he had made, and, behold, it was very good" (Gen. 1:31).

Study Outline:
I. The Heavens and Earth Created
   (Gen. 1:1-10)
II. The Heavens and Earth Filled
    (Gen. 1:11-25)
III. Human Beings Created
     (Gen. 1:26-27; 2:7; 1:28-31)

INTRODUCTION

Genesis is a book of beginnings—of the created universe, of time, of humankind, of rebellion against God, of redemptive history, and of Israel, the nation that would bring the Messiah into the world. As is true of some other titles among those of the Old Testament books, the Hebrew title *Bereshith* ("in the beginning") is the first word of the book. Our title *Genesis* originates from the translation of the Hebrew title into the Greek of the *Septuagint* version of the Old Testament.

The first book of the Old Testament appropriately begins with revelation of God's creation of the heavens and the earth. A person's account of *origins* is a strong clue as to the nature of his or her worldview. The *materialist* believes in eternally existing matter, or energy, and in self-generated life. The *pantheist* holds that the universe *is* God and that matter is illusion.

Christians are *theists*. We believe in an eternally existing triune God, who, "out of nothing," created an awesome universe, mind-boggling in its scope and complexity. This God of biblical revelation fashioned earth for habitation and dominion by human beings created "in His image" and "after His likeness." The Creation account in Genesis informs us of the nature and purpose of humankind, which is often called the "Creation Mandate." While Adam and Eve fell short of God's high purpose for humanity, this divinely communicated mandate yet stands.

Interpreters of Genesis 1 follow one of several possible approaches. Many liberal scholars read the account as myth, a creation story parallel to other Middle Eastern cultures such as Babylon. Some liberal theologians of the past century and a half have held belief in *theistic evolution*—the theory that God directed the evolution of plants and animals from single-cell organisms. Many traditional

Christians read the text literally, accepting God's creation of heaven and earth as occurring in six literal days—the "young earth" view. Others believe that once God had created heaven and earth, as reported in Genesis 1:1, a rebellion resulted in chaos and the earth was re-formed into the order of the present world—the "old earth" view. Still others believe that a "day" in Genesis 1 represents a long period of time, the six days of Creation Week being ages during which God gradually shaped the world into its present form.

The approach of this lesson is to accept the text of Scripture at face value and treat the Creation account literally, though not simplistically.

I. THE HEAVENS AND EARTH CREATED (Gen. 1:1-10)

A. Creation of the Universe (v. 1)

¹ In the beginning God created the heaven and the earth.

Scripture begins not with an explanation of God's existence, but with declaration of the mighty act which demonstrates most fully His omnipotence. *Elohim*, the Hebrew name for *God* that appears here, is a plural form which implies His supreme might and majesty and allows for His later revealed triune nature. "Beginning" refers to the beginning of the created universe. God himself has neither beginning nor end. Our triune God—Father, Son, and Holy Spirit—existed eternally before Creation and will exist eternally when the temporal order has ended. We learn in verse 2 that the Spirit of God participated in Creation, and in the New Testament we learn that Christ the Son was the active agent of God in Creation (John 1:3; Col. 1:15).

"Created" (Gen. 1:1) is the Hebrew verb *bara*, used in the Bible only of God's creation. Only God himself created in the sense of bringing into existence something from nothing. Creation by humans is always from preexisting materials and results in re-formation and often a degree of imitation. God has allowed man to analyze, synthesize, manipulate, appropriate, and exploit for good or ill the resources inherent in His original creation. Sadly, man has often destroyed or maimed elements of God's originally perfect world.

In verse 1, God brought into existence *ex nihilo* ("out of nothing") the matter composing the entire universe, and set in motion its vast array of galaxies and super galaxies. "Heaven" here includes the entire universe beyond Planet Earth. Evidently, God's purpose in Genesis 1 was not a detailed account of creation of the entire universe; rather, the focus was on God's preparation of earth for habitation by humankind.

• Why is this scripture so important?

"God dwells in His creation and is everywhere indivisibly present in all His works. He is transcendent above all His works even while He is immanent within them."—A. W. Tozer

---

B. The Initial State of Earth (v. 2)

² And the earth was without form, and void; and darkness was upon the face of the deep. And the Spirit of God moved upon the face of the waters.

Verse 2 presents earth in its unformed condition before step-by-step formation into its completed state. What is described is the "raw material" upon which God would continue to act as He made earth totally suitable for human habitation. Darkness was simply the absence of light, not yet created. The entire surface of earth was at this point covered by water. The Spirit of God, actively engaged in the divine creative acts, hovered over, or brooded upon, the water-covered surface of the earth.

• Describe the original condition of the earth.

C. Creation of Light (vv. 3-5)

³ And God said, Let there be light: and there was light. ⁴ And God saw the light, that it was good: and God divided the light from the darkness. ⁵ And God called the light Day, and the darkness he called Night. And the evening and the morning were the first day.

In verse 3, God began to speak into existence each successive stage of His ordering of earth for human existence. He also evaluated each successive step. For instance, He "saw the light, that it was good" (v. 4). He declared each step precisely right in relation to His overall purpose. The creation of light itself was distinct from creation of such light sources as the sun and moon (see vv. 14-18). Scripture later presents light as inherent in God himself. Revelation 22:5 says of the New Jerusalem, "There shall be no night there: They need no lamp nor light of the sun, for the Lord God gives them light" (NKJV).

Throughout Scripture, light serves as a powerful symbol of truth and reality (Ps. 27:1; Isa. 60:1; John 1:9; 1 Peter 2:9); in contrast, darkness is frequently symbolic of evil (Eph. 5:8; 6:12; Col. 1:13; 1 John 1:5-6). Christ declares Himself the Light of the World (John 8:12), and He calls His disciples "the light of the world" (Matt. 5:14), inasmuch as Christians are *bearers* of the Light of truth and life.

Genesis 1:3-5 records God's creative acts on the first day. The writer follows the Jewish conception of first evening and then morning as constituting a single day, since the writer and initial readers were Jewish. As one continues through chapter 1, it becomes evident that on the first three days, God prepared earth for His creative acts of the following three days, in a sense pairing days one and four, two and five, and three and six.

• How did God create light?

"Let us not ask of the Lord deceitful riches, nor the good things of this world, nor transitory honors, but let us ask for light."—Gregory Nazianaen

D. Creation of the Firmament (vv. 6-10)

⁶ And God said, Let there be a firmament in the midst of the waters, and let it divide the waters from the waters. ⁷ And God made the firmament, and divided the waters which were under the firmament from the waters which were above the firmament: and it was so. ⁸ And God called the firmament Heaven. And the evening and the morning were the second day. ⁹ And God said, Let the waters under the heaven be gathered together unto one place, and let the dry land appear: and it was so. ¹⁰ And God called the dry land Earth; and the gathering together of the waters called he Seas: and God saw that it was good.

Verse 6 implies that at the end of day one, water covered the entire earth. The word *firmament* is a translation of the Hebrew noun *raqia*, which means "expanse," or "atmosphere"—a transparent expanse, not a solid vault above the earth, as some have assumed (see *The Complete Word Study of the Old Testament*). On the second day, then, God created an expanse to divide the waters covering the earth, separating the water on earth's surface (thus below the expanse) from the water above the expanse. Verses 6 and 7 imply that a water vapor canopy now surrounded the earth above the firmament, or transparent atmosphere.

On the third day, God acted upon the waters covering the entire earth, causing them to "gather together" and cover only a part of the earth so that dry land might appear and dry land and seas be separated. He spoke this creative step into completion, declared this particular step "good" (appropriate to His purpose), and proceeded to other acts of creation on day three.

---

1. Explain the purpose of the "firmament" ("expanse," NASB) God created (vv. 6-8).
2. Describe God's actions in verses 9 and 10.

"It's wonderful to climb the liquid mountains of the sky. Behind me and before me is God and I have no fears."—Helen Keller

---

II. THE HEAVENS AND EARTH FILLED (Gen. 1:11-25)

A. Creation of Plants (vv. 11-13)

¹¹ And God said, Let the earth bring forth grass, the herb yielding seed, and the fruit tree yielding fruit after his kind, whose seed is in itself, upon the earth: and it was so. ¹² And the earth brought forth grass, and herb yielding seed after his kind, and the tree yielding fruit, whose seed was in itself, after his kind: and God saw that it was good. ¹³ And the evening and the morning were the third day.

Step-by-step, God continued to prepare the earth for its inhabitants. An ecologically balanced, habitable planet depended on usable water resources and dry continents that would support plant and animal life, though much of the surface of the planet would necessarily continue to be covered by water.

Next, God created plant life that would later support animal life—grass and trees bearing edible fruit. Creation of the entire system of plant life is implied here (and certainly is evident from verse 1), but overt emphasis in verses 11 and 12 is on the plants that would support animal life. Clearly, this account of Creation was shaped to emphasize preparation of earth for human life. God evaluated the creative acts of the third day and pronounced them perfectly appropriate to His overall purpose.

- What happened on the third day?

"Trees have their seasons at certain times of the year when they bring forth fruit, but a Christian is for all seasons."—Ralph Browning

---

B. Creation of the Sun and Moon (vv. 14-19)

[14] And God said, Let there be lights in the firmament of the heaven to divide the day from the night; and let them be for signs, and for seasons, and for days, and years: [15] And let them be for lights in the firmament of the heaven to give light upon the earth: and it was so. [16] And God made two great lights; the greater light to rule the day, and the lesser light to rule the night: he made the stars also. [17] And God set them in the firmament of the heaven to give light upon the earth, [18] And to rule over the day and over the night, and to divide the light from the darkness: and God saw that it was good. [19] And the evening and the morning were the fourth day.

The creation of light on the first day was preparatory to the creative acts of the fourth day. Scripture presents the creation of light-bearing entities in the heavens from the perspective of their effect on earth. We are presently aware of the vastness of interstellar space and of countless galaxies and super galaxies. Readers of Scripture, up until the relatively recent past, however, would have found scientific descriptions of these entities meaningless, had they occurred in the Genesis account. The progress of human knowledge has been gradual, building concept upon concept and discovery upon discovery, so that earlier readers were not prepared to conceptualize later discovered scientific facts. But those earlier readers observed the visible effect of the emission of light from sun, moon, and stars on earth. Such, therefore, is the emphasis of Scripture.

The absence of the sun would bring night, and what we now know to be the reflected light of the moon would provide a lesser amount of light at night. We know stars to be distant suns, whose light travels immense distances to earth. Earlier readers of Scripture had no conception of such distances, but understood that small discernible emissions of light from stars enhanced to a very slight degree the light they observed at night.

The Book of Genesis was written not just for recent populations of earth, but for readers throughout the last 3,400 years, and it was intended to be basically understandable by each generation of those readers—without echoing their limited, culture-bound conceptions of the world.

The lights in the heavens were created first to separate night and day, and second for signs, seasons, days, and years. Essentially, these bodies in the heavens, in addition to providing light, functioned to mark time and make possible the seasons. The Hebrews, like other ancient cultures, used a lunar calendar, periodically adjusted; thus, the moon marked *months* (from Old English *monath*, "moon"), each new moon bringing a new month and marking the passage of a year. The observable changes in the seasons could easily be related to the position of the sun in the sky; thus, the sun was seen to mark seasons. The Creation account, then, was intelligible to readers from Moses' time forward.

---

* Why did God create the world in stages?

God's Incomprehensible Creation

A light-year is the amount of time light travels during one earth year. Light travels at 186,000 miles per second. Our solar system is one of many such systems composing our galaxy. Our galaxy is over 100,000 light years across—about 600,000,000,000,000 miles. Our galaxy is only one of about 100,000,000,000 galaxies we can view through current telescopes. Such vastness of scope of the universe God created is beyond the ability of ordinary people to fully conceptualize. We merely stand in awe and offer praise.

C. Creation of Sea Creatures and Birds (vv. 20-23)

20 And God said, Let the waters bring forth abundantly the moving creature that hath life, and fowl that may fly above the earth in the open firmament of heaven. 21 And God created great whales, and every living creature that moveth, which the waters brought forth abundantly, after their kind, and every winged fowl after his kind: and God saw that it was good. 22 And God blessed them, saying, Be fruitful, and multiply, and fill the waters in the seas, and let fowl multiply in the earth. 23 And the evening and the morning were the fifth day.

On the third day, God had created the seas and, on dry land, plants suitable for sustaining animal life. On day five He would first fill the seas with animal life capable of surviving in water: mammals, such as whales; fish, from large sharks to shellfish to each variety of small fish; and sea reptiles, such as turtles. Also, when each kind was blessed and instructed to "be fruitful and multiply," we can assume that the plant life beneath the water was provided as a part of its food supply.

God then created the various kinds of birds, both on land and sea, having on day three provided their food and nesting places, and having previously made the atmosphere a suitable environment for their flight (day two). Verse 22 records God's first blessing of creatures He had just created. He blessed them by providing a suitable environment, by creating a food supply, by allowing their prolific reproduction, but also by verbally affirming and "smiling upon" their existence. They were to flourish under God's benevolent care.

---

* Describe the blessing God pronounced on the fish and the birds (v. 22).

"God's providence is His constant care for and His absolute rule over all His creation for His own glory and the good of His people."—Jerry Bridges

---

D. Creation of Land Animals (vv. 24-25)

24 And God said, Let the earth bring forth the living creature after his kind, cattle, and creeping thing, and beast of the earth after his kind: and it was so. 25 And God made the beast of the earth after his kind, and cattle after their kind, and every thing that creepeth upon the earth after his kind: and God saw that it was good.

On the third day, God had prepared the dry land for habitation by land animals of all the various kinds. On the fourth day He had created the sun, which was not only a light source but also a source of energy and heat. In fact, earth was now a perfect environment for animal life—appropriate temperatures, an environment suitable to growth of those plants necessary to sustain animal life, and availability of water necessary to sustain life as God had created it. On the sixth day, God created land animals—from the tiniest life forms to insects to reptiles to mammals of various sizes. The text emphasizes "after his kind"—not an evolution from "kind" to "kind," but the individual creation of every life form after its kind. Having completed this series of creative acts, God was now ready for His crowning work of creation.

• Explain the phrase "after their kind" (v. 25).

III. HUMAN BEINGS CREATED (Gen. 1:26-27; 2:7; 1:28-31)

A. In the Image of God (1:26)

26 And God said, Let us make man in our image, after our likeness: and let them have dominion over the fish of the sea, and over the fowl of the air, and over the cattle, and over all the earth, and over every creeping thing that creepeth upon the earth.

God had now formed earth into the perfect environment for high-order physical existence. Evolutionists see human beings (*homo sapiens*) as having evolved ultimately from a single-cell life form which had emerged spontaneously from nonliving matter. Humans, then, are viewed as the result of a series of purposeless accidents occurring over an immense amount of time that nonetheless result in amazing complexity. In contrast, the inspired writer of Genesis presents man as the result of the crowning creative act of a benevolent Creator.

Man (Hebrew, *adam*) was to have dominion over the world God had just created; therefore, God made him in His "image" (v. 26). This does not refer to physical likeness. John 4:24 asserts that "God is Spirit (NKJV)." Father, Son, and Holy Spirit existed in the eternal past as triune Spirit. When the Son became incarnate in human flesh, Father and Holy Spirit remained entirely Spirit, but the Son of God, Jesus Christ, would now live forever as one person with a divine spirit nature and a sinless, post-resurrection, glorified human nature. In light of this theological reality, man, when created, could not have borne physical resemblance to his Creator. *The*

New Spirit-Filled Life Bible suggests that creation in God's image "likely refers to such qualities as reason, personality, and intellect, and to the capacity to relate, to hear, to see, and to speak. All of these are characteristics of God which He chose to reproduce in mankind."

God desired a being with whom He could have fellowship; therefore, man would need the ability to respond to the divine initiative—the ability to "relate, to hear, to see, and to speak." God planned for humans to have dominion over earth; therefore, they would need "reason, personality, and intellect."

• What does it mean to be made in God's image?

"No human being . . . is ever conceived outside God's will or ever conceived apart from God's image. Life is a gift from God created in His own image."—John MacArthur

---

B. From the Dust of the Earth (2:7; 1:27)

2:7 And the Lord God formed man of the dust of the ground, and breathed into his nostrils the breath of life; and man became a living soul.

1:27 So God created man in his own image, in the image of God created he him; male and female created he them.

Genesis 2 provides a more detailed account of God's creation of man. We are told that the Lord God "formed" (Hebrew, *yatsar*) man out of the dust of the ground. The image is that of a sculptor shaping an object from clay—a loving act by a meticulous Creator. Humans, then, are of the earth—made from earth for earth. But, having formed man (Hebrew, *adam*), God breathed His life into him. Humans, then, are also spiritual beings—made by God for God.

God created other life forms by fiat: He spoke them into existence—both male and female, where appropriate. But He sculpted man from the earth. Later, the reader is told that Adam, the first man, was allowed to name every living creature. Having surveyed the animal kingdom, Adam did not find "a helper comparable to him" (2:20 NKJV). Then, after causing a "deep sleep to fall upon Adam" (v. 21), the Lord God removed one of his ribs and fashioned from it a suitable helper for man. Evident here is God's intense care in creating humans of complementary genders—both man and woman made in His image for intimacy with Himself and for intimate loving, living, working, and sharing side-by-side.

• How does Genesis 2:7 contradict the theory of evolution?

"God commands these people, made in His image, to multiply so that they, and thus God's image, will fill the earth."—Daniel Fuller

---

C. To Exercise Dominion (vv. 28-31)

28 And God blessed them, and God said unto them, Be fruitful, and multiply, and replenish the earth, and subdue it: and have dominion over the

fish of the sea, and over the fowl of the air, and over every living thing that moveth upon the earth. ²⁹ And God said, Behold, I have given you every herb bearing seed, which is upon the face of all the earth, and every tree, in the which is the fruit of a tree yielding seed; to you it shall be for meat. ³⁰ And to every beast of the earth, and to every fowl of the air, and to every thing that creepeth upon the earth, wherein there is life, I have given every green herb for meat: and it was so. ³¹ And God saw every thing that he had made, and, behold, it was very good. And the evening and the morning were the sixth day.

Having created humankind, God gave to this crowning work of His creation a blessing—that is, a specific mandate accompanied by divine resources and divine approval. First, man was to populate the earth; he was to reproduce, to multiply, and thereby to continually "replenish" the earth. Man also was to "subdue" the earth—that is, bring it under his control. He, moreover, was to exercise dominion over the earth—organize it, rule it, make it subject to his care. Every creature of sea and land would be under his dominion.

In order for humankind and the animals to thrive physically, God provided a plentiful food supply. At this point, all creatures were to consume plant life; only after the Flood would animals be mandated as a source for food (see 9:1-3). God had given man perfect resources to assure bountiful living. He would also offer man His abiding presence—physical blessings and challenges, as well as divine fellowship and sustenance. God surveyed the completed work of creation and pronounced it "very good"—a perfect world created by an omniscient Creator with a loving touch. What more could one wish?

---

1. What did God give humanity dominion over, and why (vv. 28-30)?
2. What did God call His creative work, and why (v. 31)?

"Whatsoever is good, the same is also approved of God."—Richard Hooker

---

CONCLUSION

Hebrews 11:3 declares that "by faith we understand that the worlds were framed by the word of God, so that the things which are seen were not made of things which are visible" (NKJV). Our triune God spoke into existence light, heavenly bodies, seas and dry land, and the infinite variety of plant and animal life on the planet. Then He fashioned in His image intelligent human beings capable of mastery and supervision, under God, of all He had created on Planet Earth. Having completed this awesome series of loving tasks, on the seventh day our omnipotent, benevolent Creator rested (Gen. 2:1-3; Heb. 3:7-15).

GOLDEN TEXT CHALLENGE

"GOD SAW EVERY THING THAT HE HAD MADE, AND, BEHOLD, IT WAS VERY GOOD" (Gen. 1:31).

God's complete satisfaction and approval in regard to His total creation is harmonious with the fact that God himself is "very good." God is the Creator, and His perfection was manifested in everything that He made.

Daily Devotions:
M. Fearfully and Wonderfully Made
    Psalm 139:13-18
T. Remember Your Creator
    Ecclesiastes 12:1-7
W. Wait on the Creator
    Isaiah 40:25-31
T. God Made the World
    Acts 17:22-28
F. Created by and for Christ
    Colossians 1:14-20
S. Worship the Creator
    Revelation 4:6-11

The Fall

Genesis 3:1-24; Romans 5:8-19

Unit Theme:
Great Events in Genesis

Central Truth:
Sin entered the world through the disobedience of Adam and Eve.

Focus:
Study how sin entered the world and accept salvation from sin provided through Christ.

Context:
Humanity's descent into sin answered by God's promise of a Savior

Golden Text:
"God commendeth his love toward us, in that, while we were yet sinners, Christ died for us" (Rom. 5:8).

Study Outline:
I. Yielding to Temptation
   (Gen. 3:1-6)
II. God Confronts Sinners
   (Gen. 3:7-13)
III. Far-Reaching Consequences of Sin
   (Gen. 3:14-24; Rom. 5:18-19, 8)

INTRODUCTION

Canonized Scripture, even with multiple writers and a writing span of sixteen centuries, under superintendence by the Holy Spirit, contains closely knit and interlocking themes and motifs which stretch across its entirety. Creation of the universe and of humanity by a sovereign God, introduced at the beginning of the first book, directly underlies much of the truth that unfolds gradually throughout the sixty-five succeeding books. High purposes for God's crowning creation, man and woman, are enunciated immediately and are in accord with creation of humankind in the image of God. Humankind was divinely designed to exercise dominion over earth, and evidence throughout Scripture shows a flawed, often spiritually ignorant humanity still attempting to exercise that divine mandate.

Our current study considers a crucial interruption of God's initial intention for humankind. God invested in the first human beings an innate moral sense, gave to them moral choice, and announced a penalty for violation of His single divine command. God conceivably could have created men and women as automatons unable to exercise moral freedom. Like puppets, they would then have obeyed divine injunctions without any possibility of deceit or departure from the divine will. But could intelligent beings have truly glorified their Creator without choice?

That first human failure, considered in the current lesson, set in motion two major motifs of Bible history—*redemption* of fallen humankind and their ultimate *restoration* to every prerogative lost as a result of initial disobedience. We can trace throughout Scripture the "scarlet thread" of redemption—from Genesis 3:15 to the seed of Abraham, to the lineage of David, to the prophecies of the Psalms and prophets, to proclamation in the Gospels, to Jesus Christ's redeeming death and authenticating resurrection and ascension, followed by the continuing building of God's church and the promise of its final glorification.

The terrible reality of sin—rebellion against divinely revealed moral and ethical truth—is clearly portrayed in Scripture; but, despite the ever-present ugliness of moral rebellion and denial of truth, the hope of redemption never dims.

Adam and Eve's lapse into disobedience is neither myth nor symbol but, necessarily, literal history; for the precise nature of our redemption through Christ, as presented in New Testament Scripture (see Rom. 5), is specifically keyed to this primordial biblical event.

I. YIELDING TO TEMPTATION (Gen. 3:1-6)

A. The Deceitful Serpent (v. 1)

¹ Now the serpent was more subtil than any beast of the field which the Lord God had made. And he said unto the woman, Yea, hath God said, Ye shall not eat of every tree of the garden?

Adam and Eve were placed in an idyllic setting with pleasant duties to perform and daily fellowship with their Creator to enjoy (see v. 8). Before Eve was created, Adam had received this single ethical injunction from his Creator: "Of every tree of the garden you may freely eat; but of the tree of the knowledge of good and evil you shall not eat, for in the day that you eat of it you shall surely die" (2:16-17 NKJV).

Satan, already expelled from heaven, found the cunning serpent suitable for his ploy to deceive Eve and defeat the plan of God. That Satan was directly behind this assault on Adam and Eve is clear from later Scripture (Rev. 12:9). One would think that Eve should have been immediately suspicious of a talking snake. The serpent, controlled by Satan, immediately began to call into question the propriety of God's single command. In John 8:44, Jesus himself insisted that the devil "was a murderer from the beginning, and does not stand in the truth, because there is no truth in him. When he speaks a lie, he speaks from his own resources, for he is a liar and the father of it" (NKJV).

---

1. Why did Satan speak through a snake?
2. Why did Satan approach Eve with a question?

"It strikes some as odd to say that Satan has a strategy. They mistakenly conclude that because our Enemy is atrociously sinful he must be equally stupid. Such reasoning has been the downfall of many in the body of Christ."—Sam Storms

---

B. The Gullible Woman (vv. 2-6)

² And the woman said unto the serpent, We may eat of the fruit of the trees of the garden: ³ But of the fruit of the tree which is in the midst of the garden, God hath said, Ye shall not eat of it, neither shall ye touch it, lest ye die. ⁴ And

the serpent said unto the woman, Ye shall not surely die: [5] For God doth know that in the day ye eat thereof, then your eyes shall be opened, and ye shall be as gods, knowing good and evil. [6] And when the woman saw that the tree was good for food, and that it was pleasant to the eyes, and a tree to be desired to make one wise, she took of the fruit thereof, and did eat, and gave also unto her husband with her; and he did eat.

Eve's reply to the serpent was only partially accurate, since God had not specifically instructed Adam to avoid *touching* the Tree of Knowledge of Good and Evil, although leaving it alone would certainly have been wise. At this point, Eve likely had no idea of the meaning of the word *die*. But the reference here was evidently to more than merely physical death, since Adam and Eve did not immediately experience physical death after their disobedience.

From later Scripture (see Rom. 5:12-14), we know that spiritual death occurred immediately after Adam and Eve's sin. This death of relationship and an ever-deepening alienation from God led ultimately to emptiness, hopelessness, and distortion and/or destruction of God's purposes for every aspect of human life, whether moral, social, intellectual, or spiritual.

The serpent planted doubt in Eve's mind regarding the veracity of God and the validity of His command. Satan, through the serpent, directly contradicted God's spoken word to Adam, saying that the pair would not die but receive moral and ethical insight, becoming "like God" (NKJV). This deliberate contradiction of God's spoken word should have been sufficient cause to deflect Eve from her downward course.

The three forms of allurement toward Satan's planned anti-God word system are "the lust of the flesh, the lust of the eyes, and the pride of life" (1 John 2:16). Eve was first tempted by "pride of life"—the desire to be "like God." She was then enticed by hunger ("lust of the flesh") and the fruit's desirable appearance ("lust of the eyes")—arousal of two powerful senses. Thus, Satan employed each of the three above forms of temptation. In James 1:14-15, Scripture gives the deadly sequence followed first by Eve and then by Adam: "Each one is tempted when he is drawn away by his own desires and enticed. Then, when desire has conceived, it gives birth to sin; and sin, when it is full-grown, brings forth death" (NKJV).

Was Adam present throughout the temptation, or did he appear only after Eve had succumbed? "With her" (Gen. 3:6) seems to imply the former. In any case, as the federal head of the human race and being undeceived, Adam was held primarily responsible (see 2 Cor. 11:3; Rom. 5:14), a point made clear in the apostle Paul's discussion in Romans 5.

---

1. Compare Eve's version of what God said (3:2-3) with what He actually said (2:16-17). What's the same? What is different?
2. According to Satan, why did God not want them to eat from the Tree of Knowledge (v. 5)?
3. What made the fruit appealing to Eve (v. 6)?

"Satan, like a fisher, baits his hook according to the appetite of the fish.—Thomas Adams

II. GOD CONFRONTS SINNERS (Gen. 3:7-13)

A. Guilt (v. 7)

⁷ And the eyes of them both were opened, and they knew that they were naked; and they sewed fig leaves together, and made themselves aprons.

Adam and Eve experienced an immediate consequence of their sin—the knowledge of their nakedness, which can be interpreted as loss of innocence and an accompanying sense of guilt. Before, they had no knowledge of sin, only open relationship with their Creator. Afterward, their guilt before God—an objective fact, not merely a subjective experience—was initially interpreted by the pair as embarrassment from being unclothed. They were indeed unclothed, their guilty hearts transparent before their Creator. They sought to make themselves a covering from fig leaves, inevitably inadequate as is any human effort to erase objective guilt without the divine remedy.

• What feelings drove the couple's actions?

"All men alike stand condemned, not by alien codes of ethics, but by their own, and all men therefore are conscious of guilt."—C. S. Lewis

---

B. Hiding (v. 8)

⁸ And they heard the voice of the Lord God walking in the garden in the cool of the day: and Adam and his wife hid themselves from the presence of the Lord God amongst the trees of the garden.

We learn of Adam and Eve's intimate daily fellowship with the Creator only after it had been interrupted by sin and guilt. What a privilege they had lost! Before their transgression, they would have welcomed such daily communion with God. Of the precise nature of this sharing, we cannot be certain; but any consecrated believer can testify to the joy of private communion with God as he or she hears Him speak through His written Word, prays with assurance of being heard by Him, and receives a very personal sense of spiritual direction.

After their transgression, Adam and Eve, aware of their violation of God's command, attempted to hide from His presence. Disobedience always leads to interruption of relationship with God. When consciously out of harmony with God's Word, we are likely to avoid the spiritual disciplines, particularly prayer and worship.

• What did Adam and Eve try to do?

"Perhaps the reason you feel guilty is because you are guilty. The answer to your guilt problem is not rationalization or self-justification, but forgiveness. The price of forgiveness is repentance. Without it, there is no forgiveness and no relief from the reality of guilt."—R. C. Sproul

C. Confrontation (vv. 9-11)

⁹ **And the Lord God called unto Adam, and said unto him, Where art thou?** ¹⁰ **And he said, I heard thy voice in the garden, and I was afraid, because I was naked; and I hid myself.** ¹¹ **And he said, Who told thee that thou wast naked? Hast thou eaten of the tree, whereof I commanded thee that thou shouldest not eat?**

God, of course, knew exactly where Adam and Eve were, but He was forcing them to confront their transgression. Sadly, Adam at this point voiced another new emotion—a cringing fear of the Creator. References to *fear of the Lord* occur throughout Scripture (e.g., Deut. 6:2; Ps. 34:9; Prov. 3:7; Matt. 10:28). Individuals in relationship with God fear Him in the sense of awe or reverence; they also fear in the sense of reluctance to displease Him, and thereby experience loss of relationship with Him. However, those in rebellion against God often deny His true nature or even His existence and ignore His ethical requirements, but, finally, without repentance, will cower before an angry God of judgment (1 John 4:18; Rev. 6:12-17).

Adam's fear was rooted in his loss of innocence and his objective guilt before his Creator. Before they transgressed, Adam and Eve could enjoy God's presence; now, they dreaded contact with a loving heavenly Father. God immediately pinpointed the source of Adam's fear—guilt and expected punishment because of disobedience.

---

1. How did Adam describe his feelings (v. 10)?
2. Why did God question Adam (v. 11)?

"Fear is born of Satan, and if we would only take time to think a moment we would see that everything Satan says is founded upon a falsehood."—A. B. Simpson

---

D. Excuses (vv. 12-13)

¹² **And the man said, The woman whom thou gavest to be with me, she gave me of the tree, and I did eat.** ¹³ **And the Lord God said unto the woman, What is this that thou hast done? And the woman said, The serpent beguiled me, and I did eat.**

A repentant spirit is always accompanied by full acknowledgment of the transgression. But Adam and Eve were not yet repentant. So they sought to transfer their guilt to someone or something else—typical human behavior. Even a naughty child will sometimes resort to casting blame—on a sibling or a pet or a playmate. Criminals, in order to lead investigators down false paths, often construct complex alibis to conceal their law-breaking. Because of lies of concealment, human relationships often suffer or are completely ruptured.

Adam, not yet ready to accept responsibility for his sin, blamed Eve, his intimate helper and companion. Eve sought to transfer her guilt to the serpent. She was gullible and therefore was deceived by the serpent, but could not absolve herself of guilt since she knew well the divine instructions regarding the Tree of Knowledge of Good and Evil. Adam, according to 1 Timothy 2:14, was not deceived; he knowingly succumbed to the allurement of the fruit; therefore, he bore the greater responsibility. Additionally, he had heard directly God's injunction, as Eve apparently had not, receiving it from Adam.

Once repentant and ready for restoration of relationship, one who has sinned against God has "godly sorrow," which "produces repentance leading to salvation, not to be regretted; but the sorrow of the world produces death" (2 Cor. 7:9-10 NKJV). Such "godly sorrow" involves the recognition that we live in a moral universe, are answerable to its Creator, and have violated His clearly seen ethical mandates. The Holy Spirit will activate the informed conscience of a Christian and cause him or her to repent, forsake the sinful behavior, and restore the ruptured relationship with God and with any injured person. Judas Iscariot illustrates well that worldly sorrow which leads to death.

---

1. Whom did Adam blame for his sin? Whom did Eve blame?
2. Why didn't they take personal responsibility for their actions?

III. FAR-REACHING CONSEQUENCES OF SIN (Gen. 3:14-24; Rom. 5:18-19, 8)

A. The Serpent (Gen. 3:14-15)

¹⁴ And the Lord God said unto the serpent, Because thou hast done this, thou art cursed above all cattle, and above every beast of the field; upon thy belly shalt thou go, and dust shalt thou eat all the days of thy life: ¹⁵ And I will put enmity between thee and the woman, and between thy seed and her seed; it shall bruise thy head, and thou shalt bruise his heel.

Sin brings consequences. Even the serpent, the tool of Satan, suffered results: he was "cursed" (v. 14). The serpent was not necessarily upright before the curse; "dust shalt thou eat" indicates his lowly position among animals, perhaps the most feared and despised of all by humans. There is the implication that other animals were also placed under a divine curse (note "above all cattle"). The apostle Paul states that "the creation was subjected to futility," that "the whole creation groans and labors with birth pangs together until now," and that "we ourselves groan within ourselves, eagerly waiting for the adoption, the redemption of our body" (Rom. 8:20-23 NKJV). Clearly, there were far-reaching consequences of the sin of Adam and Eve.

Genesis 3:15 reaches beyond the serpent himself to the Enemy who had possessed him. Satan hates the God-created humanity, whose fall into rebellion he orchestrated. Therefore, the "enmity" is not just between the serpent and Eve as progenitor with Adam of the human race, but between every human being and the chief Enemy of the human soul. "Her seed" ultimately refers to the "seed of Abraham" (see Gal. 3:16), the Messiah, who bruised the *head* of Satan through His sacrifice on Calvary, efficacious for every human transgression brought to the cross.

The prophecy of Isaiah 53:4-6 depicted with remarkable detail its actual fulfillment in the passion of Jesus Christ: "Surely he hath borne our griefs, and carried our sorrows: yet we did esteem him stricken, smitten of God, and afflicted. But he was wounded for our transgressions, he was bruised for our iniquities: the chastisement of our peace was upon him; and with his stripes we are healed.

All we like sheep have gone astray; we have turned every one to his own way; and the Lord hath laid on him the iniquity of us all." Because of Christ's victory at Calvary, the apostle Paul could say to the saints in Rome, "The God of peace shall bruise Satan under your feet shortly" (Rom. 16:20).

1. Describe the curse placed on the serpent (v. 14).
2. What does verse 15 prophesy about the coming Redeemer?

Amazing Grace

The early life of John Newton, the wicked captain of a slave ship, was characterized by filthy language, harsh behavior, and lack of humaneness. Eventually, however, Newton accepted Christ as his personal Savior, experienced a total transformation, and spent years as an Anglican pastor. In one of the best-known hymns of Christendom, he expressed the essence of redemption:

> Amazing grace, how sweet the sound
> That saved a wretch like me!
> I once was lost, but now am found,
> Was blind, but now I see.

B. The Woman (v. 16)

16 Unto the woman he said, I will greatly multiply thy sorrow and thy conception; in sorrow thou shalt bring forth children; and thy desire shall be to thy husband, and he shall rule over thee.

Scripture never says that Adam and Eve themselves were cursed, but they did undergo specific consequences as a result of their sin, and many theologians believe there was a diminishing of the image of God in humankind. For Eve and her successors, childbearing would prove to be more difficult than would otherwise have been. The mother's joy in bringing children into the world would be lessened somewhat by complications often associated with pregnancy and childbirth. During most of human history, because of the absence of aids from modern medicine, such difficulties occurred often. American history alone shows the high frequency of death of either the mother or infant, or both, during childbirth before fairly recent times. The emotional and sexual bond between wife and husband may also be alluded to in verse 16, as well as a possible change in relationship of husband to wife due to brutalizing results from the fall of man.

1. How would Eve's sin affect women's relationship with men?
2. How would motherhood be linked with sorrow?

"Eve's heart was sinless and yet she received Satan's suggested thoughts. She was thus beguiled through his deception into forfeiting her reasoning and tumbling into the snare of the enemy."—Watchman Nee

C. Adam (vv. 17-19)

(Genesis 3:18-19 is not included in the printed text.)

¹⁷ And unto Adam he said, Because thou hast hearkened unto the voice of thy wife, and hast eaten of the tree, of which I commanded thee, saying, Thou shalt not eat of it: cursed is the ground for thy sake; in sorrow shalt thou eat of it all the days of thy life. Adam, undeceived, allowed himself to be persuaded by his wife to partake with her of the fruit of the Tree of Knowledge of Good and Evil. The consequences to Adam from his sin relate primarily to his work, crucial to any male's self-concept. Work itself was not cursed. In fact, it can be a source of fulfillment and indeed a blessing from God for both genders. There is the strong likelihood that Adam and Eve enjoyed pleasant work in the Garden of Eden before their fall. Also, particularly after the Fall, work could have brought a measure of comfort and satisfaction, despite attendant difficulties and frustrations.

But the circumstances under which Adam must accomplish his work, tilling the ground, became more difficult because the ground had been cursed, resulting in such negative factors as thorns and thistles, pests, drought, floods, and bad results from overworking the soil. Only gradually would increased human knowledge mitigate some of these conditions. Adam's sorrow would flow not only from the hardness of his tasks but also from tragic events inevitable to life in a fallen world due to death, disease, ignorance, crime, and the gradual physical decline associated with aging. Even though human ingenuity has lessened some of those effects, other woes always seem to arise to replace them.

Physical death did not come to Adam and Eve immediately, but as a direct result of the Fall, it would eventually come upon them and upon all humanity. God said to Adam, "In the sweat of thy face shalt thou eat bread, till thou return unto the ground; for out of it wast thou taken: for dust thou art, and unto dust shalt thou return" (v. 19).

* How would man's life become more difficult?

"Why seekest thou rest, since thou art born to labor?"—Thomas à Kempis

D. Covering (vv. 20-21)

(Genesis 3:20-21 is not included in the printed text.)

Even though death had now entered the world, Adam prophetically called his wife *Eve*, "the mother of all living" (v. 20), for through her the human race would begin to be propagated; and in God's perfect timing, the life-giving Messiah would be born.

Adam and Eve had inadequately covered themselves with fig leaves upon awareness of their nakedness. Now God killed animals to make "tunics of skin" (v. 21 NKJV) to clothe the pair. Some believe there is here the strong suggestion of a blood sacrifice provided by God as a covering for the sin of Adam and Eve. However, there is no overt mention in Genesis 3 of repentance by Adam and Eve.

The English poet John Milton, in his highly influential seventeenth-century epic *Paradise Lost*, imagines beautifully such repentance, but without specific warrant from Scripture: "both confessed / Humbly their faults, and pardon beg'd" (see Book 10, lines 1097-1104).

---

1. What is significant about the name "Eve" (v. 20)?
2. How did God show mercy to Adam and Eve (v. 21)?

E. Ejection (vv. 22-24)

(Genesis 3:22, 24 is not included in the printed text.)

²³ Therefore the Lord God sent him forth from the garden of Eden, to till the ground from whence he was taken.

Would immediate repentance, instead of casting of blame, have mitigated the effects of the sin of Adam and Eve? One could only speculate. Certainly, no evidence of their immediate restoration of fellowship exists in the Genesis record. Instead, God acknowledged that now, "like one of Us" (v. 22 NKJV—a reference to the Trinity), Adam and Eve possessed knowledge of good and evil—gained through sad experience.

Also present in the Garden of Eden was the Tree of Life. The fallen human pair must not be allowed to partake of its fruit and live forever with the effects of their fall. God therefore ejected Adam and Eve from the Garden of Eden with the assigned task of sustaining themselves through cultivation of the soil. But we can see an aspect of ultimate human restoration in Revelation 22:1-2, when in the New Jerusalem the Tree of Life will bear multiple fruit on the banks of the river of life.

Verse 23 of our text states that God "sent," or "drove" (v. 24) Adam and Eve out of the garden, suggesting their reluctance to leave a pleasant place of habitation for a more difficult existence outside the garden. To guard its entrance, God "placed cherubim at the east of the garden of Eden, and a flaming sword which turned every way, to guard the way to the tree of life" (v. 24 NKJV). A *cherub*, according to *The Complete Word Study: Old Testament*, is "a winged celestial being whose primary function seems to have been to guard and protect, oftentimes signifying the unapproachability of God, which was removed by Christ on the cross." Genesis 3:15, often called the *Proto-evangelium* (Latin)—the highly veiled first proclamation of redemption—inaugurated the long, slow history of human recovery, rooted in divine love and holiness.

---

1. In what sense had Adam become more like God, and how was this bad (v. 22)?
2. Explain the significance of the statement "to cultivate the ground from which he was taken" (v. 23 NASB).
3. What was the purpose of the "flaming sword" (v. 24)?

"Satan gives Adam an apple, and takes away Paradise. Therefore, in all temptations, let us consider not what he offers, but what we shall lose."—Richard Sibbes

---

F. Redemption and Restoration (Rom. 5:18-19, 8)

[18] Therefore as by the offence of one judgment came upon all men to condemnation; even so by the righteousness of one the free gift came upon all men unto justification of life. [19] For as by one man's disobedience many were made sinners, so by the obedience of one shall many be made righteous.

[8] But God commendeth his love toward us, in that, while we were yet sinners, Christ died for us.

In Romans 5:12-19, Paul declares that the sin of Adam, as the federal head of the human race, and the death which resulted from Adam's sin became the sad heritage of every man and woman born into this world. Even though one may not be guilty of Adam's specific kind of sin, our propensity to sin and our inevitability of falling into sin resulted from the sin of Adam.

Even though Adam and Eve together fell into sin, Adam is assigned chief responsibility.

Jesus Christ, of whom the first Adam was a "type" (v. 14 NKJV), was able to live without sinning since He, conceived by the Holy Ghost and born of the Virgin Mary, did not partake of the results of the Fall (v. 19). Jesus, therefore, fully God and fully man, became the all-sufficient sacrifice for our sins, thereby redeeming every accepting individual from the results of the Fall. Christ will ultimately restore fully to redeemed humanity all that was lost through the lapse of Adam and Eve into sin.

In the first Adam, the *type*, man suffered enormous loss; in the second Adam (Jesus Christ), the *antitype*, man potentially enjoys marvelous restoration as a "free gift" (v. 18). That gift of God—the greatest demonstration of God's love (v. 8)—must be individually accepted to become effective in a given person's life.

"Embrace in one act the two truths—thine own sin, and God's infinite mercy in Jesus Christ."—Alexander MacLaren

---

CONCLUSION

A loving Creator placed Adam and Eve in a well-appointed environment. There they could enjoy together their daily activities, free from anxiety, and experience regular communion with their Maker. A single prohibition was given them—not to eat of the Tree of Knowledge of Good and Evil. Deceived by a serpent possessed by Satan, Eve disobeyed and persuaded Adam to join her. Thereby, the first human pair forfeited the joys of innocence and lost their fellowship with God. This primordial sin of our original forebears brought upon the human race sin and sorrow. But a loving God provided redemption and restoration through the sacrifice of His Son and our Savior Jesus Christ. At the end of the age, those who willingly accept God's offer will enjoy full restoration in postresurrection bodies like that of our resurrected and ascended Lord.

GOLDEN TEXT CHALLENGE

"GOD COMMENDETH HIS LOVE TOWARD US, IN THAT, WHILE WE WERE YET SINNERS, CHRIST DIED FOR US" (Rom. 5:8).

Those outside of Christ cannot possibly comprehend the scope of God's redeeming love. Neither can we who have experienced His forgiveness understand how this transformation is accomplished, but we must never lose our sense of wonder that heaven's choicest treasure was willingly sacrificed to buy back souls fit only for eternal destruction. When this overwhelming reality has lost its poignancy, it is time in vision to go back to Calvary until the heinous scenes that transpired on that barren hillside are branded indelibly on our spiritual consciousness.

If we could find in unregenerate man one redeeming quality to account for God's grace, we could better understand Christ's ultimate sacrifice. Since that thought is forever outside the realm of possibility, we must concede that our redemption remains a mystery sealed in the courts of heaven until our glorified minds and bodies are given the capacity to understand its miraculous nature.

Daily Devotions:

M. Portrait of a Sinner
    Psalm 10:1-13
T. God's Provision for Salvation
    Isaiah 53:4-12
W. The Soul That Sins Dies
    Ezekiel 18:1-4
T. All People Are Sinners
    Romans 3:9-20
F. One Man's Offense
    Romans 5:12-17
S. Wages of Sin; Gift of God
    Romans 6:17-23

The Flood

Genesis 6:1 through 9:17

Unit Theme:
Great Events in Genesis

Central Truth:
God judges the sinful while extending mercy to the righteous.

Focus:
Review the biblical account of the Flood and praise God for His mercy.

Context:
The Flood could have occurred as early as 8000 BC or as late as 2400 BC.

Golden Text:
"[God] spared not the old world, but saved Noah the eighth person, a preacher of righteousness, bringing in the flood upon the world of the ungodly" (2 Peter 2:5).

Study Outline:
  I. Wickedness Brings Destruction
     (Gen. 6:5-7, 11-13, 17)
 II. God Offers Mercy Amid Judgment
     (Gen. 6:8-10, 14, 18—7:4, 11-12, 23-24)
III. Divine Promise and Restoration
     (Gen. 8:1, 18-22; 9:8-17)

INTRODUCTION

After Adam and Eve were ejected from the Garden of Eden because of disobedience, they established a home in the fallen world outside Eden and soon gave birth to two sons, Cain and Abel (Gen. 4). That Adam and Eve taught their sons to honor God appears in their sons' offering of sacrifices to God out of their productivity—acts of worship which might well have exemplified the norm in their home.

God *respected* Abel and his sacrifice of the firstborn from his flock (v. 4). But God *rejected* Cain and his sacrifice because of his unacceptable attitude (vv. 5-7). Cain then murdered Abel and was sentenced by God to a nomadic existence separated from his family. Yet even in his unrepentant state, Cain received divine mercy (v. 15).

Cain produced descendants of high intelligence and talent, but also of willfulness and wickedness. He passed down to his descendants a heritage of rebellion, violence, and vengefulness, evident in Lamech, who asserted that "if Cain shall be avenged sevenfold, then Lamech seventy-sevenfold" (v. 24 NKJV).

Adam and Eve eventually produced a third son, Seth (vv. 25-26), progenitor of a line of descendants that included godly men and would eventually lead, through Noah, to the birth of Messiah. The history of Seth and his descendants (see 4:25-26; 5:1-32) offers some crucial highlights that contrast diametrically with the genealogy of Cain. For example, we are told that, after Seth's son Enos was born, "men began to call on the name of the Lord" (4:26 NKJV).

Eventually, Jared, the fourth in the line of descendants from Seth, produced Enoch, whose remarkable walk with God led to his *translation* from earth to heaven in his 365th year (5:21-24)—but not before he produced Methuselah, whose life span reached 969 years, making him the oldest person who ever lived. Methuselah's son, Lamech, fathered Noah, "a just man and perfect in his generations," who "walked with God" (6:9).

There is no indication in the Genesis record that any descendants of Cain had a positive relationship with God; instead, they formed an unbroken chain of ever-increasing wickedness.

But it also seems apparent from the biblical record that most of the descendants of Seth also gradually descended into heinous evil; otherwise, people other than the family of Noah would have been spared from the Flood. However, the direct line from Seth to Noah listed in chapter 5, which includes two outstanding examples of godliness, was an exception.

The worldwide flood in our current lesson shows the just exasperation of a merciful and loving God when confronted with intolerable depths of human wickedness.

I. WICKEDNESS BRINGS DESTRUCTION (Gen. 6:5-7, 11-13, 17)

Genesis 6 begins with an example of the depth of evil to which the society existing before the Flood sank. Various speculations regarding the identity of the "sons of God" who intermarried with "the daughters of men" (v. 2) appear in the commentaries—fallen angels, for instance, or descendants of Cain. Some even suggest that evil men possessed by demons cohabited with these alluring women. What is evident from the text is moral corruption that produced genetic freaks of enormous physical stature, wide reputation, and tendencies toward violence (v. 4).

Although these pre-Flood men and women drifted far from the divine intention for humankind, the Holy Spirit continued to work within their hearts, attempting to draw them back toward righteousness. God nonetheless set time limits on His wooing of human hearts, perhaps by establishing a definite time for the coming of the Flood—120 years from the divine pronouncement of verse 3, "My spirit shall not always strive with man." An alternative view is that God set a limit on the human life span. In any case, while false deities typically were propitiated by their suppliants, the God of biblical revelation sought to draw human beings to Himself—to reconciliation and restoration of fellowship. And, always, His justice was tempered with mercy.

A. Human Depravity (v. 5)

⁵ **And God saw that the wickedness of man was great in the earth, and that every imagination of the thoughts of his heart was only evil continually.**

The depth of human wickedness reached in the relatively brief period from the fall of man to this generation just prior to worldwide disaster is mind-boggling. Yet, we can see ample parallels in postmodern culture—traditional norms breached, sexual mores shattered, basic institutions of culture threatened, and divinely given moral absolutes ignored or contested. The point humanity had reached in verse 5 was a state from which there would be no return—no inner restraints remained to prevent the worst evil; no wholesome values were left to pull against the tide of immorality.

- What was the condition of humanity (v. 5)?

_____

B. Divine Retribution (vv. 6-7, 11-13, 17)

(Genesis 6:11-12, 17 is not included in the printed text.)

⁶ And it repented the Lord that he had made man on the earth, and it grieved him at his heart. ⁷ And the Lord said, I will destroy man whom I have created from the face of the earth; both man, and beast, and the creeping thing, and the fowls of the air; for it repenteth me that I have made them.

¹³ And God said unto Noah, The end of all flesh is come before me; for the earth is filled with violence through them; and, behold, I will destroy them with the earth.

After God created men and women in His own image, He evaluated the entirety of creation and pronounced it "very good" (1:31). Now God surveyed human wickedness throughout the earth and "was sorry that He had made man on the earth, and He was grieved in His heart" (6:6 NKJV). Human violence and moral corruption are central reasons for the divine decision to destroy human and animal life on the earth's surface (vv. 5, 11-13). The method is stated explicitly: "I am bringing a flood of water on the earth" (see v. 17). Given the love and mercy of God, this decision to destroy life in itself indicates the "point of no return" reached by humankind—no lesser remedy would suffice.

The apostle Paul, in Romans 1:18, writes of people who "suppress the truth in unrighteousness" (NKJV). Then, in verses 20 and 21, he states: "Since the creation of the world [God's] invisible attributes are clearly seen, being understood by the things that are made, even His eternal power and Godhead, so that they are without excuse, because, although they knew God, they did not glorify Him as God, nor were thankful, but became futile in their thoughts, and their foolish hearts were darkened" (NKJV).

_____

1. Explain the Lord's grief (vv. 6-7).
2. Compare the world today with its description in verses 11-12.
3. What did God reveal to Noah (vv. 13, 17)?

_____

Incomparable Righteousness

In Ezekiel 14:13-14, the Lord made a remarkable statement regarding any land that sinned against Him by "persistent unfaithfulness." He stated, "Even if these three men, Noah, Daniel, and Job, were in it, they would deliver only themselves by their righteousness" (NKJV). Genesis 6:9 declares that Noah was "just," "perfect in his generations," and that he "walked with God." Job is described as "blameless and upright, and one who feared God and shunned evil" (Job 1:1 NKJV). An angel sent to Daniel called him a "man greatly beloved" (Dan. 10:11, 19). Each of these Old Testament heroes of faith made an enormous spiritual impact on his own and succeeding generations. But only the righteousness of Christ avails to atone for sin and prevent divine judgment.

II. GOD OFFERS MERCY AMID JUDGMENT (Gen. 6:8-10, 14, 18—7:4, 11-12, 23-24)

A. The Righteousness of Noah (6:8-9)

⁸ But Noah found grace in the eyes of the Lord. ⁹ These are the generations of Noah: Noah was a just man and perfect in his generations, and Noah walked with God.

Noah's name in Hebrew suggests *rest,* or *comfort* (5:29). Noah found "favor" (6:8 NIV) with God, not arbitrarily but for three specific reasons: (1) He was "a *just* man"; that is, "a person . . . honest with other men and obedient to the laws of God" (*The Complete Word Study Old Testament*). According to Hebrews 11:7, Noah "became heir of the righteousness which is according to faith" (NKJV), because of his obedience through faith. (2) Noah was "perfect in his generations" (Gen. 6:9); that is, he was blameless in his moral conduct (not flawless but mature and exemplary). (3) He "walked with God," living in daily relationship with the Divine with sensitivity to His word and will. In the fallen pre-Flood world, only Enoch and Noah are said to have "walked with God"—Enoch was translated; Noah and his family were preserved.

———————————————

1. How does verse 9 characterize Noah?
2. What does it mean to find "grace in the eyes of the Lord" (v. 8)?

———————————————

B. The Purpose and Design of the Ark (vv. 10, 14)

¹⁰ And Noah begat three sons, Shem, Ham, and Japheth.
¹⁴ Make thee an ark of gopher wood; rooms shalt thou make in the ark, and shalt pitch it within and without with pitch.

Beginning in his five hundredth year, Noah fathered three sons—Shem, Ham, and Japheth (5:32; 6:10). In 7:6, we are told that in his six hundredth year Noah and his family entered the ark. For approximately one hundred years, Noah reared his sons and then guided his family as its patriarchal leader while preparing for the coming catastrophe. Hebrews 11:7 states, "Noah, being divinely warned of things not yet seen, moved with godly fear, prepared an ark for the saving of his household, by which he condemned the world and became heir of the righteousness which is according to faith" (NKJV).

In 2 Peter 2:5, Noah is called a "preacher of righteousness"; therefore, we can assume that during this century before the Flood, he proclaimed the word and will of God, though with no positive results. Meanwhile, in obedience to God's instructions, he continued to construct the ark.

In Luke 17:26-27, Jesus himself asserted, "As it was in the days of Noah, so it will be also in the days of the Son of Man: They ate, they drank, they married wives, they were given in marriage, until the day that Noah entered the ark, and the flood came and destroyed them all" (NKJV). The implication here is that the lives of Noah's contemporaries were consumed with self-centered, materialistic pursuits—with no thought of God or attention to Noah's warnings of coming disaster.

Noah, meanwhile, received from God precise instructions as to the proper design for the ark. It was to be constructed out of *gopher wood*, a word occurring only here (Gen. 6:14) in the Bible, but traditionally considered to be cypress, or perhaps cedar (*Hastings' Dictionary of the* Bible; Derek Kidner, *Genesis*). Considering a cubit to be equivalent to about 18 inches, the ark was to be approximately 450 feet long, 75 feet wide, and 45 feet high, with a window all around it close to the roof and a door on one side (vv. 15-16). It was to have three decks and was to be covered "inside and outside with pitch" (v. 14 NKJV). It would have "a capacity exceeding that of 500 railroad cars," and its "barge-like shape" would make "it difficult to capsize" (*New Spirit-Filled Life Bible*).

This huge construction project would necessarily take Noah and his three sons many years to complete, during which time Noah continued to warn the populace of the judgment by water to come.

---

1. How had God blessed Noah (v. 10)?
2. What did God command Noah to do (v. 14)?

"The safe place lies in obedience to God's word, singleness of heart and holy vigilance."—A. B. Simpson

---

C. God's Covenant With Noah Predicted (v. 18)

18 But with thee will I establish my covenant; and thou shalt come into the ark, thou, and thy sons, and thy wife, and thy sons' wives with thee.

Verse 18 contains the first reference to *covenant* (Hebrew *berit*) in Scripture. Such covenants are God-initiated agreements, guaranteeing certain rights and sometimes setting forth responsibilities. Ideally, they were internally characterized by mutual *covenant love* (Hebrew *hesed,* or *chesed*). After giving instructions for the building of the ark and informing Noah of the coming worldwide deluge (v. 17), God promised in verse 18 that He would—after the Flood—establish His covenant with Noah, his wife, his sons, and his sons' wives (in effect, an assurance that, in the ark of safety, they would survive the Flood). The detail of God's covenant with Noah, like some of the other biblical covenants unconditional, occurs in 9:9-17.

• Who would be blessed by God's covenant with Noah?

"The promises of the Bible are nothing more than God's covenant to be fruitful to His people. It is His character that makes these promises valid."—Jerry Bridges

---

D. The Preservation of the Animals (6:19-22; 7:1-3)

(Genesis 6:19-22; 7:1-3 is not included in the printed text.)

Noah was instructed to bring into the ark a single pair of every *kind* of *unclean* animal (6:19-20) and seven pairs of every *kind* of *clean* animal (7:2-3). Apparently, a tradition regarding clean and unclean animals already existed long before being formalized in the Mosaic Code. The additional clean animals would be available for sacrifice after the Flood. The clear implication in 7:8-9 is that

God would cause the animals to go into the ark at the appropriate time. Also, one need not suppose that every sub-species was preserved in the ark—just the basic *kinds* created by God in Genesis 1.

---

1. What did God plan to preserve (vv. 19-21)?
2. How did Noah respond to God's command (v. 22)?
3. Why were more of certain animals taken aboard the ark than other types (7:2-3)?

E. Total Calamity Through the Flood (7:4, 11-12, 23-24)

⁴ For yet seven days, and I will cause it to rain upon the earth forty days and forty nights; and every living substance that I have made will I destroy from off the face of the earth.

¹¹ In the six hundredth year of Noah's life, in the second month, the seventeenth day of the month, the same day were all the fountains of the great deep broken up, and the windows of heaven were opened. ¹² And the rain was upon the earth forty days and forty nights.

²³ And every living substance was destroyed which was upon the face of the ground, both man, and cattle, and the creeping things, and the fowl of the heaven; and they were destroyed from the earth: and Noah only remained alive, and they that were with him in the ark. ²⁴ And the waters prevailed upon the earth an hundred and fifty days.

Stories of catastrophic floods exist in numerous, widely separated cultures. *Hastings' Dictionary of the Bible* notes that such stories have been found among American Indians and "in India, Kashmir, Tibet, China, . . . Australia, some of the Polynesian Islands, Lithuania, and Greece." Various explanations are given for this wide occurrence, but believers in biblical revelation see such stories as cultural memory, however distorted, of the ancient worldwide flood recorded in Genesis. The Bible clearly portrays this deluge not as local but as covering the entire earth (see Gen. 7:19-23; Luke 17:27; 2 Peter 2:5; 3:5-6). If the Flood had been merely local, the populace could simply have relocated, thereby avoiding extinction.

At the appropriate moment, God summoned Noah and his family to enter the ark with the assembled animals, stating that after seven days a massive onslaught of water would lead to total destruction of all living beings on land (Gen. 7:1, 4). A supply of food for people and animals had already been stored in the ark (6:21). Floodwaters came not only from rain; in fact, on that day "all the fountains of the great deep [were] broken up, and the windows of heaven were opened" (7:11).

First, however, the Lord shut Noah and his family in with the animals (v. 16). Then, for forty days the waters kept increasing until the ark began to float on their surface. The waters rose to a height of twenty-two feet above the highest mountain peaks and remained at this height for 150 days. All human and animal life was destroyed, except for that of Noah and his family and the animals in the ark.

---

1. What was Noah's age when the rain began (v. 11)?
2. How long did it rain (v. 12), and what was the result (v. 23)?

"God sometimes in infinite patience adjourns His judgments and puts off the sessions a while longer. He is not willing to punish."—Thomas Watson

---

III. DIVINE PROMISE AND RESTORATION (Gen. 8:1, 18-22; 9:8-17)

A. God Remembers Noah (8:1)

¹ And God remembered Noah, and every living thing, and all the cattle that was with him in the ark: and God made a wind to pass over the earth, and the waters asswaged.

The ark, with its human and animal inhabitants, had never been absent from the omniscient attention of God. Their preservation was central to His plan. The writer (very likely Moses) was speaking in human terms to indicate God's shift in primary focus to the next step He was now ready to take. His primary attention now turned to the inhabitants of the ark. By this time, living conditions aboard the ark likely were far less than ideal. The stench was great; the air was stagnant; the food supply, decreasing. But humans and animals had survived under divine care and were now preparing to live in a renewed world, as a mighty wind helped to dry up the remaining waters.

The waters began to recede after 150 days (v. 3) until, by the tenth month, tops of mountains were visible (v. 5). After nearly thirteen months the earth was dry, and God directed Noah to leave the ark with his family and the animals (vv. 14-17).

• Explain the phrase "God remembered Noah" (v. 1).

"We may sometimes think we are a forgotten commodity, but God remembers every one of us who serve Him."—Shelton Smith

---

B. Humans and Animals Leave the Ark (vv. 18-19)

¹⁸ And Noah went forth, and his sons, and his wife, and his sons' wives with him. ¹⁹ Every beast, every creeping thing, and every fowl, and whatsoever creepeth upon the earth, after their kinds, went forth out of the ark.

The divine directions were specific. It was time for all inhabitants of the ark to disembark, although there might have been some hesitance to step forth into a world subjected to total upheaval by the Flood. At this point, God began to renew the Creation mandate of Genesis 1:28—"be fruitful and multiply" (see also 9:7). In 8:17 the writer uses the same language to name the liberated animals that he had used in 1:24-25—"birds and cattle and every creeping thing . . . so that they may abound on the earth, and be fruitful and multiply" (NKJV). The originally created life forms had survived the Flood and would gradually be distributed across the globe according to the divine will.

• What do you suppose Noah and his family's feelings were as they left the ark?

"Worship is a believer's response to God's revelation of Himself. It is expressing wonder, awe, and gratitude for the worthiness, the greatness, and the goodness of our Lord. It is the appropriate response to God's person, His provision, His power, His promises, and His plan."—Nancy Leigh DeMoss

---

C. Noah Worships God (vv. 20-22)

20 And Noah builded an altar unto the Lord; and took of every clean beast, and of every clean fowl, and offered burnt offerings on the altar. 21 And the Lord smelled a sweet savour; and the Lord said in his heart, I will not again curse the ground any more for man's sake; for the imagination of man's heart is evil from his youth; neither will I again smite any more every thing living, as I have done. 22 While the earth remaineth, seedtime and harvest, and cold and heat, and summer and winter, and day and night shall not cease.

Noah's first action upon leaving the ark was to prepare to worship God. When any human being of whatever era is walking in fellowship with God, worship "in spirit and in truth" (John 4:23) is not a rare or unusual activity. It is a frequent, highly valued and anticipated time with the Maker, as well as the first order of business at the outset of any day or of any enterprise. We worship not out of fear or dread, but out of love and gratitude. God had preserved Noah and his family; therefore, his first priority was to employ the divinely prescribed form for worship—both for a sin covering and for fellowship with the Divine. Evidently, one reason for preservation of multiple pairs of clean animals had been to provide for sacrifice to God.

God was pleased with Noah's worship—its high priority, its accepted form, and its sincere motivation. God, in His grace, now made a determination in His heart regarding both the earth and its inhabitants. First, there would be no additional curse placed on the ground as a response to human disobedience, although He recognized that "the imagination of man's heart is evil from his youth" (Gen. 8:21). As a result of the fall of man in the Garden, a sinful predisposition existed in the human heart, to be mitigated only by God's love and mercy—indeed, ultimately, by the sacrifice of His Son.

The renewal of the earth through the Flood and the survival of only eight human beings could not solve the sin problem; the pull toward disobedience within the human heart could not be eradicated by an act of judgment. Nonetheless, as a second divine determination, God would not again destroy all life. Instead, "While the earth remains, seedtime and harvest, cold and heat, winter and summer, and day and night shall not cease" (v. 22 NKJV). This promise is not merely part of the Noachian covenant, but has, without exception, been kept by God, standing as an example of His unremitting faithfulness.

---

1. After leaving the ark, what did Noah do first (v. 20)?
2. What did God promise (vv. 21-22)?

D. God Establishes His Covenant With Noah (9:8-17)

(Genesis 9:8-10, 12-17 is not included in the printed text.)

¹¹ And I will establish my covenant with you; neither shall all flesh be cut off any more by the waters of a flood; neither shall there any more be a flood to destroy the earth.

God now established his first explicit covenant with humankind. It was universal and unconditional—"with you and with your descendants after you" (v. 9 NKJV). It also included all living creatures other than humans. This covenant specified that never again would God destroy all life on the earth through a flood. He provided the rainbow as a sign of this covenant. Every time a rainbow appeared, God's unconditional promise would thereby be reiterated. He said, "The rainbow shall be in the cloud, and I will look on it to remember the everlasting covenant between God and every living creature of all flesh that is on the earth" (v. 16 NKJV).

————————

1. Describe the covenant God made (vv. 8-11).
2. Why is the rainbow an appropriate symbol of God's promise (vv. 12-17)?

————————

"God's love is the most awesome thing about Him. It is not His justice, nor His majesty, nor even His blazing holiness, but the fact that He has made and keeps a covenant of personal commitment and love to His people."—Sinclair B. Ferguson

————————

CONCLUSION

After the fall of Adam and Eve in the Garden of Eden, the vast majority of men and women living on the earth—all the descendants of Cain and most descendants of Seth—became increasingly immoral, rebellious, corrupt, and violent. Only the direct line from Seth to Noah was an exception. Finally, God determined that He must bring judgment by a universal flood on the wicked, degenerate human race. Only Noah and his family were deemed worthy to survive. Noah and his family and representative animals were preserved in the ark. After the floodwaters subsided, Noah, his family, and the animals left the ark under divine direction, and Noah immediately worshiped God. God then proclaimed post-Flood conditions for human life and established His first explicit covenant—universal and unconditional. Never would all life on earth again be destroyed by water, and the rainbow would be a frequently appearing sign of this covenant. Salvation history, leading ultimately to the advent of Messiah, would now continue through the line of Shem, Noah's first son.

GOLDEN TEXT CHALLENGE

"[GOD] SPARED NOT THE OLD WORLD, BUT SAVED NOAH THE EIGHTH PERSON, A PREACHER OF RIGHTEOUSNESS, BRINGING IN THE FLOOD UPON THE WORLD OF THE UNGODLY" (2 Peter 2:5).

It is hard to imagine only one family on earth being righteous in God's eyes, but that was exactly the case in Noah's day. Only the eight members of Noah's family were spared when God flooded the earth, while probably millions of un-righteous people were swept away in divine judgment. Noah was a "preacher of righteousness," but his warnings went unheeded in a world where everyone's desires and thoughts were focused on sin.

This reference to Noah is second in a list of three judgments recounted in 2 Peter 2:4-8. The other two are the rebellious angels being sentenced to hell, and Sodom and Gomorrah being overthrown. The message is twofold: Sinners will inevitably come to judgment in God's time and way, yet faithful believers (like the obedient angels, Lot, and Noah) will be spared (see v. 9).

No matter how many unbelievers populate one's neighborhood, town, state, or nation, God will deliver His children from their evil influence and save them from the storm of judgment.

Daily Devotions:
M. God Judges the First Murder
   Genesis 4:1-12
T. The Lord Is Merciful
   Psalm 103:8-14
W. Kindness and Peace Promised
   Isaiah 54:5-10
T. As in the Days of Noah
   Matthew 24:36-44
F. Deliverance and Judgment
   2 Peter 2:4-9
S. God Keeps His Promise
   2 Peter 3:1-9

God's Covenant With Abraham

Genesis 12:1-9; 15:1-21; 17:1-22; 21:1-5; Galatians 3:6-29

Unit Theme:
Great Events in Genesis

Central Truth:
God's covenant with Abraham is fulfilled in Jesus Christ.

Focus:
Examine the implications of God's covenant with Abraham for our lives and believe in Christ.

Context:
God makes covenant with Abraham, and Paul explains its application to Christians.

Golden Text:
"If ye be Christ's, then are ye Abraham's seed, and heirs according to the promise" (Gal. 3:29).

Study Outline:
  I. God Calls Abraham Into Covenant
     (Gen. 12:1-9)
 II. God Reaffirms the Covenant
     (Gen. 15:1-7, 18-21)
III. God Fulfills the Covenant
     (Gen. 17:1-7; 21:1-3; Gal. 3:6-9, 16, 29)

INTRODUCTION

After Adam and Eve's transgression and ejection from the Garden of Eden, God's chief purpose in relation to humankind was redemption and restoration. The earliest expression of this divine purpose is the cryptic *proto-evangelium* of Genesis 3:15: "I will put enmity between you and the woman, and between your seed and her Seed; He shall bruise your head, and you shall bruise His heel" (NKJV). In the line of Seth, third son of Adam and Eve, we can see the beginning of renewed relationship of humanity with God. Following the birth of Enos, son of Seth, people "began to call upon the name of the Lord" (4:26); also, Enoch and Noah "walked with God" (5:22-24; 6:9), living in close daily fellowship with Him.

God chose to forward His redemptive and restorative purposes for humankind by instituting *covenants* (Hebrew, *berith*). Ancient human cultures understood well the concept of covenant because such agreements were common between both individuals and groups (see 13:7-12; 21:22-32). A victorious king might impose on a conquered people a set of stipulations with penalties for violation.

The word *covenant* first appeared in Scripture in Genesis 6:18 when God was giving Noah instructions regarding constructing and entering the ark: "I will establish My covenant with you; and you shall go into the ark—you, your sons, your wife, and your sons' wives with you" (NKJV). After the Flood, God established the unconditional Noachian covenant with man and animals, stipulating that God would no more destroy the earth by water; He also included a sign of the covenant's permanent validity—the rainbow.

Throughout Scripture, salvation history is marked by covenants that gradually unfold God's full plan for restoration of humankind to their original position before God—the Abrahamic covenant, discussed extensively in this lesson; the Mosaic covenant (Ex. 19:3-6); the Davidic covenant (2 Sam. 7:1-17); and that "new covenant" based in the blood and righteousness of Jesus Christ, prophesied in Jeremiah 31:31-34 and described in Hebrews 8:7-13.

As Abraham walked with God by faith (Gen. 15:6), God revealed to him in ever-fuller detail various elements of that covenant first instituted in chapter 12.

I. GOD CALLS ABRAHAM INTO COVENANT (Gen. 12:1-9)

A. Abram's Call (v. 1)

¹ Now the Lord had said unto Abram, Get thee out of thy country, and from thy kindred, and from thy father's house, unto a land that I will shew thee.

Abram (a Hebrew name meaning "exalted father") was a descendant of Shem, the first son of Noah (9:18; 10:1), through the Semitic line of Arphaxad (11:10). Abram, a son of Terah, lived in Ur of the Chaldeans, a pagan city filled with moon worshipers (Kent Hughes, *Genesis*). Abram was married to *Sarai* (a Hebrew name meaning "princess"). We can assume that Abram participated in the idolatrous religion of his culture until, at some point, while still in the city of Ur, he received a remarkable communication from the Lord (*Yahweh*).

Yahweh (traditionally written and pronounced as *Jehovah* in English) was one designation for the eternally existent God of biblical revelation (also known in early Genesis as *Elohim* and *El Shaddai*), whose nature was gradually revealed throughout the Old Testament to godly patriarchs and prophets, including, most notably, Abram and Moses. Stephen, the first Christian martyr, began his defense before the Sanhedrin by asserting that "the God of glory appeared to our father Abraham when he was in Mesopotamia, before he dwelt in Haran" (Acts 7:2 NKJV). The verb "had said" in English translations of Genesis 12:1 implies what Stephen stated directly. Abram, while yet in Ur, received his first revelation from God and took his first step of obedience.

When Abram first heard the voice of God, he had no tradition of revealed truth against which to test this experience; he must act on faith alone, trusting in the reliability of a Deity of whom he initially knew nothing. Abram's family accompanied him as far as Haran, and he lingered there until his father's death (11:31-32). The divine directive to leave family behind implied the total abandonment of the pagan cultural tradition which they embodied. Abram must listen to the voice of the Lord and act accordingly—the one requirement of the initial covenant made with him by God. As Abram stepped out in faith, further revelation gradually ensued.

• What was God's command to Abram?

"Faith is taking the first step, even when you don't see the whole staircase."—Martin Luther King Jr.

B. The Lord's Promises (vv. 2-3)

² And I will make of thee a great nation, and I will bless thee, and make thy name great; and thou shalt be a blessing: ³ And I will bless them that bless thee, and curse him that curseth thee: and in thee shall all families of the earth be blessed.

The Book of Genesis, like the other four books of the Pentateuch, is about the *land* and the *blessing* (*The Expositor's Bible Commentary*). The initial statement of the Abrahamic covenant in verses 1-3 contains, in succinct summary form, God's unalterable intention to form and direct a chosen nation (Israel) and place it on divinely selected land so that its inhabitants could walk in obedience to God and become the light of the nations, pointing them to the true God. The nation of Israel's repeated disobedience did not alter God's purpose. That divine plan is, in fact, still in process of fulfillment today.

In verses 2-3, the Lord gave to Abram seven promises contingent only on his taking the God-mandated-and-directed venture of faith of verse1:

1. God would, from Abram's posterity, create "a great nation"—a prophecy fulfilled in the genesis and growth of Israel.
2. Abram would be "blessed"; he would enjoy the favor of God, evident both in his spiritual walk and his material prosperity.
3. Abram's "name"—his reputation, or fame, based on his godly character and providentially guided actions—would be "great," or highly noteworthy.
4. Abram would be a source of "blessing" to others because of God's favor radiating out from his life.
5. The Lord would "bless" those who "blessed" Abram; that is, individuals and groups in interaction with Abram who behaved favorably toward him would themselves enjoy God's favor.
6. Those who "cursed" Abram by their words and/or actions would remove themselves from divine favor and might possibly experience the judgment of God.
7. Through Abram "all families of the earth [would] be blessed," a promise to be fully realized only through the coming of Messiah from Abram's lineage.

---

1. What did God promise Abram (v. 2)?
2. How would Abram's descendants influence the world (v. 3)?

"You cannot obey God without your obedience spilling out in a blessing to all those around you."—Adrian Rogers

---

C. Abram's Initial Adventure (vv. 4-9)

(Genesis 12:4, 6-9 is not included in the printed text.)

⁵ And Abram took Sarai his wife, and Lot his brother's son, and all their substance that they had gathered, and the souls that they had gotten in Haran; and they went forth to go into the land of Canaan; and into the land of Canaan they came.

God's Covenant With Abraham

In obedience to the divine call, seventy-five-year-old Abram, Sarai, Abram's nephew Lot, and their servants journeyed southward from Haran with all their possessions. Their initial trek took them throughout the entire expanse of the land of Canaan in a north-to-south direction. In Shechem, God, in a second brief revelation, said to Abram, "To your descendants I will give this land" (v. 7 NKJV). Abram consistently responded to the divine initiative with appropriate worship. He built in Shechem his first altar to "the Lord, who had appeared to him" (v. 7 NKJV), an act that revealed the high priority given by Abram to communion with the Lord. He moved eventually to *Bethel* (Hebrew, "House of God"), where he "pitched his tent," apparently settling in there for a while. In a second recorded act of consecration, Abram built an altar in Bethel and "called upon the name of the Lord" (v. 8). Abram next made an unfortunate trip to Egypt to escape famine, where his faith seemed to falter or, at least, where he relied too much on his own ingenuity, uncharacteristically led by carnal motives, rather than trusting in the Lord who had commissioned and preserved him (vv. 10-20). After being dismissed by Pharaoh, Abram returned to Bethel and resumed his worship of God (13:3-4).

Eventually, the now-prosperous Abram settled in Hebron, where he sojourned for a long while, owning no land there or anywhere else in Canaan, but negotiating with long-term inhabitants of the land for grazing and watering rights. In Hebron, as was now his established custom, he built another altar to the Lord (v. 18).

The writer of Hebrews speaks of Abram's obedience through faith: "By faith Abraham obeyed when he was called to go out to the place which he would receive as an inheritance. And he went out, not knowing where he was going. By faith he dwelt in the land of promise as in a foreign country, dwelling in tents with Isaac and Jacob, the heirs with him of the same promise; for he waited for the city which has foundations, whose builder and maker is God" (11:8-10 NKJV).

---

1. List everyone who migrated with Abram (vv. 4-5).
2. What did God promise Abram, and how did he respond (v. 7)?
3. What did Abram do between Bethel and Ai (v. 8)?

"The Bible recognizes no faith that does not lead to obedience, nor does it recognize any obedience that does not spring from faith. The two are at opposite sides of the same coin."—A. W. Tozer

---

II. GOD REAFFIRMS THE COVENANT (Gen.15:1-7, 18-21)

A. Promise of an Heir (vv. 1-6)

(Genesis 15:2-4 is not included in the printed text.)

¹ After these things the word of the Lord came unto Abram in a vision, saying, Fear not, Abram: I am thy shield, and thy exceeding great reward.

⁵ And he brought him forth abroad, and said, Look now toward heaven, and tell the stars, if thou be able to number them: and he said unto him,

So shall thy seed be. ⁶ And he believed in the Lord; and he counted it to him for righteousness.

In chapter 14, Abram rescued his nephew Lot from a confederation of kings who had defeated Sodom and surrounding cities and taken them captive. It is possible that Abram was afterward beset with anxiety because of expected reprisal, for the Lord, in a vision, reassured him with these powerful words: "Do not be afraid, Abram. I am your shield, your very great reward" (15:1 NIV). Abram was promised protection and prosperity that would flow from the abiding divine presence.

But Abram fretted about the identity of his heir. He had no biological son, so custom dictated that his steward Eliezer inherit his property. The Lord, in a reiteration of the covenant promise of 12:2-3, specifically pledged that Abram's heir would come from his "own body" (15:4 NKJV). The Lord directed Abram's eyes to the stars above him and assured him that as the stars were innumerable, so would be his descendants. God was revealing His plan to Abram step-by-step and challenging him to trust Him fully in the midst of the process.

Abram's response to this divine revelation is one of the most significant texts of Scripture: "He believed in the Lord, and He accounted it to him for righteousness" (v. 6 NKJV). Both the apostle Paul (Rom. 4:1-25; 5:1) and James, the brother of our Lord (James 2:14-26), anchored the New Testament doctrine of justification by faith in this remarkable passage of early Genesis.

Abram's dedication to God was never in question, though his external rectitude (usually highly exemplary) could (because of his fallen human nature) never be completely unflawed. Abram's judgment was also imperfect at times, but his faith, his trust in God tested by the daily vicissitudes of life, remained firm. His friendship with God (James 2:23)—his intimate walk and unremitting reliance—was constant. His standing before the Lord, then, was based not on performance but on faith—a living faith that propelled him forward in God.

The apostle Paul affirmed that Abram "did not waver at the promise of God through unbelief, but was strengthened in faith, giving glory to God, and being fully convinced that what He had promised He was also able to perform" (Rom. 4:20-21 NKJV). Paul castigated believers who were allowing Judaizers to sway them toward legalism, quoting Genesis 15:6 and asserting that "only those who are of faith are sons of Abraham" (Gal. 3:6-7 NKJV).

---

1. How did the Lord describe Himself (v. 1)?
2. What wrong conclusion did Abram make (vv. 2-3)?
3. What did God reveal to Abram (vv. 4-5)?
4. How did God respond to Abram's faith (v. 6)?

"If the Lord be with us, we have no cause of fear. His eye is upon us, His arm over us, His ear open to our prayer—His grace sufficient, His promise unchangeable."—John Newton

---

B. Cutting a Covenant (vv. 7, 18-21)

(Genesis 15:19-21 is not included in the printed text.)

⁷ And he said unto him, I am the Lord that brought thee out of Ur of the Chaldees, to give thee this land to inherit it.

God's Covenant With Abraham

¹⁸ In the same day the Lord made a covenant with Abram, saying, Unto thy seed have I given this land, from the river of Egypt unto the great river, the river Euphrates.

In this setting, in a formal covenant with Abram, the Lord affirmed His identity as the One who had brought Abram out of the city of Ur to give him "this land to inherit it" (v. 7). In this divine communication, Abram received the broad boundaries of the yet-to-be-formed nation that would arise from Abram's posterity.

Then the Lord had Abram bring a three-year-old heifer, a female goat, a ram, a turtledove, and a young pigeon. He was then instructed to cut the heifer, goat, and ram in halves and arrange all the animals in two rows with space in between (vv. 9-10). The Lord now caused Abram to fall into a deep sleep and gave him a remarkable vision—a *theophany*, or appearance of God in an earthly form. A smoking oven and a burning torch, symbolic representations of God, passed between the pieces of the animals as Abram lay in "horror of great darkness" (vv. 12, 17). Through this unforgettable enactment of covenant, God was pledging Himself to keep covenant with Abram perpetually.

Only God himself walked between the animals, since God was binding Himself in an unbreakable, unconditional covenant to bring into being step-by-step the nation of Israel. In this vision the future sojourn of the Israelites in Egypt was revealed, and their return to Canaan to form a nation was assured. Centuries later, the prophet Jeremiah (34:18) briefly described such a cutting of covenant, confirming that knowledge of the divinely sanctioned ritual had existed in Israel throughout the centuries from Abram to Jeremiah.

---

1. How does God describe Himself in verse 7?
2. What details did God give concerning the covenant (vv. 18-21)?

"Take courage. We walk in the wilderness today and in the Promised Land tomorrow."—D. L. Moody

---

III. GOD FULFILLS THE COVENANT (Gen. 17:1-7; 21:1-3; Gal. 3:6-9, 16, 29)

A. Renaming of Abram (17:1-7)

¹ And when Abram was ninety years old and nine, the Lord appeared to Abram, and said unto him, I am the Almighty God; walk before me, and be thou perfect. ² And I will make my covenant between me and thee, and will multiply thee exceedingly. ³ And Abram fell on his face: and God talked with him, saying, ⁴ As for me, behold, my covenant is with thee, and thou shalt be a father of many nations. ⁵ Neither shall thy name any more be called Abram, but thy name shall be Abraham; for a father of many nations have I made thee. ⁶ And I will make thee exceeding fruitful, and I will make nations of thee, and kings shall come out of thee. ⁷ And I will establish my covenant between me and thee and thy seed after thee in their generations for an everlasting covenant, to be a God unto thee, and to thy seed after thee.

In Genesis 16, Abram allowed Sarai to persuade him to accept her Egyptian servant Hagar as a concubine so that she could bear an heir to Abram in Sarai's place. This lapse in trust and obedience caused much anguish of soul to all concerned. Both Hagar and her son Ishmael were victims of this misjudgment by Sarai and Abram, who, rather than wait for God to perform His spoken word, sought to accomplish a divinely ordained result through willful human means. God protected and preserved Hagar and Ishmael, and eventually proceeded with His plan for Abram and Sarai.

After approximately twenty-four years in Canaan and about thirteen years after the birth of Ishmael, the Lord appeared to Abram again, revealing Himself as *El Shaddai*, "Almighty God" (17:1). This designation, according to Robert Youngblood, "describes the God who makes things happen by means of His majestic power and might" (*The Book of Genesis*, Baker). In this awe-inspiring encounter, God impressed upon Abram His omnipotence; the fact that no impediment, no contrary force, was sufficient to circumvent the will of the God who had called Abram, directed his steps, and preserved and prospered him in a land populated by idolatrous ethnic groups.

Abram was challenged to walk in fellowship with God and be *perfect* (Hebrew, *tamim*), a word connoting wholeness, or integrity. "*Tamim* is the divine standard which man must attain" (*The Complete Word Study Old Testament*). Abram was to so consecrate himself to God that his daily walk would be without blame. Would he attain this ideal without flaw? He likely would not. But as he kept before him this revelation of God that caused him to fall on his face in worship, he would lead a life of exemplary righteousness.

God renewed His covenant with Abram and changed his name to *Abraham*, which meant "father of a multitude" (see v. 5). Whenever any person called his name, that person would remind Abraham of God's covenant, His irrevocable promise. A reading of the Book of Genesis reveals that Abraham was the progenitor of peoples, or nations, coming from both Ishmael and Isaac. A broader reading in Scripture reveals that the Messiah, Son of David, comes from the loins of Abraham (Matt. 1:1-17) and that He will rule over many nations.

God also, in Genesis 17:15, changed the name of *Sarai* to *Sarah*, an altered form which did not change its basic meaning, "princess." Sarah's faith did not persist as strongly as did that of Abraham (see 18:9-15). Nonetheless, her newly designated role, "mother of nations" (17:16), would be recalled by mention of her new name. She too would remember God's irrevocable promise to give her and Abraham a son and to bring forth a vast multitude from her descendants.

---

1. How did the Lord tell Abram to "walk" (v. 1)?
2. Explain Abram's name change (vv. 4-5).
3. List the details in the covenant from verses 6 and 7.

A Plan for Every Life

God has a purpose and a plan for every believer, not only for great Bible figures such as Abraham. God can take a small lad born to a poor family in the rural South, save him and fill him with His Spirit, and guide him through various possible pitfalls, whether intellectual, moral, or spiritual. He can guide him step-by-step, move him geographically, and prepare him for a lifetime appointment as a teacher in a Christian college. He can put him in unlikely places, given his background, and train his mind and will so that he can make a worthwhile contribution to young men and women of his generation. That is what God did for, in, and with me, and He can work out His individual plan for the life of every willing believer.—Sabord Woods

---

B. Birth of Isaac (21:1-3)

¹ And the Lord visited Sarah as he had said, and the Lord did unto Sarah as he had spoken. ² For Sarah conceived, and bare Abraham a son in his old age, at the set time of which God had spoken to him. ³ And Abraham called the name of his son that was born unto him, whom Sarah bare to him, Isaac.

Abraham was instructed to name his and Sarah's son *Isaac*, meaning "laughter," completing a wonderful motif that underlines the parents' tests of faith. In 17:17, Abraham "laughed" out of sheer astonishment when God promised him that his ninety-year-old wife would bear a son. In 18:12, "Sarah laughed within herself" in outright unbelief when she overheard the Lord reassuring Abraham that one year later she would bear a son (not grasping the fact that age is no barrier to God's blessing).

When God visited Sarah as He had promised and she became a mother, she said, "God has made me laugh, and all who hear will laugh with me" (21:6 NKJV). Now every time Isaac's name was called, the laughter of doubt and unbelief, succeeded by the laughter of spontaneous joy, would be recalled.

• Describe the miracle that took place.

C. Blessing From Abraham (Gal. 3:6-9, 16, 29)

⁶ Even as Abraham believed God, and it was accounted to him for righteousness. ⁷ Know ye therefore that they which are of faith, the same are the children of Abraham. ⁸ And the scripture, foreseeing that God would justify the heathen through faith, preached before the gospel unto Abraham, saying, In thee shall all nations be blessed. ⁹ So then they which be of faith are blessed with faithful Abraham.

¹⁶ Now to Abraham and his seed were the promises made. He saith not, And to seeds, as of many; but as of one, And to thy seed, which is Christ.

²⁹ And if ye be Christ's, then are ye Abraham's seed, and heirs according to the promise.

The apostle Paul was a trained rabbi who had sat at the feet of Gamaliel, a renowned rabbinic scholar of the first century AD. Paul therefore had deep, rich knowledge of the Old Testament and, particularly, of the Abrahamic covenant and its relationship to the Mosaic covenant. But Paul also understood that new covenant rooted in the redemptive sacrifice of Christ on the cross. When the apostle was faced with inroads made by purveyors of Jewish legalism among Christians in the province of Galatia, he confronted confused and backsliding believers with Old Testament truth viewed in the light of new covenant reality.

In Galatians 3, Paul first questioned why they would allow themselves to fall back toward legalism when they had received the Holy Spirit through faith. He grounded his challenge to the Galatians in the initial statement of the Abrahamic covenant in Genesis 12:1-3 and asserted that, long before the Mosaic Law was given to Israel, Abraham "believed God, and it was accounted to him for righteousness" (Gal. 3:6; see Gen. 15:6). Paul insisted that the core of the gospel lay in God's promise to Abraham that "in you all the nations shall be blessed" (Gal. 3:8 NKJV), since the promise of the coming of the Messiah rested in the fulfillment of that prophecy.

"The promise of the Spirit through faith" (v. 14) came to "Abraham and his Seed . . . who is Christ" (v. 16 NKJV). Now, through Christ, we are free from the legal bondage of the Mosaic Law and are, with Abraham, justified by faith and granted all the privileges of sons of God, whether Jew or Greek, slave or free, male or female, since we are "all one in Christ" (v. 28). We, therefore, must not place ourselves under a system that demands a perfect adherence to external laws and rituals impossible to keep and that therefore only brings condemnation. Instead, belonging to Christ, we are "Abraham's descendants, heirs according to promise" (v. 29 NASB).

---

1. Who are considered "children of Abraham" today (vv. 6-9)?
2. What is the connection between Jesus Christ and Abraham (vv. 16, 29)?

"The new covenant is the bond between God and man, established by the sacrificial death of Jesus Christ under which all who have been effectively called to God in all ages have been formed into the one body of Christ in New Testament times, in order to come under His law during this age and to remain under His authority forever."—Tom Wells

---

CONCLUSION

As Abraham walked with God by faith, God gradually unfolded to him the full covenant that guaranteed the land and the blessing. Through the *seed* (posterity) of Abraham, God would form a nation to convey the light of biblical revelation until, in the fullness of time, the Messiah came to purchase full redemption for all people—regardless of the age in which one lived, the social status one attained, or the gender role assigned by God. Ultimately, God's plan to restore fully the position of humankind previous to the fall into sin in the Garden of Eden will be completely realized at the end of the gospel age. We stand in awe at the love and mercy of our Creator and Redeemer when we comprehend even basically the fullness of redemption and restoration inherent in God's ancient, yet presently valid, covenant with Abraham.

GOLDEN TEXT CHALLENGE

"IF YE BE CHRIST'S, THEN ARE YE ABRAHAM'S SEED, AND HEIRS ACCORDING TO THE PROMISE" (Gal. 3:29).

Believers in Christ are "truly heirs of God, and this is in accordance with the promise made to Abraham. It is not by the obedience of the Law; it is by faith—in the same way that Abraham possessed the blessing; an arrangement before the giving of the Law, and therefore one that may include all, whether Jews or Gentiles. All are on a level; and all are alike the children of God, and in the same manner, and on the same terms that Abraham was."—**Albert Barnes**

Daily Devotions:

M. God Chose Abraham
   Nehemiah 9:5-8
T. God Called Abraham
   Isaiah 51:1-6
W. The Covenant-Keeping God
   Micah 7:18-20
T. God Remembers His Holy Covenant
   Luke 1:67-75
F. Heirs of the Covenant
   Acts 3:17-26
S. Abraham: Father of Believers
   Romans 4:16-25

Judgment on Sodom and Gomorrah

Genesis 18:16—19:29; Ezekiel 16:49-50; Matthew 11:20-24

Unit Theme:
Great Events in Genesis

Central Truth:
God judges sin but will forgive all who repent.

Focus:
Consider why God judged Sodom and Gomorrah, and turn to God in repentance.

Context:
Old and New Testament insights on Sodom and Gomorrah's destruction

Golden Text:
"The Lord is not slack concerning his promise, as some men count slackness; but is longsuffering to us-ward, not willing that any should perish, but that all should come to repentance" (2 Peter 3:9).

Study Outline:
  I. Investigation Into Sodom's Sin
     (Gen. 18:16-22; Ezek. 16:49-50)
 II. Abraham's Intercession and God's Mercy
     (Gen. 18:23-33)
III. Judgment for Sin
     (Gen. 19:24-29; Matt. 11:20, 23-24)

INTRODUCTION

Sodom, Gomorrah, and three smaller nearby cities named Admah, Zeboiim, and Zoar, closely aligned and located near the Dead Sea, were marked for destruction by God because of heinous wickedness. The larger cities, Sodom and Gomorrah, became symbols of the worst possible evil because of disregard of basic principles of moral decency and respect for human life, but this extreme wickedness was characteristic of all five.

In post-Genesis references, Sodom and Gomorrah serve as warnings to subsequent cultures regarding the dire judgment that can befall them should they reject righteousness, justice, and morality and descend into deep social and sexual depravity (see Deut. 29:23; Lam. 4:6; Matt. 11:23-24; 2 Peter 2:6).

When the wealth of Abraham and Lot increased and their servants quarreled, Abraham offered his nephew first choice as to what part of Canaan he might live in so they might separate and avoid further strife. Lot's choice was "the plain of Jordan" near the corrupt cities named above (Gen. 13:1-13). Lot first settled *near* Sodom; soon he was living *in* Sodom; finally he was *at home* there, "sitting in the gate" (19:1 NKJV), often indicative of leadership.

Abraham's loyalty to his nephew is well-illustrated in chapter 14. The five cities of the plain that included Sodom rebelled against their overlord, refusing to pay assigned tribute. A coalition of kings led by this overlord devastated the entire area, attacking the five cities and taking spoils and captives. Abraham, with 318 trained servants, pursued the victorious kings and recovered captives and spoils, including "Lot, and his goods, and the women also, and the people" (v. 16). Lot had gotten himself into trouble, and he had to be rescued by that uncle whose loyalty and generosity he had taken for granted. Afterward, Lot foolishly returned to Sodom, where he remained despite that city's moral corruption.

The apostle Peter, in 2 Peter 2:6-8 (NKJV), wrote of Sodom and Gomorrah that God "condemned them to destruction, making them an example to those who afterward would live ungodly," but also declared that God "delivered righteous Lot, who was oppressed by the filthy conduct of the wicked." The apostle observed that Lot had "tormented his righteous soul from day to day by seeing and hearing their lawless deeds." It was an avoidable torment. Lot had chosen material wealth and worldly prestige at the cost of his personal and family welfare.

Lot was "righteous" in the sense that he shared the faith of Abraham and had a conscience trained in godliness. But he had stayed in Sodom so long that Sodom had gotten into him, and as a result he barely escaped with his own life and that of his daughters—as we see in the current lesson.

I. INVESTIGATION INTO SODOM'S SIN (Gen. 18:16-22; Ezek. 16:49-50)

In a remarkable theophany, the Lord (*Yahweh*) (Gen. 18:1) and two angels (see 19:1) appeared to Abraham as he sat in the door of his tent at Mamre in the vicinity of Hebron. The patriarch quickly prepared a sumptuous meal for the visitors, in line with customary hospitality. The Lord honored Abraham signally by dining with him, then conversed with him, assuring him He would keep His promise to give him and Sarah a son. Abraham soon discerned the supernatural identity of his guests.

A. The Angels' Investigative Mission (Gen. 18:16-22)

16 And the men rose up from thence, and looked toward Sodom: and Abraham went with them to bring them on the way. 17 And the Lord said, Shall I hide from Abraham that thing which I do; 18 Seeing that Abraham shall surely become a great and mighty nation, and all the nations of the earth shall be blessed in him? 19 For I know him, that he will command his children and his household after him, and they shall keep the way of the Lord, to do justice and judgment; that the Lord may bring upon Abraham that which he hath spoken of him. 20 And the Lord said, Because the cry of Sodom and Gomorrah is great, and because their sin is very grievous; 21 I will go down now, and see whether they have done altogether according to the cry of it, which is come unto me; and if not, I will know. 22 And the men turned their faces from thence, and went toward Sodom: but Abraham stood yet before the Lord.

The two angels accompanying the Lord continued their journey to Sodom, sent on their way by the ever-gracious Abraham. They would observe firsthand the deplorable conditions and direct "on the ground" the preparations necessary before the coming destruction. The Lord, meanwhile, determined to share with His "friend" (2 Chron. 20:7) Abraham that act of judgment being determined for these wicked cities. The Lord recognized the covenant position of Abraham, mentioned His intimate relationship with him, and noted his "righteousness and justice" (Gen. 18:19 NKJV).

The "cry," or "outcry," coming from the inhabitants of Sodom and Gomorrah was that of the oppressed and brutalized (v. 20). The Hebrew word for *outcry* occurs often in Scripture to express the oppression of widows, orphans, or servants (Kent Hughes, *Genesis*). Not only, then, were these cities guilty of abominable sexual perversity; they also were perpetrators of gross social injustice. It becomes apparent that their wickedness had reached such an extent that no remedy short of destruction remained.

Our omniscient Lord was obviously aware of the extent of the evil of these cities, so He must have been speaking in terms easily comprehensible by humans when He spoke of determining the extent of their guilt (v. 21). In any case, Abraham now stood with the Lord (v. 22) on a height from which he could view at a distance all the cities of the plain (see 19:27-28).

---

1. What did the Lord "know" about Abraham (v. 19)?
2. Explain the phrase "their sin is very grievous" (v. 20).

"Do not be deceived; happiness and enjoyment do not lie in wicked ways."—Isaac Watts

---

B. An Inventory of Sodom's Sins (Ezek. 16:49-50)

⁴⁹ Behold, this was the iniquity of thy sister Sodom, pride, fulness of bread, and abundance of idleness was in her and in her daughters, neither did she strengthen the hand of the poor and needy. ⁵⁰ And they were haughty, and committed abomination before me; therefore I took them away as I saw good.

Long after the patriarchal age, at a time when the gradual devastation of the southern kingdom (Judah) by King Nebuchadnezzar of Babylon had already begun, the prophet Ezekiel uttered an inspired oracle that presented, in some detail, the wickedness of Sodom. Chapter 16 of the prophecy of Ezekiel includes an extended parable in which the Lord himself traced the history of Judah. In essence, this striking message from God declared that the southern kingdom had repaid the favor of the Lord with spiritual adultery (idolatry), social injustice, moral corruption, and alliances with pagan foreign powers.

In a shocking comparison, the Lord asserted that Judah was guilty of the sins of Sodom—pride, gluttony, extreme idleness, neglect of the poor and needy, haughtiness, and abomination. Because of these sins, Sodom was destroyed by God; and because of the same sins, Judah was now being devastated by Babylon, which was acting unwittingly as God's instrument of judgment.

• List the sins of Sodom.

"Though selfishness hath defiled the whole man, yet sensual pleasure is the chief part of its interest, and, therefore, by the senses it commonly works; and these are the doors and windows by which iniquity entereth into the soul."—Richard Baxter

---

II. ABRAHAM'S INTERCESSION AND GOD'S MERCY (Gen. 18:23-33)

A. The Heart of Intercession (v. 23)

23 And Abraham drew near, and said, Wilt thou also destroy the righteous with the wicked?

Intercession is the heart-cry of a compassionate spirit. Despite his exasperation with the rebellious children of Israel, Moses interceded with the Lord for them after they had fallen into idolatry while he was on Mount Sinai and God threatened to destroy them and make a great nation from Moses' own descendants. The leader of Israel pleaded for God to spare them and forgive them, saying, "Yet now, if You will forgive their sin—but if not, I pray, blot me out of Your book which You have written" (Ex. 32:32 NKJV).

Jesus Christ himself, our great Intercessor in the presence of God the Father, just hours before His passion prayed fervently for the sanctification, unity, and preservation of His disciples and of all who would come to believe in Him (John 17). Also, a few years later, the apostle Paul expressed his "great sorrow and grief" for his fellow Jews, even wishing himself "accursed" in exchange for their salvation if such could be possible (see Rom. 9:1-5). Later, the apostle directed in his first letter to Timothy (2:1) that "supplications, prayers, intercessions, and giving of thanks, be made for all men."

Exactly *how* intercessory prayer works, I do not know. But I know firsthand that it reaches the heart of God and results in changed lives and circumstances.

• What did Abraham ask the Lord?

"God is not obligated to save anybody to make any special act of grace, to draw anyone to Himself. He could leave the whole world to perish, and such would be a righteous judgment."—R. C. Sproul

---

B. The Merciful Divine Response (vv. 24-33)

(Genesis 18:27-33 is not included in the printed text.)

24 Peradventure there be fifty righteous within the city: wilt thou also destroy and not spare the place for the fifty righteous that are therein? 25 That be far from thee to do after this manner, to slay the righteous with the wicked: and that the righteous should be as the wicked, that be far from thee: Shall not the Judge of all the earth do right? 26 And the Lord said, if I find in Sodom fifty righteous within the city, then I will spare all the place for their sakes.

Abraham was anxious regarding the fate of his nephew Lot and Lot's family; moreover, compassion for fellow human beings, and particularly for innocent persons caught in a general overthrow, would be consistent with Abraham's walk with God as portrayed extensively in Genesis 12—25. Abraham interceded earnestly with the Lord on behalf of the wicked cities. He inquired of God, "Would You destroy the righteous with the wicked?"

Scripture contains examples of culture-wide divine judgment in which the righteous perished with the wicked. One can conclude from the examples of Daniel, Jeremiah, and Ezekiel that righteous Jews lived in Judah among the wicked when Babylon devastated that culture. They, in many cases, lost their lives or were removed to Babylon; but they never lost their souls, and they had the comfort of the divine presence—whether dead or alive.

Alexander Maclaren states: "In widespread calamities the righteous are blended with the wicked in one bloody ruin; and it is the very misery of such judgments that often the sufferers are not the wrongdoers. . . . The whirlwind of temporal judgments makes no distinctions between the dwellings of the righteous and the wicked, but levels them both" (*Expositions of the Holy Scripture: The Book of Genesis*). However, when considering the entire biblical record, we become aware that the righteous, while they may suffer with the wicked on earth, upon death enter the presence of God and escape the ultimate punishment of the wicked.

The Lord nonetheless mercifully entertained Abraham's repeated entreaties as a result of which initially fifty, then forty-five, forty, thirty, twenty, and finally only ten supposed righteous persons in the cities of the plain would have caused God to hold back destruction. In the words of Derek Kidner, "Abraham [was] feeling his way forward in a spirit of faith . . . humility . . . and . . . love" (*Tyndale Old Testament Commentaries*).

Abraham said to the Lord, "Shall not the Judge of all the earth do right?" (18:25). This rhetorical question assumes that because God is just, He could not include righteous persons in a general act of judgment. According to *Hastings Dictionary of the Bible,* the justice of God means that "He acts at all times consistently with his own nature and His own good and gracious purposes." That divine nature is characterized by both selfless love and perfect holiness. God, therefore, will not allow gross injustice and immorality to continue endlessly with impunity.

The justice of God, then, in light of the conditions existing in the cities of the plain, did not necessitate His granting of Abraham's request. But the Lord did promise conditional mercy in answer to Abraham's sincere entreaty. The shocking reality is that there were not even ten righteous people living in the cities of the plain. In fact, if Lot was not to be considered a permanent resident of Sodom (see 19:4), the case could be made that there were no righteous residents in these cities.

---

1. How did Abraham begin his intercession (v. 24)?
2. How is the Lord described in verse 25?
3. How does Abraham describe himself in verse 27, and why?
4. What does verse 32 reveal about God's mercy?

Miraculous Intercession
When a beloved relative of mine was devastated by a staph infection that affected both her heart and her brain, individuals and churches across the entire region began to intercede for her deliverance. At one point she

was not expected to survive through the day. But she, in fact, did survive. She survived an unusual emergency open-heart surgical procedure and experienced healing of the brain with the aid of powerful antibiotics but without brain surgery and without brain damage. When her leading physician dismissed her months later, he said, "You can tell your church that the only reason you are alive is God. It certainly wasn't anything we did." Our compassionate, merciful Lord is still moved by intercession.

III. JUDGMENT FOR SIN (Gen. 19:24-29; Matt. 11:20, 23-24)

The two angels who had accompanied the Lord and shared Abraham's hospitality arrived in Sodom late in the day (Gen. 19:1). Lot invited them to be his guests overnight, offering accepted tokens of hospitality. The depth of perversity of the men of Sodom was soon demonstrated, for the entire male population of the city surrounded Lot's house and demanded that he bring out his guests to them so that they might "know them carnally" (v. 5 NKJV) or, according to NIV, "have sex with them." Essentially, their aim was to commit mass homosexual rape. Thus, we see the wholesale perversity of the entire city culture, called *abomination* in Ezekiel 16.

The men of the city now threatened Lot himself, and the two angels quickly pulled him inside and closed the door. The men of Sodom demonstrated their contempt for Lot, and particularly his leadership position in the city (v. 9), as well as their own total lack of decency. The angels now struck the men with blindness, perhaps through a "brilliant flash of light" (*New Spirit-Filled Life Bible*) that created "a dazzled state" (Kidner), similar to the effect of the light from heaven on the apostle Paul (Acts 9:1-9).

The angels next instructed Lot to assemble all members of his family and prepare to get them out of Sodom, warning of the coming destruction—"we will destroy this place, because the outcry against them has grown great before the face of the Lord, and the Lord has sent us to destroy it" (v. 13 NKJV). The social and sexual depravity of Sodom and the other associated cities had reached such a degree that God would now obliterate them. The angels had been sent as agents of destruction.

A. The Destruction of Four Cities (Gen. 19:24-29)

24 Then the Lord rained upon Sodom and upon Gomorrah brimstone and fire from the Lord out of heaven; 25 And he overthrew those cities, and all the plain, and all the inhabitants of the cities, and that which grew upon the ground. 26 But his wife looked back from behind him, and she became a pillar of salt. 27 And Abraham gat up early in the morning to the place where he stood before the Lord: 28 And he looked toward Sodom and Gomorrah, and toward all the land of the plain, and beheld, and, lo, the smoke of the country went up as the smoke of a furnace. 29 And it came to pass, when God destroyed the cities of the plain, that God remembered Abraham, and sent Lot out of the midst of the overthrow, when he overthrew the cities in the which Lot dwelt.

Commentaries offer natural explanations for the fiery destruction of the four cities—usually an earthquake or a volcanic eruption. But the explanation in verse 24 is quite specific: The Lord himself "rained brimstone and fire on Sodom and Gomorrah, from the Lord out of the heavens" (NKJV). When the Bible is so specific, even repeating "the Lord," it is only interpretively invalid to resort to alternative explanations, if one accepts the accuracy and reliability of Scripture. The "overthrow" of the four cities was supernatural. It was also total—all buildings, inhabitants, and plant life.

Some contemporary thinkers consider *Yahweh* in the Old Testament to be a vengeful deity thundering from heaven, in contrast with the God of love of the New Testament. But such would be a false dichotomy. The God of biblical revelation is consistently revealed throughout both Testaments to be a God of love, justice, and righteousness who acts mercifully. But He is also revealed finally with judicial anger against gross injustice and immorality when there is clearly no intention of repentance and reform. The sin described in Sodom was not only abominable in the extreme; it was also characteristic of the city as a whole, making any change highly improbable.

Why did Lot's wife look back, and what is implied by this backward look? Some speculate that Lot had married a woman of Sodom who loved the luxurious life of a wealthy man of the city and who, therefore, with great longing and reluctance, was pulled away from the city by the angels. Regardless of her origins, Lot's wife lingered when specifically instructed not to look back. Perhaps, like her sons-in-law, she found it difficult to believe that God would actually overthrow the wicked cities and bring to an end the life she cherished. "She stood," according to *Wycliffe Bible Commentary*, "a silent sentinel to sordid selfishness," encased in that salt so common to the region.

Jesus cautioned, in teaching concerning circumstances preceding His second coming, that His disciples should "remember Lot's wife" (Luke 17:32)—warning against becoming enmeshed in a sinful culture and, as a result, being unprepared or even unhopeful for His return.

Lot and his daughters first found refuge in Zoar, the small city spared as the angels had promised (Gen. 19:20-22). Lot and his daughters had been afraid to flee to the mountains, but now became afraid to remain in Zoar, perhaps because they feared that destruction might finally come to that wicked little place. They finally settled in a cave in nearby mountains (v. 30).

---

1. Describe the punishment of Sodom and Gomorrah (vv. 24-25).
2. Explain the fate of Lot's wife (v. 26).
3. What did Abraham's intercession accomplish (v. 29)?

"We need to follow our Lord's admonition to remember Lot's wife, for she was one who did not forget her possessions even in a time of the greatest peril. She was not guilty of having retraced a single step towards Sodom. All she did was look back. But how revealing was that backward glance! Does it not speak volumes concerning the condition of her heart?"—Watchman Nee

B. Judgment for Rejection of Truth (Matt. 11:20, 23-24)

20 Then began he to upbraid the cities wherein most of his mighty works were done, because they repented not:

23 And thou, Capernaum, which art exalted unto heaven, shalt be brought down to hell: for if the mighty works, which have been done in thee, had been done in Sodom, it would have remained until this day. 24 But I say unto you, That it shall be more tolerable for the land of Sodom in the day of judgment, than for thee.

Capernaum was the center of the Galilean ministry of Christ. Even the enemies of Jesus could not deny the authenticity of the miracles wrought there—remarkable healings, exorcisms of demons, and even the raising from the dead of the daughter of Jairus. Establishment groups such as scribes and Pharisees, without an iota of logic, sought to explain Jesus' divinely produced cures and deliverances by accusations that Jesus consorted with evil. The Pharisees, scribes (experts in Old Testament law), Herodians, and Sadducees led privileged lives and often consorted with the Roman conquerors so as to keep intact their positions. So who was really consorting with evil? These leaders of the Jews rejected their Messiah, often refusing to accept His claims when they knew better, for fear of reprisal by the Romans.

To deny divinely given truth despite overwhelming evidence, and finally to seek the death of the Truth-giver, is to invite divine judgment. Even Sodom, however wicked, did not behave so heinously as these first-century-establishment Jews, who rejected the Son of God when He came in fulfillment of messianic prophecy and demonstrated conclusively His origin and nature. In fact, Jesus stated that Sodom would have repented and avoided judgment had they seen and heard what Capernaum had witnessed.

Eventually, Capernaum ceased to exist. But Jesus' denunciation pointed toward the final judgment, not a temporal judgment. All human beings will answer to God, whether they hail from Sodom or Capernaum or whatever human culture. God is no respecter of persons; therefore, the moral law, expressed succinctly by the apostle Paul in Galatians 6:7, still stands: "Do not be deceived, God is not mocked; for whatever a man sows, that he will also reap" (NKJV)—a principle that applies to individuals, groups, cities, and nations alike.

---

1. Why did Jesus rebuke certain cities (v. 20)?
2. What did Jesus declare about Capernaum (vv. 23-24)?

"The New Testament reveals how close one may come to the kingdom—tasting, touching, perceiving, understanding. And it also shows that to come this far and reject the truth is unforgivable."—D. A. Carson

---

CONCLUSION

Contemporary ethicists often deny the existence of moral absolutes; instead, they posit that moral values are formed within cultures and change from generation to generation. They therefore would seek to explain away the sin of Sodom, suggesting that the reason for divine overthrow lay in violation of laws of hospitality rather than in the sins cited specifically in Scripture—social and sexual depravity. But Scripture consistently, in both the Old and the New Testament, upholds social and sexual mores rooted in the Ten Commandments, which, in turn, are rooted in the holiness and justice of God. We will answer to these moral absolutes, binding today as surely as they were three millennia ago.

GOLDEN TEXT CHALLENGE

"THE LORD IS NOT SLACK CONCERNING HIS PROMISE, AS SOME MEN COUNT SLACKNESS; BUT IS LONGSUFFERING TO US-WARD, NOT WILLING THAT ANY SHOULD PERISH, BUT THAT ALL SHOULD COME TO REPENTANCE" (2 Peter 3:9).

When people, after a considerable period of time, fail to fulfill their promises, we conclude that they have changed their minds, have forgotten their promises, or do not have the ability to perform them. We can draw no such conclusion from the apparent delay in the fulfillment of God's promises or purposes. What He has promised, what He has purposed, *will* come to pass—everything, including (for example) the return of Christ and the judgment of the wicked.

God often allows sinners to continue to sin, causing heartache to themselves and to others. Why? He is patient and long-suffering. He does not want anyone to be lost. He desires that all people repent.

Sin will be punished, if one does not repent. Judgment is certain. God has not changed His mind, but He waits in patience and love for the individual to repent, often longer than we may feel is necessary. How wonderful it is that He waited so patiently for many of us!

This verse does not teach that all sinners eventually will be saved. It *does* teach that God is ready to honor any and all instances of genuine repentance. People will be lost only if they turn their backs on Jesus Christ.

Daily Devotions:
M. A Change of Heart
   1 Kings 8:46-50
T. God Will Judge
   Ecclesiastes 12:10-14
W. Sin Punished
   Jeremiah 8:4-12
T. Repent or Perish
   Luke 13:1-5
F. God Shows Mercy
   1 Timothy 1:12-17
S. Mercy Triumphs Over Judgment
   James 2:1-12

Abraham's Faith Tested

Genesis 21:1-7; 22:1-19

Unit Theme:
Great Events in Genesis

Central Truth:
Christians can stand strong when their faith is tested.

Focus:
Discuss the testing of Abraham's faith and stand strong in our faith when we are tested.

Context:
Events occurring around 2065 to 2050 BC in Beersheba and on Mount Moriah.

Golden Text:
"By faith Abraham, when he was tried, offered up Isaac: and he that had received the promises offered up his only begotten son" (Heb. 11:17).

Study Outline:
  I. Sacrifice Commanded by God
     (Gen. 21:1-7; 22:1-2)
  II. Obedience to God Displayed
     (Gen. 22:3-10)
III. Obedience to God Rewarded
     (Gen. 22:11-19)

INTRODUCTION

Two principal figures are prominent in the narrative composing the subject of the present lesson—the patriarch Abraham and his supernaturally promised and provided heir, Isaac. By the time of our lesson text, Abraham had journeyed with God for decades. Initially, Abraham, in a signal act of obedience to an invisible Deity unknown to his idolatrous city Ur, had left that place, allowed himself to be detoured temporarily while he tarried with his father, Terah, in Haran, and then eventually migrated to Canaan, where he sojourned in various locales before settling finally in Beersheba.

Abraham had several remarkable encounters with God in which He promised him posterity and a national home—the land and the blessing. The great patriarch developed spiritually through hard experience. His basic faith in that God who had revealed Himself to him was unshakeable (Gen. 15:6). His practical walk, however, was on two occasions marked by reversion to solutions characteristic of his cultural past (12:10-20; 20:1-18) and on a third occasion by an attempt, suggested by Sarah, to "assist" God in the producing of an heir by resorting to a solution not divinely ordained (16:1-16). Finally, through direct divine intervention, the aged Abraham and Sarah produced Isaac, the son and heir of God's intention.

Ishmael was Abraham's first son—the son of Sarah's handmaiden Hagar, but not the child of promise. Ishmael was in his teens when Isaac was born. His mockery of the infant Isaac led to his ejection, along with his mother, Hagar, from Abraham and Sarah's home. This was an act that seems cruel, but which was necessary to bring about God's preordained purposes for the yet-to-be-born nation of Israel. God, in His inscrutable wisdom, preserved and prospered Ishmael even as He prepared Isaac for his destined patriarchal role. Isaac would prove himself obedient to his father (22:6-9), though willing later to resort to a failed stratagem already employed twice by his father (26:6-11). However, he was peace-loving and perhaps somewhat passive (vv. 12-33), meditative (24:63), prayerful (25:21; 26:25), and receptive to communication from God (vv. 2-5). Isaac's life was far less colorful than that of his father and of his son Jacob, yet critical to the unfolding of God's covenant promises.

The outcome of the test of Abraham's faith discussed in the current lesson depended crucially on the willing obedience of the young Isaac, by this time no longer a small child but, at the least, a strapping youth in his mid-teens. (In fact, one Jewish tradition holds that he was 37.) Isaac's placid disposition (suggested above), coupled with an implicit trust in his father and his father's God, likely caused him to undergo without any apparent resistance the ordeal (analyzed below) which, while in process, must have been mystifying and incomprehensible.

I. SACRIFICE COMMANDED BY GOD (Genesis 21:1-7; 22:1-2)

A. The Birth of Isaac (21:1-7)

¹ And the Lord visited Sarah as he had said, and the Lord did unto Sarah as he had spoken. ² For Sarah conceived, and bare Abraham a son in his old age, at the set time of which God had spoken to him. ³ And Abraham called the name of his son that was born unto him, whom Sarah bare to him, Isaac. ⁴ And Abraham circumcised his son Isaac being eight days old, as God had commanded him. ⁵ And Abraham was an hundred years old, when his son Isaac was born unto him. ⁶ And Sarah said, God hath made me to laugh, so that all that hear will laugh with me. ⁷ And she said, Who would have said unto Abraham, that Sarah should have given children suck? For I have born him a son in his old age.

We revert to the conception and birth of Isaac, about which Scripture is most explicit. The Lord *visited* Sarah and enabled the conception, gestation, and normal birth of a child when the mother had been unable previously to bear a child and was now far beyond the child-bearing age. The emphasis of Scripture is on God's supernatural intervention and precise timing. The Bible, in widely separated contexts, tells of previously barren women who were supernaturally enabled to conceive sons important to God's purposes—Joseph, Samson, Samuel, John the Baptist.

The couple named their son not after the father or an ancestor, but according to God's specific direction. The name *Isaac*, "laughter," reminded Abraham and Sarah of their laughter of astonishment and unbelief, and appropriately marked the birthday as a day of laughter out of sheer delight. Abraham followed divine instructions by performing upon Isaac the rite of circumcision, sign of God's covenant.

After the departure of Hagar and Ishmael, we read nothing of Isaac until the narrative of our current lesson. We can assume, however, that a father and mother with rich cultural and spiritual experience would nurture and cherish a much-desired and loved child. Isaac, then, like Jesus of Nazareth, would increase "in wisdom and stature, and in favour with God and man" (Luke 2:52)—mental, physical, spiritual, and social growth under godly tutelage.

---

1. How did the Lord keep His promise to Sarah (vv. 1-3)?
2. How did Abraham dedicate Isaac to the Lord (v. 4)?
3. Describe Sarah's state of mind (vv. 5-6).

"Have you been asking God what He is going to do? He will never tell you. God does not tell you what He is going to do; He reveals to you who He is. Do you believe in a miracle-working God, and will you 'go out' in complete surrender to Him until you are not surprised one iota by anything He does?"—Oswald Chambers

---

B. The Testing of Abraham (22:1-2)

¹ And it came to pass after these things, that God did tempt Abraham, and said unto him, Abraham: and he said, Behold, here I am. ² And he said, Take now thy son, thine only son Isaac, whom thou lovest, and get thee into the land of Moriah; and offer him there for a burnt offering upon one of the mountains which I will tell thee of.

After a number of years had passed, during which Scripture is silent regarding Isaac, God spoke chilling words to Abraham. He "tempted," or "tested" (NKJV), him. According to *The Word Study Old Testament*, "The word in question is *nasah* . . . , which means to 'put to the test.'" Our Creator and Redeemer has the right to *test* us to determine the extent of our dedication and obedience. God, however, does not *tempt* us in the sense of temptation to sin. James 1:13 says, "Let no one say when he is tempted, 'I am tempted by God'; for God cannot be tempted by evil, nor does He Himself tempt anyone" (NKJV).

Abraham recognized readily the by-now familiar voice of God. Three phrases in Genesis 22:2 (NKJV) are nonetheless knife-like in effect—"your only son," "whom you love," "offer him there"—and, quite frankly, they are incredible in terms of human logic. God, furthermore, did not explain or justify His command; Abraham must obey without understanding, for such was basic to the test.

Abraham had walked with God for decades and formed a concept of the nature of God as revealed to him in repeated encounters. This divine directive seemed to conflict with everything he had learned about God—wisdom, justice, compassion, reliability, faithfulness. Abraham knew about child sacrifice, but it was imposed by cruel false deities, and it would later be prohibited by the Law of Moses (Lev. 18:21; Deut. 18:10).

We, moreover, are told nothing about whether Sarah was aware of this divine appointment. While Abraham, in this ancient patriarchal culture, was complete master of his house, Sarah certainly would have boldly voiced her disbelief and dismay, as we know about her from previous narratives.

Abraham was instructed to go to the mountains of Moriah and offer there this unbelievable sacrifice. In 2 Chronicles 3:1, we are told that "Solomon began to build the house of the Lord at Jerusalem in Mount Moriah." Mount Calvary was close by. So Abraham was to go to the locale of what would later be the central city of the nation of Israel, where the Temple would stand and near the site where Jesus Christ would one day be crucified.

• How did the Lord test Abraham?

"Obedience to the revealed will of God is often just as much a step of faith as claiming a promise from God."—Jerry Bridges

---

II. OBEDIENCE TO GOD DISPLAYED (22:3-10)

A. Initial Obedience (v. 3)

³ And Abraham rose up early in the morning, and saddled his ass, and took two of his young men with him, and Isaac his son, and clave the wood for the burnt offering, and rose up, and went unto the place of which God had told him.

Verse 3 recounts Abraham's straightforward obedience; there is not a hint of hesitation. But we learn nothing from the text of what must have been in Abraham's heart—nothing of the inevitable human response. He must have winced, even gasped, upon hearing God's command in verse 2. He was probably confused, and he must have wrestled with negative emotions.

Then he would have recalled God's faithfulness under all previous circumstances and rehearsed the successive encounters with God in which He had clearly promised and then made possible through supernatural means the birth of this beloved son. But what would have propelled him forward was the knowledge that God had always acted benevolently and within the framework of His gradually revealed covenant that depended on the survival of the heir of Abraham and Sarah. So he trudged onward with a breaking heart, but not devoid of hope.

• How did Abraham respond to God's command?

"There's some task which the God of all the universe, the great Creator, your redeemer in Jesus Christ, has for you to do, and which will remain undone and incomplete until by faith and obedience you step into the will of God."—Alan Redpath

---

B. An Expression of Faith (vv. 4-5)

⁴ Then on the third day Abraham lifted up his eyes, and saw the place afar off. ⁵ And Abraham said unto his young men, Abide ye here with the ass; and I and the lad will go yonder and worship, and come again to you.

Abraham and Sarah now lived in Beersheba, about fifty miles south of the divinely appointed site of the sacrifice. The means of travel for Abraham was a slow-paced donkey and, apparently, Isaac and the two servants traveled on foot. (Did the two servants carry the supplies, or were there additional donkeys to carry wood and other necessary items?) The trip consumed two full days, with the destination being reached only well into the third day. Abraham, then, had a number of slowly passing hours in which to ponder, question, and grieve before the appointed site came into view.

The servants, of course, could not be allowed at the site of the sacrifice. Their behavior could not be predicted during the course of such an event. Abraham told them that he and "the lad" would go a bit farther and "worship," concealing the specific act of obedience required by God. But Abraham also expressed submission to God and remarkable faith: they would "go yonder and . . . come back" (NKJV). Everything Abraham had previously learned about God caused him to speak with confidence of an outcome consonant with divine love and justice. We recall the statement regarding Abraham's faith in 15:6, "He believed in the Lord: and he [God] counted it to him for righteousness."

• What do these verses reveal about Abraham's faith?

"If we walk in righteousness, He will carry us through."—A. B. Simpson

---

C. Unfaltering Obedience (vv. 6-8)

6 And Abraham took the wood of the burnt offering, and laid it upon Isaac his son; and he took the fire in his hand, and a knife; and they went both of them together. 7 And Isaac spake unto Abraham his father, and said, My father: and he said, Here am I, my son. And he said, Behold the fire and the wood: but where is the lamb for a burnt offering? 8 And Abraham said, My son, God will provide himself a lamb for a burnt offering: so they went both of them together.

Abraham continued without any apparent hesitation to act in accord with the divine command, and the reader is spared none of the excruciating detail. He transferred the wood from the back of the servant (or the donkey) to Isaac's back, picked up a means for lighting the fire (maybe flint), and did not forget the knife for slaying the sacrificial victim. Abraham must have hoped against hope now for divine permission to abandon his agonizing mission, and Isaac must have by now been filled with consternation. Nonetheless, Abraham moved toward the site, at a suitable distance from the servants and already designated by God, and Isaac accompanied him without any known protest.

Abraham's unflagging obedience justified him in God's sight, for James 2:21-22 states: "Was not Abraham our father justified by works when he offered up Isaac his son on the altar? You see that faith was working with his works, and as a result of the works, faith was perfected" (NASB).

Isaac, puzzled and mystified, asked his father about the missing lamb for the sacrifice (Gen. 22:7). Abraham replied out of desperate faith, born of everything he had previously learned about God. He gave an answer that, given the nature of God, *must* be true—"God will provide" (v. 8). Abraham's response anticipates the lesson regarding God's character to be made explicit in verse 14.

---

1. What did Abraham and Isaac do "together" (v. 6)?
2. What perplexed Isaac (v. 7)?
3. Explain Abraham's response to Isaac's question (v. 8).

"Though troubles assail, and dangers affright, though friends should all fail, and foes all unite; yet one thing secures us, whatever betide, the Scripture assures us, the Lord will provide."—John Newton

---

D. Utter Compliance (vv. 9-10)

⁹ And they came to the place which God had told him of; and Abraham built an altar there, and laid the wood in order, and bound Isaac his son, and laid him on the altar upon the wood. ¹⁰ And Abraham stretched forth his hand, and took the knife to slay his son.

Abraham reached the appointed place, gathered and arranged stones to make an altar, put the wood in place, bound the unresisting (but certainly unquestioning) Isaac so that he would remain on the altar, picked up the knife, and drew back his arm to wield the fatal blow. Abraham was, at this point, utterly compliant with God's command. What God had demanded (inexplicably to him), Abraham was performing to the letter. If the possibility of disobeying entered his mind, it was not translated into action, and the Scripture gives no notice of it. Rather, Abraham was utterly obedient.

Hebrews 11:17-19 says, "By faith Abraham, when he was tested, offered up Isaac, and he who had received the promises offered up his only begotten son, of whom it was said, 'In Isaac your seed shall be called,' concluding that God was able to raise him up, even from the dead, from which he also received him in a figurative sense" (NKJV). We observe from this passage that God treated Abraham's sacrifice of Isaac as complete because Abraham's intention to obey was without reservation. We, moreover, perceive that Abraham's faith was unswerving to the point of foreseeing a possible resurrection of his son, once dead. If he must die, then God must ask him and Sarah to produce another heir or raise Isaac up—because of His unconditional covenant promises.

• How far did Abraham go in obeying the Lord (vv. 9-10)?

"O that unbelievers would learn of faithful Abraham, and believe whatever is revealed from God, though they cannot fully comprehend it! Abraham knew God commanded him to offer up his son, and therefore believed, notwithstanding carnal reasoning might suggest many objections."—George Whitefield

---

III. OBEDIENCE TO GOD REWARDED (22:11-19)

A. Divine Intervention (vv. 11-12)

¹¹ And the angel of the Lord called unto him out of heaven, and said, Abraham, Abraham: and he said, Here am I. ¹² And he said, Lay not thine

hand upon the lad, neither do thou any thing unto him: for now I know that thou fearest God, seeing thou hast not withheld thy son, thine only son from me.

Just as Abraham was about to wield the fatal blow, "the *angel of the Lord* called unto him out of heaven" (v. 11). *Hastings Bible Dictionary* views this figure as a special representative of *Yahweh*, but *Wilson's Old Testament Word Studies* sees him as "an uncreated being, and the designation of the Messiah." The phrase "for now I know that . . ." (v. 12) implies that the speaker is not "God," but is yet the object of Abraham's act of dedication, or worship—that is, the recipient of his required ultimate sacrifice. It appears that we have here an intimation of plurality of persons in God, clearly apparent in the New Testament. This clearly divine Person could say to Abraham, "You have withheld nothing; therefore, I know that you revere Me" (paraphrased).

Abraham's sacrifice of his son, seen as complete in Hebrews 11:17, serves as a type of God's giving of His only begotten Son as a sacrifice for the sins of humankind. Isaac resembled Jesus in his humble trust in his father and acquiescence in his assigned role; he also bore the wood for the sacrifice, even as Jesus would bear the instrument of His sacrificial execution.

• What did God declare about Abraham (v. 12)?

"Nothing of spiritual significance comes without sacrifice. Your spirituality will always be measured by the size of your sacrifice."—Jerry Falwell

---

B. Substitute Sacrifice (v. 13)

13 And Abraham lifted up his eyes, and looked, and behold behind him a ram caught in a thicket by his horns: and Abraham went and took the ram, and offered him up for a burnt offering in the stead of his son.

Abraham now saw a suitable animal to be a substitute, obviously placed in the exactly right spot at precisely the right moment. Abraham quickly unbound Isaac, killed the ram, and offered the animal to the Lord.

There is a sense in which Jesus Christ became our substitute. In Exodus 13:2, 11-14, the Israelites were commanded to "consecrate" to God every firstborn "both of man and beast" (NKJV). The firstborn human males were to be redeemed by the offering of a suitable animal sacrifice. These Old Testament sacrifices are types of Christ, who became our substitute, bearing our sins. The apostle Paul says, "[God] made Him who knew no sin to be sin for us, that we might become the righteousness of God in Him" (2 Cor. 5:21 NKJV).

• Describe the events of verse 13.

"If Jesus Christ be God and died for me, then no sacrifice can be too great for me to make for Him."—C. T. Studd

---

C. Revelation (v. 14)

14 And Abraham called the name of that place Jehovah-jireh: as it is said to this day, In the mount of the Lord it shall be seen.

Abraham called the "place"—the area in the vicinity of Jerusalem divinely selected as the exact spot for the interrupted sacrifice—*Jehovah-Jireh,* meaning, "The Lord will provide." The Lord provided an appropriate sacrifice in the place of Isaac. He also provided Abraham with a victorious conclusion to a harrowing experience, nonetheless excruciating for being divinely ordered and miraculously concluded.

The Lord, however, also provided the ultimate answer to the human dilemma—the only viable answer—sending Jesus Christ into the world as "the way, the truth, and the life" (John 14:6). He is the exclusive *way* because no other solution exists and no other savior could satisfy divine justice; the *truth,* in the sense of reality versus falsehood, as well as the Word of Truth; and abundant *life,* slated to become eternal *life.* Jesus provides for us as we journey through life, even as God walked with Abraham through a series of experiences that showed to him His divine nature and His plan for that nation to come from his loins. The greatest form of provision is our Lord himself—to walk with us through this life of challenges as He readies us for eternal life in that New Jerusalem which will come down out of heaven.

• How has the Lord proven Himself to be "Jehovah-Jireh" in your life?

"Don't ever think there are many ways to the Divine. Jesus is the one qualified mediator, the only qualified sacrifice, and the only qualified Savior."—Erwin Lutzer

---

D. Renewal of Covenant (vv. 15-19)

15 And the angel of the Lord called unto Abraham out of heaven the second time, 16 And said, By myself have I sworn, saith the Lord, for because thou hast done this thing and hast not withheld thy son, thine only son: 17 That in blessing I will bless thee, and in multiplying I will multiply thy seed as the stars of the heaven, and as the sand which is upon the sea shore; and thy seed shall possess the gate of his enemies; 18 And in thy seed shall all the nations of the earth be blessed; because thou hast obeyed my voice. 19 So Abraham returned unto his young men, and they rose up and went together to Beersheba; and Abraham dwelt at Beersheba.

Abraham experienced a second message from heaven—a final renewal of God's covenant with him (v. 15). God had no superior authority by which He could affirm His divine intention for Abraham and his seed, so He must swear by Himself, the eternal Rock of Ages (v. 16). The very literal King James translation carries over into English the Hebrew idioms "in blessing I will bless" and "in multiplying I will multiply" (v. 17), which emphasize through repetition (*Wuest's Word Studies*). Abraham would indeed be blessed, and his blessing is still in process of fulfillment (v. 18). We, as Christians, enjoy the blessings of Abraham presently through Jesus Christ the Messiah, and we will enjoy their ultimate fulfillment upon the return of Christ to catch us away with Him in the air to ever be with Himself in the presence of His Father.

After God provided Himself to be Jehovah-Jireh on Mount Moriah, can you imagine the conversation between father and son and the servants? For Abraham, the walk back home must have been a parade of praise!

- How did the Lord reward Abraham's obedience?

Supernatural Provision

Once in my family, the refrigerator stopped running, with the week's supply of perishable foods in it and no way to get a repairman out to fix it—no vehicle and no telephone. We prayed, and after two or three hours it started running again—and never stopped, though we had it for about thirty-two years. God also provided our pastor with a dream that saved the life of my father when he had a strangulated hernia and gangrene had already set in. The next day, the surgeon told us Dad would have been dead within twenty-four hours had help not been secured. His death would have left several small children fatherless.—Sabord Woods

---

CONCLUSION

God tested Abraham in such an unusual and unexpected way that he suffered excruciating mental and emotional agony for two-and-a-half days as he journeyed from Beersheba to Moriah to offer his beloved son as a sacrifice. But God witnessed Abraham's total obedience and reverence for Himself, and He provided a substitute sacrifice for Isaac, Abraham's promised heir. God also revealed Himself as Provider—ultimately through the Messiah, Jesus Christ—but also through daily provision for His chosen people, whether the nation of Israel in the Old Testament (by preservation to this day) or His church (from inception until her translation to glory). The ultimate provision, the ultimate blessing, is yet to come; but it is just as sure as if we were already experiencing it.

GOLDEN TEXT CHALLENGE

"BY FAITH ABRAHAM, WHEN HE WAS TRIED, OFFERED UP ISAAC: AND HE THAT HAD RECEIVED THE PROMISES OFFERED UP HIS ONLY BEGOTTEN SON" (Heb. 11:17).

Abraham is accredited with having actually offered up Isaac. If God had not intervened and suspended Abraham's act of slaying him, Isaac would have been killed. God accepted Abraham's obedience as proof of his absolute devotion to Him. This verse cites Abraham's faith, whereas Genesis 22:18 cited his obedience as giving him the victory. Actually, faith and obedience accompany each other where they are genuine. One does not exist independently of the other.

Daily Devotions:

M. Obedience Better Than Sacrifice
1 Samuel 15:12-23
T. Hezekiah Tested
2 Chronicles 32:24-31
W. Trust in God
Jeremiah 17:5-8
T. Abraham: A Man of Faith
Hebrews 11:8-12, 17-19
F. Receiving the Crown of Life
James 1:2-12
S. Faith Tried
1 Peter 1:3-9

Principles for Kingdom Living

Matthew 5:1-48

Unit Theme:
Discourses in Matthew

Central Truth:
Christians live as Kingdom citizens by following Christ's teachings.

Focus:
Observe and adhere to essential principles for living as Kingdom citizens.

Context:
Early in AD 28 on a high hill or mountain near Capernaum

Golden Text:
"Blessed are the poor in spirit: for their's is the kingdom of heaven" (Matt. 5:3).

Study Outline:
I. Embrace True Blessedness
(Matt. 5:1-12)
II. Be True Kingdom Citizens
(Matt. 5:13-16)
III. Pursue True Righteousness
(Matt. 5:17-24, 27-30, 43-45, 48)

INTRODUCTION

A division of opinion exists as to the exact location where the Sermon on the Mount was delivered. Some identify the Horns of Hattin, a short distance south of the Sea of Galilee, as the place. Others say a hilly region not far from Capernaum, toward the west, a place that is now called the Mount of Beatitudes, is the spot. However, we cannot be certain about the exact location.

What is the purpose of the Sermon on the Mount? It was not an effort to present the way of salvation. It was rather a message to those who were members of the family of God. In *The Bible Knowledge Commentary*, Louis A. Barbieri Jr. succinctly writes: "The sermon showed how a person who is in right relationship with God should conduct his life."

The standard of righteousness set forth in Jesus' sermon applies to believers today. Only those who are a part of the kingdom of God are capable of walking in obedience to these precepts. The benefits of this manifesto are reserved for them. To build one's life on these principles is to live life on the highest possible plane. It is to taste heaven while still on earth.

I. EMBRACE TRUE BLESSEDNESS (Matt. 5:1-12)

A. The Occasion (vv. 1-2)

¹ **And seeing the multitudes, he went up into a mountain: and when he was set, his disciples came unto him: ² And he opened his mouth, and taught them, saying.**

The more Jesus preached and performed miracles, the larger the crowds became that gathered to hear Him. On this occasion, He went up on a mountain to teach His followers the principles of the kingdom of God. What followed is a masterpiece of ethics and righteous living unequaled by any other person.

In *A Few Buttons Missing*, J. T. Fisher wrote:

> If you were too take the sum total of all authoritative articles ever written by the most qualified of psychologists and psychiatrists on the subject of mental hygiene, if you were to combine them and refine them and leave out the excess verbiage, if you were to take the whole of the meat and none of the parsley, and if you were to have these unadulterated bits of pure scientific knowledge concisely expressed by the most capable of living poets, you would have an awkward and incomplete summary of the Sermon on the Mount. And it would suffer immeasurably through comparison. For nearly two thousand years the Christian world has been holding in its hands the complete answer to its restless and fruitless yearning. Here rests the blueprint for successful human life, with optimum mental health and contentment.

• Why did Jesus go to a mountainside?

"Jesus does not give recipes that show the way to God as other teachers of religion do. He is Himself the way."—Karl Barth

---

B. The Poor in Spirit (v. 3)

3 Blessed are the poor in spirit: for their's is the kingdom of heaven.

The Beatitudes have a twofold significance. They describe the inner condition of a believer, and they promise blessings in the future. Their standards are unattainable by personal effort, but may be attained by the work of the Holy Spirit within.

Each beatitude begins with the word *blessed*. It involves more than just being happy; it includes being in harmony with God and the security and blessedness that spring from that relationship.

This first beatitude speaks of the "poor in spirit." Who are they? William Barclay says they are those who have fully realized their own inadequacy, their own worthlessness, and their own destitution, but who have put their whole trust in God. They have discovered that the way to power is through the realization of helplessness. The way to independence is through dependence.

The "poor in spirit" are assured a place in the kingdom of heaven, a society in which God's will is as perfectly done on earth as it is in heaven.

• How does a person become "poor in spirit" (v. 3)?

"Faith is two empty hands held open to receive all of the Lord."—Alan Redpath

C. Those Who Mourn (v. 4)

4 Blessed are they that mourn: for they shall be comforted.

The road to God is marked by a broken heart. The psalmist said: "I will declare mine iniquity; I will be sorry for my sin" (38:18). The apostle Paul wrote: "Godly sorrow worketh repentance to salvation" (2 Cor. 7:10). The first step toward the Christian life, then, is utter dissatisfaction with life apart from Christ. That dissatisfaction leads to a brokenness that produces repentance and ultimately results in salvation.

Those who are truly sorry for their sins shall be comforted, Jesus said. The word translated "comforted" is related to the word that Jesus used when He promised the coming of the Holy Spirit (see John 14:16-18). The Holy Spirit as an ally, a helper, and a counselor will bring comfort to those who mourn.

_____

• What type of mourning is Jesus talking about in verse 4?

_____

"Thou canst not tell how rich a dowry sorrow gives the soul, how firm a faith and eagle sight of God."—Henry Alford

_____

D. The Meek (v. 5)

5 Blessed are the meek: for they shall inherit the earth.

The meek person is truly humble and gentle. He has a proper perspective of himself and his position. He is an imitator of Jesus Christ, who said, "I am meek and lowly in heart" (11:29). He shows kindness to all people because he remembers that he too was one time alienated from God (see Titus 3:1-7). The meek person no longer takes matters into his own hands. Mistreatment and suffering do not call up revenge. Rather, he commits himself to Him who deals righteously (see 1 Peter 2:19-23). Pride, wrath, and revenge have no place in his life. He is submitted to God's guidance and accepts whatever God sends to him.

To the meek a promise is given: "they shall inherit the earth." Many years before the time of Christ, the psalmist had made that same promise (37:11). He listed several other promises in combination with this one: the meek will dwell in the land; they will be fed; they will have the desires of their heart; they will see evildoers cut off; they will enjoy abundance of peace (see vv. 1-11).

_____

• How was Jesus "meek" (v. 5)?

_____

"If thou desire the love of God and man, be humble, for the proud heart, as it loves none but itself, is beloved of none but itself."—Francis Quarles

_____

E. Searchers for Righteousness (v. 6)

6 Blessed are they which do hunger and thirst after righteousness: for they shall be filled.

What the heart hungers for tells you much about the person. If the desire is only for possessions and material things, the person is out of step with the kingdom of God. If the desire is for righteousness and spiritual things, the person is moving in the right direction.

When this inner longing for righteousness is satisfied, it is reflected in outward character and conduct. It also responds to the need for righteousness in the lives of others.

God honors those who have a healthy, hearty, spiritual appetite. Ultimately their hunger and thirst will be fully satisfied in that land where they "shall hunger no more, neither thirst any more. . . . For the Lamb . . . shall feed them, and shall lead them unto living fountains of waters" (Rev. 7:16-17).

• For what do you "hunger and thirst" (v. 6)?

"What [others] most need to see in you is a reflection of what God is like and of the transforming power of the gospel. Your life can create hunger and thirst for God in others' lives and can be a powerful instrument in the hand of the Holy Spirit to draw their hearts to Christ."—Nancy Leigh DeMoss

---

F. The Merciful (v. 7)

7 Blessed are the merciful: for they shall obtain mercy.

The first three beatitudes deal with our spiritual awareness in approaching God. The fourth beatitude speaks of the promise of God's provision. The last three beatitudes address the character of the believer. Each of these characteristics is an essential, divine quality.

Those who have obtained God's righteousness are to show mercy. It is to God that mercy belongs (see Isa. 16:5) and He is rich in mercy (Eph. 2:4). To be *merciful*, therefore, is to "bear toward others that outgoing love which reflects and reproduces the outgoing love of God." It "is to have the same attitude to men as God has, to think of men as God thinks of them, to feel for men as God feels for them, to act toward men as God acts toward them" (*Barclay*).

Those to whom mercy has been shown are themselves to show mercy. When this quality characterizes one's life, it is much easier to be tolerant toward others, to freely forgive others, and to lend a helping hand wherever there is a need. These Christlike traits are the product of an attitude of mercy.

• How can a person "obtain mercy" (v. 7)?

"*Mercy* is forebearance to inflict harm under circumstances of provocation, when one has the power to inflict it; compassionate treatment of an offender or adversary; clemency."—Daniel Webster

G. The Pure in Heart (v. 8)

8 Blessed are the pure in heart: for they shall see God. Those to whom Jesus was speaking were more familiar with ceremonial purification than they were with purity of heart. This purity of heart is obtained only through the blood of Christ. The writer of Hebrews declares: "How much more shall the blood of Christ, who through the eternal Spirit offered himself without spot to God, purge your conscience from dead works to serve the living God?" (9:14). Something that is pure has nothing mixed with it; it is untainted in any way. A heart that is pure is a heart whose thoughts, motives, desires, and attitudes are completely genuine and absolutely unmixed with anything that would defile in any way.

Even the psalmist understood the pure in heart will see God. He wrote: "As for me, I will behold thy face in righteousness: I shall be satisfied, when I awake, with thy likeness" (17:15). Certainly, the vision of the future in the Book of Revelation foretells a time when the Lord's "servants shall serve him: and they shall see his face; and his name shall be in their foreheads" (22:3-4). John says that believers will see Jesus as He is and be like Him (see 1 John 3:2-3).

_____

• Who will not "see God" (v. 8)?

_____

"Everything we do is to be offered to the Lord; and if done so with a pure heart of love, it becomes holy."—Joyce Meyer

_____

H. The Peacemakers (v. 9)

9 Blessed are the peacemakers: for they shall be called the children of God. *Peacemaker* is not a negative term. It is not speaking of someone who evades trouble and allows a matter to drift until the situation becomes harder to solve. A peacemaker takes positive action to bring about the highest good for another. He or she is willing to face difficulty, unpleasantness, and unpopularity in order to produce peace. A peacemaker works for right relations between individuals.

The peacemakers shall be called the "children of God." Literally, they are called *sons of God*. This expression carries with it a certain virtue or quality. For example, Barnabas was called "the son of consolation" (Acts 4:36). This meant that he was a consoling and a comforting man. To say that a man is a *son of God* is to say that he is a godlike man doing a godlike work, which, in this instance, is making peace.

_____

• Are you a "peacemaker" (v. 9)?

_____

"When our lives are filled with peace, faith, and joy, people will want to know what we have."—David Jeremiah

I. Persecution (vv. 10-12)

¹⁰ Blessed are they which are persecuted for righteousness' sake: for theirs is the kingdom of heaven. ¹¹ Blessed are ye, when men shall revile you, and persecute you, and shall say all manner of evil against you falsely, for my sake. ¹² Rejoice, and be exceeding glad: for great is your reward in heaven: for so persecuted they the prophets which were before you.

Jesus never tried to conceal the difficulties and problems His followers would face. Thus, He tells them that they will be reviled, persecuted, and have all manner of evil said against them falsely because they are following Him. The world hated Him, and it will feel no different toward them (see Matt. 10:16-22).

One of the chief reasons that believers in the early church faced persecution was the spread of emperor worship. The time came when all people under the province of Rome were expected to declare, "Caesar is Lord." No Christian could ever do that. To Christians, Jesus Christ and He alone was Lord. Rome felt threatened by this refusal to bow to its demands and severely persecuted the believers.

There is a positive side to persecution. To persecute a person is to sow that he and his claims are taken seriously. Persecution offers an opportunity to demonstrate loyalty. To endure persecution is to walk with the saints, the prophets, and the martyrs. To suffer for Christ means that we will also reign with Him (2 Tim. 2:12). For this reason we can rejoice in persecution.

---

1. What does it mean to be "persecuted for righteousness' sake" (v. 10)?
2. In verse 11, how does Jesus describe the opposition Christians can expect?
3. Describe ways prophets in Bible times were persecuted.

"If we suffer persecution and affliction in a right manner, we attain a larger measure of conformity to Christ, by a due improvement of one of these occasions, than we could have done merely by imitating His mercy, in abundance of good works."—John Wesley

---

II. BE TRUE KINGDOM CITIZENS (Matt. 5:13-16)

A. The Salt of the Earth (v. 13)

¹³ Ye are the salt of the earth: but if the salt have lost his savour, wherewith shall it be salted? it is thenceforth good for nothing, but to be cast out, and to be trodden under foot of men.

When Jesus said that believers are "the salt of the earth," He meant that we are to influence our world in a positive way. The various uses of salt illustrate how we are to be effective. For instance, *salt preserves*. This quality was of special importance in Jesus' day. The tropical climate, without cooling systems, made salt essential to keep things from spoiling. In a world that is bad and getting worse, there is a need for believers to allow God to work through them in a preserving way. This calls for Christians to be Christians at work, in politics, at home, and everywhere else. This work of preservation is desperately needed. Also, *salt provides flavor*. Others need to see the life of God in us. They need to perceive us as a people who possess within us the Spirit of the living God. Finally, *salt makes one thirsty*. Do we make anyone thirsty for Jesus Christ? Do we give such evidence of peace and joy that others say, "That's what I want to be like"?

The down side of this verse is that if the salt has lost its strength, it is worthless. Have we been guilty of losing our spiritual strength?

• How can a believer "become tasteless" (see v. 13)?

"We are the salt of the earth, mind you, not the sugar. Our ministry is to truly cleanse and not just to change the taste."—Vance Havner

---

B. The Light of the World (vv. 14-16)

(Matthew 5:15 is not included in the printed text.)

**¹⁴ Ye are the light of the world. A city that is set on an hill cannot be hid.
¹⁶ Let your light so shine before men, that they may see your good works, and glorify your Father which is in heaven.**

Are we living such a radiant life that it causes others to ask, "Why are you the way you are?"

Is the manifestation of God at work in the painful, practical, personal areas of life so obvious that all can see? Are we living and letting the light of our life shine? Are we living in such a way that others are pressing us for the key to our life? If not, are we really alive?

Believers are to be like the beacon in a lighthouse that points the ships toward the harbor. We are to be a beacon who points the way to God. We do not point to ourselves.

B. F. Westcott wrote: "We lose the light if we do not follow Christ, and move as He moves. . . . But the Light, which lightens because it lives . . . , burns on with changeless splendor. And this only is required of us if we would know its quickening, cheering, warming energies, that we should follow it." Let us walk in the light that we may bring glory to our heavenly Father.

---

1. Is your church shining like "a city that is set on a hill" (v. 14 NKJV)?
2. How is your life shining as a "light . . . before men" (v. 16)?

"We should not ask, 'What is wrong with the world?' for that diagnosis has already been given. Rather, we should ask, 'What has happened to the salt and light?'"—John Stott

---

III. PURSUE TRUE RIGHTEOUSNESS (Matt. 5:17-24, 27-30, 43-45, 48)

A. The Law (vv. 17-20)

(Matthew 5:17-19 is not included in the printed text.)

²⁰ For I say unto you, That except your righteousness shall exceed the righteousness of the scribes and Pharisees, ye shall in no case enter into the kingdom of heaven.

Since Jesus opposed the traditions of the Pharisees, there was the danger that His disciples might conclude that He intended to abolish the Old Testament. He wanted them to understand that His mission was not to destroy but to fulfill. The Law and the Prophets (v. 17) refer to the entire Old Testament, and Jesus has come to fulfill them completely. When His Word is done, the whole Old Testament will be fulfilled.

Jesus' fulfillment would extend to the smallest Hebrew letter—the "jot," and even the "tittle" (v. 18). In English, "a *jot* would correspond to the dot above the letter 'i' (and look like an apostrophe), and a *tittle* would be seen in the difference between a 'P' and an 'R.' The small angled line that completes the 'R' is like a tittle. These things are important because letters make up words, and even a slight change in a letter might change the meaning of a word" (*The Bible Knowledge Commentary*).

Further, Jesus taught that anyone who made the Old Testament teaching invalid by a vicious system of misinterpretation, and taught others to do the same, would be relegated to a degrading position in the kingdom of heaven. On the other hand, those who exalt the authority and honor of God's law shall be esteemed great in the kingdom of heaven (v. 19).

What did Jesus mean when He said that the righteousness of His disciples was to surpass that of the scribes and Pharisees (v. 20)? Did He mean that the disciples were to observe the ceremonies and rituals of the Law more earnestly than they? Were they merely to work harder at keeping the Law?

The commitment of the scribes and Pharisees was to the observance of external rules without an accompanying change of heart. Entrance into the kingdom of heaven, however, is not dependent merely on observing external rules, but rather on finding true inner righteousness through faith in God's Word (see Rom. 3:21-22). This is what Jesus was telling Nicodemus: "Except a man be born of water and of the Spirit, he cannot enter into the kingdom of God" (John 3:5). Our righteousness, then, must be inward, vital, and spiritual to surpass that of the scribes and Pharisees.

---

1. How did Jesus describe His relationship with the Old Testament law (vv. 17-18)?
2. Who will be "called great in the kingdom of heaven" (v. 19), and why?
3. Describe pharisaical righteousness (v. 20).

"No man taketh away sins (which the law, though holy, just and good, could not take away), but He in whom there is no sin."—Venerable Bede

B. The Heart (vv. 21-24)

²¹ Ye have heard that it was said by them of old time, Thou shalt not kill; and whosoever shall kill shall be in danger of the judgment: ²² But I say unto you, That whosoever is angry with his brother without a cause shall be in danger of the judgment: and whosoever shall say to his brother, Raca, shall be in danger of the council: but whosoever shall say, Thou fool, shall be in danger of hell fire. ²³ Therefore if thou bring thy gift to the altar, and there rememberest that thy brother hath ought against thee; ²⁴ Leave there thy gift before the altar, and go thy way; first be reconciled to thy brother, and then come and offer thy gift.

Six times Jesus said, "Ye have heard that it was said. . . . But I say unto you" (vv. 21-22, 27-28, 31-34, 38-39, 43-44). In each instance, what Jesus says is vastly different from what the scribes and Pharisees taught. He shows what Moses really meant in contrast to the way his words had been interpreted.

In this passage, Jesus dealt with the sixth commandment (Ex. 20:13). He sought to show that this is more than a civil law for a civil court to administer. It has rather to do with the heart.

While the Pharisees viewed murder as taking someone's life, Jesus taught that the internal attitude behind the act was involved as well. Anger, and its most common manifestation of calling ugly names, is also sin. John wrote, "Whosoever hateth his brother is a murderer: and ye know that no murderer hath eternal life abiding in him" (1 John 3:15).

Jesus said the destiny of all such sinners is hell. Sin is a violation against God and will be judged in His court, not in some civil court. Who but God could sentence anyone to hell? No civil court could do that!

In Matthew 5:23-24, Jesus illustrates the proper conduct of a believer toward others where reconciliation is needed, whether the believer is the innocent party or the offending party. The settling for the account is a public worship service after the Old Testament order. The believer brings his offering to the altar and, as he prepares to worship God, he remembers that his brother has something against him. It may be something he did or did not do, something he said or did not say. He knows in his heart that he has done his brother wrong, whether or not his brother holds it against him, and he must make it right.

---

1. In verses 21 and 22, what does Jesus teach about the heart?
2. How does our relationship with others impact our relationship with God (vv. 23-24)?

"Holiness of heart and life. This is not the perfection of the human nature, but the holiness of the divine nature dwelling within."—A. B. Simpson

---

C. Sexual Purity (vv. 27-30)

(Matthew 5:27, 29-30 is not included in the printed text.)

²⁸ But I say unto you, That whosoever looketh on a woman to lust after her hath committed adultery with her already in his heart.

The treatment given to the sixth commandment Jesus now gives to the seventh. The Pharisees interpreted this commandment only in terms of the outward act. Jesus said that adultery begins in the heart and is followed by the act. "The man who casts lustful looks," Richard C. H. Lenski wrote, "is an adulterer to begin with. The *sin* is already 'in his heart' and only comes out in his lustful look. If the heart were pure, without adultery, no lustful look would be possible. . . . The man's very heart and nature must be so changed by divine grace that lustful looks will become impossible for him."

What is said of a man in this passage may also be said of a woman. And what applies to a married man also applies to an unmarried man.

Jesus underscores the fact that the lust problem is a heart problem. He addresses the idea that the problem is in the eye or the hand or the foot (Matt. 5:29-30; see also 18:8-9). If that is where the problem is, He declares, then get rid of that part of the body. If some part of the body is so diseased with sin as to sink one into hell, then pluck it out or have it amputated. That is a small price to pay to save you from hell.

But where does the amputation end? If the right eye looks lustfully and is plucked out, what about the left eye? Is it not capable of sin as well? Is this not also true of the left hand and the left foot? If sin is in the members of the body, will not the whole body be mutilated eventually?

Is not Jesus seeking to teach that the seat of lust and sin is in the heart? His call is for a pure heart which keeps even the eyes pure. Such a pure heart is the result of regeneration and sanctifying grace alone. When a new heart is created in us, it will take care of any eye problem or hand problem or any other problem.

---

1. Describe adultery of the heart (vv. 27-28).
2. Explain Jesus' teaching about the eye and hand (vv. 29-30).

"God made everyone of us a sexual being, and that is good. Attraction and arousal are the natural, spontaneous, God-given responses to physical beauty, while lust is a deliberate act of the will."—Rick Warren

---

D. Christlike Love (vv. 43-45, 48)

43 Ye have heard that it hath been said, Thou shalt love thy neighbour, and hate thine enemy. 44 But I say unto you, Love your enemies, bless them that curse you, do good to them that hate you, and pray for them which despitefully use you, and persecute you; 45 That ye may be the children of your Father which is in heaven: for he maketh his sun to rise on the evil and on the good, and sendeth rain on the just and on the unjust.

48 Be ye therefore perfect, even as your Father which is in heaven is perfect.

The Pharisees took the teaching of Leviticus 19:18—"Thou shalt love thy neighbour as thyself"—and added the thought that you shall hate your enemies (Matt. 5:43). They ignored the portion of the verse that admonished not to avenge or hold a grudge. They interpreted their "neighbor" to be their fellow Israelites. All others were regarded as their enemies and were subject to their hatred.

Now Jesus tells them that this is a flagrant perversion of what Moses meant. Jesus' message is that we are to love our enemies (v. 44). In spite of their wickedness and hatefulness, they are to be loved. Even if they are actively persecuting us, we are to love them. Jesus is our best example. Even on Calvary, He prayed for His executioners. Likewise, we should pray that the grace of God will reach our enemies, convict them of their sins, and bring them to repentance and pardon.

We should not forget that God causes His sun to rise on all people, and He sends rain to produce their crops: to the evil and the good, the righteous and the unrighteous. Since His love reaches out to all, so should we love all people. In doing so, we are demonstrating that we are children of God (v. 45).

In contrast to the murder, lust, hate, deception, and retaliation condemned by our Lord, believers are to be "perfect," like their Father (v. 48). We are to make God our model and follow Him in spirit and in truth. We are to be completely devoted to the will of God as revealed in His Word. As we put our trust in Him, He reproduces His righteousness in us. His greatest saints are found among the common believers who respond to His grace and strive to live by His standards.

---

1. Whom does Jesus describe as the believer's "enemy"? How should that person be treated (vv. 43-44)?
2. Explain Jesus' statement about the sun and rain (v. 45).

"Through the death of Christ on the cross making atonement for sin, we get a perfect standing before God. That is justification, and it puts us, in God's sight, back in Eden before sin entered. God looks upon us and treats us as if we had never sinned."—A. C. Dixon

---

CONCLUSION

Carl Bates, respected pastor and seminary professor, once wrote about an experience of Michelangelo as related by a tour guide. The great artist was explaining his current work to a visitor. He pointed out how he had retouched one part, softened a certain feature, given more expression to a muscle, and more energy to a limb. The visitor commented that those things seemed to be mere trifles. The master replied that trifles made perfection, and perfection was no trifle.

Striving for Godlikeness brings tension into Christians' lives, but it is a tension that is needful and productive. Perhaps, as Michelangelo indicated, growing into what God wants us to be does not come by large leaps but by careful attention to the seemingly trivial activities and responsibilities of life.—**From Illustrating the Gospel of Matthew, by James E. Hightower Jr.**

GOLDEN TEXT CHALLENGE

"BLESSED ARE THE POOR IN SPIRIT: FOR THEIR'S IS THE KINGDOM OF HEAVEN" (Matt. 5:3).

The word *blessed* denotes happiness in terms of moral quality in contrast to the pagan idea of good luck or outward prosperity. Back of this word is the recognition of sin as the source of all human misery, and of holiness of heart as the one effectual cure for human woes. But this blessedness is conditioned upon a certain attitude of heart: "the poor in spirit." The same word *poor* is used in Luke 16:20, 22 of the beggar Lazarus. This word in a temporal sphere implies a daily bread. It signifies destitution, literally, "to crouch under, to cover." Translate this into spiritual terms and you have a heart attitude that qualifies one to enter "the kingdom of heaven," for the reign of God in heart and life.

Daily Devotions:
M. Characteristics of the Righteous
   Psalm 1:1-6
T. Benefits of Righteousness
   Psalm 34:11-22
W. Witnesses of God
   Isaiah 43:8-13
T. More Blessed to Give
   Acts 20:33-35
F. Live as a Kingdom Citizen
   Ephesians 5:3-10
S. Run From Evil; Pursue Righteousness
   2 Timothy 2:20-26

Practices for Kingdom Living

Matthew 6:1-34

Unit Theme:
Discourses in Matthew

Central Truth:
Kingdom living requires making choices that honor and please God.

Focus:
Identify and adopt practices that shape the lifestyle of Kingdom citizens.

Context:
Near Capernaum, Jesus teaches form a high hill or mountain in AD 28.

Golden Text:
"Seek ye first the kingdom of God, and his righteousness; and all these things shall be added unto you" (Matt. 6:33).

Study Outline:
I. Choose God's Rewards
   (Matt. 6:1-8, 16-18)
II. Live Free From Materialism
   (Matt. 6:19-24)
III. Give God's Kingdom Priority
   (Matt. 6:25-34)

INTRODUCTION

In the previous chapter, Jesus dealt with the Law and the false teachings which the Pharisees had added to it. In this chapter, He deals with a holier-than-thou attitude toward certain religious practices. Three perfectly legitimate practices—almsgiving, prayer, and fasting—were reduced to hypocritical exercises by many. Although they were encouraged by Old Testament example (see Deut. 26:12-15), there were no guidelines about their practice in ordinary and daily life. Since these were matters of custom and tradition, the Law did not directly address them. The scribes and Pharisees, therefore, added instructions which sometimes resulted in acting out of the wrong motives.

Hypocrisy is a form of deception. In Matthew 6:1-8, Jesus speaks of deceiving others. In verses 19-34, He turns His attention to self-deception. We deceive ourselves, He says, when we seek perishable items instead of the imperishable. We deceive ourselves when we think that life consists only of what we eat, what we drink, and what we wear. We deceive ourselves when we concern ourselves with those things that people outside of Christ seek, and neglect the things of the Lord.

The cure for the problem of deception is to keep our eyes on God. He takes care of the birds of the air and the lilies of the field. He knows what we need before we ask Him; He asks only that we seek His kingdom and His righteousness, and He will add the other things that we need. The Lord is mightier than any difficulty we will face. Trusting Him, He will bring us through.

I. CHOOSE GOD'S REWARDS (Matt. 6:1-8, 16-18)

A. Righteous Acts (vv. 1-4)

¹ Take heed that ye do not your alms before men, to be seen of them: otherwise ye have no reward of your Father which is in heaven. ² Therefore when thou doest thine alms, do not sound a trumpet before thee, as the hypocrites do in the synagogues and in the streets, that they may have glory of men. Verily I say unto you, They have their reward. ³ But when thou doest alms, let not thy left hand know what thy right hand doeth: ⁴ That thine alms may be in secret: and thy Father which seeth in secret himself shall reward thee openly.

Jesus admonished His followers that their righteousness should surpass that of the scribes and Pharisees. The righteousness Jesus speaks of is not the imputed righteousness which we have from Him, but the acts of righteousness which we may do. Such acts spring from a regenerated heart and are done unto God and not as a display before people (v. 1).

This does not mean that our works are not to be seen of others. Jesus said we should let our light shine before the world (5:16). But these works are to glorify our Father who is in heaven. Even great and wonderful deeds done to impress people will not be rewarded in God's sight.

The word *therefore* (6:2) refers to the principle Jesus set forth in the previous verse. The specific act which must be governed by this principle is almsgiving, or acts of charity. The disciples of Jesus were not to follow the example of the Pharisees, who were known for advertising their deeds. They chose the public places—the synagogues and the streets—to show off their deeds of charity. Much of what they did was good and needed to be done, but they did it for the wrong reasons.

Jesus called them "hypocrites." *Hypocrisy* is to "willfully and continuously attempt to produce a false impression." It is the opposite of the attitude one should have in relation to a truth-loving God. Those who do their deeds to gain the applause of people may receive that applause—but that is all they will ever get.

When Jesus said that, in giving, one should not so much as let their left hand know what their right hand is doing (v. 3), He meant that it should be so secret that the giver readily forgets what he gave. In contrast to making a public display of his giving, the giver does not even dwell on it in his own thought, lest it should lead to spiritual pride. In doing this, he shows that his giving is before God and not before people.

---

1. How should your "charitable deeds" (NKJV) not be carried out (vv. 1-2)?
2. How is it possible to do charitable deeds "in secret," and what is the benefit (vv. 3-4)?

"Noble deeds that are concealed are most esteemed."—Blaise Pascal

B. Proper Prayer (vv. 5-8)

5 And when thou prayest, thou shalt not be as the hypocrites are: for they love to pray standing in the synagogues and in the corners of the streets, that they may be seen of men. Verily I say unto you, They have their reward. 6 But thou, when thou prayest, enter into thy closet, and when thou hast shut thy door, pray to thy Father which is in secret; and thy Father which seeth in secret shall reward thee openly. 7 But when ye pray, use not vain repetitions, as the heathen do: for they think that they shall be heard for their much speaking. 8 Be not ye therefore like unto them: for your Father knoweth what things ye have need of, before ye ask him.

Jesus warned His disciples to avoid the practice of the hypocrites in prayer. The hypocrites loved to pray while standing in public places. Their prayers were offered for the ears of people, not the ears of God. They hoped to impress others with their devotion and righteousness. That others were impressed constituted their reward (v. 5).

On the other hand, believers are encouraged to go into a room by themselves and fasten the door and pray to their Father privately (v. 6). Thus the worshiper is alone with God. Such private communion will aid believers in their participation in public prayer. Also, the Father will hear and answer openly their prayer offered in secret.

Jesus also cautioned against repeating empty phrases or the same words over and over again (v. 7). Some think that long prayers spoken with a lofty tone indicate true spirituality. Jesus denied that. He said that God knows our needs even before we ask (v. 8). It is not necessary to inform Him of every detail, for He is omniscient. Yet He does encourage us to pray to Him, draw near Him, and stay near to Him—indeed, to talk and walk with Him.

---

1. How do hypocrites pray, and why (v. 5)?
2. From verses 6-8, list three principles of effective praying.

"Prayer is not so much an act as it is an attitude—an attitude of dependency, dependency upon God."—A. W. Pink

---

C. Fasting Guidelines (vv. 16-18)

16 Moreover when ye fast, be not, as the hypocrites, of a sad countenance: for they disfigure their faces, that they may appear unto men to fast. Verily I say unto you, They have their reward. 17 But thou, when thou fastest, anoint thine head, and wash thy face; 18 That thou appear not unto men to fast, but unto thy Father which is in secret: and thy Father, which seeth in secret, shall reward thee openly.

Fasting, which usually means total abstinence from food, frequently accompanied the practice of prayer in Bible times. It was practiced in times of mourning, as a sign of repentance, and as a kind of reinforcement for urgent supplication. At certain times, prophets called an entire nation to a solemn fast (see Joel 2:12, 15). Devout Pharisees fasted twice a week (see Luke 18:12). The disciples of

John the Baptist engaged in fasting (Mark 2:18). Inasmuch as Jesus gave His followers instructions about fasting, we may conclude that He assumed they would fast, just as He assumed they would pray.

The fasting Jesus addressed was to be of a private and voluntary nature and was to be regulated by each individual. But the Pharisees practiced private fasting as a means to secure the reputation of holiness among the people. To make sure people were aware they were fasting, they disfigured their faces with ashes and maintained a gloomy countenance. This recognition by men was all the reward they would ever get.

In contrast to the open display of the hypocrites in fasting, Jesus instructed His followers to give no external sign of fasting. They were to dress and appear as usual, thereby attracting no notice to themselves. Christ's teaching that they were to anoint their head indicates that instead of appearing sad, they were to maintain a countenance of joy and gladness.

"What really makes a treasure valuable," Richard C. H. Lenski wrote, "is the affection of the heart. He whose treasures are on the earth has his heart anchored to the earth; he whose treasures are in heaven has his heart anchored there. The earth and all its treasures must pass away; what, then, about the heart that loses all its treasures? Heaven alone abides forever; the heart whose treasures are there will never lose them." Where is your treasure—on earth or in heaven?

---

1. Why do hypocrites fast (v. 16)?
2. Describe effective fasting (vv. 17-18).

"When we fast, we slow down to move forward."—Billy Wilson

II. LIVE FREE FROM MATERIALISM (Matt. 6:19-24)

A. Treasures in Heaven (vv. 19-21)

[19] Lay not up for yourselves treasures upon earth, where moth and rust doth corrupt, and where thieves break through and steal: [20] But lay up for yourselves treasures in heaven, where neither moth nor rust doth corrupt, and where thieves do not break through nor steal: [21] For where your treasure is, there will your heart be also.

Earthly treasures are subject to destructive forces. In the Middle East, treasures often took the form of costly dresses and other fine garments. These items were liable to be consumed or at least damaged by moths. Other treasures might rust away. The thought here is of any power that eats, corrodes, or wastes. Then, treasures could be lost by thieves digging through the houses made of mud or sunburned bricks and carrying the goods off. James comments on this subject in his book (5:1-6).

Treasures that are laid up in heaven are unassailable and imperishable. In Luke 12:33, Jesus said, "Sell that ye have, and give alms; provide yourselves bags which wax not old, a treasure in the heavens that faileth not, where no thief approacheth, neither moth corrupteth." Paul commented, "Set your affection on things above, not on things on the earth" (Col. 3:2).

---

1. Contrast earthly treasure with heavenly treasure (vv. 19-20).
2. Where is your treasure (v. 21)?

"He who lays up treasures on earth spends his life backing away from his treasures. To him, death is loss. He who lays up treasures in heaven looks forward to eternity; he's moving daily toward his treasures. To him, death is gain. He who spends his life moving toward his treasures has reason to rejoice. Are you despairing or rejoicing?"—Randy Alcorn

---

B. Full of Light (vv. 22-23)

²² The light of the body is the eye: if therefore thine eye be single, thy whole body shall be full of light. ²³ But if thine eye be evil, thy whole body shall be full of darkness. If therefore the light that is in thee be darkness, how great is that darkness!

The eye is the one member of the body that acts as a lamp by which a person sees. Our perspective, then, depends on the spiritual quality of the eye. If the eye gazes constantly on the things of the world, the soul will tend to respond to those things. If, on the other hand, the eye is fixed on heavenly things, the soul will move toward those things. Therefore, Jesus urged His disciples to find the proper objective and, with singleness of purpose, to pursue it.

Solomon said: "Let thine eyes look right on, and let thine eyelids look straight before thee. Ponder the path of thy feet, and let all thy ways be established. Turn not to the right hand nor to the left: remove thy foot from evil" (Prov. 4:25-27).

When the eye is sound and the object is clear, the path is easy to follow. Likewise, when one resolves to serve and please God in everything, his or her whole character and conduct will give evidence of it. The Lord is looking for that kind of simple and persistent purpose.

On the other hand, if the eye is "evil" (Matt. 6:23)—wicked and godless—the entire body will be full of darkness. When that is the case, the individual puts everything ahead of God and His kingdom. In such darkness, the soul perceives nothing as it is but is deceived into thinking that earthly treasures are more important than heavenly treasures.

Our inward purpose—our scope, our aim in life—determines our character. If that light within us has become darkness, distorting our perspective, what kind of direction will our life take? What kind of character will we develop? How terrible is the nature and effects of that darkness? The total absence of light leaves room only for sin and evil—nothing positive, only negative.

• Where should our focus be, and where should it not be?

"There is a road from the eye to the heart that does not go through the intellect."—G. K. Chesterton

---

C. Two Masters (v. 24)

24 No man can serve two masters: for either he will hate the one, and love the other; or else he will hold to the one, and despise the other. Ye cannot serve God and mammon.

It is in the nature of slavery that a slave's being and his work belong wholly to his master. It is in the nature of humanity that no person is his own master: "It is ingrained in our very nature that our heart, will, and work be governed by another. The only question is who this other shall be" (Lenski). The choice in this verse is God or money.

"What you own, owns you" is a slogan once used by a large insurance company in its advertising campaign. Ours is among the most materialistic cultures the world has ever known. Many appear to have more faith in their business, their trade union, their stocks and bonds, their property, or even the "American way" than they do in Christ. Even the poor are not free of this malady of materialism; for those who have it want to keep it, and those who don't want to get it.

We could learn a great deal from a colonial Quaker Christian, John Woodman. Woodman was a successful merchant, but he operated his business each year only long enough to accumulate enough money to care for his family's needs for the year. The rest of the time he gave to the service of the Lord, traveling about the young nation at his own expense to share the good news (Raymond H. Bailey). (*Illustrating the Gospel of Matthew*, by James E. Hightower Jr.)

• What happens to the person who tries to "serve two masters"?

"Good conscience is sometimes sold for money, but never bought with it."—Jack Hyles

---

III. GIVE GOD'S KINGDOM PRIORITY (Matt. 6:25-34)

A. Anxious for Nothing (vv. 25-29)

25 Therefore I say unto you, Take no thought for your life, what ye shall eat, or what ye shall drink; nor yet for your body, what ye shall put on. Is not the life more than meat, and the body than raiment? 26 Behold the fowls of the air: for they sow not, neither do they reap, nor gather into barns; yet your heavenly Father feedeth them. Are ye not much better than they? 27 Which of you by taking thought can add one cubit unto his stature? 28 And why take ye thought for raiment? Consider the lilies of the field, how they grow; they toil not, neither do they spin: 29 And yet I say unto you, That even Solomon in all his glory was not arrayed like one of these.

If we set our mind upon spiritual things and become occupied with them, how will we care for the ordinary needs in life, such as food, clothing, and shelter? It seems that Jesus' disciples were worrying about these things. The concern about drink alludes to the hot climate of Palestine and to the lack of water in that region. Food and drink represent daily needs. Clothes last longer and are mentioned last. Will He who gave us our life and the body fail to give us the little food we need and the few garments we require? Where is our faith?

When Jesus said to "take no thought" (v. 25) about these things, He meant not to be anxiously concerned about them. He did not mean that we were to give no forethought or consideration to temporal things. We are to avoid anxiety and doubtful misgivings. Paul summed it up beautifully: "Be anxious for nothing, but in everything by prayer and supplication with thanksgiving let your requests be made known to God" (Phil. 4:6 NASB). Jesus called attention to the birds of the air (Matt. 6:26). They do not sow, reap, or gather food into barns, yet God takes care of them. We, He said, are much more valuable than they.

Most translators see verse 27 as referring to one's life span rather than to one's height. That interpretation is consistent with the context. The prolonging of life by the supply of its necessities of food and clothing is the subject being discussed. Jesus cautions that all the worry in the world cannot add so much as a step to the length of our life's journey. Worry does not lengthen life, it usually shortens life.

Jesus said it is needless and useless to worry about what we will wear, for the best we can make or purchase cannot compare to a single lily (v. 28). Someone said the lily is "the most gorgeously painted, the most conspicuous in spring, and the most universally spread of all the floral treasures of the Holy Land." So, Jesus said, there is something to be learned from the lily. It grows wild, without human care, without labor of any kind, and without spinning a thread. Yet the lilies come to wear garments so exquisite that they exceed all that Solomon at the height of his royal glory ever wore (v. 29). Dressed in a regal robe, Solomon did not compare in splendor with the lily of the field.

---

1. Explain the phrase "take no thought" (v. 25).
2. What does Jesus want us to learn from the birds and flowers (vv. 26, 28-29)?
3. Answer Jesus' question in verse 27.

"Worry does not empty tomorrow of its sorrow. It empties today of its strength."—Corrie ten Boom

---

B. 'Ye of Little Faith' (v. 30)

30 Wherefore, if God so clothe the grass of the field, which to day is, and to morrow is cast into the oven, shall he not much more clothe you, O ye of little faith?

As gorgeous as is the array of the flowers that deck the fields, they are only there for a short time. Then, they are cut and wither and are used for fuel. If God so beautifully dresses the grass which is green today but dry tomorrow, how much more likely is He to clothe His followers? They are of much greater worth to Him. His disciples should trust in His faithfulness.

On four different occasions in Matthew's Gospel, Jesus referred to His disciples as men of "little faith." The first reference was the occasion in this text. The second time was when He and His disciples were caught in a great tempest on the Sea of Galilee (8:26). Next, He used this term when Peter attempted to walk on the water and failed (14:31). Then, He used this expression when His disciples did not understand His warning to beware of the leaven of the Pharisees (16:8). In each instance, their lack of faith came under the pressure of earthly trials. It was His way of gently chiding them to shake off the spirit of unbelief and put their trust in Him.

- Why did Jesus call His listeners people of "little faith"?

"Faith is made up of belief and trust. Many people believe God, but they do not trust themselves into His keeping and care; consequently, they are filled with worry and fear."—Lee Roberson

C. The Father's Awareness (vv. 31-32)

31 Therefore take no thought, saying, What shall we eat? or, What shall we drink? or, Wherewithal shall we be clothed? 32 (For after all these things do the Gentiles seek:) for your heavenly Father knoweth that ye have need of all these things.

In verse 25, Jesus called on His disciples to stop worrying. In verse 31, He urges them not to worry at all. No matter what need may arise, including the three things He mentioned—food, drink, and raiment—nothing is ever to trouble our heart.

Worry is *irreverent*, wrote Myron S. Augsburger, for it fails to recognize the God who gave us life and is sustaining it. Worry in *irrelevant*—it does not change things, nor does it help us cope with problems. And worry is *irresponsible*—it burns up energy without using it to apply constructive action to our problem.

To worry about these things, and a thousand others, is to do as unbelievers do. They are unacquainted with proper dependence on divine Providence, and so their chief anxiety centers on life-sustaining objects. Believers, on the other hand, have a knowledge of the heavenly Father and know that He will provide tor their needs. Therefore, they have no cause to be anxious.

- How does God want us to think about our daily needs?

"Worry is the cross which we make for ourselves by overanxiety."—Francois Fenelon

D. The Kingdom of God (vv. 33-34)

33 But seek ye first the kingdom of God, and his righteousness; and all these things shall be added unto you. 34 Take therefore no thought

for the morrow: for the morrow shall take thought for the things of itself. Sufficient unto the day is the evil thereof.

While unbelievers are seeking things that pertain to this life, believers are to be seeking the kingdom of God. This quest for the Kingdom, described earlier as "hunger and thirst" (5:6), is the mark of all true disciples. It consists of a longing to enter ever more fully into union with God. It recognizes God's royal rule, which is a rule of grace leading to a rule of glory.

Believers are also to seek to be righteous and to obtain the favor of the Father. They are to bring themselves, by His grace, to personal conformity to God's standard of righteousness. Righteousness is the character trait of all those who are spiritually recovered from sin and are subjects of the King.

To seek first God's kingdom and His righteousness does not mean that believers are to seek nothing more. They do seek other things from the Father, but they seek in the right way—by humble and submissive prayer, without worry, and without a false estimate of these things. God has control over all things, and He can give us everything we need. He will give us what He deems best for us.

Verse 34 calls for a life of daily faith, a life committed to God, and a life in which there is no room for anxiety. It offers the same advice Paul gave in Philippians 4:6, when he said in effect, "Don't worry about anything, but pray about everything." This is the thought Peter had in mind when he wrote: "Casting all your care upon him; for he careth for you" (1 Peter 5:7).

Jesus also warns against borrowing trouble from the future. Every day brings its own cares, and to anticipate is only to double them. It is not even certain that you will live to see another day. If you do, that day will bring its own troubles and needs. God will be the same Father then as He is today, and He will provide then, as He does now, the proper supply of your needs.

---

1. What does it mean to seek God's righteousness (v. 33)?
2. Why does Jesus say we should not worry about tomorrow (v. 34)?

"In all things seek to know God's will, and when known obey at any cost."—Jonathan Goforth

---

CONCLUSION

Each day will have cares and anxieties of its own, but it will also bring the proper provisions for those cares. Although you have needs, God will provide for them as they occur. Do not, therefore, increase the cares of this day by borrowing trouble from the future. Do your duty faithfully now, and depend on the mercy of God and His divine help for the troubles which are yet to come. As you care each day for the things God has entrusted to you, your heavenly Father cares for your daily needs. God is faithful and will not fail to meet your needs.

GOLDEN TEXT CHALLENGE

"SEEK YE FIRST THE KINGDOM OF GOD, AND HIS RIGHTEOUSNESS; AND ALL THESE THINGS SHALL BE ADDED UNTO YOU" (Matt. 6:33).

What is the most valuable possession you have? Think about it. Be honest in your evaluation.

How much is physical life worth? What would you give to spare the life of your closest loved one?

What about the value of spiritual life? It lasts forever and therefore is of infinitely more value than anything in the physical.

The wise person makes provision to protect what is valuable to him or her. We put locks on our doors, have safe-deposit boxes, and invest in insurance policies to guard what we feel is important. In Matthew 6:33, Jesus is talking about how to persevere in the spiritual as well as the physical.

If we will prioritize Christ's kingdom and do things His way, the secondary matters will fall into place.

Daily Devotions:

M. Serve the Lord
   Deuteronomy 10:12-21
T. A Gift of God
   Ecclesiastes 5:13-20
W. True Fasting
   Isaiah 58:1-14
T. To Live Is Christ
   Philippians 1:20-26
F. Reward From the Lord
   Colossians 3:22-25
S. Godliness With Contentment Is Gain
   1 Timothy 6:6-10

Choose to Obey Christ's Teachings

Unit Theme:
Discourses in Matthew

Central Truth:
Basing our decisions on Christ's teachings results in a godly and secure lifestyle.

Focus:
Realize the importance of choices we make in life and base our decisions on God's Word.

Context:
Jesus' Sermon on the Mount in AD 28

Golden Text:
"Whosoever heareth these sayings of mine, and doeth them, I will liken him unto a wise man, which built his house upon a rock" (Matt. 7:24).

Study Outline:
I. Choose to View Others Wisely
   (Matt. 7:1-6)
II. Choose to Trust God
   (Matt. 7:7-12)
III. Choose to Follow Christ
   (Matt. 7:13-27)

INTRODUCTION

In this section of the Sermon on the Mount, Jesus employs a teaching method that was common in Judaism and Greco-Roman philosophy. It is the "two-ways method." Thus, He speaks of the two ways (vv. 13-14), two trees (vv. 15-20), two professions (vv. 21-23), and two builders (vv. 24-29).

In the previous verses, Jesus deals with two negatives that show who we are: We will not judge (vv. 1-5), and we will not give what is holy to dogs (v. 6). He also deals with two positives: We will ask with trust (vv. 7-11), and we will do unto others what we would have them do unto us (v. 12). In the remainder of the chapter, He presents a positive plus a negative: We will enter the narrow gate and will keep away from the broad gate, and so forth.

To follow the principles set forth by Jesus may involve a separation from the majority (vv. 13-14). Many people will claim to know and reveal the Lord's mind, but their true nature will be made known by their actions (vv. 15-20). Those who practice lawlessness have neither present nor future union with Christ (vv. 21-23). Those who build on a weak and wrong foundation are solemnly warned of the inevitable consequences (vv. 24-27).

At every turn in this passage, we are faced with a decision: Will we follow the path of ease and self-indulgence which will end in ruin? Or, will we take the way that leads to eternal safety no matter the cost? Each of us must decide for ourself. Therefore, each of us bears personal responsibility for the course and consequence of our life.

I. CHOOSE TO VIEW OTHERS WISELY (Matt. 7:1-6)

A. The Seriousness of Unjust Judgment (vv. 1-2)

¹ Judge not, that ye be not judged. ² For with what judgment ye judge, ye shall be judged: and with what measure ye mete, it shall be measured to you again.

The present negative imperative "judge not" (v. 1) must be limited to that rash, thoughtless, censorious, unjust, and self-righteous judgment of others, which can only harm. It is that arrogant condemnation or condemning spirit which delights to criticize and find fault in others.

There is legitimate judgment, as expressed by Jesus' own words: "Judge not according to the appearance, but judge righteous judgment" (John 7:24). The judgment by magistrates in court, the disciplinary judgment in the church family (1 Cor. 5:3, 12-13), and the forming of an opinion regarding the conduct of others is not here prohibited. Judgment here is an unkind, critical, fault-finding spirit and gossip. We have no right, personally, to condemn others, lest we become victims of similar censure by them, or perhaps the retributive judgment of God.

The reason for the Lord's warning in Matthew 7:1 is stated in a general principle in verse 2. It was probably a proverb among the Jews, but it expressed a truth that Jesus Christ adapted to teach His audience. As to quality, the unfair critic will be judged on like basis—perhaps from other people; or, in due time, they may receive chastisement from the righteous and divine Judge. As to quantity, the one who sets up his own standard of judging others will himself be judged by the same rule. "Therefore thou art inexcusable, O man, whosoever thou art that judgest: for wherein thou judgest another, thou condemnest thyself; for thou that judgest doest the same things" (Rom. 2:1).

• What rule of judgment does Christ explain?

"Yes, let God be the Judge. Your job today is to be a witness."—Warren Wiersbe

---

B. A Beam and a Mote (vv. 3-5)

³ And why beholdest thou the mote that is in thy brother's eye, but considerest not the beam that is in thine own eye? ⁴ Or how wilt thou say to thy brother, Let me pull out the mote out of thine eye; and, behold, a beam is in thine own eye? ⁵ Thou hypocrite, first cast out the beam out of thine own eye; and then shalt thou see clearly to cast out the mote out of thy brother's eye.

It is insincere to criticize others without self-judgment. The symbolism is intentional exaggeration, designed to emphasize the force of the teaching. The "mote," or speck, is of the same material as the "beam." The man with the great beam in his eye has an obstruction to sight that hinders him from seeing anything accurately. Yet, he proposes to remove the little splinter from his brother's eye— a delicate operation requiring clear sight.

Choose to Obey Christ's Teachings

The Pharisaic sin of hypocrisy was more serious and more dangerous to spiritual life than the sins which the Pharisees condemned in others. Yet, like them, we are often quicker to judge the small offences in others than we are the much larger offences in ourselves. "When men look for motes, the passion that makes them do so is a beam, more guilty in the sight of heaven than the mote for which they look" (G. C. Morgan). But it is as impossible for us to correct the faults of others without self-judgment as it is for the blind to attempt to lead the blind.

Verse 5 clearly states it is imperative to judge self before attempting to correct others. There will then be no hypocrisy in our conduct, and we will not be so quick to look for the faults in others. Self-judgment, in the light of the Word of God and the convicting influence of the Holy Spirit, will make us candid and consistent in our judgment of others, and will "enable us to see things as they are, and to make proper allowances for frailty and imperfections" (Albert Barnes).

Note the change of emphasis from the teaching in verses 3 and 4. After self-judgment, the onetime judge will see clearly, not the mote or fault, per se, but rather how to remove it.

• What is easy to see, and what is hard to see? Why?

"Hypocrisy can plunge the mind of a man into a dark abyss when he believes his own self-flattery instead of God's verdict."—John Calvin

C. Pearls and Swine (v. 6)

⁶ Give not that which is holy unto the dogs, neither cast ye your pearls before swine, lest they trample them under their feet, and turn again and rend you.

Judicious discrimination is exhorted by the Lord. This discrimination concerns the nature of those who hear the truth, and the nature of the truth itself. It is a warning against careless preaching of the Word of God, for His Word is "holy." "Dogs" refers to individuals who spurn, oppose, abuse, and proudly reject the sacred doctrines of spiritual truth.

The second metaphor is a picture of a rich person recklessly casting costly pearls to half-tamed and unclean hogs. "Pearls" illustrate the costliness of spiritual truth. The message of salvation and sanctification in God's Word is free, but to God it is costly and precious, and must be dispensed with discrimination and wisdom.

As swine can have no appreciation for costly pearls, but are only irritated to trample upon them and sometimes attack the giver, so there are individuals who will resolutely set themselves against the things of God and trample them in the mire of profanity, obscenity, unbelief, and mockery. Similar warnings are found in Proverbs 9:7-8; 23:9. Recall the warning of the apostle Paul: "Beware of dogs, beware of evil workers, beware of the concision" (Phil. 3:2). And Peter, speaking of false teachers, applied a proverb: "The dog is turned to his own vomit again; and the sow that was washed to her wallowing in the mire" (2 Peter 2:22).

- Explain Jesus' warning.

_____

"Don't be flip with the sacred."—Eugene Peterson

_____

II. CHOOSE TO TRUST GOD (Matt. 7:7-12)
A. Praying With Persistency (vv. 7-8)

⁷ Ask, and it shall be given you; seek, and ye shall find; knock, and it shall be opened unto you: ⁸ For every one that asketh receiveth; and he that seeketh findeth; and to him that knocketh it shall be opened.

In verses 7 to 11, the Lord exhorts His disciples to pray and thus seek the divine answer to their common needs. The difficulties raised in the foregoing context—the seriousness of fault-finding and the importance of judicial discrimination—are met by the divine resources in prayer.

Here the Lord employs a triple formula for effective praying, followed by a triple assurance that an answer to the requests made will be forthcoming. "Ask" is simply to beg in dependence on God to whom we are directing our prayer. We *ask* for what we *wish*, and God will give what is best for us. Further explanation for effective praying is given in James 1:5-7 and 4:3.

The command "seek" marks anxiety and urgency with great desire. We *seek* for what we *miss*, and discovery is assured. God said, "Then shall ye call upon me, and ye shall go and pray unto me, and I will hearken unto you. And ye shall seek me, and find me, when ye shall search for me with all your heart" (Jer. 29:12-13; cf. Isa. 55:6).

"Knock" indicates persistency in prayer. We *knock* for that from which we feel ourselves *shut out*. Again we have the assurance of heaven's response.

_____

- What is the difference between asking, seeking, and knocking? How are they the same?

_____

"It is hard to wait and press and pray, and hear no voice, but stay till God answers."—E. M. Bounds

_____

B. Praying With Confidence (vv. 9-11)

⁹ Or what man is there of you, whom if his son ask bread, will he give him a stone? ¹⁰ Or if he ask a fish, will he give him a serpent? ¹¹ If ye then, being evil, know how to give good gifts unto your children, how much more shall your Father which is in heaven give good things to them that ask him?

Speaking directly to His hearers in the form of questions, Jesus employs illustrations from human nature to show how we can pray with confidence in the goodness of God. As human father will not always give the very thing for which a child asks, but that which he, as a mature and loving parent, thinks will be the best for his child.

The goodness of fatherhood will not mock a child, but will recognize a child's dependence and bestow according to his needs. It would be an incredible action, says the Lord, on the part of an earthly father to mock his child by handing him a stone instead of bread, or a serpent instead of a fish. If, then, we can trust the natural goodness of a parent, we can surely trust in the supernatural goodness of our heavenly Father.

God is not bound by the limitations of finite man. He is infinitely holy, for "God is light, and in him is no darkness at all" (1 John 1:5). The loving fatherhood of God must also be understood to transcend that of any human parent. Our spiritual relationship to Him assures us of His love, concern, and provision. We can, therefore, depend on the goodness of our heavenly Father to "give good things to them that ask him" (Matt. 7:11). These *good things* are primarily spiritual (Luke 11:13), but include also the material (Phil. 4:19).

---

1. What might an abusive earthly father do (vv. 9-10)?
2. What will the heavenly Father do (v. 11)?

"If you pray for bread and bring no basket to carry it, you prove the doubting spirit, which may be the only hindrance to the boon you ask."—D. L. Moody

---

C. Considering Personal Responsibility (v. 12)

12 Therefore all things whatsoever ye would that men should do to you, do ye even so to them: for this is the law and the prophets.

This is the so-called Golden Rule of the Christian faith. The maxim is somewhat similar to that of several other religions and philosophies, but with this general distinction: whereas the so-called golden rules of non-Christian religions are negative in form, the words of Jesus are positive. It is a summary of the preceding text which began at 5:17, as is confirmed by the subsequent clause: "for this is the law and the prophets." This connection is evident from the initial word "therefore," which emphasizes the connection between a right relationship to God and a right relationship to humanity.

The Golden Rule is the practical expression of Christian love, and is, therefore, an obligation for all who believe and love Jesus Christ. This obligation raises some questions: *What are my personal desires as a Christian? What are my responsibilities to others? How can I fulfill them? Am I the kind of person that I think others ought to be? Suppose everybody were like me in spirit . . . would this then be the kind of world that God could smile on?*

• What is taught in "the Law and the Prophets" (v. 12 NKJV)?

"The one who loves knows better than anyone else how to conduct himself, how to serve the one he loves. Love prescribes an answer in a given situation as no mere rule can do."—Elisabeth Elliott

III. CHOOSE TO FOLLOW CHRIST (Matt. 7:13-27)

A. The Two Ways (vv. 13-14)

¹³ Enter ye in at the strait gate: for wide is the gate, and broad is the way, that leadeth to destruction, and many there be which go in thereat: ¹⁴ Because strait is the gate, and narrow is the way, which leadeth unto life, and few there be that find it.

Every person faces two portals in life. One is wide; the other is narrow. The wide gate opens to a broad way; the narrow gate opens to a narrow way. The wide gate may be entered with any baggage one cares to carry. Sins, self-righteousness, false notions, vices, follies—all will pass through this portal easily.

The Bible makes a clear distinction of destiny between those who enter the narrow gate and those who enter the broad gate. Those destinies are graphically described in Jeremiah 21:8: "And unto this people thou shalt say, Thus saith the Lord; Behold, I set before you the way of life, and the way of death" (see also 1 Cor. 1:18).

Entrance through the narrow gate leads to life. This gate must be approached with contrition and faith. This passageway is bounded on either side by the principles of Christianity. The life this entrance offers begins in regeneration, and culminates in a blessed and eternal existence in heaven.

The narrow gate is not as obvious as the wide gate. We do not just drift into it—we have to find it. We do not find it by our own searching; we are brought to it by the marvelous grace of our God. His great grace draws us by its attracting power. Jesus declared, "No man can come to me, except the Father which hath sent me draw him: and I will raise him up at the last day" (John 6:44).

Jesus said that only a few find the narrow gate; the majority enters the wide gate. This is another case where the majority is wrong.

-----

1. What is called "wide" and "broad," and why?
2. What is called "narrow" and "difficult" (NKJV), and why?

"The door to heaven is as narrow as Jesus."—Elmer Towns

B. Two Fruits (vv. 15-20)

(Matthew 7:17-19 is not included in the printed text.)

¹⁵ Beware of false prophets, which come to you in sheep's clothing, but inwardly they are ravening wolves. ¹⁶ Ye shall know them by their fruits. Do men gather grapes of thorns, or figs of thistles?
²⁰ Wherefore by their fruits ye shall know them.

In the Old Testament, the people of God were constantly subjected to the pernicious influence of false prophets. Moses warned the people that if any prophet arose who sought to draw them away from God, they were not to heed his message. Further, they were to put him to death (see Deut. 13:1-5). God gave Ezekiel (ch. 8) a vision of the abominations that the house of Israel committed at the hand of false prophets. In the house of God, he saw "every form of creeping things, and abominable beasts, and all the idols of the house of Israel, portrayed upon the wall" (v. 10). In response, God said that He would deal with them in fury. He would not spare them nor pity them. Even though they cried to Him, He would not hear them (vv. 17-18).

False prophets continued to pester God's people in New Testament days. Paul described them in this way: "For such are false apostles, deceitful workers, transforming themselves into the apostles of Christ" (2 Cor. 11:13). Jesus also warned of the presence of false prophets in the last days (Matt. 24:24).

False prophets are always deceitful. Verse 15 of the text says they wear sheep's clothing, but inwardly they are ravenous wolves. They make it their business to come to us, but they are never sent by God. They are as destructive as men who, with smooth and flattering speech, deceive the hearts of the unsuspecting (Rom. 16:18). They are as harmful as those who deceive with empty words (Eph. 5:6) and persuasive arguments (Col. 2:4).

Jesus said we are to recognize a false prophet by his fruits (Matt. 7:16). The fruits of the prophets have reference to their teaching. We cannot always tell by their works (see 24:24), but their teaching can be measured by the Word of God. Every prophet, true or false, appeals to the Word. Therefore, the prophet is judged as to his teaching by the Word to which he himself is constrained to appeal. If his teaching is true, we find grapes and figs—true spiritual food; if not, we will find briars and thistles—human wisdom.

---

1. How do false prophets try to fool people (v. 15)?
2. How do you recognize a false prophet (vv. 16-20)?
3. List some "good fruit" (v. 17) a genuine prophet will produce.

"Truth is so obscure in these times, and falsehood so established, that, unless we love the truth, we cannot know it."—Blaise Pascal

---

C. The Will of God (vv. 21-23)

(Matthew 7:22-23 is not included in the printed text.)

²¹ Not every one that saith unto me, Lord, Lord, shall enter into the kingdom of heaven; but he that doeth the will of my Father which is in heaven.

Not everyone who addresses Jesus as Lord will enter the kingdom of heaven. Some will because they have experienced the relationship to Jesus that this title expresses. In fact, Jesus expects His disciples to address Him in this fashion. When He washed their feet, He said, "Ye call me Master and Lord: and ye say well; for so I am" (John 13:13). The duplication of the title, "Lord, Lord," denotes zeal and is for the purpose of urgency in prayer and in worship. The objection Jesus registers is toward those who, using this title, claim a connection with Him that does not exist except in their imagination. Since there is no real relationship to Christ, there can be no entrance into the kingdom of heaven.

On the other hand, Jesus said that those who obey the heavenly Father, thus doing His will, will enter the kingdom of heaven. Doing the will of God shows that the relationship with Jesus is real. Doing the will of God begins with repentance and faith, and leads to works that please the Lord. Jesus Christ is the source of this new life (John 6:39-40). Those who have walked and worked to glorify Him benefit from His gracious, saving will (see v. 40).

A day of judgment is coming when all pretenders and false prophets will be tried. In that day, many will parade their works before the Lord as evidence that they belong to Him. Their approach to Him will be in that zealous double designation, "Lord, Lord" (Matt. 7:22). As they made His name prominent to give credibility to their earthly activities, then they will use His name to gain His favor.

These pretenders will mention that they prophesied in His name. Again, they clothed their pretense in the name and revelation of God. They proclaimed their false doctrines to be true and appealed to the Word for support. In so doing, they deceived many people. Also, they will say that they cast out demons and performed many miracles in Christ's name. In 24:24, these miracles are described as being so astonishing they would deceive, if it were possible, the very elect. This is further proof that the apparent miracle is not the criterion of a true prophet, but the Word is.

These false prophets will stand before Jesus, the Son of God, as their Judge in the last day. They have abused His name and His Word, now they must answer to Him. He will tell them that though they used His name, He never acknowledged them at any time. He orders them out of His sight and labels them practitioners of lawlessness.

---

1. Who will inherit heaven (v. 21)?
2. How can a person both perform "many wonderful works" (v. 22) and "work iniquity" (v. 23)?

"A clear conscience is absolutely essential for distinguishing between the voice of God and the voice of the enemy. Unconfessed sin is a prime reason why many do not know God's will."—Winkie Pratney

---

D. Wise or Foolish (vv. 24-27)

24 Therefore whosoever heareth these sayings of mine, and doeth them, I will liken him unto a wise man, which built his house upon a rock: 25 And the rain descended, and the floods came, and the winds blew, and beat upon that house; and it fell not: for it was founded upon a rock. 26 And every one that heareth these sayings of mine, and doeth them not, shall be likened unto a foolish man, which built his house upon the sand: 27 And the rain descended, and the floods came, and the winds blew, and beat upon that house; and it fell: and great was the fall of it.

Jesus concluded the Sermon on the Mount with a powerful illustration which called for a personal application of the truths He taught. They must not only hear what He says, but act on His words.

There is only one difference in the two men described in this parable. One acted on the words of Jesus, and one did not. Both heard the Word. Also, both built a house. And there is no indication that one house was less elaborate than the other. It is only that one built on rock, and the other on sand. The irony is that the folly of building on the sand may not be immediately apparent. As long as the sun is shining and the winds are calm, no danger appears. But when the tempest stirs, the house will crash and be swept away by the swirling floodwaters. Similarly, a life built on false teachings may not feel their damaging effects immediately. As long as things are going well, it may appear that one is on solid ground. But all of that changes when tests and trials and temptations storm in.

Can you picture the scene at the conclusion of Jesus' sermon? Throughout the message, every eye and every ear have been fixed on Him in undivided attention. They did not want to miss a single word. Perhaps now a hush fell over the audience. Maybe they expected something more from Him. When they realized that this mighty warning was His last word in this message, an amazement swept over the multitude. They were dumbfounded at what they had heard (v. 28).

Jesus' hearers were not accustomed to hearing anyone speak so clearly, and with such authority (v. 29). He spoke as One who was filled with authoritative power. His deity revealed itself in all that He said. The scribes had to rely on tradition for authority; Christ's authority was His own.

• What is the firm foundation we must build upon, and how can we do so?

"May I govern my passions with absolute sway, and grow wiser and better as life wears away."—Isaac Watts

---

CONCLUSION

Years ago, the federal government erected a multimillion-dollar courthouse in Philadelphia. The building was almost completed when inspectors noticed cracks in the brick facing the inner walls. Tests determined the building was beginning to tilt on its foundation. An extra $10 million was spent repairing the damage and providing adequate support for the building.

The foundation is crucial in construction and in life. The wise build "upon a rock," which will provide stability in the storm. The wise person will build on the sayings of Jesus and be obedient to His Word.—*Illustrating the Gospel of Matthew*, by James E. Hightower Jr.

GOLDEN TEXT CHALLENGE

"WHOSOEVER HEARETH THESE SAYINGS OF MINE, AND DOETH THEM, I WILL LIKEN HIM UNTO A WISE MAN, WHICH BUILT HIS HOUSE UPON A ROCK" (Matt. 7:24).

Being a follower of Christ is more than just professing obedience to Him. It requires action: *doing* the will of God. A personal relationship with Christ is the beginning of all good work.

Individuals may deceive other people with their profession of obedience. However, no one fools Christ. Under His eyes all disguises must drop off, and individuals will be known for what they really are. Everything we do, short of doing the will of God, is merely saying, "Lord, Lord!"

Putting the sayings of Christ into action is the *only* way to build a Christlike life. We must learn to do our Father's will here on earth so that one day we may enter into that blessed place where everyone does His will, lovingly and perfectly.

Daily Devotions:
M. Judge Fairly
   Leviticus 19:15-18
T. Choose Whom You Will Serve
   Joshua 24:14-24
W. Trust Wholeheartedly in the Lord
   Proverbs 3:5-10
T. Choose to Follow Jesus
   John 6:60-69
F. God Is for Us
   Romans 8:28-39
S. Why Judge Your Brother?
   Romans 14:1-12

Sent on a Mission

Matthew 10:1-42

Unit Theme:
Discourses in Matthew

Central Truth:
Christians are commissioned to proclaim the gospel.

Focus:
Examine Jesus' mission for the Twelve and confidently proclaim the kingdom of God.

Context:
Galilee in AD 28

Golden Text:
"As ye go, preach, saying, The kingdom of heaven is at hand" (Matt. 10:7).

Study Outline:
I.   Instructions for the Mission
     (Matt. 10:1-15)
II. Opposition to the Mission
     (Matt. 10:16-25)
III. Encouragement to Fulfill the Mission
     (Matt. 10:26-39)

INTRODUCTION

After resurrecting the daughter of Jairus (Matt. 9:23-26), Jesus was immediately followed by two blind men who pled with Him to have mercy on them. In response to their faith, Jesus healed their eyes (vv. 27-29). No sooner had these men left than others brought in a demon-possessed man whose tongue was paralyzed because of the presence of this demon. When the demon fetter was broken by its expulsion, the man was freed, his tongue was loosed, and he could speak normally (vv. 32-33).

While many people commented that no such miracle had ever been done in Israel, the Pharisees could see no good in it and resorted to the use of blasphemy to discredit Christ. They admitted that He cast out demons, but they said He did so as a representative of Satan with whom He was actually in union (v. 34).

Jesus was not about to be hindered by any Pharisaic opposition to His mission: He "went about all the cities and villages, teaching in their synagogues, and preaching the gospel of the kingdom, and healing every sickness and every disease among the people" (v. 35). The reason Jesus could not be hindered is given in verse 36—people were leaderless and uncared for, and Jesus "was moved with compassion on them."

Jesus then concludes chapter 9 with a charge to His disciples to pray for new workers to be sent into the fields since "the harvest truly is plenteous, but the labourers are few." In today's lesson, He sends out the Twelve into the harvest field.

I. INSTRUCTIONS FOR THE MISSION (Matt. 10:1-15)

A. Empowered by Christ (vv. 1-4)

(Matthew 10:2-4 is not included in the printed text.)

¹ And when he had called unto him his twelve disciples, he gave them power against unclean spirits, to cast them out, and to heal all manner of sickness and all manner of disease.

The twelve disciples had already been selected by Jesus (see 5:1). Matthew introduced us to five of their number earlier (4:18-22; 9:9). Jesus' purpose here, then, is to call them out from among the crowds following Him in order to assign them a special mission. They were to go into towns where later He himself would go, and this forerunning mission would help to train them for their future ministry. There is no better training in the work of witnessing and ministering than that gained by actual experience.

From the last half of 10:1, we can see that the disciples were to work miracles on a grand scale. Jesus delegated to them the power to cast out unclean spirits and to heal all kinds of disease. Prior to this time, the disciples had been traveling with Jesus and receiving instruction from Him (Mark 3:14). Adam Clarke notes, "Those who were Christ's apostles were first His disciples, to intimate that men must be first taught by God before they can be sent by God."

In Matthew 10:2, Peter is listed as "the first," not because he was the first chosen, nor even because he was the first on the list, but perhaps because of his prominence in the apostolic circle. But this is only the order of "first among equals," for the New Testament knows nothing of the Catholic doctrine of the supremacy of Peter over the other apostles (see Gal. 2:11; 1 Peter 5:1).

Matthew lists these names in pairs, probably because this is the way Christ sent them out—two by two (Mark 6:7). This method has proved through the years to be the most effective means of evangelism. The number is small enough so as not to lose individuality, but yet large enough to minimize any individual bias and provide for mutual encouragement when needed.

---

1. How did Jesus equip His disciples (v. 1)?
2. In the listing of the twelve disciples, what is the significance of the order (vv. 2-4)?

"How easy it is to live more or less in the enjoyment of God's free grace, and yet not realize that we are called to fulfill a divinely appointed purpose."—Duncan Campbell

---

B. Commanded to Go (vv. 5-7)

⁵ These twelve Jesus sent forth, and commanded them, saying, Go not into the way of the Gentiles, and into any city of the Samaritans enter ye not: ⁶ But go rather to the lost sheep of the house of Israel. ⁷ And as ye go, preach, saying, The kingdom of heaven is at hand.

Jesus prohibits the disciples on this particular mission to go either to the Gentiles or to the Samaritans; they were to confine their activity to the Jews. This may have been a concession to the inexperience of the apostles whose mission would later be enlarged, or it may have been that the Lord only wanted the first offers of salvation to be made to the chosen people, and then later offered to the heathen when the work itself became stronger.

Our Lord's compassion comes through His referring to His people as "the lost sheep of the house of Israel" (v. 6). They were the covenant people, and the light of the gospel must first be ignited in the Holy Land before it could be diffused throughout the world.

This is always the proper approach. The gospel must first be preached at home before it can be carried forth in missionary enterprise. Every Christian must be able to witness in their own immediate circle, from which they may draw strength and encouragement, before they dare to enlarge their efforts in the world.

In verse 7, Jesus tells the disciples they are not to be sightseers, but they are to begin with a simple declarative message clearly summarized in "The kingdom of heaven is at hand." No doubt, this early preaching involved personal testimony: "This He has done for me"; "I heard Him speak these words." This type of preaching has been, and will always be, the most effective kind of ministering. God means for us not only to *bear* the message, but to *be* the message.

---

1. What were the Twelve told *not* to do (v. 5)? Why not?
2. What was their mission (vv. 6-7)?

"Jews have God's promise, and if we Christians have it too, then it is only as those chosen with them, as guests in their house, that we are new wood grafted onto their tree."—Karl Barth

---

C. Guidelines Given (vv. 8-15)

(Matthew 10:10-12 is not included in the printed text.)

⁸ Heal the sick, cleanse the lepers, raise the dead, cast out devils: freely ye have received, freely give. ⁹ Provide neither gold, nor silver, nor brass in your purses.

¹³ And if the house be worthy, let your peace come upon it: but if it be not worthy, let your peace return to you. ¹⁴ And whosoever shall not receive you, nor hear your words, when ye depart out of that house or city, shake off the dust of your feet. ¹⁵ Verily I say unto you, It shall be more tolerable for the land of Sodom and Gomorrha in the day of judgment, than for that city.

Christ is here empowering His disciples to do the works He has done Himself (see chs. 8-9). He did not want their ministry to stop at their lips; He wanted their message to have verification through miraculous acts.

The principle "freely ye have received, freely give" (10:8) succinctly states the absolute law that must guide all Christian ministers in their labor for God. Everyone is worthy of support from those to whom he ministers, but his inward motivation must not be influenced by economic considerations lest he inadvertently secularize a spiritual work.

Jesus did not want His disciples to travel as if involved in business or pleasure. He knew that if the disciples on this training mission would take no provisions with them, they would better learn how to live by faith. They were entitled to enough food and clothing to enable them to accomplish their mission, but they were not to take more than enough. It is implied in verse 10 that the ministers are to be supported in their mission by those who benefit by their ministry (see 1 Cor. 9:14; 1 Tim. 5:17-18).

Mode of travel in New Testament times was mainly on foot, and twenty miles was the average distance a person could cover in a day's time. Naturally, the disciples could not be expected to operate out of their homes. After entering a village, they would have to look for and depend on people who saw enough value in their ministry to extend the hand of hospitality and to provide them with the extras they were not permitted to bring with them, as well as the necessities of bed and shelter. For those who were "worthy" (Matt. 10:11), such service would not be a burden, but a privilege. And once they found the worthy person in a given town, the disciples were not to move about, lest they become involved in favoritism and rivalry, or needlessly waste time; but they were to "abide" with their host until they left for another destination.

The "salute" (v. 12) which the disciples were to use was the rich and meaningful word *shalom*, meaning, in this situation, "Peace be to this house." Involved here, too, is more than a formal courtesy; this salute was to carry the connotation also for the spiritual peace which the kingdom of Christ brings with it.

Christ recognized that there was always the possibility of a mistake being made, so the worthiness of a house is left as uncertain (v. 13). Where they were to meet with inhospitality on the part of the host, they were assured that the word of peace would not be spoken in vain. While there would be no gain of peace on the part of the host, neither would there be a loss of spiritual peace on the part of the guest. Christ knew that if the disciples allowed themselves to be provoked by any poor treatment on the part of the intended host, the success of the mission would be hindered and the spread of the gospel would be delayed. Jesus knew that if anyone was so narrow-minded as to refuse the disciples hospitality, there would always be another who would open his home. They were not to stay and argue with the reluctant, but were to give their time to the willing.

The disciples were to speak the simple truth, and if that truth was met with either denial or abuse on the part of a home or a city, they were to "shake off the dust" (v. 14) from their feet. The Lord did not mean for this act to be done in anger, pride, or wounded irritation, but rather in love, suggesting that they had done all they knew to do and were free of the responsibility of the reaction, and were content to leave all issues to the judgment of God. Such an act, if necessary, and if done in sadness rather than in anger, would certainly be a last word of warning to those who had refused the disciples.

Rejection of truth is a very serious offense (v. 15). But why would those who reject the message of the disciples receive a greater punishment than the licentious people of Sodom and Gomorrah? Because of the principle involved: the greater the privilege rejected, the greater the punishment. These ancient cities could at least plead some measure of ignorance, but the Jews of Jesus' day had been prepared for centuries for the revealing of the truth they were now being given.

---

1. Explain the double use of the word "freely" (v. 8).
2. List the items the disciples were *not* to take with them (vv. 9-10). Why not?

3. What guidelines did Jesus give for the disciples' housing as they traveled (vv. 11-15)?

_____

"It is the glory of the true religion that it inculcates and inspires a spirit of benevolence. It is a religion of charity, which none other ever was. Christ went about doing good; He set the example to His disciples, and they abounded in it."—Thomas Fuller

_____

II. OPPOSITION TO THE MISSION (Matt. 10:16-25)

A. Sheep Among Wolves (v. 16)

16 Behold, I send you forth as sheep in the midst of wolves: be ye therefore wise as serpents, and harmless as doves.

At the beginning of their mission, Jesus desired that the disciples have some idea of what it would cost them to accept the work to which they were being called. If they chanced to meet "wolves," they were to act like sheep who had the wisdom of serpents and the harmlessness of doves.

The rabbis had taught that Jews were to act like doves to their own people of Israel, but to act like serpents to non-Jews. They no doubt had in mind a contrived simplicity of doves and more the cunning than the wisdom of serpents; but this is not Christ's meaning. He did not want them to invite martyrdom by provoking the ungodly to violence. Their high motivation was to deliver their message and not to allow unnecessary exposure to danger prevent the delivery of it.

_____

1. How were the disciples like sheep?
2. What other animals were they to act like, and how?

_____

"His voice leads us not into timid discipleship but into bold witness."—Charles Stanley

_____

B. Opposition (vv. 17-23)

(Matthew 10:17-22 is not included in the printed text.)

23 But when they persecute you in this city, flee ye into another: for verily I say unto you, Ye shall not have gone over the cities of Israel, till the Son of man be come.

The remainder of the chapter is given to the warning Jesus gave to His disciples as to the kind of reception they would receive. Though they would be delivered up before councils, governors, and kings, and though they would be scourged in the synagogues, yet they need not become preoccupied in their thinking as to what they should say or do in such circumstances; for in that hour they would be given the things to say at the appropriate time (v. 19). This instruction was obviously necessary lest their message become tainted with fearful anticipation of expected punishment, and lest as a result they might "pull their punches."

Jesus frankly told them they would be "hated" simply because they were followers of Christ, but He assured them that "he that endureth to the end shall be saved" (v. 22). If they were persecuted in one city, they should go to another. The Lord then assured them that they would not have gone over all the cities of Israel before He would join them (v. 23).

---

1. Describe the opposition the disciples would face (vv. 17-18).
2. How would the Holy Spirit help them (vv. 19-20)?
3. Describe the division that the gospel can cause (v. 21).
4. Who will "be saved" (v. 22)?

"The vital Christian arouses opposition because he is a standing rebuke to the selfishness and sin of those around him."—John Hagee

---

C. Like the Master (vv. 24-25)
²⁴ The disciple is not above his master, nor the servant above his lord. ²⁵ It is enough for the disciple that he be as his master, and the servant as his lord. If they have called the master of the house Beelzebub, how much more shall they call them of his household?

The disciple-master relationship was a sort of apprenticeship that aimed to help prepare the disciple to take on the characteristics of the master. So it was inevitable that the Twelve, having fulfilled that objective, could expect reaction from the world much like that directed to their Master. The disciples could never hope to be equal with Jesus, but they could emulate His qualities and be willing to suffer with Him.

Among the abuse directed to Jesus by the Jewish people was the assigning of His miracles to Satan. They called Jesus "Beelzebub," who they designated as the "prince of demons" (see 12:24). They were saying, in effect, that satanic power was behind Jesus' supernatural deeds. Jesus here assured the disciples that similar accusations would be directed to them.

• As Christ's servants, what must His disciples expect?

"The kingdom of heaven is worth infinitely more than the cost of discipleship, and those who know where the treasure lies joyfully abandon everything else to secure it."—D. A. Carson

---

III. ENCOURAGEMENT TO FULFILL THE MISSION (Matt. 10:26-39)
A. Whom to Fear (vv. 26-31)
²⁶ Fear them not therefore: for there is nothing covered, that shall not be revealed; and hid, that shall not be known. ²⁷ What I tell you in darkness, that speak ye in light: and what ye hear in the ear, that preach ye upon the housetops. ²⁸ And fear not them which kill the body, but are not able to kill the soul: but rather fear him which is able to destroy both soul and body in hell. ²⁹ Are not two sparrows sold for a farthing? and one of them shall not fall on the ground without your Father. ³⁰ But the very hairs of your head are all numbered. ³¹ Fear ye not therefore, ye are of more value than many sparrows.

The Lord assured the disciples that any fears they had of their persecutors should be overshadowed by their knowledge that in due time the full truth about all matters would be disclosed. For instance, the just character of Jesus and the divine power behind His miraculous works would come to light. The day will come when truth will triumph and things will be seen as they really are.

In verse 27, Jesus told the disciples that the information He shared with them "in darkness," or in whispered tones, was not merely for their own edification, but was God's saving grace to be shared with all people. Jesus urged them to share the truth without fear (v. 28).

Jesus' disciples need not tremble before those whose power is merely temporal. His disciples knew who was the final power and what He would do to those who defy His Word and ignore His will. The disciples were admonished to fear Him whose power is supreme.

The disciples were assured that the heavenly Father would care for them. He knows of the fall of the sparrow and takes note of even the hairs of the head of His children (vv. 29-30). If God sees the sparrow's plight, certainly He will be attentive to the needs of the human family. Humanity is central to God's purpose on earth, and He will not ignore a single legitimate concern.

---

1. What should believers fear, and what should they not fear (vv. 26-28)?
2. Describe the worth of a human being (vv. 29-31).

"Live in Christ, live in Christ, and the flesh need not fear death."—John Knox

---

B. Mutual Loyalty (vv. 32-33)

32 Whosoever therefore shall confess me before men, him will I confess also before my Father which is in heaven. 33 But whosoever shall deny me before men, him will I also deny before my Father which is in heaven.

In these verses is laid down the double loyalty of the Christian life. If a Christian is loyal to Jesus Christ in this life, Christ will be loyal to that person in the life to come.

The church of today is built on the unbreakable loyalty of those who held fast to their faith, regardless of circumstances. If there had not been men and women in the early church who, in the face of death and agony, refused to deny their Master, where would the church be today?

In *A History of the Christian Church*, Philip Schaff declares:

They live, each in his native land, but as though they were not really at home here. They share in all duties like citizens and suffer all hardships like strangers. Every foreign land is for them a father land, and every father land a foreign land. They dwell on earth but are citizens of heaven. They obey the laws that men make, but their lives are better than the laws. They love all men but are persecuted by all men.

---

1. What does Jesus promise (v. 32)?
2. What warning does Jesus give (v. 33)?

"A wife who is 85 percent faithful to her husband is not faithful at all. There is no such thing as part-time loyalty to Jesus Christ."—Vance Havner

---

C. Divine Mission (vv. 34-39)

(Matthew 10:34-36 is not included in the printed text.)

37 He that loveth father or mother more than me is not worthy of me: and he that loveth son or daughter more than me is not worthy of me. 38 And he that taketh not his cross, and followeth after me, is not worthy of me. 39 He that findeth his life shall lose it: and he that loseth his life for my sake shall find it.

Jesus' purpose in redeeming humanity from the forces of evil caused humanity a clash with the demonic forces of the world. Likewise, His disciples encounter ungodly forces coming against them as they attempt to set at liberty those bound by Satan.

In stating that He had "not [come] to send peace, but a sword" (v. 34), it appears at first glance that His words are a contradiction to His title in Isaiah 9:6—"Prince of Peace." Christ did come to bring peace—peace between the believer and God, and peace among believers. Yet the inevitable result of Christ's coming is conflict (sword)—between Christ and the Antichrist; between light and darkness; between Christ's children and those who give their allegiance to the devil.

The Spirit of Christ can have no union with the spirit of the world. Even a father, while unconverted, will oppose a godly child, wife, or daughter-in-law. A mother and daughter might be out of harmony because one is aligned with Christ, and the other with the forces of evil. The same is true of any combination of relationships in a household (vv. 35-36).

The divine mission of Christ made necessary a total commitment of His disciples. The disciples were to choose between love of Christ and love of the family (v. 37). Although children should love their father and mother, they are not to love them more than they love Jesus. Parents must love their children, but not more than they love Christ, or they are not worthy of Christ.

The first mention of the "cross" in Matthew's Gospel appears in verse 38. The cross was an instrument of death, and here it symbolizes the necessity of total commitment—even unto death—on the part of Jesus' disciples.

Jesus reminded the disciples that the person who found his life would lose it, and the one who lost his life would find it (v. 39).

There is no place for a life of ease and safety in the Christian life. We are sent into this world to serve God and fellow human beings. The way to fulfill God's purpose for us is to spend life selflessly, for only thus will we find life both here and hereafter.

---

1. What challenges can one's devotion to Christ bring to a family, and why (vv. 34-37)?
2. What does Jesus require of His disciples (vv. 38-39)?

"Those who have a saving interest in Christ must be willing to part with all for Him, leave all to follow Him. Whatever stands in opposition to Christ, or in completion with Him for our love and service, we must cheerfully quit it, though ever so dear to us."—Matthew Henry

---

CONCLUSION

It is the intention of Jesus to attract people to the kingdom of heaven, but never with false impressions. The way to the Kingdom is by way of the cross. Listen to the words of Christ in Matthew 16:24: "If any man will come after me, let him deny himself, and take up his cross, and follow me." Christ is explicit in stating the hardships for all who accept His invitation to follow Him.

GOLDEN TEXT CHALLENGE

"AS YE GO, PREACH, SAYING, THE KINGDOM OF HEAVEN IS AT HAND" (Matt. 10:7).

You know how to *go*: to work, to school, to the mall, to someone's home, to a restaurant, to the bank . . . and the list goes on. But how well do you represent the kingdom of heaven as you go?

Even if you are not called to sermonize from a pulpit, as a Christian you are called to "preach" by being Christ's witness in your daily world. People should hear and see, through your words and actions, that you are a citizen of the heavenly kingdom. And you should always be ready to tell others how they too can enter Christ's kingdom.

Daily Devotions:
M. The Discouraged Are Encouraged
   1 Kings 19:3-5, 9-18
T. Commissioned for Service
   Jeremiah 1:4-10, 17-19
W. Opposition Faced
   Jeremiah 26:1-11
T. Go and Teach
   Matthew 28:16-20
F. Fearlessly Contend for the Faith
   Philippians 1:27-30
S. Disarm Opposition
   Titus 2:1-10

Parables About the Kingdom

Matthew 13:1-52

Unit Theme:
Discourses in Matthew

Central Truth:
God's kingdom is the expression of His reign in this world.

Focus:
Explore the meaning of Jesus' kingdom parables and tell others about the Kingdom.

Context:
Jesus teaches from the Sea of Galilee.

Golden Text:
"The kingdom of God is not meat and drink; but righteousness, and peace, and joy in the Holy Ghost" (Rom. 14:17).

Study Outline:
  I. Growth in the Kingdom
      (Matt. 13:18-23, 31-33)
 II. Surpassing Value of the Kingdom
      (Matt. 13:44-46)
III. Future of the Kingdom
      (Matt. 13:24-30, 36-43, 47-50)

INTRODUCTION

At the beginning of His ministry, Jesus taught in the synagogues, but in Matthew 13 we find Him teaching on the seashore. It is not that the door of the synagogue was completely shut to Him, but it was closing. In the open countryside and sea-shores, He chose to use unique methods in teaching.

Even before the use of parables, Jesus used a way of teaching which had the germ of the parable in it. The simile of the salt and light (5:13-16), the picture of the birds and lilies (6:26-30), and the story of the wise and foolish builder (7:24-27) are embryo parables, but in this chapter we find Jesus' way of using parables fully developed.

The purpose and importance of this teaching method, according to Jesus' own words (13:10-17), was to make spiritual truth clearer to His disciples; to lure and attract the unbelievers to inquiry and, hopefully, to intelligent faith; and also to remind His hearers of their great privilege and responsibility to hear and heed the message of Christ.

Three principles may be observed in the interpretation and application of Jesus' parables: (1) each parable has one central truth or emphasis; (2) each has some details of spiritual value that are related to the central truth; and (3) each contains some details that are a part of the story but which seem to have no special spiritual significance.

I. GROWTH IN THE KINGDOM (Matt. 13:18-23, 31-33)

A. The Wayside (vv. 18-19)

¹⁸ Hear ye therefore the parable of the sower. ¹⁹ When any one heareth the word of the kingdom, and understandeth it not, then cometh the wicked

one, and catcheth away that which was sown in his heart. This is he which received seed by the way side.

The disciples expressed a sincere interest to know why Jesus was teaching in parables (v. 10). This interest sprang from hearts that wanted to understand more truth. Jesus emphatically used "ye" and its connection with "therefore" (v. 18). Therefore, He is saying, "You are the privileged ones and, therefore, deserve to know the mystery of truth tied up in this parable." Jesus implies here that the seed is the Word of God, that He himself is the sower, and that the different kinds of soil represent the differing conditions of the hearers.

The wayside hearers listened to the Word but did not give heed. It did not generate any enthusiasm in their minds and, therefore, could not reach the depths of their hearts. The reason for this is twofold. First, their heart is hard, as hard as the beaten footpath that led through the field. Such willful hardness refuses to receive the Word, thus they cannot receive the truth. Second, the fowls came and devoured the seed. When the Word is not received into the depths of the heart, the "wicked one" (v. 19) snatches it up and takes it from the heart in which it otherwise might have germinated. Those who will not heed Christ's Word automatically expose themselves to the wiles of the devil. Their hardened hearts, already cold and unbending, care not for the good seed, and it is lost.

• Describe the thievery of the devil (v. 19).

"The Word of God well understood and religiously obeyed is the shortest route to spiritual perfection. And we must not select a few favorite passages to the exclusion of others. Nothing less than a whole Bible can make a whole Christian."—A. W. Tozer

---

B. The Stony Heart (vv. 20-21)

20 But he that received the seed into stony places, the same is he that heareth the word, and anon with joy receiveth it; 21 Yet hath he not root in himself, but dureth for a while: for when tribulation or persecution ariseth because of the word, by and by he is offended.

There are some people who, not counting the cost, and taking little thought of the demands that will be made upon their life, happily receive the Word with a quickness of apprehension, a liveliness of interest, and a quickly expressed excitement.

In the lives of these stony hearers, the real test comes not in the manner in which they receive the Word, but in the depth of their commitment to it. When the root of that seed reaches down, desiring a greater selflessness, a more encompassing love, and a deeper self-denial, it finds that underneath that open reception is a heart still unchanged, unconverted, and stone-cold.

• Why do some people quickly fall away from Christ (vv. 20-21)?

"A divided heart loses both worlds."—A. B. Simpson

C. The Thorny Hearer (v. 22)

22 He also that received seed among the thorns is he that heareth the word; and the care of this world, and the deceitfulness of riches, choke the word, and he becometh unfruitful.

It appears there is nothing basically wrong with the soil in this case; it is good and the seed sinks deeply into its warm bed. Much is promised; much is hoped for. But there were also the seeds of thorns that had been left in the ground. As the good grain began to grow, so did the thorns which stole the needed nourishment and grew above the grain—taking away, too, the needed light and heart. The grain continued to grow and produced a stalk and leaves, in dwarf fashion, but there was no production of fruit.

The heart the Lord is thinking of here exhibits character, purpose, and depth of thought—all the elements that are required to bring one to a holy life. The Word stays in this person's heart, and he or she makes a profession of religion. However, the thorny seed of sin produces the roots of the cares of this world that increasingly demand the good soil of his or her heart. The person finds less time, less thought, and less love for the things of God.

• How common is the scenario described here? Why?

"The joy of Christ and the joy of the world cannot consist together. A heart delighted with worldly joy cannot feel the consolations of the Spirit; the one of these destroys the other: but in sanctified trouble, the comforts of God's Word are felt and perceived in a most sensible manner."—Abraham Wright

---

D. The Good Hearer (v. 23)

23 But he that received seed into the good ground is he that heareth the word, and understandeth it; which also beareth fruit, and bringeth forth, some an hundredfold, some sixty, some thirty.

The rich ground of this heart knows no inner defilement or outward restrictions. When the divine seed is planted, it does not have to struggle with thorny roots, shallow ground, stony depth, or hardened surfaces. Growth develops and maturation continues. The fruit appears and ripens; and, depending on the natural gifts and the degree of devotion and self-denial, it blossoms into the produce of righteousness, "yielding a hundred, sixty or thirty times what was sown" (NIV).

• How can we lead a productive Christian life?

E. The Parable of the Mustard Seed (vv. 31-32)

31 Another parable put he forth unto them, saying, The kingdom of heaven is like to a grain of mustard seed, which a man took, and sowed in his field: 32 Which indeed is the least of all seeds: but when it is grown, it is the greatest among herbs, and becometh a tree, so that the birds of the air come and lodge in the branches thereof.

The "grain of mustard seed" stands for the small Christian society which appears as the firstfruits of the Word. In this parable the seed is not the Word but rather represents the small flock who received it. The "sower," though not identified, seems certain to represent the Lord; the field is the world.

Like the minute mustard seed, which quickly grows up to be a rather large herb, so the Christian movement developed from very small beginnings to a so-called universal church, from a state of insignificance to a position of power.

• How do these verses describe the growth of Christ's church?

"So never lose an opportunity of urging a practical beginning, however small, for it is wonderful how often in such matters the mustard seed germinates and roots itself."—Florence Nightingale

---

F. The Parable of the Leaven (v. 33)

33 Another parable spake he unto them; The kingdom of heaven is like unto leaven, which a woman took, and hid in three measures of meal, till the whole was leavened.

Adam Clarke observed: "As the property of leaven is to change, or assimilate to its own nature, the meal or dough with which it is mixed, so the property of the grace of Christ is to change the whole soul into its own likeness; and God intends that this principle should continue in the soul till all is leavened—till the whole bear the image of the heavenly, as it before bore the image of the earthly. Both these parables [including the mustard seed] are prophetic, and were intended to show, principally, how, from very small beginnings, the gospel of Christ should pervade all the nations of the world, and fill them with righteousness and true holiness."

"Today, worldwide, wherever most of the ministry that matters is entrusted to laity, the church grows and is sometimes a contagious, unstoppable movement."—George Hunter III

II. SURPASSING VALUE OF THE KINGDOM (Matt. 13:44-46)

A. The Parable of the Hidden Treasure (v. 44)

44 Again, the kingdom of heaven is like unto treasure hid in a field; the which when a man hath found, he hideth, and for joy thereof goeth and selleth all that he hath, and buyeth that field.

This brief parable has been given two interpretations. First, Christ is the treasure for whom we must sell all that we have in order to gain. Second, Christ has given His all to purchase the world for the sake of the treasure—the kingdom of heaven in the world. Consistency requires the second meaning. G. Campbell Morgan explained this treasure as "the kingdom of God hidden in the world, the divine government, in its principles, its order, and its exceeding beauty."

How is Jesus Christ like the man in this parable?

_____

B. The Parable of the Costly Pearl (vv. 45-46)

45 Again, the kingdom of heaven is like unto a merchant man, seeking goodly pearls: 46 Who, when he had found one pearl of great price, went and sold all that he had, and bought it.

This parable of the "one pearl of great price" (v. 46), like the preceding one, emphasizes the value of the Kingdom. It, too, has been given two interpretations. First, some believe that Christ is the pearl for whom the sinner sells all in order to acquire. Second—the interpretation which is consistent with the principles of Christ's own teachings—is that Christ is the merchant seeking pearls among humanity in the world, and having found one, He sacrifices all to acquire it.

The costly pearl then is the Church, for whose salvation and glory Christ gave His all to acquire. Since the "one pearl" cannot be divided as another stone might be, it is thus a symbol of the spiritual unity of the Church. This unity is affirmed by Scripture (John 17:20-21; 1 Cor. 10:17; 12:12-13; Eph. 4:1-3, 11-13).

This pearl of "great price" is also symbolic of the great value of the Church. Sought and then purchased with Christ's own blood, it has been formed by the painful accretion of Christ's suffering and the tears and persecutions of the saints of history. Then, too, as the costly pearl was destined to adorn some monarch, so the glorious destiny of the Church is for "the praise of his [Christ's] glory" (Eph. 1:12), to be presented "to himself a glorious church, not having spot, or wrinkle, or any such thing" (5:27).

_____

• What is the "pearl of great price," and how was it purchased?

_____

"See that you buy the field where the Pearl is; sell all, and make a purchase of salvation. Think it not easy: for it is a steep ascent to eternal glory: many are lying dead by the way, slain with security."—Samuel Rutherford

_____

III. FUTURE OF THE KINGDOM (Matt. 13:24-30, 36-43, 47-50)

A. The Wheat and the Tares (vv. 24-30)

(Matthew 13:26-29 is not included in the printed text.)

24 Another parable put he forth unto them, saying, The kingdom of heaven is likened unto a man which sowed good seed in his field: 25 But while men slept, his enemy came and sowed tares among the wheat, and went his way.

30 Let both grow together until the harvest: and in the time of harvest I will say to the reapers, Gather ye together first the tares, and bind them in bundles to burn them: but gather the wheat into my barn.

Again Jesus is making use of a parable to teach about the "kingdom of heaven" (v. 24). Just as a harvest comes with sowing seed, plowing ground, and a growing season, so does the kingdom of God. The gospel must be planted in people's hearts; they must respond with acceptance and love. This begins life and starts the growth process toward the mature stages.

In verse 25 the enemy's strategy of operation is unfolded. He does his work while people sleep. Also, the enemy takes advantage of the labors of others. The hard labor of preparing the ground had already been done. All the enemy had to do was scatter the bad seed.

But the enemy's strategy also includes deception. This is evidenced by the use of "tares." The word *tares* is a translation of a Greek word meaning "darnel," a poisonous plant or spurious wheat.

The pictures in this parable would be clear and familiar to Palestinian farmers. Tares were one of the curses against which they had to labor.

In their early states, the tares so closely resembled the wheat that it was impossible to distinguish the one from the other. When both had ripened, it was easy to distinguish them (v. 26); but by that time the roots were so intertwined that the tares could not be removed without uprooting the wheat.

From the characteristics of the tares, it is apparent that the growing was well under way when the servants detected an unusual amount of tares growing in the wheat. When the tares were noticed, the servants questioned the householder about the possible contamination of the seed that had been sown (v. 27). The householder explained that he had sown only good seed and that an enemy had sown the bad seed (v. 28).

The servants appear to have been ready to go gather the tares but were cautioned by the householder to let them grow together with the wheat till harvest (vv. 29-30). A. M. Hunter suggests this point: "The parable sounds like Jesus' reply to a critic—probably a Pharisee (the very name means 'separatist')—who had objected: 'If the kingdom of God is really here, why has there not been a separating of sinners from saints in Israel?'" (*Interpreting the Parables*).

At the harvest the tares would be gathered, bound in bundles, and burned. The wheat would be gathered and stored in the barn. What makes for a good harvest is not the absence of tares, but the presence of rich, golden grain.

- When did the farmer decide to root out the tares in his field, and why then?

"My principal method for defeating error and heresy is by establishing the truth. One purposes to fill a bushel with tares; but if I can fill it first with wheat, I may defy his attempts."—John Newton

---

B. The Parable Explained (vv. 36-39)

(Matthew 13:36-39 is not included in the printed text.)

After some intervening parables and the dismissing of the multitudes, Jesus entered into a home—probably Peter's in Capernaum—perhaps for some rest and privacy. There the disciples requested an explanation of the parable of the tares. Again Jesus gave an allegorical interpretation as in the case of the parable of the sower.

The sower is Jesus himself, here called the "Son of man" (v. 37). This parable reveals how the kingdom of God grows. It does not come by military conquest, political revolution, or social change. It was begun and continues to grow because the truth of God is sown in the world. The truth of God's Word, when sown, produces more good seed which in turn is planted and produces more good seed. The more the seed is sown, the more the Kingdom grows.

The field is the world, where the sowing and reaping takes place; where the contest is waged between the forces of evil and Jehovah. It is also where the Enemy, bent on his vicious efforts to frustrate the redemptive plan, sows evil seed.

The good seed are the children of the Kingdom. They are the redeemed who have responded in faith and obedience to the Word of God by the power of the Holy Spirit.

As one grain of wheat has the power to make a stalk on which will grow many grains, so the Christian has the power and potential to produce a life which will multiply many times into other Christians for the great harvest.

The tares are the children of the Wicked One. They are the people whose fruit is produced from the seeds sown by the Enemy. The children of the Wicked One have refused to respond to the gospel of Christ but are rather influenced by Satan. The tares live, grow, and produce their own kind of fruit—fruit that is worthless and poisonous. Their active cooperation with the forces of evil explains why the kingdom of Satan expands.

The enemy is the devil. This evil one attempts to frustrate God's plan and is active in deceiving the human family. He uses every possible means not only to attack on the children of the Kingdom, but also to keep those who have sided with him.

The harvest is "the end of the world" (v. 39). The word *world* used here is better translated "age." At the end of the age, there will be a final separation of the evil from the righteous.

The reapers are the angels who "will weed out of [Christ's] kingdom everything that causes sin and all who do evil" (v. 41 NIV).

---

1. What are the "good seed," and who plants them (vv. 37-38)?
2. What are the tares, and who plants them (vv. 38-39)?

"Only Christianity and its teachings can explain the purpose and meaning of this world—and also gives the basis for right and wrong, good and evil, and so on."—Ken Ham

---

C. The Parable Applied (vv. 40-43)

(Matthew 13:40-43 is not included in the printed text.)

At the end of the age, the angels of God will be sent forth as reapers to gather the tares. These *tares* are identified in verse 41 as "all things that offend, and them which do iniquity."

Those who have helped to further the growth of the kingdom of the devil and joined in the rebellion against the laws of God will be gathered, bound, and cast into "a furnace of fire: there shall be wailing and gnashing of teeth" (v. 42).

In contrast to the end of the wicked is the reward of the righteous, who will "shine forth as the sun in the kingdom of their Father" (v. 43). Human minds cannot conceive the happiness and eternal peace that awaits those who have cast their lot with the kingdom of God, but Jesus assures us such splendor awaits the righteous.

1. Describe the harvest of the tares (vv. 40-42).
2. Describe the fate of the righteous (v. 43).

D. The Parable of the Dragnet (vv. 47-50)

⁴⁷ Again, the kingdom of heaven is like unto a net, that was cast into the sea, and gathered of every kind: ⁴⁸ Which, when it was full, they drew to shore, and sat down, and gathered the good into vessels, but cast the bad away. ⁴⁹ So shall it be at the end of the world: the angels shall come forth, and sever the wicked from among the just, ⁵⁰ And shall cast them into the furnace of fire: there shall be wailing and gnashing of teeth.

This parable, exclusive to Matthew, is taken from the experiences of the commercial fishermen of Jesus' day, and would be easily understood by His followers, His fisherman disciples. It is the picture of a great net being let down into the sea, and being left to swing to the moving of the waters till the close of day, or perhaps even early morning. The fishermen draw in the net and proceed to sort and sift the great haul of mixed fish, casting out the worthless and saving the good.

The Lord's explanation of this parable, as introduced by the word "so" (v. 49), emphasizes the separation of the evil from the good at the end of the age. The *sea* is the world and the *net* is Christendom, with its mixture of converted and unconverted people, of sincerity and hypocrisy.

Nothing is said here of the destiny of the righteous; the emphasis is on the eternal fate of the wicked. Their anguish in the "furnace of fire" is described as "wailing and gnashing of teeth" (v. 50). The *wailing* speaks of sorrow and remorse, while the *gnashing of teeth* speaks of impenitence and bitterness. Therefore, it behooves us all to "make [our] calling and election sure" (2 Peter 1:10), so that we may be prepared for the consummation of God's kingdom.

• How is the parable of the dragnet similar to the parable of the wheat and the tares?

"Make us more dead to the world, and separate in spirit from it."—William Tiptaft

CONCLUSION

When Jesus concluded His series of parables on the mysteries of the kingdom of heaven, He called for a response from His disciples (v. 51). Had they understood His teachings? An intellectual apprehension of Kingdom truth and a spiritual experience of the same are the conditions for growth in grace and knowledge of Christ.

We should now ask ourselves the same question: *Have we studied these parables with a heart to understand? Have we allowed the Holy Spirit to teach us? How will we respond to what we have learned?*

GOLDEN TEXT CHALLENGE

"THE KINGDOM OF GOD IS NOT MEAT AND DRINK; BUT RIGHTEOUS-NESS, AND PEACE, AND JOY IN THE HOLY GHOST" (Rom. 14:17).

We tend to become preoccupied with nonessential matters in the Christian life. This was true of the Roman Christians (and the Corinthians as well). They had become embroiled in controversy about holy days and the eating of meats. The "strong" in faith were eating and manifesting contempt for those who did not. The "weak" in faith were abstaining and condemning those who did. Who was wrong? Both, says Paul, because each was taking a judgmental stand on a nonessential issue. "The kingdom of God is not meat and drink."

One of the most important (and difficult) distinctions for people to make is the one between essentials and nonessentials. On the former there must be unity, and on the latter there must be love. Pettiness of spirit causes us to elevate private whims to the level of universal law and attempt to measure everyone else by our own "half-bushel."

How much better it is to accept our brother in doubtful matters (14:1) and to focus on cultivating among ourselves righteousness (justice), peace, and joy of fellowship "in the Holy Ghost." As we live according to the values of Christ's kingdom, our lives will spread good seed and be productive.

Daily Devotions:
M. The Righteous King
   Psalm 45:1-7
T. The Enduring Kingdom
   Daniel 2:44-47
W. The Indestructible Kingdom
   Daniel 6:25-27
T. Entrance Into the Kingdom
   John 3:1-8
F. Priority of the Kingdom
   Luke 9:57-62
S. Far-Reaching Kingdom
   Luke 13:23-30

Kingdom Values

Matthew 18:1-35

Unit Theme:
Discourses in Matthew

Central Truth:
Christians must align themselves with Kingdom values.

Focus:
Recognize and accept the value God places on humility, believers, and the practice of forgiveness.

Context:
AD 29 in Capernaum

Golden Text:
"It is not the will of your Father which is in heaven, that one of these little ones should perish" (Matt. 18:14).

Study Outline:
I. Embrace Humility
   (Matt. 18:1-5)
II. Value Every Believer
   (Matt. 18:6-14)
III. Practice Forgiveness
   (Matt. 18:15-35)

INTRODUCTION

Jesus' answer to His disciples' question concerning the nature of true greatness is an especially rich one. Like the facets of a diamond, as one turns it first one way and then another, it reveals first one series of truths and then another.

The recurring references to "child" and "little ones" indicate that here we have a revelation concerning the worth of a child. The child is an example of greatness, a channel through which Christ can be received. The child is so highly regarded in heaven that to suffer mutilation or even death is better than to be guilty of leading one astray spiritually. The child even has an angelic representative in the presence of God and is the object of Christ's compassion—His greatest joy is to restore the straying child.

Some Bible scholars believe that "little ones" also refer to the newly converted, or "babes in Christ," and that here is to be found Christ's instructions on the tender care and concern to be shown by the church toward those added to its number.

But the disciples' question puts the entire passage in the context of the topic for this lesson—those who live by the values of Christ's kingdom discover true greatness. He reveals five aspects of greatness: (1) childlikeness, (2) condescension, (3) carefulness, (4) compassion, and (5) forgiveness.

I. EMBRACE HUMILITY (Matt. 18:1-5)

A. Who Is the Greatest? (v. 1)

¹ At the same time came the disciples unto Jesus, saying, Who is the greatest in the kingdom of heaven?

At first glance, this seems to be an innocent question. It is quite normal for men, particularly young men (in which group at least some of Jesus' disciples would have been included), to be ambitious and to want to excel. But the parallel accounts reveal that the disciples' question arose out of a carnal, shameful argument among themselves as to which of them was the greatest (Mark 9:33ff.; Luke 9:46ff.). It was no doubt that, to heighten their sense of embarrassment, Jesus made His answer so graphic, so extended, and so revealing.

Wilbur Williams said, "If ambition is allowed a carnal infection, it will warp into a horrible monster which is not satisfied until it destroys the very person it embodies. . . . The only safe kind of ambition to have is the kind that is cleansed of all the taint of sin, that seeks God and His will first and foremost."

• Why did the disciples ask Jesus this question?

B. Greatness in Childlikeness (vv. 2-4)

² And Jesus called a little child unto him, and set him in the midst of them, ³ And said, Verily I say unto you, Except ye be converted, and become as little children, ye shall not enter into the kingdom of heaven. ⁴ Whosoever therefore shall humble himself as this little child, the same is greatest in the kingdom of heaven.

Jesus apparently gave attention to children quite regularly—in an age when they were customarily relegated to the background (Matt. 19:13-15). Because of this, they were attracted to Him and seemed to have been frequently near Him. Now He called one to Him, to be used as an object lesson in answering the disciples' question.

Jesus made His answer quite emphatic by pointing out that without a change in their hearts and attitudes, the disciples would not have to worry about who was greatest in the Kingdom—they would not be in it at all! In other places, He had demanded *repentance*—a change of mind. Here, He demands a change of direction and objectives. And in terms similar to those in which He demanded of Nicodemus a new birth (John 3:3-7), He demands here of His own disciples a new beginning.

Jesus does not mean one must "humble himself in the same way a child humbles himself." A child is not consciously humble. Rather, Jesus means one must "humble himself so as to assume the role and manner of a child"—be truly childlike, submissive, unassuming, blissfully unaware of the accolades for which adults strive. Only by abandoning the kind of interests which led to their question, and by experiencing a new beginning, could the disciples assume the place of a child and be possessed of these traits.

---

1. Who "shall not enter into the kingdom of heaven" (v. 3)?
2. Explain the humility Christ commands (v. 4).

"When our Lord says we must be converted and become as little children, I suppose He means also that we must be sensible of our weakness, comparatively speaking, as a little child."—George Whitefield

---

C. Greatness in Condescension (v. 5)

⁵ **And whoso shall receive one such little child in my name receiveth me.**
Jesus points out that anyone who ignores the "exalted" level of adult interests, and stoops as it were to open his heart to a child—in the name of Christ—was actually the one who would receive Christ. The shortest route to influence on the highest levels was the route of condescension to those ignored by the world. Wess Stafford wrote:

> A new topic took over at this moment. Up to this point, Jesus had been talking about greatness in His kingdom, using the boy as an illustration. Now the child became the central focus as He forged ahead with renewed passion: "And whoever welcomes a little child like this in my name welcomes me" (Matt. 18:5 NIV).
>
> Luke's account adds, "For he who is least among you all—he is the greatest" (Luke 9:48 NIV). Mark takes it even a step further: "Whoever welcomes me does not welcome me but the one who sent me" (Mark 9:37 NIV).
>
> Well, that certainly derailed the roadside debate! No doubt the disciples were stunned and reeling as Jesus' words sank in. An act of kindness to a child is the same as doing that act to Jesus Christ—indeed, to God himself! (*Too Small to Ignore*).

• How should we treat children?

"No man or woman ever had a nobler challenge or a higher privilege than to bring up a child for God, and whenever we slight that privilege or neglect that ministry for anything else, we live to mourn it in heartache and grief."—Vance Havner

---

II. VALUE EVERY BELIEVER (Matt. 18:6-14)

A. Greatness in Carefulness (vv. 6-10)

(Matthew 18:7-9 is not included in the printed text.)

⁶ **But whoso shall offend one of these little ones which believe in me, it were better for him that a millstone were hanged about his neck, and that he were drowned in the depth of the sea.**

¹⁰ **Take heed that ye despise not one of these little ones; for I say unto you, That in heaven their angels do always behold the face of my Father which is in heaven.**

Jesus turned now to the negative counterpart of verse 5. Just as the person would be blessed who would receive the child in Christ's name, so a terrible fate awaited the one who was responsible for leading the child astray or causing the child to fall into sin. A sudden, violent, and inescapable death would be easier to face than the wrath of God under such circumstances (v. 6).

Jesus recognized that temptations or snares that trap people into sinning are the source of the world's woe (v. 7). He takes a practical view of temptation—it is inevitable in this present age. But He pronounces woe upon the head of the person who becomes the instrument or agent of temptation.

In verse 8, the Lord applies the negative side of His answer. If true greatness is shown in receiving a child in His name, it must also be shown in the care taken to avoid misleading the child. And if one is to avoid being the source of temptation to the child, he must apply the strictest of discipline to himself so that he himself can avoid temptation. Self-denial of one's rights in the interest of avoiding personal or influential temptation is illustrated even to the extreme of cutting off the offending hand or foot—a hyperbole, as the message is emphasized that much more dramatically.

What a rebuke to ministers and church members who live below par spiritually! What a rebuke to hypocrisy and inconsistency—the claiming of Christ's name as a canopy for a life that reflects nothing of His purity, His love, and His grace, but much of self, the carnal mind, and depravity of heart!

The hyperbole of the hand and the foot is expanded to include the offending eye (v. 9). Just as earlier Jesus had pictured a violent death as being preferable to being the recipient of the wrath of God (v. 6), so now He declares that mutilation would be preferable to an eternity spent in hell.

Jesus sums up His warning in verse 10—apply carefulness in personal life and public influence, with an exhortation not to lightly disregard the "little ones." This time He bases it not on the danger of consequent judgment, but on the fact that these little ones have angels who represent them before the heavenly Father. The Jews commonly believed there were angelic counterparts in heaven of some people and some groups of people on earth—of nations (see Dan. 10:13), and of individuals (Acts 12:15). This idea was carried over into the Christian era to include churches (Rev. 1:20; 2:1). But Jesus demonstrates His understanding of the importance of children by declaring that each of them also has an angel in God's presence.

---

1. How serious is the sin of misleading children (v. 6)?
2. Upon whom does Jesus pronounce "woe" (v. 7)?
3. What point is Jesus making in verses 8 and 9?
4. What does verse 10 reveal about God's care for "little ones"?

"We will never bring in the Kingdom by simply seeking to save an adult generation. We must give God a chance at the children or the cause of righteousness is going to be defeated. But if we will save the child, we will surely save the world."—Clovis G. Chappell

---

B. Greatness in Compassion (vv. 11-14)

11 For the Son of man is come to save that which was lost. 12 How think ye? if a man have an hundred sheep, and one of them be gone astray, doth he not leave the ninety and nine, and goeth into the mountains, and

seeketh that which is gone astray? ¹³ And if so be that he find it, verily I say unto you, he rejoiceth more of that sheep, than of the ninety and nine which went not astray. ¹⁴ Even so it is not the will of your Father which is in heaven, that one of these little ones should perish.

Jesus has explained greatness in terms of little children: characteristics, the importance of opening oneself to them, the serious consequences of being responsible for their ensnarement by sin. Now He carries it one step further. True greatness is still concerned even when a child has gone astray. This, in fact, is the ultimate purpose in Jesus' coming—"to save that which was lost" (v. 11).

Luke's account puts the parable of the lost sheep in the context of two other similar parables—those of the lost coin and the lost son (ch. 15). Matthew puts it in the context of Jesus' discourse on the "little ones." If just one of these sheep (like the little ones) strays, the shepherd (like the Good Shepherd) considers it to be sufficiently important to necessitate his leaving the others who are safe in the fold and exposing himself to the danger of the mountain wilderness, giving of himself to the utmost that the lost may be found (v. 12).

There is the throb of deep emotion in "rejoiceth more" (v. 13). The shepherd could have found normal contentment in the possession of his flock, could have been better satisfied if none had strayed, but he could have known joy only through the fact that the lost had been found.

The shepherd's care of the sheep becomes the picture of the Father's care for His little ones—whether children, young converts, or those whom the world counts unimportant.

---

1. Why did Jesus come to earth (vv. 11-13)?
2. What is the will of the heavenly Father (v. 14)?

"When we stray from His presence, He longs for you to come back. He weeps that you are missing out on His love, protection, and provision. He throws His arms open, runs toward you, gathers you up, and welcomes you home."—Charles Stanley

---

III. PRACTICE FORGIVENESS (Matt. 18:15-35)

A. A Sinning Believer (vv. 15-20)

(Matthew 18:17-18, 20 is not included in the printed text.)

¹⁵ Moreover if thy brother shall trespass against thee, go and tell him his fault between thee and him alone: if he shall hear thee, thou hast gained thy brother. ¹⁶ But if he will not hear thee, then take with thee one or two more, that in the mouth of two or three witnesses every word may be established.

¹⁹ Again I say unto you, That if two of you shall agree on earth as touching any thing that they shall ask, it shall be done for them of my Father which is in heaven.

Jesus says that if a brother has offended us, we should go to that brother and tell him about it. In the Sermon on the Mount, Jesus told His hearers that if they came to the place of worship and remembered that their brother had something against them, they were to leave their gift in front of the altar, go first and be reconciled to the offended party, and then come back to complete the act of worship

(5:23-24). It is thus apparent that whenever I, as an individual Christian, have a strained relationship with another Christian, it is my responsibility to go to him and seek reconciliation—whether it is his fault or mine. Strict adherence to these twin rules would end a lot of "church fusses" before they got a start!

Jesus pointed out that the person-to-person approach might well win the brother. If it did not, then one or two others should be brought into the picture to try to effect a reconciliation (18:16). If this was not successful, then and only then should the entire congregation be brought into the picture (v. 17). If the offending brother would hear neither his brother, nor the small group, nor the church, then he was to be put out of the fellowship. He would still be the object of prayer and concern.

Jesus reinforced this disciplinary power of the church by enlarging an earlier commitment of great power to Peter (16:19) to include the entire Twelve—what they would bind or loose on earth would accordingly be bound or loosed in heaven. And He strengthened it even more by connecting with it two of the most precious promises in the New Testament—one concerning a prayer agreed to by two Christians, and the other concerning His guaranteed presence in the smallest of congregations (18:19-20). Both are connected with the church's power to discipline its members.

---

1. If a Christian offends you, what should you do (v. 15)?
2. Explain the church discipline process in verses 16-18.
3. How important is it for believers to be unified (vv. 19-20)?

"Nothing so clearly discovers a spiritual man as his treatment of an erring brother."—Augustine

---

B. The Greatness of Forgiveness (vv. 21-22)

²¹ Then came Peter to him, and said, Lord, how oft shall my brother sin against me, and I forgive him? till seven times? ²² Jesus saith unto him, I say not unto thee, Until seven times: but, Until seventy times seven.

Peter wanted to explore this area of spiritual truth a bit further. The scribes regularly taught that one should forgive another three times. A few, on the basis of Amos' formula, "for three transgressions . . . and for four" (Amos 1:3), had stretched this to "seven times." Peter is feeling quite expansive under the Lord's influence, and is no doubt proud of his improving spirituality! He allows the largest number of forgiveness he has ever heard—surely this will please the Lord!

We may be contemptuous of Peter's narrow view of forgiveness until we bring it into focus in a practical way. What if a brother comes out of church and finds the air has been let out of all four tires? After he gets them repaired, a brother comes and asks forgiveness for his meanness. It is granted. But this is repeated the second Sunday, and the third, until the seventh. About the third time, the reasonableness of the scribes might become apparent! Surely by the seventh time, we would be ready to give Peter due credit!

Jesus' answer surely shocked Peter and the others: "Not seven times, Peter, but multiply the *seven* by *ten* and then by *seven* again." It is quite apparent that Jesus did not mean a mere 490 times. Rather, He was trying to tell Peter that forgiveness is not a matter of math, not something to be tallied until obligations have been met. Rather, forgiveness is supposed to be an attitude—a basic way of looking at others—a forgetting of personal rights and slights and a loving of others for what God has designed them to be and what they can potentially become.

- What limits does Jesus place on forgiving others (vv. 21-22)?

"You are nothing better than deceitful hypocrites if you harbor in your minds a single unforgiving thought. There are some sins which may be in the heart, and yet you may be saved. But you cannot be saved unless you are forgiving. If we do not choose to forgive, we choose to be damned."—Charles Spurgeon

---

C. A Demonstration of Forgiveness (vv. 23-27)

(Matthew 18:23-25 is not included in the printed text.)

26 The servant therefore fell down, and worshipped him, saying, Lord, have patience with me, and I will pay thee all. 27 Then the lord of that servant was moved with compassion, and loosed him, and forgave him the debt.

Jesus proceeds to illustrate what He means. He likens God's kingdom to that of an Oriental despot who has called in the servants who have labored under him in the affairs of state, and wants to check up on the way they have handled the accounts (v. 23).

One servant was brought in who owed him a staggering sum (v. 24). The only way that such a debt could have been accumulated in that day would have been through willful or careless mismanagement of the king's funds, taxes, or estates. The size of the debt is intended to picture the enormity of humanity's sin—our unpaid obligations to God.

Certainly the enslavement of the man and his family, and the sale of his goods, would not bring in enough to pay the debt. But it was all that could be done, and it was in full accord with the custom of the day (v. 25).

The threat of losing his freedom, his family, and his all, brought about his cry for "patience" (v. 26). He did not ask for forgiveness, but rashly promised what he could never do—to repay the debt.

In keeping with the dramatic way in which Oriental despots either pronounced extreme judgments or a manifested astonishing mercy, the king not only was moved to patience, but went far beyond the servant's request—canceling the entire obligation, looking upon it not as a theft or an embezzlement, but as a loan (v. 27).

- How is Jesus like the "certain king" in this parable?

"When you forgive, you must cancel the debt. Do not spend your life paying and collecting debts."—Joyce Meyer

---

D. A Lack of Forgiveness (vv. 28-34)

(Matthew 18:28-31 is not included in the printed text.)

32 Then his lord, after that he had called him, said unto him, O thou wicked servant, I forgave thee all that debt, because thou desiredst me:

---

³³ Shouldest not thou also have had compassion on thy fellowservant, even as I had pity on thee? ³⁴ And his lord was wroth, and delivered him to the tormentors, till he should pay all that was due unto him.

The focus shifts from royal or divine forgiveness to human forgiveness—or rather the lack of it. In contrast with the impossible debt he had owed the king, the forgiven servant remembered a manageable sum owed him by one of his peers (v. 28). The sum would have represented perhaps three months' income in that day. Although he had not the authority to call this servant in as his master had done, he took the matter into his own hands—and the matter included the other fellow's throat! Instead of being humbled, softened, and made grateful, he became arrogant, misinterpreting entirely his master's act of mercy.

"His fellowservant" (v. 29) went to great lengths to express his repentance. And the promise he made, in contrast to the one made by the first servant to the king, was one which he could have kept.

What a picture of the poverty and narrowness of a hard heart we find in verse 30! While God can forgive sin, which is beyond our ability fully to measure as to its repulsiveness to Him, we cannot even forgive the slight of a brother, a joking word, or a misunderstood attitude. Not only do we refuse to forgive, but just as this servant put his fellow beyond the ability of repaying by putting him in prison, we seal our grudge in such a way as to make reconciliation impossible.

We can always see the incongruity and injustice of the hardness of another man's heart! So a group of "fellowservants" told their "lord" about their unforgiving coworker (v. 31). The king called the erring servant to account, reminding him both of the size of his debt and of the magnanimity of the royal forgiveness (v. 32).

Forgiveness should naturally lead to forgiveness; the gifts of God to us should lead to responsive gifts by us to others (v. 33). Eleanor Doan asked:

> How can we gain a forgiving heart? Only by going to the Cross, and there seeing how much our Lord has forgiven us and at what a cost. Then we shall see that the utmost we are called upon to forgive, compared with what we have been forgiven, is a very little thing.

In verse 34 we see that the unforgiving spirit of the servant canceled his own forgiveness. That the judgment was a final one is evident from the fact that he was put in the hands of the jailers until he should have paid everything that was due: something that was impossible, both from the enormous amount used in the illustration and from what it represented—the sin of humanity.

- To which character in this parable can you best relate?

"He that cannot forgive others breaks the bridge over which he himself must pass if he would ever reach heaven; for everyone has need to be forgiven."—George Herbert

---

E. The Principle of Forgiveness (v. 35)

³⁵ So likewise shall my heavenly Father do also unto you, if ye from your hearts forgive not every one his brother their trespasses.

Jesus makes certain that the moral of the story is not lost. He lays down a principle of forgiveness: God will forgive as we forgive others; God will withhold forgiveness if we withhold it. It is not that God's attitude toward us is anything less than forgiving. Rather, by the very nature of forgiveness, we make ourselves incapable of receiving divine forgiveness when we do not let that forgiveness flow through our life to rule in our relations to others. To fail to forgive is to cause a short-circuit of the forgiveness which God longs to make a reality in our life.

• What warning does Jesus give us?

CONCLUSION

In today's lesson, Jesus used a little child as an illustration of what His followers should be like. Children are born in a state of innocence; they do not sin and become guilty of that sin until they reach the age when they become accountable and know their actions to be rebellion against God. Childhood, then, is a period of innocence—a kind of innocence that should be a part of all adult actions, where God, through Christ, has declared us "not guilty."

GOLDEN TEXT CHALLENGE

"IT IS NOT THE WILL OF YOUR FATHER WHICH IS IN HEAVEN, THAT ONE OF THESE LITTLE ONES SHOULD PERISH" (Matt. 18:14).

Jesus summarizes the Father's attitude toward the individual soul. The Father's will precludes the loss of even "one of these little ones." And since Jesus came to earth expressly to do the Father's will, He could not allow even one little child to be despised or destroyed by some thoughtless or evil-minded adult without sounding the terrible warnings herein contained. Let those who persist in sinning against little children beware!

Daily Devotions:
M. God Forgives
   Psalm 32:1-5
T. Arrogant People Will Be Humbled
   Isaiah 2:11-17
W. Lack of Caring Denounced
   Ezekiel 34:1-10
T. Care for Each Other
   1 Corinthians 12:12-25
F. Follow Christ's Example of Humility
   Philippians 2:1-11
S. Forgive as You Are Forgiven
   Colossians 3:12-14

Christ-Focused Living

`Matthew 24:1-51`

Unit Theme:
Discourses in Matthew

Central Truth:
Faithfulness to Christ is necessary for victorious Christian living.

Focus:
Reflect on challenges to living for Christ and be faithful to Him.

Context:
Jesus' discourse on the Mount of Olives shortly before His death

Golden Text:
"For to me to live is Christ, and to die is gain" (Phil. 1:21).

Study Outline:
I.   Remain Committed to Christ
     (Matt. 24:1-13)
II. Maintain Confidence in Christ's Words
     (Matt. 24:23-35)
III. Faithfully Serve Christ
     (Matt. 24:36-51)

INTRODUCTION

It is natural that Matthew follows up Jesus' reference to the coming judgment upon Jerusalem with a lengthy discourse by the Lord on the future. It seems that when He turned from His denunciation of the scribes and Pharisees and departed from the Temple area, His disciples were so shocked at His suggestion (which they could not reconcile with the beauty and permanence which was evident all around them) that they followed Him with their questions.

Jesus replied with one of His longer discourses, recorded in its fullest form in Matthew 24—25. In it, He attempts to answer the disciples' twofold question (24:3)—first with some principles about the Christian's proper attitude toward the future (vv. 4-14), then with some predictions about the coming destruction of Jerusalem (vv. 15-22) and His own return (vv. 23-31). Then He exhorts them regarding their conduct relative to the destruction of Jerusalem (vv. 32-35) and His return (vv. 36-44), and finally illustrates the attitudes that should be exhibited by the Christian with four parables: (1) on the servants, calling for faithfulness to duty rather than self-indulgence (vv. 45-51); (2) on the ten virgins, calling for personal readiness (25:1-13); (3) on the talents, calling for total investment of the Master's trust for the furtherance of the Master's purpose (vv. 14-30); and (4) on the judgment of the sheep and the goats, calling for a life of Christlike service to others (vv. 31-46).

This week's lesson concentrates on the disciples' questions and the Lord's principles and revelations concerning the future. As His coming draws closer, our focus should be on living for Him.

I. REMAIN COMMITTED TO CHRIST (Matt. 24:1-13)

A. Jesus' Warning (vv. 1-2)

(Matthew 24:1-2 is not included in the printed text.)

As Jesus departed from the Temple area, His disciples tried to call His attention to the marvelous buildings which had been erected there. Surely judgment would not be visited upon this city and this Temple. The Temple was indeed an awe-inspiring sight. The sanctuary proper was about 150 feet high, and some of the stones in its walls were 40 feet long. It was built of white or greenish-white marble, and gilded with gold. It was one of the most beautiful houses of worship in the ancient world. But Jesus responded that the time was coming when not one stone would be left in its place. Josephus' record of the destruction of Jerusalem in AD 70 assures us that Jesus' prediction was literally fulfilled.

_____

• What did Jesus reveal to His disciples?

_____

B. Disciples' Question (v. 3)

³ **And as he sat upon the mount of Olives, the disciples came unto him privately, saying, Tell us, when shall these things be? and what shall be the sign of thy coming, and of the end of the world?**

When Jesus and His disciples had reached the quiet slopes of the Mount of Olives and paused for a period of rest, four of the disciples (Mark 13:3) came to Him privately, to ask Him again about the predictions He had just made concerning the judgment on Jerusalem and the destruction on the Temple. The Holy Spirit must have guided the disciples' framing of their questions, for they asked far more than they could have intelligently expressed at this time. Subsequent events prove that they did not yet understand about Jesus' resurrection and ascension, so "thy coming" for them probably meant only His coming to power. And they probably thought the predictions of judgment, His occupation of Israel's throne, and the end of the old age were all parts of the same grand event.

Jesus' answer treated their question as being twofold: (1) "When shall these things be?" (i.e., the destruction of Jerusalem), and He used the term "these things" twice to make His answer to this part of their question (24:33-34). (2) "What shall be the sign of thy coming, and of the end of the world?" Jesus used the terms "the end" (vv. 13-14), "that day" (v. 36), and various other terms to speak about His own coming (vv. 27, 30, 37, 39, 42; 25:13, 31) to mark His answer to that part of their question.

_____

• What did the disciples want to know?

_____

"You may not be able to predict the time of a tornado, earthquake, or the Lord's return. But you can know for a fact that He is coming back. Work today to share the escape route of God's grace with others, before the night cometh."—David Jeremiah

C. False Christs (vv. 4-5)

⁴ And Jesus answered and said unto them, Take heed that no man deceive you. ⁵ For many shall come in my name, saying, I am Christ; and shall deceive many.

If Jesus had divided all of His answer to the disciples' questions as clearly as He did part of the answer, the exposition of this chapter would be relatively simple. But it is difficult to tell whether some parts refer to the destruction of Jerusalem or to the Second Coming. Some of them seem to apply to both. And it was in this manner that Jesus began, cautioning the disciples not to be deceived with relation to prophecy, whether in matters near at hand or those distant in the future.

False messiahs arose during the first generation of the church's history (cf. Acts 5:36-37; 8:9-11; 21:38; 1 John 2:18). There have, of course, been countless ones in the many generations which have followed. Christ's followers are not to be deceived by the counterfeit. Apparently, when He returns, He will need to make no vocal claims to His messiahship. Who He is will be self-evident.

• Describe the deception about which Jesus warned. Why do we need to pay attention to this warning today?

D. Beginning of Sorrows (vv. 6-8)

⁶ And ye shall hear of wars and rumours of wars: see that ye be not troubled: for all these things must come to pass, but the end is not yet. ⁷ For nation shall rise against nation, and kingdom against kingdom: and there shall be famines, and pestilences, and earthquakes, in divers places. ⁸ All these are the beginning of sorrows.

"Wars and rumours of wars" (v. 6) have characterized practically every generation. Jesus spoke during the great peace established by the Roman Empire. But even within it, there were insurrections and violence. Later the barbarians overthrew Rome, and petty lords warred with each other incessantly. Then came great nations and war on a grander scale. Then alliances between nations have led to global war, and scientific advances have made possible speculation about war fought in outer space. Christ's prediction has been fulfilled in a crescendo pattern. But wherever we find ourselves on the pattern, we are not to be unduly distressed. "The end is not yet" (v. 6).

Not only political disturbances but natural ones, as well, will take place. "Famines, and pestilences, and earthquakes" (v. 7) occurred with unusual frequency and severity during the first century and are occurring again in this century. As with war, they have characterized practically every generation.

With His words "the beginning of sorrows" (v. 8), it is as though Jesus had repeated, "The end is not yet." Undue anxiety should not victimize God's child, whatever the severity of life's disturbances. Not only will things be worse before the end, but the conditions which will exist just prior to His coming will prepare the way for the glorious reign of the Messiah.

- What are the "beginning[s] of sorrows" (vv. 6-8)?

_____

"The signs that mark the beginning of the end are not given for us to calculate the date of the Second Coming but to watch and wait for the return of Christ."—French Arrington

_____

E. Persecution (vv. 9-13)

⁹ Then shall they deliver you up to be afflicted, and shall kill you: and ye shall be hated of all nations for my name's sake. ¹⁰ And then shall many be offended, and shall betray one another, and shall hate one another. ¹¹ And many false prophets shall rise, and shall deceive many. ¹² And because iniquity shall abound, the love of many shall wax cold. ¹³ But he that shall endure unto the end, the same shall be saved.

Just as Jesus had warned His followers to be on their guard at all times against false christs and great political and natural disturbances—both in connection with the destruction of Jerusalem and with His own return—so He warns them now that they must be prepared to face persecution of the most intense form. This certainly came to pass prior to the destruction of Jerusalem, as the Book of Acts and Paul's epistles record, but the worst persecutions of Christians have occurred since Jerusalem's destruction. In fact, more Christians are being persecuted now than ever before.

"Offended" (v. 10) is better translated "caused to be caught" or "caused to fall." Persecution would cause some Christians to fall into the snare of self-preservation, of giving up Christ to avoid trouble. Once they had turned their backs on Christ, they would go on to "betray one another" to the persecutors, and perhaps join in the persecuting. Paul compelled some to turn back before he was himself converted (Acts 26:11), and many others weakened after the fall of Jerusalem under Roman persecution.

Not only false christs from without but also false prophets from within the church will lead Christ's followers astray (Matt. 24:11). The tenacity of sin will discourage some, and the appeal of sin will turn the affections of still others (v. 12).

Through the peculiar temptations of each of the things Jesus had mentioned—persecution, false teachings, the assault of sin itself—one thing was called for: faithfulness (v. 13). Each Christian was to be loyal through every changing circumstance, until the end—whether that was the end of the age or the end of his or her own personal pilgrimage.

_____

1. How did Jesus portray end-times persecution (vv. 9-10)?
2. Name two things that will cause some people to turn away from Christ (vv. 11-12).
3. How can Christians "endure unto the end" (v. 13)?

_____

"The best way in the world to deceive believers is to cloak a message in religious language and declare that it conveys some new insight from God."—Charles Stanley

II. MAINTAIN CONFIDENCE IN CHRIST'S WORDS (Matt. 24:23-35)

A. Discernment Necessary (vv. 23-26)

(Matthew 24:25-26 is not included in the printed text.)

²³ Then if any man shall say unto you, Lo, here is Christ, or there; believe it not. ²⁴ For there shall arise false Christs, and false prophets, and shall shew great signs and wonders; insomuch that, if it were possible, they shall deceive the very elect.

Jesus returned to His caution against deception, implying that such caution will be needed after the destruction of Jerusalem as well as before it . . . and until He returns. Superhuman power is sometimes exercised by evil forces as well as by God (v. 24). But even this must not be permitted to deceive those who are committed to the Lord.

These false christs and false prophets would try to lure the Christians into clandestine meetings out in the wilderness or in the inner compartments of houses—secret, private, or hidden places (v. 26). But when Christ comes back, He will not be in hiding; nor will He try to come secretly or incognito.

---

1. How can "signs and wonders" be deceptive (vv. 23-25)?
2. What lie must believers overcome (v. 26)?

"As Christ has a Gospel, Satan has a gospel too; the latter being a clever counterfeit of the former. So closely does the gospel of Satan resemble that which it parades, multitudes of the unsaved are deceived by it."—A. W. Pink

---

B. Christ's Awesome Return (vv. 27-31)

(Matthew 24:28-29 is not included in the printed text.)

²⁷ For as the lightning cometh out of the east, and shineth even unto the west; so shall also the coming of the Son of man be.
³⁰ And then shall appear the sign of the Son of man in heaven: and then shall all the tribes of the earth mourn, and they shall see the Son of man coming in the clouds of heaven with power and great glory. ³¹ And he shall send his angels with a great sound of a trumpet, and they shall gather together his elect from the four winds, from one end of heaven to the other.

Christ's return will be open and evident to all, sudden but inescapable (v. 27). In verse 28, Jesus seems to repeat this inescapable aspect of His return with an Oriental proverb. Just as vultures will feed on a carcass, so those who are spiritually dead will be subject to a terrible fate when Christ returns.

In verse 29, Christ describes cataclysmic changes that will occur. The sun will stop shining, the moon will give no light, the stars will fall from heaven, and the forces of the heavens will be convulsed. All that holds the heavenly bodies in their orbits and enables the sun and moon to light the earth will give way. What is described is utterly beyond human conception.

Immediately following these things, the sign that heralds the Son of Man will appear in the heavens. This manifestation of the Son of Man in glory will be observed by the tribes of the earth.

Their reaction will be one of wringing their hands and beating their breasts—the Oriental expression of grief, fear, or despair that overwhelms the heart. They will react in this way because of the judgment of God facing them. This Son of Man whom they despised, this appearance which they thought to be a dream, and this convulsion of the world which they never believed would happen will then be a reality, and they will be overwhelmed.

Then they will see Christ coming on the clouds of heaven, as was promised in Acts 1:9-11. The "clouds" are God's chariot, the symbol of His heavenly majesty. The "power" is Christ's omnipotence, which was manifested in the heavenly bodies; His "glory" is the sum of all His divine attributes which were displayed before men (Matt. 24:30). His angels will "gather together His elect from the four winds" (v. 31 NASB).

---

1. How will Christ return (v. 27)?
2. How will nature be shaken during the end times (v. 29)?
3. What will cause worldwide mourning, and why (v. 30)?
4. What will cause indescribable joy among many (v. 31)?

"We should be holy people eager to greet our Lord when He returns, ready at any moment for the trumpet's call, people of optimism, busy in evangelism, hands to the plow, eyes on the prize."—David Jeremiah

---

C. The Certainty of Christ's Words (vv. 32-35)

(Matthew 24:32-34 is not included in the printed text.)

35 Heaven and earth shall pass away, but my words shall not pass away.

The fig tree's indication of approaching summer was considered highly dependable and is used as a symbol of all the signs by which the progression of time toward the return of Christ may be judged (v. 32). Consequently, this parable should be interpreted in relation to all the prophecies that Christ had just given.

By the use of this figure in relation to approaching summer and its application of His own second coming, Christ is teaching an important lesson. Believers should be as alert to spiritual signs as the natural person is to the signs of summer. By such attentiveness to signs of Christ's return, the believer remains ever vigilant. It is clear that this is Christ's intention by His warning, "Know that it is near, even at the doors" (v. 33). The sense of immediacy is conveyed and is essential to every generation of Christians.

Verse 34 is variously understood by Bible scholars. The difficulty hinges on the interpretation of the word *generation*. Some understand this to mean "race, nation, kind, family, breed"; hence they interpret this to mean the Jewish race. Others believe the word refers to the people to whom Jesus was speaking. Still others see it to mean the generation that will be living at the end of the age when Christ will return.

Probably the correct interpretation is to apply this scripture first to the destruction of Jerusalem. The generation to which Christ spoke did see this event occur. In the broader sense, however, the destruction of Jerusalem was a prophetical type of the events leading up to the second advent of Christ.

Of special assurance in these statements of Christ is the authority of the divine Word, which He contrasts with all things temporal (v. 35). When He says "Heaven and earth shall pass away," He refers to the physical universe. The physical universe is by nature decaying, changing, and doomed for destruction. The Word of God issues from an eternal God and is not subject to time and its changes. It is, by its nature, permanent.

---

1. Explain the parable of the fig tree (vv. 32-34).
2. How should verse 35 encourage Christians?

"Failure to see Jesus Christ as the final revelation of truth is a major error that will open the door of the church to a multitude of heresies, taught in the name of truth. Every true movement initiated by the Spirit of God leads men back to the words of Christ which were inscripturated by His own inspiration."—Walter J. Chantry

---

III. FAITHFULLY SERVE CHRIST (Matt. 24:36-51)

A. An Unknown Date (vv. 36-41)

(Matthew 24:38-40 is not included in the printed text.)
³⁶ But of that day and hour knoweth no man, no, not the angels of heaven, but my Father only. ³⁷ But as the days of Noah were, so shall also the coming of the Son of man be.

⁴¹ Two women shall be grinding at the mill; the one shall be taken, and the other left.

Verses 37-39 show that the period preceding the Flood was a time of self-centeredness and self-indulgence. The activities listed here—eating, drinking, marrying—are not in themselves illegitimate. However, a study of the Genesis account of the days preceding the Flood indicates it was a time of excess to the point of unrestrained sexual activities and a time of drunkenness. People were completely preoccupied with their own affairs.

Because of everyone's preoccupation with themselves and the pursuit of pleasure, they were taken by surprise in the Flood. Noah had been a faithful minister of God and had preached the warnings of divine wrath. The people had not heeded because of their self-centeredness. They had no idea of the nature of the judgment that was to come, nor of its imminence.

It is not so much the conduct of the people the Lord has in mind, but rather the suddenness of His return (Matt. 24:39). Paul said, "For yourselves know perfectly that the day of the Lord so cometh as a thief in the night. For when they shall say, Peace and safety; then sudden destruction cometh upon them, as travail upon a woman with child; and they shall not escape" (1 Thess. 5:2-3).

As the Lord first delivered Noah before He sent the Flood, so likewise He shall catch up into the heavens those who "love" and wait for His "appearing" (2 Tim. 4:8). This act of God—the taking away of the one group, while leaving behind another (Matt. 24:40-41)—expresses approval on the one and disapproval and

---

judgment on the other. It is clear that this separation will be sudden, unexpected, and physical.

---

1. What has God not revealed to humanity, and why not (v. 36)?
2. How are the end times like the days of Noah (vv. 37-39)?
3. How do verses 40 and 41 depict the suddenness of Christ's return?

"I know that some are always studying the meaning of the fourth toe of the right foot of some beast in prophecy and have never used either foot to go and bring men to Christ. I do not know who the 666 is in Revelation but I know the world is sick, sick, sick, and the best way to speed the Lord's return is to win more souls for Him."—Vance Havner

---

B. Be Watchful (vv. 42-44)

42 Watch therefore: for ye know not what hour your Lord doth come. 43 But know this, that if the goodman of the house had known in what watch the thief would come, he would have watched, and would not have suffered his house to be broken up. 44 Therefore be ye also ready: for in such an hour as ye think not the Son of man cometh.

The exhortation to watch is a strong one. It means to be alert and to watch with meticulous care. This watchfulness requires attention to details.

The watchman cannot afford to make a judgment concerning the time of danger. He must assume every hour is an hour of danger. The attempt to make this decision by human ingenuity in relation to the coming of Christ is to apply human wisdom to a divinely determined decree.

Christ illustrated the futility of humanity's attempt to discern the times of watchfulness by the parable of the steward of the house. Continual watching was the only approach to safety because the thief would attempt to figure out the times of vulnerability.

• Why must Christians "watch" and "be ready?" How can we do this?

"The promise to the Church is a promise of persecution, if faithful in this world, but a promise of a great inheritance and reward hereafter. In the meantime, she is to be a pilgrim body, passing through this scene, but abiding above."—C. I. Scofield

---

C. The Reward of Faithful Stewardship (vv. 45-47)

45 Who then is a faithful and wise servant, whom his lord hath made ruler over his household, to give them meat in due season? 46 Blessed is that servant, whom his lord when he cometh shall find so doing. 47 Verily I say unto you, That he shall make him ruler over all his goods.

The steward in this illustration is responsible to run the household and to see that all his responsibilities are met. This position is one of great trust, and it demands faithfulness even in the absence of the owner. This, the very time of the steward's greatest temptation, is no time for him to be slack. Christ is illustrating to the believers the pattern of responsibility and of temptation which they will face in His physical absence.

The servant who is faithful under these trying circumstances is blessed because of his faithfulness. He has the happiness of the approval of his master and the consequent reward. The reward takes the form of increasing the trust given to this servant. The final result is an appointment over all the master's property.

• How does verse 46 answer the question in verse 45?

D. The Judgment of Forfeited Stewardship (vv. 48-51)

48 But and if that evil servant shall say in his heart, My lord delayeth his coming; 49 And shall begin to smite his fellowservants, and to eat and drink with the drunken; 50 The lord of that servant shall come in a day when he looketh not for him, and in an hour that he is not aware of, 51 And shall cut him asunder, and appoint him his portion with the hypocrites: there shall be weeping and gnashing of teeth.

The decision of the evil servant that the lord of the house delayed his coming assumed he was away at a great distance. He further assumed the distance was too great to bring about any immediate accounting of his stewardship. This assumption also ignored the master's promise to return.

Having made this presumptuous decision, the evil servant began to use the estate in a way contrary to the wishes of the owner. He abused his fellow servants and squandered the wealth of the household. Thus the servant revealed his character. It is clear that he thought he could correct his error at a time of his own choosing. However, he was caught at a time that he could not.

The judgment of this servant was harsh. He was fiercely lashed and then rejected as servant from the household. Christ draws a parallel between the judgment of the parable and the eternal judgment of God on the wicked.

• Who will be assigned "a place with the hypocrites" (v. 51 NIV), and why (vv. 48-50)?

"Hell is the highest reward that the devil can offer you for being a servant of his."—Billy Sunday

CONCLUSION

The hope of the return of Christ is an exercise in faith and in holiness. The believer is asked to keep on believing in this promise of our Lord Jesus and to live in holiness, despite the course of the world. The world takes the fact that the return has not yet taken place as proof that the promise is of no value. These scoffers say, "Where is the promise of his coming? for since the fathers fell asleep, all things continue as they were from the beginning of the creation" (2 Peter 3:4). It is the privilege and obligation of faith to resist this reasoning and to proclaim fearlessly that Christ will come, keeping our focus on Him.

GOLDEN TEXT CHALLENGE

"FOR TO ME TO LIVE IS CHRIST, AND TO DIE IS GAIN" (Phil. 1:21). Writing as a prisoner of Rome caused Paul to recognize that physical death was not a vague dream but a present probability. Moved with emotion, he declared, "I have a desire to depart, and to be with Christ" (see v. 23).

The Greek text strongly suggests that Paul, a seagoing man, utilized a nautical metaphor in expressing his desires. Depicting himself as a sea captain aboard his vessel in a foreign port, he was strongly tempted to hoist the anchor and set sail for home. However, ship's orders required that he do everything within his power to successfully complete his itinerary.

Paul's natural desire was to be with Christ in glory. There his travels would be terminated. However, he humbly recognized that his counsel and guidance were still needed by the struggling churches. Trying to determine and select priorities, while emotionally stirred, created a serious dilemma for Paul.

Nevertheless, his personal commitment was complete, and he was ready to anticipate a sudden, violent death or a continued ministry. In either case, Paul felt he would not lose.

We are called to follow Paul's example of Christ-focused living to the end of our days on earth—whether we die or are alive when our Lord returns.

Daily Devotions:
M. Serve God Only
   Deuteronomy 6:13-19
T. God's Word Is Sure
   Psalm 19:7-11
W. Commit Yourself to God
   Psalm 37:1-11
T. God's Enduring Word
   1 Peter 1:22-25
F. Perseverance Needed
   Hebrews 10:32-39
S. Faithfulness Rewarded
   Revelation 2:8-11

Introduction to Winter Quarter

"Songs and Hymns in the New Testament" comprise the first unit (lessons 1-3, 5-7), first focusing on songs surrounding the birth of Christ (Mary's hymn, Zachariah's praise, the angels' declaration, and Simeon's song). The final two lessons cover baptismal/creedal hymns and doxologies.

The expositions were written by the Reverend Dr. J. Ayodeji Adewuya (Ph.D., University of Manchester). Dr. Adewuya is an associate professor of New Testament at the Church of God Theological Seminary in Cleveland, Tennessee. Prior to joining the seminary, Dr. Adewuya served as a missionary in the Philippines for seventeen years. He is an active member of the Society for Biblical Literature, Wesleyan Theological Society, and the Society for Pentecostal Studies. He is the author of Holiness and Community in 2 Corinthians 6:14–7:1.

The Christmas lesson (4) was compiled by Lance Colkmire (see biographical information on page 16).

The second unit (lessons 8-13), "Wisdom From Ecclesiastes and Proverbs," explores ancient advice that is still needed today. Themes are time and eternity, relationships, daily wisdom, purity, financial guidelines, and the power of words.

The expositions were written by the Reverend Joshua F. Rice (B.A., M.A., Th.M.), associate pastor of Mount Paran North Church of God in Marietta, Georgia. Formerly a state youth and Christian education director (Great Lakes Region) and youth pastor, Josh and his wife, Johanna, have two children.

Magnify the Lord (*The Magnificat*)

Luke 1:26-56

Unit Theme:
Songs and Hymns in the New Testament

Central Truth:
God is to be praised for the gift of His Son, Jesus.

Focus:
Appreciate Mary's role as the mother of Jesus and praise God for the gift of His Son.

Context:
Jerusalem, about 5 BC

Golden Text:
"O magnify the Lord with me, and let us exalt his name together" (Ps. 34:3).

Study Outline:
  I. Jesus' Birth Foretold
     (Luke 1:26-33)
 II. Mary's Submission and Faith
     (Luke 1:34-45)
III. Mary Magnifies the Lord
     (Luke 1:46-55)

INTRODUCTION

The birth of Jesus Christ is an amazing story, one that is both glorious and mysterious. It begins by telling how God sent a celestial being to the earth with the news of the impending incarnation of the Son of God. Just as the angelic message of a wondrous birth made known the character and special role of John to his father, Zacharias, so the announcement of the more wondrous birth of Jesus to Mary revealed His identity and role.

Before God revealed to Mary her unique place in the world, she was on a different track altogether, looking forward to a good life with Joseph. She was busy making her own plans. But God called her to let go of her own plans and to enter into His will. God sent the angel Gabriel to Mary with startling news. The announcement was not only dramatic but was also a declaration of the character of the Child that was to be born and of divine involvement in His origin.

Mary's response was that she lived to do God's will. There was no argument, no complaining, no "But what will the neighbors say?" or "How will Joseph take the news?" Mary did not consider her earthly reputation or relationships; she was only concerned with her relationship with God. Mary trusted God.

I. JESUS' BIRTH FORETOLD (Luke 1:26-33)

A. Mary and Joseph (vv. 26-31)

26 And in the sixth month the angel Gabriel was sent from God unto a city of Galilee, named Nazareth, 27 To a virgin espoused to a man whose name was Joseph, of the house of David; and the virgin's name was Mary. 28 And the angel came in unto her, and said, Hail, thou that art highly favoured, the Lord is with thee: blessed art thou among women. 29 And when she saw him, she was troubled at his saying, and cast in her mind what manner of salutation this should be. 30 And the angel said unto her, Fear not, Mary: for thou hast found favour with God. 31 And, behold, thou shalt conceive in thy womb, and bring forth a son, and shalt call his name JESUS.

The story of Mary and Joseph begins in the region of Galilee and the town of Nazareth, where Jesus grew up. The angel Gabriel was sent from God to Mary. This was Gabriel's second mission surrounding the birth of Jesus. His first was to the Temple in Jerusalem, where he announced to Zacharias that his wife, Elizabeth, would give birth to the forerunner of the Messiah (vv. 5-17).

It was six months after Elizabeth's conception that Gabriel was sent to an obscure village, Nazareth of Galilee. Galilee bordered Gentile or heathen nations; therefore, it was sometimes called "Galilee of the Gentiles." Nazareth in particular was a despised city, considered inferior by the rest of Israel. Its residents were a conquered people especially despised by the Romans. The city and its citizens were derided and were the object of deep prejudice by Jews and Romans alike. Yet God had a vessel of choice, Mary, in an unlikely place.

There are two important lessons to learn from this episode. First, God is no respecter of persons or places. He sends a message to Nazareth as readily as He does to Jerusalem, and to a virgin in Nazareth as quickly as He does to a righteous person in Jerusalem (Zacharias). Second, as we are apt to do, we must refrain from our quickness to judge places, cities, or nations by their institutions and advantages, and instead consider their godliness and righteousness.

The phrase "house of David" (v. 27) prepares for the Davidic descent of the Child to be born. David was the greatest king that Israel had, and God promised that David's throne would be everlasting (Isa. 9:7). The everlasting kingdom of David is fulfilled in Jesus.

Mary was "espoused" (Luke 1:27), or betrothed, to Joseph. Betrothal is similar to a marriage engagement, but in that time the engagement signified that the two parties had already entered into a binding commitment. Betrothals in a girl's thirteenth year of life were usual, with marriage to be consummated about a year later. Mary had already committed to marry Joseph, but she had not entered into sexual relations with him. In the espousal period, sexual contact by either of the espoused with another person was regarded as adultery. The espousal was so serious a matter that if it was broken, a divorce had to be secured.

Mary was "troubled" (v. 29) not only because of the sudden, unexpected appearance of an angel, but also for the weight of the message that the angel came to convey. She did not understand how God could so greatly favor a person like herself. Mary probably never dreamed she was anyone special. How could she, so ordinary and humble, do anything special for God? That is the essence of grace.

What a striking example Mary was! She did not have need to fear because she had found favor with God. Mary's favor was only by the grace of God. It was a surprising action for God to choose Mary. God reversed the human expectations in Mary's situation. God was willing to use the lowest in that time to be the bearer of the King, and today God continues to use the poor, the powerless, the helpless, and the weak.

The virgin birth of Christ by Mary is a central truth of the Christian faith. Jesus, although divine, is human. He was born like every other human that has come into existence. Jesus was flesh and blood like every other person. The miraculous act was in Jesus' conception.

---

1. Who was sent to Mary, and why?
2. What do verses 27 and 28 reveal about Mary?
3. What "troubled" her (v. 29)?
4. How did Gabriel encourage Mary (vv. 30-31)?

"Mary's virginity protected a great deal more than her own moral character, reputation, and the legitimacy of Jesus' birth. It protected the nature of the divine Son of God."—John MacArthur

---

B. One Greater Than John (vv. 32-33)

32 He shall be great, and shall be called the Son of the Highest: and the Lord God shall give unto him the throne of his father David: 33 And he shall reign over the house of Jacob for ever; and of his kingdom there shall be no end.

In verses 13-19, Luke just described the announcement of John the Baptist's birth. He then proceeded with the announcement of Jesus' impending birth. This passage assumes and builds upon the previous one. The mighty work God did in John the Baptist's conception would be surpassed by a greater miracle in the virginal conception of Jesus, God's Son. The mighty work God foretold He would do through John the Baptist's ministry would be surpassed by an even greater work through His Son's ministry.

Whereas John would be "great in the sight of the Lord" (v. 15), Jesus would be great without qualification and would be called "the Son of the Highest" (v. 32). An even more important tie between the accounts is that the whole significance of John's ministry, as pointed out in verse 17, is found in his preparation for the One coming after him who was more powerful than he (3:16).

---

1. What is Jesus called (v. 32)?
2. Describe the kingdom of Jesus (v. 33).

"Rejoice that the immortal God is born, so that mortal man may live in eternity."—John Huss

II. MARY'S SUBMISSION AND FAITH (Luke 1:34-45)

A. Believing the Impossible (vv. 34-38)

³⁴ Then said Mary unto the angel, How shall this be, seeing I know not a man? ³⁵ And the angel answered and said unto her, The Holy Ghost shall come upon thee, and the power of the Highest shall overshadow thee: therefore also that holy thing which shall be born of thee shall be called the Son of God. ³⁶ And, behold, thy cousin Elisabeth, she hath also conceived a son in her old age: and this is the sixth month with her, who was called barren. ³⁷ For with God nothing shall be impossible. ³⁸ And Mary said, Behold the handmaid of the Lord; be it unto me according to thy word. And the angel departed from her.

Mary's question, "How will this be?" (v. 34 NIV) is probably due to being puzzled rather than a question that arises from doubt or mistrust. She was not asking for some sign or proof like Zacharias (v. 18). She was simply asking for more information. She was single and had never known a man sexually. How could she possibly bear a child without knowing a man?

Mary's statement that she had not been with a man reveals the miraculous action of God that took place in Jesus' conception through the Holy Spirit. God's action reveals that "nothing is impossible with God" (v. 37 NIV). If a woman is able to have a child despite not having any sexual relations, God is able to do anything.

Mary's response to the angel is that she is only a servant of the Lord (v. 38), which reveals her humility, and further strengthens the reason why she had been chosen to bear the Messiah of Israel. Mary is a servant of God and will follow the words of God.

How do we respond to the words of God when those words seem impossible? Do we accept them with faith, remembering that we are humble servants of God? Or do we reject the words of God as impossible and therefore fail to follow God's plan?

To assuage any lingering apprehensions that Mary might have, the angel informs her of another seemingly and humanly impossible situation: Elizabeth's pregnancy in her old age (v. 36). Jesus is a king in the line of David, and He is the unique Son of God. Jesus is the fulfillment of the expectation of a Savior (v. 35).

---

1. How did Gabriel explain the miracle that would occur (v. 35)?
2. How was Elizabeth a sign to Mary (vv. 36-37)?
3. Explain Mary's response (v. 38).

"The Almighty appeared on earth as a helpless human baby, needing to be fed and changed and taught to talk like any other child. The more you think about it, the more staggering it gets. Nothing in fiction is as fantastic as this truth of the Incarnation."—J. I. Packer

---

B. Receiving Prophetic Encouragement (vv. 39-45)

³⁹ And Mary arose in those days, and went into the hill country with haste, into a city of Juda; ⁴⁰ And entered into the house of Zacharias, and saluted

Elisabeth. **⁴¹ And it came to pass, that, when Elisabeth heard the salutation of Mary, the babe leaped in her womb; and Elisabeth was filled with the Holy Ghost: ⁴² And she spake out with a loud voice, and said, Blessed art thou among women, and blessed is the fruit of thy womb. ⁴³ And whence is this to me that the mother of my Lord should come to me? ⁴⁴ For, lo, as soon as the voice of thy salutation sounded in mine ears, the babe leaped in my womb for joy. ⁴⁵ And blessed is she that believed: for there shall be a performance of those things which were told her from the Lord.**

After the departure of the angel, Mary paid a memorable visit to Elizabeth. She probably went so she and Elizabeth could encourage each other. God had acted upon their bodies, performing a miracle for both. Elizabeth's womb was made alive for the son of Zacharias to be conceived, and Mary's virgin womb had conceived. Mary in particular could be encouraged, for Elizabeth was already six months pregnant.

It should be noted that Mary knew about Elizabeth's miraculous conception, but Elizabeth did not know about Mary's pregnancy. This provides an important context for understanding Elizabeth's prophetic pronouncements that follow.

Upon Mary's entry to the house and the greetings, three unusual things immediately happened. First, the babe leaped in Elizabeth's womb (v. 41). Although the baby might previously have leaped or kicked in Elizabeth's womb, this leap was different from previous ones. It was a sign to Elizabeth that the Babe within Mary was someone unique—someone whose identity was about to be revealed to her under the inspiration of the Holy Spirit.

Second, Elizabeth was instantly "filled with the Holy Spirit" (v. 41 NKJV), and a special spirit of prophecy was given her. Third, the Holy Spirit led Elizabeth to greet Mary as the mother of the Messiah, the coming Lord. Elizabeth called Mary "the mother of my Lord" (v. 43), a most dramatic statement of faith about the child to whom Mary would give birth.

Through divine anointing, Elizabeth assured Mary, "Blessed is she who believed that there would be a fulfillment of what had been spoken to her by the Lord" (v. 45 NASB).

---

1. Why did Mary act "with haste" (v. 39)?
2. Explain the amazing events in verses 41-44.
3. Restate Elizabeth's prophecy (v. 45).

"Only when the Holy Spirit comes in is there any life and force and power."—Charles Spurgeon

---

III. MARY MAGNIFIES THE LORD (Luke 1:46-55)

A. Praise From a Humble Heart (vv. 46-48)

⁴⁶ And Mary said, My soul doth magnify the Lord, ⁴⁷ And my spirit hath rejoiced in God my Saviour. ⁴⁸ For he hath regarded the low estate of his handmaiden: for, behold, from henceforth all generations shall call me blessed.

Mary's faith was reassured and confirmed. We may learn from this that God assures and confirms our faith. We believe and trust, and as the need arises, God moves to confirm the reality of what we believe.

Mary responds to Elizabeth's Spirit-inspired utterances in a song that is commonly known as the Magnificat. Although it has some similarity to Hannah's song in 1 Samuel 2:1-10, there are also striking differences between the two songs. Whereas Hannah proclaimed a triumph over her enemies, Mary proclaimed God and His glorious mercy to humanity. Mary proclaimed the salvation of God—a salvation wrought through the promised Messiah, her Savior (Luke 1:47).

How different are contemporary songs! Mary's song was not self-centered. She was not praising herself. The Lord was the subject of her praise and rejoicing. She magnified the Lord (v. 46). To *magnify* means to make something appear larger than what it already is in order to have a better and proper perception. Think of a magnifying glass that a child uses to see an ant. The ant is small, but when the child looks through the glass, the picture of the ant becomes large. Yet, God cannot appear larger because God is already bigger than we could ever imagine. Magnifying demands that we enlarge our picture of God. We often have a picture of God that is too small and contrived. Therefore, we need to magnify the Lord so we can have a better and bigger picture of God.

Why do we magnify the Lord? It is because God is Savior. The Messiah was a symbol of liberation, freedom, and salvation to the Israelites. They believed the coming of the Savior meant that God was saving their people from oppression. This Savior had bestowed grace on Mary, and she responded to the Savior with humility (v. 48). She restated that she was only a servant of the Lord—one of the lowest and most powerless people in that world—yet God used her to bring salvation to all. The grace God had given her is more than she deserved, so Mary praised the Lord with a humble heart.

---

1. How does Mary worship the Lord (vv. 46-47)?
2. What does Mary say about the present, and what does she say about the future (v. 48)?

"Adoration is the spontaneous yearning of the heart to worship, honor, magnify, and bless God."—Richard J. Foster

---

B. Praise to Almighty God (vv. 49-55)

⁴⁹ For he that is mighty hath done to me great things; and holy is his name. ⁵⁰ And his mercy is on them that fear him from generation to generation. ⁵¹ He hath shewed strength with his arm; he hath scattered the proud in the imagination of their hearts. ⁵² He hath put down the mighty from their seats, and exalted them of low degree. ⁵³ He hath filled the hungry with good things; and the rich he hath sent empty away. ⁵⁴ He hath helped his servant Israel, in remembrance of his mercy; ⁵⁵ As he spake to our fathers, to Abraham, and to his seed for ever.

The Messiah's coming is a universal blessing. The salvation that Jesus brought is not for one person, or for one people group, but is available for everyone. God blesses all because He is mighty and holy (v. 49). The King had come to bring salvation because of God's mercy (vv. 50, 54).

Mary's song turned from looking at what God had done in her life to what He had done in history. God has done mighty works throughout history, and He continues to do these mighty works even into our own time. With the Lord's strong "arm" He has shown His mighty power (v. 51), and God would take Israel by the hand and lead them to salvation.

The term for *hearts* (v. 51) refers to human thoughts, intents, or attitudes. The arrogance of humankind blocks vision of seeing when God is present. Mary was lowly and humble in her heart, and thus she was able to hear the word of the Lord, obey it, and receive the grace of God. Mary is an example of those whom God wishes to use. God does not use the rich, powerful, and full because they are arrogant in their hearts, and thereby miss the words of God (vv. 52-53). Those that are needy, hungry, and weak are open to hearing the word of the Lord and are in a position to be used by Him.

---

1. What "great things" has God done for you (v. 49)?
2. What does God do "from generation to generation" (v. 50)?
3. How does God deal with the proud (vv. 51-52)?
4. What does God do for the lowly and the hungry (vv. 52-53)?

We have been a most favored people.
We ought to be a most grateful people.
We have been most blessed people.
We ought to be most thankful people.
—Calvin Coolidge

CONCLUSION

The life of Mary, the mother of our Savior, stands out as an example of trust, commitment, and gratitude. She was a humble and lowly woman who followed the word of the Lord. In her humility and grace, she found favor with God, which would allow her to bear Jesus, the King of Israel. Yet, the grace of God did not give her a prideful heart. Instead, she worshiped and praised God because of His holiness, grace, and goodness.

How do we respond when God uses us? Do we worship with a humble heart? Mary was given the opportunity to bear the Son of God, and she remained humble. How much more should we remain humble when God uses us? When God bestows grace upon us, we should magnify the Lord. Our picture of God should become larger and we should be able to see God more clearly.

GOLDEN TEXT CHALLENGE

"O MAGNIFY THE LORD WITH ME, AND LET US EXALT HIS NAME TOGETHER" (Ps. 34:3).

Our worship is a witness of the God we serve. The psalmist urges us to magnify the Lord and exalt His name so others may see and understand His greatness.

It is not that we make the Lord greater by "magnifying" His name, for He is Almighty. However, as we declare His attributes, others hear about His incomparable awesomeness.

When we praise the Lord with our lives and not just our lips—when we lift up His name by giving Him supreme devotion through the way we live—He receives the highest praise.

Daily Devotions:

M. God's Name Be Magnified
    2 Samuel 7:22-29
T. The Lord Be Magnified
    Psalm 40:11-17
W. God Magnifies Himself
    Ezekiel 38:18-23
T. Magnifying God in the Spirit
    Acts 10:44-48
F. The Name of Jesus Magnified
    Acts 19:13-20
S. Desiring Christ to Be Magnified
    Philippians 1:14-21

Blessed Be the Lord God (*The Benedictus*)

Luke 1:5-25, 57-80

Unit Theme:
Songs and Hymns in the New Testament

Central Truth:
We bless God by using words of thanksgiving and praise.

Focus:
Acknowledge God's goodness and faithfulness, and bless His name.

Context:
Hebron, about 5 BC

Golden Text:
"I will bless the Lord at all times: his praise shall continually be in my mouth" (Ps. 34:1).

Study Outline:
  I. John's Naming and Zacharias' Miracle
     (Luke 1:57-66)
 II. Blessing God for Salvation
     (Luke 1:67-75)
III. Blessing God for Messiah's Forerunner
     (Luke 1:76-80)

INTRODUCTION

The story of John the Baptist's birth manifests the favor or mercy that God shows to His people in removing the stigma of barrenness—a special burden for Elizabeth as the wife of a priest. It also emphasizes the manifestation of God's mercy in the bestowal of the name *John*, which means "Yahweh has shown favor."

The account of John the Baptist's birth is within the larger story of God sending Jesus to the world. The grace that God shows to Elizabeth favors not only His people Israel but is given to the whole world. Luke recounts the events surrounding the births of Jesus and John by setting them side by side. Such a technique enables him to highlight the unique role each will have in God's plan and to show Jesus' superiority to John.

Just as the angel Gabriel announces the birth of John to the husband, Zacharias, of the barren Elizabeth, he later announces the birth of Jesus directly to the Virgin Mary. Then Mary visits Elizabeth, who joyfully witnesses to the incomparable superiority of the baby in Mary's womb compared to the one in her own. Mary sings a canticle, and so does Zacharias. Both sons are divinely named before their birth and circumcision, although their names are not made public until eight days had passed. There are many other parallels as well. However, Luke clearly wants to show that Jesus, not John, is the Messiah.

Before Christ and His mighty ministry burst upon the world, there had to be a period of preparation. John was born for this purpose. He had to be a rough diamond to cut through the hard surface of carnality that gripped the world. He was an extraordinary man, much like the prophets before him and much like the apostles after him. He was, in fact, a blending of the two—he can be called the last prophet and the first apostle.

I. JOHN'S NAMING AND ZACHARIAS' MIRACLE (Luke 1:57-66)

In Luke's comparison between the mission of John the Baptist and Jesus, he repeatedly shows the superiority of Jesus. This is even seen in the amount of space given to John's birth (1:57-58) in comparison to the amount devoted to Jesus' birth (2:1-20). Whereas John is described as "a prophet of the Most High" (1:76 NIV), Jesus is "the Son of God" (v. 35), "an horn of salvation" (v. 69), and "the Lord" (v. 76), who through His life and death will "redeem" God's people (v. 68). John is described by the question "What . . . ?" (v. 66), for his greatness is seen in how he serves the greater One. On the other hand, Jesus is described by the question "Who . . . ?" (5:21; 7:49; 9:9).

Another emphasis involves the dawn of a new stage in salvation history (1:68-79) and John the Baptist's role in it. Clearly John's conception, birth, and ministry (vv. 76-77) are part of the coming of God's kingdom in fulfillment of God's covenantal promises (vv. 68-75).

A. The Miracle Baby Is Named (vv. 57-63)

57 Now Elisabeth's full time came that she should be delivered; and she brought forth a son. 58 And her neighbours and her cousins heard how the Lord had shewed great mercy upon her; and they rejoiced with her. 59 And it came to pass, that on the eighth day they came to circumcise the child; and they called him Zacharias, after the name of his father. 60 And his mother answered and said, Not so; but he shall be called John. 61 And they said unto her, There is none of thy kindred that is called by this name. 62 And they made signs to his father, how he would have him called. 63 And he asked for a writing table, and wrote, saying, His name is John. And they marvelled all.

Luke here resumes the story of 1:5-25. The time for Elizabeth to give birth has now come. Apparently Elizabeth had remained in seclusion throughout her pregnancy, but now neighbors and relatives came to rejoice with her.

Luke continues the story by giving an account of the naming ceremony of John. In faithful observance of the Law, and true to the righteous character of Zacharias, John is circumcised on the eighth day (v. 59; see also Gen. 17:11-12; Lev. 12:3). As became usual in later Judaism, the day of circumcision was also the day of naming. Luke points out John the Baptist's Jewish origin. He does the same thing with Jesus' circumcision and naming in 2:21. Circumcision was the covenant mark (cf. Gen. 17:12-14; 21:4; Lev. 12:3).

Today, it seems irrational for a non-Jewish believer to be anti-Semitic when a hero of the faith such as John the Baptist and, more importantly, Jesus Christ were Jewish.

The neighbors and relatives wanted to honor stricken Zacharias by naming the child after him, but Elizabeth insisted it was not to be. She, but not they, knew the child was to bear a divinely given name that marked his destiny (Luke 1:13). How Elizabeth knew that the name to be given was *John* is not stated. Zacharias probably revealed this to her along with what happened to him in the Temple.

Turning from Elizabeth, the well-intentioned relatives and friends appealed to Zacharias. He was deaf and mute (v. 22), so they appealed to him by means of signs. He responded by writing (v. 63). Having once disbelieved the angelic word (v. 20), a chastened and more experienced Zacharias showed confident faith in fulfilling the angelic word by naming the child. He is *John*, not *Zacharias*.

The people did not understand, but they were obviously impressed by the insistence of Elizabeth and Zacharias. To everyone's astonishment he wrote, "His name is John." Why the astonishment? Probably because "John" was not a name used in their family and because Zacharias was not able to hear Elizabeth's choice of this name.

---

1. How did the neighbors and relatives respond to Elizabeth's miracle (vv. 57-58)?
2. How did Elizabeth and Zacharias surprise everyone (vv. 59-63)?

Not mine, not mine the choice,
In things great or small:
Be though my guide, my strength,
My wisdom, and my all.
—Horatius Bonar

B. Zacharias Speaks (vv. 64-66)

[64] And his mouth was opened immediately, and his tongue loosed, and he spake, and praised God. [65] And fear came on all that dwelt round about them: and all these sayings were noised abroad throughout all the hill country of Judaea. [66] And all they that heard them laid them up in their hearts, saying, What manner of child shall this be! And the hand of the Lord was with him.

The direction of the angel having now been followed, Zacharias' curse was now withdrawn. Zacharias' speaking further heightened the miraculous nature of this event, and thus its importance. It also fulfilled the angel Gabriel's word in verse 20. The neighbors realized that God would work great things through this child (v. 66).

No more the skeptic, Zacharias gave praise to God (v. 64). One commentator noted, "A totally unlikely pregnancy, a strange insistence on a completely unexpected name, and the subsequent instantaneous recovery of Zacharias combine to produce that involuntary response of fear in the presence of the divine activity (5:26; 7:16; 8:37; etc.)."

The public impact of these events is not contained in the Temple, but spread by word of mouth to a much larger circle. People concluded that, in some way, this was a child of destiny—an opinion confirmed by Luke's statement, "The hand of the Lord was with him" (v. 66).

---

1. What happened "immediately" (v. 64), and why (vv. 13, 20)?
2. What was "noised abroad" (v. 65)?
3. What did the people wonder (v. 66)?

December 8, 2013   157

"A miracle is an extraordinary event wrought by God through human agency, an event that cannot be explained by natural forces."—John MacArthur

---

II. BLESSING GOD FOR SALVATION (Luke 1:67-75)

This is the first part of the second major song in Luke. Commonly called the *Benedictus*, it translates the Greek word *eulogetos* ("blessed"). This part of the song gives praise to God for salvation or deliverance.

A. A Spirit-Inspired Song (vv. 67-70)

67 And his father Zacharias was filled with the Holy Ghost, and prophesied, saying, 68 Blessed be the Lord God of Israel; for he hath visited and redeemed his people, 69 And hath raised up an horn of salvation for us in the house of his servant David; 70 As he spake by the mouth of his holy prophets, which have been since the world began.

Just as Elizabeth was filled with the Spirit (v. 41), so was Zacharias. He now prophesies. There is an important lesson from the story of Zacharias: his previous doubt about the angelic pronouncement concerning John's birth and his discipline through loss of speech did not mean the end of his spiritual ministry. So today, when a believer has submitted to God's discipline, she or he may go on in Christ's service.

Verses 68-75 consist of a single sentence in Greek. Zacharias' prophetic words begin in the form of a familiar Old Testament blessing of God (1 Sam. 25:32; 1 Kings 1:48; Ps. 41:13), and the content of the song spells out the reason God is to be blessed. God is to be blessed fundamentally because He has set in motion the salvation of His people through the Messiah, as promised through the prophets (Luke 1:68b-70).

Specifically, the conception of Jesus has taken place, and this is spoken of as a visitation by God (cf. Gen. 21:1). God has now acted for the redemption of His people in that He has begun to activate the final phase of His promise to the house of David (Luke 1:69; see 2 Chron. 21:7). He has "raised up a horn of salvation for us" (Luke 1:69 NKJV)—*horn* being a frequent Old Testament image for strength or power (2 Sam. 22:3; Ps. 132:17).

Although the redemption awaits the future work of the Son of God, its certainty is such that a past tense corresponding to a prophetic perfect can be used to describe this future event. Implied in this beginning that God has made is the full flowering of the salvation He intends for His people. This prospect is anticipated in the outbursts of praise that now follow.

---

1. What enabled Zacharias to prophesy (v. 67)?
2. Explain the term "redeemed" (v. 68).
3. What had God "raised up" (v. 69)?

"The certainty of our salvation rests on the character of God."—F. B. Meyer

B. Outbursts of Praise (vv. 71-75)

71 That we should be saved from our enemies, and from the hand of all that hate us; 72 To perform the mercy promised to our fathers, and to remember his holy covenant; 73 The oath which he sware to our father Abraham, 74 That he would grant unto us, that we being delivered out of the hand of our enemies might serve him without fear, 75 In holiness and righteousness before him, all the days of our life.

The first outburst identifies salvation negatively as rescue from enemies, and probably echoes Psalm 106:10. From the beginning, Israel was surrounded by enemies who wanted to annihilate them. However, God, through the mighty hand of His Messiah, would preserve His people. The same hatred for Israel exists today; yet, God will not allow His people to be overwhelmed.

This ministry of the Messiah is "mercy . . . to our fathers" (Luke 1:72) in that it fulfills God's commitment made to them. All God had promised to Abraham, He would now perform. In Genesis 22:15-18, God gave Abraham a promise of seed that would bless the earth. This promise had been the Jewish hope in times of near extinction, and all generations had longed for its fulfillment. Now the messianic day was about to dawn.

In verses 74 and 75 of our text, Zacharias sums up the national hope for holiness and righteousness. His prayer was that all Israel might share in these godly qualities, for this was the messianic expectation. Here the language of Joshua 24:14 is echoed: what had been, for many centuries, the scantily fulfilled hope for life in the Promised Land was now to become a reality. Luke's terminology of salvation comes from such Old Testament passages as Psalms 18:17; 106:10; and 2 Samuel 22:18. Salvation encompasses not just political and nationalistic deliverance from enemies, but personal and corporate deliverance from sin and judgment.

---

1. What did God "remember" (vv. 71-73)?
2. What would enable God's people to "serve him without fear" (v. 74)?
3. How does God want us to live (v. 75)?

"To be assured of our salvation is no arrogant stoutness. It is faith. It is devotion. It is not presumption. It is God's promise."—Augustine

---

III. BLESSING GOD FOR MESSIAH'S FORERUNNER (Luke 1:76-80)

A. The Dayspring From on High (vv. 76-79)

76 And thou, child, shalt be called the prophet of the Highest: for thou shalt go before the face of the Lord to prepare his ways; 77 To give knowledge of salvation unto his people by the remission of their sins, 78 Through the tender mercy of our God; whereby the dayspring from on high hath visited us, 79 To give light to them that sit in darkness and in the shadow of death, to guide our feet into the way of peace.

Verse 76 begins the second major part of the hymn of Zacharias. There is a change of tense at this point—from the past tense, which describes what God had already begun to do, to the future tense, which speaks specifically of John the Baptist's future mission. This is not simply a prediction of what John would be *called* but primarily of what he would *be*. God would make John His prophet. The One whom John announced, however, would be called "the Son of God" (v. 35). John is to be the preparer who goes ahead (v. 76; Mal. 3:1). As in verse 69, the text implies a preparatory role for John. He will give human beings a "knowledge of salvation" (v. 77), but Jesus will visit them in their darkness to bring them light (v. 79).

John's task is to make known to his compatriots the coming salvation in Davidic lineage. His role was described to Zacharias as one of preparing a people fit for the Lord. John will come ahead of that visitation of God, which will be the ultimate sunrise from heaven (v. 78) in which messianic salvation will reach its full realization.

Although there are various interpretations of the phrase "dayspring from on high" (v. 78), or literally "the dawn from on high," it is best understood as a reference to Christ. And, as preparer, he will be able to extend to the people God's forgiveness of their sins. John, in a preliminary way, and Jesus, in an ultimate way, will be the instruments of the end-time outpouring of the tender mercies of God (v. 78). Salvation is possible because of the tender mercies of God.

---

1. How would John "prepare the way" (NIV) for the Messiah (vv. 76-77)?
2. How would God bless those who accepted Jesus Christ (vv. 78-79)?

"Grace comes into the soul, as the morning sun into the world; first a dawning; then a light; and at last the sun in his full and excellent brightness."—Thomas Adams

---

B. John's Maturation (v. 80)

⁸⁰ And the child grew, and waxed strong in spirit, and was in the deserts till the day of his shewing unto Israel.

John the Baptist experienced normal physical growth, and he became "'strong in spirit'; that is, in courage, understanding, and purposes of good, fitting him for his future work" (*Albert Barnes' Notes*). However, he spent his youth in the wilderness. He remained there until the word of the Lord came to him (3:2), and God began ministering through him as a prophet (v. 3).

• Describe the development of young John.

"One of the special marks of the Holy Ghost in the apostolic church was the spirit of boldness."—A. B. Simpson

CONCLUSION

The parents of John rejoiced in his coming. It was a cause for celebration for them, their family, and friends. Someone said that if the greatest human need

---

had been information, God would have sent an educator. If the greatest need had been technology, God would have sent us a scientist. But humanity's greatest need is forgiveness and the restoration of relationship with God, so God sent us a Savior. That was the message that John came to herald, preparing the way for the coming Messiah.

GOLDEN TEXT CHALLENGE

"I WILL BLESS THE LORD AT ALL TIMES: HIS PRAISE SHALL CONTINUALLY BE IN MY MOUTH" (Ps. 34:1).

When should the believer worship the Lord through praise? David answered from a personal perspective by saying "at all times." Worship exceeds the boundaries of circumstance and time limitations. There is no setting or situation when worship through praise is out of order. In fact, by virtue of David's beginning this psalm with the subject of worship, he implied that worship is one of the major steps we must take in order to receive deliverance by God's power.

Praise in trying times is possible because of the nature and character of God, who is the stimulus as well as the recipient of our praise. Praise is possible when threatened by disease, the economy, war, and other results of sin, because we boast in God rather than in ourselves. Praise flows when we dwell on who God is and what He has done for us through Jesus Christ. Praise lifts us beyond our momentary limitations and enables us to see who we are—the children of God.

Daily Devotions:
M. Blessing God in Trouble
    Job 1:1, 13-21
T. Thank God; Bless His Name
    Psalm 100:1-5
W. Thanking and Praising God
    Daniel 2:13-23
T. Praising God Loudly
    Luke 19:33-40
F. Praising God at Midnight
    Acts 16:16-25
S. Praise Be to God Forever
    1 Peter 4:7-11

Glory to God (*Gloria in Excelsis*)

Luke 2:1-20

Unit Theme:
Songs and Hymns in the New Testament

Central Truth:
All glory, honor, and praise belong to God.

Focus:
Be informed about the birth of Jesus Christ and glorify God.

Context:
About 4 BC, Christ is born in Bethlehem.

Golden Text:
"Give unto the Lord the glory due unto his name; worship the Lord in the beauty of holiness" (Ps. 29:2).

Study Outline:
I. Christ Born at Bethlehem
   (Luke 2:1-7)
II. Angels Sing Glory to God
   (Luke 2:8-14)
III. Christ Found and Proclaimed
   (Luke 2:15-20)

INTRODUCTION

Caesar Augustus was the ruler of the great Roman Empire. He had reigned as an absolute monarch for more than forty years, and maintained a high degree of order and peace. This helped to prepare the way for the rapid spread of Christianity. However, the so-called *Pax Romana* (Roman peace) was attained by force and did not bring true peace to the world.

This was the state of affairs when Jesus Christ, the Prince of Peace, was born. Augustus decreed that a census should be taken. Since the Jews were exempt from military service, for them the census would be predominantly for taxation purposes.

The supreme power figure of the Roman world was instrumental in the fulfillment of messianic prophecy, although he did not realize it. Ordinarily the call for census was a state affair, but God was working out His plan and purposes. The birth of Christ happened at the right time and at the right place (in Bethlehem), all in fulfillment of prophecy.

The fact that God made the announcement of Christ's birth to shepherds helps us to understand the real meaning of Christmas. Shepherds were at the opposite end of the social strata from all the influential people of the day. Shepherds lived in the fields with their animals. They were not respected; they had no power or prestige. Yet, God's angel came to them.

The chord of the "lowly" had already been struck in Mary's song in Luke 1:52. Combined with the angelic announcement to the shepherds, we see that God's interest in the marginalized, oppressed, poor, and outcasts is a major thread that runs through the Gospel of Luke.

Luke 2:1-20 consists of two distinct parts: (1) the historical setting—which explains how Mary, whose home was Nazareth (1:26), gave birth to God's Son in Bethlehem, and describes the birth (2:1-7)—and (2) the angelic announcement to the shepherds (vv. 8-20).

I. CHRIST BORN AT BETHLEHEM (LUKE 2:1-7)

A. The Census (vv. 1-5)

¹ And it came to pass in those days, that there went out a decree from Caesar Augustus that all the world should be taxed. ² (And this taxing was first made when Cyrenius was governor of Syria.) ³ And all went to be taxed, every one into his own city. ⁴ And Joseph also went up from Galilee, out of the city of Nazareth, into Judaea, unto the city of David, which is called Bethlehem; (because he was of the house and lineage of David:) ⁵ To be taxed with Mary his espoused wife, being great with child.

Having detailed the fact of the birth of John the Baptist, the Messiah's forerunner (ch. 1), Luke narrates the story of the birth of the Messiah himself in chapter 2. He furnishes facts left out by the other writers of the Gospels. Just as the pronouncement to Mary of Jesus' birth was superior to that given to Zacharias about John the Baptist's birth, and just as Jesus' conception was more wonderful, so was His birth.

Under the power and genius of the celebrated Julius Caesar, the imperial government of Rome was established. His nephew, Augustus Caesar, who ruled from 30 BC to AD 14, succeeded him. During Augustus' reign, he ended most of the war in the Roman Empire and became known as the one who brought peace to the world. During his reign, the temple of Janus (a Roman god) was shut as a sign of universal peace, and the Prince of Peace made His advent. He was not born in a palace, but in a lowly manger. Jesus brought a new message of peace to every person, and He did not use war to accomplish the peace of God. Instead, He used self-sacrifice on the cross.

The Roman government used the census to count people and properties in Judea that would allow levying proper taxes. The census was used by God to fulfill His plan for the birth of the Messiah. It had been prophesied that the Messiah was to be born in Bethlehem (Mic. 5:2), and Scripture had to be fulfilled. The scribes understood it (Matt. 2:5-6), and so did the common people (John 7:42). Joseph and Mary lived in Galilee, and Mary was now pregnant. How was God going to make sure that the Child was born in Bethlehem? The taxation happened just at the right time and in the right way; that is, everyone had to return to the city of his birth to pay his taxes. The taxation forced Joseph to Bethlehem.

Bethlehem was David's birthplace, and Jesus was in the line of David. He was born in Bethlehem as the first step in establishing an everlasting kingdom.

- The NASB translates verse 1, "A decree went out from Caesar Augustus, that a census be taken of all the inhabited earth." How did God use this decree for His purpose?

"There were only a few shepherds at the first Bethlehem. The ox and the donkey understood more of the first Christmas than the high priests in Jerusalem. And it is the same today."—Thomas Merton

---

B. The Manger (vv. 6-7)

⁶ And so it was, that, while they were there, the days were accomplished that she should be delivered. ⁷ And she brought forth her firstborn son, and wrapped him in swaddling clothes, and laid him in a manger; because there was no room for them in the inn.

Mary and Joseph were unable to find room in an inn, so they had to turn to whatever lodging they could find. The place was most likely filled with animals, and Jesus' bed was a feeding trough. This was the most humble beginning for the King of Israel to be born.

The "swaddling clothes" was the Oriental garment for the first year of a baby's life. The mother would place the cloth under the baby diagonally; fold the cloth's corners over the baby's feet and body and under the head; then with two or more bandages, she tied the cloth in place. Thus clothed, the Son of God was laid in a manger.

The birth of Jesus is one of the greatest events in the history of humankind. God became a human, but not a man—a baby. Jesus was born in the lowliest of circumstances, in poverty. Christ humbled Himself and became a human being in order that He could identify with every class in humanity and bring salvation to all.

• If God had planned for Jesus Christ to be born on earth in 2013, what town might He have chosen? Instead of a manger, where might Christ have been born?

"He was born in another man's house, and buried in another man's tomb."—John Boys

---

II. ANGELS SING GLORY TO GOD (Luke 2:8-14)

A. The Shepherds' Fear (vv. 8-9)

⁸ And there were in the same country shepherds abiding in the field, keeping watch over their flock by night. ⁹ And, lo, the angel of the Lord came upon them, and the glory of the Lord shone round about them: and they were sore afraid.

God continued to use the humble and lowly in society, reaching out to shepherds. In the words of J. Marshall Lang:

It is not to supercilious Pharisee, not to Sadducee cold and dry as dust, not to Essene ascetic and separatist, not to Herodian worldly and crafty, not to the mighty or the noble that the first tidings of the great joy are brought. The first preacher is the heavenly angel, and the first congregation some lowly, simple men, who are doing their duty in the place which God has appointed to them. Thence comes the lesson to us. Heaven is always near the dutiful (*Pulpit Commentary*).

Glory to God (*Gloria in Excelsis*)

Shepherds being in the field argues against the traditional winter date for the birth of Christ. In the winter the sheep would be in the fold and the grass would be scarce. It is in spring, around Passover time, that grass is at its best in Israel.

The appearance of the angel and the glory of God—which signified the presence of God—brightened the night sky. In the midst of the glory or presence of God, the shepherds were afraid. This is not surprising, for fear was an accepted response to God's presence. Shepherds were the lowest caste in ancient society—paid low wages and living in poverty. Yet, the angels, the divine messengers, appeared to them and proclaimed the arrival of the Christ. The term *Christ* comes from the Greek word used for the Jewish word *Messiah*, and means "the anointed one."

The coming of the Messiah, or Christ, signified to Israel a King that would deliver them from all their oppressions, and He would bring peace to the nation. The Messiah was expected to follow in the footsteps of His forefather David, bringing salvation, peace, prosperity, and stability to the nation.

The angels announced the birth of a Savior, which is exactly what humankind needs. We do not need another adviser, a reformer, or a committee, but a Savior. Jesus was and still remains the answer to humanity's yearning for peace and freedom.

---

1. What were some nearby shepherds doing when Jesus was born (v. 8)?
2. Describe the angel's appearance and the shepherds' reaction (v. 9).

Hark! the herald angels sing,
"Glory to the newborn king.
Peace on earth, and mercy mild,
God and sinners reconciled!"
—Charles Wesley

B. The Angel's Message (vv. 10-14)

10 And the angel said unto them, Fear not: for, behold, I bring you good tidings of great joy, which shall be to all people. 11 For unto you is born this day in the city of David a Saviour, which is Christ the Lord. 12 And this shall be a sign unto you; Ye shall find the babe wrapped in swaddling clothes, lying in a manger. 13 And suddenly there was with the angel a multitude of the heavenly host praising God, and saying, 14 Glory to God in the highest, and on earth peace, good will toward men.

The angels brought "tidings of great joy" (v. 10) because God had acted on humanity's behalf, bringing salvation to all people—the Messiah had finally come. Their good news is the most important message ever proclaimed: a message of unspeakable blessedness, bringing joy that has no bounds, and having a geographical reach no one can measure. This good news has no thought of class, race, or sect—it is joy to all the world's peoples.

The word rendered as "good tidings" is the source of the word *evangelize*. The angel evangelized the shepherds with the joyful news. And the message was intended for everyone.

Verse 11 clearly communicates the identity of Jesus. He is not only a "Savior" but also the long-awaited Messiah—the "Christ." And He is "Lord"—the same title as the One whose glory shone around the shepherds. To deny the deity of Jesus is to reject the angelic message.

The promise of end-time salvation that the people of Israel had hoped was being fulfilled in the birth of this Child. The sign of salvation was not outward splendor, wealth, or glory, but a Child wrapped in cloth and lying in a feeding trough. God reversed the expectations of humanity. He used the lowly, the oppressed, the weak, and the poor to bring about His salvation.

These events led to more angels appearing, and they all gave glory and praise to God. They praised God because in the birth of Jesus the greatest revelation of God had happened. Because of God's greatness, God is worthy of all praise, glory, and honor.

The birth of Jesus signifies peace on earth. This is true peace, not peace accomplished by weapons and fighting. Even the unbelievers of the first century sensed this need for peace and a savior. Epictetus, a first-century pagan writer, said, "While the emperor may give peace from war on land and sea, he is unable to give peace from passion, grief, and envy; he cannot give peace of heart, for which man yearns for more than even outward peace."

God's peace in Christ affects the entire social order, bringing about peace in every area of human life. God deserves glory because of the divine actions that lead to salvation to all. Since God lowered Himself and became a human, we can now participate in the salvation and peace made available in the coming of Jesus. Therefore, let us give glory to God for the greatest gift that He gave.

---

1. What are the "good tidings of great joy," and who should receive them (vv. 10-11)?
2. What "sign" was given to the shepherds (v. 12)?
3. Who can receive the peace of God (v. 14)?

"The immense step from the Babe at Bethlehem to the living, reigning, triumphant Lord Jesus, returning to earth for His own people—that is the glorious truth proclaimed throughout Scripture. As the bells ring out for Christmas, may we also be alert for the final trumpet that will announce His return."—Alan Redpath

---

III. CHRIST FOUND AND PROCLAIMED (Luke 2:15-20)

A. The Shepherds' Proclamation and Praise (vv. 15-18, 20)

15 And it came to pass, as the angels were gone away from them into heaven, the shepherds said one to another, Let us now go even unto Bethlehem, and see this thing which is come to pass, which the Lord hath made known unto us. 16 And they came with haste, and found Mary, and Joseph, and the babe lying in a manger. 17 And when they had seen it, they made known abroad the saying which was told them concerning this child. 18 And all they that heard it wondered at those things which were told them by the shepherds.

20 And the shepherds returned, glorifying and praising God for all the things that they had heard and seen, as it was told unto them. The shepherds left an astounding encounter with angels in the field, but then they found the Savior of the world. Bubbling with excitement, coupled with a sense of urgency, they immediately sought for the Child. They found the Baby just as the angel had said; and having found Him, they decided to share their experience and the message wherever they went, thus becoming the first people to bear witness to the Savior of the world. This is ironic since shepherds were so lowly regarded by society that their testimony was not even allowed in court!

The shepherds were effusive in their praise to God for what they had heard and seen. God had spoken to them and they had received the message. They obeyed God's instructions to seek out the Savior; therefore, they had been privileged to see the Messiah. They had reason to praise God.

We should ask: How many hear and see, yet never respond and never praise God? As Matthew Henry observed, the zeal of the shepherds in praising and glorifying God "is an implied reproof of our indolence, or rather of our ingratitude. If the cradle of Christ had such an effect upon them, as to make them rise from the stable and the manger to heaven, how much more powerful ought the death and resurrection of Christ to be in raising us to God?"

It is clear that in the Gospel of Luke, this spirit of doxology is the proper response to the mighty works of God (cf. 5:25-26; 7:16; 13:13; 17:15; 18:43; 23:47).

---

1. Where did the shepherds go, and what did they find (vv. 15-16)?
2. Describe how the shepherds became evangelists (vv. 17-18).

"It is here, in the thing that happened at the first Christmas, that the most profound depths of the Christian revelation lie."—J. I. Packer

---

B. Mary's Pondering (v. 19)

19 But Mary kept all these things, and pondered them in her heart. Mary was awe-stricken, and she responded by meditating on all the wonderful things that had happened to her and to the shepherds. She had good reason to muse on these events. What had brought this ordinary Galilean peasant to Bethlehem? Ostensibly, an emperor's decree from Rome . . . but behind it all was the divine King's plan. God works through all kinds of people and events to accomplish His plan.

In view of whatever limited explanation about the events that she might have been able to proffer, Mary bowed again in humble adoration to God and quietly entrusted all these things into God's keeping. Mary could easily have identified with Paul's declaration in Romans 8:28 that "God causes all things to work together for good to those who love God, to those who are called according to His purpose" (NASB).

Mary is a great and beautiful picture of a humble, trusting, and obedient heart. She had seen much that night and the days before, so she continued to wonder concerning the significance of her Son and the affect that He would have on the world. What she clung to in simple faith would become more and more clear as the ministry and sacrifice of Jesus unfolded.

• How did Mary respond to all that happened around the manger?

———————————

"He was created of a mother whom He created. He was carried by the hands that He formed. He cried in the manger in wordless infancy, He the Word, without whom all human eloquence is mute."—Augustine

———————————

CONCLUSION

The story of the shepherds is an encouragement to all those who seek the Savior. However, there were others in the story who missed the Savior. The first person who missed Jesus was the innkeeper. If he had known that the baby to be born that night was the Creator of the world, he probably would have found room.

King Herod and the religious leaders also missed the Baby. He was right under their noses, but they missed Him. They had their own concerns. Mary and Joseph's fellow travelers knew she was with child, but they also missed the Savior's coming. They were probably in a hurry, or they were just too worn out from the journey. We must be careful not to miss the Savior by being too busy. The shepherds received news about the Gift that still goes on. Like them, we should rejoice that the Savior has come, and spread the good news to others.

GOLDEN TEXT CHALLENGE

"GIVE UNTO THE LORD THE GLORY DUE UNTO HIS NAME; WORSHIP THE LORD IN THE BEAUTY OF HOLINESS" (Ps. 29:2).

We should give God glory because of His astonishing deed of redemption of lost humanity through the incarnation, death, resurrection, and exaltation of Jesus Christ our Lord. This is the supreme reason why both heaven and earth should give honor and worship to the Lord.

But what is meant by the expression "in the beauty of holiness"? The Lord himself is the beauty of holiness! What a wonderful title for God! How descriptive of His essential and inner being, describing the totality of His great attributes. We are called to worship the One who is "majestic in holiness" (Ex. 15:11 NIV) and who enables us to share in His holiness through the gift of His Son.

Daily Devotions:

M. The Heavens Declare God's Glory
   Psalm 19:1-6
T. The Lord's Glory Revealed
   Isaiah 40:1-5
W. Vision of God's Glory
   Ezekiel 43:1-5
T. God's Glory in Christ
   John 17:1-5
F. Glory to God Forever
   Galatians 1:1-5
S. Glory to God by Christ
   Ephesians 3:14-21

The Birth of the King (Christmas)

Matthew 1:18 through 2:23

Unit Theme:
Birth of Jesus Christ

Central Truth:
Because He is the King, Jesus is worthy of our adoration and praise.

Focus:
Recognize Jesus as the King and worship Him.

Context:
Matthew's account of Jesus Christ's birth

Golden Text:
"Behold, a virgin shall conceive, and bear a son, and shall call his name Immanuel" (Isa. 7:14).

Study Outline:
I. The King Is Born
   (Matt. 1:18-25)
II. The King Is Sought
   (Matt. 2:1-8)
III. The King Is Worshiped
   (Matt. 2:9-12)

INTRODUCTION

The most significant event in the history of humanity was the birth of Jesus Christ, the Savior of the world. Had it not been for that birth, there could have been no Calvary, no resurrection, and no ascension. Indeed, "the hinge of history is on the door of the Bethlehem stable."

At first thought, it seems most unworthy that the Son of God had to be conceived, born, and to pass through all the stages of human development. But the interval between God and humanity is so vast that the difference between childhood and manhood is of little consequence. The greatest marvel is that He would consent to become man at all, not that He would consent to become an infant.

Sometime after the birth of Jesus in Bethlehem, mysterious visitors from the East arrived in Jerusalem with strange tidings. Matthew calls them "wise men," or Magi—probably priest-sages, students of astrology and religion. They had come from an eastern country, probably Persia, Arabia or Media, in quest of the "King of the Jews." Contrary to popular belief, we have no certainty as to their number or their names. But their quest was probably motivated by a holy desire and inspired by the appearance of a heavenly beacon or "star." The purpose of their coming was to pay homage to a newborn "King of the Jews," and to worship Him as a deliverer.

The Magi represent the countless hungry hearts of the heathen world who, seeing the light of God revealed in nature, yearn for the Light of the World. The Magi coming as Gentiles to pay homage in Judea is a strong proof of the messiahship of Jesus.

I. THE KING IS BORN (Matt. 1:18-25)

A. A Shocking Discovery (vv. 18-19)

[18] Now the birth of Jesus Christ was on this wise: When as his mother Mary was espoused to Joseph, before they came together, she was found with child of the Holy Ghost. [19] Then Joseph her husband, being a just man, and not willing to make her a publick example, was minded to put her away privily.

Here we have a concise and conclusive statement as to how Jesus was conceived. Matthew makes no attempt to explain how it happened, since, no doubt, he himself could not fully understand it; he makes a plain statement of the facts.

The phrase "was espoused" might better be translated "had been betrothed." In biblical times the marriage ceremony began with a betrothal, which was almost equivalent to marriage (see Deut. 22:23-24), and which could not be broken off without a formal divorce. The betrothal ended after a period of time, generally a one-year interval, with the groom going to the bride's house and taking her home with him. During this year's interval, the betrothal was considered legal and binding on both sides, and a violation of that trust was considered as a case of adultery and was punished in that way (see vv. 25, 28).

Imagine the surprise of both Joseph and Mary when Mary "was found with child." Nothing could have been more distressing and humiliating to them. And what sustained them during this time? Adam Clarke said, "Nothing but the fullest consciousness of her own integrity and the strongest confidence in God could have."

Joseph now knew his wife was pregnant, but he did not know as yet that this child was conceived "of the Holy Ghost." The *Pulpit Commentary* states, "Christianity starts with a miracle. It is a miracle altogether so stupendous and so unique that its reception settles the whole question of the possibility of the miraculous. He who can believe that God shadowed Himself to our apprehension in the likeness of a man, he who can recognize in the Babe of Bethlehem, both the Son of God and the Son of Mary, will find that no equal demand is ever afterwards made upon his faculty of faith. Both Testaments begin with a miracle. A world of order and beauty arising out of chaos is a miracle as truly as is the birth of a divinely human Saviour by the divine overshadowing of Mary."

What was Joseph to do? The legal penalty for Mary's supposed fault was stoning (John 8:5). Joseph loved his wife; but, as a betrothed man, he had a duty in the matter. Being just and righteous, he observed all the law of Moses, and he could not overlook the apparent fault. Yet, Joseph was motivated by a loving desire to deal with Mary as tenderly as possible. He had two alternatives: he could expose her to public repudiation, or he could quietly cancel the bond of betrothal without stating any reason. A Jewish husband could divorce his wife just because she did not please him; and he could do so simply by giving her divorce papers in the presence of witnesses. He did not have to specify the cause. Because of his loyal love and deep devotion, Joseph chose the latter of the two courses.

1. What was Joseph's primary concern in these verses? What does this say about him?
2. How important is the doctrine of the Virgin Birth to the Christian faith? Why?

"God did not send a subordinate to redeem us. He chose to do it Himself."—Alister McGrath

---

B. A Surprising Dream (vv. 20-21)

20 But while he thought on these things, behold, the angel of the Lord appeared unto him in a dream, saying, Joseph, thou son of David, fear not to take unto thee Mary thy wife: for that which is conceived in her is of the Holy Ghost. 21 And she shall bring forth a son, and thou shalt call his name Jesus: for he shall save his people from their sins.

The processes of thought that went through Joseph's mind during these hours must have been most painful and distressing. Righteous as he was, we can be sure that he prayed. He certainly had trusted his betrothed wife, and he, no doubt, still wanted to. Yet, how could the present circumstance be explained? God, not desiring to leave His servants in perplexity any longer than necessary, sent His special representative, probably Gabriel (see Luke 1:19, 26), to appear unto and to clarify for Joseph how this situation had developed.

Perhaps desiring that Joseph be approached in his calmest moments, the angel chose to make his revelation in a dream. The angel addressed Joseph by name and identified him as "thou son of David." Joseph, no doubt, had been aware of the promise that God made to David in 2 Samuel 7:12-16, and the angel was well aware that Joseph wanted to keep the family line pure, but Joseph did not know all the circumstances of this situation. So the mission of the angel was to reveal the true circumstances of Mary's pregnancy and to urge Joseph to take her so the promise made to David might be fully carried out in his family instead of in another.

In a concise statement the angel related the greatest fact in the world's history: "That which is conceived . . . is of the Holy Ghost." This was the birth of all births; this was a truth above the reach of human thought. This was the miracle of all miracles, for the blood that was now beginning to flow through this Baby's veins would soon be made available to atone and cleanse all humanity who, born in sin, like ourselves, would accept His death for their sin and in their place.

The name *Jesus* was the personal name of our Lord and was derived from the Greek equivalent of the old Hebrew name of *Joshua*. It was a familiar name to the Jewish mind; other mothers had named their boys Jesus. But, from this announcement on, with every word, every act of the Savior, the name would take on a new significance and be elevated to a higher value.

And what was His mission to be? That of a great teacher? Certainly so; He became the greatest teacher that ever lived. To be a king? Most definitely, He came to set up a universal kingdom. To be a friend? Yes, in the most absolute way, one that sticks closer than a brother. But, first and foremost, He came to be a Savior. This is why, as a personal name, *Jesus* comes before His official title, *Christ.* It was, and still is, His nature to save. He came to teach in order that He might save; He came to rule over those who would be saved; and He came to establish an eternal friendship with those who were saved.

F. B. Meyer said, "This is the mission of Immanuel. He came, not as the News expected, to break the yoke of Caesar and to re-establish the kingdom of David; He came to break the yoke of sin, and to set up the sinless kingdom of God. The Church has too often misunderstood the object of His advent, as though He meant simply to save from the consequences and results of sin. This was too limited a program for the Son of God: to cancel the results and leave the bitter cause; to deliver from the penalty, but not from the power; to rescue His people from the grasp of a broken law, but confess Himself unable to deal with the bad virus of the blood—this was to fail. No. Dare to take this announcement in its full and glorious meaning, written, as it is, on the portico of our Saviour's life."

• List everything you can know about Jesus from these two verses.

"In Christ two natures met to be thy cure."—George Herbert

C. A Fulfilled Prophecy (vv. 22-23)

²² Now all this was done, that it might be fulfilled which was spoken of the Lord by the prophet, saying, ²³ Behold, a virgin shall be with child, and shall bring forth a son, and they shall call his name Emmanuel, which being interpreted is, God with us.

The statement "all this was done" is in the past tense, making the birth of Jesus and the saving of His people from their sins as already having taken place. This was a tool of speech to impress it upon Joseph's mind. Throughout the Old Testament this manner of speaking was used by prophets who saw the thing that was going to happen in the future with such clarity and certainty that when they uttered the prophecy, they put everything in the past tense.

The phrase "that it might be fulfilled" is one Matthew uses ten times in his Gospel, but it is not found anywhere else in the New Testament. Matthew particularly wanted to emphasize that the events of Christ's life were taking place in order to fulfill God's gracious promises, made in the Old Testament through the prophets.

"The prophet," to Matthew, was Isaiah; and, in many ways, Isaiah is considered the greatest of all of the Hebrew prophets. His writings are more often quoted in the New Testament than those of any other and are sometimes referred to as the fifth Gospel.

The quotation is taken from Isaiah 7:14, words that were uttered by Isaiah to King Ahaz. Ahaz was anticipating war with King Rezin of Assyria and Pekah of Israel, and was contemplating the establishment of an alliance with Assyria to effectively deal with this challenge. On command of the Lord, Isaiah went to Ahaz to try to convince him that the best course was not in a foreign alliance, but in trusting in the Lord to effectively defeat his enemies. Isaiah tried to get Ahaz to ask for a sign from the Lord that He would do as Isaiah had said He would do, but Ahaz refused. Isaiah gave the sign anyway, which was the Virgin Birth statement, quoted here by Matthew. However, this prophecy had to wait about seven hundred years for its complete fulfillment, which was realized in the virgin birth of Christ.

_____

• Explain how Jesus lives up to the name *Immanuel* in our day.

_____

"God surprises earth with heaven, coming here on Christmas Day."— John Bell

_____

D. Joseph's Acceptance (vv. 24-25)

24 Then Joseph being raised from sleep did as the angel of the Lord had bidden him, and took unto him his wife: 25 And knew her not till she had brought forth her firstborn son: and he called his name Jesus.

Verse 25 shows Mary's pregnancy was enveloped in such sanctity that Joseph refused to normalize his marriage until after Jesus was born. At this point Catholic theologians through the centuries have declared that Joseph never did fully consummate his marriage, and that Mary lived in perpetual virginity. There is nothing here or anyplace in the Bible to suggest this, and the wording here intends to suggest that the marriage was fully consummated after Jesus was born.

_____

• Why was Joseph so quick to obey the angel?

_____

II. THE KING IS SOUGHT (Matt. 2:1-8)

A. The Wise Men From the East (vv. 1-2)

1 Now when Jesus was born in Bethlehem of Judaea in the days of Herod the king, behold, there came wise men from the east to Jerusalem, 2 Saying Where is he that is born King of the Jews? for we have seen his star in the east, and are come to worship him.

Verse 1 at once identifies the place and the time of Jesus' birth. He was born in Bethlehem ("House of Bread"), a little town about five miles south of Jerusalem. Since it was the native town of David, it has also been called the "city of David" (Luke 2:11). Matthew omits reference to the circumstances that brought Mary and Joseph to Bethlehem, details recorded by Luke only. The time was during the reign of King Herod in Jerusalem and, according to Luke, the rule of Caesar Augustus in Rome.

The arrival of these Magi from the East very likely took place a year or so after the birth of Jesus, since the distance of travel required considerable time. Then too, Herod's decree to destroy the Bethlehem infants up to the age of two years seems to suggest that at least a year had passed since Jesus' birth. It was natural for the Magi to come to Jerusalem, the capital, in their quest for the infant King.

The question put by the Magi expresses the expectation prevailing throughout the East of the advent of a great king who was to rise from among the Jews. These expectations were probably based on some acquaintance with the Hebrew

Scriptures, probably the Book of Daniel, and also the influence of the dispersed Jews throughout the East.

The title "King of the Jews" is applied to no one but the Messiah, and it appears later in accord with Jesus' own claims in the inscription on the cross (Matt. 27:37). What prompted the venture of these Magi at this time was the sight of "his star in the east." Although it has not been definitely ascertained whether this star was a peculiar astronomical appearance or a supernatural manifestation, it is safe to assume that it was by divine arrangement so that the Magi were thus inspired to venture out on a religious quest. Their expectations were high, for they had "come to worship him."

---

1. Why did the wise men go to Jerusalem?
2. Why was Jesus born in Bethlehem?

Unusual Alignment

The great astronomer Kepler discovered that in Christ's birth year there was an unusual occurrence among the planets. He found that in that year Jupiter and Saturn, which are generally in remote parts of the sky, came three times so near together that to the unassisted eye the rays of one were absorbed by the other, and their combination gave an extraordinary brilliant light, which continued for some months.—F.B. Meyer

---

B. King Herod's Agitation (vv. 3-4)

[3] When Herod the king had heard these things, he was troubled, and all Jerusalem with him. [4] And when he had gathered all the chief priests and scribes of the people together, he demanded of them where Christ should be born.

The agitation of King Herod over the inquiry of the Magi was due to his jealous and suspicious nature. After his appointment to kingship by the Roman Senate in 40 BC, he besieged Jerusalem and took it in 37 BC, and then established his authority by force of Roman arms. His constant fear of displeasing his overlords in Rome and the suspicion of some rival to his throne made him cruel and tyrannical, and outbursts of rage and consequent massacres were not uncommon in Jerusalem. His knowledge of Israel's expectations and rumors of Messiah's nearness made him tense, so that the Magi's quest further irritated him. It is probable that Jerusalem's disturbance was due to fear of a new outbreak of violence, a revolution or a massacre.

The king at once summoned the religious leaders of the city for a consultation. It is not clear whether these chief priests and scribes of the people represented a formal meeting of the Sanhedrin or an informal gathering of religious leaders to get the desired information as soon as possible. The chief priests could have been those who had served the office of high priest, and also the heads of the twenty-four courses into which the priests were divided, or they could have been the Sanhedrin. The scribes were the transcribers and interpreters of the Mosaic Law. The former represented the ecclesiastical and Sadducean part, the latter the more literary and probably the Pharisaic part of the nation. With character-istic cleverness, as though he too shared the messianic hopes, he courteously inquired of them, as the authorized interpreters of Scripture, where the Christ should be born.

---

1. What does the title "Christ" mean?
2. Why was Herod "troubled"?

"He who has no Christmas in his heart will never find Christmas un-der a tree."—Roy L. Smith

---

C. The Prophetic Light (vv. 5-6)

⁵ And they said unto him, In Bethlehem of Judaea: for thus it is written by the prophet, ⁶ And thou Bethlehem, in the land of Juda, art not the least among the princes of Juda: for out of thee shall come a Governor, that shall rule my people Israel.

This gathering of religious leaders without hesitation informed the king that Bethlehem was the predicted birthplace of the Messiah. And they quoted from the prophet Micah (5:2) who, seven hundred years before the event, predicted the place and importance of the One to be born. It is recorded for us as the scribes quoted it, not as Matthew himself may have quoted the prophecy. The prophet Micah contrasts the outward insignificance of the birthplace with the spiritual and divine greatness of the One born there. And although, for some reason, they did not fully and accurately quote it, Herod got his answer. Then, too, although they knew the Scriptures, they did not act upon their knowledge. This indifference to divine truth is characteristic of many who are religious but lack in spiritual life and power.

• What does verse 6 reveal about Jesus' ministry? Why would this both-er Herod?

D. King Herod's Hypocrisy (vv. 7-8)

⁷ Then Herod, when he had privily called the wise men, enquired of them diligently what time the star appeared. ⁸ And he sent them to Bethlehem, and said, Go and search diligently for the young child; and when ye have found him, bring me word again, that I may come and worship him also.

Having ascertained from the Jewish theologians the prophetic information as to the place of the Messiah's birth, Herod's next step in his murderous design was to determine from the Magi themselves the probable age of the infant. He supposed that the birth of the child happened simultaneously with the first appearance of the star. For this information accuracy was important and secrecy was doubly neces-sary, for the public must not think that Herod could give any recognition to a pos-sible rival, nor must the parents learn of his knowledge of the event.

The unsuspecting strangers must have told the king all he wanted to know, for they now got his royal mandate to make a diligent search for the child and report back their discovery. Lest anyone, whether the Magi or the Jews, would suspect Herod's intentions, he hypocritically assured them that his desire was to join them in this reverent homage to the royal child.

---

1. Why did Herod talk with the wise men privately?
2. What did Herod tell the wise men to do, and why?

"Alexander, Caesar, Charlemagne, and myself founded empires; but on what foundation did we rest the creations of our genius? Upon force. Jesus Christ founded an empire upon love; and at this hour millions of men would die for Him."—Napoleon Bonaparte

---

III. THE KING IS WORSHIPED (Matt. 2:9-12)

A. The Guiding Light (vv. 9-10)

9 When they had heard the king, they departed; and, lo, the star, which they saw in the east, went before them, till it came and stood over where the young child was. 10 When they saw the star, they rejoiced with exceeding great joy.

It must have been a disappointing and disturbing experience for the Magi to find such ignorance and indifference in the capital city of Judaism. But having traveled so far in their quest, they must not give up now. So the weary Magi ventured forth toward Bethlehem in accord with the king's mandate. Over and above the royal direction was the sure word of prophecy that Bethlehem was the place. God's Word is a sure guide to the discovery of the Christ and His salvation (2 Tim. 3:15). But as soon as they passed the city wall, the heavenly beacon appeared again. The star which had aroused their hopes now appeared as a guide to the very place where the new King was to be found. "Its reappearance was the pledge of the full answer to their search, the full reward of their toilsome journey" (*Pulpit Commentary*). So their temporary perplexity turned to exuberant joy, and they went on their way rejoicing.

• How much did God want the wise men to find Jesus? Why?

B. The Worship of the King (v. 11)

11 And when they were come into the house, they saw the young child with Mary his mother, and fell down, and worshipped him: and when they had opened their treasures, they presented unto him gifts; gold, and frankincense, and myrrh.

Upon their arrival at Bethlehem the wise men found the infant King, not in the manger where the shepherds found Him (Luke 2:16), but in the house. At the sight of the Child with His mother, Mary, they bowed in reverent worship—not of Mary, but of the Child. For this purpose the Magi had traveled far; now the time had come for reverent homage to the divine King. Only Deity deserves our worship; and since Jesus Christ was (and is) the Son of God, He was often worshiped (Matt. 8:2; 9:18; 14:33; 28:9, 17).

Next in order was the consecration, and this was fittingly expressed by the Magi in their presentation of gifts to Christ. In full accord with Eastern usage, they opened their treasure chests and presented the three traditional gifts of homage to a ruler. As an expression of their faith in the King, these gifts gave both meaning and increase to their faith.

The King's Gifts

Bring Him thy precious things
And lay them at His feet;
The gold of love, the hope that springs
The unknown ways to meet.

Bring Him thy lovely things;
The joy that conquers care,
The faith that trusts and sings,
The frankincense of prayer.

Bring Him thy bitter things;
The myrrh of grief and fears,
The aching heart that stings
With pain of unshed tears.

These for thy gifts to Him;
And for His gifts to thee,
The comfort of His steadfast love,
His tender sympathy.
—Annie Johnson Flint

———————

1. How do you suppose this event affected Mary?
2. What was the significance of the wise men's gifts?

———————

"Some gifts you can give this Christmas are beyond monetary value: Mend a quarrel, dismiss suspicion, tell someone 'I love you.' Give something away—anonymously. Forgive someone who has treated you wrong. Turn away wrath with a soft answer. Visit someone in a nursing home. Apologize if you were wrong. Be especially kind to someone with whom you work. Give as God gave to you in Christ, without obligation, or announcement, or reservation, or hypocrisy."—Charles Swindoll

———————

C. Supernatural Message (v. 12)

¹² **And being warned of God in a dream that they should not return to Herod, they departed into their own country another way.**

It was probably during the night following their visit to the infant King that the warning dream came to these Magi. Whatever plans they may have had to return with a report to Herod were suddenly changed by divine intervention. Thus both the Magi and the Christ were protected from the immediate tyranny and wrath of Herod. Those who have found the Christ always return another way—a new and living way.

• How did God protect His Son?

CONCLUSION

The visit of the wise men to the Christ child in Bethlehem was motivated by a holy desire. Their own wisdom and research having failed to satisfy, they hoped for something better in Israel. They were encouraged by the heavenly light which aroused their hopes and gave guidance on the way. Although temporarily delayed in Jerusalem by human apathy, they obeyed the direction from Holy Scripture and came to Bethlehem. There they were rewarded by the holy discovery of the Christ. In faith they worshiped Him and consecrated to Him their treasures, and with confirmed faith they returned to their home.

GOLDEN TEXT CHALLENGE

"BEHOLD, A VIRGIN SHALL CONCEIVE, AND BEAR A SON, AND SHALL CALL HIS NAME IMMANUEL" (Isa. 7:14).

King Ahaz had rejected God's offer for immediate deliverance; he also refused the sign God had promised. But Isaiah told him that in spite of his refusal, God would still give a sign to His people, and He would provide redemption for them. He was saying to the king, "By rejecting the promise, you would endeavor to overturn the decree of God; but God's purposes will remain inviolable, and your treachery and ingratitude will not hinder God from being continually the Deliverer of His people; for He will at length raise up His Messiah."

What sign would the Lord give? "Behold, a virgin shall conceive." The word *behold* was used emphatically, to denote the greatness of the event. A virgin would conceive, not by the ordinary course of nature, but by the gracious influence of the Holy Spirit (see Matt. 1:18-25). This is the mystery Paul extolled in lofty terms, that "God was manifest in the flesh" (1 Tim. 3:16).

The prophet said that the mother would designate His name: "[she] shall call." This was contrary to custom. The father was always assigned the right of giving a name to a child. But here that responsibility was given to the mother. Therefore, it follows that this Son was to be conceived in such a manner as not to have a father on earth.

His name was to be *Immanuel*. This name indicates He was to be the only-begotten Son of God, clothed with our flesh, and united to us by partaking of our nature. *Immanuel*, which means "God with us," or "united to us," was a name that could not apply to a man who was not God. By this name He was to excel all that were before and all that were to come after Him. Immanuel was a title expressive of some extraordinary excellence and authority that He would possess above all others.

The Birth of the King

Daily Devotions:

M. Prince of Peace
   Isaiah 9:2-7
T. God Is Savior
   Isaiah 43:1-7
W. Christ's Birth Announced
   Luke 1:26-31
T. Sought by Shepherds
   Luke 2:8-18
F. The Word Becomes Flesh
   John 1:1-14
S. Imitate Christ's Humility
   Philippians 2:5-11

Song of Salvation (*Nunc Dimittis*)

Luke 2:21-40

Unit Theme:
Songs and Hymns in the New Testament

Central Truth:
All who believe in Jesus Christ are saved by Him.

Focus:
Recognize Jesus as the Savior and rejoice in the salvation He provides.

Context:
The infant Jesus is brought to the Temple in Jerusalem in 5 BC.

Golden Text:
"The Lord hath made known his salvation: his righteousness hath he openly shewed in the sight of the heathen [Gentiles]" (Ps. 98:2).

Study Outline:
I.   Jesus Dedicated to God
     (Luke 2:21-24)
II. Song About Jesus the Savior
     (Luke 2:25-35)
III. Thanksgiving for Redemption
     (Luke 2:36-40)

INTRODUCTION

According to Exodus 13:2, every firstborn male, "both man and beast," was sacred to God (NKJV). That law recognized the gracious power of God in giving human life. In the case of a firstborn son, there was also a requirement that he be acknowledged as belonging to the Lord in a special way (vv. 12, 15). The child had to be redeemed by the payment of five shekels (Num. 18:15-16). Though this payment could be made anywhere in the land, the ideal was to present the child at the Temple (Neh. 10:35-36). When this was done, the purification and presentation would be done together. To use two turtledoves or young pigeons for the sacrifice (instead of the usual lamb and one turtledove or pigeon) was a concession for poorer families (Lev. 12:8).

The story of the bringing of baby Jesus to the Temple has parallels with the story of the dedication of Samuel (Luke 2:22; cf. 1 Sam. 1:24, 28). Young Jesus was dedicated to the service of God as was Samuel. Luke, in 2:23, modifies the quotation of Exodus 13:2, 12 in order to lift up the holiness of Jesus, "[the] Holy One" (Luke 1:35 NKJV).

The shepherds recognized the Christ child by a sign, but now the spiritual eyes of Simeon and Anna perceive directly the place of the Child in God's purpose and the eschatological hopes of Israel. Where the dramatic movement of John the Baptist's story was *from* the Temple, that of Jesus' story is *to* the Temple. Where conformity to the Law had been noted in passing in the case of

John (John 1:23), now in the case of Jesus the fulfilling of all righteousness as required by the Law is made prominent (1:17).

While Mary, Joseph, and Jesus are at the Temple, Simeon's dream comes true—He sees the Messiah. We do not know a lot about Simeon. He is not mentioned anywhere else in Scripture, but we know that he was "waiting for the consolation of Israel: and the Holy Ghost was upon him" (Luke 2:25). Simeon's dream was that someday he would meet the One whom God sends to be Savior of Israel.

In today's Scripture text, we study Jesus' circumcision and naming (2:21-24), Simeon's and Anna's prophetic encounter and pronouncements (vv. 25-38), and a summary of Jesus' growth (vv. 39-40).

I. JESUS DEDICATED TO GOD (Luke 2:21-24)

A. Naming and Circumcision (v. 21)

21 And when eight days were accomplished for the circumcising of the child, his name was called JESUS, which was so named of the angel before he was conceived in the womb.

When Mary's firstborn son was eight days old, He was circumcised and given the name *Jesus*. The Hebrew form of *Jesus* was *Joshua*, which means "savior." The chosen name was communicated to Mary by the angel Gabriel, even before He was conceived (1:31). Mary and Joseph obeyed God's command in naming the child (Matt. 1:21).

Through His circumcision, Jesus was marked in the same way as John, with the sign of the covenant (Gen. 17:11) and incorporated into Israel, the people of God (Josh. 5:2-9).

---

1. Why was the Savior named "Jesus"?
2. What was the purpose of circumcision (see Gen. 17:10-14)?

> How sweet the name of Jesus sounds
> In a believer's ear!
> It soothes his sorrows, heals his wounds,
> And drives away his fear.
> —John Newton

B. Parental Fidelity (vv. 22-24)

22 And when the days of her purification according to the law of Moses were accomplished, they brought him to Jerusalem, to present him to the Lord; 23 (As it is written in the law of the Lord, Every male that openeth the womb shall be called holy to the Lord;) 24 And to offer a sacrifice according to that which is said in the law of the Lord, A pair of turtledoves, or two young pigeons.

These verses focus on the fidelity of Mary and Joseph as devout and pious Jews to all the requirements of the Mosaic Law. They carry out on behalf of Jesus all the things required by the Law for the birth of a child.

According to the Law, a woman became ceremonially unclean on the birth of a child. She remained unclean for an additional thirty-three days after circumcision of a male child, or a total of eighty days after the birth of a daughter (Lev. 12:1-5). At the conclusion of this period, the mother offered a sacrifice, either a lamb and a dove or pigeon; or, if she was poor, two doves or two young pigeons (vv. 6-8).

So, Luke (2:22-24) recounts the two important events that necessitate the eventual manifestation of Jesus: the purification of Mary (forty days after Jesus' birth) and the redeeming of Jesus (the firstborn, a month after his birth). The purification was the occasion for bringing Jesus to Jerusalem to present Him to the Lord, just as in verse 21 the circumcision was the occasion for the naming.

The latter is treated by Luke as the presentation of Jesus in the Temple, without a mention of the five shekels required by the Law. In his narrative, Luke shows how Jesus was brought up in conformity with the Law and suggests just how poor Joseph and Mary might have been. Joseph was a carpenter, not a prosperous merchant or landowner. For God's purposes, Jesus began His earthly life in ordinary and humble conditions.

Just as Jesus' earthly parents were committed to rearing Jesus according to the ways of God, so Christian parents today are obligated to bring up their children in accordance with God's Word.

---

1. Why was young Jesus brought to the Temple again (v. 22)?
2. What had God declared about the firstborn male (see Ex. 13:2)?
3. What did Mary and Joseph sacrifice (Luke 2:24)?

"While bringing up your children, you are to remember that they are not your 'possessions' but instead are the Lord's gift to you. You are to exercise faithful stewardship in their lives."—John C. Broger

---

II. SONG ABOUT JESUS THE SAVIOR (Luke 2:25-35)

A. The Long-Awaited Messiah (vv. 25-32)

25 And, behold, there was a man in Jerusalem, whose name was Simeon; and the same man was just and devout, waiting for the consolation of Israel: and the Holy Ghost was upon him. 26 And it was revealed unto him by the Holy Ghost, that he should not see death, before he had seen the Lord's Christ. 27 And he came by the Spirit into the temple: and when the parents brought in the child Jesus, to do for him after the custom of the law, 28 Then took he him up in his arms, and blessed God, and said, 29 Lord, now lettest thou thy servant depart in peace, according to thy word: 30 For mine eyes have seen thy salvation, 31 Which thou hast prepared before the face of all people; 32 A light to lighten the Gentiles, and the glory of thy people Israel.

Through the song of Simeon, Luke assures us of the credentials of Jesus as Messiah, taking care to show that Simeon is an authentic representative of Judaism. The utterances of Elizabeth, Mary, and Simeon flow from one to the other, each beginning where the other ends. Mary sings about God choosing her to bear the Messiah (1:46-56); Zacharias celebrates the triumph of Israel (vv. 68-75); and Simeon announces the hope of the Gentiles (2:29-35).

Simeon is described as a "just" (upright), "devout," and aged Jew, who is reminiscent of the aged priest Eli (1 Sam. 1—2) and of Zacharias, who prophesied about the greatness of his son, John (Luke 1:76-79). In the same way, Simeon will now predict the greatness of Jesus in his hymn.

Luke describes Simeon as not only just and devout, but also as one who lived in expectation of the consolation of Israel. There is an important lesson here for believers today. We ought to live in the light of Christ's return. Simeon is further described as particularly endowed with the Holy Spirit, who made it known to him that he would not die until he sees the Lord's Messiah. Guided by the Holy Spirit, without any sign such as was given to the shepherds, Simeon came to the Temple area at the right time, took the Child from Mary, and pronounced his song.

Few people in the Temple would likely have paid any attention to the infant in Mary's arms. The fact that His parents had given the offering of the poor would have made Him even less noticed by either the people or religious leaders. However, the one who did notice Him lived in anticipation of the coming of the Messiah. That is the meaning of the phrase "waiting for the consolation of Israel."

In the Book of Isaiah, the idea of the consolation of Israel is associated with God's end-times restoration of His people (40:1; 49:13; 51:3; 52:9; 57:18; 66:10-11). Simeon's attitude of expectant waiting was shared by the people around Anna "who were looking for the redemption of Jerusalem" (Luke 2:38 NASB) and by Joseph of Arimathea, who was "waiting for the kingdom of God" (23:51 NASB). As believers living in the twenty-first century, we must live in expentancy of the second coming of Christ.

Simeon saw the Messiah, the One who was to bring salvation to the world— "a light to bring revelation to the Gentiles, and the glory of Your people Israel" (2:32 NKJV). To see Jesus is to see salvation embodied in Him. Simeon rejoices that his eyes saw the word of the Lord fulfilled. He recognizes in Jesus the promised bearer of messianic peace, joy, and light. The Messiah was expected to bring salvation not only for the Jewish nation but, as Simeon says, for "all people" (v. 31). Social class and ethnicity do not matter when it comes to God's salvation because Jesus came so that all could be saved. We should give thanks to God because salvation has become available to all who will receive it by faith.

---

1. List three characteristics of Simeon (v. 25).
2. What had the Holy Spirit shown Simeon (v. 26)?
3. Why did Simeon take Jesus in his arms (vv. 27-30)?
4. What did Simeon prophesy about Jesus' ministry (vv. 31-32)?

"There were many who saw the babe, but did not see the salvation."
—Author unknown

B. Division and Suffering (vv. 33-35)

³³ And Joseph and his mother marvelled at those things which were spoken of him. ³⁴ And Simeon blessed them, and said unto Mary his mother, Behold, this child is set for the fall and rising again of many in Israel; and for

a sign which shall be spoken against; [35] (Yea, a sword shall pierce through thy own soul also,) that the thoughts of many hearts may be revealed.

Joseph and Mary's amazement (v. 33) is twofold: (1) They marvel that a devout stranger such as Simeon should recognize the divine nature of their Son. (2) They are amazed at such deep insight into the things He is destined to do.

Simeon declares the Messiah child is destined to cause the falling and rising of many in Israel (v. 34). Simeon's oracle is ominous and looks to the future. He makes it known that the coming of the Messiah not only means salvation, but also division in the nation of Israel—a message that foreshadows Jesus' own saying in Luke 12:51-53. People would be brought to a moral decision. Sooner or later they would choose for or against Jesus.

A person's attitude toward Christ reveals and defines the quality of his or her character. Jesus would be a stumbling block to Israel. Simeon's saying reflects the critical mission of the Messiah and points to the future rejection of Jesus by His own people. The nation would be divided into two: those who responded to Jesus' message and those who opposed it.

Jesus' life will not be easy. Instead, His life will be filled with suffering and rejection. There will be a cost to Jesus. As the ultimate "sign" from God—the visible affirmation of God's declared intentions—Jesus will be vulnerable to the hostility of unbelievers.

After the blessing of the parents (2:34), the focus of Simeon's attention narrows to Mary, who will also suffer. The image of a sword piercing through Mary's soul means she will feel a mother's pain as she watches her Son suffer rejection. Mary bore the pain of giving birth to the Messiah, and she will have to share in His rejection. A sword will pierce her soul as she suffers the loss of her Son in death. The rejection and opposition to her Son will reach such a pitch that a literal sword will pass through His being.

To identify with Jesus will bring pain, because as they rejected Him, they will also reject His followers (see John 15:20). We are called to follow in the footsteps of Jesus, and those footsteps lead to suffering and ultimately to death. Are we living a life that is journeying toward the cross? Or, are we avoiding this path?

---

1. How would Jesus cause "the fall and rising" of many (v. 34)?
2. What would be "revealed" (v. 35)?
3. What warning did Simeon give to Mary (v. 35)? What did it mean?

"The Christmas message is that there is hope for a ruined humanity—hope of pardon, hope of peace with God, hope of glory—because at the Father's will Jesus became poor, and was born in a stable so that thirty years later He might hang on a cross."—J. I. Packer

---

III. THANKSGIVING FOR REDEMPTION (Luke 2:36-40)

A. The Prophetess Anna (vv. 36-37)

[36] And there was one Anna, a prophetess, the daughter of Phanuel, of the tribe of Aser: she was of a great age, and had lived with an husband seven years from her virginity; [37] And she was a widow of about fourscore

and four years, which departed not from the temple, but served God with fastings and prayers night and day. Luke's attention to the renewal and fulfillment of prophecy at the coming of the Messiah continues with the introduction of Anna as a "prophetess" (v. 36). Zacharias had been "filled with the Holy Spirit, and prophesied" (1:67 NKJV). However, Jesus' manifestation is made not only to a pious, upright, and devout Jewish man, but also to a woman.

Anna was an extraordinary woman, a widow of about eighty-four years of age, who never left the Temple (2:36-37). She likely lived in a small chamber of the Temple. She "served God with fastings and prayers night and day" (v. 37). The kingdom of God has been greatly advanced by saintly women who make precious their latter years by devoting themselves to intercession.

Anna looked and longed for the coming of the promised Redeemer. She never ceased to worship and pray. She spent her life in God's house with God's people. Though she was old, the years had left Anna without bitterness or rancor, but in steadfast hope, she kept her contact with Him who is the source of strength (Ps. 28:7) and in whose strength weakness is made perfect (2 Cor. 12:9).

1. Who was Anna?
2. Describe Anna's ministry.

"God is pleased with no music below so much as with thanksgiving songs of relieved widows and supported orphans; or rejoicing, comforted, and thankful persons."—Jeremy Taylor

B. Anna's Prophecy (vv. 38-40)

38 And she coming in that instant gave thanks likewise unto the Lord, and spake of him to all them that looked for redemption in Jerusalem. 39 And when they had performed all things according to the law of the Lord, they returned into Galilee, to their own city Nazareth. 40 And the child grew, and waxed strong in spirit, filled with wisdom: and the grace of God was upon him.

The providence of God so ordering it, when Anna saw the child Jesus, her eyes were open to His identity. She responded by offering praise and gratitude to God, as Simeon had done, for sending the long-expected Messiah. The expression "all them that looked for redemption in Jerusalem" (v. 38) seems to be a reference to Simeon's speech, and it might intimate that Anna's song was a kind of response (or counterpart) to his. She shared the same hope as Simeon did and was looking to the completion of God's redemption.

On that day, Anna found the One she was looking for. The Child had come, and the promises of God were being fulfilled. She continued speaking afterward of the newborn Messiah to all her acquaintances at Jerusalem. She declared that Jesus would bring redemption to Israel.

Having obeyed the law of Moses, Jesus' parents returned to their home in Nazareth (v. 39). Jesus grew in strength and wisdom, receiving the favor of God (v. 40).

1. What two things did Anna declare (v. 38)?
2. Describe the maturing process of Jesus (v. 40).

"Christ's yesterday was the accomplishment of redemption—His tomorrow is having His church with Himself in glory. But He is a living Christ for today."—G. V. Wigram

---

CONCLUSION

More than two thousand years have passed since Simeon saw Jesus in the Temple. What does this story have to say to us today?

Seeing Jesus meant everything to Simeon; it was his longing and hope. We must not be satisfied to go through life without Christ. Knowing Jesus is more important than anything we can imagine, yet it is a dream within our grasp. In a sense, Simeon's dream can come true in each of our lives.

Although we cannot hold Jesus in our arms or see Him with our physical eyes during this lifetime, we can know the Messiah personally. We can have a relationship with Jesus as our Savior, Friend, Brother, Lord, and King.

GOLDEN TEXT CHALLENGE

"THE LORD HATH MADE KNOWN HIS SALVATION: HIS RIGHTEOUSNESS HATH HE OPENLY SHEWED IN THE SIGHT OF THE HEATHEN [GENTILES]" (Ps. 98:2).

Psalm 98 begins with a call to "sing unto the Lord a new song" (v. 1). This psalm celebrates the salvation the Messiah offers to all people.

Orthodox believers sing verses 2 and 3—"The Lord has made known His salvation. . . . All the ends of the earth have seen the salvation of our God" (NKJV)—when they celebrate the Feast of Christ's Presentation in the Temple.

As we conclude this Christmas season, we should join in praising the Messiah for saving us.

Daily Devotions:
M. Salvation Announced to Abraham
    Genesis 12:1-3; Galatians 3:8
T. Salvation for the Gentiles
    Isaiah 45:20-23
W. Salvation by the Messiah
    Isaiah 59:16-21
T. Salvation Through God's Love
    John 3:14-18
F. Salvation by Jesus Christ
    Acts 15:7-11
S. Salvation by God's Grace
    Ephesians 2:4-10

Songs of Faith (Baptismal/Creedal Hymns)

1 Corinthians 15:53-58; Ephesians 5:8-14; Philippians 2:5-11;
1 Timothy 3:16; 2 Timothy 2:11-13; Revelation 15:3-4

Unit Theme:
Songs and Hymns in the New Testament

Central Truth:
Belief and confession affirm our faith in Christ.

Focus:
Examine confessional songs in Scripture and affirm our faith in Christ.

Context:
New Testament confessions of faith in Christ

Golden Text:
"If thou shalt confess with thy mouth the Lord Jesus, and shalt believe in thine heart that God hath raised him from the dead, thou shalt be saved" (Rom. 10:9).

Study Outline:
 I. Confessions of Faith
    (1 Tim. 3:16; 2 Tim. 2:11-13; Rev. 15:3-4)
 II. Song of Incarnation and Exaltation
    (Phil. 2:5-11)
III. Victory Over Death
    (Eph. 5:8-14; 1 Cor. 15:53-58)

INTRODUCTION

We do not have any recordings of first-century Christian vocal groups or soloists to listen to, and thereby discuss various aspects of the early music of the church. Yet there are a number of Scripture texts that are considered to be hymns of the early church.

In general, these songs confess various aspects of the life, work, and ministry of Christ. The heart of the New Testament and, in particular, of Paul's understanding of the person and place of Jesus Christ as the church's Lord and creation's head is to be found in the hymns.

The evidence of the songs in the Gospel of Luke (1:46-55; 68-79; 2:29-32) and certain hymn fragments in the Book of Revelation (e.g., 15:3-4) supports the conclusion that messianic psalms were being sung in Jewish-Christian circles that treasured those hymns. The significance of these compositions was partly celebratory but chiefly apologetic, and formed an important component of the early Christians' way of justifying their conviction that, in spite of the suffering and opposition they had to endure, God was sovereign in their affairs.

The hymns served an apologetic purpose in a culture where there were not only many lords and many gods, but also heresies (such as *Gnosticism* and *Docetism*) that were threatening the early Christian communities. According to the Gnostics, God is pure spirit who, by definition, is both untouched by matter and has no direct dealings with the material order. Thus, Jesus could not have been God. On the other hand, according to the Docetists, Jesus did not become a human, but remained only a spiritual being.

Christian hymns expressed gratitude to God for all He had done for the world's reconciliation and the church's salvation. The hymns celebrated (1) who Christ was and what He did before Creation, (2) His mission of incarnation and reconciliation, and (3) His installation and exaltation as Lord of all worlds and ruler of every agency—heavenly, human, and demonic.

I. CONFESSIONS OF FAITH (1 Tim. 3:16; 2 Tim. 2:11-13; Rev. 15:3-4)

A. Beyond All Question (1 Tim. 3:16)

16 And without controversy great is the mystery of godliness: God was manifest in the flesh, justified in the Spirit, seen of angels, preached unto the Gentiles, believed on in the world, received up into glory.

The phrase "without controversy"—or "beyond all question," as some modern translations render it—suggests that Paul is writing about something on which there is common consent among believers. The phrase introduces an outline of Christian faith expressing the unanimous conviction of Christians.

It is described as "the mystery of godliness." The term *mystery* also appears in verse 9 (translated "deep truths," NIV) and refers to truth that is now revealed. This mystery of the Christian religion is God's redemptive plan which had been a secret but was now revealed. Paul was extolling God's powerful actions that form the basis of the gospel and the transforming results that derive from accepting it.

Paul's outline is presented in the form of an early hymn. It contains six distinct statements, with Christ as the understood subject of each line. First, Paul asserts the humanity of Christ—He was "manifest in the flesh"; that is, He appeared in a body. The term *flesh* is a reference to Christ's humanness (except sin; cf. Rom. 8:3). Paul was asserting that in Christ, God himself had appeared in a human body. The incarnation of Christ comes first.

Second, He was "justified in the Spirit" or, literally, *vindicated* by the Holy Spirit—possibly a reference to the resurrection of Christ (cf. Rom. 1:3-4; 1 Peter 3:18).

Third, He "was seen by angels" (NKJV). The verb "was seen" is used in the New Testament to describe Jesus' post-resurrection appearances (1 Cor. 15:5-8). The expression of Paul is likely a reference to the worship given by angels to the ascended Christ.

Fourth, Christ was "preached unto the Gentiles"—He purchased salvation for all people.

Fifth, He was "believed on in the world"—a reference to the spread of the gospel in the Roman Empire.

Last, He was "received [taken up] into glory." Having finished His redemptive work, He was enthroned at the right hand of God. Jesus Christ is exalted—amen!

---

1. What does "great is the mystery of godliness" mean?
2. How was God "manifest in the flesh"?
3. How was Jesus "vindicated in the Spirit" (NASB)?

4. What is still being "preached"?

5. How is Jesus still being "believed on in the world"?

_____

"There is no mystery in heaven or earth so great as this—a suffering Deity, an almighty Savior nailed to a cross."—Samuel Zwemer

_____

B. A Faithful Saying (2 Tim. 2:11-13)

11 It is a faithful saying: For if we be dead with him, we shall also live with him: 12 If we suffer, we shall also reign with him: if we deny him, he also will deny us: 13 If we believe not, yet he abideth faithful: he cannot deny himself.
Paul begins these verses with his "faithful saying" formula. Each saying of verses 11-13 has four "if" clauses, each describing an action of a believer and with conclusions that present the results in terms of either Christ's individual action or joint action with the believer. The initial two sayings describe positive actions; the final two sayings refer to negative actions.

The initial line of the first saying, "If we died with Him" (v. 11 NKJV), reads like Romans 6:8. Paul presented Christian conversion as a dying and rising with Christ. The future tense of "we shall also live" suggests this is a reference to life in heaven. Although the reference is to heavenly life, there is a sense in which believers experience a beginning of eternal life now (John 5:24).

The first "if" clause of verse 12 of the text encouraged Timothy to remain loyal, even in the face of suffering. To "suffer" refers to a continuing experience of bravely bearing up under the hardships and afflictions heaped upon believers because of their relation to Christ. The conclusion promises a victory both for Timothy and in the end times for faithful believers. Believers will participate in the reign of the glorified Messiah after His return—a probable allusion to the millennial reign described in Revelation 20:1-6.

The second "if" clause of verse 12 of the text was a warning to Timothy and to all believers. The emphasis now shifts from positive actions of believers to negative actions. The language echoes that of Matthew 10:33. The disavowal of Christ is a verbal or behavioral denial to avoid suffering. Those who deny Christ in or because of persecution will face denial by Him in the Final Judgment (Mark 8:38). Those whom Christ denies in the Judgment will enter eternity as lost people.

Paul's dreadful warning did not apply to a temporary denial such as Peter demonstrated (Luke 22:54–62), but to a permanent denial such as Judas illustrated (Acts 1:15-19). The threat of disavowal would have been a warning to Timothy and other believers and a threat of judgment to the Asians of 2 Timothy 1:15 who had deserted.

Paul's statement in 2:13 has raised varied interpretations. To "believe not" ("faithless," NKJV) is a present tense, implying that the readers were developing a pattern of failure to live up to their profession or were proving unstable and disobedient in trials. Paul's point is that, despite human unfaithfulness, God's saving purpose has not retreated. Timothy and all those with him were to continue their endurance that they might experience God's blessing. Paul did not state these words to open the door to backsliding, careless living, and disobedience, but to soothe a troubled conscience and to provide encouragement to return to God.

Paul's warnings in these verses promise that God will reward loyalty to Christ and steadfastness in persecution. Disloyalty will receive punishment. May these warnings not fall on deaf ears! God will never change, will always be true to His character, and will continue to be faithful as He has promised regardless of the believer's faithlessness. God's omnipotence does not include the possibility of self-contradiction. God's divine faithfulness is immutable; for God not to be faithful would be to cease being Himself.

In these three verses, Paul's certainty of reward derived largely from the certainty that God was faithful to care for and love His people. God's faithfulness means future life and glory for believers. The warning of verse 12b presents relevant truth. Those who persist in a denial of God by a refusal to suffer for Him can expect to enter eternity separated from fellowship with God.

---

1. Explain the "faithful saying" (v. 11).
2. What is promised to those who suffer for Christ (v. 12)?
3. Whom will Christ "disown" (v. 12 NIV)?
4. What can Christ not deny (v. 13)?

"When you look at the Cross, what do you see? You see God's awesome faithfulness. Nothing—not even the instinct to spare His own Son—will turn Him back from keeping His Word."—Sinclair B. Ferguson

---

C. Song of Celebration (Rev. 15:3-4)

³ And they sing the song of Moses the servant of God, and the song of the Lamb, saying, Great and marvellous are thy works, Lord God Almighty; just and true are thy ways, thou King of saints. ⁴ Who shall not fear thee, O Lord, and glorify thy name? for thou only art holy: for all nations shall come and worship before thee; for thy judgments are made manifest.

This is a song of celebration, offering praise to God. The saints declare the righteous and redemptive activity of the Lord, beginning from Moses and culminating in the death and exaltation of the Lamb, which resulted in a new exodus.

The "song of Moses" (Ex. 15:1-18) celebrated the victory of the Lord in the defeat of the Egyptians at the Red Sea. Moses, as the leader of God's people and as a type of the Redeemer, who himself is part of the redeemed community, brought God's people out of Egypt. The deliverance from Egypt, with its divine plagues of judgment on Israel's enemies, was for the Jew a signpost of God's just rule over the world. In like manner, God's eschatological judgment and the deliverance of the followers of the Lamb bring forth from the victors over the Beast exuberant songs of praise to God for His righteous acts in history. The saints were praising God for His mighty deliverance and judgment on their enemies. Revelation 15:3-4 has a prophetic and messianic sense and points to resurrection. In their prophetic symbolism, the "song of Moses" and the "song of the Lamb" are identical.

---

1. List some of the Lord's "great and marvelous" works (v. 3).
2. How have you seen His ways to be "just and true" (v. 3)?
3. Why must we reverence and worship God (v. 4)?

"When God does it, we do more than remember it—we celebrate it."—
Woodrow Kroll

II. SONG OF INCARNATION AND EXALTATION (Phil. 2:5-11)

A. Christ's Humiliation (vv. 5-8)

5 Let this mind be in you, which was also in Christ Jesus: 6 Who, being in the form of God, thought it not robbery to be equal with God: 7 But made himself of no reputation, and took upon him the form of a servant, and was made in the likeness of men: 8 And being found in fashion as a man, he humbled himself, and became obedient unto death, even the death of the cross.

Philippians 2:5-11 is one of the lofty peaks of the entire New Testament. It narrates the story of Christ more fully than virtually any other passage in Paul's writings. The goal of these verses is to call the Philippians to embody the pattern of Christ's story in their own lives and relationships (v. 5).

Most interpreters understand verses 6-11 to be an early Christian hymn in honor of Christ, composed either by Paul or by someone else. The passage features exalted language and a poetic, rhythmic character. It tells the story of Jesus in summary form.

Verses 6-8 focus on Christ's incarnation. He voluntarily humbled Himself to the point of death. Rather than taking advantage of His rights, He humbled Himself in sacrificial love, showing us the character of God. Christ embraced the human condition in all its lowliness. This is the significance of the self-emptying action of Christ. Jesus, the Son of God, stands in solidarity with the poor, powerless, and oppressed—the suffering and the vulnerable, the lowly and the marginalized—because He has shared our fate. He indeed is *Immanuel*, "God with us." As one songwriter penned, "He walked where I walked . . . He understands."

---

1. What does it mean to have the "mind" of Christ (v. 5)?
2. How did the Son of God empty Himself (vv. 6-7)?
3. Describe the extremeness of Christ's obedience (v. 8).

"To achieve the divine purpose of becoming the Savior, the divine glory needed to be veiled. Christ voluntarily, moment by moment, submitted to human limitations apart from sin. The humiliation was temporary. The Incarnation was everlasting."—John F. Walvoord

---

B. Christ's Glorification (vv. 9-11)

9 Wherefore God also hath highly exalted him, and given him a name which is above every name: 10 That at the name of Jesus every knee should bow, of things in heaven, and things in earth, and things under the earth; 11 And that every tongue should confess that Jesus Christ is Lord, to the glory of God the Father.

These verses speak about the exaltation of Christ. He is exalted because He emptied Himself and embraced the cross in obedience to the Father. Because

He willingly gave up His position of honor and His life, He was given a name that is above every name, at the mention of which every knee shall bow and every tongue must confess.

What a reversal of fortune—the Suffering Servant is exalted as the unique Lord of the universe. Confessing Jesus as Lord means giving Him our obedience and love that belongs to Him and no one else. In saying that "every knee should bow" and "every tongue should confess that Jesus Christ is Lord" (vv. 10-11), Paul does not imply a universal salvation but indicates a universal acknowledgment of Christ's sovereignty, even by His enemies. Paul's point is that the whole gamut of created beings will bend the knee and acclaim the supremacy of Lord Jesus—nothing or no one is excluded.

When will this universal worship of Jesus take place? Is it simply a future event reserved for the final day? Or is it a current possibility, based on the present exaltation of Jesus? Surely we do not need to choose between the two. Since God has already exalted Jesus and given Him "[the] name which is above every name" (v. 9), the Church worships Jesus as Lord even now. But God's ultimate purpose that all would submit and confess Christ's lordship will occur only in the end-time future. Every creature will eventually recognize the dignity and divine prerogatives that the name *Lord* implies. When we acknowledge the lordship of Christ, we bring glory to God the Father who exalted Him.

---

1. Explain the loftiness of Jesus' name (v. 9).
2. Describe the authority in Jesus' name (vv. 10-11).

"On the head of Christ are many crowns: He wears the crown of victory . . . sovereignty . . . creation . . . providence . . . grace . . . glory."—James H. Aughey

---

III. VICTORY OVER DEATH (Eph. 5:8-14; 1 Cor. 15:53-58)

A. Singing as Children of Light (Eph. 5:8-14)

8 For ye were sometimes darkness, but now are ye light in the Lord: walk as children of light: 9 (For the fruit of the Spirit is in all goodness and righteousness and truth;) 10 Proving what is acceptable unto the Lord. 11 And have no fellowship with the unfruitful works of darkness, but rather reprove them. 12 For it is a shame even to speak of those things which are done of them in secret. 13 But all things that are reproved are made manifest by the light: for whatsoever doth make manifest is light. 14 Wherefore he saith, Awake thou that sleepest, and arise from the dead, and Christ shall give thee light.

Not only did all believers once live in darkness, they *were* darkness (cf. 4:18). But the good news is that now they have been rescued from the dominion of darkness and inherit the kingdom of light (Col. 1:12-13). They not only live in the light, they *are* light. This is something to sing about!

The parenthetical statement in verse 9 of the text explains the command at the end of verse 8. Light is known by its effects. Verse 10 completes the exhortation in verse 8. Christians are to conduct their lives in a morally discriminating way, and this requires that they put all their actions to the test of what is acceptable to the Lord.

Furthermore, Christians are to have no share in "the unfruitful works of darkness" (v. 11). Christians must dissociate both from evil works and evil persons. Paul is not advocating pharisaical separatism—his language does not necessarily exclude association with the children of darkness in the daily routines of life. Followers of Christ will go where their Master went and meet those their Master met. But though they do not withdraw from the world, they refuse to adopt its standards or fall in with its ways. We must beware of joining or assisting those who do wrong. Far from participating in them, believers should "reprove" ("expose," NASB) these practices.

Paul expresses why the works of darkness must be exposed (v. 12). First, they are unspeakably abominable—exceedingly sinful. Second, they are hidden.

Paul appeals to the effect of light in the natural world (v. 13). It penetrates wherever it shines, causing everything to be lit up by it. In the same way, whenever the light of Christ appears, it shows sin for what it is. Evil can no longer masquerade as anything else. The effect of Christian goodness on the society must be first to shame and then purify it.

Verse 14 is generally considered to be a baptismal hymn, sung to symbolize the transformation of a believer from a life of darkness into the radiant and awakening light of Christianity. It is not a direct quotation of Old Testament Scripture, though it contains echoes of Isaiah 60:1 and possibly other passages. Whatever the source of the hymn, its intent and purpose are clear—to praise Christ, the Light of the World, who gives light to all humanity.

---

1. What do the "children of light" produce (vv. 8-10)?
2. What do sinners produce (vv. 11-12)?
3. How does righteousness expose evil (vv. 11, 13-14)?
4. How does Christ want believers to live (v. 14)?

"I live and love in God's peculiar light."—Michelangelo

B. Celebrating Final Victory (1 Cor. 15:53-58)

53 For this corruptible must put on incorruption, and this mortal must put on immortality. 54 So when this corruptible shall have put on incorruption, and this mortal shall have put on immortality, then shall be brought to pass the saying that is written, Death is swallowed up in victory. 55 O death, where is thy sting? O grave, where is thy victory? 56 The sting of death is sin; and the strength of sin is the law. 57 But thanks be to God, which giveth us the victory through our Lord Jesus Christ. 58 Therefore, my beloved brethren, be ye stedfast, unmoveable, always abounding in the work of the Lord, forasmuch as ye know that your labour is not in vain in the Lord.

Our human body is not made to last forever. It will eventually die, no matter how much we exercise, eat right, and take care of it. Unless Jesus returns first, every one of us will die—it is just a question of when.

The resurrection body, on the other hand, will never die; it is imperishable. The laws of physics will be suspended in this new realm. The corruptible body will become incorruptible. The mortal—that which is subject to death—will put on immortality, so it will not be subject to death. Paul used the term *must* with these terms to emphasize the necessity of the change (v. 53).

Resurrection is the final defeat of death. A resurrected body is not a resuscitated corpse. It is a new order of life that will never die again. Death will be "swallowed up in victory" (v. 54).

Death is the result of sin. However, if a person's sin has been forgiven, death is but a step toward life eternal in a heavenly, resurrected body. Christ's sacrifice and resurrection has removed the sting of death.

Sigmund Freud, the well-known psychologist, once said, "And finally there is the painful riddle of death, for which no remedy at all has yet been found, nor probably ever will be." But he was dead wrong! Paul triumphantly taunts death: "O death, where is your victory? O death, where is your sting?" (v. 55 NASB).

Paul concludes with an encouragement to Christian workers: "Your toil is not in vain in the Lord" (v. 58 NASB). The hope of resurrection means that ministry carried out in the name of the Lord is not worthless.

---

1. When will believers "put on incorruption, and . . . immortality" (vv. 53-54)?
2. Where does death get its "sting" and "power" (vv. 55-56 NASB)?
3. How does God give victory (v. 57)?
4. What should motivate us to be faithful in our service to God (v. 58)?

"Jesus became mortal to give you immortality; and today, through Him, you can be free."—David Jeremiah

---

CONCLUSION

In our postmodern culture, the question frequently arises, "Why do you say Jesus is the only way?" or "Who are you to say Jesus is the only way?" We can expect the culture to ask questions like these, but sad to say, in the last few years the Christian church itself has begun to ask these same questions.

The divinity and incarnation of Christ are cardinal truths of the Christian faith. These are irreducible cores of convictions that we must maintain and affirm. God reveals Himself to us, and we receive His truth and experience a relationship with our Creator. Only Jesus can forgive sins because only Jesus Christ was God manifested in the flesh. He became the Son of Man so that we can become the sons and daughters of God. It is worth our celebration and song.

GOLDEN TEXT CHALLENGE

"IF THOU SHALT CONFESS WITH THY MOUTH THE LORD JESUS, AND SHALT BELIEVE IN THINE HEART THAT GOD HATH RAISED HIM FROM THE DEAD, THOU SHALT BE SAVED" (Rom. 10:9).

Upon hearing the gospel message, our requirement begins as we confess that Jesus is the Lord of Creation, our lives, and all that exists in heaven and in earth.

Throw yourself off the throne of your heart and establish Jesus as Lord and Master. Confess to yourself and to everyone around you that Jesus reigns supreme in your life. Acknowledge each day that you are His servant. Your happiness will be complete in knowing He is truly Lord.

Our faith in the fact that He rose from the grave is another essential of salvation. Without the resurrection of Jesus, the sacrifice on Calvary would have profited nothing; so the completion of our salvation, even though Christ paid the price, will depend on our belief in the open tomb.

Daily Devotions:
M. Confidence in the Living Redeemer
   Job 19:21-27
T. Expecting the Righteous King
   Isaiah 11:1-10
W. Seeing the Suffering Savior
   Isaiah 53:1-12
T. Believing in God's Son
   John 9:30-38
F. Fearing to Confess Christ
   John 12:37-43
S. Boldly Testifying of Christ
   Acts 4:5-13

Songs of Praise to God (Doxologies)

Revelation 4:8-11; 5:9-13; 7:9-12; 11:15-18; 19:1-7

Unit Theme:
Songs and Hymns in the New Testament

Central Truth:
God is worthy of our continual praises.

Focus:
Reflect on songs of praise to God in Scripture and praise Him continually.

Context:
From the island of Patmos in the first century AD, John the Revelator writes about worship in heaven.

Golden Text:
"While I live will I praise the Lord: I will sing praises unto my God while I have any being" (Ps. 146:2).

Study Outline:
I. Praise the Omnipotent God
    (Rev. 4:8-11; 7:11-12)
II. Praise Christ the Redeemer
    (Rev. 5:9-13; 7:9-10)
III. Worship God Who Reigns
    (Rev. 11:15-18; 19:1-7)

INTRODUCTION

Few books of the Bible hold as much mystery and fascination as does Revelation. It is filled with incredible images, animations, and symbols. Amid all the drama, the theme that repeatedly appears is *worship and praise to God*. Worship is neither incidental nor accidental, but forms an intricate part of the overall pattern and purpose of the book.

Whether dealing with the final crisis regarding those who worship the Beast and its image, or revealing living creatures and other beings in heaven who sing praises to God, Revelation comes back again and again to the worship of Him who "liveth for ever and ever" (5:14). He is "the One who is and who was and who is to come" (11:17 NKJV), and is deserving of all "glory and honour and power" (4:11).

The worship of God is always offered by true believers or angelic beings (11:1; 19:4-7). He is given the chief place, and worshipers take the low. In Revelation, worship is given to both God the Father and Jesus Christ. This would have been scandalous to first-century Jewish people, who were good monotheists. But those who became Christians, also strict monotheists, found room within their monotheism for worship of Jesus.

God is worshiped in Revelation for several reasons: He is omnipotent, omniscient, and omnipresent; He is worthy, eternal, sovereign, and holy; He is the

Creator, Redeemer, and the Judge. His plan is coming to pass, regardless of human and satanic oppositions. He is the Lamb who was slain yet who lives!

I. PRAISE THE OMNIPOTENT GOD (Rev. 4:8-11; 7:11-12)

A. Glory and Honor (4:8-11)

8 And the four beasts had each of them six wings about him; and they were full of eyes within: and they rest not day and night, saying, Holy, holy, holy, Lord God Almighty, which was, and is, and is to come. 9 And when those beasts give glory and honour and thanks to him that sat on the throne, who liveth for ever and ever, 10 The four and twenty elders fall down before him that sat on the throne, and worship him that liveth for ever and ever, and cast their crowns before the throne, saying, 11 Thou art worthy, O Lord, to receive glory and honour and power: for thou hast created all things, and for thy pleasure they are and were created.

John's letters to the seven churches of Asia (chs. 2-3) are followed by a dramatic scene shift in which the apostle is invited to ascend from earth to heaven (4:1). Here we see John's throne-room vision. Readers are given a sneak peek into God's world. We see a throne and the One sitting on it (vv. 2-5). We see the four beasts, which could be thought of as the worship leaders, in the throne room (v. 8). The number *four* was known to represent the "four corners" of the earth (cf. 7:1), and the four creatures represent parts of the created order.

The first words that the six-winged creatures sing are "Holy, holy, holy." This threefold praise is given in Trinitarian form. God the Father, the Lamb, and the Holy Spirit are all holy and worthy of praise. The phrase "which was, and is, and is to come" symbolizes that, in the throne room of God, past, present, and future merge together because the eternal God has no beginning and no end.

The four creatures continuously give praise because God is worthy of constant worship. God is worthy of praise simply because He is the enthroned One. A throne is a symbol of power and sovereignty. God is the Almighty and powerful One who is ruling over the heavens and the earth.

As the four living creatures praise God, the twenty-four elders begin to praise Him (vv. 9-10). They bow and cast their crowns before the Lord Almighty, and they sing praise to Him. Whatever power they have to wear crowns in the throne room of God ultimately belongs to Him, so they bow down and cast their crowns before the throne. Their praise covers another aspect of God's greatness—His creative power (v. 11). God is worthy off all praise because He is the holy, eternal, all-powerful Creator.

When is the last time we praised God simply because He is the Almighty? When is the last time we expressed appreciation to God for His creation and worshiped Him for His creative power?

---

1. Why do you suppose "holy" is used three times (v. 8)?
2. Explain the phrase "was, and is, and is to come" (v. 8).
3. How do the twenty-four elders respond to "him that liveth for ever and ever" (v. 10)?
4. Describe the Lord's relationship to the creation (v. 11).

"How divinely full of glory and pleasure shall that hour be when all the millions of mankind that have been redeemed by the blood of the Lamb of God shall meet together and stand around Him, with every tongue and every heart full of joy and praise!"—Isaac Watts

B. Eternal Worship (7:11-12)

¹¹ And all the angels stood round about the throne, and about the elders and the four beasts, and fell before the throne on their faces, and worshipped God, ¹² Saying, Amen: Blessing, and glory, and wisdom, and thanksgiving, and honour, and power, and might, be unto our God for ever and ever. Amen.

The angels, elders, and the four living creatures join the triumphant song of the multitude. Those worshiping God put their faces to the ground. This prostration is the appropriate response because of God's greatness.

There is a sevenfold doxology of praise given to God: *blessing, glory, wisdom, thanksgiving, honor, power,* and *might*. The number *seven* is considered the number of completeness in the Bible. It shows that the angels, the twenty-four elders, and the four living creatures are worshiping God to the full extent, and for all time. They worship God because of His greatness.

The praise begins and ends with "Amen" (v. 12). The phrase "unto our God" puts the praise in the context of personal relationship with God. He is not an abstract principle but a personal, relational, and interactive God whom all creation is meant to praise.

- List the seven words the angels ascribe to God in their worship (v. 12).

"Praise now is one of the great duties of the redeemed. It will be their employment forever."—Albert Barnes

II. PRAISE CHRIST THE REDEEMER (Rev. 5:9-13; 7:9-10)

A. 'Worthy Is the Lamb' (5:9-13)

⁹ And they sung a new song, saying, Thou art worthy to take the book, and to open the seals thereof: for thou wast slain, and hast redeemed us to God by thy blood out of every kindred, and tongue, and people, and nation; ¹⁰ And hast made us unto our God kings and priests: and we shall reign on the earth. ¹¹ And I beheld, and I heard the voice of many angels round about the throne and the beasts and the elders: and the number of them was ten thousand times ten thousand, and thousands of thousands; ¹² Saying with a loud voice, Worthy is the Lamb that was slain to receive power, and riches, and wisdom, and strength, and honour, and glory, and blessing. ¹³ And every creature which is in heaven, and on the earth, and under the earth, and such as are in the sea, and all that are in them, heard I saying, Blessing, and honour, and glory, and power, be unto him that sitteth upon the throne, and unto the Lamb for ever and ever.

Before we explore those praising the Lamb, we should examine what provoked such magnificent praise in the throne room of God. The Lamb is "standing in the center of the throne" (v. 6 NIV). The author, John, often refers to Jesus as the Lamb, which illustrates the Passover Lamb. Jesus is the sacrificial Lamb, but here He is also the Lamb who is now standing. He is risen! The Cross and Resurrection are the central reason to praise the Lamb.

Since the Lamb is standing in the seat of authority, He is worthy to take the book and open it (v. 9). This book is sealed with seven seals (v. 1). When it is opened, divine judgments leading to the Final Judgment are released on the earth.

The fourfold phrase "kindred, and tongue, and people, and nation" represents the whole earth. The praise begins around the throne and moves in an outward fashion. It begins with the four living creatures, then to the twenty-four elders, to the angels, to more and more angels (v. 11), and finally, to all creation.

As the redeemed people of all ages praise God, they express thanks for being made "kings and priests" (v. 10). This is reminiscent of 1 Peter 2:4-5, where believers are called "chosen by God and precious . . . living stones . . . a holy priesthood, to offer up spiritual sacrifices acceptable to God through Jesus Christ" (NKJV).

Blessing, honor, glory, and power are ascribed to the One on the throne (Rev. 5:12). Today, will you join in worship of the sacrificed, resurrected, reigning Lamb of God?

---

1. What is the Lamb of God "worthy" to do, and why (v. 9)?
2. What will Christ do for His followers (v. 10)?
3. Describe the sights and sounds around the throne of God (vv. 11-12).
4. Compare the universal praise pictured in verse 13 with your current worship of the Lord.

"If you had a thousand crowns, you should put them all on the head of Christ! And if you had a thousand tongues, they should all sing His praise, for He is worthy!"—William Tiptaft

---

B. 'Salvation to Our God' (7:9-10)

⁹ After this I beheld, and, lo, a great multitude, which no man could number, of all nations, and kindreds, and people, and tongues, stood before the throne, and before the Lamb, clothed with white robes, and palms in their hands; ¹⁰ And cried with a loud voice, saying, Salvation to our God which sitteth upon the throne, and unto the Lamb.

Again, the fourfold designation of nation, kindred, people, and tongue—illustrating men and women from the whole earth—is seen worshiping God and the Lamb before the heavenly throne. The "palms" (v. 9) are a reminder of Jesus' triumphal entry into Jerusalem, when the people proclaimed, "Hosanna to the son of David: Blessed is he that cometh in the name of the Lord; Hosanna in the highest" (Matt. 21:9).

The *palm branches* are a sign of Jesus' victory and kingship that was accomplished through the Cross and the Resurrection, thereby bringing salvation to humanity. *Salvation* is the victory accomplished through the Lamb of God by the will of God.

---

1. Describe (1) the number, (2) the diversity, and (3) the clothing of the worshipers (v. 9).
2. Thank God and the Lamb of God for providing salvation (v. 10).

"Does not all nature around me praise God? If I were silent, I should be an exception to the universe."—Charles Spurgeon

---

III. WORSHIP GOD WHO REIGNS (Rev. 11:15-18; 19:1-7)

A. God's Universal Reign (11:15-18)

15 And the seventh angel sounded; and there were great voices in heaven, saying, The kingdoms of this world are become the kingdoms of our Lord, and of his Christ; and he shall reign for ever and ever. 16 And the four and twenty elders, which sat before God on their seats, fell upon their faces, and worshipped God, 17 Saying, We give thee thanks, O Lord God Almighty, which art, and wast, and art to come; because thou hast taken to thee thy great power, and hast reigned. 18 And the nations were angry, and thy wrath is come, and the time of the dead, that they should be judged, and that thou shouldest give reward unto thy servants the prophets, and to the saints, and them that fear thy name, small and great; and shouldest destroy them which destroy the earth.

Instead of the silence in heaven, which follows the breaking of the seventh seal (8:1), the seventh trumpet precipitates the sound of "great" (loud) voices in heaven (11:15). Here is a victory chorus sung at the end of time when God comes to earth. The kingdom of humanity becomes the kingdom of God, and God will rule His people forever. Humanity will no longer have to deal with unjust and oppressive rulers.

The kingdoms of this world have always opposed God. Yet, the day is coming when God will establish a new kingdom that is ruled by peace, justice, and righteousness. The world will finally submit to the demands of God's sovereign kingdom. The coming of His kingdom to earth will provoke the twenty-four elders to worship Him as "Lord God Almighty" who will rule over the people of earth in His great power (v. 17). They will worship Him as the eternal God who has never changed and never will change.

The coming of God provokes anger from the nations of the earth (v. 18). There will be a final assault on God's authority, but the nations will lose their power to rule and will be judged for their evil works. God will destroy those who have brought destruction on the earth.

Meanwhile, those who have faithfully served God will be rewarded. The righteous from all walks of life—the "saints" both "small and great"—will be rewarded. The greatest reward will be that God will rule over them. "He will dwell with them, and they shall be his people" (21:3).

Songs of Praise to God (Doxologies)

1. Explain the reason for the praises in verses 15-17.
2. When God judges the earth, who will be rewarded, and who will be condemned (v. 18)?

"Jesus will come bathed in radiant splendor, enveloped within an atmosphere of indescribable brilliance, surrounded by the ear-piercing praise of angels and saints."—Sam Storms

---

B. The Marriage Supper of the Lamb (19:1-7)

[1] And after these things I heard a great voice of much people in heaven, saying, Alleluia; Salvation, and glory, and honour, and power, unto the Lord our God: [2] For true and righteous are his judgments: for he hath judged the great whore, which did corrupt the earth with her fornication, and hath avenged the blood of his servants at her hand. [3] And again they said, Alleluia. And her smoke rose up for ever and ever. [4] And the four and twenty elders and the four beasts fell down and worshipped God that sat on the throne, saying, Amen; Alleluia. [5] And a voice came out of the throne, saying, Praise our God, all ye his servants, and ye that fear him, both small and great. [6] And I heard as it were the voice of a great multitude, and as the voice of many waters, and as the voice of mighty thunderings, saying, Alleluia: for the Lord God omnipotent reigneth. [7] Let us be glad and rejoice, and give honour to him: for the marriage of the Lamb is come, and his wife hath made herself ready.

Revelation 19 begins with a celebration of divine justice and victory after the judgment of Babylon in chapters 17 and 18. The crowd praises God for salvation, His righteous judgment of Babylon, and His vengeance for the blood of the martyrs. Babylon—the evil worldly system—has corrupted the kings of the earth and spilled the blood of the martyrs. The victory of God celebrated in 19:1-5 is inclusive of those who have suffered for God through the ages. The servants of God are all those who belong to Him by faith, some of whom have died for that faith. All of His servants will be qualified to enter the heavenly city and to share in the Tree of Life (22:14).

The fall of Babylon caused a great multitude to sing a hallelujah chorus. God judges the "great whore" and those who are committing adultery with her (19:2). God is able to judge because He is "true and righteous" in His judgments. Since God is the righteous Judge, He is worthy of our praise.

The smoke that rises "for ever and ever" (v. 3) is representative of a city that has been set on fire and its smoke continues to rise as it burns. The fact that the smoke ascends unendingly shows the finality and totality of the devastation.

God will punish the wicked and vindicate the righteous. In verse 4, the twenty-four elders and four creatures, in their final appearance in the book, join in the rejoicing over the destruction of Babylon. As in previous appearances, they respond to God's actions with praise and worship.

In verse 5, there is a voice from the throne room with a command to praise God. A great multitude responds (v. 6). This is one of the greatest instances of worship throughout Revelation. The multitude comprises of all God's servants—not just a select group. The description of the sound alone is overwhelming, since thunder and a waterfall are some of the loudest natural sounds.

The saints praise because God is ruling sovereignly. Another reason for the saints in heaven and on earth to praise God is that the marriage feast of the Lamb has arrived—their salvation has been consummated (v. 7).

Right now, the Church is espoused to Christ and waiting for His return. We must maintain our commitment, keep ourselves pure, and trust in His promise to return.

---

1. How is God worshiped in verses 1-4, and why?
2. What do the "small and great" have in common (v. 5)?
3. What is "the marriage of the Lamb" (v. 7)?

"Very soon the shadow will give way to reality. The partial will pass into the perfect. The foretaste will lead to the banquet. The troubled path will end in paradise. A hundred candle-lit evenings will come to their consummation in the marriage supper of the Lamb."—John Piper

---

CONCLUSION

God is worthy of our worship. Our lives ought to be characterized by worship, not just because of what He does but because of who He is. He is the Creator, the sin-bearing Savior, and the coming King. We should follow the example of the four beasts and the twenty-four elders by falling prostrate at the Lord's feet in total worship.

GOLDEN TEXT CHALLENGE

"WHILE I LIVE WILL I PRAISE THE LORD: I WILL SING PRAISES UNTO MY GOD WHILE I HAVE ANY BEING" (Ps. 146:2).

The psalmist laid out his plan for the future—he would praise the Lord as long as he had the breath to do so. He could not predict the ups and downs he might experience with his health, his work, or his family, but he determined that whatever happened, he would continue to praise the Lord.

He knew the Lord would always be there to receive his praise, for "the Lord shall reign forever . . . to all generations" (v. 10 NKJV). Praise the Lord!

Daily Devotions:
M. Praising God for Victory
   Exodus 15:1-7
T. Exhortation to Praise God
   1 Chronicles 16:23-34
W. Sing Praises to God
   Isaiah 42:8-12
T. Glorifying God for Healing
   Luke 5:18-26
F. Glorifying God for Life Restored
   Luke 7:11-16
S. Glorifying God for Cleansing
   Luke 17:11-19

Time and Eternity

Unit Theme:
Wisdom From Ecclesiastes and Proverbs

Central Truth:
God rules supremely over time and eternity.

Focus:
Reflect on the brevity of life and the reality of eternity, and submit to God's sovereignty.

Context:
Ecclesiastes was probably written by Solomon during his long reign (970-931 BC).

Golden Text:
"I know that, whatsoever God doeth, it shall be for ever: nothing can be put to it, nor anything taken from it: and God doeth it, that men should fear before him" (Eccl. 3:14).

Study Outline:
  I. A Time for Everything
     (Eccl. 3:1-8)
 II. Eternity in Our Hearts
     (Eccl. 3:9-15)
III. God's Sovereignty and Human Mortality
     (Eccl. 9:1-10)

INTRODUCTION

The scriptural view of time is rooted in the Hebrew tradition. It is special and distinct. In fact, there are many different ways humanity thinks about time. Hindus believe in reincarnation—that a person's time marches onward into the future, changing and transforming as time moves on. Buddhists see time as not much more than a blip on the radar screen of the life cycle. They believe that after death, they can rejoin the cosmic life force, absorbed "like a drop in the ocean" into some universal consciousness. Atheists see time as linear, moving in one direction, with a beginning and an ending for all things. Christians view time as a precious gift, sanctified by God himself.

From the beginning of creation, God sanctified time. Genesis 2:3 says, "God blessed the seventh day, and sanctified it. . . ." This sanctification of time makes the God of the Bible different from other gods. Most gods have been hard at work sanctifying temples. The creation of sacred space is central to the human experience. In fact, some of the wonders of the world are temple complexes, built centuries ago to put people in touch with divinity. The God of the Bible, however, isn't that concerned about sacred spaces. Even when King David expresses the desire to build a temple for Him, God responds, "Are you the one to build me a house to dwell in? I have not dwelt in a house from the day I brought the Israelites up out of Egypt to this day. I have been moving from place to place with a tent as my dwelling" (2 Sam. 7:5-6 NIV). Rather than focusing on sacred space, God desires that humanity should see time as our most sacred gift.

In the Hebrew tradition, time is circular. We see this in the overarching story of the Bible, as God works to reverse the effects of the fall of man so that the entire creation is restored to God's original intent. The Garden of Eden will one day prevail again. Until then, the Book of Ecclesiastes assures us that God is involved in every detail of our time.

I. A TIME FOR EVERYTHING (Eccl. 3:1-8)

Ecclesiastes is a book of philosophy, theology, and practicality. It describes the different value systems people choose, and guides us in the best choices. In the first two chapters, Solomon describes the various pursuits of his own life. He had tried the pursuit of wisdom, knowledge, and learning (1:12-18), the pursuit of personal pleasure (2:1-3), the pursuit of great projects (vv. 4-7), and the pursuit of wealth (vv. 8-10). However, these pursuits led to the same problem which is the mantra of Ecclesiastes: "Everything was meaningless, a chasing after the wind" (v. 11 NIV). This conclusion is common among people who achieve great wealth, fame, and success. After Solomon has it all, he questions what any of it is really worth. He asks what will last and what is meaningless. In so doing, he takes us on a theological journey.

In chapter 3, Solomon turns to begin a new section of the Book of Ecclesiastes. Now that he has spent so much time devoting himself to these different pursuits, he addresses the reality of time itself. His conclusions about time lay the foundations for his answer to the problem of meaninglessness. Time spent wisely, pursuing the life God has purposed for humanity, solves the problem of vanity.

A. A Time for Life and Death (vv. 1-3)

¹ To every thing there is a season, and a time to every purpose under the heaven: ² A time to be born, and a time to die; a time to plant, and a time to pluck up that which is planted; ³ A time to kill, and a time to heal; a time to break down, and a time to build up.

In Scripture, as in the history of human thought, death always threatens to render life meaningless. One of the central issues Solomon deals with in Ecclesiastes is the problem of death. This subject may have been the catalyst that caused him to write in the first place. He notes in 2:14 that death overtakes both the wise and the foolish. He observes in verse 21 that even a skilled worker leaves the fruits of his labor to another generation. He revisits the subject in an extended essay in 9:1-12. In chapters 1 and 2, this is all seen as depressing information. In chapter 3, however, Solomon begins to incorporate an all-knowing God into these realities.

In the first two chapters, Solomon recounts periods of his life where he devoted all of his time to pursuing success in different forms. At the end of this pursuit, he found only meaninglessness. In chapter 3, however, Solomon recognizes the need to see the diversity of time. No one's time should be directed toward the pursuit of one thing, for God is present in all forms of time. Being sovereign, God is even present in death.

Solomon had only known a compartmentalized life in which he tried to block out elements of life that he found unpleasant. In verses 1-3, he admits the futility of this. Instead of trying to bend time to his demands, he recognizes that God has set time in place to order human life. This ordering includes birth and death, planting and uprooting, killing and healing, tearing down and building.

In Solomon's society, most laborers were farmers. The people had a close relationship with the earth. They were not disconnected from the sources of their food, their meat, and their water, as modern societies often are. Solomon's language of life and death reflects this background and communicates to this kind of society.

He begins by reflecting on birth and death. There were no hospitals in Solomon's society. People were very familiar with the realities of birth and death.

Solomon then describes planting and uprooting. A farmer would uproot a crop if it was diseased or threatening to the life of the healthy crop. This is part of the life cycle of growing crops.

Next, Solomon sets up a contrast between killing and healing. This is the language of livestock. Solomon's original audience knew the bloodiness of killing an animal in order that it might sustain their own lives. They also knew the compassion of caring for their sick animals in order to help them heal.

Finally, Solomon describes a time to tear down and a time to build. This is the language of primitive home construction. When a home had outlived its capacity and begun to rot, it was torn down. Likewise, new-home construction was common. Solomon's point is to help us see the darker sides of life in a new light. Tearing down, killing, uprooting, and death do not have to lead to depression. They can be seen in the light of their opposites: building, healing, planting, and birth. Solomon reminds us that God is sovereign over all of this—both the joys and the sorrows of life.

---

1. Why is life seasonal (v. 1)?
2. Are you currently in a season of planting and building or uprooting and breaking down (vv. 2-3)?

A Secret Society?

In a letter written to the Roman emperor Trajan during the New Testament time period, a local governor named Pliny writes about the problem of Christianity. Interestingly, Pliny tells the emperor that he had prohibited Christian worship gatherings because he considered them a "secret society." In the ancient world, no one could conceive of a God without a temple. Early Christians, however, knew their God was focused not on sacred space, but sacred time. This message is beautifully presented by Solomon in the Book of Ecclesiastes.

B. A Time for Relationships (vv. 4-8)

⁴ A time to weep, and a time to laugh; a time to mourn, and a time to dance; ⁵ A time to cast away stones, and a time to gather stones together;

a time to embrace, and a time to refrain from embracing; ⁶ A time to get, and a time to lose; a time to keep, and a time to cast away; ⁷ A time to rend, and a time to sew; a time to keep silence, and a time to speak; ⁸ A time to love, and a time to hate; a time of war, and a time of peace.

The Book of Ecclesiastes places healthy human relationships at the center of God's will for humanity. One of the most inspiring passages of the book centers on friendship and community (4:9-12). In the second half of Solomon's poem about time in 3:4-8, the king builds the foundation for this inspiration. He speaks of relational time.

Solomon knows that the subject of human relationships is as important to people as is the subject of time and eternity. In fact, these subjects are intertwined. The quality of a person's life depends on the quality of his or her relationships. Therefore, Solomon depicts the action of God in creating "relational time."

The beauty of this passage is its depiction of God's providence over human relationships in times of happiness *and* sadness. What relevance to marriage, family, and friendship! Between people, Solomon says, there is both crying and laughter, mourning and dancing. Each of these should take place in community. He cautions us from thinking that God has somehow withdrawn Himself when a key relationship in our lives breaks down. Instead, there are times to embrace and times to let a relationship cool. What is more, there are times to break away from a relationship, and times to keep up the fight. There are even times to be silent.

The most dramatic couplet in the stanza occurs in verse 8, as Solomon addresses war/hate and peace/love. Relationships between nations are not much different than relationships between individuals. The destruction caused by war has caused many people to question God's providence. Indeed, Christians are charged to oppose unjust war. But Solomon reminds us of human history and God's sovereignty over it. There have been times of war, just as there have been times of peace. When difficulty comes, God is not suddenly absent.

Solomon's poem reminds us that God is the giver and dispenser of the most sacred gift we have: *time.* Time is the great equalizer. For people at war or peace, laughing or mourning, building or uprooting, young or old, each person is given by God the same amount of time each day. As Derek Kidner states, time "is a gift from God, an allotted portion in life, whose purpose is known to the Giver and is part of His everlasting work; for God does nothing in vain" (*The Message of Ecclesiastes: A Time to Mourn, and a Time to Dance*). The passage is an encouragement to look to God as the One who gives man the ability to even ask the questions posed in Ecclesiastes. These abilities would be nonexistent if it were not for the gift of time.

---

1. What has caused mourning and weeping in your life (v. 4)? What has brought about laughter and dancing?
2. How do you know when to "keep silence" and when to "speak" (v. 7)?
3. Are you currently experiencing "war" or "peace" in your personal life (v. 8)?

"In everyone's life, at some time, our inner fire goes out. It is then burst into flame by an encounter with another human being. We should all be thankful for those people who rekindle the inner spirit."—Albert Schweitzer

---

II. ETERNITY IN OUR HEARTS (Eccl. 3:9-15)

It is impossible to speak of time without speaking of its limitations. For the atheist, those limitations are narrow: time exists for each person from birth until death, with nothing before nor after. For the Christian, however, time's boundaries are expanded to embrace eternity—the furthest reaches of time. We see this in the character of God as revealed in the Old Testament. He is sometimes called the God who is "from everlasting to everlasting" (1 Chron. 16:36 NIV; Ps. 41:13). In Genesis 1, He is the originator of all of creation who Himself was not created. He simply *is*. Because God is the creator of time, Solomon turns to Him to understand how to wisely use it.

A. The Mystery of Time (vv. 9-11)

⁹ What profit hath he that worketh in that wherein he laboureth? ¹⁰ I have seen the travail, which God hath given to the sons of men to be exercised in it. ¹¹ He hath made every thing beautiful in his time: also he hath set the world in their heart, so that no man can find out the work that God maketh from the beginning to the end.

Throughout Ecclesiastes, Solomon is fascinated by the problem of toil. In his agrarian society, hard work was necessary for survival; and even then, things did not always pan out for the poor. In the Hebrew tradition, difficult toil is part of the curse upon Adam's sin. God declared, "Cursed is the ground . . . through painful toil you will eat of it all the days of your life" (Gen. 3:17 NIV). We should not confuse all work with toil. Adam and Eve were given work to do in the Garden. Productive work is sanctified by God throughout Scripture. Toil, however, is work without end that does not produce the sustenance for a fulfilling life. This is the problem Solomon sees all around him (Eccl. 3:9-10). Solomon asks, "What does the worker gain from his toil?" (v. 9 NIV) from the context of the problem of time. He recognizes that even the fruits of successful labor will be left for another generation (2:21). He attributes this reality to God.

But there is another side of the coin. The same God who demands hard labor also creates beauty, wonder, and mystery that inspires people's hearts (3:11). Even among the realities of toil, there is beauty all around. Even when toil seems to reduce people to machines, there is something that sets us apart from the animals: we can conceive eternity.

This is important because the conception of eternity sets men and women apart as the beings who can commune with God. Also, the ability to understand eternity brings meaning to the time we have on this earth, even this toil! We recognize that everything we do is under the watchful eye of an eternal God. This does not mean we can fathom God. Solomon says plainly that this is ludicrous. But the fact that we can dialogue with one another about eternity speaks to our own eternal nature alongside God.

1. Answer the question in verse 9.
2. How does God make "everything beautiful in its time" (v. 11 NKJV)?
3. What quandary is presented in verse 11?

> Our toil is sweet with thankfulness,
>   Our burden is our boon;
> The curse of the earth's gray morning is,
>   The blessing of its noon.
> —John Greenleaf Whittier

B. The Significance of Time (vv. 12-15)

¹² I know that there is no good in them, but for a man to rejoice, and to do good in his life. ¹³ And also that every man should eat and drink, and enjoy the good of all his labour, it is the gift of God. ¹⁴ I know that, whatsoever God doeth, it shall be for ever: nothing can be put to it, nor any thing taken from it: and God doeth it, that men should fear before him. ¹⁵ That which hath been is now; and that which is to be hath already been; and God requireth that which is past.

This conception of eternity begins to turn the discussion into a hopeful direction. Because we can conceive eternity, there is hope for us! There is meaning for our life, even in the midst of toil (vv. 12-13). We can experience happiness, satisfaction, and plenty. Solomon recognizes these qualities for what they are— a gift. They are not earned by us. They are not begrudgingly given. They are God's free gift to us all.

As the passage comes full circle, Solomon finally depicts God's active involvement in human time. Indeed, God sanctifies time (vv. 14-15). The glory of time is that God owns it and has chosen to act within human time. What is more, His actions are eternally enduring. We cannot affect them or delete them. And God does this to bring us closer to Himself! This brings time meaning in a way that Solomon's vainglorious pursuits did not. The fact that God makes demands of the way we spend our time infuses it with a sacred character. He "will call the past to account" (v. 15 NIV), indicating that time is not meaningless—it is the domain of God. Time matters to God, and this ends Solomon's search for time's meaning. God orders it, sanctifies it, and holds man accountable for the way it is spent.

---

1. What is "the gift of God" (vv. 12-13)?
2. How is God's work superior to humanity's work (v. 14)?

"Oh, how precious is time, and how it pains me to see it slide away, while I do so little to any good purpose."—David Brainerd

III. GOD'S SOVEREIGNTY AND HUMAN MORTALITY (Eccl. 9:1-10)

In Solomon's day, classes separated populations of people. Typical societies were led by a small percentage of wealthy elites, while the vast majority of the population was primitive and even poor. In the Book of Ecclesiastes, Solomon brings separated groups of people together. He shows how they are the same. They have been given the same time, the same anxiety, and the same God. In chapter 9, Solomon writes about the same destiny for all people. He destroys the categories that people have set up to create insiders and outsiders, and levels the human playing field beneath the demands of life and God.

A. The Futility of Death (vv. 1-6)

¹ For all this I considered in my heart even to declare all this, that the righteous, and the wise, and their works, are in the hand of God: no man knoweth either love or hatred by all that is before them. ² All things come alike to all: there is one event to the righteous, and to the wicked; to the good and to the clean, and to the unclean; to him that sacrificeth, and to him that sacrificeth not: as is the good, so is the sinner; and he that sweareth, as he that feareth an oath. ³ This is an evil among all things that are done under the sun, that there is one event unto all: yea, also the heart of the sons of men is full of evil, and madness is in their heart while they live, and after that they go to the dead. ⁴ For to him that is joined to all the living there is hope: for a living dog is better than a dead lion. ⁵ For the living know that they shall die: but the dead know not any thing, neither have they any more a reward; for the memory of them is forgotten. ⁶ Also their love, and their hatred, and their envy, is now perished; neither have they any more a portion for ever in any thing that is done under the sun.

Ecclesiastes is a book of meandering questions. Solomon often holds contradictory truths on the same page, and slowly works them out by bending them toward God. He does this with death—the ultimation of human time—in chapter 9.

Solomon begins by questioning whether morality matters, given that death will find every sort of person (vv. 1-2). Death operates just like time—it levels the playing field. It destroys the walls we set up that make some people superior and others inferior. Every kind of person has it coming. As a result, Solomon is driven to despair. There is no reason to prefer righteousness, because the righteous cannot fight death. Because of this harsh reality, he calls the problem of death an "evil" (v. 3). All this leads to the further despair of verses 4-6. The dead are characterized as hopeless and nonexistent.

For the New Testament Christian, Solomon's treatise on death is a bit shocking. We must keep in mind two points. First, the Old Testament does not have a developed view of the afterlife. In fact, throughout the Bible, God is incredibly pro-world, pro-now, and anti-death. Paul calls death "the last enemy" (1 Cor. 15:26) God will destroy. So there is no biblical sentiment that God's goal is to get us to the afterlife, but rather God's new creation is breaking into the old. In the Old Testament, we catch glimpses of life after death, but these are not central to Old Testament theology. As Old Testament scholar Lawrence Boadt writes, "The most striking feature in Israel's thinking about the question of death was how *final* death was thought to be throughout most of the Old Testament period" (*Reading the Old Testament: An Introduction*). Solomon reflects this view of death.

The second point is that the Bible is a progressive revelation of God's plan. That is, the Bible does not tell us everything we need to know in one page. It is a history spanning thousands of years, and over that time period we come to know God's revelation. Indeed, His full revelation is in the person and teachings of Jesus. So we should not pass judgment on Solomon's view of death given the historical time period he fills. Yet even centuries before the resurrection message of Easter, Solomon catches glimpses of death's hope.

---

1. What is "in the hand of God" (vv. 1-2)?
2. Explain the phrase "a living dog is better than a dead lion" (v. 4).

"To contemplate all things as God sees them, as Christ beholds them, overcomes sin, defies Satan, dissolves perplexities, lifts us above trials, separates us from the world, and conquers fear of death."—A. B. Simpson

---

B. The Hope of Death (vv. 7-10)

⁷ Go thy way, eat thy bread with joy, and drink thy wine with a merry heart; for God now accepteth thy works. ⁸ Let thy garments be always white; and let thy head lack no ointment. ⁹ Live joyfully with the wife whom thou lovest all the days of the life of thy vanity, which he hath given thee under the sun, all the days of thy vanity: for that is thy portion in this life, and in thy labour which thou takest under the sun. ¹⁰ Whatsoever thy hand findeth to do, do it with thy might; for there is no work, nor device, nor knowledge, nor wisdom, in the grave, whither thou goest.

The reality of death, somber as it is, still provides reason for Solomon to hope. He says there are two ways of looking at this harsh reality of death: (1) fall into hopelessness or (2) drink deep of the joys of life! God's favor is now, so Solomon champions a full life, a fulfilling marriage, and productive work. He is not recommending, of course, debauchery, but simply the recognition that God's gift of time has been given right now and is not guaranteed tomorrow. Therefore, he finds meaning in a fulfilling life.

This fulfilling life is first described in eating, drinking, and even dressing beneath God's hand of favor (vv. 7-8). The reality of death is a cause for true life! In Solomon's culture, wine, white clothes, and anointing oil were symbols of prosperity and peace.

Next, Solomon encourages healthy marriages as a gift of enjoyment (v. 9). Finally, Solomon speaks of the joy that comes from personal development, from pushing oneself toward excellence (v. 10). He presents this way of life as a strategy for dealing with what we cannot know. Since we can never truly comprehend death, we should be driven to truly live life.

We may not be used to reading the Bible this way, but one simple message of Ecclesiastes rings out loud and clear: living a happy, fulfilling life is a gift from God. Present Christianity still lives beneath the shadow of medieval Catholic Christianity, when the images for life with God were images of pain and suffering. Indeed, the early monastic movement elevated suffering to an idol all itself.

Suffering certainly has a place in Christian experience, but Ecclesiastes tells us that so does a full life. This too is a gift from God.

---

1. Explain the blessing of verse 8.
2. What does verse 9 say about the married life?
3. Explain the work ethic in verse 10.

"A human being does not cease to exist at death. It is change, not destruction, which takes place."—Florence Nightingale

---

CONCLUSION

In Ecclesiastes 3 and 9, Solomon dives into difficult topics: the limits of time and the reality of death. Whereas these subjects could be disillusioning, Solomon finds reason to hope. This hope is centered in an eternal God who is above all time. This eternal God sanctifies time on earth so that it can be meaningful and enjoyed by humanity.

GOLDEN TEXT CHALLENGE

"I KNOW THAT, WHATSOEVER GOD DOETH, IT SHALL BE FOR EVER: NOTHING CAN BE PUT TO IT, NOR ANY THING TAKEN FROM IT: AND GOD DOETH IT, THAT MEN SHOULD FEAR BEFORE HIM" (Eccl. 3:14).

We see things from an earthbound perspective, but God sees the beginning and the end of all things. What God does, He does with eternity and our best in mind.

The *Orthodox Study Bible* comments, "'That men should fear before him' expresses the writer's understanding of why the world is the way it is. God uses the world to turn us to Himself, for at the end of the age the time will come for judgment."

Daily Devotions:
M. The Eternal Refuge
   (Deut. 33:26-29)
T. The Brevity of Life
   (Eccl. 12:1-7)
W. The One Who Inhabits Eternity
   (Isa. 57:15-18)
T. Eternal Blessings for the Faithful
   (Mark 10:28-31)
F. An Eternal Home
   (2 Cor. 5:1-8)
S. An Eternal Inheritance
   (Heb. 9:11-15)

Authorities and Friends

Ecclesiastes 3:16-17; 4:1-12; 8:1-5, 11-13

Unit Theme:
Wisdom From Ecclesiastes and Proverbs

Central Truth:
Godly wisdom is needed in our relationships with authorities and friends.

Focus:
Explore and follow wise advice concerning authorities and friendship.

Context:
Ecclesiastes was probably written by Solomon during his long reign (970-931 BC).

Golden Text:
"Wisdom strengtheneth the wise more than ten mighty men which are in the city" (Eccl. 7:19).

Study Outline:
  I. Dealing With Injustice
     (Eccl. 3:16-17; 4:1-6)
 II. Obeying Authorities
     (Eccl. 8:1-5, 11-13)
III. Benefits of Companionship
     (Eccl. 4:8-12)

INTRODUCTION

As human beings, we are thoroughly relational creatures. We navigate our time on earth through the network of relationships we are born into and that we continue to develop. It is interesting that even before sin entered the world through the disobedience of Adam and Eve, God observed a problem: "It is not good that the man should be alone" (Gen. 2:18). This is astounding! God looks at His perfect creation and proclaims that something is "not good"—something is incomplete. So, with the addition of Eve, the human community is born.

Since that day, the human community has grown increasingly complex. We can no longer relate to God as a single family. Instead, we navigate thousands of relationships across the span of our lives. In the twenty-first century, the human family is more interconnected than ever before. We are aware that the decisions we make affect people in other parts of the world whom we will likely never meet. These layers of complexity demand relationships that take a different form than Adam and Eve knew in the Garden, namely, friendship and authority. Without friendship, we would remain a tribal society, stuck within each of our extended family networks. Without authority, society would dive into anarchy, and sheer chaos would result. Although these were not issues in the Garden of Eden, we still see God laying a foundation for the dynamics of friendship and authority.

First, God relates to Adam and Eve as a friend. He cares for them, watches over them, and guides them. He is no tyrant demanding to be appeased, but a friend who walks with them each day. It is only when they choose to listen to the wrong voice—the voice of the serpent, who poses falsely as a friend—that they have problems. Second, the fall of Adam and Eve shows that God set the world up to adhere to His authority alone. Although God mercifully makes clothes for the first man and woman (3:21), He also banishes them from the Garden, never to return. God's authority is nothing to be toyed with. As we turn to these two themes (friendship and authority) in the Book of Ecclesiastes, we should remember that they are rooted throughout the Bible from its first pages.

I. DEALING WITH INJUSTICE (Eccl. 3:16-17; 4:1-6)

Justice is one of the most prominent themes in the Old Testament. It is unfortunate that many contemporary Christian understandings of God's judgment treat it as a negative thing. For example, God's "retributive justice" is the basis of the sacrificial system, where the guilt of humans is transferred to the death of animals. In certain New Testament passages, Jesus' death is compared to this retributive justice. However, this is not the entire story. God's justice in the Bible is not only about God's wrath, it is also about His mercy. This second type of justice is called "distributive justice." It is a form of justice that is graciously distributed to the whole of creation. This justice celebrates the destruction of sin, evil, and oppression, so that everyone may live in a fully restored creation that is full of God's glory. It is the ultimate expression of this justice that the New Testament looks forward to, a time when "there will be no more death or mourning or crying or pain, for the old order of things has passed away" (Rev. 21:4 NIV).

A. The Ultimate Judge (3:16-17)

16 And moreover I saw under the sun the place of judgment, that wickedness was there; and the place of righteousness, that iniquity was there. 17 I said in mine heart, God shall judge the righteous and the wicked: for there is a time there for every purpose and for every work.

Because the Scriptures are rooted in the concept that God desires a just society, there is a tremendous focus on just leaders. This was a time before the world's modern judicial system. Kings, governors, priests, and local political leaders were often charged with mediating legal disputes. We see this in the early stories about the author of Ecclesiastes. In 1 Kings 3, two prostitutes are brought before the king, arguing over a baby. Each woman claims to be the mother. Solomon wisely determines the real mother, and the story makes him famous. Verse 28 summarizes: "When all Israel heard the verdict the king had given, they held the king in awe, because they saw that he had wisdom from God to administer justice" (NIV). So we see that the capacity to rightly administer justice is a very significant part of proper rulership.

This fixation in biblical thought about the just ruler obviously stems from the fact that such rulers were probably rare. Even in Israel's history, not to mention her neighbors', we see rulers claiming to follow God yet consistently perverting justice. Not even King David is immune, as the shock of his affair with Bathsheba is more about justice than it is about sexual immorality (David—the most powerful man in the East—knocks off the "little guy" and takes his wife).

As David's son, Solomon is well aware of these dynamics. In Ecclesiastes 3:16-17, Solomon makes a common lament in the literature of this time period—a complaint about unjust rulers.

The places of "judgment" and "righteousness" (v. 16) should be considered one and the same. Solomon was writing about political leaders who were charged to order a just society. This is a time period in which religion, politics, and the legal system were intertwined. Therefore, the "place of judgment" could refer to the administration of a king, the ministry of a priest, or the power of a local tribal leader. These were all places where ancient peoples might turn for justice in mediating their disputes with one another.

It is important to remember that this observation about unjust rulers comes from the king who asked God, above all, for "a discerning heart to govern your people and to distinguish between right and wrong" (1 Kings 3:9 NIV). Solomon himself was a champion of justice. Scholars tell us that the stability of his governance led to the most unprecedented economic boom in Israel's ancient history. Solomon was successful in ordering a just society, and the results were peace and prosperity for Israel's citizens. Therefore, it is easy to understand why he would admit shock at seeing wickedness in the place of judgment.

Solomon's response to this observation about unjust leadership (Eccl. 3:17) is unlike Old Testament passages where unjust leaders are immediately condemned. In Psalm 58, David calls for God to "break the teeth" of those rulers who "devise injustice" (vv. 2, 6 NIV). Such violent refrains are common in the Bible's criticism of injustice. Here, however, Solomon is more measured. He takes a theocentric, or "God-centered," approach to the problem.

Instead of issuing a royal edict or proclaiming his opinion from the rooftops, Solomon lays out a basic theology for responding to unjust rulers. It is simple: God will judge every person, from the least to the greatest. The New Testament echoes this great biblical truth that "every one of us shall give account of himself to God" (Rom. 14:12). It was a revolutionary idea that the ruling class would be given no favoritism in the divine realm after death. Remember the pharaohs of Egypt, whose pyramids are stocked with their wealth to assist them in their dealings with the gods. There is no such favoritism in God's viewpoint, Solomon says. The problem of unjust rulers is solved by a just God. He will not leave wickedness unpunished. Their time will end. Their time will bend its knee to God's time, and God's justice will ultimately prevail, for He is the ultimate judge.

---

1. What frustrated the writer (v. 16)? When do you have a similar frustration?
2. What encouraged the writer (v. 17)?
3. How do you practice justice?

"Justice and power must be brought together, so that whatever is just may be powerful, and whatever is powerful may be just."—Blaise Pascal

Authorities and Friends

B. The Problem of Power (4:1-3)

¹ So I returned, and considered all the oppressions that are done under the sun: and behold the tears of such as were oppressed, and they had no comforter; and on the side of their oppressors there was power; but they had no comforter. ² Wherefore I praised the dead which are already dead more than the living which are yet alive. ³ Yea, better is he than both they, which hath not yet been, who hath not seen the evil work that is done under the sun.

In biblical thought, the result of unjust power is called *oppression*. Oppression is what happens when one class of people are denied basic rights by a higher class of people. It's not surprising, then, that Solomon turns to observations about oppressed people in the wake of his observations about unjust rulers.

On first glance, the situation appears to be hopeless for those who are oppressed (vv. 1-3). Solomon sat in the most privileged position in the nation and the world. Yet he had the ability to stoop down from his throne and to observe that his just society still had an underclass. As much as he strove for justice, he was unable to fully eradicate injustice. In the tears of the oppressed, he sees there was still much work to be done.

This observation leads to a state of depression in verse 2. The situation is so dire, Solomon says, that perhaps the dead are better off than those living persons who are relegated to this class of oppressed people. Solomon has built his entire administration around achieving justice. It is his "campaign platform." Although he is heartbroken when he sees that it has failed many people and that they still languish under the power of oppressors, he holds out hope for the future (v. 3). There is a new generation yet to be born. This generation holds the most privileged position. In these words, Solomon expresses faith that God will continue to lead this nation and continue to lead him. He believes his emphasis on just leadership will create a better society for the next generation. Things may be dark for an entire class of people now, but Solomon believes a brighter day awaits.

---

1. Where is oppression currently taking place (v. 1)?
2. In what sense are the unborn better off than the living (vv. 2-3)?

"According to [the Bible], a leader is first and foremost a servant. His concern is not for himself; his concern is not to give orders, to boss other people around, to have his own way. His concern is to meet the needs of others."—Wayne Mack

---

C. How Much Is Enough? (vv. 4-6)

⁴ Again, I considered all travail, and every right work, that for this a man is envied of his neighbour. This is also vanity and vexation of spirit. ⁵ The fool foldeth his hands together, and eateth his own flesh. ⁶ Better is an handful with quietness, than both the hands full with travail and vexation of spirit.

Solomon's observation of oppression leads to a new observation on the problem of *self*-oppression. He sees some people toiling because they have no choice. He sees others toiling in oppression because they have voluntarily chosen such a path (v. 4). This is nothing less than the ancient equivalent of what we might call "keeping up with the Joneses." Solomon's primary subject here is laborious toil. He traces way too much of that toil back to the problem of envy. He calls this pursuit exactly what it is—meaninglessness and vanity.

In the ancient world, envy was considered particularly dangerous. Social scientists have studied a phenomenon they call "the perception of limited goods" in peasant communities. Solomon's community would have shared this perception, that all things are limited. Therefore, if someone is envious of someone else's goods or status, the whole society is put under threat. In the face of this instability, Solomon moves to strike a balance.

In verses 5 and 6, Solomon sets up two extremes. There is one type of person who avoids toil altogether. This person will not put his hands to work, and so ruins himself. But Solomon does not champion the opposite! Throughout Ecclesiastes, he criticizes the pursuit of constant toil. Instead, his balanced and wise viewpoint comes through in verse 6. It is better to have one handful, or to have one's basic needs met, and be at peace, than to have two handfuls with constant toil.

Such a lesson applies to the powerful, because no doubt Solomon is narrating how he himself has learned it. We saw in 2:9 that his pursuit of wealth made his name great around the world, but this was meaningless. It is Solomon who has learned the pathway of balance, and he shares this throughout the wisdom of Ecclesiastes.

---

1. What does envy produce (v. 4)?
2. When is less better than more (v. 6)?

"It's about time we stopped buying things we don't need with money we don't have to impress people we don't like."—Adrian Rogers

---

II. OBEYING AUTHORITIES (Eccl. 8:1-5, 11-13)

The subject of the believer's stance toward authority figures comes up repeatedly in Scripture. The early Christians dealt with it in the face of state-sponsored persecutions. The Old Testament Jews dealt with it when they were sent into exile into Babylon. In Ecclesiastes 8, Solomon deals with the issue from the standpoint of a just and orderly society. His counsel is invaluable to Christians today who are charged to be a force for good in their cultures. We are called to "make the teaching about God our Savior attractive" (Titus 2:10 NIV) no matter the cost. This calling includes maintaining a proper relationship with authorities.

A. Obeying the King (vv. 1-5)

1 Who is as the wise man? and who knoweth the interpretation of a thing? a man's wisdom maketh his face to shine, and the boldness of his face shall be changed. 2 I counsel thee to keep the king's commandment, and that in regard of the oath of God. 3 Be not hasty to go out of his sight: stand not in an evil thing; for he doeth whatsoever pleaseth him. 4 Where the word of a king is, there is power: and who may say unto him, What doest thou? 5 Whoso

keepeth the commandment shall feel no evil thing: and a wise man's heart discerneth both time and judgment.

One of the occasional difficulties in reading the Old Testament is the total lack of democracy. Most of us do not live in a society where a king or queen is present. Ancient societies, however, including Israel, were monarchies. A single ruler controlled absolute power. When that ruler was just and godly, the system worked. When that ruler was unethical and ungodly, horrible things resulted for the entire population. In this chapter, Solomon writes from the perspective of his own time period and even his own administration. He knows the difference between successful and unsuccessful approaches to petitioning a king, and so he offers helpful guidance to his readers.

Interestingly, Solomon's advice on how to properly come before the king is introduced with a poem about wisdom (v. 1). Court customs were complicated in Solomon's time. People privileged to come before the king had one chance to successfully make their case to the one person in the land who possessed absolute authority. The immensity of such a task cannot be exaggerated.

Everything Solomon has to say about successfully petitioning the king falls under the umbrella of obedience (v. 2). While we do not know of an "oath" of allegiance to the king in the Old Testament, we assume that such oaths were common, and that becomes the basis of Solomon's advice to obey.

Next, Solomon gives some practical advice about coming before the king (vv. 3-4). No doubt he had observed thousands of such petitioners. There are certain citizens who become so nervous in the presence of the king that they hurry the entire exchange. Doing so causes suspicion. What is more, one should examine his or her motives before approaching the king. If the cause is unjust, a righteous king will know and respond in kind. Being confident about one's message and stance, however, is not cause for arrogance. Solomon reminds his readers that no one is empowered to question the king except for his advisers. So, in all things caution should be the rule.

In verse 5, Solomon ties his instruction back to the wisdom introduced in verse 1. He brings the passage into focus with two bottom lines. First, obeying a righteous king always has a positive result. The petitioner should not become so impassioned with his or her own point of view that this simple fact is forgotten. Second, it takes a wise heart to find success with a king. Solomon trusts that the wisdom of God will light the path of the successful petitioner.

---

1. What does wisdom do for a person (v. 1)?
2. List three wise principles for responding to an authority figure (vv. 2-4).
3. What does "a wise man's heart" know (v. 5)?

Moral Decisions

In a 2005 Gallup poll, 74 percent of American Christians claimed that when facing "difficult moral questions" they would follow their own conscience over church teaching. This poll is a poignant depiction of the state of our world today. By spurning biblical authority, moral truth is left up in the air.

B. Crime and Punishment (vv. 11-13)

11 Because sentence against an evil work is not executed speedily, therefore the heart of the sons of men is fully set in them to do evil. 12 Though a sinner do evil an hundred times, and his days be prolonged, yet surely I know that it shall be well with them that fear God, which fear before him: 13 But it shall not be well with the wicked, neither shall he prolong his days, which are as a shadow; because he feareth not before God.

We have seen that ancient kings functioned as judges. There were certainly written laws as we have today, but the king was the chief justice. He was the foremost interpreter of the law for various situations that might come up among the kingdom's subjects. In this passage, Solomon deals with crime and punishment in the country's judicial system.

Solomon begins with a simple observation which might also be considered instruction. For a king to successfully wield power, his word must be obeyed quickly, especially with regard to legal determinations (v. 11). This is all the more serious as it relates to criminal behavior.

If a king is to be an adequate judge, the sentences he delivers should take place speedily. This is not meant to deny justice. Instead, as a result of swift consequences for crimes, society as a whole will be preserved. Otherwise, those inclined to do evil will pollute the entire population.

Next, Solomon takes a pass at an age-old problem: how to think about the evil person who never gets caught red-handed (vv. 12-13). As ruler, Solomon saw it all the time. It is easy to look at wicked people who prosper and to imagine that is a great course of life. Solomon admits that any judicial system is broken. No judge and jury can catch every criminal. Nonetheless, injustice catches up with everyone. Solomon sees that the legacy of the righteous eventually overshadows the vapor of the wicked.

---

1. How is the truth of verse 11 seen today?
2. Contrast the fate of the wicked and the righteous (v. 12).
3. What can the wicked person expect (v. 13)?

"Do not be deceived; happiness and enjoyment do not lie in wicked ways."—Isaac Watts

---

III. BENEFITS OF COMPANIONSHIP (Eccl. 4:8-12)

Friendship is the other side of the coin of authority. Both deal with human relationships. Authority deals with vertical relationships; friendship deals with horizontal relationships. Navigating each with success brings specific rewards. It is the rewards of friendship that Solomon describes in Ecclesiastes 4:8-12.

A. The Pain of Isolation (v. 8)

8 There is one alone, and there is not a second; yea, he hath neither child nor brother: yet is there no end of all his labour; neither is his eye satisfied with riches; neither saith he, For whom do I labour, and bereave my soul of good? This is also vanity, yea, it is a sore travail.

Solomon begins his poem on friendship with a familiar motif. He records his observation of one man who becomes the vivid touchstone that sets up what comes next. The man lives in total isolation—he is alone with his toil.

This isolated man is a pitiful creature, especially in the worldview of the ancients—a society that is communal, communitarian, and collectivist. Unlike modern Western societies, people do not perceive themselves primarily as individuals, but as part of a group. This man can never be content, for he has no one with whom to share his life and wealth.

• What is tragic about this scene?

"God created us as social creatures with a need to belong. He never intended that any Christian should live in isolation."—David Jeremiah

---

B. The Gift of Community (vv. 9-12)

9 Two are better than one; because they have a good reward for their labour. 10 For if they fall, the one will lift up his fellow: but woe to him that is alone when he falleth; for he hath not another to help him up. 11 Again, if two lie together, then they have heat: but how can one be warm alone? 12 And if one prevail against him, two shall withstand him; and a threefold cord is not quickly broken.

Ecclesiastes is a book of observations, thoughts, and theories. In it, Solomon does not often lay down hard-and-fast rules of instruction. When it comes to the gift of human friendship and community, however, Solomon writes in the mode of proverbs. He specifically prefers community over isolation.

Many benefits of companionship are covered in this passage. First, there is better pay for workers who partner together (v. 9). As they work, they can help one another, particularly if one is injured on the job (v. 10). Second, the coldness of isolation cannot touch those who gird themselves with the gift of community (v. 11). They will experience the perpetual warmth of friendship. Third, companionship brings protection (v. 12). People can join together for their common defense. The result of these benefits is a beautiful picture of an unbreakable cord. If two are better than one, three are even stronger.

---

1. How are "two . . . better than one" (vv. 9-10)?
2. Describe a relationship that brings you warmth (v. 11).
3. How are three better than two (v. 12)?

" 'I am going down into the pit; you hold the ropes,' said William Carey, the pioneer missionary. They that hold the ropes, and the daring miner that swings away down in the darkness, are one in the work, may be one in the motive, and, if they are, shall be one in the reward."—Alexander MacLaren

---

CONCLUSION

The Book of Ecclesiastes has much to say about the significance of human relationships. Solomon's teachings apply to marriages, friendships, families, and even governing authorities. Throughout his teachings, however, Solomon places wisdom and a reverence for God as the foremost qualities that will bring people success in their relationships. His counsel is completely relevant to our lives today.

GOLDEN TEXT CHALLENGE

"WISDOM STRENGTHENETH THE WISE MORE THAN TEN MIGHTY MEN WHICH ARE IN THE CITY" (Eccl. 7:19).

Wisdom strengthens the wise, strengthens their spirits, and makes them bold and resolute, by keeping them always on sure grounds. It strengthens their interest, and gains them friends and reputation. It strengthens them for their services under their sufferings, and against the attacks that are made upon them, more than ten mighty men, great commanders, strengthen the city. Those that are truly wise and good are taken under God's protection, and are safer there than if ten of the mightiest men in the city, men of the greatest power and interest, should undertake to secure them, and become their patrons.—Matthew Henry

Daily Devotions:
M. Cry Against Injustice
   Psalm 43:1-5
T. Respect of Royal Authority
   Proverbs 20:2, 8, 26, 28
W. Sweetness of Friendship
   Proverbs 27:5-6, 9-10
T. Confidence in a Friend
   Luke 11:5-8
F. Hope in Divine Justice
   Acts 24:10-16
S. Submission to Government Authorities
   Romans 13:1-7

Wisdom for Daily Living

Ecclesiastes 5:10-17; 10:1-12; 11:1-6

Unit Theme:
Wisdom From Ecclesiastes and Proverbs

Central Truth:
God's Word guides us in making wise choices.

Focus:
Realize wrong choices have consequences and make wise decisions.

Context:
Ecclesiastes was probably written by Solomon during his long reign (970-931 BC).

Golden Text:
"Ponder the path of thy feet, and let all thy ways be established. Turn not to the right hand nor to the left: remove thy foot from evil" (Prov. 4:26-27).

Study Outline:
I. Futility of Chasing Possessions
   (Eccl. 5:10-17)
II. Necessity of Wise Decisions
   (Eccl. 10:1-12)
III. Work Wisely; Trust God
   (Eccl. 11:1-6)

INTRODUCTION

One of the central themes of the Old Testament is wisdom. This is seen especially in the writings of Solomon. In fact, the books of Job, Proverbs, and Ecclesiastes are often referred to as "Wisdom Literature." This kind of literature is not only found in the Bible; it flourished in the ancient Near East during the Old Testament period. The major cultures of this time had their own wisdom literature. In later Greek and Roman culture, this focus on wisdom would be transformed into the study of philosophy, which was largely a different endeavor altogether. Philosophy was focused more on knowing and less on doing. In the Bible, however, the focus on wisdom is practical and worshipful. Wisdom keeps a person following the commandments of God and living a productive life.

Christian author and pastor Barbara Brown Taylor captures the biblical definition of *wisdom*:

> In biblical terms, it is wisdom we need to live together in this world. Wisdom is not gained by knowing what is right. Wisdom is gained by practicing what is right, and noticing what happens when that practice succeeds and when it fails. . . . Wisdom atrophies if it is not walked on a regular basis (*An Altar in the World: A Geography of Faith*).

This is the difference between early Christianity and its clash with Greek philosophy. Christian wisdom is about practicing righteousness, not endlessly debating abstract truths. Wisdom is not a philosophy; it is a lifestyle. In the Old Testament, wisdom is sometimes personified as a woman (Prov. 4:6). In 1:20-33, wisdom calls out to the simple-minded to improve their paths. Some Christians argue that many Old Testament references to wisdom as a person speak of Jesus Christ. This leap is unnecessary. We can say with authority that wisdom is an important part of the Scriptures. Through the teachings of the Bible, God sets before us the pathway of wisdom—a pathway of fruitful living under the light of God.

I. FUTILITY OF CHASING POSSESSIONS (Eccl. 5:10-17)

King Solomon was a man of unparalleled wealth. In 1 Kings 10:23, we read that he "was greater in riches and wisdom than all the other kings of the earth" (NIV). This is not a man who writes about chasing possessions as an outsider. Instead, he knows about the allure of wealth from personal experience. In Ecclesiastes 5:10-17, he contemplates the merit of his own pursuit of wealth. Although he does not criticize success and God's blessing, Solomon makes it clear that greed leads to misery. The fact that Solomon sits atop the financial pyramid of his day gives us reason to pay attention to his counsel.

A. The Rich Man and the Laborer (vv. 10-12)

¹⁰ He that loveth silver shall not be satisfied with silver; nor he that loveth abundance with increase: this is also vanity. ¹¹ When goods increase, they are increased that eat them: and what good is there to the owners thereof, saving the beholding of them with their eyes? ¹² The sleep of a labouring man is sweet, whether he eat little or much: but the abundance of the rich will not suffer him to sleep.

Solomon has already addressed the futility of wealth before we arrive at Ecclesiastes 5. At the beginning of chapter 2, we find a list of some of his accomplishments, which included gaining vast treasures of land, slaves, and precious metals (vv. 4-9). Yet we find there that Solomon made a conscious decision to not throw away his wisdom (v. 9). In chapter 5, he turns to address the other side of wealth—the darker side. He introduces the subject by referring to the exploitation of the poor by the rich (vv. 8-9). He observes the unfairness of the system, and roots it in the vain and wasteful pursuit of money.

Solomon directs us toward the great irony of wealth. Its promises are so great, but one often winds up miserable from the pursuit (v. 10). Solomon's observation has been echoed for thousands of years. When tycoon John D. Rockefeller—one of the richest men of the early twentieth century—was asked how much money would be enough, his response was infamous: "Just a little bit more." This is precisely the attitude Solomon is criticizing. His focus is on the *love* of wealth. The Hebrew word is *ahav*, and it refers to a range of passionate forms of love, including that between a man and woman. The person who sets his or her complete passion on gaining more money, Solomon says, is never satisfied, because no amount of money is enough. He summarizes this predicament with the hallmark poetic refrain of Ecclesiastes: it is "vanity"—pure meaninglessness.

In verse 11, Solomon moves away from observing individual pursuers of wealth toward the problems with the system at large. As king, he has a special advantage in the ability to see how decisions affect the entire society. Solomon refers to the merchant class that had boomed under his administration. The society at this time is still overwhelmingly agrarian. Most people farm small plots of land. However, as Solomon opened up new trade routes, goods from all over the world poured into the nation of Israel. Many people looked to "get rich quick" by selling such goods. Solomon notices the strange paradox. The more goods there are, the more buyers line up. This is exactly what merchants want to see. However, Solomon asks if it is really a worthwhile life, since the merchants themselves do not get to partake of the luxury goods they sell. They simply sell them off for a profit, and success in such a business was not easy.

Finally, Solomon contrasts the problems of the wealthy with the problems of the poor (v. 12). What an amazing difference! Solomon knows from personal experience that along with wealth goes the need to preserve wealth. This is a time-consuming enterprise. A common laborer, however, knows no such stress. He rests peacefully at night, shielded from the anxieties of the rich. It is a contrast that largely carries the Book of Ecclesiastes. Solomon consistently moves toward basic truths that are most applicable to a working-class environment. These are the people Solomon hopes to impact most.

---

1. Who "never has money enough," and why not (v. 10 NIV)?
2. What causes some people to lose sleep, and why (v. 12)?

"When Jesus wants us not to store up treasures on earth, it's not just because wealth might be lost; it's because wealth will always be lost. Either it leaves us while we live, or we leave it when we die."—Randy Alcorn

---

B. The Limits of Wealth (vv. 13-17)

13 There is a sore evil which I have seen under the sun, namely, riches kept for the owners thereof to their hurt. 14 But those riches perish by evil travail: and he begetteth a son, and there is nothing in his hand. 15 As he came forth of his mother's womb, naked shall he return to go as he came, and shall take nothing of his labour, which he may carry away in his hand. 16 And this also is a sore evil, that in all points as he came, so shall he go: and what profit hath he that hath laboured for the wind? 17 All his days also he eateth in darkness, and he hath much sorrow and wrath with his sickness.

In the former passage, Solomon lays out some of the problems that befall the wealthy person. Now he turns to the limitations that wealth brings. Although wealth appears to open up countless options, it adds little to our human experience. In this regard, humans are equal, no matter our earning power.

Solomon first points out the limitation of wealth's temporary nature. It can be here today and gone tomorrow (vv. 14-15).

It is Old Testament passages like this one that Jesus is calling to mind in His parable of the rich fool in Luke 12:13-21. In that story, a person in the crowd involves Jesus in a dispute over his family inheritance. Jesus then tells a story that illustrates Solomon's observation here. It is a short story about a rich man who hoards his wealth in barns, only to quickly die. Centuries before Jesus, King Solomon noticed this problem. Even savings could be lost in so many different ways, and any rich person might be reduced to poverty in an instant. This is an ongoing limitation of wealth. Something so impermanent cannot be the answer to all of life's problems.

In the next verses in Ecclesiastes 5, Solomon begins to level the human playing field. His language here has become famous in the life of the church. As we read them, we should remember that this was a time period long before the conception of modern democracy. The people of the ancient world did not live with the belief that "all men are created equal." Instead, a hard system of separate classes governed society. Here, Solomon challenges such an understanding of humanity (v. 15).

Not only are the rich denied the luxury of carrying their wealth into the afterlife, they will not even take the clothes from their backs. The richest people in the world will go to the grave in the same manner as the poorest. The fruits of their labor will be gone—a blip on the radar screen of history.

Solomon's closing words to the passage (vv. 16-17) set up his exhortation toward contentment in verses 18-20. The evil which Solomon points out should be compared to duplicity. Wealth looks so satisfying, but in the end it is unsatisfying. What's more, it leads to a particular way of looking at people that is not God's way. God does not separate classes into rich and poor. We know this because of birth and death—it is the same for everyone. Death reminds us that all profit from wealth will one day be gone. The person who fails to recognize this will one day lie beneath a mountain of regret.

What wise words from such a wealthy man! Solomon does not back down from the truth. The Bible frequently affirms that the pursuit of wealth for the purposes of gaining more and more is a dead-end road.

---

1. What can cause health problems (v. 13)?
2. What can happen to an inheritance (v. 14)?
3. How will a person's coming be like his or her leaving (vv. 15-16)?

"Riches have never yet given anybody either peace or rest."—Billy Sunday

---

II. NECESSITY OF WISE DECISIONS (Eccl. 10:1-12)

The foundation of Ecclesiastes is the proper pursuit of wisdom. In the first chapter, *wisdom* is defined against the futile pursuit of knowledge. Solomon recounts how he sought out to understand everything around him, yet this did not lead to wisdom; instead, it led to vanity (1:12-18). In the following chapters, however, Solomon deals with practical wisdom. He notes in numerous places that the proper pursuit of wisdom brings amazing benefits. Some of these benefits are explained in 10:1-12.

Wisdom for Daily Living

A. Wisdom Versus Folly (vv. 1-3)

¹ Dead flies cause the ointment of the apothecary to send forth a stinking savour: so doth a little folly him that is in reputation for wisdom and honour. ² A wise man's heart is at his right hand; but a fool's heart at his left. ³ Yea also, when he that is a fool walketh by the way, his wisdom faileth him, and he saith to every one that he is a fool.

The passage actually begins with 9:13. There, Solomon notices that the wisdom of the poor can overcome the power of the rich (vv. 13-18). This observation launches him into a comparison between wisdom and foolishness (10:1). Here we see the heart of wisdom literature, and it comes down to a choice between wisdom and folly. For Solomon, this choice is all-or-nothing. One cannot stockpile both wisdom and folly in the same life. Folly is weightier; it will overtake any life that gives in to it.

Keeping with the subject of the demand of wisdom, Solomon turns to a familiar Old Testament refrain (v. 2). In ancient Jewish culture, a person's right hand was associated with authority and uprightness. These are lacking in the posture of the foolish. They are off-course at the level of the heart. This contrast is extended in verse 3. Like wisdom, foolishness is on open display. Solomon, the great observer, encourages his readers to look around and test his words. The choice of wisdom or folly is easy to illustrate. It is all around us in the actions of others.

---

1. With what does the writer compare "dead flies [in] a perfumer's oil" (v. 1 NASB)?
2. Describe the foolish person's sense of direction (vv. 2-3).

Smart Yet Stupid

Yale professor Robert J. Sternberg is famous for his study on the "psychology of folly." The work he has collected, titled *Why Smart People Can Be So Stupid*, finds that unwise people share one common quality: pride. He notes that the fallacies of perceiving oneself as invulnerable and omnipotent lead to a life of folly. The Wisdom Literature of the Bible is a case study of the life of wisdom vs. folly. Its message is simple: God desires that we choose the path of wisdom.

B. The Problem of Foolish Leadership (vv. 4-7)

⁴ If the spirit of the ruler rise up against thee, leave not thy place; for yielding pacifieth great offences. ⁵ There is an evil which I have seen under the sun, as an error which proceedeth from the ruler: ⁶ Folly is set in great dignity, and the rich sit in low place. ⁷ I have seen servants upon horses, and princes walking as servants upon the earth.

Throughout Ecclesiastes, Solomon pulls out real-world examples that are familiar to his audience to illustrate what he is trying to get across. In this passage, as he explains the contrast of wisdom and folly, he finds a well-known example in the problem of foolish leadership. Leadership mattered to people in the ancient world as it does to the modern. Back then, however, there were limited options of resisting an unjust leader. There was no formal democratic process. As a result, people were at the whim of their governmental leaders.

In verse 4, Solomon warns his readers that the problem of foolish leadership does not open the door for disrespect and disobedience. In all things, he champions wisdom. Flying off the handle in the face of an angry ruler is unproductive and unhelpful. Solomon uses this precept as a springboard for an observation in favor of the "little guy."

This observation is that people in high leadership positions are not always wise, while people with no influence are not always foolish (vv. 5-7). The foolish decisions of a leader have a greater effect than the foolish decisions of a common person. Solomon lays out the telltale signs: The foolish leader ignores the natural influencers of his society, and installs fools to the highest rank. What is more, his slaves occupy positions of influence, because the ruler assumes he can exert greater control over his own property. These things, Solomon notes, are evil and full of error. They do not provide the conditions for a peaceful society.

---

1. How should we respond to a hot-tempered leader (v. 4)?
2. What kind of leadership does Solomon bemoan (vv. 5-6)?

"A competent leader can get efficient service from poor troops, while on the contrary an incapable leader can demoralize the best of troops."—General John J. Pershing

---

C. The Contradiction of Skill (vv. 8-12)

Solomon has been discussing the tyranny of an unskilled ruler. He notes that in such an environment, those who do have great skill—the wealthy and the princes—are relegated to inferior positions. In the following verses, Solomon explains how this paradox applies to the common laborer. In short, skill can be a contradiction. It does not cure every problem.

⁸ He that diggeth a pit shall fall into it; and whoso breaketh an hedge, a serpent shall bite him. ⁹ Whoso removeth stones shall be hurt therewith; and he that cleaveth wood shall be endangered thereby. ¹⁰ If the iron be blunt, and he do not whet the edge, then must he put to more strength: but wisdom is profitable to direct.

Solomon lists a series of tragic parallels from the world of skilled manual labor—digging a well and demolishing a wall (v. 8), working in a quarry and chopping wood (v. 9). Even the great builder can find failure on the other side of the task. This calls for wisdom.

Wisdom is superior to skill. In fact, without wisdom no skill can bring a person true success. Wisdom overcomes inferior tools—telling the ax man to sharpen his blade (v. 10). Still, the artisan should be cautious.

¹¹ Surely the serpent will bite without enchantment; and a babbler is no better.

Some skills are worthy of mockery. Here Solomon makes fun of the person who tries to make a profit by charming a snake, but instead is snake-bitten. This kind of work is contrasted with the one who deftly swings an ax. The skill that a person chooses is as important as the way it is managed.

¹² The words of a wise man's mouth are gracious; but the lips of a fool will swallow up himself.

Solomon has reflected on an array of wise and foolish choices. He now circles back to wise and foolish words. Speech is the best way to pick out the wise person from the fool. The wise person's speech is full of grace; the fool's speech leads to his or her undoing.

---

1. How could "skill . . . bring success" (NIV) in the various scenarios given in verses 8-10?
2. Contrast wise words with foolish ones (v. 12).

"Vigilance in watching opportunity; tact and daring in seizing upon opportunity; force and persistence in crowding opportunity to its utmost of possible achievement—these are the martial virtues which must command success."—Austin Phelps

---

III. WORK WISELY; TRUST GOD (Eccl. 11:1-6)

The call to work wisely is central to the Book of Ecclesiastes. It is a common refrain to "find satisfaction in toil" (see 3:13; 5:18). We know that God himself instituted work in the Garden of Eden. He gave Adam and Eve the daily responsibility to "subdue" His good creation and to "rule over it" (Gen. 1:28 NIV). It is only with man's choice of disobedience that his work is cursed as toilsome (3:17-19). The Book of Ecclesiastes explores this dynamic between work as gift and work as toil. In this exploration, Solomon offers helpful instruction about how to balance work, rest, and achievement.

A. A Balanced Approach to Work (vv. 1-4)

³ If the clouds be full of rain, they empty themselves upon the earth: and if the tree fall toward the south, or toward the north, in the place where the tree falleth, there it shall be. ⁴ He that observeth the wind shall not sow; and he that regardeth the clouds shall not reap.

Solomon has already criticized the mindless and exhausting pursuit of wealth. His words here, toward the end of the Book of Ecclesiastes, are serene and peaceful. They speak directly to the common man (vv. 1-2).

¹ Cast thy bread upon the waters: for thou shalt find it after many days. ² Give a portion to seven, and also to eight; for thou knowest not what evil shall be upon the earth.

Instead of a mentality of hoarding, Solomon encourages an openness to the fruits of labor. God promises to provide bread. We can trust that the result of our labor will eventually return to us. Because of this, we can be giving people. We can dole out portions to eight people at our table, and we should. This is a lavish household banquet! When times are plentiful, we should enjoy them, because we cannot know the future.

Such words call to mind Jesus' teaching on worry and work in the Sermon on the Mount. He says candidly, "Do not worry about your life, what you will eat or drink; or about your body, what you will wear" (Matt. 6:25 NIV). Elsewhere Jesus says to His disciples, "Do not be afraid, little flock, for your Father has been pleased to give you the kingdom. Sell your possessions and give to the poor" (Luke 12:32-33 NIV). Jesus echoes the faith of Solomon: we can trust in God to honor the fruits of our labors and to provide for our needs. Therefore, we should not feel guilty about enjoying them.

This faith in God, however, does not imply inaction on our part. Solomon calls his audience's attention to the cause-and-effect cycle in the natural world to remind them of the necessity of hard work (vv. 3-4).

Solomon paints a picture of the logic of the natural world. The facts that clouds produce rain and trees stay where they fall are obvious. In the same way, the person who does not work will not reap the benefits of work. Paul lays down the rule in 2 Thessalonians 3:10: "If a man will not work, he shall not eat" (NIV).

---

1. Explain the "casting" principle in verse 1.
2. What is Solomon proposing in verse 2?
3. What is the trouble with being overcautious (vv. 3-4)?

"Get all you can, save all you can, and give all you can."—John Wesley

---

B. Remaining Steady Under God's Care (vv. 5-6)

5 As thou knowest not what is the way of the spirit, nor how the bones do grow in the womb of her that is with child: even so thou knowest not the works of God who maketh all. 6 In the morning sow thy seed, and in the evening withhold not thine hand: for thou knowest not whether shall prosper, either this or that, or whether they both shall be alike good.

In an agrarian society, there are many interruptions to the cause-and-effect cycle of work. Farmers do not log their hours and get paid accordingly. They make a profit based on the harvest. In the ancient world, famines, pestilences, and draughts were not uncommon. A farmer could lose everything within a matter of weeks. As a result, Solomon calls attention to the fact that the ways of God are similarly mysterious (v. 5).

Solomon admits a hard truth: we cannot know many of the answers we want to know. Although medical science has discovered tremendous insights about the growth of a fetus in the womb, no one knows what exactly makes it grow; it is a miracle of life. God is the same way; we do not know how He works. We know there are no limits to His power, yet we still see destruction—natural and human. Solomon's point is that God can be trusted even when His ways are a mystery to us. This is why each worker should not hesitate to put his or her hand to the plow under the watchful eye of God (v. 6).

We do not have a guarantee of God's decisions, but we do have a guarantee of God's goodness. Therefore, the worker should labor in faith.

1. What can we not know (v. 5)?
2. How should we approach daily living (v. 6)?

"If there is one single reason why good people turn evil, it is because they fail to recognize God's ownership over their kingdom, their vocation, their resources, their abilities, and above all their lives."—Erwin Lutzer

---

CONCLUSION

The Book of Ecclesiastes is full of wisdom, written by one of the wisest men to ever live. This wisdom applies to our daily lives even thousands of years after the life of King Solomon. This wisdom includes instructions on wealth, priorities, work, and a relationship with God. By following this wisdom, we will live the productive, balanced, and fruitful lives that God has for us.

GOLDEN TEXT CHALLENGE

"PONDER THE PATH OF THY FEET, AND LET ALL THY WAYS BE ESTABLISHED. TURN NOT TO THE RIGHT HAND NOR TO THE LEFT: REMOVE THY FOOT FROM EVIL" (Prov. 4:26-27).

Humans are the only creatures God made with the capacity for reflection, self-evaluation, and goal-setting. We can look back on past decisions, judge what they accomplished and how they affected our integrity, and then set a new course. These verses encourage us to make those reflections wisely.

If we make decisions based on personal wants, desires, and temptations, we will stray from the righteous path and set a disastrous course. The result will be a loss of integrity. We must keep our eyes focused on the right goal—heaven, and dwelling eternally in God's presence.

Daily Devotions:
M. Esau's Rash Choice
  Genesis 25:29-34
T. A Pattern of Stubbornness
  Judges 2:11-19
W. The Legacy of Fools
  Proverbs 3:31-35
T. Two Kinds of Servants
  Matthew 24:45-51
F. Wise in Their Own Eyes
  Romans 1:22-32
S. Wisdom From Above
  James 3:13-18

Plea for a Pure Lifestyle

Proverbs 1:10-33; 7:1-5, 21-27

Unit Theme:
Wisdom From Ecclesiastes and Proverbs

Central Truth:
Divine blessings outlast sensual pleasures.

Focus:
Review the danger of a sensual lifestyle and pursue God's way.

Context:
Solomon gives fatherly advice concerning purity.

Golden Text:
"Whoso hearkeneth unto me [Wisdom] shall dwell safely, and shall be quiet from fear of evil" (Prov. 1:33).

Study Outline:
 I. Reject the World's Call
    (Prov. 1:10-19)
 II. Heed Wisdom's Call
    (Prov. 1:20-33)
III. Abstain From Immoral Pleasures
    (Prov. 7:1-5, 21-27)

INTRODUCTION

One of the primary teachings of the Bible is that something has gone wrong. This problem affects not only everything about people but also everything about creation. Scripture affirms that forces and decisions that cause harm were not the original intent of God. They did not come from Him; they stem from what the Bible calls *sin*.

Sin is a word that is rarely used in popular speech today. This term has been replaced by others, such as *dysfunction*, *addiction*, and *disorder*. These words certainly have their place, but Christian author and pastor Barbara Brown Taylor cautions the church from moving away from the biblical language of sin: "There are words in the Christian language that have no equivalent in the other languages we speak, such as the languages of business, law, or psychology. When we lose the religious words, we lose the hold they have on the realities they represent" (*Speaking of Sin: Lost Language of Salvation*). We should not shy away from these "religious words." We should instead reclaim their power.

The Book of Proverbs is an amazing overview of the power of theological language. Because it is laid out in short, pithy statements, the book's power hangs on the usage of major biblical terms. These terms include *commandment*, *obey*, *love*, *worship*, *instruction*, *life*, *death*, and *sin*, along with many others. From the beginning of the collection, Solomon is concerned to impart the knowledge necessary to remain pure from sin. Without this emphasis, Proverbs has no theological foundations, but is only a book of advice. With this emphasis on the problem of sin, the counsel of the Proverbs is transformed into an arm of God's salvation. It is this salvation that Solomon preaches.

Paul takes a similar approach in the letter of 1 Corinthians. There, he was being attacked by people who laid special claim to divine wisdom that they felt made them superior to Paul and other Christians. Paul is clear that God's wisdom doesn't work that way. It is not like the graduate degrees of this world for the superior. Instead, it is "a wisdom that has been hidden and that God destined for our glory before time began" (2:7 NIV). It is a wisdom that testifies to God's plan to save the world through the death and resurrection of Jesus. As we turn to the wisdom of the Proverbs, let us keep this definition of *wisdom* in the forefront.

I. REJECT THE WORLD'S CALL (Prov. 1:10-19)
Right after Solomon's introduction to his book of Proverbs in 1:1-7, the king launches into a series of warnings to his son. We see, then, that one of the primary functions of this book is to instruct the next generation of the monarchy. Through the Proverbs, Solomon teaches his lineage about the morality, ethics, and spirituality required for proper leadership and upright government. However, we can imagine that these words were also used by many families in the upbuilding of young men throughout the ancient Jewish community. These teachings were meant to be imparted from parent to child. They represent a powerful centerpiece to the life of any family.

A. The Call of Sinners (vv. 10-15)
(Proverbs 1:11-14 is not included in the printed text.)
¹⁰ My son, if sinners entice thee, consent thou not.
¹⁵ My son, walk not thou in the way with them; refrain thy foot from their path.
Children are often susceptible to the opinion of the group. Solomon knows the trap of such peer pressure, so he paints a vivid picture of the kind of group that his son should avoid. For the person desiring evil, opportunity for evil always knocks. This vivid word picture begins with a simple injunction to stay away from the call of sinners. "Do not consent" (v. 10 NASB) is the foundation to what comes in the following nine verses. A person in the royal court might be particularly targeted by a variety of groups. A person in such an esteemed position could provide resources and "cover" for all kinds of unethical activity. This is exactly what the "sales pitch" of these sinners leads us to believe. They are on the search for a powerful partner to ensure their heartless success.

The next verses clarify the enticement of this group of sinners. They are out for no less than blood. Solomon is describing some sort of assassination attempt in verses 11 and 12. Political assassinations were not uncommon in the ancient world. This is precisely why we see the position of "cupbearer" in many of the royal courts illustrated in the Bible. Remember that Nehemiah was cupbearer to the Persian king (Neh. 1:11). The most undetectable way to assassinate a political leader was by secretly poisoning his food or drink. Solomon probably has such an assassination in mind. A group of sinners have approached his son, promising great gain by the assassination of a rival to the throne.

The promise of the enticers is attractive. Their motivations are not primarily political, but financial. Perhaps what is in view in verses 13 and 14 of the text is knocking off a political opponent that would result in a great transfer of royal wealth to a new ruling party. We can only guess. Solomon paints this group as nothing but a lynch mob. They promise an equal share of the purse, but they do not have fair morals. Therefore, they cannot be trusted in any way.

Solomon's advice to his son is as direct as the introduction to the matter in verse 10. In verse 15, we can hear the desperate plea of a father in Solomon's intense words. His language is clear: Do not have any associations with such people or their ways! Such associations are offensive to the pathway of wisdom.

---

1. When do "sinners entice you" (v. 10 NKJV)?
2. How do some people get caught up in a violent lifestyle (vv. 11-14)?
3. What advice does the writer give (v. 15)?

"Associate with sanctified persons. They may by their counsel, prayers, and holy example be a means to make you holy."—Thomas Watson

---

B. The Consequences Faced by Sinners (vv. 16-19)

16 For their feet run to evil, and make haste to shed blood. 17 Surely in vain the net is spread in the sight of any bird. 18 And they lay wait for their own blood; they lurk privily for their own lives. 19 So are the ways of every one that is greedy of gain; which taketh away the life of the owners thereof.

In the Bible, virtue is never its own reward. The writers of Scripture did not hesitate to clarify the rewards and the consequences of certain forms of behavior. They encouraged their readers to decide on the course of action based on these rewards or consequences. The Bible is written directly toward human nature. It is not abstract philosophy. It is practical wisdom, especially in the Proverbs.

After Solomon forbids his son to pursue the path of murderous sinners, he launches into a vivid description of the consequences that wait for them. Although they may not be presently reaping the fruit of their actions, such consequences are not far away (vv. 16-18). Solomon uncovers the true reality behind their sinful behavior. They believe they are killing others for gain. In actuality, they are killing themselves. They have set a trap that will wreck their own lives.

This is the great paradox of the power of sin: Sinners attempt to inflict harm on others, but in reality they harm themselves. We get a picture of this conflict in Romans 7:11. Paul writes, "For sin, seizing the opportunity afforded by the commandment, deceived me, and through the commandment put me to death" (NIV). The power of sin is the power of suicide. Sin is deadly to its users. It warps a person's mind and judgment.

Solomon summarizes these consequences in the final verse of the Proverbs passage (v. 19). Ill-gotten gain seems like the easiest road. It appears to be a shortcut to wealth. Solomon states that it is a ticking time bomb. Wealth that is achieved illegally is lethal and should be avoided.

This summary on ill-gotten gain lays the foundation for all that Solomon will say about wealth. Indeed, many of the proverbs expound the limitations and advantages of wealth, along with the choices and disciplines necessary to creating wealth. He begins in this passage by emphasizing that wealth must not be achieved immorally or unethically; that is a recipe for disaster.

• What will eventually befall those who victimize others?

The Powers of Sin

Dietrich Bonhoeffer was a famous theologian who openly resisted Hitler's regime in Germany. As a consequence, he was jailed and killed by the Nazis. His resistance was rooted in a strong belief in the powers of sin that he saw at work in the politics of his day. In his book *Life Together*, Bonhoeffer remarks: "The most experienced psychologist or observer of human nature knows infinitely less of the human heart than the simplest Christian who lives beneath the cross of Jesus. The greatest psychological insight, ability, and experience cannot grasp this one thing: what sin is."

II. HEED WISDOM'S CALL (Prov. 1:20-33)

In this passage wisdom is *personified*, meaning it is transformed into a person for Solomon's writing purposes. It is a vivid way to get a point across. Rather than simply writing *about* wisdom, Solomon writes from the standpoint *of* wisdom, as if wisdom were a person. The speech of Wisdom calls the simple-minded to listen, to change their ways, and to live.

A. Wisdom's Generous Offer (vv. 20-21)

20 Wisdom crieth without; she uttereth her voice in the streets: 21 She crieth in the chief place of concourse, in the openings of the gates: in the city she uttereth her words, saying.

One of the goals of the Book of Proverbs is to make the offer of wisdom clear, simple, and open. For Solomon, wisdom is not a secret. It is not the primary possession of the rich, powerful, or smart. It certainly did not originate with him. It is equally available to all who will reverence the Lord (v. 7). As a result, in this passage Wisdom makes a public speech to anyone who will listen.

We have seen in previous lessons that the reign of Solomon was a time of economic expansion and financial boom. Closely linked to this is the urbanization of Solomon's time period. With the increased spending of the royal court came an influx of workers into the capital city. This is the setting of Wisdom's speech—a bustling metropolis filled with a diverse population (vv. 20-21).

The speech by Wisdom is not a singular event in one place. Instead, Wisdom covers the breadth of the city, shouting out in the streets, in the public square, and even at the gates. Solomon wants to be clear: no one is exempt from the demands of Wisdom. Anyone hearing his wise words in Proverbs ignores them at his own peril.

Wisdom's speech is completely directed toward those who have a wisdom deficiency. Similar to Solomon's words to his son in the preceding passage, Wisdom's words are a warning. They are full of shock and awe in the attempt to turn the unwise from their paths.

- Where is Wisdom calling out in our society? Who is listening?

"Wisdom is the power to see and the inclination to choose the best and highest goal, together with the surest means of attaining it."—J. I. Packer

---

B. Wisdom Makes an Offer (vv. 22-23)

22 How long, ye simple ones, will ye love simplicity? and the scorners delight in their scorning, and fools hate knowledge? 23 Turn you at my reproof: behold, I will pour out my spirit unto you, I will make known my words unto you.

In verse 22, Solomon introduces three stock characters that he turns to throughout the Book of Proverbs. The first are the "simple ones." Derek Kidner characterizes this Hebrew designation as "the kind of person who is easily led, gullible, silly. Mentally, he is naïve; morally, he is willful and irresponsible. He is a person whose instability could be rectified, but who prefers not to accept discipline in the school of wisdom" (*Proverbs: An Introduction and Commentary*). Second are the "scorners," or mockers. This character appears seventeen times in the book and he shares qualities with the simple and the fool. The difference is this: "The mischief he does is not the random mischief of the ordinary fool, but the deeper damage of the 'debunker' and the deliberate trouble-maker" (Kidner). The mocker is smart, cynical, superior, and full of sinful pride.

Third are the "fools"—the most important designation in Proverbs. The fool is set against everything that is wise. There are multiple Hebrew words to describe this person, each possessing different connotations: stupidity, malevolence, bad motives, and others.

Wisdom addresses each of these groups, noting that they "love" their present state (v. 22). That is the chief problem—they do not want to improve. They enjoy their lifestyle.

In the face of the stubbornness of the simple, the mocker, and the fool, Wisdom cries aloud. If these people would stop rejecting, and simply accept godly wisdom, their entire lives could change quickly (v. 23)! Wisdom promises immediate rewards and full disclosure. It is amazing that anyone could choose rejection when given this generous promise.

---

1. What characterizes "simple ones," "scorners," and "fools" (v. 22)?
2. What does Wisdom desire (v. 23)?

"No mind, no wisdom; temporary mind, temporary wisdom; eternal mind, eternal wisdom."—Adoniram Judson

---

C. Wisdom Rejected (vv. 24-26)

24 Because I have called, and ye refused; I have stretched out my hand, and no man regarded; 25 But ye have set at nought all my counsel, and would none of my reproof: 26 I also will laugh at your calamity; I will mock when your fear cometh.

These verses illustrate the problem with human nature. Even with Wisdom holding out this generous offer, most have rejected Wisdom's advances. This rejection is amplified by the image in verse 24 of Wisdom stretching out her hand, reaching out in the attempt to bring everyone into her fold, but it is no use. Most people ignore the advice and rebuke of the wisdom of Proverbs.

As a result of this rejection, the language of verse 26 turns ironic and sarcastic. Because the fools laughed at Wisdom, she will one day laugh at their calamity. Because the mockers mocked her, Wisdom will one day mock them in the day of destruction.

• What warning is given here?

"Where do you run for help? When you are in trouble, what is your first instinct? Do you run to others or to God? Is it usually the counsel of another rather than the counsel found on waiting upon God in prayer?"—Kay Arthur

----

D. Destruction Promised (vv. 27-33)

(Proverbs 1:27-31 is not included in the printed text.)

32 For the turning away of the simple shall slay them, and the prosperity of fools shall destroy them. 33 But whoso hearkeneth unto me shall dwell safely, and shall be quiet from fear of evil.

The day of destruction is vividly illustrated in verse 27. Note that God does not hand out this punishment. It is simply the natural result of rejecting the life of wisdom.

In the day of calamity, when fools reap the consequences of their action, Wisdom cannot undo those consequences (v. 28). The fool will fully own them. This is primarily because of the worst indictment of all in verse 29—the fool refuses to "fear the Lord" (NIV). The commandment to fear the Lord is the thesis statement of the entire book, as stated in verse 7. The wisdom-rejecting fool of Solomon's Proverbs has no relationship with God, and thus reaps what he or she sows.

The final two verses of the chapter summarize the two choices set before the readers of Proverbs. Life or death is at stake. In this regard, *wisdom* is not a schoolhouse topic. We often use the term in that way, but Solomon does not. In fact, he sometimes draws a distinction between *wisdom* and *knowledge*. Wisdom is not simply information. Information will not save anyone. *Wisdom* is godly information that is immediately put into practice. Without this habit of wise daily living, one can expect destruction.

The other side of the coin, however, is triumphant and hopeful. If one will but listen to Wisdom, the results will be safety, ease, and a freedom from fear. These great promises from the Book of Proverbs should lead us to heed Wisdom's call.

----

1. What happens to those who steadfastly reject Wisdom's call (vv. 28-31)?
2. What does Wisdom promise those who listen to her (v. 33)?

In verse 32, "prosperity" is better translated as "complacency."

III. ABSTAIN FROM IMMORAL PLEASURES (Prov. 7:1-5, 21-27)

The Bible takes special interest in the destruction caused by the sin of adultery. The prohibition against adultery is one of the Ten Commandments (Ex. 20:14; Deut. 5:18). Jesus himself teaches that adultery is the only acceptable grounds for divorce (Matt. 5:32; 19:9). Interestingly, although adultery does not make the list of seven sins that are most detestable to God in Proverbs 6:16-19, the Book of Proverbs is filled with instructions on avoiding adultery. This is due to the fact that adultery is such a destructive form of sin. It does not harm the sinner alone. It destroys relationships, families, the body, and the human soul. It is not surprising, then, that Solomon warns his son against the dangers of adultery.

A. Wisdom Is Supreme (vv. 1-5)

¹ My son, keep my words, and lay up my commandments with thee. ² Keep my commandments, and live; and my law as the apple of thine eye. ³ Bind them upon thy fingers, write them upon the table of thine heart. ⁴ Say unto wisdom, Thou art my sister; and call understanding thy kinswoman: ⁵ That they may keep thee from the strange woman, from the stranger which flattereth with her words.

The foundation of Solomon's warning against adultery is rooted in wisdom. Proverbs, along with the rest of the Bible, always addresses the problem in terms of the solution. Adultery cannot be avoided apart from a holistic lifestyle founded on wisdom. Therefore, Solomon carefully builds up his argument against adultery with a poem proclaiming the supremacy of wisdom.

Throughout the Old Testament, there is a stated love for the commands of God. God's commands are not meant to be woodenly followed without any emotions. Instead, the writers speak passionately of God's commandments as the key to true life. We see this especially in the Psalms. Here in Proverbs 7, Solomon extols the life-giving wisdom of God.

The English word *law* (v. 2) translates the word *Torah* in the Hebrew. The Torah referred to the first five books of the Old Testament. Another word for these books is *Pentateuch*. These were the most sacred books for Old Testament Jews. In fact, the Sadducees of Jesus' time *only* recognized the Torah as inspired. Solomon means to invoke the entire Torah in what follows. He refers to it as "my law." He has taken it into himself. He is responsible for keeping it. He wants his son to know this example.

Solomon will not stop by simply admonishing his son to obey the Torah. In verse 3, he uses a vivid example that calls to mind Deuteronomy 6:4-9, which is the most important Jewish recitation, normally used as a prayer. The Jews call this passage the *Shema*, meaning "hear" in Hebrew. It is the passage that Jesus identified as the greatest of all the commandments (Matt. 22:37-38). Solomon's instruction to his son to "bind" the Torah on his fingers is a reference to Deuteronomy 6:8: "Tie them as symbols on your hands and bind them on your foreheads" (NIV). By the time of Jesus, religious leaders were taking this passage literally, wearing boxes filled with Scripture on their wrists and foreheads (Matt. 23:5). Solomon, however, couples this injunction with a metaphor that would later become most popular in the Prophets. Jeremiah, for instance, prophesies that God "will put [His] law in their minds and write it on their hearts"

(31:33 NIV). Solomon's dual metaphor depicts the Torah governing both outward (fingers) and inward (heart) disposition and behavior.

Solomon continues to encourage his son to pursue wisdom (Prov. 7:4). He tells his son to treat wisdom like a cherished family member—like a sister. Protect her, love her, and nurture her. The result will be a freedom from anxiety over waywardness.

Wisdom is a barrier between Solomon's son and the dangerous adulteress (v. 5). A member of the royal court would be a special prize for any wayward woman. Solomon knows of this temptation. Ironically, it would be his many wives that led him to fall away from God (1 Kings 11:3). Here we get a glimpse into his certainty before his choice of wives led him astray. He warns his son of the seductive words of the adulteress. He must continue holding to the path of wisdom to remain free of her grasp.

---

1. What does it mean to keep God's law as "the apple of thine eye" (v. 2)?
2. How did the Jews remind themselves of God's law (v. 3)? How could we do something similar?
3. How should we look at Wisdom (v. 4), and how can she save us (v. 5)?

"If any occupation or association is found to hinder our communion with God or our enjoyment of spiritual things, then it must be abandoned. . . . Whatever I cannot do for God's glory must be avoided."—A. W. Pink

---

B. The Way of the Adulteress (vv. 21-27)

²¹ With her much fair speech she caused him to yield, with the flattering of her lips she forced him. ²² He goeth after her straightway, as an ox goeth to the slaughter, or as a fool to the correction of the stocks; ²³ Till a dart strike through his liver; as a bird hasteth to the snare, and knoweth not that it is for his life. ²⁴ Hearken unto me now therefore, O ye children, and attend to the words of my mouth. ²⁵ Let not thine heart decline to her ways, go not astray in her paths. ²⁶ For she hath cast down many wounded: yea, many strong men have been slain by her. ²⁷ Her house is the way to hell, going down to the chambers of death.

The Proverbs are written to be memorized and easily taught. They are written to capture the mind and the imagination. Nowhere is this on greater display than when Solomon observes the way of the adulteress. In his description, Solomon goes into colorful detail to warn his son of the calamities of adultery.

Throughout chapter 7, Solomon takes upon himself the role of narrator. He carefully describes the steps that an adulteress might take to capture her prey. He describes a simple youth who is unaware of her dangers (vv. 21-23). The simple man is under a spell. Solomon compares him to a beast of the field unknowingly walking directly into the slaughterhouse. He also compares him to the fool who is incarcerated. The result is that his liver is speared. We might expect Solomon to refer to the heart, but in ancient Hebrew thought the liver was the seat of the emotions. The man's emotional life is wrecked. He is trapped like an animal, with no knowledge of the destruction that awaits him.

After this memorable illustration, Solomon turns back to address his son. He wants to be sure that the image sticks (vv. 24-27). Solomon turns his plea to address all of his "children." He demands that they guard their heart from such a woman so as to avoid her path of destruction. His language is powerful. Her ways are the very ways of death and hell.

---

1. How do verses 21-23 characterize the adulterous woman?
2. How can the allure of adultery be overcome (vv. 24-25)?
3. What is the fate of the adulterer (vv. 26-27)?

"When adultery walks in, everything worth having walks out."—Woodrow Kroll

---

CONCLUSION

The wisdom of the Proverbs guides the servant of God to make wise choices. Solomon reminds us that those choices often come down to life and death. After all, what more is life but the summation of our choices? Solomon repeatedly depicts the consequences of wise and unwise choices in order to encourage the reader to choose rightly. We can be sure that living a life of purity will always lead us along this wise path.

GOLDEN TEXT CHALLENGE

"WHOSO HEARKENETH UNTO ME [WISDOM] SHALL DWELL SAFELY, AND SHALL BE QUIET FROM FEAR OF EVIL" (Prov. 1:33).

The man who hears the voice of wisdom in preference to the enticements of the wicked . . . shall dwell in safety, he shall inhabit safety itself . . . and shall be quiet from the fear of evil, having a full consciousness of his own innocence and God's protection.—**Adam Clarke**

Daily Devotions:
M. Purity Rewarded
   Psalm 18:20-27
T. A Legacy of Impurity
   2 Chronicles 22:1-9
W. Impure Religion
   2 Chronicles 28:22-27
T. Moses' Wise Choice
   Hebrews 11:23-29
F. The Lust of the World
   1 John 2:15-17
S. Hope of the Pure
   1 John 3:1-3

Financial Wisdom

Proverbs 6:1-11; 11:16, 24-26; 15:16-17; 22:1-2, 7, 9; 26:13-16; 28:19, 22

Unit Theme:
Wisdom From Ecclesiastes and Proverbs

Central Truth:
Our level of trust in God is reflected in our handling of money.

Focus:
Assess financial advice from Proverbs and manage money wisely.

Context:
Financial advice from King Solomon

Golden Text:
"If therefore ye have not been faithful in the unrighteous mammon, who will commit to your trust the true riches?" (Luke 16:11).

Study Outline
I. Adopt a Biblical Work Ethic
(Prov. 6:6-11; 26:13-16; 28:19, 22)
II. On Lending and Borrowing
(Prov. 6:1-5; 22:7; 15:16-17)
III. Build a Good Reputation
(Prov. 22:1-2, 9; 11:16, 24-26)

INTRODUCTION

Finances are one of the most common subjects in the Bible. This is surprising to many people today. Others expect the Bible to be a book of spiritual wisdom alone. Some believe the writers of Scripture were only concerned with the afterlife. This is all false. God's Word speaks to the daily routines of real life, and finances play a vital part of this daily routine.

Overall, the Bible looks at finances from every angle. We will see in the Proverbs, for example, that building wealth is the product of a disciplined life of wisdom. This echoes the promises of Deuteronomy that obedience to God results in financial blessing (28:1-8).

After the fall of Jerusalem to the Babylonians in 587 BC, the prophets arise with a strong word against the oppression of the poor by the rich (see Isa. 10:1-3). This message continues in the ministry of Jesus and the New Testament period. In Jesus' time, the Jews are no longer living in the prosperity of the new Promised Land, but under the oppression of the Roman Empire. Scarcity, not prosperity, is the rule of the day. In this environment, Jesus cautions the people about attempts to gain wealth (Matt. 6:24; Luke 16:13). With so many people in need, Jesus champions a life of giving, not saving.

The New Testament letters encourage congregations to incorporate both rich and poor without favoritism (see James 2:1-9). To take a biblical vantage point, then, means the Scriptures speak to all aspects of our financial lives. Nowhere is this vantage point more helpful than in the Book of Proverbs. When we read the teachings of Proverbs on finances, we are reading the counsel of an expert. Solomon was the wealthiest person of his time (1 Kings 10:23). He knew what it takes to build and manage successful finances. His advice stems from the great wisdom given to him by God, who also blessed Solomon with enormous financial wealth.

I. ADOPT A BIBLICAL WORK ETHIC (Prov. 6:6-11; 26:13-16; 28:19, 22)

In the Bible, work is a gift from God. God instituted work as a blessed duty of man in the Garden of Eden, charging Adam to subdue the earth and rule over it (Gen. 1:28). A strong work ethic is part of life under God's rule. However, the lack of a strong work ethic is a product of sin and often leads to even greater sin. As one of the most productive people in history, Solomon spends ample time in the Book of Proverbs setting out the ways of a biblical work ethic. For all of us who can work, we should see it as a privilege and a responsibility, not a burden. In fact, one of the hallmarks of Western society is "Protestant work ethic." Scholars believe the rise in wealth in the Christian West was largely the cause of a biblical work ethic.

A. The Example of the Ant (6:6-11)

⁶ Go to the ant, thou sluggard; consider her ways, and be wise: ⁷ Which having no guide, overseer, or ruler, ⁸ Provideth her meat in the summer, and gathereth her food in the harvest. ⁹ How long wilt thou sleep, O sluggard? when wilt thou arise out of thy sleep? ¹⁰ Yet a little sleep, a little slumber, a little folding of the hands to sleep: ¹¹ So shall thy poverty come as one that travelleth, and thy want as an armed man.

The first nine chapters of Proverbs set the stage for Solomon's sayings in chapters 10-29. These opening chapters are written in poetic form. They introduce the major themes that Solomon returns to after chapter 9 in his list of short, pithy proverbs. Often in these opening chapters, those themes are built around a stock character: the fool, the adulteress, personified wisdom. In chapter 6, Solomon introduces another example of waywardness from the path of wisdom—the sluggard. As Derek Kidner describes, "The sluggard in Proverbs is a figure of tragic comedy, with his sheer animal laziness, his preposterous excuses and his final helplessness" (*Proverbs: An Introduction and Commentary*). The total impact of Solomon's portrayal of the sluggard is direct and pointed— the sluggard is completely unwise. He will reap the fruit of his sluggishness.

Solomon introduces the subject of the sluggard in Proverbs 6 by telling the story of a common problem. He frames this story in a discourse to his son. The problem is the person who pledges security for his neighbor. This referred to the process of a loan, whereby one person would guarantee the loan of another. Solomon recognizes this as the road to potential financial ruin. He encourages the person trapped in such an arrangement to do whatever he can to free himself from these bonds. Such bonds were the goal of a sluggard who refused to provide for himself, choosing instead to seek loans from those around him. It is to this person that Solomon directs the vivid illustration of the ant, who needs no outside stimulus to provide for itself.

The Bible often refers to the natural world to illustrate a spiritual or moral truth. We see this in both Testaments. Jesus referred to the fig tree as an example of how to discern the signs of the times (Matt. 24:32). Paul talks about the visible natural world as a signpost that points to an invisible, perfect God (Rom. 1:20). Solomon directs his reader to examine the habits of one of God's smallest creatures as a prerequisite to learning the ways of financial freedom (Prov. 6:6-9).

The ant has no boss. It has no external pressure or counselor demanding that it be productive. It has an internal drive to provide for itself. The sluggard, however, acts in the opposite way, sleeping away his time. The following verses show the result of such a lifestyle. The quick road to poverty is the path of the sluggard.

Although Solomon rules over a prosperous economy, the ancient world remained a world of tough financial situations. Most farmers were just one bad crop away from starvation. Hard work was a life-or-death matter. Any person who ignored Solomon's words did so at great risk to themselves and their families. These words are not only for children, but for working adults as well. They are the key to financial prosperity.

---

1. What should we learn from ants (vv. 6-8)?
2. What results in personal poverty (vv. 9-11)?

"He lives long that lives well; and time misspent is not lived, but lost."
—Thomas Fuller

B. The Excuses of the Sluggard (26:13-16)

¹³ The slothful man saith, There is a lion in the way; a lion is in the streets. ¹⁴ As the door turneth upon his hinges, so doth the slothful upon his bed. ¹⁵ The slothful hideth his hand in his bosom; it grieveth him to bring it again to his mouth. ¹⁶ The sluggard is wiser in his own conceit than seven men that can render a reason.

Proverbs 25 begins a new section of Solomon's proverbs, copied by Hezekiah's court (see v. 1). Solomon's wisdom was so great that foreign rulers sought his wisdom (1 Kings 10:1). Therefore, multiple collections of his proverbs existed. In this section, Solomon turns again to the sluggard, and illuminates his futile excuses. Those excuses only keep him on the road toward poverty and destruction.

Solomon opens the segment of four proverbs with a wild depiction of how a sluggard will find any excuse to avoid hard work: "There is a lion in the way" (Prov. 26:13). Some proverbs are made memorable through humor. This is a great example of a truly humorous proverb. The sluggard is so dedicated to his course of laziness that he will make up ridiculous excuses to remain dormant.

The next two proverbs (vv. 14-15) continue in this humorous mode. A door, of course, moves back and forth but never travels anywhere. Its position never changes, because it is fixed to hinges. The sluggard is portrayed as a person fixed to his bed. This laziness is so ridiculous that the sluggard cannot even summon the energy to feed himself. He buries his hand in the food dish, but does not lift it up to his mouth to eat. What a picture of the calamity of laziness! All of the tools are available to the sluggard to feed himself. The food is right in front of him! But he would rather make excuses and go hungry.

The irony of the sluggard's excuses is that he eventually convinces himself that he is in the right (v. 16). He is a smooth talker. He is "wiser in his own conceit" (v. 16), even more so than seven wise men. The sluggard is actually guilty of the sins of pride and arrogance. By eschewing work, he convinces himself that he is somehow better than those who work hard for a living. In reality, the sluggard is guilty of an offense against God. Laziness is a profoundly theological problem. It is God who gave man a working body, an acute mind, and the ability to achieve amazing things. To ignore those abilities is to ignore God and to replace the true God with human selfishness.

---

1. What similar excuse might a lazy person use today (v. 13)?
2. How is a lazy person like a door (v. 14)?
3. What do some lazy people think about themselves (v. 16)?

C. The Way of Prosperity (28:19, 22)

19 He that tilleth his land shall have plenty of bread: but he that followeth after vain persons shall have poverty enough.

22 He that hasteth to be rich hath an evil eye, and considereth not that poverty shall come upon him.

Thankfully, Solomon's proverbs do not only deride the lazy; they also teach the way of prosperity. In verse 19, Solomon champions the cause of the common farmer. While some might have considered farming to be an inferior occupation, Solomon knows better. A good farmer could adequately provide for his needs and for the needs of his family. The person who chased after get-rich-quick schemes and other fantasies in the attempt to get around hard work was sure to come to poverty. Such schemes were as common in the ancient world as they are in the modern.

On the other hand, Solomon recognizes the limitations of the pursuit of wealth. A farmer knows the limits of the crops that his land can produce. Ignoring these limits is a road to financial ruin.

Another path to financial ruin is having an "evil eye" (v. 22)—an eye for greed. The greedy person who wants to get rich quick is likely to find poverty instead. This desire for quick riches is addressed in the New Testament as well. Jesus cautioned, "You cannot serve both God and Money" (Matt. 6:24 NIV). He challenged the Pharisees as people "who loved money" (Luke 16:14 NIV). Paul told Timothy to beware of "lovers of money" (2 Tim. 3:2 NIV). Greed is such a grievous evil because it turns a person away from trusting God toward trusting himself. It also takes away goods from those who need them.

---

1. How does verse 19 contrast two approaches to life?
2. What is a danger of get-rich-quick schemes (v. 22)?

"Work is not the result of the Fall. Man was made to work, because the God who made him was a 'working God.' Man was made to be creative, with his mind and his hands. Work is part of the dignity of his existence."—Sinclair B. Ferguson

---

II. ON LENDING AND BORROWING (Prov. 6:1-5; 22:7; 15:16-17)

In Solomon's world, lending and borrowing was a personal business matter. There were no institutions that worked like our modern, impersonal banks. Loans were personal exchanges with high risks. We see in the parables of Jesus that unpaid debts could land a man in prison (Matt. 18:34). If a man borrowed more than he could repay, all of his possessions, including the members of his family, could be obtained as partial payment. This is why Solomon takes pains to carefully warn his readers about the potential dangers of borrowing and lending.

A. Pitfalls of Lending and Borrowing (6:1-5; 22:7)

(Proverbs 6:3-5 is not included in the printed text.)

6:1 My son, if thou be surety for thy friend, if thou hast stricken thy hand with a stranger, 2 Thou art snared with the words of thy mouth, thou art taken with the words of thy mouth.

22:7 The rich ruleth over the poor, and the borrower is servant to the lender.

As a member of the royal court, and potentially the future king, Solomon's son would have had ample opportunity to invest his personal finances into an array of business opportunities. Solomon is not criticizing such investment, per se, but the habit of putting personal funds on the line for a venture that is totally outside of the investor's control (6:1). The greatest danger for Solomon's son would be to make a loan to a friend. This is a sure way to be taken advantage of. We can only imagine the number of people who attempted to worm their way into relationships with the royal family in the hopes of financial profit.

Solomon is warning against what we would call "cosigning for a loan." The deal is made where the lender shakes hands with the borrower (v. 1). Verbal oaths were often part of such proceedings, legally binding the agreement.

Solomon realizes that no matter how common these handshakes and verbal agreements might be, they are tremendously risky. His son should steer completely clear of them and aim for financial independence. If such an arrangement has already been made, in verses 3-5 Solomon pleaded for his son to do everything he can to release himself—"press your plea with your neighbor!" (v. 3 NIV).

In another proverb, Solomon explains the flipside of borrowing and lending. He has already warned his son about foolish lending. Now he turns to foolish borrowing (22:7).

There is no reason to conclude that this proverb prohibits borrowing money. Solomon is simply making an accurate and general observation. People in the position to loan money are always in better condition than people in the position to borrow. Both lenders and borrowers should keep this truth in mind before any exchange of money. It is a general rule that is consistent throughout every culture and time period.

---

1. What does Solomon say about cosigning a loan (6:1-5)?
2. What is the relationship between a lender and a borrower (22:7)?

"Two-thirds of all the strifes, quarrels, and lawsuits in the world arise from one single cause—money!"—J. C. Ryle

---

B. The Importance of Contentment (15:16-17)

16 Better is little with the fear of the Lord than great treasure and trouble therewith. 17 Better is a dinner of herbs where love is, than a stalled ox and hatred therewith.

The Proverbs by and large take a positive view of wealth. Solomon understands wealth as part of the blessing of God. However, he also writes candidly about its dark side. There is more to life than trying to achieve wealth.

The greatest theme of Proverbs is the "fear of the Lord" (v. 16). In fact, the thesis statement of the entire collection proclaims the fear of the Lord as the true source of wisdom and knowledge (1:7). Solomon puts wealth in proper perspective. Compared with one's relationship to God, wealth is absolutely unimportant. Failing to recognize this skews anyone's priorities, whether he or she is rich or poor.

Not only does Solomon compare wealth to a relationship with God, but also to loving family relationships (15:17). Solomon sees the dissension that wealth can cause between family members. Contention over inheritance rights was a common source of dispute among the wealthy households of this time. Typically the older children, especially the firstborn, were given the greater share of the inheritance. As a result, jealousy and grudges could break out within the family. Solomon sets such dispute in proper perspective. Meals of only vegetables in a loving household trump sumptuous feasts in a difficult household. Peacefulness and healthy relationships are much more important than the size of the family bank account.

---

1. What is "better" (v. 16)?
2. What else is "better" (v. 17)?

"Contentment is one of the most distinguishing traits of a godly person, because a godly person has his heart focused on God rather than on possessions or position or power."—Jerry Bridges

---

III. BUILD A GOOD REPUTATION (Prov. 22:1-2, 9; 11:16, 24-26)

In the Book of Proverbs, a good reputation is a precious treasure to be maintained and preserved. This is connected to finances because Solomon realizes that a good reputation is vital to successful financial dealings within the community. Israel at this time is still a village-based community. People with good reputations are well known, as are people with bad reputations. Business is transacted based on these reputations. No one will do business with a shady character. Once again, Solomon has the acute ability to set wealth in its proper perspective. The way of prosperity is connected to other paths: the paths of contentment and a good name in the community.

A. The Priority of a Good Reputation (22:1-2)

¹ A good name is rather to be chosen than great riches, and loving favour rather than silver and gold. ² The rich and poor meet together: the Lord is the maker of them all.

In the Book of Proverbs, wealth is a result of other decisions. This is quite revolutionary in Solomon's time. Because of the way wealth was typically concentrated into the hands of families who passed it down from generation to generation, wealthy people were sometimes seen as the product of a divine right. Solomon knows better. He sees a society where wealth is created and lost based on the everyday decisions of everyday people.

These everyday decisions add up over time to create a person's reputation. When a good reputation is earned, the ability to prosper is increased. If a person owns a bad reputation, they will struggle to do business in the community (v. 1). A good reputation is not the product of wealth. The opposite is true.

This is the differentiation Jesus makes when describing the Pharisees. While the common people revered them because of their wealth, Jesus saw through their duplicity. In Luke 16:15, He proclaims to them, "What is highly valued among men is detestable in God's sight" (NIV). Jesus is speaking in agreement with Solomon's proverbs, which consistently affirm that wealth does not infer any kind of special status. A good reputation, a loving home, and a life of honor are much more important.

This standpoint makes it easy for Solomon to caution the wealthy against arrogance (v. 2). He does so because of his strong faith in God's providence. When dealing with people of lesser financial status, the rich should not think that God has given them a special position. God has created both sorts of people, allowing some to be extravagantly blessed. This reminds us that the proverbs are not worldly advice, but are rooted in biblical theology. Apart from faith in the Creator God of the Bible, the Proverbs are useless.

---

1. Why is a "good name" so valuable (v. 1)?
2. What do the wealthy and the poor have in common (v. 2)?

Three Conversions

Martin Luther, the great leader of the Protestant Reformation in the sixteenth century, wrote, "There are three conversions necessary: the conversion of the heart, the mind, and the purse." As we seek to communicate the gospel of Jesus Christ, we should not forget this latter conversion.

B. Grace Versus Greed (11:16)

11:16 A gracious woman retaineth honour: and strong men retain riches.

The "strong man" mentioned here is one who does whatever to hold on to the material goods he can gather. He looks out only for himself, taking advantage of others and forcefully grasping everything his greedy hands can hold.

In contrast stands the "gracious woman," from whom flows wisdom, modesty, and humility. "Her grace is not merely the perishing grace of the body, but the enduring grace of the soul. It is not by dress, worldly vanities, or admiration of lovers that she obtains and retains 'honor,' but by spiritual and internal graces" (*Jamieson, Fausset, and Brown Commentary*). Such a woman will be generous and discerning with her finances.

"One gains by losing self for others and not by hoarding for oneself."
—Watchman Nee

C. The Result of Generosity (22:9; 11:24-26)

22:9 He that hath a bountiful eye shall be blessed; for he giveth of his bread to the poor.

11:24 There is that scattereth, and yet increaseth; and there is that withholdeth more than is meet, but it tendeth to poverty. 25 The liberal soul shall be made fat: and he that watereth shall be watered also himself. 26 He that withholdeth corn, the people shall curse him: but blessing shall be upon the head of him that selleth it.

There is the consistent expectation in Scripture that the rich will share their blessings with those around them, especially with those of lesser means. This is a time before modern welfare systems. Governments did not dole out much assistance to the poor. In times of famine, crisis, and need, entire populations looked to wealthy benefactors to contribute to the plight of the poor. Solomon shares this outlook and likely followed this path as king, ensuring the ongoing prosperity of his kingdom.

Solomon understands that wealth is a tool. It is a means to an end, not an end in itself. The end to which wealth aims is the harmony and peace of the society, the family, and the individual. Blessing comes to the wealthy one who has a "bountiful eye" (22:9)—a tendency toward generosity. The wealthy man of good reputation is not looking to hoard, but to give. He sees opportunities to spread his bounty all around him. The blessing he receives from God parallels the character of God himself. God is ever bountiful, doling out His blessings to the whole of creation. Those blessings never run dry.

Solomon contrasts this "bountiful eye" with those who take the course of stinginess. It seems counterintuitive that a stingy person would have less than a generous one, but this is exactly the case (11:24-25). Somehow the generous who scatter their wealth in many directions increase their wealth. The one who expects to save will lose out. This reminds us of Jesus' parable of the barns. In that story, the one who builds bigger barns to hoard his goods says to himself, "You have plenty of good things laid up for many years. Take life easy; eat, drink and be merry" (Luke 12:19 NIV). Jesus attacks this posture, calling him a fool in the next verse. The man has forgotten the proverbs of Solomon. It is only in giving that we can find God's financial blessings.

Not only does generosity unlock the blessings of God, it also leads to a great reputation in the community (Prov. 11:26). In times of famine, it was certainly a temptation for the wealthy to store their own provisions. This will lead to ruin, for the community will suffer. Note that Solomon here does not call upon the withholder to freely give, but to sell his supplies. The stingy life is a road to a poor reputation. But the wealthy man who cares for the poor will find greater levels of blessings.

---

1. What principle of giving is lifted up (22:9; 11:24-25)?
2. Who will be cursed, and who will be blessed (11:26)?

"We are not cisterns made for hoarding, we are channels made for sharing."—Billy Graham

---

CONCLUSION

The financial wisdom of the Proverbs comes to us from one of the wealthiest men of all time. King Solomon knows the necessity of a strong work ethic, careful lending and borrowing, and the merits of a good reputation in the community. He also keeps the blessing of wealth in proper perspective. Although recognizing wealth to be a blessing from God, he notes the responsibility that comes along with it. By remaining generous, one gains a good reputation and thus builds his or her wealth for the future.

GOLDEN TEXT CHALLENGE

"IF THEREFORE YE HAVE NOT BEEN FAITHFUL IN THE UNRIGHTEOUS MAMMON, WHO WILL COMMIT TO YOUR TRUST THE TRUE RICHES?" (Luke 16:11).

Most Bible scholars agree that the "unrighteous mammon" (v. 11) means "money." The "true riches" means treasure in heaven. It is generally agreed that the meaning of this verse is, "He who is dishonest and unfaithful in the discharge of his duties on earth need not expect to have heavenly treasure, or to be saved."

Daily Devotions:
M. Generosity to the Poor
    Exodus 22:21-27
T. A Mind to Work
    Nehemiah 4:1-6
W. Wrong Motivation
    Micah 3:9-12
T. A Generous Spirit
    Matt. 5:38-42
F. Lovers of Money
    Luke 16:13-15
S. A Good Reputation
    Acts 6:1-7

The Mighty Tongue

Proverbs 15:1-2, 4, 7, 23, 28; 16:23-24; 18:21; 20:25; 26:17-26, 28; 27:1-2, 5, 21

Unit Theme:
Wisdom From Ecclesiastes and Proverbs

Central Truth:
Our words are a powerful force for good or evil.

Focus:
Acknowledge the power of words and guard our speech.

Context:
Wisdom from Proverbs about the power of speech

Golden Text:
"A wholesome tongue is a tree of life: but perverseness therein is a breach in the spirit" (Prov. 15:4).

Study Outline:
I. Use Words Properly
   (Prov. 18:21; 20:25; 27:1-2, 5, 21)
II. Avoid Destructive Words
   (Prov. 26:17-28)
III. Choose Life-Giving Words
   (Prov. 15:1-2, 4, 7, 23, 28; 16:23-24)

INTRODUCTION

The power of speech is a recurring biblical theme. Its power is connected to the Hebrew tradition that sees speech as a creative force. We tend to understand speech as simply the way to relay accounts of things that happen around us. The ancient Jews understood speech as the means *by* which things happen around us.

We see this power of speech in two primary ways. First, the Hebrew term for *word* (*dabar*) means both "word" and "deed." At the basic level of vocabulary, words were connected to actions. Second, the Creation story affirms that God created the cosmos by speaking it into existence. This is particular to the Hebrew tradition. There were many other creation stories floating around in ancient cultures, with various gods creating the world in all kinds of ways. The Bible, though, affirms the power of divine speech: "God said, Let there be light: and there was light" (Gen. 1:3). In fact, each day of the Creation begins with, "And God said. . . ."

The writers of Scripture demand that the people of God recognize the seismic influence of words. They are loaded with possibilities for both good and evil, therefore they should be used carefully and intentionally. We see this in the teachings of Jesus: "By your words you will be acquitted, and by your words you will be condemned" (Matt. 12:37 NIV). We see this in the teachings of James, the brother of Jesus: "If anyone is never at fault in what he says, he is a perfect man, able to keep his whole body in check" (James 3:2 NIV). We see this in the power of New Testament confession: "If you confess with your mouth, 'Jesus is Lord' . . . you will be saved" (Rom. 10:9 NIV). In fact, there is no conversion in the New Testament apart from verbal confession. Speech has positive power. Speech also has the power to do boundless harm, as Solomon observes repeatedly in the Book of Proverbs. His words of wisdom are applicable to anyone who can speak, whether young or old, rich or poor. They are practical, insightful, logical, and helpful. No Christian can go wrong by adhering to Solomon's proverbs about speech. They are easy to memorize and will never lead us astray.

I. USE WORDS PROPERLY (Prov. 18:21; 20:25; 27:1-2, 5, 21)

Propriety is significant in the proverbs of Solomon. King Solomon sees that the fittingness, appropriateness, setting, and timing of one's words make all the difference in their success. Words have proper and improper usages. The same words may work one time and fail another. Because of the sensitivity of knowing how and when to use proper words, Solomon carefully crafts proven proverbs to guide us.

A. The Power of Words (18:21)

21 Death and life are in the power of the tongue: and they that love it shall eat the fruit thereof.

Three of the seven deadly sins listed in Proverbs 6:16-19 involve the misuse of words. In 18:21, Solomon summarizes the high stakes of using words properly. The power of life and death is not in one's income, social status, or even physical health. This level of power is reserved for the tongue.

We see this truth at work in modern medicine. Doctors have proven time and time again that our attitude, reflected by our words, makes a tremendous difference in our physical health. Jesus said in Luke 6:45, "Out of the abundance of the heart, the mouth speaks" (NKJV). Solomon recognizes this. He also teaches that good fruit can come from the tongue for those who "love" the tongue. The Hebrew word here is *ahav* and refers to a variety of loving relationships, including that between God and man and between man and wife. For Solomon to love wisdom is to love the tongue for the amazing good that it can do. When one possesses this love for the potential capacity of the tongue, incredible fruit will result.

In a farming society such as ancient Israel, the subject of fruit is a powerful image. People know that successfully developing good fruit takes time, patience, and the blessing of God. Fruit represented one of life's "finer things" in these ancient communities. The image that Solomon paints here works from this farming metaphor. Through taking proper time, remaining patient, and trusting in the blessing of God, we can learn to cultivate the power of the tongue. When we do this, our reward will be the good fruit that such verbal discipline produces.

• How have you found this proverb to be true?

Silence Prescribed

"If I could prescribe just one remedy for all the ills of the modern world, I would prescribe silence. For even if the Word of God were proclaimed in the modern world, no one would hear it; there is too much noise." Incredibly, he wrote these words at the beginning of the nineteenth century—Soren Kierkegaard

B. The Seriousness of Vows (20:25)

²⁵ It is a snare to the man who devoureth that which is holy, and after vows to make enquiry.

Solomon is perhaps most famous for building the first great temple to Yahweh. We know that this temple was destroyed by the Babylonians in 587 BC, and that Solomon reigned during the tenth century BC. This means that the Temple stood for almost five centuries. First Kings 7 describes the remarkable furnishings of the Temple and the astounding amount of money paid for its construction. Artists have often painted a replica of Solomon's temple based on these texts, and even the paintings evoke awe. Truly, visiting the Temple must have been an incredible experience of worshiping God.

As the builder of the Temple, Solomon knew its opulence could be overwhelming to the common person. Most worshipers would never see a building so grand. As a result, he set out Proverbs 20:25. This saying indicates a key feature of temple worship. It was common for worshipers to make a vow to God, along with their sacrifice. This would involve dedicating the animal unto the Lord, along with a stated vow of commitment. This vow would be communicated to the priest. When the animal was cooked and eaten by the worshiper, this solidified the vow. This is partially what Jesus had in mind in the Sermon on the Mount when He instructed His disciples to avoid making vows:

> "Again, you have heard that it was said to the people long ago, 'Do not break your oath, but keep the oaths you have made to the Lord.' But I tell you, Do not swear at all: either by heaven, for it is God's throne; or by the earth, for it is his footstool; or by Jerusalem, for it is the city of the Great King. And do not swear by your head, for you cannot make even one hair white or black. Simply let your 'Yes' be 'Yes,' and your 'No,' 'No'; anything beyond this comes from the evil one" (Matt. 5:33-37 NIV).

Solomon, however, does not criticize the *practice* of vows to the Lord, but the *hastiness* of such vows. He sees the danger of peasants who find themselves so overwhelmed by the presence of God at the Temple that they make vows they cannot keep. These vows would probably consist of some sort of financial donation to the Temple, but they might be more personal. In Solomon's worldview, once a vow is uttered, it cannot be taken back—especially a vow before God. Vows should be carefully considered before the time of sacrifice, not afterward, for vows are solemn and serious.

• What is a "snare," and why?

"Devoureth that which is holy" means "dedicate something rashly" (NIV).

C. Praise From Others (27:2, 21)

(Proverbs 27:2 is not included in the printed text.)

²¹ As the fining pot for silver, and the furnace for gold; so is a man to his praise.

Throughout the Book of Proverbs, Solomon differentiates between the type of speech that is appropriate for one's self, and the type of speech appropriate for others. Some speech is, of course, prohibited altogether, but other speech is slotted into its proper category. In short, the person who speaks about a subject is often as important as the subject itself. We see this especially in verse 2: "Let another man praise thee, and not thine own mouth; a stranger, and not thine own lips."

Self-praise is looked down upon in Solomon's world. Jesus echoes this sentiment in His parable of the praying Pharisee in Luke 18:11-12. The Pharisee He introduces is the model of self-praise. He prays, "God, I thank you that I am not like other men—robbers, evildoers, adulterers—or even like this tax collector. I fast twice a week and give a tenth of all I get" (NIV). The shock of Jesus' parable is that the humble sinner—the tax collector—finds the mercy of God, while the "righteous" Pharisee finds God's judgment.

Solomon is not prohibiting praising others, of course. Encouragement is a gift that God gives to us. His point is that if our character and behavior deserve praise, it is not our job to make this known. Others will praise us if we are patient.

In verse 21, Solomon teaches that the praise we receive is a refining ingredient that God uses to shape our overall character. The refining pot was the crucible for separating precious metals from outside agents. Pure gold or silver would go through an elaborate refining process to ensure its quality. This would involve heating the metal until it melted, and then filtering out all impurities. Solomon says the praise we receive works in this way; it tests us and refines our character. This is not an instruction to explain away the praise of others, or to shy away from it. Solomon's counsel is, instead, to utilize praise to test ourselves. The praise of others can be a means of sinful arrogance or productive refinement; the choice is ours.

Solomon not only examines the power of positive speech, but also the power of negative speech. Flattery was a common subject in ancient literature. During the New Testament period, a Greek author named Plutarch wrote a popular book titled *How to Tell a Flatterer From a Friend*. Interestingly, Plutarch does not add much to the words of Solomon. One thousand years previously, this king of Israel had already laid out the wisdom of listening to negative speech.

---

1. What kind of praise has meaning (v. 2)?
2. How does praise from others test us (v. 21)?

"The person who prays more in public than in private reveals that he is less interested in God's approval than in public praise. Not piety but a reputation for piety is his concern."—D. A. Carson

---

D. Rebuke and Boasts (27:5, 1)
⁵ Open rebuke is better than secret love.
¹ Boast not thyself of to morrow; for thou knowest not what a day may bring forth.
The Bible's term for negative speech is *rebuke*. This form of speech, though painful at times, is always to be cherished and utilized (v. 5).

Solomon's emphasis is on the public nature of this rebuke. Hebrew culture was very relational and verbal. An angry rebuke might take place in public. Solomon shows that such a rebuke has uses, whereas secret love has none. He encourages the wise to embrace such rebukes as a further opportunity to grow.

As we see in verse 1, the proverbs consistently prohibit boasting. This prohibition is echoed throughout the Scriptures. Paul quotes Jeremiah 9:24 in 1 Corinthians 1:31 and 2 Corinthians 10:17: "Let him who boasts boast in the Lord" (NIV). The sin of boasting is the sin of pride. The one who boasts does so as if he or she has achieved success apart from God's empowerment, blessings, and providence. Solomon wants to nip such sin in the bud.

Proverbs 27:1 is echoed by the apostle James in his letter:

Now listen, you who say, "Today or tomorrow we will go to this or that city, spend a year there, carry on business and make money." Why, you do not even know what will happen tomorrow. What is your life? You are a mist that appears for a little while and then vanishes. Instead, you ought to say, "If it is the Lord's will, we will live and do this or that." As it is, you boast and brag. All such boasting is evil (4:13-16 NIV).

So we see that the Old Testament Proverbs are as rooted in the character of God as are the documents of the New Testament. They are not just proverbs of practice, but proverbs of theology and spirituality.

---

1. How is "open rebuke" better than "love that is concealed" (v. 5 NASB)?
2. What type of boasting is foolish, and why (v. 1)?

"It is difficult to rebuke well; that is, at a right time, in a right spirit, and in a right manner."—John Henry Newman

---

II. AVOID DESTRUCTIVE WORDS (Prov. 26:17-28)

There are some words and forms of speech that should be avoided at all costs. Solomon is never afraid to advise what should be completely avoided. He knows that people can so easily rationalize their way around sin and error. In Proverbs 26, he demands that quarreling, doublespeak, and gossip be avoided in order to pursue the path of God's wisdom.

A. The Stupidity of Quarreling (vv. 17, 21)

17 He that passeth by, and meddleth with strife belonging not to him, is like one that taketh a dog by the ears.

21 As coals are to burning coals, and wood to fire; so is a contentious man to kindle strife.

What is it about human nature that loves to argue? Solomon recognizes the dangers of this tendency. He begins in verse 17 with a humorous word-picture. Some people love a good fight so much that they will leap into a quarrel that they are unfamiliar with. They are simply a passerby, jumping into an argument. This person does not even know the people involved in the discussion. Solomon compares this to seizing an unknown dog by the ears. Such behavior is sure to earn a terrible bite.

In verse 21, Solomon paints another vivid word-picture, this time centering on a cooking fire. Solomon's ancient readers were skilled in the art of building a fire to cook their food. They used wood or charcoals to keep the fire hot. For whatever reason, some people love to stoke the fires of strife between others. They prefer strife to peace. Solomon warns against such behavior. He encourages his readers to stay away from such people. They simply make the uncomfortable fire of dissension burn ever hotter.

---

1. Why is meddling so dangerous (v. 17)?
2. Why do some people love to "kindle strife" (v. 21)?

"If a man has a quarrelsome temper, let him alone. . . . He will soon meet with someone stronger than himself, who will repay him better than you can."—Richard Cecil

---

B. Beware of Doublespeak (vv. 18-19, 23-28)

(Proverbs 26:18-19, 26-27 is not included in the printed text.)

²³ Burning lips and a wicked heart are like a potsherd covered with silver dross. ²⁴ He that hateth dissembleth with his lips, and layeth up deceit within him; ²⁵ When he speaketh fair, believe him not: for there are seven abominations in his heart.

²⁸ A lying tongue hateth those that are afflicted by it; and a flattering mouth worketh ruin.

The culture of Solomon was an oral, not a written, culture. This seems like a contradiction, given that we are studying a written book that maintained a central place in Hebrew life. However, the Proverbs were not primarily written to be read, but to be heard and memorized. This is why they are short and vivid. Scholars estimate that in ancient peasant societies such as Solomon's, perhaps 5 percent of the population was literate. As a result, business transactions, stories, and spiritual truths were communicated orally. If oral communications could not be trusted, the entire society would fall apart.

This is precisely what is at stake when Solomon warns his society against doublespeak (v. 23). If a person has ulterior motives, he or she should be avoided. Truth-telling was vital and foundational to a healthy society.

Solomon first attacks the smooth talker, the one gifted at impassioned and convincing speech. If this person's talk does not match up with their heart, trouble is sure to follow. They are like a common, dirty, clay pot that would be covered with a more expensive glaze to protect the pot. Solomon wants his hearers to differentiate between the two. They must see through a person's words to the attitude of the heart. Sometimes this is easy to do, such as depicted in verses 18-19: "Like a madman shooting firebrands or deadly arrows is a man who deceives his neighbor and says, 'I was only joking!'" (NIV). A person who contradicts himself by claiming to be joking is showing the clear sign of hypocrisy. Others, though, are more skilled in the art of disguise.

The significance of the "seven abominations" (v. 25) connects back to Solomon's list of the seven most detestable sins (6:16-19). The second of these deadly sins is a "lying tongue." Solomon claims that the liar is sure to be guilty of the rest of the abominations. Just as James 3:2 ascribes a perfect character to the man able to keep his tongue in check, the opposite is also true. Liars are completely infected with ignoble character, and should not be trusted at all. Their wickedness will be exposed eventually (Prov. 26:26). Verse 27 illustrates the self-destructiveness of such individuals: "If a man digs a pit, he will fall into it; if a man rolls a stone, it will roll back on him" (NIV). The liar is not just destructive, but also vengeful (v. 28). Lying words are the best indicators of hatred. Those who are able to deceive their lying heart through flattery are even more ruinous. They should heed Solomon's word to align their speech with their true motivations.

_____

1. When is "Was I not joking?" (NASB) a lame excuse (vv. 18-19)?
2. What is "like a coating of glaze over earthenware" (v. 23 NIV)?
3. If a person "disguises it [hatred] with his lips" (NASB), what will eventually happen (vv. 24-26)?
4. How are lying and flattery similar (v. 28)?

_____

"God has given us two ears, but one tongue, to show that we should be swift to hear, but slow to speak."—Thomas Watson

_____

C. Avoid Gossip (vv. 20, 22)

20 Where no wood is, there the fire goeth out: so where there is no tale-bearer, the strife ceaseth.

22 The words of a talebearer are as wounds, and they go down into the innermost parts of the belly.

The basic practicality of the proverbs is seen in the number of times Solomon addresses the problem of gossip. In the small village communities of Israel, gossip always threatened to damage relationships and separate families. Solomon desires a kingdom of peace, so he opposes the evils of gossip. Although he is king, village gossip is no small matter.

Verse 20 parallels the one that comes next. In the same way that a quarrelsome man stirs up dissension, refusing to gossip can stop a quarrel in the first place. Solomon is saying, "Just let the potential fire go out by refusing to gossip!" We can only imagine the relationships that would be preserved if this simple advice were consistently followed in our communities.

The problem is that gossip is delicious (v. 22). People have an appetite for it. It is interesting, entertaining, and captivating. Like choice cuts of meat, gossip goes down smooth and temporarily satisfies. Unfortunately, the end results are wounds. Digesting gossip may seem fun and harmless, but it packs a brutal punch.

_____

1. What will quiet contention and quarreling (v. 20)?
2. Why is gossip alluring (v. 22)?

"A real Christian is a person who can give his parrot to the town gossip."—Billy Graham

---

III. CHOOSE LIFE-GIVING WORDS (Prov. 15:1-2, 4, 7, 23, 28; 16:23-24)

We have seen that in the Hebrew tradition, words have the power to create life. In fact, this is on display in the first verses of the Bible, as God speaks life into existence. In the healing ministry of Jesus, there is always a spoken word that directs the healing. It is no surprise, then, that Solomon's proverbs instruct us to speak life-giving words.

A. Gentle Words (15:1-2, 4)

¹ A soft answer turneth away wrath: but grievous words stir up anger. ² The tongue of the wise useth knowledge aright: but the mouth of fools poureth out foolishness.

⁴ A wholesome tongue is a tree of life: but perverseness therein is a breach in the spirit.

Solomon often focuses on the power of gentle words. By "soft" (v. 1), he means words that are carefully chosen to have a positive impact. They take into account the emotions of the other person, especially if those emotions are fragile. Someone with the discipline to answer gently trumps someone who lashes out in anger.

The fool cannot harness the power of gentle words because he cannot control his tongue (v. 2). Solomon paints the picture of a gushing waterfall that cannot be contained. So pours silly speech from the mouth of the fool.

Although Solomon is relentless in depicting the consequences of foolish speech, he is even more graphic when describing the benefits of healthy speech (v. 4). The "tree of life," of course, comes from the Garden of Eden in Genesis. Wholesome speech is filled with the power of God to create life. Perverse speech, however, breaks down the human soul.

---

1. What can a "soft answer" accomplish (v. 1)?
2. Contrast the foolish tongue with the wise one (v. 2).
3. How can you be "a tree of life" (v. 4)?

"Kind words do not cost much. Yet they accomplish much."—Blaise Pascal

---

B. Thoughtful Words (15:23, 28; 16:24)

¹⁵:²³ A man hath joy by the answer of his mouth: and a word spoken in due season, how good is it!

²⁸ The heart of the righteous studieth to answer: but the mouth of the wicked poureth out evil things.

¹⁶:²⁴ Pleasant words are as an honeycomb, sweet to the soul, and health to the bones.

In great contrast to the pouring mouth of the fool is the studied speech of the wise (15:28). As if preparing for a test, the heart of the righteous ponders the right words to use. It is in this pondering that life-giving words are chosen. Such words are joyous and delightful, especially as they are spoken at just the right time (v. 23).

Thoughtful words are not just life-giving in an abstract sense; they affect the soul and the body, encourage the weak, and strengthen the downtrodden (16:24). They are full of real, life-giving power.

---

1. When and how has "a timely word" helped you (15:23 NIV)?
2. Contrast the words of the righteous with the words of the wicked (v. 28).
3. Are you an ongoing source of "pleasant words" (16:24)?

C. Knowledgeable Words (15:7; 16:23)

15:7 The lips of the wise disperse knowledge: but the heart of the foolish doeth not so.

16:23 The heart of the wise teacheth his mouth, and addeth learning to his lips.

In order to be life-giving, words must be filled with knowledge (15:7). Solomon portrays the words of the wise in just this way. They are not idle or full of meaninglessness. They are always carefully chosen to make a positive impact on the hearer.

In 16:23, we see that the person with a wise heart "speaks as it dictates; and therefore his speeches are all speeches of wisdom" (Adam Clarke). "Wisdom in the heart suggests to the mouth what, how, where, and when one ought to speak" (Jamieson, Fausset, and Brown).

---

1. How can you tell a wise person from a foolish one (15:7)?
2. How do your words reveal what is in your heart (16:23)?

"Remember that the tongue only speaks what is in the heart."— Theodore Epp

---

CONCLUSION

The Bible is clear that the tongue has incredible power—the power of life and of death, of healing and of destruction. In the Proverbs, King Solomon brings this power to the forefront. By encouraging us to use words properly, to avoid destructive words, and to choose life-giving words, we are given a textbook on successful speech. The New Testament follows this pattern, illustrating the tremendous power for good, or for evil, that each of us possess in the way we use our words.

GOLDEN TEXT CHALLENGE

"A WHOLESOME TONGUE IS A TREE OF LIFE: BUT PERVERSENESS THEREIN IS A BREACH IN THE SPIRIT" (Prov. 15:4).

A perverse tongue reveals "a breach in the spirit." Deceit, error, reviling, filthy speaking, and frivolity not only do not heal the sick in soul, but increase their spiritual malady, and corrupt those whole, tainting their integrity, and affecting them with various evils.—*Jamieson, Fausset, and Brown Commentary*

Daily Devotions:

M. Speak Words From the Lord
     Numbers 22:1-12
T. Do Not Make Rash Vows
     Judges 11:29-40
W. Communicate the Truth
     Ecclesiastes 12:9-14
T. Words Reveal the Heart
     Matthew 12:33-37
F. Beware of Smooth Talk
     Romans 16:17-20
S. Use Sound Speech
     Titus 2:6-8

Introduction to Spring Quarter

"Hope in the Book of Isaiah" (lessons 1-6) starts with the story of Isaiah's call to prophetic ministry. The remaining weeks address five of Isaiah's prophecies about the Messiah, hope in God, holiness and restoration, salvation, and God's eternal kingdom.

The lessons were written by Dr. Lee Roy Martin (D.Th., University of South Africa; M.Div., Pentecostal Theological Seminary), professor of Hebrew and Old Testament at the Pentecostal Theological Seminary in Cleveland, Tennessee. He has pastored for eighteen years, and has written books on Jonah and the Book of Judges.

The Easter lesson (8) was compiled by Lance Colkmire (see biographical information on page 16).

The second unit, "Principles for Christian Living" (lessons 7, 9-13), merges theological and practical truths from the apostle John's three letters.

This unit was written by Dr. Homer G. Rhea (L.H.D.), who has served the church in many capacities, including editor in chief of Church of God Publications, pastor, district overseer, and chairman of the Ministerial Internship Program (Mississippi). An ordained minister since 1966, Dr. Rhea is the author of three books, has contributed to other books, and has written numerous magazine articles.

Life-Changing Encounter With God

Isaiah 6:1-13

Unit Theme:
Hope in the Book of Isaiah

Central Truth:
Encountering God's glory can lead to repentance and service.

Focus:
Examine Isaiah's response to God's call and obey His call on our lives.

Context:
About 750 BC in Jerusalem, Isaiah is divinely commissioned.

Golden Text:
"I heard the voice of the Lord, saying, Whom shall I send, and who will go for us? Then said I, Here am I; send me" (Isa. 6:8).

Study Outline:
I. A Vision of God
    (Isa. 6:1-4)
II. Cleansed for Service
    (Isa. 6:5-8)
III. Commissioned to Prophesy
    (Isa. 6:9-13)

INTRODUCTION

This is the first of six lessons devoted to the study of the Book of Isaiah, which is described as "the vision of Isaiah the son of Amoz" (1:1). Isaiah's ministry spanned a generation (740 to 701 BC) and overlapped the days of Hosea and Micah. Isaiah prophesied during the reigns of four kings of Judah (Uzziah, Jotham, Ahaz, and Hezekiah). His most important prophecies were addressed to the Israelites during the days of Ahaz and Hezekiah.

Although Isaiah lived more than 700 years before the birth of Jesus Christ, his words are as relevant today as they were when first uttered to the ancient inhabitants of Jerusalem. Isaiah addressed questions that we continue to wrestle with in the twenty-first century. What does it mean to be God's people? What is the nature of judgment and salvation? How does Israel fit into God's mission to the world? What is the future of this world? How can God's people learn to trust Him when it seems that everything is falling apart all around them? These and other important questions will be addressed as we study the Book of Isaiah.

Isaiah's message is a warning of judgment and a call to repentance. As early as chapter 1, Isaiah presents the Lord's invitation, "Come now, and let us reason together, saith the Lord: though your sins be as scarlet, they shall be as white as snow; though they be red like crimson, they shall be as wool" (v. 18). Israel was a people who had strayed from God and who now faced a crossroads. If they chose to disobey God, they would encounter judgment; but if they chose to repent, they would enjoy God's forgiveness. The name *Isaiah* means "Jehovah is salvation," and the hopeful theme of salvation is prominent throughout the sixty-six chapters of this powerful prophetic book.

This week's lesson comes from chapter 6, which tells of Isaiah's vision of the heavenly throne room and his commission to carry God's Word to Israel. In a vision Isaiah encounters the Holy One of Israel, the King of kings; and as a result of the divine encounter, Isaiah volunteers to serve as the Lord's messenger to the Israelites.

I. A VISION OF GOD (Isa. 6:1-4)

Chapter 6 is Isaiah's testimony of God's call upon his life. We might expect Isaiah to begin his book with the story of his calling, but instead, he begins with a summary of the prophetic message that will unfold throughout the book. The first five chapters of Isaiah take the form of a covenant lawsuit that sets the stage for Isaiah's call. In His "lawsuit" against Israel, God accuses them of being a nation of disobedient children who have engaged in rebellion and hypocritical worship. Furthermore, Israel is like a vineyard that the Lord had planted, watered, and tended. But the vineyard brought forth only sour grapes. Therefore, the Lord has set His hand against Israel and promises to bring judgment upon her unless she repents.

A. The King on His Throne (v. 1)

¹ In the year that king Uzziah died I saw also the Lord sitting upon a throne, high and lifted up, and his train filled the temple.

In chapters 1–5, the Lord comes down to Israel and holds court, accusing His people of disobedience. In chapter 6, Isaiah is given a vision of the heavenly court, the throne room of God. He sees God high and exalted, with heavenly beings uttering constant praise and adoration to God.

The vision takes place "in the year that king Uzziah died." A comparison of Isaiah's method of dating his prophecies (see 14:28; 20:1) with other Old Testament writers reveals that the vision occurred immediately prior to Uzziah's death, not after it, as many people assume. If the vision had happened after Uzziah's death, the date would have been written in a different fashion. It would have read, "And it came to pass after the death of Uzziah . . ." (see Gen. 25:11; Josh. 1:1; Judg. 1:1; 2 Sam. 1:1). Or, it would have made reference to the new king, using this formula: "And in the first year of Jotham, king of Judah . . . ," because biblical dating always mentions the reigning king, not the dead king (see Isa. 7:1; 1 Kings 16:23; 2 Chron. 29:3; 36:22; Jer. 25:1; Dan. 9:1).

Therefore, Isaiah's vision was not given to him in the aftermath of the death of Uzziah. It was not given as a response to Isaiah's grief and loss. Rather, the vision was given as a way of preparing Isaiah for the transition that was on the horizon. Uzziah had been stricken with leprosy (2 Chron. 26:19-21) and would soon die. A new era was about to begin, and it was an era in which Isaiah and his prophecies would play a significant role.

In his vision, Isaiah saw God as majestic, magnificent, and exalted. He was "sitting upon a throne, high and lifted up." The Israelites believed that the Jerusalem Temple was the dwelling place of God, and that God sat enthroned in the Holy of Holies between the cherubim upon the ark of the covenant (Ps.

80:1; 99:1). Isaiah saw God there, and His majesty was so great that the entire Temple was filled with the skirt of His kingly robe.

• What is the significance of "the Lord sitting upon a throne"?

"To say that God dwells in heaven is not to say that He is contained there. But it is uniquely His home, His center of operations, His command post. It is the place where His throne resides. And it is where the most perfect worship of Him occurs."—John MacArthur

---

B. The Seraphim and Their Praise (vv. 2-3)

2 Above it stood the seraphims: each one had six wings; with twain he covered his face, and with twain he covered his feet, and with twain he did fly. 3 And one cried unto another, and said, Holy, holy, holy, is the Lord of hosts: the whole earth is full of his glory.

Above the throne of God were stationed the seraphim (we are not told how many there were), each with six wings. With two wings they covered their faces, so as not to look upon God directly; and with two wings they covered their feet, so as to hide the least presentable part of their bodies from God's view. With the remaining two wings they flew.

The seraphim are winged creatures who attend to God and His throne, but their outward appearance is not described fully. Some people think of them as angels, but the function of angels is to serve as God's messengers, carrying out God's will. The Hebrew word *seraphim* is found in only five biblical passages. In Numbers 21:6-8 and Deuteronomy 8:15, the seraphim are "fiery serpents." In Isaiah 14:29 and 30:6, they are "fiery flying serpents." If these passages can be taken as a guide, then the seraphim of Isaiah 6 must be understood as some kind of winged serpent with feet, perhaps resembling a dragon. The presence of strange creatures around God's throne is not unusual in Scripture. The seraphim remind us of Ezekiel's cherubim, which were animal-like winged creatures with four faces—the face of a man, the face of an ox, the face of an eagle, and the face of a lion. The cherubim had four wings and had feet like a calf (Ezek. 1:5-11). We also read of heavenly creatures in the Book of Revelation: "Round about the throne, were four beasts full of eyes before and behind. And the first beast was like a lion, and the second beast like a calf, and the third beast had a face as a man, and the fourth beast was like a flying eagle. And the four beasts had each of them six wings about him; and they were full of eyes within: and they rest not day and night, saying, Holy, holy, holy, Lord God Almighty, which was, and is, and is to come" (4:6-8).

Whatever the appearance of the seraphim, their function is clear. They cry out to one another in unceasing praise to God. They proclaim God's majesty, shouting, "Holy, holy, holy, is the Lord of hosts: the whole earth is full of his glory" (Isa. 6:3). Thirty times in the Book of Isaiah, God is described as the "Holy One of Israel." God's awesome holiness stands in stark contrast to the sinfulness of disobedient Israel. Not only is God holy, but His glory fills the earth. From the human perspective, the earth is filled with sin, violence, uncertainty, idolatry, and vice. Our eyes are unable to perceive the pervasive presence of God's Holy Spirit and His glory that covers the earth. For His holiness and for His glorious presence, we should praise God continually, just as the seraphim praise Him.

---

1. How did Isaiah describe the seraphim ["fiery, burning ones"]?
2. Since our world is sinful, how is "the whole earth . . . full of [God's] glory" (v. 3)?

"The more clearly we see the infinite chasm between God's glory and our sinful falling short thereof, the greater will be our appreciation of His grace and love in bridging that guilt to redeem us."—Dave Hunt

---

C. The Power of God's Presence (v. 4)

⁴ And the posts of the door moved at the voice of him that cried, and the house was filled with smoke.

Isaiah's vision is multisensory. He first tells us what he saw—he saw the Lord, the Lord's throne, the Lord's robe filling the Temple, and the seraphim. Then, he tells us what he heard—he heard the seraphim crying out in praise to God. Now, he describes another sensation—he felt the shaking of the Temple. The voices of the seraphim were so powerful that the very foundations of the Temple trembled. Not only did the Temple shake, but it also was filled with smoke. In the Bible, God's appearance is often accompanied by smoke, which is intended in part to obscure and hide His face from human onlookers. The smoke may also represent worship that ascends to God from the brazen altar and from the altar of incense.

The scene reminds us of the time when God came down upon Mount Sinai and gave to Israel the Ten Commandments. When God descended, the earth shook, the mountain was covered with thick smoke, lightning flashed, God's voice thundered from heaven, and the people were terrified. The shaking of the Temple also reminds us of an episode in the Book of Acts when the early church gathered together to pray: "The place was shaken where they were assembled together; and they were all filled with the Holy Ghost" (4:31). From the very beginning of the Pentecostal Movement, God has appeared in our midst with powerful signs and wonders. We should expect no less today.

• What is the significance of the smoke?

"I had an overwhelming experience of the Lord's presence. I felt so powerfully overcome by the nearness of the Holy Spirit that I had to ask the Lord to draw back lest He kill me. It was so glorious that I couldn't stand more than a small portion of it."—Mordecai Ham

II. CLEANSED FOR SERVICE (Isa. 6:5-8)

A. Isaiah Made Aware of His Sin (v. 5)

⁵ Then said I, Woe is me! for I am undone; because I am a man of unclean lips, and I dwell in the midst of a people of unclean lips: for mine eyes have seen the King, the Lord of hosts.

It is impossible for a human being to stand in the presence of God without being deeply affected. Therefore, as soon as Isaiah comes face-to-face with God's holiness, he also comes face-to-face with his own sinfulness. The holiness of God stands in stark contrast to the sinfulness of humanity.

We would not be surprised that Isaiah recognizes the sin of his people because we have already heard of their rebellion in the previous five chapters of the book. However, Isaiah not only points to the sin of Israel, but he confesses his own sin as well. Isaiah and his people have "unclean lips." Unclean lips are an outward manifestation of an unclean heart, and the lips are mentioned because Isaiah stands in the presence of the worshiping seraphim. In chapter 1, we hear that the worship of the Israelites is unacceptable to God. In chapter 6, we find Isaiah confessing that their lips are too unclean to join with the seraphim in praising and worshiping God.

Isaiah feels the weight and heaviness of his impurity, and he cries out, "Woe is me! for I am undone." In chapter 5, Isaiah had pronounced "woes" upon all those who were living in rebellion against God. But now, as he stands before God's holiness, he pronounces the same "woe" upon himself. He feels a deep sense of condemnation and imminent doom. Isaiah knows that no one can look upon God and live; therefore, he expects to fall down dead at any moment.

Isaiah states that the vision occurred within the last year of the life of King Uzziah, but Uzziah is not the king that really matters. Uzziah is just one of many earthly, human kings, but the Lord of Hosts is *the* King, the true King, the ultimate King. *Lord of hosts* literally means "Lord of armies." Uzziah may be the king over Israel's armies, but the Lord is King over the armies of heaven.

• How did Isaiah feel, and why?

"I am convinced that the first step toward attaining a higher standard of holiness is to realize more fully the amazing sinfulness of sin."—J. C. Ryle

---

B. Isaiah's Sin Cleansed (vv. 6-7)

⁶ Then flew one of the seraphims unto me, having a live coal in his hand, which he had taken with the tongs from off the altar: ⁷ And he laid it upon my mouth, and said, Lo, this hath touched thy lips; and thine iniquity is taken away, and thy sin purged.

As soon as Isaiah confessed his impurity, one of the seraphim flew to him, carrying a hot coal that had been taken from the altar of the Temple. In a symbolic act, the seraphim placed the burning coal on Isaiah's unclean lips. This painful scorching of Isaiah's lips represented the taking away of his iniquity and the purging of his sin. Throughout the Bible, fire is used as a means of cleansing and purification. Isaiah learned that submitting to the judgment of God can be painful. In the same way, the people of Israel would be asked to submit to God's judgment so they might be cleansed and made fit for God's service.

If we will yield to God's judgment rather than resist it, we can be transformed just as Isaiah was transformed. Perhaps it is not accidental that on the Day of Pentecost the mouths of the apostles were touched by fire. The fire of Pentecost transformed the apostles into mighty witnesses of Jesus.

---

1. How did one of the seraphim minister to Isaiah?
2. Compare Isaiah's experience here with Jeremiah's (see Jer. 1:9).

"To confess your sins to God is not to tell [God] anything [God] doesn't already know. Until you confess them, however, they are the abyss between you. When you confess them, they become the bridge."—Frederick Buechner

---

C. Isaiah Called Into Service (v. 8)

⁸ Also I heard the voice of the Lord, saying, Whom shall I send, and who will go for us? Then said I, Here am I; send me.

After he is cleansed, Isaiah for the first time hears the voice of the Lord. In light of the other call narratives in the Bible, we would expect the Lord to speak to Isaiah directly and to designate him as a prophet, a messenger of the Lord. But instead of calling Isaiah directly, the Lord gives an invitation, asking, "Whom shall I send, and who will go for us?" The question signifies that the Lord is looking for an ambassador, a messenger who will carry God's word to its intended audience. The Lord is looking for a person who will speak on His behalf.

Apparently without hesitation, Isaiah immediately volunteers for the task. "Here am I," he says, "send me." At this point, Isaiah is probably overwhelmed by the awesomeness of his encounter with God, and he is oblivious to the many obstacles that might stand in the way of carrying out the divine commission. Isaiah's vision of God fills his mind and his heart, and makes him willing to do anything God would ask of him.

- To whom does "us" refer (v. 8)?

Instant Volunteers

On Monday, August 29, 2005, Hurricane Katrina struck New Orleans. The city and surrounding areas were devastated. Christians from all over the country recognized the great need and volunteered to help relieve the suffering. Some volunteers took time off without pay from their jobs. Others used vacation time. College students left their classrooms. Volunteers brought in food, water, clothing, and medical care. They cleaned up debris,

---

cleared roads, and ministered to broken hearts. Overcoming the many inconveniences and hardships, they declared, "Here am I, send me."

III. COMMISSIONED TO PROPHESY (Isa. 6:9-13)
A. Isaiah's Unresponsive Audience (vv. 9-10)

⁹ And he said, Go, and tell this people, Hear ye indeed, but understand not; and see ye indeed, but perceive not. ¹⁰ Make the heart of this people fat, and make their ears heavy, and shut their eyes; lest they see with their eyes, and hear with their ears, and understand with their heart, and convert, and be healed.

The Lord accepts Isaiah as His messenger and begins to make him aware of the message that he is to deliver to Israel. It is not a joyous message, but one of judgment that will be delivered to an unresponsive audience. The Lord informs Isaiah that the Israelites will not hear his message; they will not see what is before their eyes; they will not understand God's word; and they will not perceive the truth. They are hard-hearted and will not repent. Therefore, the doom of Israel is certain.

These verses are quoted repeatedly by Jesus Christ, who used them to explain why He spoke in parables. By speaking in parables, Jesus made the Kingdom more difficult to understand for those whose hearts were hardened. In the same way, Isaiah's preaching will make the heart of the people "fat," which means dull and insensitive. His message makes their ears "heavy," or stopped up, so that they cannot hear the word. They will willfully "shut their eyes" against the truth. The apostle Paul warns that the preaching of the gospel brings life to those who hear and death to those who refuse to hear (see 2 Cor. 2:16). Similarly, Isaiah's audience will not see, hear, or understand; therefore, they will not "convert, and be healed."

• How would the people respond to Isaiah's prophetic ministry?

"The most tremendous judgment of God in this world is the hardening of the hearts of men."—John Owen

---

B. Isaiah's Message of Judgment (vv. 11-12)

¹¹ Then said I, Lord, how long? And he answered, Until the cities be wasted without inhabitant, and the houses without man, and the land be utterly desolate, ¹² And the Lord have removed men far away, and there be a great forsaking in the midst of the land.

Isaiah wants to know how long he must minister under these circumstances. He wonders how long he must preach this message of doom to a hard-hearted and unresponsive audience. The answer to his question must have been difficult for him to bear. He must continue to carry God's message until the nation of Israel is destroyed, until the cities are left desolate and the homes are empty, until the entire nation has been carried away into exile—into what we call the Babylonian Captivity. The Israelites had been warned, even from the time of Moses, that if

they disobeyed God on a continual basis, the Lord would punish them by removing them from the land (Deut. 28:15-41). Now, after hundreds of years of
idolatry and unfaithfulness, the Israelites would finally receive their punishment.
God chastises those whom He loves; and Israel's exile in Babylon, though it be
judgment, is a redemptive judgment that will forever cure Israel of her idolatry.

• What did the Lord reveal to Isaiah about his nation's future?

"Today some Christians are content to merely exist until they die.
They don't want to risk anything, to believe God, to grow or mature. They
refuse to believe His Word, and have become hardened in their unbelief.
Now they're living just to die."—David Wilkerson

C. Isaiah's Promise of a Remnant (v. 13)
**13 But yet in it shall be a tenth, and it shall return, and shall be eaten: as
a teil tree, and as an oak, whose substance is in them, when they cast their
leaves: so the holy seed shall be the substance thereof.**
Isaiah's call narrative concludes with a powerful promise of a holy remnant.
Although Isaiah will be delivering his message to a generation that will refuse to
hear and that will be sent into exile, the exile will not be the end. Beyond this generation will be "a tenth," which represents another generation. This remnant will return
and will be faithful. Nevertheless, even this remnant must be further reduced by
burning. "Shall be eaten" should be translated literally as "shall be burned." This
"tenth" will be burned down like a tree that is consumed to the ground. Within the
stump, however, remains the "holy seed" of new life; for even if a tree is burned
down, the roots will shoot forth new sprouts of growth. The generation that is unresponsive will be destroyed with only a tenth remaining. That remnant will pass
through the fire of judgment once more, but within the stump will be preserved a
remnant of the remnant, a holy seed.
These final verses of Isaiah's call are the key to understanding the entire Book
of Isaiah. In chapter 7, Isaiah will confront King Ahaz and challenge him to trust
God in the midst of national crisis, but Ahaz will not hear. Ahaz, therefore, represents the unresponsive generation. Years later (ch. 37), Isaiah will bring God's
word to King Hezekiah, who is the son of Ahaz. Unlike his father, Hezekiah will
listen to Isaiah and the disaster will be averted. Hezekiah represents the remnant. But not long after Hezekiah's death, the Israelites will go into exile and the
nation will be destroyed. Against all odds, however, the holy seed will come forth
out of Babylon and bring restoration to Israel (chs. 40–66).

CONCLUSION

Divine encounters on the scale of Isaiah's experience are quite uncommon.
We are not likely to see a vision of God like Isaiah did. However, God continues to
reveal Himself quite frequently and in various ways. We should keep in mind that
Jesus promised to be in the midst of His people whenever two or three are gathered together in His name. Pentecostal believers should continue to expect God
to manifest Himself through signs and wonders. We should continue to anticipate

holy encounters that reveal our sinfulness, drive us to our knees in confession, and challenge us to serve as God's messengers in the world. The world needs to hear God's word, and even now God is asking the question, "Whom shall I send, and who will go for us?" Let us come together in the presence of God and, in spite of our weaknesses, declare wholeheartedly, "Here am I; send me."

GOLDEN TEXT CHALLENGE

"I HEARD THE VOICE OF THE LORD, SAYING, WHOM SHALL I SEND, AND WHO WILL GO FOR US? THEN SAID I, HERE AM I; SEND ME" (Isa. 6:8).

God's question, "Whom shall I send?" has the limitation of, "Who will go for us?" The Lord can only send one who is willing. Also, those who would go will not truly succeed unless they are sent of God. God has chosen to depend on the willingness of people—people must rely on the anointing, power, and guidance of the Holy Spirit.

Many want to give themselves to God only to the degree necessary to appropriate to themselves His blessings. They want to receive spiritual life and excitement, natural and material benefits, as well as physical and emotional health (and the Scriptures certainly promise these things). But when it comes to saying, "Send me," many hesitate. This, in effect, is an attempt to make the Creator their personal genie, who serves them by giving them their desires and wishes!

Let us no longer linger with the concept of God serving us, but rather say, "How and where can I serve You, Lord?" Like Isaiah, each of us should make a total commitment to God. We need to reach the place where we can say with honesty and genuine feeling, "I'll go wherever You want me to, Lord." Indeed, this is the same dedication which the apostle Paul appealed for us to make when he penned the words of Romans 12:1, "Present your bodies a living sacrifice."

Daily Devotions:
M. Abraham Encounters God
   Genesis 15:1-6
T. Samuel Encounters God
   1 Samuel 3:9-19
W. Ezekiel Commissioned to Prophesy
   Ezekiel 3:24-27
T. Disciples Encounter the Risen Lord
   Luke 24:30-39
F. Saul Encounters the Lord
   Acts 9:1-9
S. Cleansed to Serve God
   Hebrews 9:11-14

The Promised Deliverer

Isaiah 7:14-16; 8:14-15; 9:2-7; 11:1-9; Matthew 1:22-23; Luke 20:17-18

Unit Theme:
Hope in the Book of Isaiah

Central Truth:
Jesus Christ fulfills the Old Testament messianic prophecies.

Focus:
Reflect on messianic prophecies from Isaiah and rejoice in their fulfillment.

Context:
In the eighth century BC, Isaiah receives supernatural insight about the Messiah.

Golden Text:
"A virgin shall be with child, and shall bring forth a son, and they shall call his name Emmanuel, which being interpreted is, God with us" (Matt. 1:23).

Study Outline:
I. The Deliverer Is With Us
   (Isa. 7:14-16; Matt. 1:22-23; Isa. 8:14-15; Luke 20:17-18)
II. The Deliverer Governs His People
   (Isa. 9:2-7)
III. The Deliverer Reigns Righteously
   (Isa. 11:1-9)

INTRODUCTION

The Book of Isaiah has been called the "Fifth Gospel." Its many messianic prophecies, its emphasis on faith, its presentation of God as "Savior," and its frequent use by New Testament writers make it the most powerful Old Testament witness to the gospel of Jesus Christ. More specifically, the Book of Isaiah predicts the coming of the King of Israel, the Son of David, who will bring salvation to the Jews and to the Gentiles, even to the ends of the earth (49:6).

This coming Messiah is more than a mere man. Many other great religious teachers and leaders have lived and died, but all of them were only mortal humans. Confucius was just a man; Buddha was just a man; and Muhammad was just a man. However, the prophecies of Isaiah demonstrate that Jesus was more than just a man. He was more than a Jewish rabbi whose teachings are worth emulating. The birth of Jesus was a supernatural birth. The ministry of Jesus was empowered by the Holy Spirit and accompanied by miracles, signs, and wonders. According to Isaiah, Jesus is the anointed Messiah (61:1) and "The mighty God, The Everlasting Father" (9:6) who was born of a virgin (7:14). Isaiah declares that Jesus was able to take our sins upon Himself and secure our salvation: "He was wounded for our transgressions, he was bruised for our iniquities; the chastisement of our peace was upon him; and with his stripes we are healed" (53:5).

Jesus identified Himself closely with the Book of Isaiah, citing prophecies therein as referring to Himself (Matt. 11:1-5; Luke 4:18-21). The uniqueness of Jesus makes Christianity a unique religion, unlike any other religion.

In this lesson we will examine four powerful messianic passages from the Book of Isaiah, and we will observe their fulfillment in the life and ministry of Jesus Christ. As we study, we should keep in mind that Isaiah's words are relevant to us today, and that the anointed ministry of Jesus continues in the lives of His followers. We have been called of God to speak the words of Jesus, live the teachings of Jesus, and perform the works of Jesus so that His gracious gift of salvation will reach to the farthest corners of the globe.

I. THE DELIVERER IS WITH US (Isa. 7:14-16; Matt. 1:22-23; Isa. 8:14-15; Luke 20:17-18)

A. The Promise of Immanuel (Isa. 7:14-16)

14 Therefore the Lord himself shall give you a sign; Behold, a virgin shall conceive, and bear a son, and shall call his name Immanuel. 15 Butter and honey shall he eat, that he may know to refuse the evil, and choose the good. 16 For before the child shall know to refuse the evil, and choose the good, the land that thou abhorrest shall be forsaken of both her kings.

In the time of Isaiah, the Israelites were divided into two kingdoms. The northern kingdom was called Israel, with its capital in Samaria; and the southern kingdom was called Judah, with its capital in Jerusalem. In Isaiah 7, Jerusalem is attacked by the combined armies of Pekah, king of Israel, and Rezin, king of Syria (a neighboring country). Ahaz, king of Judah, is worried that Jerusalem may be defeated; therefore, the Lord directs Isaiah to go to Ahaz and give him an assurance of victory. Isaiah encourages Ahaz to "fear not" (v. 4) because the plans of his enemies will not stand. In fact, within sixty-five years, the northern kingdom of Israel will be broken into pieces and will no longer be a people (v. 8). The Lord challenges Ahaz to stand firm in his faith, but if he will not do so, his reign will not be established (v. 9). As a way of proving himself to King Ahaz, the Lord offers to show him a sign, any sign that he desires. Ahaz, however, is unwilling to cooperate, and refuses to name a sign. Isaiah then tells Ahaz, "Therefore the Lord himself shall give you a sign; Behold, a virgin shall conceive, and bear a son, and shall call his name Immanuel" (v. 14).

The word *virgin* in the Hebrew language refers to a young woman who is of age to be married. Therefore, on the day that Isaiah gave his prophecy, there was a young woman who would soon conceive a child. Isaiah goes on to say that the child will be nourished with butter and honey, the normal diet of an Israelite baby. Before this young child grows old enough to distinguish between good and evil, the threat against Jerusalem will be removed. The name *Immanuel* means "God is with us." It is a sign of God's grace and salvation; and it confirms that, for now, God is with Jerusalem and will deliver her from the attack of the enemy armies.

1. What "sign" did God promise to give Ahaz (v. 14)?
2. What would God's Son be called, and why (v. 14)?

"Immanuel God with us in our nature, in our sorrow, in our lifework, in our punishment, in our grave, and now with us, or rather we with Him, in resurrection, ascension, triumph, and Second Advent splendor."—Charles Spurgeon

---

B. God Is With Us (Matt. 1:22-23)

22 Now all this was done, that it might be fulfilled which was spoken of the Lord by the prophet, saying, 23 Behold, a virgin shall be with child, and shall bring forth a son, and they shall call his name Emmanuel, which being interpreted is, God with us.

The prophecy of Emmanuel has two meanings—one for Isaiah's day and one for later times. A son was born in Isaiah's day, but he was not the deliverer. He was a sign of God's deliverance and of God's presence with Jerusalem. The Gospel of Matthew records the birth of another son who will also signify God's presence among His people—that son is Jesus Christ.

Matthew tells us that Joseph and Mary were promised to each other in marriage, and before their marriage was consummated, Mary was found to be pregnant. Joseph was understandably shaken by this news, and he considered divorcing her privately. But the angel of the Lord appeared to him with an amazing message: Mary had conceived her child through miraculous means, by the Holy Spirit (1:20). Mary's baby would be named *Jesus*, because "he shall save his people from their sins" (v. 21).

This divine conception in the womb of Mary was a fulfillment of Isaiah's prophecy that a "virgin" would conceive and bear a son. Matthew 1:23 is best translated "the virgin" (NKJV), meaning Mary was unique—the only woman to ever become a mother by means of the Holy Spirit "overshadowing" her (see Luke 1:35). And her Son would be called *Emmanuel,* which means "God is with us." The difference in spelling between *Immanuel* in Isaiah and *Emmanuel* in Matthew results from the fact that Isaiah is written in Hebrew and Matthew is written in Greek. There is no difference in meaning between the two spellings.

The virgin birth of Jesus means that He had no human father; therefore, He is the unique Son of God (Mark 1:1). He is both human and divine at the same time. He is God "manifest in the flesh" (1 Tim. 3:16). The birth of Jesus is called the *Incarnation*—God "was made flesh, and dwelt among us" (John 1:14). Before His birth, Jesus had existed as part of the invisible Godhead (vv. 1-2). At His birth, He took upon Himself the "form of a servant, and was made in the likeness of men" (Phil. 2:7-8).

When Jesus was born, when God took on the form of humanity, He became "God with us." Jesus became a man for three reasons. First, He came to truly reveal God to us (John 14:8-10; Heb. 1:1-2). Second, Jesus came to die a sacrificial death and redeem us from our fallen state (John 3:16; Rom. 5:8; Luke 19:10). As the second Adam, Jesus "bore our sins in his own body on the [cross]" (1 Peter 2:24). Third, Jesus came to share humanity with us, to enter sympathetically into our human condition. Not only was Jesus "truly God," but He also was "truly man." God became one of us and was tempted in all points like we are, yet without sin (Heb. 4:15). Somehow, the Incarnation opened a new dimension of empathy and help for humanity (2:18). God experienced human pain and alienation, and the Son of God now intercedes on our behalf (7:25). We can come boldly to the throne of grace, because we have a High Priest who is "touched with the feeling of our infirmities" (4:15-16). Whatever we feel today, Jesus felt it; He understands. Like us, Jesus experienced hunger, pain, temptation, bodily weakness, persecution, betrayal, loneliness, and even death. During His life on this earth, Jesus was "God with us"; but even now, He continues to be and always will be "God with us."

• To whom is Isaiah 7:14 quoted here, and why (Matt. 1:23)?

False or Real?

About twenty-six years ago, former NASA engineer Edgar C. Whisenant wrote *88 Reasons Why the Rapture Will Be in 1988*. He predicted that Jesus would return sometime between September 11 and 13. Surprisingly, the book sold four million copies, and Christians everywhere debated Whisenant's prediction. Jesus, however, did not return, and Whisenant was labeled a false prophet. But Isaiah was no false prophet. His predictions of the birth, life, and death of Jesus are fulfilled in the New Testament. We can rejoice in the prophecies of Isaiah and trust in those that are yet to be fulfilled.

C. Jesus, Our Rock (Isa. 8:14-15; Luke 20:17-18)

(Luke 20:17-18 is not included in the printed text.)

Isaiah 8:14 **And he shall be for a sanctuary; but for a stone of stumbling and for a rock of offence to both the houses of Israel, for a gin and for a snare to the inhabitants of Jerusalem.** [15] **And many among them shall stumble, and fall, and be broken, and be snared, and be taken.**

Isaiah 8 continues the message from chapter 7 in which Isaiah challenged Ahaz to trust God for deliverance from the attacks of the enemy kings. Ahaz, however, refused to trust in God and chose instead to make a political alliance with the Assyrians. The message of chapter 7 was directed primarily at King Ahaz, but in chapter 8, Isaiah speaks to the people of Israel. He encourages the Israelites to fear God, honor God, and trust in God's power to deliver.

The Lord will be to them a "sanctuary"—a place of refuge to those who trust Him. A sanctuary is a holy place, a consecrated place, usually referring to the Tabernacle or to the Temple. A sanctuary can also be a refuge to which people might flee in case of danger.

However, anyone who resists or opposes God's Word will stumble, fall, and be entrapped by the Enemy. First, the Lord will be "for a stone of stumbling and for a rock of offense" to those who do not trust Him. When God sends His word into our pathway, we should receive it as a stepping-stone to a place of safety, or else we will trip over it and fall on our faces in defeat. Second, the Lord is a "gin and a snare" to these people who do not believe His word. *Gin* and *snare* refer to traps for catching small game. Anyone who refuses to hear God's Word will fall into the trap of the Enemy.

In Luke 20:17-18, Jesus applied Isaiah 8:14 to His own ministry. He is the stone that was rejected but then became "the chief cornerstone" (see Ps. 118:22), and He is the stone that will crush His enemies to powder. Those who hear the gospel will be divided into only two groups. Either we accept Jesus as the "cornerstone" or we reject Him, in which case He becomes a "rock of offense" that grinds us to powder.

---

1. How is Jesus Christ a "sanctuary" (Isa. 8:14)?
2. How is Jesus Christ "a rock to stumble over" (v. 14 NASB)?
3. What will happen to "many" (v. 15)?

"Great truths that are stumbling blocks to the natural man are nevertheless the very foundations upon which the confidence of the spiritual man is built."—Harry Ironside

---

II. THE DELIVERER GOVERNS HIS PEOPLE (Isa. 9:2-7)

A. The Deliverer Brings Light (v. 2)

2 The people that walked in darkness have seen a great light: they that dwell in the land of the shadow of death, upon them hath the light shined.

Chapter 8 concludes with a bleak picture of the Israelite people of Isaiah's time. They do not seek God (v. 19), and they do not speak according to God's word because "there is no light in them" (v. 20). They see nothing around them but "trouble and darkness" (v. 22). The tone of chapter 9, however, is entirely different. It is a message of hope and promise—a promise that "a great light" is coming. The people who need this light are characterized by two figurative statements: (1) they "walked in darkness," and (2) they "dwell in the land of the shadow of death." To walk in darkness is to stumble around without guidance, without the truth, and without God. To dwell in the land of the shadow of death means to live in such a manner that death hangs over everything as a dark cloud. To be under the shadow of death is to live in misery, ignorance, and dread of the future.

To all of those who walk in darkness and to all of those who live in the shadow of death, Isaiah has a message of hope—the light is coming! In Scripture, light is symbolic of knowledge, joy, life, and deliverance. Light is the opposite of spiritual darkness, unbelief, and judgment.

Before Jesus found us, we walked in the darkness of this world, groping about, unable to find our way. We lived underneath a heavy cloud—the shadow of death. We feared death, and always felt its presence looming over our lives. But then appeared "the light of the world" (John 8:12), who brought us out of darkness and into His marvelous light.

• Upon whom does Christ's light shine?

"The issue is now clear. It is between light and darkness and everyone must choose his side."—G. K. Chesterton

---

B. The Deliverer Brings Joyous Victory (vv. 3-5)

³ Thou hast multiplied the nation, and not increased the joy: they joy before thee according to the joy in harvest, and as men rejoice when they divide the spoil. ⁴ For thou hast broken the yoke of his burden, and the staff of his shoulder, the rod of his oppressor, as in the day of Midian. ⁵ For every battle of the warrior is with confused noise, and garments rolled in blood; but this shall be with burning and fuel of fire.

The coming of the light brings with it growth, joy, and liberty. Through the light of the gospel, the number of believers is "multiplied," and the people of God are able to rejoice as in the time of harvest and as in the time of victory when the spoils are divided among the victors (v. 3). The light of the gospel breaks the burdensome "yoke" that restricts us, the "staff" that strikes us on the shoulder, and the "rod" that is wielded by our oppressors (v. 4). We are delivered from the bondage of the Enemy.

Verse 5 is clarified by the *New King James Version*, which reads, "For every warrior's sandal from the noisy battle, and garments rolled in blood, will be used for burning and fuel of fire." The meaning here is that war will be abolished in the kingdom of God. Peace will come, and everything pertaining to battle will be destroyed by fire.

---

1. How does verse 3 describe the joy Christ gives?
2. What is the reason for rejoicing (vv. 4-5)?

"Take your stand on the Rock of Ages. Let death, let the judgment come: the victory is Christ's and yours through Him."—D. L. Moody

---

C. The Deliverer Brings an Everlasting Kingdom (vv. 6-7)

⁶ For unto us a child is born, unto us a son is given: and the government shall be upon his shoulder: and his name shall be called Wonderful, Counsellor, The mighty God, The everlasting Father, The Prince of Peace. ⁷ Of the increase of his government and peace there shall be no end, upon the throne of David, and upon his kingdom, to order it, and to establish it with judgment and with justice from henceforth even for ever. The zeal of the Lord of hosts will perform this.

The age of peace, salvation, and victory is brought in by the birth of a special child. As the comments above on Isaiah 7:14 show, the birth of this child is a miraculous event. Almighty God humbles Himself, laying aside the glories of heaven, to be born in a humble manger. Before He was the "Lamb slain," He was the "Son born" (see Luke 2:11). Let us never forget the importance of the birth of the Son of God. He will be God's chosen ruler, and "the government shall be upon his shoulder" (Isa. 9:6). The word *government* means "dominion, rule," and the word *shoulder* signifies that the Son carries the weight of this responsibility upon Himself.

The special character of the Son is embodied in His five names. Some modern translations join together the words *wonderful* and *counselor* to form one phrase, "wonderful Counselor." The usual argument is that the writer intends four pairs of words, but that argument is made invalid by the fact that the Hebrew term "everlasting Father" is only one word. Furthermore, the original Hebrew accent marks indicate that the words *wonderful* and *counselor* are intended to be two separate names.

It is appropriate that the first of these names is *Wonderful*, a word which is used throughout the Old Testament to signify an event or a person or an idea that causes great wonder and amazement. The word is often used to describe miracles, and it is tied closely to God's great acts of salvation (see Ex. 15:2; Judg. 6:13; Dan. 12:6). The Son of God is wonderful in every respect. He is wonderful in His miraculous birth . . . His sinless life . . . His unequaled teachings . . . His ministry of healing and deliverance . . . His sacrificial death . . . His powerful resurrection from the dead . . . His continued ministry of intercession for God's children.

The second name given to our deliverer is *Counselor*, a title which describes a person of high rank, a person worthy of great honor. It signifies great wisdom and the ability to guide others through times of decision and uncertainty.

The third and fourth names point directly to the divine nature of the Messiah. He is the *mighty God*, a name ascribed to the Lord in the next chapter of Isaiah's prophecy: "The remnant shall return, even the remnant of Jacob, unto the mighty God" (10:21).

The name *everlasting Father* demonstrates the eternal existence of the Son and the unity between Father and Son. Even though the Messiah is called *Son*, His eternal nature is one with the Father; therefore, He can also be called "everlasting Father."

The first and second names relate to the awesomeness and honor of the Messiah, while the third and fourth describe His divine nature. The fifth and final name, *Prince of Peace*, predicts the nature and character of His divine rule. At the time of its creation, the earth was a place of peace. But when sin entered into the world, peace became an ideal hoped for in the future. The birth of the Son of God was announced by the angels with the words "peace on earth" (see Luke 2:14). Jesus is the source of peace for every troubled heart, for every divided family, and for every warring nation. Furthermore, at His second coming, our Savior will institute a reign of peace.

Verse 7 of the text tells us the peaceful reign of the Messiah will have no end. He will sit "upon the throne of David," ruling with judgment and justice forever. The establishment of His kingdom is not the work of human politics; it is the work of the Lord of hosts.

---

1. What does "the government shall be upon his shoulder" mean (v. 6)?
2. How has Christ shown Himself to be the "Wonderful Counselor" in your life (v. 6 NIV)?
3. How have you found Him to be the "Prince of Peace"?
4. What characteristics mark the reign of Jesus Christ (v. 7)?

"There are no term limits on His reign. He has always been King and He always will be King. There is no death that threatens the perpetuity of His sovereign authority. There is no usurping of power by a lesser rival to His throne. There are no coups, no revolutions (at least, none that succeed). There is no threat of impeachment. He is a King who rules eternally."—Sam Storms

III. THE DELIVERER REIGNS RIGHTEOUSLY (Isa. 11:1-9)

A. The Deliverer Is the Son of David (v. 1)

¹ And there shall come forth a rod out of the stem of Jesse, and a Branch shall grow out of his roots.

Isaiah 11 expands on the idea of the reign of the Messiah. First, we are told His family history. He will emerge from the family of Jesse, the father of King David; therefore, the Deliverer will be called "the Son of David." The Davidic dynasty was brought to an apparent end by the Babylonians, but the roots still remained. And from those roots the Son of God will grow.

• Why is Christ referred to as a "Branch"?

B. Endowed With the Sevenfold Spirit (v. 2)

² And the spirit of the Lord shall rest upon him, the spirit of wisdom and understanding, the spirit of counsel and might, the spirit of knowledge and of the fear of the Lord.

The predicted Deliverer will be endowed special power by the Spirit of the Lord. Because the Spirit of the Lord is upon Him, the Messiah will possess special qualities that make Him an ideal ruler. He will have "the spirit of wisdom and understanding." Wisdom is an indispensable qualification for a ruler, and understanding goes hand-in-hand with wisdom. Wisdom is the ability to know what is good, and understanding is the ability to distinguish the best course of action when presented with opposing choices.

He will also have "the spirit of counsel and might." The word *counsel* is the same as we saw in 9:6 above, and the word *might* means simply "strength" or "power."

Furthermore, the Spirit will give Him the "knowledge" necessary to rule over the kingdom of God. The Holy Spirit knows all things and is able to dispense that knowledge to God's chosen ruler. Finally, the Messiah will display the "fear of the Lord," which signifies a deep reverence for the Lord and for His commandments.

• Describe the anointing on the Messiah's life.

"God is completely sovereign. God is infinite in wisdom. God is perfect in love. God in His love always wills what is best for us. In His wisdom, He always knows what is best, and in His sovereignty He has the power to bring it about."—Jerry Bridges

C. The Deliverer Reigns in Righteousness (vv. 3-5)

³ And shall make him of quick understanding in the fear of the Lord: and he shall not judge after the sight of his eyes, neither reprove after the hearing of his ears: ⁴ But with righteousness shall he judge the poor, and reprove with equity for the meek of the earth: and he shall smite the earth with the rod of his mouth, and with the breath of his lips shall he slay the wicked. ⁵ And righteousness shall be the girdle of his loins, and faithfulness the girdle of his reins.

The special attributes that are given to the Messiah by the Holy Spirit will enable Him to rule in "righteousness" (v. 4), not judging things on outward appearance and not deciding things according to the opinions of others (v. 3). He will not give preference to the rich and the powerful. Instead, He will give justice to the poor and to the meek. Because the Messiah is righteous and faithful, He will strike down the "wicked" with the "breath of his lips" (v. 4). The *New International Version* renders verse 5, "Righteousness will be his belt and faithfulness the sash around his waist."

---

1. How is Christ unlike human judges (v. 3)?
2. What can the "poor" and the "afflicted" expect from Christ (v. 4 NASB)?
3. Describe the power of Christ's words (v. 4).
4. How is the Messiah dressed (v. 5)?

"The righteousness of Jesus Christ is one of those great mysteries, which the angels desire to look into, and seems to be one of the first lessons that God taught men after the Fall."—George Whitefield

---

D. The Deliverer Reigns in Peace (vv. 6-9)

⁶ The wolf also shall dwell with the lamb, and the leopard shall lie down with the kid; and the calf and the young lion and the fatling together; and a little child shall lead them. ⁷ And the cow and the bear shall feed; their young ones shall lie down together: and the lion shall eat straw like the ox. ⁸ And the sucking child shall play on the hole of the asp, and the weaned child shall put his hand on the cockatrice' den. ⁹ They shall not hurt nor destroy in all my holy mountain: for the earth shall be full of the knowledge of the Lord, as the waters cover the sea.

These verses continue to describe the Messiah's reign of peace. In fact, the peace spoken of here is deeper than just the ceasing of hostilities between one nation and another. The peace of God's kingdom will eventually include a reordering of the entire creation, in which even animal life itself displays the perfect peace that God intends for His world. The wolf will no longer attack the lamb; the kid goat will no longer be afraid of the leopard, and "a little child shall lead them" (v. 6). Poisonous snakes will not endanger children's lives (v. 8). The earth will be restored to the pristine state that it enjoyed at the time of the original creation—the time before sin entered into the world and brought death.

When God sets up His kingdom on earth, no one will be able to deny the reality of God and His reign. Instead, just as the water fills the ocean, so the earth will be filled with people who know God and live accordingly (v. 9).

---

1. In the Messiah's restored kingdom, how would animals be different?
2. How will children be safer?
3. What will fill the earth (v. 9)?

"The story of paradise lost becoming paradise regained is the story of God's grace bringing us from alienation from Him to membership in His family. God's grace restores us to what Adam lost for us—sonship to the God who made us, loves us, and provides for us in every detail of life."—Sinclair B. Ferguson

---

CONCLUSION

Isaiah's messianic prophecies have been a source of hope and inspiration for Christians throughout the ages, and they continue to serve in that capacity today. Beginning with his prophecy of the Virgin Birth and concluding with his prophecy of the Messiah's peaceful kingdom, Isaiah paints a picture of Jesus Christ, our Savior and Deliverer. Many of Isaiah's prophecies were fulfilled in the life of Jesus, but many are yet to be fulfilled in the future. We can be sure that every word will come to pass just as the prophet predicted, for "the zeal of the Lord of hosts will perform this" (9:7).

GOLDEN TEXT CHALLENGE

"A VIRGIN SHALL BE WITH CHILD, AND SHALL BRING FORTH A SON, AND THEY SHALL CALL HIS NAME EMMANUEL, WHICH BEING INTERPRETED IS, GOD WITH US" (Matt. 1:23).

Our Lord came into this world by an extraordinary event, the Virgin Birth. His birth was a pure miracle. When Mary learned that she was to give birth to the Savior, her own reaction showed the purity and innocence of her heart. But it also revealed she did not understand how it was biologically possible for her to have a son. "How shall this be, seeing I know not a man?" (Luke 1:34). To say the least, the birth of Jesus was not of normal human conception. Mary was found to be with child of the Holy Spirit before she and Joseph came together (Matt. 1:18). The miraculous and absolutely unique birth of the Savior fulfilled the prophecy of Isaiah 7:14.

The importance of His supernatural birth cannot be overstated. First, the Virgin Birth reinforces our understanding of the person and work of Jesus. The miracle of His birth fits perfectly well with what we know about His atoning work, His bodily resurrection, and His return in glory. His miracles, teachings, and claims are in accord with what we would expect of One who had such an extraordinary entrance into the world.

Second, the supernatural birth of the Savior affirms the power of the Cross to save from sin and death. Only God can do that. The wonderfulness of Jesus' birth bears witness to the union of Deity and humanity in His person. No other kind of person could have accomplished the miracle of saving grace through the Cross. The miracle of His birth makes believable the miracle of the Cross.

Third, the uniqueness of the Savior's birth indicates that He is worthy of our worship. While on the earth, He asserted that He was the Son of God. A number of people recognized His deity and worshiped Him. The birth of the babe in Bethlehem cannot be separated from the worship of Him as our Lord. The Virgin Birth is part of the history of the One who said, "I am Alpha and Omega, the beginning and the ending, saith the Lord, which is, and which was, and which is to come, the Almighty" (Rev. 1:8).

Daily Devotions:
M. God Raises Up a Deliverer
    Judges 3:7-11
T. Song of Deliverance
    2 Samuel 22:1-4
W. The Lord Governs Righteously
    Psalm 67:3-7
T. Moses, Ruler and Deliverer
    Acts 7:35-40
F. Reject Sin's Reign
    Romans 6:11-18
S. Reigning Kings and Priests
    Revelation 5:6-10

Our Awesome Hope in God

Isaiah 25:1 through 26:4

Unit Theme:
Hope in the Book of Isaiah

Central Truth:
The Christian's hope is based on who God is and what He has done.

Focus:
Explore our hope in God and join the prophet's anthem of praise.

Context:
Probably between 740 and 738 BC in Judah, Isaiah prophesies of God's unfailing salvation.

Golden Text:
"Trust ye in the Lord for ever: for in the Lord Jehovah is everlasting strength" (Isa. 26:4).

Study Outline:
I. Rehearse God's Awesome Deeds
   (Isa. 25:1-5)
II. Praise God for Salvation
   (Isa. 25:6-12)
III. Trust in God's Strength
   (Isa. 26:1-4)

INTRODUCTION

Tragedy is a regular part of life in the fallen world, and even the most devoted Christians are not exempt from tragedy. Sometimes disasters come our way through the course of nature. The rain falls on the just and on the unjust (Matt. 5:45). Hurricanes and tornadoes destroy the homes and businesses of wicked *and* righteous people. Other types of trouble can be described as attacks of the Enemy, because "the devil, as a roaring lion, walketh about, seeking whom he may devour" (1 Peter 5:8). Job was a man who was "perfect and upright" (Job 1:1), yet God allowed him to suffer a series of severe attacks from Satan. Furthermore, even though we might not like to admit it, we also suffer a third category of trouble, what the Bible calls "chastisement"—the disciplinary tests given to us from the hand of God himself (Heb. 12:5-11).

When troubles befall us, we may find it difficult to discern the cause that lies behind it. God eventually rescued Job from all his troubles, but Job never learned that Satan was the source of his suffering. We must not give in to the temptation to expend all of our energy seeking out the source and/or reason for our suffering. While it is true that what we desire is understanding, what we really need is the presence of God. Therefore, whether our trouble is a result of the forces of nature, an attack of the Enemy, or the disciplinary hand of our heavenly Father, our response should be the same. When trouble comes we should humbly fall before God, seek His face, trust in God's grace, and hope in His promises.

As Pentecostals, we can take this approach because we live what can be called an apocalyptic spirituality. That is, we live every day in expectation of the return of Jesus, and we know that when Jesus returns He will set all things right and will establish His kingdom on the earth. We know that even though the world appears to be in chaos, God is still in control and He hears our prayers. The kingdoms of the earth are nothing and "less than nothing" (Isa. 40:17) in comparison to God; and soon, "the meek shall inherit the earth" (Ps. 37:11; Matt. 5:5).

I. REHEARSE GOD'S AWESOME DEEDS (Isa. 25:1-5)

This lesson is drawn from a section of Isaiah's prophecies that Bible scholars call "the Isaiah Apocalypse," which includes chapters 24-27. Like the Book of Revelation in the New Testament, the Isaiah Apocalypse looks beyond the writer's present time and gazes into the future. It teaches us that history is moving toward God's intended purposes. God will surely judge the nations, triumph over evil, and exalt the righteous. In the end, when God judges sin, the people of God will praise Him for their salvation and for the deliverance of Israel.

A. Exalt God for His Faithfulness (v. 1)

¹ O Lord, thou art my God; I will exalt thee, I will praise thy name; for thou hast done wonderful things; thy counsels of old are faithfulness and truth.

Chapter 25 is a song of praise to the Lord, in which His people praise Him for His mighty acts of deliverance. The song begins with a strong profession of faith—"O Lord, thou art my God"—which signifies a personal relationship, specifically a covenant relationship. The songwriter knows God as his God, and he expresses a strong commitment to glorify God. First, the writer promises to "exalt" God—to lift Him up through praise. It means literally to make God high and lifted up. Second, Isaiah promises to "praise" the name of the Lord—to publicly and audibly testify to God's great works. It means to specify out to the congregation all of God's mighty acts.

After promising to praise God, the writer gives two all-inclusive reasons for that praise. First, God has "done wonderful things." As we learned in the previous lesson, the word *wonderful* refers to something that causes great amazement and astonishment, particularly the mighty acts of God that cause us to marvel at His power, grace, and love. These wonderful things for which the writer wishes to praise God will be enumerated in the verses that follow.

Second, not only has God done mighty wonders, but His "counsels of old are faithfulness and truth." The word *counsels* means God's plans and His methods of attaining those plans. Unlike human leaders, whose plans may be based on selfishness, pride, and other evil desires, God's plans are based entirely on His "faithfulness" to His people and to His holy nature. Human plans are often carried out through deceit, manipulation, and other unscrupulous means; but God's plans are always carried out in "truth." This means that in accomplishing His plans, God can always be trusted to tell the truth.

---

1. What motivated Isaiah to praise the Lord?

---

2. Name some "marvelous things" God has accomplished that He "planned long ago" (NIV).

_____

"My attitude was and still is like that of David, who was ashamed that the armies of Israel would tremble before Goliath. Without hesitation he stepped forward with complete confidence in the God who had proven Himself to be faithful (1 Sam. 17). For David, the size of the giant was irrelevant."—Dave Hunt

_____

B. Glorify God for Defeating the Enemy (v. 2)

² For thou hast made of a city an heap; of a defenced city a ruin: a palace of strangers to be no city; it shall never be built.

With verse 2, we begin to hear of specific wonders God has performed. God has overthrown a wicked city that stood in opposition to His plans and oppressed the people of God. He reduced the city to "an heap," a pile of rubble. This enemy of God was a "defenced city," but no human defenses can stand up against the power of God. Human leaders trust in their fortifications, place their faith in their military armaments, and rely on their wealth; but God will bring it all to nothing in the end—"Babylon is fallen, is fallen, that great city" (Rev. 14:8). This great city played host to all the important leaders of the world, opening its palace to "strangers"; but when God finishes with it, it will no longer be called a city, and it will never be rebuilt.

_____

• How had God demonstrated His strength, and why did His actions motivate praise?

_____

"Many Christians estimate difficulty in the light of their own resources, and thus they attempt very little and they always fail. All giants have been weak men who did great things for God because they reckoned on His power and presence to be with them."—Hudson Taylor

_____

C. Honor God for Strengthening the Weak (vv. 3-5)

³ Therefore shall the strong people glorify thee, the city of the terrible nations shall fear thee. ⁴ For thou hast been a strength to the poor, a strength to the needy in his distress, a refuge from the storm, a shadow from the heat, when the blast of the terrible ones is as a storm against the wall. ⁵ Thou shalt bring down the noise of strangers, as the heat in a dry place; even the heat with the shadow of a cloud: the branch of the terrible ones shall be brought low.

God's wonderful deliverance of His people will not only cause them to praise Him, but it will make such an impression on the "strong people" of the world that they also will turn to the Lord and worship Him (v. 3). When other nations witness what God can do, they will "fear" Him. From a human perspective, these other nations are "terrible," but God can bring them down in a moment.

What is it that brings about such a change among these nations of the world? What do they see that causes them to "glorify" God and to "fear" Him? The answer is that they see God's care for the poor and the needy. They see that God has been "a strength to the poor, a strength to the needy in his distress" (v. 4). The people of God were afflicted, oppressed, persecuted, and tormented; but God strengthens their hearts, pours out His grace upon them, and undergirds them with His Holy Spirit. In times of distress and trouble, the Lord is their "refuge from the storm." He protects them from danger just as a place of shade protects from the heat of the sun. Even when "terrible ones" sweep down and invade the land like a storm, the Lord is a shield of protection.

Moreover, not only will the Lord be a refuge and a protection for His people, He will also "bring down" (v. 5) the enemy. The "branch" of the evil ones will be pulled down. The Hebrew word for *branch* can also mean "song," in which case the phrase would mean that "the song of the terrible ones will be humbled." That is, their songs of victory will be silenced, and their shouts of joy will be turned to despair.

The "noise of strangers" refers to the sounds of battle and songs of triumph, but this noise of the enemy will be brought down, just as the heat of the day is brought down by the "shadow of a cloud."

---

1. What three statements are made about "terrible," or "ruthless" (NASB), people (vv. 3-5)?
2. List ways God helps people who trust in Him (v. 4).

"When we sincerely seek the face of God, we gain strength. And when we do, we stand in a long line of people who have sought the same sense of strength . . . and found it."—Woodrow Kroll

---

II. PRAISE GOD FOR SALVATION (Isa. 25:6-12)

A. Praise God for His Banquet Table (v. 6)

⁶ And in this mountain shall the Lord of hosts make unto all people a feast of fat things, a feast of wines on the lees, of fat things full of marrow, of wines on the lees well refined.

Verses 1-5 spoke of God's victory over evil as characterized by His defeat of the city that oppressed God's people. And now that the victory has been gained, we learn that God prepares a great banquet feast in celebration of His awesome victories. This great feast takes place on "this mountain," which is Mount Zion, the city of God. Mount Zion is where the Temple was located—the place of God's special presence. Therefore, we can say that the victory celebration consists of a feast that takes place within God's own home.

In the Book of Revelation, this feast is called "the marriage supper of the Lamb" (19:9). The Lord is the host, and we are the guests. Even though the banquet is set in Mount Zion, it is intended for "all people" (Isa. 25:6)—for everyone who worships and serves the Lord, people "of all nations, and kindreds, and people, and tongues" (Rev. 7:9).

The Lord will prepare His banquet table with nothing but the best food and drink. "Fat things," "marrow," and "wine" are emblematic of sumptuous entertainment and of abundant provision. "Wines on the lees" refers to wine that is aged until it possesses a rich color and flavor.

"He satisfies the longing soul, and fills the hungry soul with goodness" (Ps. 107:9 NKJV).

B. Praise God for Removing the Veil (v. 7)

⁷ And he will destroy in this mountain the face of the covering cast over all people, and the vail that is spread over all nations.

The Lord celebrates His victory over evil by providing a lavish feast for all who hunger and thirst for Him. It is an occasion of great joy. But an even greater joy is realized when God removes the "covering" or the "veil" that covers the eyes of all the nations and peoples of the earth. This veil symbolizes the spiritual darkness that is spread across the world by false religions and man-made systems of belief. This veil is kept in place by the work of Satan, the great deceiver (Rev. 12:9) and the father of lies (John 8:44; 1 John 2:4). Without Christ, people in the world walk about as if blindfolded, wandering in darkness, and unable to find their way (Eph. 5:8). But God, through His Holy Spirit, reaches down to humanity and tears away the blinding veil so that the light of the gospel can be clearly seen (see Col. 1:13). In this removal of the veil, humanity is once again brought face-to-face with the Creator, just as in the Garden of Eden. Once again, men and women who have dwelt in darkness, separated from God, can look upon the face of the Lord and, in beholding Him, can be transformed into His likeness "from glory to glory" (2 Cor. 3:18).

• What is "the veil which is stretched over all nations" (NASB)?

"I simply define *glory* as the beauty of God unveiled."—Sam Storms

---

C. Praise God for Defeating Death (v. 8)

⁸ He will swallow up death in victory; and the Lord God will wipe away tears from off all faces; and the rebuke of his people shall he take away from off all the earth: for the Lord hath spoken it.

After describing God's defeat of his enemies and the great celebration banquet, Isaiah lifts his praise to a different level. For God to bring judgment and defeat upon human leaders and human kingdoms is one thing, but for God to defeat death itself is a much greater accomplishment. We read in the New Testament, "The last enemy that shall be destroyed is death" (1 Cor. 15:26). Death is the ultimate enemy, but Isaiah declares that God "will swallow up death in victory." He will abolish death and remove it forever. From the time of Adam's sin, "death reigned" (Rom. 5:14-17) over all of humanity, separating men from their families and snatching away children from the loving arms of their mothers.

But in Christ, God has determined to completely and permanently destroy death. On the cross, Jesus Christ "tasted death" for everyone (Heb. 2:9), in order that "through death he might destroy him that had the power of death, that is, the devil" (v. 14). Therefore, the apostle Paul can cite the words of Isaiah and add to them, saying, "Death is swallowed up in victory. O death, where is thy sting? O grave, where is thy victory?" (1 Cor. 15:54-55).

In addition to His victory over death and its elimination forever, God will perform two other powerful acts of grace: He will "wipe away tears" and remove "the rebuke of his people" (Isa. 25:8). We all encounter times when the tears run down our faces, and for some people those times of grief, pain, and sorrow are the daily rule rather than the exception. However, the day will come when God will give perfect comfort to those who are troubled, complete healing to the brokenhearted, and fullness of joy to those who are sorrowing. "God shall wipe away all tears from their eyes; and there shall be no more death, neither sorrow, nor crying, neither shall there be any more pain: for the former things are passed away" (Rev. 21:4).

The removal of tears is accompanied by the removal of "rebuke," which refers to reproach, contempt, and shame. In the present world, God's people suffer opposition, scorn, and persecution; but the day is coming when persecution will cease, and God's people will enjoy perfect peace. In God's presence, we will no longer be misrepresented, put to shame, ridiculed, or misunderstood. As singer/songwriter Dottie Rambo wrote, "Tears will never stain the streets of that city."

———————————

• List the promises God makes to His people here.

———————————

Hope in the Face of Death

The doctors informed Thomas Cook that his cancer was inoperable and that he had only a few months to live. When I heard the bad news, I rushed to the hospital to pray for him. As we began to pray, I was astounded at the words that burst forth from this dying man. He prayed only four words, repeating them over and over: "Praise the Lord, Hallelujah." Thomas was dying, but he had hope. He had hope for healing (whether on earth or in heaven). And he had hope that he would see his Savior face-to-face.

———————————

D. Praise God for Bringing Salvation (vv. 9-12)

⁹ And it shall be said in that day, Lo, this is our God; we have waited for him, and he will save us: this is the Lord; we have waited for him, we will be glad and rejoice in his salvation. ¹⁰ For in this mountain shall the hand of the Lord rest, and Moab shall be trodden down under him, even as straw is trodden down for the dunghill. ¹¹ And he shall spread forth his hands in the midst of them, as he that swimmeth spreadeth forth his hands to swim: and he shall bring down their pride together with the spoils of their hands. ¹² And the fortress of the high fort of thy walls shall he bring down, lay low, and bring to the ground, even to the dust.

At the return of Jesus, when God accomplishes all that Isaiah foretold, we will say, "This is our God; we have waited for him" (v. 9). It will be a day of fulfillment, a day of rejoicing, and a day of praising God for His salvation. For now, we wait patiently, knowing that He will come. In the midst of trials and temptations, we wait for Him. However, we do not wait idly. We keep ourselves busy in the work of His kingdom, shining His light in this world, and spreading the gospel to the ends of the earth. Jesus will soon return to save us from this present world, and we will rejoice in the salvation that He brings. "To those who eagerly wait for Him He will appear a second time, apart from sin, for salvation" (Heb. 9:28 NKJV). The return of Jesus will be a day of judgment for the wicked, but for God's people it will be a day of rejoicing.

On "this mountain" (Isa. 25:10)—that is, on Mount Zion—the hand of the Lord will "rest." The word *hand* signifies the power and protection of the Lord. For the Lord's power to "rest" on this mountain means it will remain there permanently as a guarantee of safety. At the same time the Lord protects His people, He will tread down His enemies, which are symbolized by the nation of Moab. Moab is chosen here to represent all evil forces because of its continuing opposition to Israel and to God's plans throughout history. The enemies of God will be subdued like the straw that is trodden underfoot by a cow or donkey in its stall. Furthermore, God will stretch out His hands like a swimmer in the water; and as easily as the swimmer's hands part the waters and push them aside, so God will displace all of His enemies, pushing them aside and bringing down their pride (v. 11). The Moabites would have been proud of the "spoils" they had taken from the Israelites and from other peoples in time of war, but God will humble the pride of Moab, and all of their possessions will be destroyed in God's judgment.

Finally, God will throw down their fortresses and their walls of protection (v. 12). He will raze the cities of Moab to the ground. All of their fortifications will be powerless against the hand of God. He will crush them into the dust. Human pride continues to lift itself up against God, but it will always be brought down.

---

1. What does it mean to "wait" for God, and what is the benefit (v. 9)?
2. Contrast God's hands with human hands (v. 11).

"Salvation is from our side a choice, from the divine side it is a seizing upon, an apprehending, a conquest by the Most High God. Our 'accepting' and 'willing' are reactions rather than actions. The right of determination must always remain with God."—A. W. Tozer

---

III. TRUST IN GOD'S STRENGTH (Isa. 26:1-4)

A. God's Strength Is an Open Door (vv. 1-2)

¹ In that day shall this song be sung in the land of Judah; We have a strong city; salvation will God appoint for walls and bulwarks. ² Open ye the gates, that the righteous nation which keepeth the truth may enter in.

With this new chapter we see the beginning of a new song—another song of praise that will be sung in the day of victory, when God has vanquished all of His enemies. It celebrates the establishment of the city of God—a "strong city" in which all of God's people dwell. The strength of the city, however, is not in the strength of its walls, nor in the height of its towers, nor in the skill of its armies. The city of God is protected by God's promise of "salvation." In a similar prophecy, Zechariah would later promise that God would be "a wall of fire" around God's people (2:5).

The gates of this city will protect the inhabitants against all evil, but the same gates will open wide to welcome all of the "righteous" who keep the "truth" (Isa. 26:2). The city of God, therefore, is built not just for the Jewish people, but for the righteous ones from every nation. God's holy city welcomes everyone who loves the truth.

1. What is the "strong city" (v. 1)?
2. Who dwells in that city (v. 2)?

"Since no man is excluded from calling upon God, the gate of salvation is open to all. There is nothing else to hinder us from entering, but our own unbelief."—John Calvin

B. God's Strength Gives Perfect Peace (vv. 3-4)

³ Thou wilt keep him in perfect peace, whose mind is stayed on thee: because he trusteth in thee. ⁴ Trust ye in the Lord for ever: for in the Lord Jehovah is everlasting strength.

Isaiah knows that as we await the coming of the Lord and the fulfillment of all these promises, we will be faced with circumstances and situations that threaten our peace. The Lord is concerned not only to give us peace in the future, but He also desires that we experience His peace in this present life. Jesus promised, "Peace I leave with you, my peace I give unto you: not as the world giveth, give I unto you. Let not your heart be troubled, neither let it be afraid" (John 14:27).

Isaiah teaches us that this "perfect peace" comes to us through a twofold process (26:3). First, peace comes to the person "whose mind is stayed on" God. This means that we lean on God as our strength and we rely on Him as our guide. When we arise every morning we place our day into the hands of God, and throughout the day we walk with Him. Second, peace comes to the person who is trusting God. Solomon put it this way: "Trust in the Lord with all thine heart; and lean not unto thine own understanding. In all thy ways acknowledge him, and he shall direct thy paths" (Prov. 3:5-6).

In order to retain the perfect peace of God, our minds must be set upon God, and our trust must be firmly in Him. We have good reason to trust in the Lord, because He is our "everlasting strength" (Isa. 26:4).

1. How can we live in "perfect peace" (v. 3)?
2. How long can we trust in God, and why (v. 4)?

"Only he who can say, 'The Lord is the strength of my life' can say, 'Of whom shall I be afraid?'"—Alexander MacLaren

CONCLUSION

As Pentecostal believers, we live differently from worldly people. Furthermore, we live differently from many other Christians. Not only have we been redeemed by the blood of Christ and forgiven of our sins, but we also have encountered the fire of Pentecost. In the Pentecostal experience, we gain a new perspective on life—a deeper hope. Through the Holy Spirit, we are made to realize that the beginning and the end of all things is God himself, and nothing else really matters. We are like the psalmist who says to God, "Whom have I in heaven but You? And there is none upon earth that I desire besides You" (73:25 NKJV). Our goal is to know God, love God, walk with God, and someday see God face-to-face.

GOLDEN TEXT CHALLENGE

"TRUST YE IN THE LORD FOR EVER: FOR IN THE LORD JEHOVAH IS EVERLASTING STRENGTH" (Isa. 26:4).

Isaiah was placed by the Lord in a strategic position to observe the rise and fall of both leaders and nations. As a trusted companion of kings and statesmen, his prophetic messages of both judgment and promised blessings carried considerable weight with his contemporaries. The pristine quality of his prophecies and promises not only stood the test of authenticity then, but continue to stand the test of time imposed upon them by the intervening centuries between Isaiah's time and our own crucial moment in human history.

As history has confirmed the accuracy of his predictions of judgment, so has it validated his promises of encouragement and hope held out to the faithful. In a transient world where families face one impending crisis after another, the words *forever* and *everlasting* have a uniquely comforting ring. For the single-parent family, the family facing relocation, the family facing the cold uncertainty of illness and death, or the family confronting a myriad of other problems, the timeless message of the prophet of God reminds them that they are not alone in their struggle. The God who rolled back the Red Sea, showered manna upon His hungry people, scattered their enemies before them, and miraculously clothed His wandering nation in the wilderness is offering His everlasting strength as the solution to our present-day problems and needs.

Daily Devotions:

M. Remember God's Goodness
Exodus 13:3-10
T. Recall God's Strength to Deliver
Deuteronomy 7:17-24
W. Hope in God's Mercy
Lamentations 3:21-26
T. Magnify the Lord
Luke 1:46-55
F. Salvation Through Jesus Christ
1 Thessalonians 5:8-11
S. Heirs of Salvation
Hebrews 1:14 through 2:4

The Lord's "High" Ways

Isaiah 35:1-10; 43:15-21; 49:7-17; 62:10-12

Unit Theme:
Hope in the Book of Isaiah

Central Truth:
God has prepared and revealed the way of righteousness.

Focus:
Discover and walk in God's "high" ways.

Context:
Isaiah writes about God's plans for His people.

Golden Text:
"I [the Lord] will do a new thing; now it shall spring forth; shall ye not know it? I will even make a way in the wilderness, and rivers in the desert" (Isa. 43:19).

Study Outline:
 I. Way of Holiness
    (Isa. 35:1-10)
 II. Path to Victory
    (Isa. 43:15-21)
III. Road to Restoration
    (Isa. 49:7-17; 62:10-12)

INTRODUCTION

In one of Frank Sinatra's most famous songs, he declares, "I did it my way." We can live life our way, or we can turn over our lives to God and live His way. Jesus proclaimed Himself as "the way, the truth, and the life" (John 14:6), but many people ignore the way of Jesus and stubbornly follow their own way. The writer of Proverbs describes those people when he says, "The way of a fool is right in his own eyes" (12:15).

When we affirm that Jesus is "the way," we often draw a sharp contrast between ourselves and people who are outside the Church. We preach (and rightly so) that Jesus is the only way of salvation. Therefore, Islam is not the way; Buddhism is not the way; Hinduism is not the way; and secularism is not the way. However, we need to dig deep and examine ourselves closely. The Church can get off track and go in directions where the Lord is not leading. It is easy for us, even as God's people, to build our own roads and ignore the highway God has laid out before us. For this reason, God said to Abraham, "I am the Almighty God; walk before me, and be thou perfect" (Gen. 17:1).

As we study these prophecies of Isaiah, we will discover and examine God's "high" ways. Along the way, let us examine our own hearts. In order to facilitate this process, perhaps we should ask ourselves the following questions: (1) Am I daily pursuing the ways of God? (2) Are there areas of my life that tend to stray away from God's ways? (3) Is my church remaining faithful to the way of the Lord? (4) How do we, as individuals or as a church body, discern that we are getting off track? Finally, let us pray along with David, "Search me, O God, and know my heart; try me and know my thoughts: and see if there be any wicked way in me, and lead me in the way everlasting" (Ps. 139:23-24).

I. WAY OF HOLINESS (Isa. 35:1-10)
A. A Place for Rejoicing (vv. 1-2)
¹ **The wilderness and the solitary place shall be glad for them; and the desert shall rejoice, and blossom as the rose.** ² **It shall blossom abundantly, and rejoice even with joy and singing: the glory of Lebanon shall be given unto it, the excellency of Carmel and Sharon, they shall see the glory of the Lord, and the excellency of our God.**

Isaiah often alternates between the themes of judgment and promise, and chapters 34 and 35 follow this pattern. In chapter 34, the judgment of God falls on all of His enemies, especially on those who have oppressed Israel. God judges evil and establishes the fact that He rules over the earth and over the governments of humanity. The judgment of chapter 34 leads us into the grace of chapter 35, where God's mighty rule over the earth reestablishes the nation of Israel to a place of prominence and blessing.

Earlier in his prophecy, Isaiah warned Israel that they would be taken into Babylonian captivity (see 5:13; 13; 14; 22:17; 39:5-7). Here in chapter 35, we learn that God will not allow His people to remain in that captivity forever. He will bring them home again, and Israel will be restored to her glory. God will not leave His people in bondage, drought, and oppression, but He will bring deliverance and restoration. Isaiah's vision of restoration begins with creation itself, which undergoes a radical transformation. The "wilderness," the "solitary place," and the "desert" will "rejoice" because God transforms them into beautiful gardens that reflect the "glory of the Lord" (vv. 1-2). The dry desert land will be made to resemble the fruitful areas of Lebanon, Carmel, and Sharon. Where there was drought, there is now rain. Where there was death, there is now life. These changes are the work of God and His Spirit, and they display the glory and majesty of God.

_____

• When God restores all things, how will His glory be displayed?

_____

"The permanence of God's character guarantees the fulfillment of His promises."—A. W. Pink

_____

B. Strengthening Each Other (vv. 3-4)
³ **Strengthen ye the weak hands, and confirm the feeble knees.** ⁴ **Say to them that are of a fearful heart, Be strong, fear not: behold, your God will come with vengeance, even God with a recompence; he will come and save you.**

The restoration continues, but its focus shifts. The subject is no longer the deprived land, but it is the weakened people. Without rain, the land is unable to fulfill its potential. Similarly, without the presence of the Spirit of Almighty God, humanity is unable to function and live according to its God-given potential. Verse 3 focuses on the physical dimensions of human frailty, speaking to those who have "weak hands" and "feeble knees." However, verse 4 shows us that the most fundamental human disability is not physical but spiritual—it is "a fearful heart," a feeling of hopelessness and despair.

The hearer of Isaiah's prophecy is encouraged to "strengthen" those who are weak and to speak a word of encouragement to those who have lost hope. Circumstances may look bleak, and prospects may be few, but "behold, your God will come." It may seem that God has been absent or far away, but He is coming. He will come to punish all enemies and to bring *recompence* to His people. The word *recompence* is translated in Psalm 103:2 as "benefits." The psalmist writes, "Bless the Lord, O my soul, and forget not all his benefits." One of the benefits that God will bring with His coming is His salvation: "he will come and save you."

• What is the status of the people mentioned here, and what does God promise them?

"Even when God deems it necessary to discipline us for persistent disobedience, He always does so out of love to restore us to the way of obedience."—Jerry Bridges

---

C. Miracles Along the Way (vv. 5-7)

⁵ Then the eyes of the blind shall be opened, and the ears of the deaf shall be unstopped. ⁶ Then shall the lame man leap as an hart, and the tongue of the dumb sing: for in the wilderness shall waters break out, and streams in the desert. ⁷ And the parched ground shall become a pool, and the thirsty land springs of water: in the habitation of dragons, where each lay, shall be grass with reeds and rushes.

When God comes, bringing His salvation, wonderful things begin to happen. Blind eyes and deaf ears will be opened (v. 5). The lame will walk and the mute will sing (v. 6). The power of illness and death is broken. Those who have been unable to hear God's Word (see 6:9-10) can now receive it. Those who have been unable to praise God can now shout with a loud voice. Those who have been unable to see the glory of God can now experience it. Jesus associated these verses with His own ministry. When asked by the disciples of John the Baptist, "Are You the Messiah?", Jesus replied, "Go your way, and tell John what things ye have seen and heard; how that the blind see, the lame walk, the lepers are cleansed, the deaf hear, the dead are raised, to the poor the gospel is preached" (Luke 7:22).

Verses 6 and 7 return to creation imagery and describe the newness of life that comes to the earth when God reigns in power. Refreshing "waters" will spring forth in the thirsty wilderness, and the "parched ground" will "become a pool" of water. Grass, reeds, and rushes will grow in the desert lands, which was the habitation of "jackals" (NJKV). Of special interest is the term "parched ground." The Hebrew term *sharav* may signify here the phenomenon that we call a mirage. The refraction of the rays of the sun on the glowing sands of the desert can give the appearance of a sea or lake of water. A mirage sometimes tempts thirsty travelers to go out of their way, but then deceives them by either moving or vanishing when they come nearer. Therefore, the message here is that God will turn the imaginary into reality. In our times of need, we will no longer be deceived by false illusions and unreal hopes. Without God, we continue to pursue hopes and promises that are as delusive as the mirage. The promises of God, however, do not recede or vanish.

• What will become of physical handicaps?

"God never made a promise that was too good to be true."—D. L. Moody

---

D. A Highway Built by God (v. 8)
⁸ And an highway shall be there, and a way, and it shall be called The way of holiness; the unclean shall not pass over it; but it shall be for those: the wayfaring men, though fools, shall not err therein.
Not only will the wilderness become fruitful as a garden, it will also contain a "highway" on which God's people will travel when they return to Israel from the Babylonian Captivity. This does not mean there will be a literal highway through the desert, but that God will make a way for His people to return home. The theme of the entire passage is the homecoming of Israel. God will ensure that His people are brought out of bondage and are returned to a place of freedom.
Most of the roads in the ancient world were quite difficult to travel, and those rulers who attempted to build empires needed a way to transport their armies and war machines over long distances. Therefore, they would have engineers build roads. They would remove obstructions, fill the valleys, and lower the hills, much as we do today. Isaiah's picture of the highway symbolizes God's intention to facilitate Israel's homecoming. The highway also stands for the gospel of Jesus Christ, which is the way out of bondage into freedom, the way out of darkness into light, and the way out of misery into joy. Therefore, the highway represents God's ability to save His people, whether they be in the captivity of Babylon, the clutches of sin, or the bondage of depression or fear. God will make a way out.
God's way, however, is a "way of holiness," and the "unclean" are not able to walk on it. God is holy, and He makes His people holy. By God's grace, He cleanses us from our sins, purifies our hearts, and places us on His highway to walk in His presence. The highway is clearly marked, and even a fool shall not "err therein."

• How is "the way of holiness" described?

"God has a course mapped out for your life, and all the inadequacies in the world will not change His mind. He will be with you every step of the way. And though it may take time, He has a celebration planned for when you cross over the Red Seas of your life."—Charles Stanley

---

E. A Harmless, Happy Highway (vv. 9-10)

⁹ No lion shall be there, nor any ravenous beast shall go up thereon, it shall not be found there; but the redeemed shall walk there. ¹⁰ And the ransomed of the Lord shall return, and come to Zion with songs and everlasting joy upon their heads: they shall obtain joy and gladness, and sorrow and sighing shall flee away.

As long as we keep our eyes on the Lord and follow Him closely, all will be well. The highway is peaceful, secure, and safe. Travelers on this highway are undisturbed by the furious beasts of destruction. Keeping on the highway elevates us from many dangers. It is built up above the surrounding terrain in order to protect its travelers from the snares of the world, the pits of destruction, and the swamps of sin that lie all around. However, if we stray from the highway, we will fall into danger.

This highway is built for only one group of people—"the redeemed" (v. 9). It is not for the sinner or the hypocrite. It is not for those who love the world, the flesh, and the devil. The redeemed are those who have been brought out of slavery, those who have been purchased by the "precious blood of Christ, as of a lamb without blemish and without spot" (1 Peter 1:19).

This is a joyous highway upon which the "ransomed of the Lord shall return" to Zion, which is Jerusalem (Isa. 35:10). The word *ransom* means essentially the same as "redeemed" in verse 9. It means that a price has been paid to reclaim one's property. The "ransomed of the Lord" are able to walk on this highway because, though they had been blind, they now can see; though they had been lame, they now can walk; though they had foolishly walked according to the flesh, they now "walk in the Spirit" (Gal. 5:16).

Words can hardly express the great joy that accompanies salvation. Captive Israel returns to Zion with "songs and everlasting joy." But there is more—returning home produces "joy and gladness." Jesus tells us there is "joy . . . in heaven" when one sinner repents (Luke 15:7); and in His parable of the prodigal son, we learn that homecoming includes great celebration (vv. 22-24). But there is still more—when God brings salvation, "sorrow and sighing shall flee away" (Isa. 35:10). Misery cannot continue to exist in the presence of God.

• What will replace "sorrow and sighing" in God's eternal kingdom, and how will it be expressed?

Safe or Perilous?

When building a highway, engineers use heavy equipment to construct a road bed that is level, straight, and elevated above the surrounding terrain. Low places must be filled in with rock and dirt. High spots must be reduced and leveled. All of this effort is expended in order to make travel easier, quicker, and safer. Similarly, God has designed and constructed a "highway" for His people. As long as we remain on the highway, our journey is spiritually safe; but if we should stray onto a path of our own making, the journey will quickly become perilous and unsafe.

II. PATH TO VICTORY (Isa. 43:15-21)

A. A Display of Divine Power (vv. 15-17)

15 I am the Lord, your Holy One, the creator of Israel, your King. 16 Thus saith the Lord, which maketh a way in the sea, and a path in the mighty waters; 17 Which bringeth forth the chariot and horse, the army and the power; they shall lie down together, they shall not rise: they are extinct, they are quenched as tow.

The Lord can not only make a highway in the wilderness, He can also make a "way in the sea, and a path in the mighty waters" (v. 16). As "creator" (v. 15), the Lord has power over both land and sea. He created the heavens and the earth, and He also created Israel. This "way into the sea" is a reference to God's miraculous opening of the Red Sea, when He led His people out of Egyptian bondage. This interpretation is confirmed by the following verse, which makes reference to chariots, horses, and "the army" (v. 17). The entire Egyptian army was "extinguished" in the Red Sea, "snuffed out like a wick" (NIV). What God has done before, He can now do again, destroying the enemies of His people.

---

1. List the titles of God in verse 15. How are they interrelated?
2. What does God's ability to create "a path in the mighty waters" (v. 16) reveal about His ability to guide your life?

"God's mighty power comes when God's people learn to walk with God."—Jack Hyles

---

B. A New Thing (vv. 18-19)

18 Remember ye not the former things, neither consider the things of old. 19 Behold, I will do a new thing; now it shall spring forth; shall ye not know it? I will even make a way in the wilderness, and rivers in the desert.

Isaiah's mention of the Red Sea, which is described here as "the former things," is a testimony of what God has done in the past. However, God declares that He will do a "new thing." The people of God must never live in the past, because God is always present to do a new thing. He is the "I AM," not the "I was." The miracles of the past testify to God's character and nature, and the remembrance of God's work in the past should create an anticipation for God's miraculous intervention in the present and in the future. God is not limited to what He has done in the past; He will do even greater works in the future. The Israelites who were in Babylonian captivity should know that the same God who made a pathway through the Red Sea will now make a highway through the wilderness.

• What does Isaiah say to "forget" (v. 18 NIV), and why?

"Never be afraid to trust an unknown future to a known God."—Corrie ten Boom

---

C. Godly Care (vv. 20-21)

²⁰ The beast of the field shall honour me, the dragons and the owls: because I give waters in the wilderness, and rivers in the desert, to give drink to my people, my chosen. ²¹ This people have I formed for myself; they shall shew forth my praise.

As Israel travels on the highway through the wilderness in their return to Zion, the "beast of the field" will give way, and "waters" will spring up "to give drink" to God's chosen people. The word *dragons* is properly translated as "jackals" (v. 20 NKJV). When passing through a desert region, one would normally be on the lookout for snakes and other wild animals and would not expect to find water there. But, where God leads He also provides. His protection and care are available, even in the places where we least expect it.

The beasts of the field honor God, and the desert places rejoice in His presence. How much more should God's people, whom the Lord has "formed" for Himself, display God's glory! Earlier, God described Himself as the "creator" of Israel, and now He adds that He formed them (v. 21). This forming of Israel refers to God's work through history, including the Babylonian Captivity, to shape Israel into the holy people of God. This molding process has the ultimate goal of showing forth God's praise. God's people were created to praise, glorify, and magnify Him (see also 1 Peter 2:9).

• What does God call His people, and what does He expect from them?

O worship the King, all glorious above,
And gratefully sing His wonderful love.
—Robert Grant

III. ROAD TO RESTORATION (Isa. 49:7-17; 62:10-12)

A. The Lord Comforts His People (49:7-17)

(Isaiah 49:7-12 is not included in the printed text.)

¹³ Sing, O heavens; and be joyful, O earth; and break forth into singing, O mountains: for the Lord hath comforted his people, and will have mercy upon his afflicted. ¹⁴ But Zion said, The Lord hath forsaken me, and my Lord hath forgotten me. ¹⁵ Can a woman forget her sucking child, that she should not have compassion on the son of her womb? yea, they may forget, yet will I not forget thee. ¹⁶ Behold, I have graven thee upon the palms of my hands; thy walls are continually before me. ¹⁷ Thy children shall make haste; thy destroyers and they that made thee waste shall go forth of thee.

For a third time Isaiah mentions the highway of the Lord. Here in chapter 49, the message is addressed once again to a despondent Israel. They are "despised" and "abhorred," but they are the "chosen" people of God (see v. 7). God has made a "covenant" with Israel, and He promises to restore them to their land (v. 8). All of those who are bound ("prisoners") and in "darkness" will be brought out and placed on the highway God has prepared (vv. 9-11).

In verse 13, this deliverance is an occasion for great joy. The heavens, the earth, and the mountains are called on to rejoice, because "the Lord hath comforted his people." Their time of suffering has ended, and their homecoming is near. During their time in Babylon, the Israelites felt as if the Lord had "forsaken" and "forgotten" them (v. 14). But here, the Lord speaks a word of assurance. He declares to them that even though a woman may forget her own child, God will never forget His people (v. 15). In fact, the Lord makes an astonishing statement: "Behold, I have graven thee upon the palms of my hands" (v. 16). It is impossible for God to forget His people, because He has carved their names into His flesh. The "walls [of Zion] are continually before" the Lord.

Once Israel returns from bondage, progress will be quick. The "children"—the younger generation—will "make haste" to rebuild Jerusalem (v. 17). Those who had opposed Israel, the "destroyers," will be forced to leave. They will "go forth" out of Israel, never to return.

---

1. What will be revealed to "kings" and "princes" (v. 7)?
2. What is the "acceptable time" (v. 8)?
3. What will God do for His people (vv. 9-13)?
4. How does God describe His relationship with His people (v. 15)?
5. Why is it impossible for God to forget His people (v. 16)?

B. The Lord Restores His People (62:10-12)

10 Go through, go through the gates; prepare ye the way of the people; cast up, cast up the highway; gather out the stones; lift up a standard for the people. 11 Behold, the Lord hath proclaimed unto the end of the world, Say ye to the daughter of Zion, Behold, thy salvation cometh; behold, his reward is with him, and his work before him. 12 And they shall call them, The holy people, The redeemed of the Lord: and thou shalt be called, Sought out, A city not forsaken.

As we draw near to the end of the prophecy of Isaiah, the perspective changes. In the earlier parts of our lesson, the highway represented the future work of the Lord in preparing deliverance for His people. Here, however, Isaiah pictures Jerusalem as already restored. The Israelites are encouraged to go out of the city, to "go through the gates," into the world carrying the gospel (v. 10). God's people should proclaim "unto the end of the world" that "salvation" has come (v. 11).

Until now, the work of restoration has been entirely God's work; but now, the people are called upon to participate in the restoration process. The people of God, inspired by God's promises, are to "build up the highway" (v. 10 NIV). The future depends not only on God's faithfulness but also on the faithfulness of the people of God as they are active in doing His will in the world. God does not intend His people to sit by passively, awaiting His return. We must be about the Father's business.

This passage concludes with the renaming of Jerusalem in the form of four titles (v. 12). These titles point to a restoration of relationship to God. "Holy" means a people totally committed to the Lord. "Redeemed" refers to those who are brought out of bondage by the power of God and through the blood of Jesus. "Sought out" signifies someone who is looked after, cared for, and valued. "Not forsaken" indicates that those who were formerly shamed, rejected, and abandoned are now restored to full relationship with the Lord.

---

1. What does God promise His people (v. 11)?
2. What does it mean to be "the redeemed of the Lord" (v. 12)?

"God means every Christian to be effective, to make a difference in the actual records and results of Christian work. God put each of us here to be a power. There is not one of us but is an essential wheel of the machinery and can accomplish all that God calls us to."—A. B. Simpson

---

CONCLUSION

When Israel went into captivity, they felt as if God had cast them off forever. Their hopes for the future were dashed into pieces, and the promises of God seemed to be an illusion. In the midst of despair, one of the captives wrote: "By the rivers of Babylon, there we sat down, yea, we wept, when we remembered Zion. We hanged our harps upon the willows in the midst thereof. For there they that carried us away captive required of us a song; and they that wasted us required of us mirth, saying, Sing us one of the songs of Zion. How shall we sing the Lord's song in a strange land?" (Ps. 137:1-4). Out of the midst of disaster, however, God brought deliverance. He built a "highway" through the wilderness and brought His people home to Jerusalem. If God made a way for His people in that day, He will also make a way for His people now.

In concluding this lesson, we should consider several questions:
- Are we walking on the Lord's highway, or have we strayed onto some other path?
- If the highway of the Lord is a pathway of joy, peace, hope, and redemption, does my life demonstrate these qualities?
- Is our church concerned more about fitting into the culture around us than about pleasing God?
- Do our young people perceive the highway of the Lord in a positive way, or do they think of serving God as a burden?
- How can we adjust our lifestyles and attitudes so the way of the Lord is desirable and sought after by our children and by unbelievers around us?

GOLDEN TEXT CHALLENGE

"I [THE LORD] WILL DO A NEW THING; NOW IT SHALL SPRING FORTH; SHALL YE NOT KNOW IT? I WILL EVEN MAKE A WAY IN THE WILDERNESS, AND RIVERS IN THE DESERT" (Isa. 43:19).

God says He will do something "unprecedented in its wonderful character. 'Now it shall spring forth'—as a germinating herb: a beautiful image of the silent but certain gradual growth of events in God's providence (Mark 4:26-28). Here, however, the growth shall be unprecedented in its rapidity. The new thing shall spring forth as it were in a day.

"Just as Israel in the wilderness, between the Red Sea and Canaan, was guided and supplied with water by Yahweh . . . the 'new' deliverance shall be attended with manifestations of God's power and love eclipsing the old (cf. Isa. 41:17-19).

"'I will open a way not merely in the Red Sea, but in the wilderness of the whole world; and not merely one river shall gush out of the rock, but many, which shall refresh, not the bodies as formerly, but the souls of the thirsty, so that the prophecy shall be fulfilled' (Jerome)."—*Jamieson, Fausset, and Brown*

Daily Devotions:

M. God's Higher Way
   2 Samuel 22:31-37
T. Teach Me Your Ways
   Psalm 27:11-14
W. A Hard Way
   Proverbs 14:8-14
T. The Right Way
   Isaiah 26:4-9
F. Christ Is the Way
   John 14:1-6
S. Walk the Righteous Way
   Romans 14:13-21

From Darkness to Light

Isaiah 59:1 through 60:22

Unit Theme:
Hope in the Book of Isaiah

Central Truth:
The light of God's glory dispels spiritual darkness.

Focus:
Become aware of spiritual darkness and reflect the light of God's glory.

Context:
In the eighth century BC, Isaiah prophesies about the light of God.

Golden Text:
"Arise, shine; for thy light is come, and the glory of the Lord is risen upon thee" (Isa. 60:1).

Study Outline:
  I. Sin Results in Spiritual Darkness
     (Isa. 59:1-2, 8-13)
 II. The Light Dispels Darkness
     (Isa. 59:19—60:3)
III. Live in the Everlasting Light
     (Isa. 60:15-22)

INTRODUCTION

Approximately 11.4 million Americans are blind or visually impaired, and an estimated 47,000 Americans go blind each year. Stated another way, one person every eleven minutes is forced to live in darkness. The blind are robbed of the ability to look on the faces of their loved ones and the beauties of creation. Because they walk in darkness, they often require assistance in traveling from one place to another. They cannot enjoy the entertainment of watching a baseball game or a television show. Blind children cannot experience the joy of running through the forest or the excitement of a snowball fight with their friends. The darkness takes away many of the pleasures and benefits of life.

It is much worse for those who walk in spiritual darkness—they are unable to enjoy a relationship with God. They cannot experience the deep peace that comes from walking in His light. As Christians, we have been brought "out of darkness" into God's light (1 Peter 2:9); therefore, we should "walk as children of light" (Eph. 5:8). Furthermore, we must "not participate in the unfruitful deeds of darkness" (v. 11 NASB). Sometimes, however, we drift away from the Lord, and in so doing, we find ourselves far away from the light. This drifting away does not happen quickly, but gradually and subtly. Without being aware of our backsliding, our small acts of disobedience lead to larger and deeper patterns of disregarding God's will, until eventually we are blind like the Laodicean church. Jesus counseled that church, "Anoint your eyes with eye salve, that you may see. . . . Be zealous and repent" (Rev. 3:18-19 NKJV). The Laodicean congregation was walking in spiritual darkness and needed a revival.

Hundreds of years before the Lord sent the corrective word to his backslidden church in Laodicea, He spoke a similar word to His people, Israel. Isaiah 59 is a stern rebuke to those who had forgotten the basic demands of living together in covenant with the Lord. Spiritual darkness covered the land, and God's truth was ignored. Thankfully, the grace, mercy, and love of God were able to overcome Israel's darkness. Because of God's faithfulness, He poured out His Spirit upon His people and restored them to a place in the light. God can do the same today. He can send a mighty revival across the world, dispelling all darkness and restoring His people to brightness so that unbelievers will see God's glory in us.

I. SIN RESULTS IN SPIRITUAL DARKNESS (Isa. 59:1-2, 8-13)

A. God's Power Not Lacking (v. 1)

¹ Behold, the Lord's hand is not shortened, that it cannot save; neither his ear heavy, that it cannot hear.

The Israelites had fasted and prayed, but God had not answered their prayers. Is God's failure to answer a sign that He has lost His power or that He has not heard their prayers? No. He is still able to stretch forth His hand to perform mighty deeds. His power is as great as ever, and it has not been reduced at all. Furthermore, it is not because of deafness that God has been silent. His ear is not "heavy, that it cannot hear." His ears have heard their prayers, and their cries have reached up to Him. God's attention continues to be turned toward His people, and His ears are always open to their cries.

• How does this scripture describe God?

"Your sigh is able to move the heart of Jehovah; your whisper can incline His ear unto you; your prayer can stay His hands; your faith can move His arm."—Charles Spurgeon

---

B. Sin Separates Us From God (v. 2)

² But your iniquities have separated between you and your God, and your sins have hid his face from you, that he will not hear.

If it is not from a lack of power or from a lack of concern that God has not answered their prayers, then what is the reason for His inactivity on their behalf? Is God at fault in some way? No, the fault is entirely Israel's. Isaiah says to them, "Your iniquities have separated between you and your God." Iniquity is an activity that is crooked and wrong. Many of Israel's iniquities had already been specified in chapter 58. Here in chapter 59, the list will be expanded, and their depths of sin will be described in greater detail.

Israel's sinful acts have created a separation—a division—like a curtain or a wall. Their iniquities were like a partition between them and God, so that no contact was possible. Apparently, they believed that the religious rituals of fasting and prayer would gain the attention of God, even if their lives did not demonstrate the kind of faithful lifestyle God demanded of them. However, Isaiah declares that no ritual can take the place of righteousness. All of their fasting and praying will result in nothing if they do not live in obedience to God's will. The only thing that will remove the wall of separation is repentance.

Not only have their sins separated them from God, but those sins have also caused God himself to turn away from them. Isaiah says, "Your sins have hid his face from you, that he will not hear." Indulgence in sin causes God to turn away His face and to withhold mercy and compassion. In the Bible, the "face of God" represents His presence, His nearness, and His approval. Therefore, to "turn away His face" means He is no longer present with His people and He disapproves of their behavior.

In verses 3-7, Isaiah lays out a scathing rebuke, naming several of Israel's most prominent sins. In order to show the depth of their depravity, he mentions various parts of the body that serve as agents through which people can commit sin: the hands, the fingers, the lips, the tongue, the feet, and the mind. First, he says, "Your hands are defiled with blood" (v. 3)—an image which can refer to murder, but which, in a broader sense, signifies any action that brings harm to another member of the community. It can refer to cruelty, extortion, violence, and other actions whereby those in power take advantage of those who are weak. The broadness of the accusation is made clear by the second phrase, "and your fingers with iniquity." As stated above, iniquity would include any activity that is crooked and wrong.

Israel's sins, however, include more than physical actions. Their "lips have spoken lies" and their tongues have "muttered perverseness" (v. 3). At least two of the Ten Commandments have obvious connections to the misuse of speech. Isaiah's condemnation of Israel's speech continues with the observation that silence can also be a sin: "None calleth for justice, nor any pleadeth for truth" (v. 4). Apparently, lies and abuse are accepted as the norm, and no one calls the wicked to account.

Isaiah accuses Israel of producing more and more evil. "They hatch cockatrice' eggs, and weave the spider's web" (v. 5) The cockatrice is a poisonous snake, and Israel is nourishing this poison in their midst. They also weave webs of deceit and wrap themselves in the webs like garments. A spider's web, however, is unfit as a garment, and the Israelites are clothed in "works of iniquity" and acts of "violence" (v. 6).

This section concludes with a mention of two other parts of the human body: the feet and the mind. Isaiah says, "Their feet run to evil" and "their thoughts are thoughts of iniquity" (v. 7). Israel is filled with wickedness from head to toe. Every part of the body is employed in doing evil. Instead of walking the paths of righteousness, and hurrying to execute God's mercy and justice, they were running to do evil. The words *run* and *haste* are significant, because they indicate Israel's enthusiastic desire to sin.

• What are "iniquities," and why do they separate a person from God?

From Darkness to Light

"The core and essence of the gospel is its tremendous and glorious revelation of how deadly is God's hatred of sin, so that He cannot stand having it in the same universe as Himself, and will go any length, and will pay any price, and will make any sacrifice, to master and abolish it."—A. J. Gossip

---

C. Sin Leads to Spiritual Blindness (vv. 8-11)

⁸ The way of peace they know not; and there is no judgment in their goings: they have made them crooked paths: whosoever goeth therein shall not know peace. ⁹ Therefore is judgment far from us, neither doth justice overtake us: we wait for light, but behold obscurity; for brightness, but we walk in darkness. ¹⁰ We grope for the wall like the blind, and we grope as if we had no eyes: we stumble at noon day as in the night; we are in desolate places as dead men. ¹¹ We roar all like bears, and mourn sore like doves: we look for judgment, but there is none; for salvation, but it is far off from us.

Isaiah portrays Israel as hopelessly evil and destructive. Their sin produces a situation in which the basic benefits of the faith community are absent: (1) They have no peace. (2) They have no light. (3) They have no salvation.

First, because they have walked on "crooked paths" and, because there is no justice in their ways, they do "not know peace" (v. 8). In the Old Testament, *peace* (*shalom*) is more than just the absence of war; it is total well-being . . . complete wholeness. This kind of peace is impossible to achieve when we allow sin, lies, and abuse of neighbor to continue unabated.

Second, a lack of equity and ongoing injustice produces darkness. There were some who said, "We hope for light" and "for brightness, but we walk in gloom" (v. 9 NASB). That is, even when someone would search for truth, it would be unavailable. Those who were searching for the right way could not find it, because there was nothing but darkness. Isaiah paints a poignant picture of spiritual darkness when he writes, "We grope for the wall like the blind . . . as if we had no eyes: we stumble . . ." (v. 10).

Third, Israel's sin makes them miserable, because they do not have the assurance of salvation. Here, Isaiah turns to unhappy animals as examples: "All of us growl like bears, and moan sadly like doves" (v. 11 NASB). Justice is nowhere to be found, and salvation is "far off"; therefore, they wail, weep, mourn, and grieve. In short, they are in deep misery that is brought about because of their sins.

---

1. Who will "not know the way of peace" (v. 8 NASB), and why not?
2. Today, who fits the sad description in verses 9-11?

Reflecting Christ's Light

The earth does not produce its own light. The bright light of day is emitted by the sun, and whatever faint light we may enjoy during the night is reflected by the moon. Without the sun and the moon, the earth would lie in total darkness. Similarly, everyone who is without Christ is living in darkness (Eph. 5:8). Even we Christians have no light within ourselves. As the moon reflects the light of the sun, we reflect the light of Jesus Christ. Let us walk in the light and reflect that light to the world.

D. Sin Multiplies Guilt (vv. 12-13)

¹² For our transgressions are multiplied before thee, and our sins testify against us: for our transgressions are with us; and as for our iniquities, we know them; ¹³ In transgressing and lying against the Lord, and departing away from our God, speaking oppression and revolt, conceiving and uttering from the heart words of falsehood.

For the first time in this chapter, the people make what appears to be a confession of their sins, speaking directly to God. The word *transgressions* refers to rebellions against God, and these rebellions are on the increase. Nothing is holding back the flood of sin. Their sins are so evident that they form a witness against the people. Their sin stares them in the face, ever with them as a constant companion. Apparently, the people are beginning to feel a sense of guilt, shame, and condemnation.

They "know" their sins (v. 12); that is, they are fully aware of their rebellion against God. They name specific sins: transgression, lying against the Lord, departing from God, speaking oppression and revolt, conceiving and speaking lies (v. 13). These are heinous sins against God and against their neighbors. It is significant that these sins began in the "heart." As Jesus said, "Out of the abundance of the heart the mouth speaketh" (Matt. 12:34).

It is important that the people know and admit their sins, but it is even more important to acknowledge that God knows. In verses 14-16, Isaiah turns his attention to the way in which God perceived Israel's situation. The Lord "saw" there was no "judgment" and no "justice," and He saw that "truth," like a wounded man, had "fallen in the street." Furthermore, when the Lord saw Israel's condition, "it displeased him," and he "wondered" why no one would stand up for the truth and why no one would intercede.

---

1. What will "testify against" a person, and how (v. 12)?
2. List the sins confessed in verse 13. How common are these sins today?

"Perhaps the reason you feel guilty is because you are guilty. The answer to your guilt problem is not rationalization or self-justification, but forgiveness. The price of forgiveness is repentance. Without it there is no forgiveness and no relief from the reality of guilt."—R. C. Sproul

---

II. THE LIGHT DISPELS DARKNESS (Isa. 59:19—60:3)

A. The Redeemer (vv. 19-20)

¹⁹ So shall they fear the name of the Lord from the west, and his glory from the rising of the sun. When the enemy shall come in like a flood, the Spirit of the Lord shall lift up a standard against him. ²⁰ And the Redeemer

shall come to Zion, and unto them that turn from transgression in Jacob, saith the Lord.

Truth has fallen to the ground, and no one cares. Nevertheless, despite human apathy, God himself continues to care, and He is stirred to action. Like a soldier going to battle, the Lord puts on His armor: the breastplate of righteousness, the helmet of salvation, and a cloak of zeal (v. 17). Truth has been struck down in battle, but the Lord himself will reach down and lift up truth from the ground, striking down His "enemies" and His "adversaries" (v. 18).

When the people see that God has suited up in His armor and is marching out to battle, they begin to fear Him (v. 19). Before now, they had not feared God; rather, they had engaged in open rebellion against Him. Israel had prayed for victory against its enemies, but, because of Israel's sins, the Lord had not answered. Now, however, in defense of His own honor, the Lord declares that "when the enemy shall come in like a flood, the Spirit of the Lord shall lift up a standard against him." The word *standard* refers to the banner that is carried at the forefront of the army as it marches into battle. That the enemy comes in like a flood implies a mighty force; therefore, an even mightier force is required to defeat this flood. The Spirit of the Lord is a force far greater than any power that can rise against God's people. By the power of His Spirit, the Lord comes to Zion as "the Redeemer." However, He does not come to redeem everyone. He redeems only those who "turn from transgression," meaning those who repent.

---

1. Who will "fear the name of the Lord" (v. 19)?
2. Whom will the Lord help, and how (v. 19)?

"Fearing God has two aspects. The first is reverence. It is a sacred awe of God's utter holiness. . . . The second aspect is fear of God's displeasure. Genuine faith acknowledges God's right to chasten, His right to punish, and His right to judge."—John MacArthur

---

B. The Lord's Covenant (v. 21)

21 As for me, this is my covenant with them, saith the Lord; My spirit that is upon thee, and my words which I have put in thy mouth, shall not depart out of thy mouth, nor out of the mouth of thy seed, nor out of the mouth of thy seed's seed, saith the Lord, from henceforth and for ever.

God intervenes and brings deliverance to His people because He remembers His "covenant." Earlier in the Old Testament, He had said to Israel, "I will never break my covenant with you" (Judg. 2:1). Even when His people are unfaithful, God remains faithful. The apostle Paul wrote to Timothy, "If we are faithless, He remains faithful; He cannot deny Himself" (2 Tim. 2:13 NKJV).

Here in Isaiah, the Lord restates His covenant in the dual terms of His Spirit and His words. Speaking to the Israelites as individuals, He says, "My Spirit . . . and My words . . . shall not depart from your mouth" (NASB). This is Isaiah's version of what Jeremiah calls "the new covenant" (see Jer. 31:31-34). It is a covenant based on God's written Word, but it is also a covenant that depends on the indwelling of the Holy Spirit and the charismatic gifts of the Spirit. This new covenant was instituted on the Day of Pentecost (Acts 2), when the Holy Spirit was poured out on the waiting disciples. This covenant of the Word and the Spirit is to be carried on from generation to generation, "from now and forever" (Isa. 59:21 NASB).

• Describe the covenant God makes here.

"How comfortable it is to have One, day and night, before the throne to control the charge of our enemy, and the despondencies of our souls."— Stephen Charnock

C. Light in the Darkness (60:1-3)

¹ Arise, shine; for thy light is come, and the glory of the Lord is risen upon thee. ² For, behold, the darkness shall cover the earth, and gross darkness the people: but the Lord shall arise upon thee, and his glory shall be seen upon thee. ³ And the Gentiles shall come to thy light, and kings to the brightness of thy rising.

This new covenant of the Spirit and of the Word is the dawning of a new day for God's people. Here in chapter 60, Isaiah calls on the Lord's people to "arise" and let their light shine across the earth. The glory of the Lord rests on those who have God's Word in their mouths and God's Spirit in their hearts. Spiritual darkness covers the earth, but the glory of the Lord will shine over God's people, and "the Gentiles shall come" to the light of the gospel. Nations will be changed, and even "kings" will be drawn to the light. The light of the gospel will reach to every dark corner of the earth, so that "whosoever will" may come to God (Rev. 22:17).

The multitude of Gentiles who will "be converted" and who will "come from far" is detailed in Isaiah 60:4-14. The Gentiles will enter God's kingdom, flowing like a mighty river. They will bring their offerings to God's house, and they will "shew forth the praises of the Lord" (v. 6). People from the ends of the earth will come to the Lord (v. 9), and the gates of the city "shall be open continually; they shall not be shut day nor night" (v. 11; cf. Rev. 21:25). Isaiah's prophecy seems to prefigure the new Jerusalem that John saw "coming down from God out of heaven" (21:2ff.).

1. Describe the power of God's glory (vv. 1-2).
2. Describe the magnetic appeal of God's light (v. 3).

III. LIVE IN THE EVERLASTING LIGHT (Isa. 60:15-22)

A. Everlasting Peace (vv. 15-20)

(Isaiah 60:15-17 is not included in the printed text.)

¹⁸ Violence shall no more be heard in thy land, wasting nor destruction within thy borders; but thou shalt call thy walls Salvation, and thy gates Praise. ¹⁹ The sun shall be no more thy light by day; neither for brightness shall the moon give light unto thee: but the Lord shall be unto thee an everlasting light, and thy God thy glory. ²⁰ Thy sun shall no more go down;

From Darkness to Light

neither shall thy moon withdraw itself: for the Lord shall be thine everlasting light, and the days of thy mourning shall be ended.

In the past, Israel had been seemingly "forsaken and hated" (v. 15), so that the country was desolate and abandoned. This was especially true during the time of the Babylonian Captivity. God, however, will turn things around, and Israel will be forever honored and exalted. The Gentiles, who were once enemies of Israel, will now contribute to and support Israel's well-being. This transformation of the Gentile world is a sign that the Lord is Israel's "Saviour and . . . Redeemer, the mighty One of Jacob" (v. 16). Israel will grow in wealth—her brass will become gold, and her iron will become silver (v. 17).

More important than the increase of riches, however, is the onset of peace. These verses seem to be talking about the future kingdom of God, where "violence" will be eliminated and no "wasting nor destruction" will be found at all (v. 18). The word *wasting* means "destruction, devastation, or ruin." A new and symbolic name will be given to Jerusalem. Her walls will be called "Salvation," and her gates will be called "Praise."

When God's kingdom comes in its fullness, the entire creation will be changed. In the new heaven and the new earth, we will no longer need the light of the sun or the moon, because the Lord himself will be our "everlasting light." In that day, there will be no more sorrow, for all "mourning shall be ended."

---

1. How will God transform His covenant people (v. 15)?
2. What "walls" and "gates" will God establish, and what will they replace (v. 18)?
3. What phrase is repeated in verses 19 and 20, and what does it mean?

"Heaven is not here, it's there. If we were given all we wanted here, our hearts would settle for this world rather than the next. God is forever luring us up and away from this one, wooing us to Himself and His still invisible Kingdom, where we will certainly find what we so keenly long for."—Elisabeth Elliot

---

B. Eternal Righteousness (vv. 21-22)

[21] Thy people also shall be all righteous: they shall inherit the land for ever, the branch of my planting, the work of my hands, that I may be glorified. [22] A little one shall become a thousand, and a small one a strong nation: I the Lord will hasten it in his time.

Isaiah's magnificent picture of the future concludes with three final points. First, everyone in the Holy City will be "righteous." Peter draws from this verse when he writes, "Nevertheless we, according to his promise, look for new heavens and a new earth, wherein dwelleth righteousness" (2 Peter 3:13). Second, the people of God "shall inherit the land forever" (Isa. 60:21), that is, they will dwell in safety and security. They will always have a place, a home that cannot be taken away, "an inheritance incorruptible" that is reserved for them (1 Peter 1:4). Third, they will be so strong that a little child will be like a thousand men, and the smallest person will have the power of a strong nation. This strength, of course, does not reside in the human being; rather, it resides in the Lord himself, who pledges Himself to the eternal protection and support of His people.

---

1. How will God "be glorified" (v. 21)?
2. What does verse 22 say about God's timing?

"He hides our unrighteousness with His righteousness, He covers our disobedience with His obedience, He shadows our death with His death, that the wrath of God cannot find us."—Henry Smith

---

CONCLUSION

At times in these last days, darkness seems to be gaining the upper hand. The battle for truth is raging, and we wrestle "against principalities, against powers, against the rulers of the darkness of this age" (Eph. 6:12 NKJV). Therefore, we should not be surprised that "evil men and impostors . . . grow worse and worse, deceiving and being deceived" (2 Tim. 3:13 NKJV). Jesus predicted that "because lawlessness will abound, the love of many will grow cold" (Matt. 24:12 NKJV). Although the world is shrouded in darkness, Isaiah's prophecy gives us hope. He declares that the darkness must flee before the Lord and before His mighty Spirit. Yes, we need a revival, and God is well able to send exactly what we need. Let us pray for a new Pentecost, so that in these last days God will pour out His Spirit on all flesh (Acts 2:17)

GOLDEN TEXT CHALLENGE

"ARISE, SHINE; FOR THY LIGHT IS COME, AND THE GLORY OF THE LORD IS RISEN UPON THEE" (Isa. 60:1).

This verse follows the prediction in Isaiah 59:20 that "the Redeemer shall come to Zion," which Paul, in Romans 11:26-27, interprets as to be fulfilled in the future salvation of Israel. Here, then, God is speaking to Israel. The light is Christ, the Redeemer who has come and who will come. He has come as earth's Savior; He will come as earth's King.

Daily Devotions:
M. God Lights the Darkness
   2 Samuel 22:25-30
T. Peril of the Wicked
   Psalm 73:12-20
W. The Light Foretold
   Isaiah 9:2-7
T. Dawning of the Light
   John 1:1-9
F. God Is Light
   1 John 1:5-7
S. Christ Is the Light
   Revelation 21:22-26

Our Ultimate Hope

Isaiah 61:1-9; 64:1-9; 65:17-25

Unit Theme:
Hope in the Book of Isaiah

Central Truth:
God promises a glorious new creation.

Focus:
Appreciate and hope in the promise of God to make all things new.

Context:
In the eighth century BC, Isaiah prophesies about God's restoration of all things.

Golden Text:
"Behold, I [the Lord] create new heavens and a new earth: and the former shall not be remembered, nor come into mind" (Isa. 65:17).

Study Outline:
I. God's Promise of Restoration
   (Isa. 61:1-9)
II. Plea for God's Intervention
   (Isa. 64:1-9)
III. What God Will Do
   (Isa. 65:17-25)

INTRODUCTION

Hope is a powerful force for good, but without hope we can lose all motivation to live. The loss of hope causes over thirty-six thousand people in the United States to commit suicide every year. It must be very difficult for an unbeliever to maintain hope in the future, but sometimes even Christians find it a challenge to sustain a hopeful attitude. The apostle Paul realized that our hope must not be based on the circumstances of this life. He said, "If in this life only we have hope in Christ, we are of all men most miserable" (1 Cor. 15:19). Rather, our hope must rest in the promises of God—promises that are based on God's love for us.

God declared through the prophet Jeremiah, "For I know the thoughts that I think toward you, says the Lord, thoughts of peace and not of evil, to give you a future and a hope" (29:11 NKJV). Our hope does not rest in what our parents can do for us, nor in our friends. Our hope for the future does not rest in the stock market, in a political party, or in our nation's military might. Our *only* hope for the future is in God's promise to create for us a new heaven and a new earth. Therefore, we continue to look up, keeping our eyes upon the eastern sky, watching and praying, and "looking for the blessed hope and glorious appearing of our great God and Savior Jesus Christ" (Titus 2:13 NKJV).

In recent years, some Pentecostals have diminished their emphasis on the return of Jesus and have chosen instead to give all of their attention to life in this world. The change is understandable, given that some Pentecostal believers have retreated into a sheltered existence within the four walls of the church. However, the strategy for revitalizing the church's mission is not to be found in de-emphasizing the future, because without an expectant hope in God's future work, the present time is meaningless. Trying to live in the present without an anticipation for the future is like reading only two-thirds of a novel, or like leaving a football game before the last quarter ends. Knowing the end gives us perspective on the present.

I. GOD'S PROMISE OF RESTORATION (Isa. 61:1-9)

A. The Mission of the Messiah (vv. 1-3)

¹ The Spirit of the Lord God is upon me; because the Lord hath anointed me to preach good tidings unto the meek; he hath sent me to bind up the brokenhearted, to proclaim liberty to the captives, and the opening of the prison to them that are bound; ² To proclaim the acceptable year of the Lord, and the day of vengeance of our God; to comfort all that mourn; ³ To appoint unto them that mourn in Zion, to give unto them beauty for ashes, the oil of joy for mourning, the garment of praise for the spirit of heaviness; that they might be called trees of righteousness, the planting of the Lord, that he might be glorified.

The birth of Jesus was the turning point of human history, and the ministry of Jesus was the inauguration of the kingdom of God on earth, the beginning of the end times. In Luke 4:18, Jesus stood up in the synagogue and read from the Book of Isaiah, acknowledging Himself as the fulfillment of Isaiah's prophecy: "The Spirit of the Lord is upon me, because he hath anointed me to preach the gospel to the poor." In the Old Testament, priests were anointed with oil as a sign of their commissioning, and so were prophets and kings. Jesus is a perfect embodiment of all three offices. More than anyone before Him or after Him, Jesus could say, "The Spirit of the Lord God is upon Me."

According to Isaiah's prophecy, the mission of the Messiah involves proclamation, healing, deliverance, and comfort. He proclaims "good tidings" (Isa. 61:1), which is the Hebrew equivalent to the word *gospel* in the New Testament. The *gospel* is the good news that God has obtained victory over the forces of evil and that He gives that victory to anyone who will confess Him as Savior and Lord. The Messiah also proclaims "liberty to the captives." Because God is victor, everyone who had been taken captive by the enemy will be set free. Furthermore, He is to "proclaim the year of the Lord's favor" (v. 2 NIV), which is the Year of Jubilee—the year when every parcel of land was returned to its original owner and every slave was released.

In His work as healer, the Messiah "bind[s] up the brokenhearted" (v. 1). The *brokenhearted* are those who are oppressed, afflicted, or distressed for any reason. It is significant that God not only forgives sins but also heals the heart and the emotions, "comforting" all who mourn" (see v. 2), which may refer to those who mourn over the loss of earthly friends and possessions or to those who mourn over sin. In both cases, the gospel offers abundant resources for comfort.

It was the custom in biblical times for mourners to place ashes on their heads and to refrain from using fragrant oil. The Messiah, however, replaces the ashes with "beauty," and adorns the mourners with holy oil (v. 3). He removes from them the "spirit of despair" and places on them "a garment of praise" (NIV). Advancing to another metaphor, Isaiah declares that the Messiah plants His people as "oaks of righteousness" (NIV). As trees planted by the Lord, His people are guaranteed to "bring forth fruit" and to "prosper" (see Ps. 1:3).

The ministry of the Messiah is the ministry of Jesus, and the ministry of Jesus is the ministry of the Church. If we want to know what the Church should be doing in the world today, we need only pay attention to Isaiah 61.

---

1. Who "anointed" the Messiah, and what does this mean (v. 1)?
2. What message did the Messiah declare (vv. 1-2)?
3. What exchanges can the Messiah make for "those who grieve" (v. 3 NIV)?
4. Describe the "planting" Christ wants to make (v. 3).

"It ought to be placed in the forefront of all Christian teaching that Christ's mission on earth was to give men life."—Henry Drummond

---

B. The Renewal of God's People (vv. 4-9)

4 And they shall build the old wastes, they shall raise up the former desolations, and they shall repair the waste cities, the desolations of many generations. 5 And strangers shall stand and feed your flocks, and the sons of the alien shall be your plowmen and your vinedressers. 6 But ye shall be named the Priests of the Lord: men shall call you the Ministers of our God: ye shall eat the riches of the Gentiles, and in their glory shall ye boast yourselves. 7 For your shame ye shall have double; and for confusion they shall rejoice in their portion: therefore in their land they shall possess the double: everlasting joy shall be unto them. 8 For I the Lord love judgment, I hate robbery for burnt offering; and I will direct their work in truth, and I will make an everlasting covenant with them. 9 And their seed shall be known among the Gentiles, and their offspring among the people: all that see them shall acknowledge them, that they are the seed which the Lord hath blessed.

The coming of the Messiah signals a new age of salvation. What's more, His coming produces a mighty revival, a renewal, a restoration. "They shall rebuild the old ruins" (v. 4 NKJV). Everything that the enemy had destroyed will be rebuilt and restored. Even those parts of the land that had been desolate for "many generations" will be repaired. This restoration will be so great that the people who were once enemies will come into the land and bear the workload of watching after the flocks, plowing the fields, and tending the grapes (v. 5). God's people, however, will be called "priests of the Lord" and "ministers" of God, devoting themselves entirely to the worship and service of God. Everyone who had suffered shame in the past will receive a double reward, and "everlasting joy" will be theirs (vv. 6-7).

When the Lord says He loves "judgment" (v. 8), He means that He loves proper and righteous judgments. He loves to render justice decisions for His people, and

He loves it when His people judge righteously. However, He hates "robbery for burnt offering," which speaks of people who use stolen animals as their offerings.

God promises to "faithfully give" His people "their recompense" (v. 8 NASB). The coming of the Messiah is part of the new "everlasting covenant" that God makes with His people.

God will ensure that His people are known for who they really are. Even among the nations, their "offspring" will be acknowledged as the children of God, whom "the Lord hath blessed" (v. 9). Apparently, this is a fulfillment of God's promise to Abraham: "And in thy seed shall all the nations of the earth be blessed" (Gen. 22:18).

———————————

1. What has God rebuilt and repaired in your life (v. 4)?
2. What does it mean to be "priests" and "ministers" of God (v. 6)?
3. Explain the double use of the word "double" (v. 7)?
4. What does God "love," and how will He express it (vv. 8-9)?

———————————

"A true revival means nothing less than a revolution, casting out the spirit of worldliness and selfishness, and making God and His love triumph in the heart and life."—Andrew Murray

———————————

II. PLEA FOR GOD'S INTERVENTION (Isa. 64:1-9)

A. Prayer for God to Come Down (vv. 1-3)

¹ Oh that thou wouldest rend the heavens, that thou wouldest come down, that the mountains might flow down at thy presence, ² As when the melting fire burneth, the fire causeth the waters to boil, to make thy name known to thine adversaries, that the nations may tremble at thy presence! ³ When thou didst terrible things which we looked not for, thou camest down, the mountains flowed down at thy presence.

Jesus instructed His disciples to pray, "Thy kingdom come" (Matt. 6:10). Our prayer for God's kingdom to come on the earth echoes Isaiah's prayer hundreds of years before Jesus. Isaiah prayed that God would "rend the heavens" (64:1) and come down to set things right on the earth. The word *rend* means "to tear"; therefore, Isaiah's prayer presents a picture of God tearing open a hole in the sky through which He can descend. When God comes down, His presence is so powerful that the mountains break open and begin to flow like a volcano (v. 2). This mighty display of God's power causes the nations to tremble and to give honor to God's name.

This awesome scene, in which God appears in fire upon the mountains, reminds us of His previous appearance on Mount Sinai. God came down upon Sinai in fire and smoke, in thunder and lightning, and in an earthquake. The people did not expect such "awesome things" (v. 3 NKJV); therefore, they trembled with fear. Isaiah prays that God will once again manifest Himself in power and glory (see 2 Thess. 1:7-9; 2 Peter 3:10-13).

———————————

1. What was Isaiah's heart cry, and why (vv. 1-2)?
2. What did Isaiah remember (v. 3)?

"Before we can pray, 'Lord, Thy Kingdom come,' we must be willing to pray, 'My kingdom go.'"—Alan Redpath

---

B. Anticipation of a Heavenly Reward (v. 4)

4 For since the beginning of the world men have not heard, nor perceived by the ear, neither hath the eye seen, O God, beside thee, what he hath prepared for him that waiteth for him.

Isaiah knows that when the Lord appears, He will come not only in judgment upon the wicked but also with a reward for the righteous. The life that God has prepared for His people will be so great that nothing can be compared to it. Even from "the beginning of the world," no one has seen or heard anything like it. At no time in the history of the world has anyone witnessed the kind of rewards that God will give to His people. What God has prepared for us is something entirely new and far beyond our greatest expectations.

• How is God unique?

Incredible Transformation

Trying to visualize God's future kingdom is much like trying to imagine a butterfly when all you have ever seen is a caterpillar. The mighty oak tree was once a small round acorn. Mysteriously, beautiful red roses emerge from a bushy plant with thorns. Similarly, out of the chaos and ugliness that we see in the world today will someday emerge God's glorious kingdom. We long to see it.

C. The Tragedy of Human Sin (vv. 5-7)

5 Thou meetest him that rejoiceth and worketh righteousness, those that remember thee in thy ways: behold, thou art wroth; for we have sinned: in those is continuance, and we shall be saved. 6 But we are all as an unclean thing, and all our righteousnesses are as filthy rags; and we all do fade as a leaf; and our iniquities, like the wind, have taken us away. 7 And there is none that calleth upon thy name, that stirreth up himself to take hold of thee: for thou hast hid thy face from us, and hast consumed us, because of our iniquities.

Isaiah's prayer for the coming of the Lord causes him to examine his heart and the heart of his people, Israel. Isaiah knows that the Lord demands "righteousness," but Israel has sinned against God. Therefore, God's anger is stirred up against Israel. The people say, "You are indeed angry, for we have sinned—in these ways we continue; and we need to be saved" (v. 5 NKJV).

Salvation cannot be gained through our righteousness, for "all our righteousnesses are as filthy rags" (v. 6). The words *filthy rags* refer to garments that have become polluted by coming in contact with menstrual blood. The garment is ceremonially unclean, and is therefore unfit to be worn in the presence of God. All of our acts of righteousness, our good deeds, our prayers, our offerings, and our sacrifices are polluted with human impurity. When we come into God's presence, we must lay aside all of our claims to righteousness and approach God only on the basis of His mercy.

Furthermore, whatever strength and vigor we possess will wither away like the falling leaves of autumn (v. 6). The leaves fall and decay, and the wind blows them away. Like dead leaves, we have been swept away by our sins. Earlier, Isaiah had described humanity in similar terms when he said, "The grass withers, the flower fades . . . surely the people are grass" (40:7 NKJV).

In 64:5-7, Isaiah records three serious accusations against us: (1) Our righteous deeds are polluted. (2) Our sins have swept us away. (3) We do not seek after God. He says, "There is none that calleth upon thy name, that stirreth up himself to take hold of thee" (v. 7). Perhaps the people had fallen into deep despair or had lost their faith in God. Whatever the reason, no one was seeking God for His favor and His Spirit. The words *stirreth up* refer to the effort that is required to rouse oneself from a deep sleep. Isaiah's point is that God's people had fallen into a state of spiritual slumber from which they could not wake themselves. The apostle Paul uses similar language when he says to the Roman church, "Knowing the time, that now it is high time to awake out of sleep" (Rom. 13:11). The Hebrew word translated *take hold* means to grasp firmly or strongly, with steadfast intent. It means that we should follow Jacob's example of wrestling with God and say with Jacob, "I will not let You go unless You bless me!" (Gen. 32:26 NKJV). It was required that Israel seek after God because it was their sins that caused God to hide from them.

---

1. Contrast the "righteousness" of verse 5 with the "righteousness" of verse 6. What is the difference?
2. Explain the desperation in verse 7.

"The stiff and wooden quality about our religious lives is a result of our lack of holy desire. Complacency is a deadly foe of all spiritual growth. Acute desire must be present or there will be no manifestation of Christ to His people."—A. W. Tozer

---

D. The Care of the Heavenly Father (vv. 8-9)

8 But now, O Lord, thou art our father; we are the clay, and thou our potter; and we all are the work of thy hand. 9 Be not wroth very sore, O Lord, neither remember iniquity for ever: behold, see, we beseech thee, we are all thy people.

Isaiah follows his stinging rebuke with a prayer of humility. The people address God as "Father," one of the few places in the Old Testament where God is addressed with this term. Despite all that the Israelites had done against the Lord and despite the punishments the Lord had measured out to them, they continued to look upon God as their Father. Therefore, in this prayer, they plead as children to their Father, hoping that God will be merciful and kind.

They surrender themselves into God's hands, recognizing that He is the "potter" and they are nothing more than "the work" of His hands. God has the right to mold and shape His people in whatever manner He sees fit; therefore, the people pray that God will not be angry and that He will not remember their sins any longer. Finally, they plead with God, "Behold, look now, all of us are Your people" (v. 9 NASB). This is a cry of utter desperation.

---

1. How is God both a "Father" and a "potter" (v. 8)?
2. What is Isaiah's plea (v. 9)?

"In our addresses therefore unto God, let us so look upon Him as a just God, as well as a merciful; and not either despair of or presume upon His mercy."—Abraham Wright

---

III. WHAT GOD WILL DO (Isa. 65:17-25)

A. God Will Create All Things New (vv. 17-22)

(Isaiah 65:20-22 is not included in the printed text.)

¹⁷ For, behold, I create new heavens and a new earth: and the former shall not be remembered, nor come into mind. ¹⁸ But be ye glad and rejoice for ever in that which I create: for, behold, I create Jerusalem a rejoicing, and her people a joy. ¹⁹ And I will rejoice in Jerusalem, and joy in my people: and the voice of weeping shall be no more heard in her, nor the voice of crying.

The Israelites prayed that God would treat them kindly as His children and that He would forgive their sins and bring salvation to the land. God, however, will do that and much more! He will "create new heavens and a new earth" (v. 17). The old heavens and earth cannot be fixed; they must be remade. The solution to humanity's problems does not reside in humanity itself. Our government cannot bring righteousness to our nation. A new president cannot stem the tide of immorality and drug addiction. Neither our military might nor our political maneuverings will bring peace to the world. Neither our charitable organizations nor our improved farming techniques will eliminate hunger. Neither our medical missions nor our pharmaceutical advances will conquer disease. The answer to these and all other problems is found in God's declaration: "Behold, I make all things new" (Rev. 21:5).

God's renewal of the earth will be so magnificent that the world as it was "shall not be remembered, nor come into mind" (Isa. 65:17). That which shall be created will be so superior that it will totally eclipse the former. The past will be forgotten completely, and God's people will be "glad and rejoice" (v. 18) in the new world that God creates. Jerusalem will be restored as a place of "rejoicing," and her people will be "a joy." Sorrow will be eliminated and the "voice of weeping shall be no more heard" (v. 19). There will be no more "crying."

Sickness will be conquered in this new earth. Infants will no longer die young, and everyone will live out their full days (v. 20). The land will be secure, and people can "build houses" and "plant vineyards" without fear that anyone will rob them of their homes or steal the fruit of their vineyards (v. 21). God's chosen people will "enjoy the work of their hands" (v. 22).

1. Why will "the former things . . . not be remembered" (v. 17 NIV)?
2. How will the sounds of Jerusalem change, and why (vv. 18-19)?
3. Describe various ways God's people will experience longevity (vv. 20-22).

"We must meet the uncertainties of this world with the certainty of the world to come."—A. W. Tozer

B. God Will Answer His People (vv. 23-24)

23 They shall not labour in vain, nor bring forth for trouble; for they are the seed of the blessed of the Lord, and their offspring with them. 24 And it shall come to pass, that before they call, I will answer; and while they are yet speaking, I will hear.

God promises a day when no one will "labour in vain." Whenever they plant seed, it will yield a good crop because the weather conditions will be perfect. When they harvest their produce, no one will steal it from them or swindle them out of their profits. Whenever they have children, they will not bring them forth "for trouble"; that is, their children will not suffer hardship and calamity as in times past. These benefits are guaranteed by the Lord, for both the parents are "the offspring of those blessed by the Lord, and their descendants with them" (v. 23 NASB).

In this new creation, God will be ever-present and ever-attentive to the needs of His people. So much so that even "before they call," He will answer them; and "while they are yet speaking," He will hear their prayers (v. 24). As soon as thoughts form in their minds, God will know them; and before their prayers are finished, God will have answered already. God will anticipate every need of His people. In the present world, we are encouraged to "wait upon the Lord" (40:31), but in the new world, there will be no waiting. Our access to the throne of God will be immediate and effective.

1. List two ways God's blessing will be evidenced in the new order (v. 23).
2. Describe God's relationship with His people in the new world (v. 24).

"God's willingness to answer our prayers exceeds our willingness to give good and necessary things to our children, just as far as God's ability, goodness, and perfection exceed our infirmities and evil."—E. M. Bounds

C. God Will Make New Paradise (v. 25)

25 The wolf and the lamb shall feed together, and the lion shall eat straw like the bullock: and dust shall be the serpent's meat. They shall not hurt nor destroy in all my holy mountain, saith the Lord.

Even the animal kingdom will be transformed to a peaceful existence. The "wolf and the lamb" will no longer be enemies. The lion will no longer seek out its prey; rather, it will "eat straw like the ox" (NASB). Creation will again be like the Garden of Eden. The punishment that was laid upon the serpent, however, is not reversed (see Gen. 3:14). Dust will continue to be his food, but his venom will not be harmful to humanity. God's kingdom will be a place of safety and security. Nothing will be able to "hurt nor destroy" the people of God.

• How will the new world be like the Garden of Eden?

"The unceasing activity of the Creator, whereby in overflowing bounty and goodwill, He upholds His creatures in ordered existence, guides and governs all events, circumstances, and free acts of angels and men, and directs everything to its appointed goal, for His own glory."—J. I. Packer

---

CONCLUSION

It is impossible for us to grasp the sorrow and disappointment that must have enveloped Adam and Eve when they heard God's pronouncement of judgment upon their sin. They had enjoyed a perfect world, but they ruined it. Into the garden of life they had brought death. However, even in the moment of this first human judgment, God spoke a word of salvation, a word of hope: "I will put enmity between thee and the woman, and between thy seed and her seed; it shall bruise thy head, and thou shalt bruise his heel" (Gen. 3:15). This seed of the woman, which would bruise the head of the Serpent, would be Jesus Christ, the Son of God.

The prophet Isaiah foretold the coming of Jesus, and He entered the world amid great promises and great announcements. Joseph was commanded to "call his name Jesus: for he shall save his people from their sins" (Matt. 1:21). When Jesus was born, the angel proclaimed, "Unto you is born this day in the city of David a Saviour, which is Christ the Lord" (Luke 2:11). Jesus fulfilled all of the Old Testament messianic prophecies concerning salvation. "He was wounded for our transgressions, He was bruised for our iniquities . . . and by His stripes we are healed" (Isa. 53:5 NKJV). However, prophecies remain whose fulfillments lie in the future. Jesus will return to rule and reign on the earth, and He will set up His kingdom of righteousness. Then, in the end, He will create "a new heaven and a new earth" (21:1). Jesus proclaims to us, "Surely I come quickly," and we respond, "Even so, come, Lord Jesus" (Rev. 22:20).

GOLDEN TEXT CHALLENGE

"BEHOLD, I [THE LORD] CREATE NEW HEAVENS AND A NEW EARTH: AND THE FORMER SHALL NOT BE REMEMBERED, NOR COME INTO MIND" (Isa. 65:17).

God has not finished His creative work. His coming masterpiece will be a new heaven and a new earth.

Create is from the Hebrew word *bara*, which can refer to the production of something new, rare, and wonderful. *Bara* can also refer to the act of renovating—remaking something already in existence into a renewed form—which is the idea expressed in this verse. Through God's re-creative powers, there will be a totally new condition of things.

April 6, 2014

Believers will inherit this new world during Christ's millennial reign. The renewed creation will be so marvelous that life as we now know it will be forgotten—just a vague memory.

In this new order, God's children "will be priests of God and of Christ and will reign with him for a thousand years" (Rev. 20:6 NIV).

Daily Devotions:
M. Hope in God
    Psalm 71:1-7
T. Hope for Renewal
    Isaiah 40:25-31
W. Hope of Restoration
    Joel 2:23-27
T. New Creation
    Colossians 3:3-10
F. Awaiting Immortality
    1 Thessalonians 4:13-18
S. New Heaven and Earth
    2 Peter 3:10-14

Principles of Fellowship

1 John 1:1 through 2:2; 3 John 1-14

Unit Theme:
Principles for Christian Living (1, 2, 3 John)

Central Truth:
Fellowship with God is affected by our relationships with others.

Focus:
Identify and apply biblical principles of fellowship with God and others.

Context:
Near the end of the first century AD, the elderly apostle John penned these epistles, probably writing from Ephesus.

Golden Text:
"If we walk in the light, as he is in the light, we have fellowship one with another, and the blood of Jesus Christ his Son cleanseth us from all sin" (1 John 1:7).

Study Outline:
I. Fellowship With God and Others
   (1 John 1:1-6)
II. Conditions of Fellowship
   (1 John 1:7—2:2)
III. Show Hospitality
   (3 John 5-11)

INTRODUCTION

The epistles of John present God as "light" (1 John 1:5). Ultimately, God is beyond our comprehension, and yet because He is Light He desires to make Himself known to humankind. So great is that desire that He sent His Son, Jesus Christ, into the world, dressed in human flesh, to live before people so they could see what God is like. As John Killinger put it, "Jesus is God's way of getting rid of a bad reputation."

Humans had many ideas about the nature of God, some of them not very good, prior to the coming of Jesus. But in Christ, God has given us a true picture of His nature. We could not climb up to Him, so He reached down to us in Jesus of Nazareth. He is the revelation of God.

John also presents God as "love" (1 John 4:8). His attitude toward humans is love. Jesus said, "For God so loved the world that He gave His only begotten Son, that whoever believes in Him should not perish but have everlasting life" (John 3:16 NKJV). This same love that God has toward us, we should have toward Him and toward each other.

John also teaches us that God is "life" (1 John 1:1). When we accept Christ as our Savior, we become partakers of the divine nature. The life of God lives within us. God is eternal, and the life we receive from Him is everlasting. This is life of the highest possible quality. No one on earth who is apart from Christ, no matter how rich or noble, enjoys the quality of life Christians have.

From this high and lofty look at the attributes of God as they relate to believers, John comes down to earth, as it were, and deals with a conflict that had arisen in the church. He has words of commendation for Gaius and Demetrius as examples of what a believer should be (3 John 1, 12), but he strongly condemns Diotrephes for his vain and corrupt ways (v. 9). John sees Diotrephes as a troublemaker in the church and vows to correct the situation when he arrives. Although we know John as the apostle of love, he could be stern when it came to defending the truth.

I. FELLOWSHIP WITH GOD AND OTHERS (1 John 1:1-6)

A. The Word of Life (vv. 1-4)

¹ That which was from the beginning, which we have heard, which we have seen with our eyes, which we have looked upon, and our hands have handled, of the Word of life; ² (For the life was manifested, and we have seen it, and bear witness, and shew unto you that eternal life, which was with the Father, and was manifested unto us;) ³ That which we have seen and heard declare we unto you, that ye also may have fellowship with us: and truly our fellowship is with the Father, and with his Son Jesus Christ. ⁴ And these things write we unto you, that your joy may be full.

In his Gospel, John describes Jesus as the Word: "In the beginning was the Word, and the Word was with God, and the Word was God. . . . In him was life" (John 1:1, 4). Being "the Word of life" (1 John 1:1), God's Son, along with the Father and the Holy Spirit, is the author and sustainer of physical life, spiritual life, and eternal life.

There were those in John's day who denied that Christ had come in the flesh. John offers the strongest possible evidence of the physical presence of Christ. He declared that he and the other disciples had heard Him with their own ears, seen Him with their own eyes, and touched Him with their own hands. John says that they "looked upon" (v. 1) Him, meaning that He captured their total attention and they gazed upon Him with admiration. There was no convincing him that Jesus was not real (v. 2). While we are not eyewitnesses of His physical presence, our encounter with Him is just as real as was that of the disciples. The Holy Spirit has brought us into joyful fellowship with Christ.

True believers walk in fellowship with Christ, and those who have fellowship with Him have fellowship with the Father through Him (v. 3). This fellowship also includes the members of the Church, the body of Christ. To continue in fellowship with Christ, we must be obedient to His commandments and faithful to His teachings.

John wanted his readers to find the joy that fellowship with Christ brings—the joy he and the disciples had found (v. 4). He knew that if they were firmly established in the Christian faith and fellowship, they would be filled with joy. The beloved disciple wrote during challenging days for the Church. He knew that if persecuted believers were to survive, they would need the joy of fellowship with Christ and with each other. No circumstance of this life could triumph over them as long as they walked close to Him and continued in unity with other believers. The same is true for believers today. We are made stronger through fellowship with other Christians.

---

1. What title is Jesus given in verse 1? What does it signify?
2. What was John's testimony (v. 2)?
3. Describe genuine fellowship (vv. 3-4).

"God is not silent. It is the nature of God to speak. The second person of the Holy Trinity is called 'The Word.'"—A. W. Tozer

---

B. God Is Light (v. 5)

⁵ This then is the message which we have heard of him, and declare unto you, that God is light, and in him is no darkness at all.

In the Book of Genesis, light is shown to be the first of God's creative acts. "And God said, Let there be light: and there was light" (1:3). The psalmist declared, "The Lord is my light and my salvation; whom shall I fear?" (27:1). John opens his Gospel with the assertion that Christ is light. He quotes John the Baptist as announcing, "The one who is the true light, who gives light to everyone, was coming into the world" (John 1:9 NLT). Jesus himself made the bold proclamation, "I am the light of the world. He who follows Me shall not walk in darkness, but have the light of life" (8:12 NKJV).

In saying that God is light and Christ is light, we are given a glimpse into the character of God which Christ lived out while on earth. God is holy and righteous; in Him there is nothing that is evil or false—"no darkness at all" (1 John 1:5). Those who walk in fellowship with "the Father, and with his Son Jesus Christ" (v. 3) will reflect the character of God in their lives.

It is the nature of light to shine, and it is the nature of God to reveal Himself. When God chooses to make Himself known, what we see is One who possesses perfect purity and displays unutterable majesty. He is "the High and Lofty One who inhabits eternity, whose name is Holy" (Isa. 57:15 NKJV). Yet, God makes Himself known and dwells with those who are lowly in heart. He says, "I dwell in the high and holy place, with him who has a contrite and humble spirit, to revive the spirit of the humble, and to revive the heart of the contrite ones" (v. 15 NKJV).

What comfort we find in knowing that God never deceives, misleads, or distorts. Those are attitudes of darkness, and there is no darkness in Him. He deals only in truth. Thus, we can trust the light He shines on our pathway and walk safely in His way.

• Why is "light" an appropriate name for God?

"The fundamental principle of Christianity is to be what God is, and He is light."—John Hagee

---

April 13, 2014   319

C. Fellowship With God (v. 6)

⁶ If we say that we have fellowship with him, and walk in darkness, we lie, and do not the truth.

To be conscious of God's presence in our life, we must walk by faith. To maintain a closeness to Him calls for living a holy life, and exhibiting purity in our daily living. Through the grace of God, we can enjoy a rich and rewarding communion with God. If we neglect to worship and obey God and fail to act according to truth, any confession of communion with God is only a pretense. Truth is the standard for righteousness. Jesus said, "I am the way, the truth, and the life. No one comes to the Father except through Me" (John 14:6 NKJV).

If we claim to have fellowship with God while we are walking in darkness, we are deceiving ourselves and others. If we consciously practice sin, a taint of darkness overshadows our heart that makes fellowship with God an impossibility. Our actions prove the truth is not in us. John bluntly says if we pretend to be a friend of God and at the same time live a wicked life, we are liars. Our profession is false and insincere. Light and darkness cannot dwell together. Holiness and wickedness are not compatible.

Those who walk in the light have nothing to hide. Jesus said, "Those who do what is right come to the light so others can see that they are doing what God wants" (John 3:21 NLT). They welcome the shining of the light on their life, and have no problem with others observing their conduct. They can pray as did the psalmist: "Search me, O God, and know my heart: try me, and know my thoughts: and see if there be any wicked way in me, and lead me in the way everlasting" (139:23-24).

Are you walking in the light? Do you have any problem with your life being an open book before God? The beauty of walking in the light is that Jesus Christ travels the road with us, enabling us to overcome difficulties and to live victoriously. Further, the Holy Spirit lives within us, teaching us the way of righteousness.

• What does it mean to "walk in darkness" (v. 6)?

"If you think you can walk in holiness without keeping up perpetual fellowship with Christ, you have made a great mistake. If you would be holy, you must live close to Jesus."—Charles Spurgeon

---

II. CONDITIONS OF FELLOWSHIP (1 John 1:7—2:2)

A. Fellowship With Others (1:7)

⁷ But if we walk in the light, as he is in the light, we have fellowship one with another, and the blood of Jesus Christ his Son cleanseth us from all sin.

There was a time when we all walked in darkness. Only by the grace of God did we find the road that is illuminated by Christ. The Holy Spirit took us out of the realm of darkness and created within us a new life. "Walking in darkness" is to believe a lie and live in hypocrisy and pretense. "Walking in the light" is to walk with God and to always walk toward Him. Our path is lighted by the Word of God. Not only do we receive Christ, we also embrace His words. After all, He is the living Word. The way of light is the way of truth, and truth is found in the Scripture. The more we know of His Word, the brighter the light shines on our path.

As we walk in the light, not only do we have fellowship with the Father and with His Son, but we also enjoy a special camaraderie with fellow believers. The common thread that knits believers together is our mutual communion with God. There are other bonds that unite individuals, but there is none so strong as our membership in the family of God. There is a uniqueness about that relationship that the world can never experience. Believers have so much in common because we love the same God, share the same beliefs, and live with the same ends in mind. In this life, our goal is to glorify Christ and win others to Him. Beyond this life, we believe there is a larger, better life and an eternal home in the presence of God. With all of this commonality, we feel at home with each other.

This fellowship is possible through the blood of Jesus Christ shed for our sins. In our state of sinfulness and rebellion, fellowship with God was impossible. Something had to remove that barrier, and only the shed blood of Jesus Christ was sufficient. The moment individuals trust Christ, they are fully forgiven and cleansed from all sin. The door of fellowship with God and others is opened wide.

• What are the benefits of walking "in the light" (v. 7)?

Christian Fellowship
Christian brotherhood is not an ideal which we must realize; it is rather a reality created by God in Christ in which we may participate. The more clearly we learn to recognize that the ground and strength and promise of all our fellowship is in Jesus Christ alone, the more serenely shall we think of our fellowship and pray and hope for it.—Dietrich Bonhoeffer

---

B. Confessing Our Sins (vv. 8-10)

8 If we say that we have no sin, we deceive ourselves, and the truth is not in us. 9 If we confess our sins, he is faithful and just to forgive us our sins, and to cleanse us from all unrighteousness. 10 If we say that we have not sinned, we make him a liar, and his word is not in us.

We can trace our plight back to Adam. When Adam fell, the human race fell with him. Paul makes it clear that "all have sinned, and come short of the glory of God" (Rom. 3:23). Since we were all born in sin, we all need a Savior. If we imagine that we have no guilt and thus no need for the blood of Jesus Christ to wash away our sin, "we deceive ourselves" (1 John 1:8). The result of such thinking is to live under the weight of sin and travel down a road that leads to hell with no remedy.

But there is a remedy; it is by way of confessing our sins. If we come before God with a deep sense of our guilt, recognizing our inability to do anything about it on our own and humbly cast ourselves on His mercy, He will "cleanse us from all unrighteousness" (v. 9). On Calvary, Christ paid the debt for our sins and purchased our redemption. When we put our trust in Christ's sacrifice, God will take away all our guilt and cleanse us from every kind of sin. We are then ready for communion with God in this world and to enjoy His presence and glory forever in the place Christ has gone to prepare for us.

There were some in the community to which John wrote who denied that they had ever sinned, or that they needed a Savior. But the apostle says that if we deny we need pardon through the blood of Christ and claim we have never sinned, "we make [God] a liar" (v. 10). This attitude also shows either that we have no understanding of the Word or that we have given no place for it in our heart. Nothing could be more important than to understand our lostness, apart from Christ, and to humbly look to Him for our salvation.

---

1. According to verse 8, how do some people deceive themselves? Why is this serious?
2. How do we receive forgiveness (v. 9)?
3. Explain the phrase "make him [God] a liar" (v. 10).

"It's Satan's delight to tell me that once he's got me, he will keep me. But at that moment I can go back to God. And I know that if I confess my sins, God is faithful and just to forgive me."—Alan Redpath

---

C. The Divine Advocate (2:1-2)

¹ My little children, these things write I unto you, that ye sin not. And if any man sin, we have an advocate with the Father, Jesus Christ the righteous: ² And he is the propitiation for our sins: and not for ours only, but also for the sins of the whole world.

The biblical standard for believers is that we do not sin. If we walk in fellowship with God, it stands to reason that we will strive to lead a holy life. After all, we have been forgiven and cleansed from all our sin by the blood of Christ. That within itself is enough to encourage us to practice holiness. Although we are imperfect, we no longer live in sin by indulging our fleshly appetites and walking contrary to the Word of God. By the grace of God, we adopt a Christ-centered lifestyle marked by good works.

While John teaches that holiness is God's standard of living for His people, he recognizes that the temptation to sin is an ongoing reality. His statement "If anybody does sin" (v. 1 NIV) acknowledges this. When a believer sins, he or she must not continue in sin as though there was no help available. Rather, the believer should repent and find the remedy God has provided through Jesus Christ. What relief there is to know that if we fail, we should not despair. "Jesus Christ, the Righteous One," will speak "to the Father in our defense" (v. 1 NIV) and restore us to fellowship with Him.

Not only did Jesus Christ die on the cross to pay the price for our sins, He sits at the right hand of the Father to make intercession for us. The writer of Hebrews said, "We have not an high priest which cannot be touched with the feeling of our infirmities; but was in all points tempted like as we are, yet without sin. Let us therefore come boldly unto the throne of grace, that we may obtain mercy, and find grace to help in time of need" (4:15-16). Although we are helpless without Christ, we are overcomers through Him.

1. Why do people need an advocate?
2. Whom is Jesus Christ willing to represent before His Father?

"The happy sequence culminating in fellowship with God is penitence, pardon, and peace—the first we offer, the second we accept, and the third we inherit."—Charles H. Brent

---

III. SHOW HOSPITALITY (3 John 5-11)

A. Modeling Hospitality (vv. 5-8)

5 Beloved, thou doest faithfully whatsoever thou doest to the brethren, and to strangers; 6 Which have borne witness of thy charity before the church: whom if thou bring forward on their journey after a godly sort, thou shalt do well: 7 Because that for his name's sake they went forth, taking nothing of the Gentiles. 8 We therefore ought to receive such, that we might be fellowhelpers to the truth.

This third epistle of John is written to Gaius, whom he refers to as his "dear friend" (v. 1 NIV) and whom he commends for his hospitality toward traveling preachers and teachers. Even though they were "strangers" to Gaius (v. 5), he must have received them into his house and entertained them at his own expense. John viewed Gaius' action as more than mere hospitality; he saw it as an expression of his faithfulness to God (v. 6). Cannot the same thing be said of the Christian congregation who supports its pastor? Christian preachers and teachers certainly have the right to be supported by those who benefit from their ministry. In doing so, the congregation is showing its faithfulness to God.

John commended Gaius for what he was doing also because these Christian missionaries had no other means of support. As a matter of policy, they did not seek help from unbelievers (v. 7). This does not mean they would not accept gifts voluntarily offered to them by those who were not serving Christ. There are unbelievers today who appreciate the cause of Christ and want to help. There is nothing wrong with accepting their contributions. But, by and large, the church should get its support from the body of believers.

A third observation John made to Gaius is that those who support the work of Christian preachers and teachers share in the results of their ministry (v. 8). When we support the ministry with our means, we sometimes accomplish more than we realize. And when we combine that support with the giving of others, we make an even greater impact.

What we could never do as individuals, we can do when we combine our giving with that of fellow believers in the local church. There is a limit as to how much one person alone can accomplish, but there is virtually no limit to what can be done when we all pitch in. Thomas Lane Butts wrote: "One of the miracles of the organized church is that you can be busy at your daily tasks at home and at the same time be preaching the gospel in Africa, feeding the hungry in Haiti, or helping the homeless in India. You can win some victory for humanity, wherever you are, by your tithe."

---

1. Describe the reputation of Gaius (vv. 5-6).
2. Describe the ministry of those to whom Gaius was a "fellow helper" (vv. 7-8).

"The challenge of hospitality, both personally and professionally, comes when we are stressed out or tired and we offer it grudgingly. The gift of hospitality comes when we find in the welcoming face of hospitality the welcoming face of God."—Cornelius Plantinga

---

B. Hindering Hospitality (vv. 9-10)

⁹ I wrote unto the church: but Diotrephes, who loveth to have the preeminence among them, receiveth us not. ¹⁰ Wherefore, if I come, I will remember his deeds which he doeth, prating against us with malicious words: and not content therewith, neither doth he himself receive the brethren, and forbiddeth them that would, and casteth them out of the church.

John's third letter was written to Gaius, who was a model Christian and a strong supporter of the apostle. Now John speaks to Gaius about a man in the local church who was malicious, power-hungry, and sought to run the church. Apparently, he had gathered enough followers to be a force to be reckoned with in the church. He apparently felt threatened by the apostle John and refused to allow his correspondence to be heard by the church. He also spread malicious rumors about John, denigrating his character.

Diotrephes took it upon himself to administer discipline in the church, and for all the wrong reasons. He sought only to perpetuate his position in the church and advance his warped and wrong beliefs. Not only did he not practice hospitality himself, but he punished those who did.

John was not one to allow something of this nature to go on unchallenged. He assured Gaius that, upon his arrival, he would confront this troublemaker and expose him to the congregation for what he really was. Diotrephes' refusal to help traveling preachers and his threat to excommunicate any church member who offered assistance to them grieved the apostle, and he promised to do something about it.

Are there still church members who seek to have the preeminence and who, through their vanity and pride, hinder the work of the Lord? Sadly, yes. God-fearing believers in the church need to recognize such an attitude and stand against it.

• Describe Diotrephes' attitude and the actions that flowed from it.

"The image of the Lord has been replaced by a mirror."—Jorge Luis Borges

---

C. Doing Good (v. 11)

¹¹ Beloved, follow not that which is evil, but that which is good. He that doeth good is of God: but he that doeth evil hath not seen God.

Having pointed out the flaws in Diotrephes, the apostle admonishes Gaius not to follow him. Rather, he suggests that if he is going to follow anyone, he should follow Demetrius because he had a good testimony and everybody spoke highly of him (v. 12). We need to choose carefully those whom we imitate or endorse. The lines are clearly drawn in this passage: believers are to shun evil and follow good. Those who do good are of God; those who do evil "are far from God" (v. 11 TLB). John spoke to this issue in his first epistle: "Dear children, don't let anyone deceive you about this: When people do what is right, it shows that they are righteous, even as Christ is righteous. But when people keep on sinning, it shows that they belong to the devil, who has been sinning since the beginning. But the Son of God came to destroy the works of the devil. Those who have been born into God's family do not make a practice of sinning, because God's life is in them. So they can't keep on sinning, because they are children of God" (3:7-9 NLT).

Believers are followers of the Father and imitators of Christ. Having been raised from death unto life, they practice kindness and mercy. They walk in God's grace, gain their strength from Christ, and depend on the Holy Spirit's guidance. One of their strongest attributes is their love for fellow believers—a love that springs from their love for Christ.

There is no joy comparable to being a member of the family of God and to enter into relationships that are rich and wholesome and Christlike. There is no higher plane to live on than to make Christ our model and to follow His example—indeed, in every situation, to ask, What would Jesus do?

• What is the connection between God and goodness?

"We can exert power for good, therefore, only if we are prepared to drum it into our heads that the church of Christ can never exert influence on civil society directly, only indirectly."—Abraham Kuyper

------

CONCLUSION

This lesson has raised several questions about our fellowship and hospitality. Who are your closest companions? Are you living in fellowship with the Father and with His Son, Jesus Christ? Do you enjoy fellowship with other believers? What expressions of hospitality do you show in your daily living? Does goodness and kindness play a major role in your life?

GOLDEN TEXT CHALLENGE

"IF WE WALK IN THE LIGHT, AS HE IS IN THE LIGHT, WE HAVE FELLOWSHIP ONE WITH ANOTHER, AND THE BLOOD OF JESUS CHRIST HIS SON CLEANSETH US FROM ALL SIN" (1 John 1:7).

If is the "big" little word in this scripture. It indicates something that may or may not happen. Here the power of choice lies with men and women, boys and girls.

"If we walk" indicates we must decide whether we will live in darkness or light. There is no middle ground—no partially lit paths. Either we follow Christ according to the light of the Scriptures or we walk in darkness.

If we are walking in the Light, we have a kinship with fellow believers that is not experienced elsewhere—not even in the bonds of human families —because this fellowship is spiritual and eternal. When we are adopted into relationship with God through faith in His Son, we become a brother or sister of every other believer in the world. And the blood of Jesus will keep on cleansing us—allowing us to lead a holy life—as we dedicate ourselves to His purposes.

Daily Devotions:
M. Fellowship With God Broken
   Genesis 3:8-13
T. Hospitality and Fellowship Demonstrated
   2 Kings 4:8-13
W. Fellowship Betrayed by a Friend
   Psalm 55:12-14
T. Fellowship in the Early Church
   Acts 2:41-46
F. The Limitations of Fellowship
   2 Corinthians 6:14-18
S. The Right Hand of Fellowship
   Galatians 2:6-10

Experiencing the Resurrection (Easter)

Luke 24:13-35; John 20:1-18; 21:1-23

Unit Theme:
Christ's Resurrection

Central Truth:
Because Christ is alive, we can experience a personal relationship with the living Lord.

Focus:
Examine the effects of Christ's resurrection on those who witnessed it and experience its impact.

Context:
Three accounts of the resurrected Christ ministering to individuals

Golden Text:
"That I may know him [Christ], and the power of his resurrection, and the fellowship of his sufferings, being made conformable unto his death" (Phil. 3:10).

Study Outline:
  I. Recognizing the Risen Christ
     (John 20:1, 11-18)
 II. Relationship With the Risen Christ
     (Luke 24:13-18, 26-35)
III. Restored by the Risen Christ
     (John 21:1-2,15-19)

INTRODUCTION

The Gospel narratives are like a jigsaw puzzle with some pieces missing. Anyone who has tried to put such a jigsaw puzzle together knows that it cannot be done if one insists he has all the parts in his possession and is determined to make them fit. The procedure ends in total frustration. Once, however, the person admits that some parts are missing, he can fit the rest together successfully, even though there are gaps in the picture.

For reasons of His own, God has seen fit not to tell us everything that happened in the life of our Lord. If a person persists that he has all the parts within the four Gospels, and keeps on attempting to make a perfect and complete picture, he will surely become frustrated. If, however, he will face the fact that God has not given us all the parts, and will work from this assumption, he will be able to trace out the broad outlines and some details of Christ's life.

Henry Alford expressed the following conviction: "I believe much that is now dark might be explained were the facts themselves, in order of occurrence, before us. Till that is the case (and I am willing to believe that it will be one of our delightful employments hereafter, to trace the true harmony of the Holy Gospels, under His teaching of whom they are the record), we must be content to walk by faith, and not by sight" (*The Greek Testament*).

Careful readers of the fourth Gospel are aware that John omits a great deal which the other three Gospels contain, and gives much which they omit. He does this in regard to the narrative of the Resurrection.

It would be a useful exercise each Easter for every Christian to read the complete account of the Resurrection in a harmony of the Gospels. Thus, we would all get all of the story which God has seen fit to leave us, in the sequence in which it occurred.

In today's lesson, drawing from accounts in Luke and John, we will see Mary Magdalene, Cleopas and his traveling companion, and Simon Peter have life-changing encounters with the risen Lord.

I. RECOGNIZING THE RISEN CHRIST (John 20:1, 11-18)

A. Mary Magdalene's Discovery (v. 1)

¹ The first day of the week cometh Mary Magdalene early, when it was yet dark, unto the sepulchre, and seeth the stone taken away from the sepulchre.

The Synoptic Gospels (Matthew, Mark, and Luke) state that several women made an early Sunday morning visit to Christ's tomb for the purpose of anointing His body with spices (Matt. 28:1; Mark 16:1; Luke 24:1). John mentions only Mary Magdalene. However, as MacGregor says, "John, with his love of individualizing, mentions but one woman, but, as is hinted in the next verse ('we'), there may have been others with her" (*Moffatt's Commentary on John*).

The Jewish Sabbath ended at sunset on Saturday. Mary and her friends were at the tomb of Christ before daybreak. John says "early, when it was yet dark" (v. 1). The word refers to the last of the four watches into which the night was divided, the watch which lasted from approximately 3:00 a.m. until sunrise.

The fact that the women went so early to the tomb is an indication of the way that love can conquer timidity and fear, and motivate one to action. Jenny Evelyn Mussey penetrated into the significance of this incident in the stanza, "Let me like Mary, through the gloom, come with a gift to Thee." It was not only gloom literally, but gloom also in Mary's soul, as of course in the souls of all the disciples. Her gloom was deepened when she found the tomb was empty. Without stopping to look inside the tomb with the other women (Mark 16:5-7; Luke 24:3-8), she at once turned and ran to tell Peter and John her own interpretation of what had happened: "They have taken away the Lord out of the sepulchre" (John 20:2).

• Why did Mary come to the tomb so early?

"With the stone in place, Mary would have had the problem of gaining access to the tomb; with the stone removed, she had a problem of another kind. To her mind, the situation had worsened."—*The Wycliffe Bible Commentary*

B. Mary's Sorrow (vv. 11-13)

¹¹ But Mary stood without at the sepulchre weeping: and as she wept, she stooped down, and looked into the sepulchre, ¹² And seeth two angels

in white sitting, the one at the head, and the other at the feet, where the body of Jesus had lain. [13] And they say unto her, Woman, why weepest thou? She saith unto them, Because they have taken away my Lord, and I know not where they have laid him.

John's record does not describe the reactions in Peter's mind to the staggering sight that confronted him in the tomb (vv. 6-7). Luke, however does so: "Then arose Peter, and ran unto the sepulchre; and stooping down, he beheld the linen clothes laid by themselves, and departed, wondering in himself at that which was come to pass" (Luke 24:12). His only reaction was wonder or amazement.

But let us now carefully notice the different reaction in John. Seeing, no doubt, the look of amazement on Peter's face, he also went into the tomb to see for himself, "and he saw, and believed" (John 20:8).

The question naturally arises, *Why was Mary not affected or influenced at all by the staggering discovery of Peter and John?* For this, it seems, was certainly the case. It may be that she was too full of her personal grief to understand what was happening. However, a simpler explanation, it seems, is that she was not present at the time. Mary had left the tomb on her first visit without seeing the "vision of angels" (Luke 24:23) which her women companions saw. She arrived back at the tomb only after Peter and John had left. And she was still ignorant of the truth. "She *continued standing* outside the sepulchre weeping" (John 20:11, Greek tense). The Greek word for *weeping* is a strong word implying audible crying—"sobbing, convulsed with tears."

It was her love for Christ that made Mary act like that, but it was love uninformed and unilluminated by the Truth. She was overwhelmed with her sense of personal loss. Jesus—though to her imagination, dead, stolen, vandalized—was still her "Lord," but she could not grasp that He was in the situation in which she imagined Him to be.

- Why was Mary crying?

"O for the touch of a vanished hand,
And the sound of a voice that is still!"
—Alfred Lloyd Tennyson

C. The Lord's Question (vv. 14-15)

[14] And when she had thus said, she turned herself back, and saw Jesus standing, and knew not that it was Jesus. [15] Jesus saith unto her, Woman, why weepest thou? whom seekest thou? She, supposing him to be the gardener, saith unto him, Sir, if thou have borne him hence, tell me where thou hast laid him, and I will take him away.

The reason why Mary turned away from the angels is not obvious. There must have been a reason. After all, people do not see angels every day! But when she turned, she "saw Jesus standing, and knew not that it was Jesus" (v. 14). She was so dominated by the sense of personal loneliness and grief that though the Lord was present with her, and present in such a glorious manner, she failed to recognize Him.

Why did Mary suppose Jesus was the gardener? That was the obvious conclusion, for who else would be there that early? Oh, the suppositions that have been made by Christian people to account for happenings—both good and evil—in their lives, when all the time it was Jesus!

• Why do you suppose Mary did not recognize Jesus?

D. The Lord's Revelation (vv. 16-18)

16 Jesus saith unto her, Mary. She turned herself, and saith unto him, Rabboni; which is to say, Master. 17 Jesus saith unto her, Touch me not; for I am not yet ascended to my Father: but go to my brethren, and say unto them, I ascend unto my Father, and your Father; and to my God, and your God. 18 Mary Magdalene came and told the disciples that she had seen the Lord, and that he had spoken these things unto her.

MacGregor calls this "the greatest recognition scene in all literature. . . . The speaking of her own name by Jesus calls up memories and awakens recognition."

Cold print can never convey to us what the spoken word conveyed to Mary. But we can imagine it. If at any time we have waited long and anxiously for the return of a loved one, or for a message from that person, and suddenly, when the mind is heavy and the heart is sick, he or she arrives or calls, what a flood of relief and joy it brings! All that, and more, the familiar word spoken in a familiar way meant to Mary. And all recognition and all ecstasy were in her one-word reply, "Rabboni" (Master or Teacher)!

Christ's statement "Touch me not" (v. 17) is acknowledged by all commentators as difficult to understand, and there are several explanations. Jesus, a week or so later, invited Thomas to touch Him (v. 27). Even on the Resurrection Day, as Matthew records, the women "came and held him by the feet" (Matt. 28:9). It is said that clinging to the knees or feet was an ancient mode of worship. Why, then, was Mary forbidden to touch Him?

The forms of the Greek may hold the clue: it should be rendered, "Don't keep on holding Me or clinging to Me." Mary, in her relief and overwhelming gladness at seeing Jesus alive, and probably not even comprehending the nature of His resurrection, was attempting to cling to His body. She needed to learn that the Christ of resurrection life and glory was to be approached and contacted in a different way from the preresurrected Christ.

The form of the prohibition suggests that it is but temporary: "Touch me not; for I am not yet ascended to my Father" (John 20:17). When He has ascended, it would be possible to touch Him again! Nevertheless, it would not be a touching of His physical body but a touching through the Spirit.

Moreover, what Jesus said to Mary, He said on behalf of us all. We are to "walk by faith, not by sight [or by ear or by touch]" (2 Cor. 5:7). This is the nature of Christ's relationship to humanity and their relationship to Him in this age. What it will be in the glorified state is yet to be revealed.

---

1. What did Mary call Jesus, and why (v. 16)?
2. What message was Mary given to deliver (v. 17)?

Experiencing the Resurrection

"Enjoying God's immediate presence, face to face, is the Christian's anticipation."—R. C. Sproul

---

II. RELATIONSHIP WITH THE RISEN CHRIST (Luke 24:13-18, 26-35)

A. Two Men (vv. 13-16)

13 And, behold, two of them went that same day to a village called Emmaus, which was from Jerusalem about threescore furlongs. 14 And they talked together of all these things which had happened. 15 And it came to pass, that, while they communed together and reasoned, Jesus himself drew near, and went with them. 16 But their eyes were holden that they should not know him.

The two men featured in this passage were not from the eleven disciples, and not necessarily from the Seventy who had been sent forth. They were more likely from that wider circle of disciples who were now together at Jerusalem. The name of one of them is given, Cleopas (v. 18). The other remains unnamed, and speculation about who this person was has yielded no definite conclusion.

These men were from a village called Emmaus. It was located about six-and-a-half miles west/northwest from Jerusalem.

Walking along amid the beauties of nature is often a means of sorting out life's puzzles. But the experience of these two men illustrates that nature alone cannot possibly satisfy the heart that has lost its Christ. Into the sanctuary of creation, these wanderers take the recollection of the scenes they have witnessed and the reports they have heard about their Lord.

Apparently they discussed in great detail what had happened, what they had hoped for, and how this hope had slipped away from them. They reasoned together how things could be this way and what they could make of it. And as they were deep in conversation, the Lord, in the form of a common traveler, came up behind them and began to walk with them.

They did not recognize it was the Lord. They were still thinking of Him in terms of His death, so the reality of His resurrection had not dawned on them. Moreover, they had no thought that He would appear to them and join them in their journey. In this frame of mind, how could they recognize this traveler as the crucified One? It also appears that through some supernatural means they were not allowed to discover who He was. Brooke Westcott wrote: "It is vain to give any simply natural explanation of the failure of the disciples to recognize Christ. After the Resurrection He was known as He pleased, and not necessarily at once. . . . Till they who gazed upon Him were placed in something of spiritual harmony with the Lord, they could not recognize Him."

These two disciples show us what disciples love best to talk about when they are intimately together—their Lord. After all, the living Christ is always the third person in every Christian friendship. Another thought from this event is that Jesus is already near to us, even when we believe Him to be far away.

---

threescore furlongs (v. 13)—seven and a half miles
holden (v. 16)—"restrained" (NKJV)

- What were the two travelers discussing (vv. 13-14)?

_____

B. Jesus' Question (vv. 17-18)

17 And he said unto them, What manner of communications are these that ye have one to another, as ye walk, and are sad? 18 And the one of them, whose name was Cleopas, answering said unto him, Art thou only a stranger in Jerusalem, and hast not known the things which are come to pass there in these days?

Jesus asked the two men what they were talking about and what had made them so sad. He desired to have them open up their heart to Him. What He already knew, He wished to hear from their own mouth. Then Jesus listened to them as they related what was on their heart. Cleopas sometimes spoke alone, at other times his companion spoke also, but together they told Him everything that lay so heavily upon the heart of both (vv. 19-24). What do you suppose were the emotions of Jesus as He listened to them? Perhaps He became silently displeased at their unbelief, but He must also have rejoiced at their love.

Apparently the two men thought Jesus a stranger who had been to Jerusalem to observe the Passover and was now headed home again (v. 18). They could not imagine that anyone could have been in Jerusalem for that purpose and not know what was going on. The news of the crucifixion of Jesus of Nazareth filled the whole capital as well as their own hearts, and how anyone could have missed it was beyond their comprehension.

If these two men could not imagine anyone not having knowledge of the events of the weekend, Jesus found it difficult to understand how they could be sad on such an occasion. This was not a day for sadness; it was a day for gladness. The greatest event in the history of the world had taken place, and these men did not comprehend its value and were therefore sad. Are we not guilty sometimes of forgetting the benefits God has made available to us? We sometimes carry burdens we should be letting Him carry. We sometimes dishonor Him through our lack of faith. We are not that different from these two men. Our Lord wants our full confidence, not for His sake but for ours.

_____

- Why didn't Jesus reveal His identity at first (vv. 17-18)?

_____

"There are no foolish questions and no man becomes a fool until he has stopped asking questions."—Charles Steinmetz

_____

C. The Necessity (vv. 26-27)

26 Ought not Christ to have suffered these things, and to enter into his glory? 27 And beginning at Moses and all the prophets, he expounded unto them in all the scriptures the things concerning himself.

Jesus would have the two disciples to understand that all these events were foretold. What they were offended by was inevitable. They would not have been in this state of confusion if they had given closer attention to what the prophets had said about the suffering Messiah. This suffering was necessary before the Lord should enter into His glory.

These men did not understand the connection between suffering and glory for Christ and the Christian. Suffering prepares the way for glory, suffering is transformed into glory, and suffering endured heightens the enjoyment and the worth of glory.

Verse 27 says Jesus began with Moses (the Pentateuch) and went on to the Prophets to explain what they had to say about His person and His work. We are not told what passages He used. However, there are many expressions of Jesus and the apostles in reference to the prophecies of the Messiah contained in the New Testament. Rather than presenting isolated passages of Scripture, it is likely that Jesus gave an overview of the great whole of the Old Testament in its typical and symbolical character. After all, Christ is the central theme of the entire Bible. We have missed its main message if we fail to find Him in its pages.

The appearance before these disciples is one of the strongest proofs of the high value which the Lord Jesus places upon the prophetic scriptures, and upon the predictions of His suffering and of His glory. Whoever denies either the existence or the importance of these passages finds himself not only in conflict with the believing church of all centuries but also with the Lord himself.

• What did Jesus explain?

D. Opened Eyes (vv. 28-32)

28 And they drew nigh unto the village, whither they went: and he made as though he would have gone further. 29 But they constrained him, saying, Abide with us: for it is toward evening, and the day is far spent. And he went in to tarry with them. 30 And it came to pass, as he sat at meat with them, he took bread, and blessed it, and brake, and gave to them. 31 And their eyes were opened, and they knew him; and he vanished out of their sight. 32 And they said one to another, Did not our heart burn within us, while he talked with us by the way, and while he opened to us the scriptures?

When Jesus and the two men arrived in Emmaus, He offered to continue on, but they insisted that He stay with them. Jesus probably offered the usual formula of benediction, but already they felt so close to Him that the thought of separation at this point was unendurable. They entreated Him with the utmost urgency; they invited Him in and reminded Him that the sun was about to set and that He could not possibly continue His journey in the night.

Jesus accepted their invitation and entered the house with them. When the meal was ready, they gathered at the table. Jesus took the bread, gave thanks to God before the meal, broke the bread, and gave it to the two men. It was not customary for the guests to break the bread and bless it, for this was the responsibility of the head of the house. There was, however, purpose in what Jesus was doing.

Do you think there was something in the manner in which Jesus broke the bread and uttered the blessing that caused them to associate it with their earlier acquaintance with Him? Or did they now discover in His opened hands the marks of the wounds? Did He refer them back to a word He had uttered before His death? Whatever the reason, their eyes were now opened. Suddenly, they were fully persuaded that the identity of this person was Jesus of Nazareth. By the time they recognized Him, Jesus had miraculously disappeared from sight.

After Jesus' departure, the two men discussed how they had felt as He spoke to them along the way. They had experienced an extraordinary emotion of soul as they listened to Him. Even by that experience they should have recognized the Lord. It was now incomprehensible to them that their eyes were not opened sooner. It speaks well for their inner growth that after His departure, it was not the breaking of bread but the opening of Scripture which stood out in their minds.

---

1. What caused the two men to recognize Jesus (vv. 30-31)?
2. Explain the phrase "burn within us" (v. 32).

"To know the road ahead, ask those coming back."—Chinese proverb

---

E. Eager Witness (vv. 33-35)

33 And they rose up the same hour, and returned to Jerusalem, and found the eleven gathered together, and them that were with them, 34 Saying, The Lord is risen indeed, and hath appeared to Simon. 35 And they told what things were done in the way, and how he was known of them in breaking of bread.

One of the arguments these men had used to persuade Jesus to stay at their house was that it was too late to travel. Well, it was later now than it was then. But this did not matter to these excited disciples. Even if it was midnight, they must return immediately to Jerusalem and announce the joyful message. What the women did at the express command of the angel, what Mary Magdalene did at the command of the Lord, these two disciples did at the impulse of their heart. Apparently they also left the meal untouched, and together they went to tell what had happened.

When they arrived at Jerusalem, they went to the place where the other disciples were staying. Even at this late hour, they were admitted to the company of believers. They were also greeted with some exciting news: "The Lord is risen indeed, and hath appeared to Simon." They answered this message with the narrative of what happened to them on the way and how the Lord had been recognized by them in the breaking of bread.

The attitude of these two men demonstrates that Christ is our life. How miserable life would be without Him, how rich and rewarding it can become through Him, and how yielded it must be to Him!

• How did Christ's appearance affect the two men?

III. RESTORED BY THE RISEN CHRIST (John 21:1-2, 15-19)

A. Seaside Appearance (vv. 1-2)

¹ After these things Jesus shewed himself again to the disciples at the sea of Tiberias; and on this wise shewed he himself. ² There were together Simon Peter, and Thomas called Didymus, and Nathanael of Cana in Galilee, and the sons of Zebedee, and two other of his disciples.

The phrase "after these things" (v. 1) usually marks off a distinct section in John's Gospel. It may or may not have any direct connection with what immediately precedes. The verb used here to describe Christ's appearance to the disciples is active in form and marks His appearance as depending on His own will. The manifestation took place somewhere near the Sea of Tiberias (or Sea of Galilee). The details of the revelation are recorded in the verses that follow. It is interesting that Matthew records only the appearances in Galilee; Luke and Mark, only those in Jerusalem; while John records some of both.

At the familiar location on the shore of the Galilean lake, with its many memories, the risen Christ appeared to a group of seven disciples. Since *seven* seems to be the number of divine completeness, the revelation here may have special significance. Simon Peter is well known as the spokesman for the apostles. Thomas, the onetime skeptic but now a true believer, is given special mention. Nathanael was the guileless Israelite (John 1:47). The sons of Zebedee are, of course, James and John, perhaps left unnamed and placed in this order out of modesty on the part of the author. The "two other of his disciples" (v. 2) may have been Andrew and Philip, but more likely they were not of the apostles but were, rather, as G. Campbell Morgan says, "the representatives of the great anonymous crowd in the Christian church, which constitutes here real strength."

Tiberias (v. 1)—another name for the Sea of Galilee

• What did Jesus do "again," and why?

"Christians! Dry your flowing tears,
Chase those unbelieving fears;
Look on his deserted grave,
Doubt no more his power to save."
—Collyer

B. Probing Question (vv. 15-17)

¹⁵ So when they had dined, Jesus saith to Simon Peter, Simon, son of Jonas, lovest thou me more than these? He saith unto him, Yea, Lord; thou knowest that I love thee. He saith unto him, Feed my lambs. ¹⁶ He saith to him again the second time, Simon, son of Jonas, lovest thou me? He saith unto him, Yea, Lord; thou knowest that I love thee. He saith unto him, Feed my sheep. ¹⁷ He saith unto him the third time, Simon, son of Jonas, lovest thou me? Peter was grieved because he said unto him the third time,

Lovest thou me? And he said unto him, Lord, thou knowest all things; thou knowest that I love thee. Jesus saith unto him, Feed my sheep.

After serving breakfast to the seven disciples, the Lord turned to the more serious business of probing Peter about his love for the Lord. Addressing him as "Simon, son of Jonas," Jesus recalled the examination given at their first meeting when the disciple had been addressed in like manner (Matt. 16:17-19).

The question "Lovest thou me more than these?" (John 21:15) has more than one possible meaning: (1) Do you love Me more than these other disciples love Me? (2) Do you love Me more than you love these things? or (3) Do you love Me more than you love these disciples? The first accords with Peter's previous boast of loyalty to Christ though all others would be offended (Matt. 26:33; John 13:37). It may then have been a painful reminder of his threefold denial, and provided the opportunity for a complete repentance and restoration by a three-fold affirmation of love. By the word Jesus uses for *love* (*agape*), He questions Peter's loyalty and devotion. In response, Peter appeals to Jesus' knowledge and uses another word for *love* (*phileo*) meaning "personal and natural affection." He makes no claim here of any superior love, and offers no comparison of his loyalty with that of his fellow disciples.

Jesus' commission is correctly rendered, "Tend my lambs." This suggests the shepherd's responsibility for giving tender care and support to children and young Christians, and for providing spiritual food for them. Christ apparently accepted Peter's answer and renewed His commission.

In the second question, Jesus omits the words "more than these" (v. 15), but makes use of the same word for *love* (v. 16), that is, "Do you very deeply love Me?" It is the love with understanding, and as required by the Law (Luke 10:27). Peter again responds with the word for personal and natural affection. His appeal to Jesus' knowledge indicates both humility and confidence united. Jesus again commands Peter to discharge his shepherd responsibility. He is called upon to shepherd the sheep. And this implies providing guidance and government as well as food. Peter would soon be doing this under the Chief Shepherd's direction.

For the third time Jesus probes Peter's love for Him. This time, however, the Lord condescends to use Peter's word for *love*. This is probably why Peter is "grieved" (John 21:17). Then, too, perhaps Peter would recall his threefold denial, an experience which would aggravate his grief still more. In his answer to the Lord, Peter casts himself entirely on the omniscience of Christ. He is certain that the Lord can read his heart and thus know even better than Peter himself the love in his heart.

The three verses just considered show that Peter used two different words in the original to express the knowledge of Christ. The two indicate supernatural intuition as well as to refer to experience and discernment. Again, Jesus commands His apostle to feed or tend His sheep. Note that each time Jesus refers to these sheep as His own ("my sheep"), not Peter's. Thus, undershepherds are the stewards of the Christians entrusted to them by the Chief Shepherd. No one is qualified as a spiritual shepherd who does not sincerely love the Lord Jesus Christ.

---

1. What "grieved" Peter (v. 17)?
2. What did Jesus tell Peter to do (vv. 15-17)?

"God created you for a reason; He has important work for you to do; and He's waiting patiently for you to do it. So why not begin today?"—Woodrow Kroll

C. Sobering Future (vv. 18-19)

¹⁸ Verily, verily, I say unto thee, When thou wast young, thou girdest thyself, and walkedst whither thou wouldest: but when thou shalt be old, thou shalt stretch forth thy hands, and another shall gird thee, and carry thee whither thou wouldest not. ¹⁹ This spake he, signifying by what death he should glorify God. And when he had spoken this, he saith unto him, Follow me.

In assigning to Peter his occupation as a shepherd of His sheep, Jesus made a prediction concerning the future. The apostle's love for the Lord and his responsibility as preacher and pastor would not exempt him from persecution in due time. The double *verily* introduces some solemn words. First, Jesus recalls for him his younger days, when he was alert, vigorous, independent, self-willed, and able to manage his own affairs. After meeting the Lord, however, Peter had learned dependence through some difficult experiences. As for the future, in later years, Peter would be compelled to stretch out his hands for help. Another would "gird" him (v. 18)—that is, bind him as a criminal and he would be taken against his will—not that he would be unwilling to die a martyr's death, but a violent execution as a criminal is what any man would naturally shrink from.

Since Peter's death would occur as a result of his obedience to the Lord, it was spoken of as glorifying God. Having predicted His apostle's persecution, Jesus exhorts him to "follow me" (v. 19). Although this exhortation might simply mean to follow Jesus on the seashore, its spiritual significance may be implied, especially in the light of its repetition in verse 22.

Jesus' personal examination of the apostle Peter, following the breakfast on the beach, served to restore him to full favor and fellowship with the Lord and to emphasize the motive and duty of Christian service. It is only those who truly love Christ that are fit to minister to His flock. After this important lesson, Christ exhorts Peter on the importance of personal responsibility on the part of a disciple—to follow Christ. To follow Christ is to have complete confidence in Him, to imitate Him as our example, to learn from Him whose yoke is easy and whose burden is light (Matt. 11:29-30), to obey His every command, and to suffer in fellowship with Him.

1. What did Jesus prophesy about Peter (vv. 18-19)?
2. Why do you suppose Jesus said, "Follow me" (v. 19; also see Matt. 4:18-19)?

God's Purpose

God intends to use you in wonderful, unexpected ways if you let Him. But be prepared: finding God's purpose and following it will undoubtedly require work and sacrifice—which is perfectly okay with God (because He knows the marvelous blessings that He has in store for you if you give yourself to Him).—Woodrow Kroll

CONCLUSION

Just as the risen Lord ministered to the believers in today's lesson in personalized ways, so He reaches out His scarred hands to each one of us at our point of need. Do we recognize Him? Do we have relationship with Him? Have we been restored by Him?

GOLDEN TEXT CHALLENGE

"THAT I MAY KNOW HIM [CHRIST], AND THE POWER OF HIS RESURRECTION, AND THE FELLOWSHIP OF HIS SUFFERINGS, BEING MADE CONFORMABLE UNTO HIS DEATH" (Phil. 3:10).

Suppose that fifteen years ago you deposited one thousand dollars in the bank. From that time you began withdrawing fifty dollars a month on that account, and are still doing so. But is such a thing possible? No, because you would have overdrawn the account years ago.

For this same reason, many Christians, spiritually speaking, are operating in the red. Years ago they received Christ into their heart. But all these years, they have been drawing on a beginner's experience. Instead of reading the Bible each morning for a new deposit in their soul's resources, they hurriedly eat breakfast and rush off to work, utterly unprepared to face the problems of the day.

On the other hand, I read of a man whose motto was, "No Bible; no breakfast." Like that man we should spend time every day with the Word and in prayer with the Lord. This is essential if we are to know Christ experientially.

Paul gave three essentials of how we may know Christ experientially. First, we must know "the power of [Christ's] resurrection." Only when the believer makes a complete commitment of his life to the will of God can he know this miraculous power. Second, we must know "the fellowship of [Christ's] sufferings." Complete submission to Christ does not exclude suffering. But the suffering we know is as nothing when compared with our future glory in Christ. Third, we must be "made conformable unto [Christ's] death." To live victoriously requires a daily crucifixion of oneself with Christ.

Daily Devotions:
M. Samson's Strength Restored
   Judges 16:25-30
T. Naomi's Hope Restored
   Ruth 4:13-17
W. David's Joy Restored
   Psalm 51:1-13
T. Lazarus' Life Restored
   John 11:38-44
F. Thomas' Faith Restored
   John 20:24-29
S. Saul Encounters the Risen Christ
   Acts 9:1-15

Principles of Knowing God

1 John 2:1-29

Unit Theme:
Principles for Christian Living (1, 2, 3 John)

Central Truth:
Obedience to God is the evidence that a person knows Him.

Focus:
Reflect on and cultivate an experiential knowledge of God.

Context:
Near the end of the first century AD, the elderly apostle John penned these epistles, probably writing from Ephesus.

Golden Text:
"Hereby we do know that we know him [God], if we keep his commandments" (1 John 2:3).

Study Outline:
I. Obey God's Commandments
   (1 John 2:3-14)
II. Love God, Not the World
   (1 John 2:15-19)
III. Continue in Christ
   (1 John 2:20-29)

INTRODUCTION

In today's lesson, John calls attention to several vital aspects of the Christian life. He begins by reminding us how important it is to obey God. The instructions set forth in the Word of God are not to be taken lightly. Obeying them is essential to our walk before the Lord. Throughout 1 John 2, the apostle urges his readers to abide in Christ by knowing and obeying the Word, which leads to eternal life.

Not only does this chapter show us the way to life, it reminds us that if we (having embraced life) falter along the way, God has made a provision for us: "we have an advocate with the Father, Jesus Christ the righteous" (v. 1). The writer of Hebrews said, "We have not an high priest which cannot be touched with the feeling of our infirmities; but was in all points tempted like as we are, yet without sin" (4:15). Christ sits at the right hand of the Father to plead our case. Having walked in human flesh, He knows our weaknesses. When we fall and acknowledge such before Christ, He intercedes on our behalf.

John also clearly names the sins that make up worldliness. They fall into three categories: "the lust of the flesh, and the lust of the eyes, and the pride of life" (1 John 2:16). The Father has nothing to do with these attitudes, and if that is where our heart is centered, we do not love Him.

The apostle John is the only writer in the Bible who names the person who personifies the spirit that defies God and seeks to destroy everything He represents.

John calls him the "antichrist" (v. 18). While the spirit of antichrist existed in his day, and has been present in every age, John points to a time when a diabolical person will come on the scene who will be bent on destroying all that God represents.

I. OBEY GOD'S COMMANDMENTS (1 John 2:3-14)

A. Keeping God's Commandments (vv. 3-6)

³ And hereby we do know that we know him, if we keep his commandments. ⁴ He that saith, I know him, and keepeth not his commandments, is a liar, and the truth is not in him. ⁵ But whoso keepeth his word, in him verily is the love of God perfected: hereby know we that we are in him. ⁶ He that saith he abideth in him ought himself also so to walk, even as he walked.

John wants his readers to have a right perspective about sin. In the previous chapter, he has observed that all have sinned. But this is not the end of the story. We are responsible for our sins, yet forgiveness is available to all (2:2). Christ paid the price for our sins on the cross. When we confess our sins, seeking forgiveness because we recognize that sin is not to be taken lightly, He pleads our case before the Father (v. 1).

To *know* Christ, to *love* Him, and to be *in Him* are expressions John uses to describe the relationship we should have with the Lord. If we expect Christ to be our advocate with the Father, we must be seeking to live a life that is pleasing to Him. The knowledge of God that John speaks of is more than opinion or speculation; it is a practical knowledge that leads to loving God and keeping His commandments (v. 3). The test of one's relationship with the Lord is that he or she keeps—and delights in keeping, and goes on keeping—the commandments of the Lord. This person is a true Christian.

When Christ is received and takes up residence in our soul, we will know that He is there. We are not speaking of a head knowledge alone, but of a heart experience. There is a difference! Someone said, "A religion you can get and not know it, you can lose and never miss it."

Somewhere I read this striking illustration: "Two men may sit at a table laden with delicious food—the one a doctor of chemistry with cancer of the stomach, the other a diligent laborer with a healthy appetite. The chemical expert may take the food into the laboratory, analyze it, and give a minute description of its ingredients and their nutritional value, but he cannot eat of it. The hungry laborer knows very little about the chemical composition of the meal, but he tastes its deliciousness, eats and digests it, and thus knows its power of nutrition by experience."

Even a child may appropriate Christ by faith, taste His goodness and mercy, and thus know Him.

Knowing God leads to obeying God. When God's Word becomes our roadmap on the journey of life, it shows how completely we love Him. Christ becomes our model, and we seek to live our life as Christ lived His. We cannot claim to abide in Him unless we behave like Him.

---

1. Who is a liar (v. 4)?
2. How do we "know" we are "in" God (vv. 5-6)?

"Every syllable of every statute, every clause of every commandment that ever proceeded from the mouth of God was divinely designed to bring those who would obey into the greatest imaginable happiness of heart. Don't swallow God's law like castor oil. For when you understand His intent, it will be like honey on your lips and sweetness to your soul."—Sam Storms

---

B. Observing a New Commandment (vv. 7-11)

⁷ Brethren, I write no new commandment unto you, but an old commandment which ye had from the beginning. The old commandment is the word which ye have heard from the beginning. ⁸ Again, a new commandment I write unto you, which thing is true in him and in you: because the darkness is past, and the true light now shineth. ⁹ He that saith he is in the light, and hateth his brother, is in darkness even until now. ¹⁰ He that loveth his brother abideth in the light, and there is none occasion of stumbling in him. ¹¹ But he that hateth his brother is in darkness, and walketh in darkness, and knoweth not whither he goeth, because that darkness hath blinded his eyes.

John assures his readers that he is not coming to them with some novel idea they had never heard. The commandment to love God came out of the Old Testament and was something they had known from the time of their conversion. What is new is the extent to which they are to love one another. John is referring to Jesus' statement in John 13:34: "Love one another; as I have loved you." Christ's followers are to love one another to the degree that Christ loved them . . . and that love extended to His death on the cross.

The apostle makes a strong statement in verse 9 of the text: A believer cannot walk in the light of Christ and hate a fellow Christian. Christ is the light of life, and light and love go hand in hand. At the same time, darkness and hatred are in the same camp. To claim to walk in the light and hate another believer is contrary to the design and nature of the gospel. The genuineness of a believer's faith is seen in a right relationship with God and with fellow believers. Jesus said, "By this all will know that you are My disciples, if you have love for one another" (John 13:35 NKJV).

There may be several reasons for disliking the ways of another believer. We may find another person to be too talkative, or too critical, or too self-absorbed, or too infatuated with their station in life, or too much of a name-dropper. But none of these reasons for disliking a person should ever be elevated to the level of not loving him or her. Jesus is our example. He loved His disciples even when their attitudes and actions were wrong. Clearly, Jesus' heart went out to them, and He longed to see them choose the right path.

The person who walks in Christ's light lays no stumbling block in the way of others, and just as important, avoids all stumbling blocks in his or her own way (v. 10). That person sees plainly the way of the Lord and walks in the light.

---

1. Explain the statement "The darkness is past, and the true light now shineth" (v. 8).

---

2. Explain the statement "There is nothing in him to make him stumble" (v. 10 NIV).
3. Who is living in darkness (v. 11)?

Follow the Light

One night, during a visit to India, journalist Lee Strobel and his group needed to travel from one rural village to another. There were no street lights or well-marked roads. Their guide was a young Indian man who carried a small lantern.

Lee became impatient with the group's slow pace, so he decided to step out of the lighted path and walk on ahead. But as soon as Lee stepped out of the light, he tumbled down a steep embankment into a dry riverbed.

Lee remarks that this experience gave him a deeper appreciation for Psalm 119:105: "Your word is a lamp to guide my feet and a light for my path" (NLT).—*God's Outrageous Claims*

C. Offering Words of Reassurance (vv. 12-14)

(1 John 2:12-14 is not included in the printed text.)

John addresses three sections of the Christian family in this passage. First, he speaks to "little children," representing all those whose sins have been forgiven, for this is the starting point of the Christian life (v. 12). All believers share the blessing of sins forgiven. Our forgiveness is based on the mercy and grace of God through the shedding of Christ's blood on Calvary, and the fact that God found His sacrifice satisfactory to cover our sins and purchase our redemption. There was no merit in us that would purchase our salvation, nor service or works that could render us acceptable before the Father; only the blood of Jesus would suffice. His redemptive work covers all our sins.

Second, John focuses on "fathers," representing those who are mature in the faith (v. 13). These have known Christ and grown in Him over a long period of time. Those who have served God the longest should have a better understanding of the reach of His love. How many of us, like Peter, would have faltered except that Christ interceded on our behalf? How many of us, like the Prodigal Son, have strayed only to have Him receive us back with open arms? How many of us, like John Mark, have given up in the heat of the battle only to be welcomed back to the battle with the sense that we are an important part of the Kingdom?

Third, he refers to "young men," representing those who are newcomers to the faith (v. 14). He rejoices that they are strong in the Word, and have overcome evil and the Evil One. From time to time, through the aid of the Holy Spirit, we all have encountered the Evil One and overcome him; but he is relentless in his efforts to destroy our witness. We must be forever vigilant in resisting the forces of evil, and always consistent in trusting in the Lord to make us overcomers.

---

1. According to verse 12, why does God forgive sins?
2. Describe the overcoming power believers have in Christ (vv. 13-14).

"God knows our situation; He will not judge us as if we had no difficulties to overcome. What matters is the sincerity and perseverance of our will to overcome them."—C. S. Lewis

---

II. LOVE GOD, NOT THE WORLD (1 John 2:15-19)
A. Warning About the World (vv. 15-16)

[15] Love not the world, neither the things that are in the world. If any man love the world, the love of the Father is not in him. [16] For all that is in the world, the lust of the flesh, and the lust of the eyes, and the pride of life, is not of the Father, but is of the world.

The term *world* can refer to the inhabitants of the planet or the creation itself. In both cases, it is the object of God's love. God loved the world so much that He gave His Son to provide redemption for humanity. Christ is both the Light of the world and the Savior of the world. He is the Lamb of God who takes away the sin of the world. As to Creation, God made the world and He made it well. Jesus acknowledged the beauty of Creation when He pointed to the lilies of the field and said, "Even Solomon in all his glory was not arrayed like one of these" (Matt. 6:29).

But the "world" John is talking about is all together different than the world described above. The "world" John speaks of is a society organized on wrong principles, based on wrong values, and devoted to false gods. John identifies three elements of the fallen world: the lust of the flesh, the lust of the eyes, and the pride of life.

The *lust of the flesh* may be described as craving physical pleasures. The apostle Paul wrote: "Now the works of the flesh are evident, which are: adultery, fornication, uncleanness, lewdness, idolatry, sorcery, hatred, contentions, jealousies, outbursts of wrath, selfish ambitions, dissensions, heresies, envy, murders, drunkenness, revelries, and the like; of which I tell you beforehand, just as I also told you in time past, that those who practice such things will not inherit the kingdom of God" (Gal. 5:19-21 NKJV).

The *lust of the eyes* may be thought of as wanting everything we see. It speaks of an appetite for great wealth and possessions, but never satisfied with what we have. It is the same attitude Solomon had when he listed the things he had gathered to himself and finally summed it up by saying, "Whatsoever mine eyes desired I kept not from them" (Eccl. 2:10). In the end, he determined that it was all "vanity and vexation of spirit" (v. 11).

The *pride of life* is an attitude that seeks to show oneself to be more than what one is; it represents an exaggerated sense of one's importance. The self-exalting posture that lords it over other people is out of step with Christ's instructions to His disciples. In contrast to the Gentiles around them, Jesus said to His disciples, "Whoever desires to become great among you, let him be your servant" (Matt. 20:26 NKJV).

• Why can we not love both God and the world?

"If loving God with one's whole being is the greatest commandment, then not to do so must be the greatest sin—indeed, the root of all sin."—Dave Hunt

---

B. Doing God's Will (v. 17)

¹⁷ And the world passeth away, and the lust thereof: but he that doeth the will of God abideth for ever.

The reader is confronted with a choice of lifestyles: to embrace this world system and the temporary pleasures it offers or to walk with God and reap eternal benefits. John realized that his world is passing away, and all the things that people desire and seek after are going with it: the lust of the flesh, the lust of the eyes, and the pride of life. None of the things that are anchored in this world can follow us beyond the grave. Why should anyone place their interests and ambitions in such a perishable order? An inordinate love of the world, when it fails, leaves people bitter and sorrowful. The objects of lust are fleeting things that are eventually taken away. Beauty fades with the passing of time; riches can be wiped out with one catastrophic illness; honors bestowed are soon forgotten; and the pleasures of sin are for but a season.

What a different picture walking in the will of God offers. When we put our trust in the never-changing God, pleasing Him and doing those things that advance His kingdom become the motivations for our life. What joy it brings to us to know we are part of a never-fading, unshakable order. When the world and all its lusts are gone, the kingdom of God will still stand. Thus, Jesus admonishes us, "Seek first the kingdom of God and His righteousness, and all these things [the basic needs of life] shall be added to you" (Matt. 6:33 NKJV).

The individual who loves God and does His will shall enjoy what he or she loves forever.

• Contrast the world with the Christian (v. 17).

"It comes to my having the mind of God, do I want to be like Christ in everything? If born of God, I have power to overcome all that is not of God, and to walk according to God."—G. V. Wigram

---

C. Coming of Antichrists (vv. 18-19)

¹⁸ Little children, it is the last time: and as ye have heard that antichrist shall come, even now are there many antichrists; whereby we know that it is the last time. ¹⁹ They went out from us, but they were not of us; for if they had been of us, they would no doubt have continued with us: but they went out, that they might be made manifest that they were not all of us.

John is the only biblical writer who uses the term *antichrist*, but the idea expressed by this term is found in other portions of Scripture. Perhaps Paul described him best in writing to the Thessalonians: "Let no one deceive you by any means; for that Day will not come unless the falling away comes first, and the man of sin is revealed, the son of perdition, who opposes and exalts himself above all that is called God or that is worshiped, so that he sits as God in the temple of God, showing himself that he is God" (2 Thess. 2:3-4 NKJV).

Long before the appearance of the Man of Sin himself, many individuals who operate in the antichrist spirit will surface. John was aware of their presence in his day. Jesus also warned about them: "For many shall come in my name, saying, I am Christ; and shall deceive many. . . . For there shall arise false Christs, and false prophets, and shall shew great signs and wonders; insomuch that, if it were possible, they shall deceive the very elect" (Matt. 24:5, 24).

Our day is no different than other times. The spirit of antichrist is seen today in the work of false teachers and false prophets. The closer we come to the end of the age, the stronger this evil influence is felt. It appears that the stage is being set for this Man of Sin to take center stage and carry out his diabolical schemes.

Some of those who showed the spirit of antichrist in John's day had identified themselves with believers. They made up part of the local church. By their departure from the local assembly, they revealed their true colors. They were not merely backsliders, they were apostates. Their purpose was to disrupt and destroy from within. They had turned their back on the truth and chosen to propagate a lie. May we be as discerning about those in our day who fall into this category as John was in his day.

- Where did the antichrists John mentions come from? What was their purpose?

"The best way in the world to deceive believers is to cloak a message in religious language and declare that it conveys some new insight from God."—Charles Stanley

---

III. CONTINUE IN CHRIST (1 John 2:20-29)

A. Knowing the Truth (vv. 20-25)

20 But ye have an unction from the Holy One, and ye know all things. 21 I have not written unto you because ye know not the truth, but because ye know it, and that no lie is of the truth. 22 Who is a liar but he that denieth that Jesus is the Christ? He is antichrist, that denieth the Father and the Son. 23 Whosoever denieth the Son, the same hath not the Father: (but) he that acknowledgeth the Son hath the Father also. 24 Let that therefore abide in you, which ye have heard from the beginning. If that which ye have heard from the beginning shall remain in you, ye also shall continue in the Son, and in the Father. 25 And this is the promise that he hath promised us, even eternal life.

We sometimes think of the anointing of the Holy Spirit as the exclusive right of the minister behind the pulpit, but the anointing is the birthright of every believer. The Holy Spirit opens up the Word to us and leads us to a knowledge of the truth. Jesus made this clear when He said, "But the Helper, the Holy Spirit, whom the Father will send in My name, He will teach you all things, and bring to your remembrance all things that I said to you" (John 14:26 NKJV). Jesus added,

"When He, the Spirit of truth, has come, He will guide you into all truth; for He will not speak on His own authority, but whatever He hears He will speak; and He will tell you things to come" (16:13 NKJV). So, the believer, taught by the Spirit, knows the difference between the truth and lies.

The greatest lie Satan has perpetrated on the human race is the denial of the truth that is the heart and soul of Christianity—Jesus is the Christ, the Son of God, who became a man, being born from a virgin's womb. Whoever denies that wonderful truth is operating in the spirit of antichrist, which not only denies Christ but also denies the Father. Such a denial strikes at the foundation of the gospel. This is a grievous error.

The only way to have continual communion with the Father and the Son is to embrace the truth about them clearly set forth in the Scripture. There are certain truths which we embraced at conversion, and we must hold on to them. Times may change; cultures may change; all things around us may change; but the Word of God remains steadfast and true. It is not enough to start well and then drift away; we must persevere in the faith and finish strong. Those who remain true to the gospel and faithful to Christ are assured of eternal life. That should be enough motivation to keep us on the right track and take us to our glorious heavenly home.

---

1. What is "an unction from the Holy One," and why is it needed (vv. 20-21)?
2. According to verse 23, who has the Son? Who has the Father?
3. What are the "beginning" truths (v. 24) to which believers must cling, and what will the result be?

"Trying to do the Lord's work in your own strength is the most confusing, exhausting, and tedious of all work. But when you are filled with the Holy Spirit, then the ministry of Jesus just flows out of you."—Corrie ten Boom

---

B. Receiving the Anointing (vv. 26-27)

26 These things have I written unto you concerning them that seduce you. 27 But the anointing which ye have received of him abideth in you, and ye need not that any man teach you: but as the same anointing teacheth you of all things, and is truth, and is no lie, and even as it hath taught you, ye shall abide in him.

In John's day as in ours, there were false teachers who were clever enough to deceive the followers of Christ and lead them astray. But John teaches here, and elsewhere, that God has given us safeguards against such destructive outside influences. The Lord has provided believers all that we need to see through those who would deceive us and to understand the truth. First, we have abiding within us the One who said, "I am . . . the truth" (John 14:6). The second safeguard we have is the presence within us of "the Spirit of truth" (16:13). Third, we have the Word of God to give us understanding of the truth, for Jesus said when praying for His disciples, "Sanctify them in the truth; Your word is truth" (17:17 NASB). The Holy Spirit unlocks the wonders of the Word.

So, we do not need the aid of some outside force to teach us the truth. But we do need to be taught by those who share the same anointing we have. The body of Christ, operating in the Spirit of God with the anointing of the Lord, is able to discern truth. As long as we abide in Christ, He will enable us to recognize and reject falsehood by discerning whatever is incompatible with the truth.

• What difference does the Holy Spirit's anointing make in a believer's life (vv. 26-27)?

"To the individual believer indwelt by the Holy Spirit there is granted the direct impression of the Spirit of God on the spirit of man, imparting the knowledge of His will in matters of the smallest and greatest importance. This has to be sought and waited for."—G. Campbell Morgan

---

C. Abiding in Christ (vv. 28-29)

28 And now, little children, abide in him; that, when he shall appear, we may have confidence, and not be ashamed before him at his coming. 29 If ye know that he is righteous, ye know that every one that doeth righteousness is born of him.

Abiding in Christ involves more than embracing a creed or endorsing a set of beliefs; it also includes living right. By righteous living, believers give evidence that they have been born again. By abiding in Christ, we will have confidence to stand before Him at His appearing. In fact, we will be able to welcome Him with open arms. Even now we are encouraged to "come boldly unto the throne of grace, that we may obtain mercy, and find grace to help in time of need" (Heb. 4:16). Imagine how wonderful it will be to meet Jesus face-to-face and bask in the glory of His presence. John gave us a glimpse of that moment when he said, "Beloved, now are we the sons of God, and it doth not yet appear what we shall be: but we know that, when he shall appear, we shall be like him; for we shall see him as he is. And every man that hath this hope in him purifieth himself, even as he is pure" (1 John 3:2-3).

The Bible speaks of a time when the wicked will flee to the rocks and mountains in fear and trembling, trying to hide from the presence of the Lord (Hos. 10:8; Luke 23:30). What a different posture believers will have! We can stand boldly in His presence not because of anything we have done, but because we have been washed in the blood of the Lamb and have been accepted in Him. Those who, by His grace, have remained faithful to Him and persevered to the end will have a joyful account to give on that day. As Paul urged, "My beloved brethren, be ye stedfast, unmoveable, always abounding in the work of the Lord, forasmuch as ye know that your labour is not in vain in the Lord" (1 Cor. 15:58).

---

1. What is the greatest "confidence" a person can have (v. 28)?
2. Who has been born again (v. 29)?

"Don't let obstacles along the road to eternity shake your confidence in God's promise. The Holy Spirit is God's seal that you will arrive."—David Jeremiah

CONCLUSION

Are you abiding in Christ? Do your lifestyle and actions support your answer? Will you stand ashamed before the Lord on that Judgment Day, or will you welcome that moment with open arms? Are you prepared to meet the Lord? A glorious day is coming, and it behooves each of us to be ready for that occasion.

GOLDEN TEXT CHALLENGE

"HEREBY WE DO KNOW THAT WE KNOW HIM [GOD], IF WE KEEP HIS COMMANDMENTS" (1 John 2:3).

God is light. The opposite of light is darkness. God's light provides us a candle by which we walk through the darkness of this life.

Also, since He is light, He exposes anything that lurks in the darkness. Sin cannot continue where His light shines. Thus, if we have a real relationship with the Lord, He is constantly exposing areas of darkness in our lives. To maintain our relationship with Him, we must put aside anything He exposes. If we don't, we are living a lie in claiming a relationship with Him. Such hypocrisy will ultimately be exposed.

However, if we confess any sin He exposes, the blood of Jesus Christ will cleanse us.

Daily Devotions:
M. Growing in Knowledge of God
   Exodus 33:12-23
T. Knowing God Through Obedience
   Deuteronomy 6:1-9
W. Knowing God Through Intimate Worship
   Psalm 100:1-5
T. Eternal Life Is Knowing God
   John 17:1-5
F. Knowing the "Unknown" God
   Acts 17:22-31
S. Knowing Christ's Power and Sufferings
   Philippians 3:7-11

Living as Children of God

1 John 3:1-18

Unit Theme:
Principles for Christian Living (1, 2, 3 John)

Central Truth:
God's children are to reflect His character.

Focus:
Realize and appreciate that Christians are children of God.

Context:
Near the end of the first century AD, the elderly apostle John penned these epistles, probably writing from Ephesus.

Golden Text:
"My little children, let us not love in word, neither in tongue; but in deed and in truth" (1 John 3:18).

Study Outline:
I. God's Children Identified
   (1 John 3:1-6)
II. God's Children Characterized by Holiness
    (1 John 3:7-10)
III. God's Children Characterized by Love
     (1 John 3:11-18)

INTRODUCTION

Today's lesson teaches the value and beauty of being children of God. We are the objects of God's love, a thought that is almost beyond our comprehension. But the world looks at Christians differently, sometimes with disdain, because we adhere to a higher standard and answer to a higher power. When we are treated adversely by those around us, we must remember that God loves us with a love we cannot fathom.

When we were received into the family of God, we became a new creation. The change that began at conversion has grown with the passing years and will culminate in a complete likeness of Christ at His appearing. There is no way for us to grasp what lies in store for us when we reach the other side.

Being a child of God calls for a life of purity. Therefore, we renounce sin and, if we do commit sin, ask for His forgiveness and turn away from any wrongdoing. As children of the Lord, we live righteously.

There are two groups of children in the world: the children of God and the children of the devil. Those who practice sin are not part of the household of God; their allegiance is to Satan. Our challenge as believers is to influence as many people as possible to abandon the kingdom of Satan for the kingdom of God.

A vital characteristic of the children of God is our love for one another. Jesus identified this attribute as a sign of true discipleship. It is also one of the standards by which the world understands we are followers of Christ. This love which emanates from Christ manifests itself in deeds of kindness toward others. No true believer can see another believer in need without showing love and compassion toward that individual. This means more than just speaking words of comfort; it involves providing for the needs of the person if we have the ability to do so. In doing good toward others, we gain the favor of God. He will not fail to reward such actions, even though it is not being done for recognition.

I. GOD'S CHILDREN IDENTIFIED (1 John 3:1-6)

A. Children of God (v. 1)

¹ Behold, what manner of love the Father hath bestowed upon us, that we should be called the sons of God: therefore the world knoweth us not, because it knew him not.

In this passage, we are confronted with two views of the believer: the view of the Father and that of the world. The Father sees believers as His children, and that view stems from His love. John would have us consider how great the love of God is that He would adopt us into His family, even though we were totally unworthy. There is no love higher than the divine love that reaches down and lifts us up. When we remember how insignificant we are and how insensitive we have been as sinners, we stand amazed at the love which would welcome us into the household of God. If the child of the poorest man in the world was adopted by the greatest monarch who ever lived, it would not be an honor as great as that of being adopted as a child of God.

What was said of Israel concerning their day of restoration can be said of all believers: "Yet the number of the children of Israel shall be as the sand of the sea, which cannot be measured or numbered. And it shall come to pass in the place where it was said to them, 'You are not My people,' there it shall be said to them, 'You are sons of the living God'" (Hos. 1:10 NKJV). God transforms "nobodies" into "somebodies"—into children of the living God.

The world does not understand who we are nor what motivates us. We are a mystery to them. Believers are not governed by the world's ways; we get our marching orders from the Lord. We look to the Word of God for our standard of living. Our principles and lifestyle are different from those of the world, and sometimes that leads unbelievers to react to us harshly. But should we be surprised? They did not understand the Lord either.

• Why can't the world understand Christians?

"What an incredible witness it is to a lost and fearful society when the Christian acts like a child of God, living under the loving sovereignty of the heavenly Father."—Henry Blackaby

---

B. Children of Hope (vv. 2-3)

² Beloved, now are we the sons of God, and it doth not yet appear what we shall be: but we know that, when he shall appear, we shall be like him;

for we shall see him as he is. ³ **And every man that hath this hope in him purifieth himself, even as he is pure.**

In our present state, it is sometimes difficult to fathom what the Lord has done in us. The change He has wrought is so great that we are incapable of fully grasping what it all means. We do know that the old life of sin has passed away and we have been given a new life of peace, love, and holiness. If we have a problem fully realizing what we are and who we are in Christ in the present, imagine how much more difficult it is to picture what we will be in the future. Presently, we have been regenerated and we are growing in our Christian walk, but then we will be completely transformed into His likeness.

John readily acknowledges that he does not know everything about our future, but he does know we will be like Christ. The apostle also knows that Christ will appear and believers will see Him with unveiled faces beholding His glory. That glimpse of Him in glory will result in our becoming finally and completely like Him. We will be with Christ, and we will be like Him.

We can face the future with the same assurance Job had, who said, "After my body has decayed, yet in my body I will see God! I will see him for myself. Yes, I will see him with my own eyes. I am overwhelmed at the thought!" (19:26-27 NLT). In heaven, we will not be dependent on secondhand knowledge as it relates to Jesus; we will see Him for ourselves.

We rejoice at the descriptions given to us by John and Paul and others about Christ, but in that day we will behold Him in His glory and personally reach our conclusions about Him. Those conclusions will lead us to fall at His feet in adoration. We will enjoy the same satisfaction the psalmist anticipated when he said, "As for me, I will see Your face in righteousness; I shall be satisfied when I awake in Your likeness" (17:15 NKJV).

This hope of seeing Him, being with Him, and being made like Him is incentive enough to live a life of purity, one that is modeled after Jesus. Eugene Peterson paraphrases it this way: "All of us who look forward to his Coming stay ready, with the glistening purity of Jesus' life as a model for our own" (1 John 3:3 TM).

---

1. What does it mean to be a child of God in this life? What will it mean after this life?
2. How does someone "purify himself" (v. 3)?

"He who counts the very hairs of our heads and suffers not a sparrow to fall without Him, takes note of the minutest matters that can affect the lives of His children, and regulates them all according to His perfect will, let their origin be what they may."—Hannah Whitall Smith

---

C. Nature of Sin (vv. 4-6)

⁴ **Whosoever committeth sin transgresseth also the law: for sin is the transgression of the law. ⁵ And ye know that he was manifested to take away our sins; and in him is no sin. ⁶ Whosoever abideth in him sinneth not: whosoever sinneth hath not seen him, neither known him.**

Whether you practice righteousness or practice sin, it defines you in relation to God. The first is acceptable in His sight; the second is not. Simply put, sin is rebellion against God. Although we live under grace, the law still defines sin and shows us God's standard of living for His people (v. 4). When we rebel against the standard God has set in His Word, we are guilty of sin. It doesn't matter who a person is—high or low, rich or poor, famous or infamous—if that person rebels against the law of God, he or she is guilty of sin.

So what do we do about this sin problem? This is where we need help from Someone who is greater than we are. Christ came into the world to take away our sins, something He alone could do (v. 5). By the shedding of His blood on Calvary, Christ accomplished what all the blood of sacrificial animals had not been able to do. When we accept Him into our heart, He washes away all our sin and makes us acceptable to the Father. Christ was guilty of no sin; therefore, His death on the cross was not in His own behalf, but rather for us that we might become like Him.

John goes a step further and says those who abide in Christ do not practice sin (v. 6). This does not mean they are incapable of sinning or that they never sin. If believers never sinned, there would be no need for the provision of an Intercessor who pleads our case before the Father (see Heb. 4:16; 7:25; 1 John 2:1-2). Clearly, the norm for the Christian life is that we do not sin; but if we do sin and confess it, God "is faithful and just to forgive us our sins, and to cleanse us from all unrighteousness" (1 John 1:9). The apostle would have us understand that those who practice a sinful lifestyle do not know Christ.

---

1. What is sin (v. 4)?
2. Why is Jesus able to take away our sin (v. 5)?

"We must keep from sin. If Christ has indeed saved us from sin, we cannot bear the thought of falling into it. Those who take delight in sin are not the children of God. If you are a child of God, you hate it with a perfect hatred, and your very soul loathes it."—Charles Spurgeon

---

II. GOD'S CHILDREN CHARACTERIZED BY HOLINESS (1 John 3:7-10)

A. Children of Righteousness (v. 7)

7 Little children, let no man deceive you: he that doeth righteousness is righteous, even as he is righteous.

What a comforting thought that believers who do what is right are righteous. They are following the example of the Lord. We do not need to be deceived about this: pretenders are not righteous. They may boast of their good deeds and may be applauded by others, but unless they are in a right relationship with God, they are not righteous.

We do right only when we are in a right relationship with the Lord. Character precedes conduct. Sometimes we are guilty of only seeing what one does without regard for the motives behind the action. *Why* something is done is as important as *what* is done. How many times did Jesus call out the Pharisees for their hypocrisy? On the surface, it appeared they were righteous, doing religious deeds—praying, tithing, giving alms—but the Lord looked deeper and saw what they were doing was only for show. They were more interested in having the approval of people than the praise of God (see Matt. 23:23-28). We do well to pause and ask ourselves why we do what we do. Are we following the example of Jesus and seeking to glorify His name? If our motives are pure and our actions designed to honor the Lord, great will be our reward. We should be ever mindful that as we travel on this journey of life, God is at the end of the journey. We will answer to Him as to how we have made the journey. If our walk is a walk of righteousness, we will hear Him say, "Well done."

• What deception has fooled some people?

"The same Christian activity can be either an expression of our own righteousness that we think earns favor with God, or it can be an expression of love and gratitude because we already have His favor through the righteousness of Christ."—Jerry Bridges

---

B. Children of the Devil (vv. 8-9)

8 He that committeth sin is of the devil; for the devil sinneth from the beginning. For this purpose the Son of God was manifested, that he might destroy the works of the devil. 9 Whosoever is born of God doth not commit sin; for his seed remaineth in him: and he cannot sin, because he is born of God.

If we trace sin back to its origin, our search takes us to the devil (v. 8). He was the first being in the universe to sin, and he hasn't stopped. He is still the primary practitioner of sin, and he seeks to get all of humanity to follow in his footsteps. Those who practice sin as the devil does are said to be his children. The reference here is to those who live in sin, who keep on sinning, who make sin a daily practice of their life. To live this way is to go against all that Christ came to eliminate. Christ will ultimately destroy the devil and his works. Satan is an eternally defeated foe; Christ took care of him on Calvary. Not only did He destroy the works of the devil, He made it possible that righteousness might be established in the hearts of people. All who are born again should practice righteousness internally, externally, and with resolute determination.

Believers become partakers of the divine nature, and thereafter sin and sinning are foreign to their nature (v. 9). Again, this does not mean we become incapable of sinning or that we will never falter along the way; otherwise, there would be no need for the many warnings in Scripture to avoid wrongdoing. However, as children of God, we long to please Him. Our whole outlook on life has changed. The things we once loved, we now hate. The grace of God sustains us, and the Spirit of God enables us to withstand the temptations of the devil. John made a comforting and powerful statement about the Lord's care for His own: "We know that God's children do not make a practice of sinning, for God's Son holds them securely, and the evil one cannot touch them" (5:18 NLT).

---

1. How did Jesus Christ "destroy the works of the devil" (v. 8)?
2. Explain the phrase "His seed remains in him" (v. 9 NKJV).

"Satan doth not tempt God's children because they have sin in them, but because they have grace in them. Had they no grace, the devil would not disturb them. . . . Though to be tempted is a trouble, yet to think why you are tempted is a comfort."—Thomas Watson

---

C. A Simple Test (v. 10)

¹⁰ In this the children of God are manifest, and the children of the devil: whosoever doeth not righteousness is not of God, neither he that loveth not his brother.

We are either the children of God or the children of the devil; and John gives us criteria by which we may distinguish one from the other. It is not determined by our belonging to a certain church or following a certain creed. Believers are set apart from unbelievers by our daily practice of righteousness. Another mark that distinguishes the true from the false is love for all Christians.

Believers demonstrate their righteousness by their works done in love. It is not enough to do good deeds; it is the love behind them that makes them acceptable to the Lord. While works of righteousness prove we are the children of God, they are not done to be seen of others. Only when they are done to the glory of God do they become a witness to our relationship with the Lord. When we do the right thing and our motive is love, it will always bring glory to God.

Righteousness and love coexist in the Father and were manifested in the Son. They are equally a part of the makeup of every Christian. Love for fellow believers is as much a part of being a child of God as is the practice of righteousness. In fact, those who call themselves believers and do not treat other Christians with love are deceiving themselves. Believers make up the body of Christ. How can we say that we love the Lord if we do not love the members of His body?

• Contrast the children of God with the children of Satan.

"A righteous man may make a righteous work, but no work of an unrighteous man can make him righteous. Now we become righteous only by faith, through the righteousness of Christ imputed to us."—Thomas Boston

---

III. GOD'S CHILDREN CHARACTERIZED BY LOVE (1 John 3:11-18)

A. Children of Love (vv. 11-15)

¹¹ For this is the message that ye heard from the beginning, that we should love one another. ¹² Not as Cain, who was of that wicked one, and slew his brother. And wherefore slew he him? Because his own works were evil, and his brother's righteous. ¹³ Marvel not, my brethren, if the world hate you. ¹⁴ We know that we have passed from death unto life, because we love the brethren. He that loveth not his brother abideth in

death. **¹⁵ Whosoever hateth his brother is a murderer: and ye know that no murderer hath eternal life abiding in him.**

The apostle continues to stress the importance of loving one another. Cain, Adam's son, is an example of what happens when jealousy, envy, and hatred take possession of an individual. Abel, Cain's brother, was a righteous man who lived righteously and, for this reason, found acceptance in God's eyes. Sensing that "the Lord had regard for Abel and for his offering," but "for Cain and for his offering He had no regard" (Gen. 4:4-5 NASB), Cain murdered his brother in a fit of rage. John uses this example to say if we hate our brother or sister, we have committed murder in our heart (1 John 3:15).

Drawing from Cain's example, John advises his readers not to be surprised if the world hates them (v. 13). By "the world," the apostle means unbelievers who oppose Christians. They subscribe to an ungodly system inspired by the devil himself. This kind of opposition did not begin in John's day, and it will not end in our day. From Adam's time, there has been enmity between the offspring of the Serpent and the offspring of the woman (Gen. 3:15). If we think our day is going to be any different than other times, we are mistaken. At the same time, whenever Satan has made war against the saints, the grace of God has been sufficient to carry them through the battle and to ultimate victory. Also, history shows that when persecution against the saints has been the greatest, believers have bonded together and grown in their love for each other.

When we have been born of God, loving our Christian brothers and sisters becomes natural (1 John 3:14). It is also evident that we have passed from spiritual death to a life of righteousness. Jesus said, "By this all will know that you are My disciples, if you have love for one another" (John 13:35 NKJV). If we do not love our brothers and sisters, we do not have the life of God in us. We may be members of the church . . . may have been baptized . . . may be doing many of the right things; but if we do not have love in our heart for others, we are still dead in our sins and do not have the favor of the Father or the Son.

---

1. What motivated Cain to murder his own brother (v. 12)?
2. How do "we know that we have passed from death unto life" (v. 14)?
3. How serious is the sin of hatred (v. 15)?

It Is Enough

According to the church father Jerome, the aging apostle John always uttered the same address to the church: "My little children, love one another." When the believers asked him why he always repeated the same thing, he replied, "Because it is the commandment of the Lord, and if this one thing be attained, it is enough."—*Jamieson, Fausset, and Brown Commentary*

B. The Outworking of Love (vv. 16-17)

¹⁶ Hereby perceive we the love of God, because he laid down his life for us: and we ought to lay down our lives for the brethren. ¹⁷ But whoso hath this world's good, and seeth his brother have need, and shutteth up his bowels of compassion from him, how dwelleth the love of God in him?

Jesus died that whoever believes on Him might be saved and enjoy eternal life. In this passage, John makes that reality very personal. He reminds his readers that Jesus died for them. We should all view Calvary in that light. He died for each of us individually. In dying for us, Jesus showed us what real love is. We should be so deeply influenced by His example as to be willing to lay down our lives for our fellow believers should He call upon us to do so. Priscilla and Aquila are examples of what John is talking about. Of them, Paul said, "They once risked their lives for me. I am thankful to them, and so are all the Gentile churches" (Rom. 16:4 NLT). Paul spoke of his willingness to be executed in the service of the Lord: "But I will rejoice even if I lose my life, pouring it out like a liquid offering to God, just like your faithful service is an offering to God. And I want all of you to share that joy" (Phil. 2:17 NLT).

In 1 John 3:17, John raises the sobering question that if we have the means to help a brother or sister who is in need and show no compassion toward them, how can the love of God reside in us? A Christian not only *desires* to do good, but as much as he has the ability to do so, he actually *does* good. If God's love lives within us, we will do what we can to make life better for others. Seeing the needs of others involves more than just a passing glance; it involves taking the time to see clearly the circumstances they are facing and then determining what we can do about it. When we do that, we are loving them like God sacrificially loved us.

• Why should we "lay down our lives for the brethren," and how (vv. 16-17)?

"The power of God through His Spirit will work within us to the degree that we permit it."—Mrs. Charles E. Cowman

---

C. Deeds of Love (v. 18)

18 My little children, let us not love in word, neither in tongue; but in deed and in truth.

John concludes this section with a strong plea that we "not merely say that we love each other; let us show the truth by our actions" (NLT). That is another way of saying that actions speak louder than words. Love is more than talk; it involves doing. It is not enough to make verbal expressions of love; those expressions need to be backed up with deeds. James addressed this issue in these words: "Suppose you see a brother or sister who has no food or clothing, and you say, "Good-bye and have a good day; stay warm and eat well"—but then you don't give that person any food or clothing. What good does that do?" (James 2:15-16 NLT).

If we love people as Jesus loved them, we will want to help them. We will not be satisfied with a pat on the back or a kindly word of well-wishing. This does not mean we should never speak words of encouragement; it only means we should not stop there. There are many ways we can help others, and it doesn't always involve finances. Loving in deed and in truth has far-reaching implications. It includes bearing one another's burdens, forgiving one another, praying for one another, and building up one another in the faith. It sometimes calls for correcting others in love and restoring with meekness. And, of course, it means ministering to the needs of others, out of our resources.

Deeds of kindness done for others is pleasing to the Lord. In fact, there is a sense in which it is done to the Lord. Solomon said, "He who is kind to the poor lends to the Lord, and he will reward him for what he has done" (Prov. 19:17 NIV).

• Why is it so much easier to "love in word" than "in deed and in truth" (v. 18)?

"God has lots of folks who intend to go to work for Him 'some day.' What He needs is more people who are willing to work for Him this day."—Marie T. Freeman

---

CONCLUSION

To what degree are you following the example of Jesus by giving sacrificially of yourself to help others? Have you been guilty of telling someone you would pray for them, but you did not pray? Is there someone in the church you attend who is in need and you have the means to meet that need? What are you going to do about it? How seriously do you take the admonition to "love . . . in deed and in truth"?

GOLDEN TEXT CHALLENGE

"MY LITTLE CHILDREN, LET US NOT LOVE IN WORD, NEITHER IN TONGUE; BUT IN DEED AND IN TRUTH" (1 John 3:18).

This word love (agape) expresses the essential nature of God. This love can only be known from the actions it prompts. It is practical love given by God that causes people to be drawn to Him.

John proclaims that this type of love cannot be shared properly with others through our "words," which are the expressions of our thoughts or our good intentions. John exhorts us that the love he is proclaiming can only be shared in "deed" and in "truth."

This is a practical Christianity which encompasses every activity undertaken for Christ's sake; it is the practical effect that faith in Christ has upon us. This "deed" expresses the "truth" that Christ is indeed Lord of our life by revealing Him in concrete ways.

Daily Devotions:

M. Being the People of God
   Leviticus 26:9-13
T. God's People Forever
   2 Samuel 7:21-24
W. Promises to God's People
   Ezekiel 36:24-29
T. Authority to Become God's Children
   John 1:6-12
F. Confirmed as God's Children
   Romans 8:16-21
S. Children of God by Faith
   Galatians 3:24-29

Test the Spirits

1 John 3:19 through 4:6; 2 John 7-11

Unit Theme:
Principles for Christian Living (1, 2, 3 John)

Central Truth:
Christians must differentiate between the Spirit of Truth and the spirit of error.

Focus:
Perceive the dangers of deception and walk in truth.

Context:
Near the end of the first century AD, the elderly apostle John penned these epistles, probably writing from Ephesus.

Golden Text:
"Beloved, believe not every spirit, but try the spirits whether they are of God" (1 John 4:1).

Study Outline:
  I. Gain Confidence Through Obedience
     (1 John 3:19-24)
 II. Discern the Spirits
     (1 John 4:1-6)
III. Beware of Deceivers
     (2 John 7-11)

INTRODUCTION

The church in John's day had to grapple with discerning between the Spirit of truth and the spirit of error. Some deceivers who operated in the spirit of antichrist had infiltrated the church, and believers had to be on guard against them. No doubt, they were smooth talkers who made their message seem very acceptable. The trouble is, they denied the most cardinal truth of the Christian faith: that Jesus is the Christ, the Son of God come in the flesh.

Many arguments in the church today have to do with the color of the carpet, the shape of the lights, the design of the pulpit (glass or wood), or other trivial things. The false teachers of apostolic times were denying the incarnation, atonement, resurrection, ascension, and intercession of Jesus Christ. These truths are the components of the gospel. This is a life-or-death struggle. The denial of these glorious truths wipes out all hope.

This is not to say that there are no gigantic struggles related to the faith going on in Christendom today; there are. We too must be on guard, lest we fall prey to those who would lead us astray. Some forms of communication, such as television, offer such a variety of interpretations of the Scripture that we can be left utterly confused about what is truth and what is error.

Three ways to be able to discern between truth and error include: (1) *Live close to God*. Once we have tasted His goodness and grace and experienced His loving-kindness in our life, we will not be so easily drawn into error. (2) *Be sensitive to the Holy Spirit*. When the Holy Spirit lives in us and in the one presenting the message to us, our spirits agree. We can recognize a right spirit and identify with it. What a wonderful safeguard the Holy Spirit is! (3) *Know the truth*. Knowing the truth necessitates reading and studying the Bible. If we don't know what God says is truth, it makes us vulnerable to believing a lie.

I. GAIN CONFIDENCE THROUGH OBEDIENCE (1 John 3:19-24)

A. Belonging to the Truth (vv. 19-22)

¹⁹ And hereby we know that we are of the truth, and shall assure our hearts before him. ²⁰ For if our heart condemn us, God is greater than our heart, and knoweth all things. ²¹ Beloved, if our heart condemn us not, then have we confidence toward God. ²² And whatsoever we ask, we receive of him, because we keep his commandments, and do those things that are pleasing in his sight.

It is not enough that we say we love one another; we must demonstrate our love by our actions. Then we know that we belong to the truth (v. 19). When that bond of love operates in our life, we can be assured that we are walking in the favor of God. There may be times when we struggle with our standing with God because of past sins. Satan stands ready to point an accusing finger at us, causing us to doubt our relationship with the Lord. But God is greater than any accusation Satan may bring against us (v. 20). When God, who knows us better than we know ourselves, forgives us for our wrongdoing, He also lifts the guilt from our heart and gives us peace within (v. 21). When that guilt is gone, we can come boldly to the throne of grace believing that He will meet our every need.

John gives us two reasons why our prayers are answered (v. 22). The first reason is because we obey the Lord's commandments. When we obey the Lord's commandments, we walk in His will. Having resigned ourselves to the will of God, our prayers are based on our faith in the wisdom and power of God to bring the desired result. Turning the matter over to Him, we wait patiently for His response.

The second reason God answers our prayers is because we do things that please Him. Our relationship with Him is genuine, without pretense or hypocrisy. What an incentive this gives us to live righteously and love God unreservedly! God honors such a life and attitude and bestows His blessings richly.

The Scripture makes it clear that whatever we ask according to His will, in the name of Jesus, for His sake, and in faith, we will receive. Jesus promised: "Ask, and it will be given to you; seek, and you will find; knock, and it will be opened to you. For everyone who asks receives, and he who seeks finds, and to him who knocks it will be opened" (Matt. 7:7-8 NKJV). Later in his writing, John reaffirms this truth: "Now this is the confidence that we have in Him, that if we ask anything according to His will, He hears us. And if we know that He hears us, whatever we ask, we know that we have the petitions that we have asked of Him" (1 John 5:14-15 NKJV).

1. What should give us "confidence toward God," and why (vv. 19-21)?
2. Who can expect to have their prayers answered (v. 22)?

Unchanging Truth

A man came to his old friend, a music teacher, and said to him, "What's the good news today?" The old teacher struck a tuning fork. As the note sounded through the room, he said, "That is A. It is A today; it was A five thousand years ago, and it will be A ten thousand years from now. That's the good news for today."

The good news for us is that the Word of God is truth. He has always been truth; it will always be truth. Jesus said, "Heaven and earth shall pass away: but my words shall not pass away" (Luke 21:33). In this battle between truth and error, truth will prevail.

B. Believing in the Son (v. 23)

23 And this is his commandment, That we should believe on the name of his Son Jesus Christ, and love one another, as he gave us commandment.

John sums up our duty as it relates to keeping Christ's commandments in two words: *believe* and *love*. John Wesley observed that this command to believe and love "is the greatest and most important command that ever issued from the throne of glory. If this be neglected, no other can be kept: if this be observed, all others are easy."

We must believe in the name of Christ. To believe in His name is to believe He is the Son of God and that He stands in a relationship with God like no other. He alone can show us the Father and demonstrate by His life what the Father is like. And, He alone has paid the price for our redemption. Because of His work on Calvary, we who believe in Him are redeemed by His precious blood, restored to favor with God, and made partakers of the divine nature.

Belief and *love* go hand in hand. Both are the will of God, and both are commanded by Him. They represent right belief and right conduct and are a test of the true believer. Jesus said, "A new commandment I give to you, that you love one another; as I have loved you, that you also love one another. By this all will know that you are My disciples, if you have love for one another" (John 13:34-35 NKJV). The love we show to one another is to be modeled after the love Christ has for us. It must be a love that puts others first and is quick to forgive others.

Love may be considered the cardinal virtue of the Christian life. More than any other characteristic, it distinguishes believers and identifies them as followers of Christ. Love so permeates the Christian life that it is unthinkable to claim to be a Christian when it is absent. No trait is more Christlike than love.

• What is the basic commandment from which all others flow (v. 23)?

"We never can thank God enough for giving us not only a whole gospel to believe, but a whole world to give it to."—A. B. Simpson

---

Test the Spirits

C. Living in Christ (v. 24)

24 And he that keepeth his commandments dwelleth in him, and he in him. And hereby we know that he abideth in us, by the Spirit which he hath given us.

The believer dwells in God, and God in him. This is evident by his or her conduct: keeping the Lord's commandments. Those who conscientiously obey God's commandments enjoy a vital relationship with Christ and the Father. The apostle Paul affirms that relationship when he speaks of Christ dwelling "in your hearts through faith; that you, being rooted and grounded in love, may be able to comprehend with all the saints what is the width and length and depth and height—to know the love of Christ which passes knowledge; that you may be filled with all the fullness of God" (Eph. 3:17-19 NKJV).

What a marvelous thought that Christ dwells in us in such fashion as to influence every aspect of our daily life. It is almost beyond our comprehension that we can live in such an endearing relationship with Him. It is sometimes difficult for us to grasp that the Lord will do for us whatever His perfect wisdom and goodness deems best to enable us to grow in grace and in our knowledge of Him. Yet, that is exactly how He deals with His faithful children.

The abiding of the Father and the Son in us, and us in them, is affirmed by the indwelling of the Holy Spirit. This is the first mention of the Holy Spirit in this book. Both the Father and the Son are involved in bestowing the gift of the Spirit. Jesus said the Father sends the Holy Spirit in Jesus' name (John 14:26), and Jesus said He would send the Spirit from the Father (15:26).

We cannot possibly fulfill the requirements of the Christian life, apart from the enabling of the Holy Spirit. He abides within to assist us in the exercise of our faith and every other grace. He inspires us to confess before others that Jesus is the Son of the living God. He provides the common bond that enables us to love one another as brothers and sisters in Christ. Furthermore, He empowers us to live a life of righteousness. Apart from the indwelling of the Spirit, we are incapable of carrying out these distinguishing marks of the Christian life.

• How does God's Spirit assure believers (v. 24)?

"Love God, and He will dwell with you. Obey God, and He will reveal to you the truth of His deepest teachings."—Frederick W. Robertson

---

II. DISCERN THE SPIRITS (1 John 4:1-6)

A. Discerning False Prophets (vv. 1-3)

1 Beloved, believe not every spirit, but try the spirits whether they are of God: because many false prophets are gone out into the world. 2 Hereby know ye the Spirit of God: Every spirit that confesseth that Jesus Christ is come in the flesh is of God: 3 And every spirit that confesseth not that Jesus Christ is come in the flesh is not of God: and this is that spirit of antichrist, whereof ye have heard that it should come; and even now already is it in the world.

The presence of false prophets is nothing new. The Old Testament gives us many examples of those who pretended to be what they were not. The criteria for determining the difference between a true prophet and a false prophet was simple: If a prophecy came to pass, it came from a true prophet. If it did not come to pass, the speaker was a false prophet (Deut. 18:21-22). The same test was true in New Testament times and is true in our time.

John admonishes his readers not to take the messages they hear for granted, but rather to test the spirits to see if the speakers are of God. Is the speaker speaking under the inspiration of the Holy Spirit, or is his inspiration coming from another spirit? When the apostle Paul preached at Berea, the people searched the Scriptures to see if the message they had heard conformed to the Word of God (Acts 17:10-11). We should be equally diligent to determine that what we are hearing is in line with the Truth, and also if the speaker is in harmony with God.

The test John wanted his readers to use was the speaker's attitude toward Jesus Christ (1 John 4:1-2). Did this individual believe that Jesus Christ was a real flesh-and-blood human being and at the same time the Son of God? If he did not believe Jesus was both human and divine, he was not a true prophet. If his faith was anchored in Christ, fully accepting every aspect of His being, he was a true prophet and his message was to be accepted.

Those who denied that Jesus was all He said He was were false prophets inspired by the "spirit of antichrist"—a spirit that existed even in John's day (v. 3). The end-time Antichrist will refuse to acknowledge Jesus Christ and will set himself up as the real Christ. That same spirit has been present in every age. But no matter how smooth or charismatic or charming or persuasive a speaker may be, if he does not embrace Christ and His message fully and completely, he is to be recognized for what he is—a false prophet.

---

1. How can a Christian "test the spirits" (v. 1 NIV)? Why is this necessary?
2. To be a Christian, what must a person believe and confess concerning Jesus Christ (vv. 2-3)?

"The first point of wisdom is to discern that which is false; the second, to know that which is true."—Lucius Caelius Lactantius

---

B. Belonging to God (vv. 4-5)

4 Ye are of God, little children, and have overcome them: because greater is he that is in you, than he that is in the world. 5 They are of the world: therefore speak they of the world, and the world heareth them.

How do believers overcome false teachers and false teaching? First, we do so by the grace of God. What comfort to know that we belong to God and that if we truly depend on Him, He will enable us to be overcomers. Second, we do so by remaining steadfast in the faith. False teachers soon learn that we will not be turned away from the truth, and so they depart. There may be times when it seems that truth is in retreat and error has the ascendancy, but in the end, truth will prevail. Third, the Spirit of truth that is in us, the anointing that abides in us, is greater than the spirit of error that is in the world. The spirit of error emanates from the devil himself. While we cannot defeat the devil in our own strength, we become conquerors through the Holy Spirit who lives in us. He illuminates our minds, leads us into all truth, and teaches us how to apply the truth to our daily lives. The spirit of evil may be strong, but the Holy Spirit is stronger.

The world embraces false teachers because they speak their language. The problem with those who will not hear the truth is that they are not of God. Jesus said, "Anyone who belongs to God listens gladly to the words of God. But you don't listen because you don't belong to God" (John 8:47 NLT). The apostle Paul added, "The natural man does not receive the things of the Spirit of God, for they are foolishness to him; nor can he know them, because they are spiritually discerned" (1 Cor. 2:14 NKJV). How fortunate we are to have learned this truth and therefore trust the Spirit to guide us into all truth. This is something the world can never experience.

• Whom must believers "overcome," and how can this happen (vv. 4-5)?

"God has defeated Satan through the death and resurrection of the Lord Jesus Christ. Through this overwhelming victory, God has also empowered you to overcome any temptation to sin and has provided sufficient resources for you to respond biblically to any problem of life. By relying on God's power and being obedient to His Word, you can be an overcomer in any situation."—John C. Broger

---

C. Understanding the Truth (v. 6)

⁶ We are of God: he that knoweth God heareth us; he that is not of God heareth not us. Hereby know we the spirit of truth, and the spirit of error.

John speaks for himself and for those who teach the same doctrines he did, saying, "We are of God." It was a declaration they could easily defend. Their allegiance to God was evident by the holy lives they lived and supported by the purity of the doctrine they preached. Their message and their ministry centered on Jesus Christ. They embraced Him as the Son of God and the Savior of the world. Further, God worked through them with the exercise of spiritual gifts and miraculous powers—works that could only be attributed to the Lord. When they claimed they belonged to God, they were not being boastful but truthful. They understood God had chosen them, called them, and sent them forth to preach the gospel.

When the apostles went out to represent the Christian faith, they spoke of the things that pertain to God and truth. Contrarily, worldly people speak a language the world understands and accepts, which contradicts God and truth. When the true messenger of God speaks, his message rings true to those who have the Holy Spirit abiding within. The Spirit of God in them recognizes the truth and bears witness to it.

So, by the grace of God and the Spirit of God within, believers have the ability to discern between truth and error. Since they have that ability, they can distinguish between true ministers of the gospel and false teachers. Sometimes this distinction can be made just by observing who their followers are. Those who operate by the spirit of the world will be embraced by the world; those who minister through the Spirit of God will have the approval of those who know Christ and walk worthy of Him.

- How will "he that is not of God" respond to Christian teaching (v. 6)?

"In the last analysis, this is what preaching to the heart is intended to produce: inner prostration of the hearts of our listeners through a consciousness of the presence and the glory of God. This distinguishes authentic biblical, expository preaching from any cheap substitute for it; it marks the difference between preaching about the Word of God and preaching the Word of God."—Sinclair B. Ferguson

---

III. BEWARE OF DECEIVERS (2 John 7-11)

A. Recognizing the Antichrist Spirit (vv. 7-8)

⁷ For many deceivers are entered into the world, who confess not that Jesus Christ is come in the flesh. This is a deceiver and an antichrist. ⁸ Look to yourselves, that we lose not those things which we have wrought, but that we receive a full reward.

John repeats his former warning about the coming of messengers who represent the spirit of antichrist—messengers who are deceivers whose mission is to lead people astray. These messengers refuse to acknowledge that Jesus Christ has come in the flesh, thus completely denying the Lord's incarnation.

Notice that John said these deceivers went "into the world" with their false teachings (v. 7). The implication is that, as the apostles went forth proclaiming the gospel of truth, these "antichrists" went out to spread a message based on falsehoods. They presented themselves as Christian missionaries when in reality they were impostors. So whatever churches they visited in their travels, they sought to create confusion and raise doubts about the divinity of Christ.

Let it be clearly stated that Jesus did not become the Son of God at His birth nor at His baptism; neither did He cease to be the Son of God at His death on the cross. He is the Son of God from eternity to eternity. He is Christ come in the flesh, both man and God from the time of His birth and forevermore.

Now John issues a warning to the believers that they be careful not to be taken in by this spirit of error and thus lose the fruit of their labors in the Kingdom (v. 8). Rather than being taken in and spreading the false teaching they are hearing, they need to continue to preach and teach the doctrine they have heard and embraced from the beginning of their Christian sojourn. If they remain faithful to the truth, they will receive the full benefits of the rewards due to them. The message John is sharing with his readers agrees with the teaching of the apostle Paul, who wrote to the Corinthians: "Now he who plants and he who waters are one, and each one will receive his own reward according to his own labor. . . . If anyone's work which he has built on it endures, he will receive a reward" (1 Cor. 3:8, 14 NKJV).

---

1. What is the goal of the "deceivers" mentioned here (v. 7)?
2. Explain the warning in verse 8.

Test the Spirits

"The gospel is not speculation but fact. It is truth, because it is the record of a Person who is the Truth."—Alexander MacLaren

---

B. Teaching the Doctrine of Christ (v. 9)

⁹ Whosoever transgresseth, and abideth not in the doctrine of Christ, hath not God. He that abideth in the doctrine of Christ, he hath both the Father and the Son.

Whoever walks out on the teachings of Christ, or adds to His teachings more than He intended, has transgressed against God and cannot call Him his God and Father. The apostle Paul wrote in an astonishing tone and with a strong warning to the Galatians about embracing anything other than the truth: "I am shocked that you are turning away so soon from God, who called you to himself through the loving mercy of Christ. You are following a different way that pretends to be the Good News but is not the Good News at all. You are being fooled by those who deliberately twist the truth concerning Christ. Let God's curse fall on anyone, including us or even an angel from heaven, who preaches a different kind of Good News than the one we preached to you" (1:6-8 NLT). Furthermore, Jesus said: "If anyone takes away from the words of the book of this prophecy, God shall take away his part from the Book of Life, from the holy city, and from the things which are written in this book" (Rev. 22:19 NKJV).

This danger of denying Christ is just as real today as it was in John's day. There are plenty of people who declare they believe in God and express their allegiance to Him, but who want to have nothing to do with Jesus Christ. No true Christian can take that position, because the Christian faith has its foundation in the incarnation, atonement, and finished work of Christ that makes salvation possible. To believe otherwise is not progress, but apostasy; not enlightenment, but darkness.

The other side of this coin is that those who remain faithful to the truth enjoy a rich relationship with Jesus Christ as Savior and Lord, as well as a vital communion with God as their Father.

• How can someone have "both the Father and the Son" (v. 9)?

"You must not do, you must not even try to do, the will of the Father unless you are prepared to 'know of the doctrine.'"—C. S. Lewis

---

C. Sharing in Evil Deeds (vv. 10-11)

¹⁰ If there come any unto you, and bring not this doctrine, receive him not into your house, neither bid him God speed: ¹¹ For he that biddeth him God speed is partaker of his evil deeds.

False teachers are not to be allowed to speak from the Christian pulpit or to be encouraged to enjoy the fellowship of the church. They are to be denied the hospitality that is common to true believers, both publicly and privately. Furthermore, they are not to be extended a salutation that suggests they have the blessing of the church upon their departure. To say to them "God be with you" may suggest to them that they have gained some favor in the church. It can also be a stumbling block to weaker Christians who may conclude they can embrace some of their teaching or even become followers of these false teachers. The apostle's language could not be clearer. We are not only to reject the false teaching, we are also to reject the false teacher. To do less than this is to identify with the false teacher and to give him a platform to continue to spread his false teachings. In short, it is to become a partner with him in his evil ways.

Irreparable damage has been done to local churches when wolves dressed in sheep's clothing have been allowed to remain in the midst of the flock, propagating their erroneous message and perusing their chaotic ways. Churches have been split, lifelong friends have become alienated, and sometimes churches have been forced to close because leaders of the congregation failed to deal with the disrupters and deceivers. No wonder John is so harsh in his denunciation of those who pretend to be followers of Christ but who are acting in the spirit of antichrist.

• How should the church and individual Christians respond to false teachers?

"The mind of him that worketh ill is not always corrupt; but the mind of him that defendeth evil is ever corrupt."—Lancelot Andrewes

---

CONCLUSION

To recognize false teaching, it is necessary to be familiar with the truth. Are you knowledgeable enough with the teachings of Christ to know when they are being misrepresented? Do you live close enough to Christ, and are you sensitive enough to the Holy Spirit that you can discern between the Spirit of truth and the spirit of error? Though he or she may be smooth-talking and clever, can you sense when an individual is a deceiver? If you can, what a blessing you are to the kingdom of God!

GOLDEN TEXT CHALLENGE

"BELOVED, BELIEVE NOT EVERY SPIRIT, BUT TRY THE SPIRITS WHETHER THEY ARE OF GOD" (1 John 4:1).

The apostle John admonished his readers to try, or to test, the spirits to see if they were of God, for many false prophets had gone out into the world. Not everyone who claims to have a message from God really has a word from Him. Jesus said, "Beware of false prophets, which come to you in sheep's clothing, but inwardly they are ravening wolves" (Matt. 7:15).

Perhaps as never before in the history of the church, Christians today need to be on guard, lest we be taken in by smooth-talking people who are propagating various erroneous doctrines. May none of us be in the group prophesied about in 1 Timothy 4:1—"The Spirit speaketh expressly, that in the latter times some shall depart from the faith, giving heed to seducing spirits, and doctrines of devils." We have the Scriptures and the Holy Spirit to direct us. All ideas, all beliefs, all doctrines should be submitted to the test of scriptural authority and to the witness of God's Spirit.

Daily Devotions:

M. Pharaoh's Deception
   Exodus 9:25-35
T. Discerning God's Way
   Job 34:1-12
W. Judgment Against False Prophets
   Jeremiah 23:25-32
T. Revelation From the Father
   Matthew 16:13-17
F. Let No One Deceive You
   2 Thessalonians 2:1-4
S. Be on Your Guard
   2 Peter 3:14-18

Evidences of Loving God

1 John 4:7-21; 2 John 1-11

Unit Theme:
Principles for Christian Living (1, 2, 3 John)

Central Truth:
Christians express God's love by loving others.

Focus:
Examine and emulate God's love.

Context:
Near the end of the first century AD, the elderly apostle John penned these epistles, probably writing from Ephesus.

Golden Text:
"Beloved, let us love one another: for love is of God; and every one that loveth is born of God, and knoweth God" (1 John 4:7).

Study Outline:
I. Love as God Loves Us
    (1 John 4:7-12)
II. Dwell in God's Love
    (1 John 4:13-18)
III. Walk in God's Love
    (1 John 4:19-21; 2 John 1-6)

INTRODUCTION

In both his Gospel and his Epistles, John has much to say about love. He reminded us God's love for the world was so great that He gave His only begotten Son so we could be reconciled to Him. This is understandable when we realize God is the personification of love. He does not just *do* acts of love; He *is* love. Love is the essence of His nature, making Him the source of all genuine love.

God loves all humanity. The greatness of His love is seen in that He loved us when we were sinners, alienated from Him. God expresses His love for those who have become His children through faith in Christ by ministering to their needs, filling their heart with joy, and protecting them from the Evil One. He also shows His love to His children by correcting them when they make a misstep. Furthermore, God identifies with them in their afflictions, rejoices with them when they rejoice, and remains faithful to them under all circumstances.

Because God first loved us, we love Him and our brothers and sisters in Christ. In fact, Christ set the standard of our love for one another as the way outsiders will know we are His followers. John even wonders how we can love God whom we have not seen, if we don't love our fellow believers whom we have seen. When Christ abides in two people, they enjoy a kindred spirit. They discover that, in spiritual matters, they have much in common. They may be different in many ways, but their love for God and His Word forms in them a common bond.

The love of God in the heart of believers manifests itself in a love for the lost and a passionate desire to see them turn to the Lord. Since Jesus came into this world to seek and to save the lost, how can we possibly have His love in our heart and not long to see others saved?

I. LOVE AS GOD LOVES US (1 John 4:7-12)

A. God Is Love (vv. 7-9)

7 Beloved, let us love one another: for love is of God; and every one that loveth is born of God, and knoweth God. 8 He that loveth not knoweth not God; for God is love. 9 In this was manifested the love of God toward us, because that God sent his only begotten Son into the world, that we might live through him.

In the previous verses, John talks about the spirit of antichrist and the spirit of error and how these manifest themselves in man's inhumanity to man. He calls on his readers to distance themselves from this kind of behavior and to exhibit that which is most Godlike; that is, to love one another. The love the apostle is talking about shows itself through a consuming passion for what is best for others. There is nothing selfish or self-serving about this love; rather, it is always reaching out and finding ways to be a blessing to those it encounters.

John gives a compelling reason for loving one another—"love is of God" (v. 7). It is God's nature to love, and if we have become partakers of the divine nature, then it becomes natural for us to love also. Love is both a gift of God's grace and a fruit of the Holy Spirit. It pleases the Lord when believers demonstrate this trait toward one another and toward those outside the circle of the saints.

Showing love to one another is also a sign that we Christians have been born into the family of God, and that we truly know God. Some may boast of their knowledge of God, but true knowledge manifests itself in love for God and others. If love is absent, then no true knowledge of God is present. How can it be otherwise, since God is love? God demonstrated how remarkable His love is when He gave His only, well-beloved Son on the cross that people might have redemption. The fountain from which His love flows never fails. It should flow just as freely from us to others, and especially to our brothers and sisters in Christ.

The plan of redemption was born in the love of God, and it was carried out when Jesus Christ freely suffered and died to make this glorious salvation available to us. Christ dying on the cross means we who were dead in trespasses and sin may now enjoy abundant, eternal life.

---

1. Why is love an essential part of the Christian life?
2. Why did God love us first? How did He prove His love?

"Because God is love, the most important lesson He wants you to learn on earth is how to love."—Rick Warren

---

B. Real Love (vv. 10-11)

10 Herein is love, not that we loved God, but that he loved us, and sent his Son to be the propitiation for our sins. 11 Beloved, if God so loved us, we ought also to love one another.

We did not initiate the love between God and ourselves. God loved us first. In fact, we were sinners and enemies of God. The apostle Paul recognized this when he wrote: "God demonstrates His own love toward us in that, while we were still sinners, Christ died for us. Much more then, having now been justified by His blood, we shall be saved from wrath through Him. For if when we were enemies we were reconciled to God through the death of His Son, much more, having been reconciled, we shall be saved by His life" (Rom. 5:8-10 NKJV).

This is love that cannot be matched. Because we were hopelessly lost in trespasses and sins, we needed a Savior to become our "atoning sacrifice" (1 John 4:10 NIV). So great was God's love for us that He sent His Son to die on our behalf so we might enter into eternal life. This is the only way the justice of God could be satisfied. Christ paid the price for us, although we were utterly undeserving.

Since God loved us in such a magnificent manner, we are under obligation to love one another. If God loved us when we were unlovable and alienated from Him, how much more should we love one another now that we are redeemed by the blood of Christ? The greatest motive we have for loving one another is God's love for us. We walk in holiness because He is holy; we show mercy because He is merciful; and we love one another because He is love. We should love one another for God's sake. There may be some things about the personality of some believers that we do not like, but that does not free us from the call to love them. They are God's children, our brothers and sisters in Christ, members of the same family, and therefore deserving of our love.

- Why must we love other people? Does this include people we don't like?

"What binds us together is not common education, common race, common income levels, common politics, common nationality, common accents, common jobs, or anything else of that sort. Christians come together because they have all been loved by Jesus himself. They are a band of natural enemies who love one another for Jesus' sake."—D. A. Carson

---

C. Complete Love (v. 12)

12 No man hath seen God at any time. If we love one another, God dwelleth in us, and his love is perfected in us.

In his Gospel, John made this same assertion about God: "No one has seen God at any time. The only begotten Son, who is in the bosom of the Father, He has declared Him" (1:18 NKJV). Jesus provides the clearest revelation of God that we have. John Killinger put it this way: "Jesus is God's way of getting rid of a bad reputation." People had many ideas about the nature of God, not all of them good, prior to the coming of Jesus. But Jesus shows us what God is really like. He said, "He who has seen Me has seen the Father" (14:9 NKJV).

Since God is invisible, and Christ has returned to heaven, the best way people can see God now is through His children. The world sees God most clearly in His children when they love one another. However, nothing turns people away from the Christian religion more readily than when they see believers fighting among themselves. If we cannot show love to one another, how can we expect to attract a lost world to our Savior?

When people see the love of God in us as we show love to one another, they perceive that God dwells in us. Loving one another also brings His love to full expression in us. Showing our love to others is another way of showing our love for God. We cannot claim to be mature Christians until love for others is a central part of our confession. The importance of love is expressed by Paul in 1 Corinthians 13:13: "Three things will last forever—faith, hope, and love—and the greatest of these is love" (NLT).

• How do we know if God is living in us?

"Until we know Jesus, God is merely a concept, and we can't have faith in Him. But once we hear Jesus say, "He who has seen Me has seen the Father" (John 14:9 [NKJV]) we immediately have something that is real, and our faith is limitless."—Oswald Chambers

---

II. DWELL IN GOD'S LOVE (1 John 4:13-18)

A. Proof in the Spirit (vv. 13-14)

13 Hereby know we that we dwell in him, and he in us, because he hath given us of his Spirit. 14 And we have seen and do testify that the Father sent the Son to be the Saviour of the world.

John speaks of the mutual habitation between God and us. Not only does God dwell in us, but we also dwell in Him. By faith, we enjoy a union with God that has been made possible by the work of Christ on our behalf. The assurance of this relationship is the indwelling of the Holy Spirit. He is not only the Spirit of love, He is also the Spirit of truth. The primary truth He imparts to us is that Jesus Christ is the Savior of the world. Jesus said, "When the Helper comes, whom I shall send to you from the Father, the Spirit of truth who proceeds from the Father, He will testify of Me" (John 15:26 NKJV).

John could speak as an eyewitness to events surrounding the life of Christ. He had seen the life He lived, the miracles He performed, and the suffering He endured. John was also witness to the voluntary nature of Jesus' death. Jesus willingly gave up His life that He might give life to humankind. Not only was John at the cross when Jesus died, he also saw Him after His resurrection. Furthermore, he recorded one of the strongest statements relative to the coming again of the Lord to be found in Scripture. The apostle would remind us that through the work of the Holy Spirit in our lives, we too are witnesses to the saving grace of our Lord.

Observe that "the Father sent the Son to be the Saviour of the world" (1 John 4:14). The triune God works in unison to provide salvation. Christ came under the blessing and authority of the Father. There is no division among the Trinity; they work in harmony to make the various aspects of salvation a reality.

The term "Saviour of the world" only appears in John's writings—once in this epistle and once in his Gospel. The Samaritans who heard and believed the witness of the woman at the well referred to Christ as "the Saviour of the world" (John 4:42). They had no interest in a message of salvation that was for the Jews only, but they had considerable interest in a message that spoke to people everywhere—including Samaritans.

1. How can we live in God while He lives in us?
2. What is the message the Holy Spirit wants to communicate through us? How can we communicate it?

"Christianity is a love relationship between a child of God and His Maker through the Son Jesus Christ and in the power of the Holy Spirit."—Adrian Rogers

B. A Life of Love (vv. 15-16)

15 Whosoever shall confess that Jesus is the Son of God, God dwelleth in him, and he in God. 16 And we have known and believed the love that God hath to us. God is love; and he that dwelleth in love dwelleth in God, and God in him.

Previously, John has said that if we love one another, God abides in us. Now he gives another evidence of the abiding presence of God in our life—our confession that Jesus Christ is the Son of God. This confession is to be made openly and publicly, even if it means we face the prospect of persecution. If we do not make this confession that Jesus is the Son of God and that His atonement covers all our sins, we have no message to proclaim and no hope of eternal life. Paul expressed it plainly: "If you confess with your mouth the Lord Jesus and believe in your heart that God has raised Him from the dead, you will be saved. For with the heart one believes unto righteousness, and with the mouth confession is made unto salvation" (Rom. 10:9-10 NKJV). This call to confession involves more than mental assent—the demons believe . . . some unrepentant people believe. But, in both cases, there is no communion with God. They believe in vain. Faith that saves means a surrender of the heart to Christ, followed by a walk of obedience that takes His commands seriously. When our faith is anchored in Christ, He dwells in us and we dwell in Him.

As we "know and rely on the love God has for us" (1 John 4:16 NIV), His "love becomes a working force in us" (*Wycliffe Bible Commentary*). As Paul recorded: "I am convinced that nothing can ever separate us from God's love. Neither death nor life, neither angels nor demons, neither our fears for today nor our worries about tomorrow—not even the powers of hell can separate us from God's love. No power in the sky above or in the earth below—indeed, nothing in all creation will ever be able to separate us from the love of God that is revealed in Christ Jesus our Lord" (Rom. 8:38-39 NLT).

God's love is poured out into our hearts by the Holy Spirit (5:5), but it is not to lay dormant there; it must flow out to others. Without the Holy Spirit, our hearts are cold and indifferent, but His work is to warm our hearts and enhance our love for God and for others. That love evidences that the Holy Spirit is at work in us.

- What does it fully mean to "confess that Jesus is the Son of God" (v. 15)?

_____

"Love and pity and wish well to every soul in the world; dwell in love, and then you dwell in God."—William Law

_____

C. Perfect Love (vv. 17-18)

[17] Herein is our love made perfect, that we may have boldness in the day of judgment: because as he is, so are we in this world. [18] There is no fear in love; but perfect love casteth out fear: because fear hath torment. He that feareth is not made perfect in love.

The longer we serve God and the closer we grow in Him, the more perfect our love becomes. As our love matures, our confidence grows so that we can stand calmly and boldly on the Day of Judgment. This does not lessen our awe of God. It does mean when God looks at us believers in the final judgment, He will see Christ in us and deal with us accordingly. This is the assurance Jesus expressed in John 5:24: "I tell you the truth, those who listen to my message and believe in God who sent me have eternal life. They will never be condemned for their sins, but they have already passed from death into life" (NLT). In that day, the sins of our past cannot condemn us, for the blood of Jesus has washed them away. No wonder we can face God with confidence in that day. We understand that we are nothing and Christ is everything.

For believers who fear the Day of Judgment, love has not been perfected. There is no fear in love; the two are incompatible. We cannot approach God in love and hide from Him in fear at the same time. If Christ is living in us in this world, we have no need to fear. After all, that is what being a Christian is all about—being Christlike. Many are the testimonies from loved ones of believers who faced death and judgment in perfect calmness and confidence. They understood their place in Christ and looked forward to His warm embrace upon their arrival on the other side. Of these, it could be said they had been "perfected in love" (v. 18 NASB).

_____

1. How can we have confidence now ("in this world") about the coming "day of judgment" (v. 17)?
2. Why do love and fear not live together (v. 18)?

_____

"He who loveth God with all his heart feareth not death, nor punishment, nor judgment, nor hell, because perfect love giveth sure access to God. But he who still delighteth in sin, no marvel if he is afraid of death and judgment."—Thomas á Kempis

_____

III. WALK IN GOD'S LOVE (1 John 4:19-21; 2 John 1-6)

A. Loving People (1 John 4:19-21)

[19] We love him, because he first loved us. [20] If a man say, I love God, and hateth his brother, he is a liar: for he that loveth not his brother whom he

hath seen, how can he love God whom he hath not seen? ²¹ And this commandment have we from him, That he who loveth God love his brother also.

"We love." John states this affirmation in contrast to *we fear*. The reason we love, or even have the capacity to love, is that God first loved us and the Holy Spirit has poured His love into us. God's love for us is from eternity to eternity. Out of His love, He gave His only begotten Son to die for our sins and make reconciliation to Himself a possibility. In return for the love God has shown us, He is the first object of our love. Out of our love for God, we follow the pattern He has established in loving one another.

There is no way we can love God and not love our brothers and sisters in Christ. Jesus said the two greatest commandments are to love God and to love one's neighbor (Matt. 22:37-40). The thought that we can love God and show an ungodly attitude toward His followers is preposterous. If such an attitude exists, it must be eradicated and replaced with the same love shown to God. Jesus makes it clear in Matthew 25 that behavior toward His brethren will be equated with behavior toward Him on Judgment Day.

We may not like everything about certain Christians, but this does not take away our Christian duty to love them. We should remember that we were unlikable and unlovable when God saved us. We were sinners and enemies of God, but He loved us in spite of what we were.

---

1. Why is it possible to love God?
2. Who is a "liar" (v. 20)?

Practical Love

Some years ago, a wealthy Christian woman saw a little ragged homeless boy gazing into the window of a shoe store. She asked him what he was doing. "I was praying that God would give me some shoes," he said.

The lady took the little boy into the store, summoned a bowl of water, and washed the little fellow's feet. She then bought for him a pair of strong, comfortable boots. The boy, amazed at what had been done, looked at the kind woman's face and said, "Please. Ma'am, are you Christ's wife?"

May our love for others show to the extent that others might ask us, "Are you a brother or sister in Christ?"—Author unknown

---

B. Living Out the Truth (2 John 1-4)

(2 John 1-3 is not included in the printed text.)
⁴ I rejoiced greatly that I found of thy children walking in truth, as we have received a commandment from the Father.

John addressed this second epistle to "the elect lady and her children." We are not told who this lady is or where she lived. She appears to be an individual of great distinction who was devoted to the service of Christ. The apostle praises her for the manner in which she has raised her family and the principles she has instilled in them. Some scholars do not see this woman as a person, but rather as a personification of a local church, and her children as individual members of the church.

The apostle commends the elect lady for the spirit and conduct he had seen in some of her children. Their life brought honor to the gospel of Christ which they had embraced. Not only had they received the truth, but John found them walking in the truth. It is not enough for us to know the truth; we must live it out daily.

---

1. What must Christians do "for the truth's sake" (v. 2)?
2. What two qualities does verse 2 reveal about truth?
3. What brought great joy to the apostle John (v. 4)? Why?

"In our manner of speech, our plans of living, our dealings with others, our conduct and walk in the church and out of it—all should be done as becomes the gospel."—Albert Barnes

---

C. Loving One Another (vv. 5-6)

5 And now I beseech thee, lady, not as though I wrote a new commandment unto thee, but that which we had from the beginning, that we love one another. 6 And this is love, that we walk after his commandments. This is the commandment, That, as ye have heard from the beginning, ye should walk in it.

John reminds the elect lady how important it is to love one another. This is not some new requirement he is putting on her, but rather something that has been expected all along. The idea that we should love one another is so simple, yet so profound, that it has been common knowledge. This is not some newfangled approach to Christianity, but the living out of a principle found in both Testaments.

The commandment "which we had from the beginning" probably means the one they had from the start of their experience with the Lord. "Love one another" was not a new commandment when John was writing; it was as old as the gospel. It was not even new to his readers; they had known it from the first days of their Christian walk. It is possible to fake belief, and confession can be made with the lips only, but love is more difficult to counterfeit.

In verse 6, John declared the interrelationship of love and obedience. Obedience finds its expression in love, and love finds its expression in obedience. "Walk in it" refers to God's command to love. When all of God's precepts have been condensed into one, we are left with the command to love God and one another.

• We know God's command to love one another. Why can it be difficult to "walk in it" (v. 6)?

"We are obliged to love one another. We are not strictly bound to 'like' one another."—Thomas Merton

---

CONCLUSION

Is our love for our fellow believers of such character that we will stand with them against evil? Do we love God and truth enough to stand up for the right, no matter the consequences?

GOLDEN TEXT CHALLENGE

"BELOVED, LET US LOVE ONE ANOTHER: FOR LOVE IS OF GOD; AND EVERY ONE THAT LOVETH IS BORN OF GOD, AND KNOWETH GOD" (1 John 4:7).

Beloved is the beautiful word that John begins with. It appears five times in 1 John (3:2, 21; 4:1, 7, 11). The word is beautiful because it tells us that, as believers in Christ, we are being loved. Jesus proved once and for all that God loves all people. And there is nothing that can separate us from His love (Rom. 8:35-39).

John knew God loves us, and he in turn was directed by the Holy Spirit to tell us that we ought to love one another. If we know God, we know what love is. And if we know what love is, we know how to love. If we relate to others as God relates to us, we are showing love. God through Christ is our example.

Daily Devotions:

M. God's Love for the Rejected
   Genesis 29:31-35
T. Understanding God's Love
   Psalm 103:1-12
W. God's Loving-Kindness
   Psalm 63:1-4
T. Love's Sacrifice
   John 3:14-17
F. Love's Attributes
   1 Corinthians 13:4-7
S. Walk in Love
   Ephesians 4:29—5:4

Principles of an Overcoming Life

1 John 5:1-21

Unit Theme:
Principles for Christian Living (1, 2, 3 John)

Central Truth:
Faith in Jesus Christ produces a life of victory.

Focus:
Consider and practice principles of a victorious Christian life.

Context:
Near the end of the first century AD, the elderly apostle John penned these epistles, probably writing from Ephesus.

Golden Text:
"Who is he that overcometh the world, but he that believeth that Jesus is the Son of God?" (1 John 5:5).

Study Outline:
I. We Must Be Born Again
   (1 John 5:1-5)
II. Trust the Testimonies of God
   (1 John 5:6-13)
III. Live With Confidence in God
   (1 John 5:14-21)

INTRODUCTION

In chapter 5, the apostle John summarizes all he has taught in his first epistle. He begins by reminding us of the need to be born again. The new birth comes about by believing on the Lord Jesus Christ and receiving Him as our personal Savior. Through the shedding of His blood, Jesus made salvation available to all humanity.

John also confronted the false teachers of his day. Many false teachers had arisen who denied that Jesus Christ is the Son of God. The apostle is careful to declare that these impostors have no part in the kingdom of God. They were to be resisted and rejected. There was to be no place for them in the community of believers—neither in the church nor in the houses of the saints.

John also addressed the issue of living victoriously. Throughout this book, he reminds us that if we are to live an overcoming life, we must base our life on the truth—the Word of God. The principles set forth in the Word will enable us to live triumphantly in the midst of a world that opposes all that is Christian. It is important that we search the Word daily, asking God for guidance.

There is victory in Jesus. We sing about it, but do we live it out so that others see Christ in us? Our lifestyle will either draw others to Christ or turn them away from Him. What an awesome responsibility we have to live in a way that unbelievers will want to experience what we have found in Christ! We need to be able to say with the apostle Paul: "I have been crucified with Christ; it is no longer I who live, but Christ lives in me; and the life which I now live in the flesh I live by faith in the Son of God, who loved me and gave Himself for me" (Gal. 2:20 NKJV).

I. WE MUST BE BORN AGAIN (1 John 5:1-5)

A. Children of God by Faith (v. 1)

¹ Whosoever believeth that Jesus is the Christ is born of God: and every one that loveth him that begat loveth him also that is begotten of him.

Believing that Jesus is the Christ, the Messiah, is a recurring theme in John's writing. In fact, he gave this theme as the reason for the writing of his Gospel. Although he could not record everything Jesus did, his writing was designed to aid the reader in believing in Jesus as the Christ. He declared: "Jesus did many other signs in the presence of His disciples, which are not written in this book; but these are written that you may believe that Jesus is the Christ, the Son of God, and that believing you may have life in His name" (John 20:30-31 NKJV).

When we put our personal faith in Jesus Christ as the Messiah, we become the children of God. John wrote, "As many as received Him, to them He gave the right to become children of God, to those who believe in His name: who were born, not of blood, nor of the will of the flesh, nor of the will of man, but of God" (1:12-13 NKJV).

The message of the false prophets who troubled the church in John's day was a denial of the messiahship of the Lord. John makes it clear that anyone who believes in his or her heart that Jesus is the Christ is a child of God. Also, anyone who loves God the Father also loves Christians, because they are His children. So, not only do we love the only begotten Son of God; we love all God's children. When we are born again, we enter into a new family—the family of God. We are surrounded by brothers and sisters in Christ. The common bond of Christ within draws us to one another. We enjoy a holy love for one another that this world knows nothing about. They can only wonder and marvel at the bond that exists between believers.

- Who is "born of God"? What is the born-again person's relationship with Jesus Christ? With God the Father?

"When we have accepted Jesus Christ, we have become akin to the Father; having become real children of God, we then have the spirit of sonship by which we can come into His presence and make known our wants in a familiar way."—A. C. Dixon

---

B. God's Commandments and Love (vv. 2-3)

² By this we know that we love the children of God, when we love God, and keep his commandments. ³ For this is the love of God, that we keep his commandments: and his commandments are not grievous.

We frequently hear that our love for other believers is an evidence of our love for God. But now the apostle is saying the opposite: Our love for God is evidence of our love for His children. Why is this important? Friendships in the world may be formed for a variety of reasons, some of them less than noble. The motivation is as important as the friendship itself. If our love for Christians stems from our love for God, we know it is based on pure and genuine motivation. When our love for fellow believers is based on love for God, it has an unfathomable quality. As Christians we relate to each other through the grace of God, and find common ground for our respect and admiration.

There is a second factor in this relationship. This love for God is coupled with obedience to God: keeping His commandments. When we obey the commandments of God, we show our love is more than a mere profession. Our deeds prove it is genuine.

Some people have the wrong idea about the commandments of God. They view them as hard and difficult to obey. They do not realize we walk in His commandments by the grace of God. When we look at obedience in that light, we understand that His commandments are not burdensome. Jesus himself made that clear in the beautiful invitation He extended to all who will hear: "Come to Me, all you who labor and are heavy laden, and I will give you rest. Take My yoke upon you and learn from Me, for I am gentle and lowly in heart, and you will find rest for your souls. For My yoke is easy and My burden is light" (Matt. 11:28-30 NKJV).

Paul gave us assurance that the difficulties we face in this life are nothing compared to the glory we will share with Christ in the world to come. Furthermore, he assured us that God's grace will sustain us in the trials of life. He wrote, "No temptation has overtaken you except such as is common to man; but God is faithful, who will not allow you to be tempted beyond what you are able, but with the temptation will also make the way of escape, that you may be able to bear it" (1 Cor. 10:13 NKJV).

---

1. How do God's children live?
2. Why are God's laws not considered burdensome?

"To love God does not mean to meet His needs, but rather to delight in Him and to be captivated by His glorious power and grace, and to value Him above all other things on earth. All the rest of the commandments are the kinds of things that we will do from our hearts, if our hearts are truly delighted with and resting in the glory of God's grace."—John Piper

---

C. God's Children Overcoming the World (vv. 4-5)

⁴ For whatsoever is born of God overcometh the world: and this is the victory that overcometh the world, even our faith. ⁵ Who is he that overcometh the world, but he that believeth that Jesus is the Son of God?

The apostle speaks here of overcomers and identifies them as those who are born of God. Apart from the new birth, we cannot hope to be triumphant in this life or in the life to come. But being born from above, we can stand face-to-face with the world and all it can throw at us and come out victorious. The god of this world is no match for the Spirit-filled believer. He who is within us is greater than he who is in the world. The lustful things of this world lose their appeal to those who are living a Christ-centered life. As long as our faith is anchored in Christ, the promises or threats of this world do not move us. Walking in obedience to the Lord, we are assured that we are "more than conquerors" through Christ who loves us (Rom. 8:37).

There is nothing within ourselves that enables us to overcome the world; however, when our faith is in Jesus Christ as the Son of God, we are united with Him and His victory becomes our victory. We conquer by faith because we derive our strength from Christ. Paul said, "I can do all things through Christ who strengthens me" (Phil. 4:13 NKJV). We can be victorious over Satan, the world, and our own flesh by total surrender to Christ and total dependence on His power. Thus, the formula for victory is spelled out in Revelation 12:11: "And they overcame him [Satan] by the blood of the Lamb, and by the word of their testimony; and they loved not their lives unto the death."

What we believe about Jesus and the extent of our trust in Him determine the degree to which we live an overcoming life. Do we believe He is the Messiah? Do we embrace the supernatural nature of His birth? Do we fully accept Him as Savior and Lord of our life? Only when we come to grips with these truths can we expect to receive the benefits of His passion. Only then can we give thanksgiving to God "who gives us the victory through our Lord Jesus Christ" (1 Cor. 15:57 NKJV).

• Who overcomes the world, and how is it accomplished?

"Let us never give up, but, in our thoughts knit the beginning, progress and end together, and then we shall see ourselves in heaven out of the reach of all enemies."—Richard Sibbes

---

II. TRUST THE TESTIMONIES OF GOD (1 John 5:6-13)

A. Witness to the Son of God (vv. 6-8)

6 This is he that came by water and blood, even Jesus Christ; not by water only, but by water and blood. And it is the Spirit that beareth witness, because the Spirit is truth. 7 For there are three that bear record in heaven, the Father, the Word, and the Holy Ghost: and these three are one. 8 And there are three that bear witness in earth, the Spirit, and the water, and the blood: and these three agree in one.

John continues to assert that Jesus is the Son of God and that believing in Him is essential to salvation. In support of this declaration is the witness of water (v. 6), representing Jesus' baptism and attested to by God the Father. What greater witness could there be than to have God himself say, "This is my beloved Son, in whom I am well pleased" (Matt. 3:17)? Not only did the Father voice His approval, but the Holy Spirit descended in the form of a dove and lighted upon Him (v. 16). Jesus' baptism was one of the first steps in His journey toward fulfilling all righteousness (see v. 15).

The proof that Jesus is the Son of God is seen not only in water, but also in blood (1 John 5:6). On the cross, He accomplished what He had come to do—

make salvation available to all people. The apostle wants us to know that the One who died at Calvary was the same One whom John the Baptist baptized in the Jordan. The blood shed on that hill was precious blood, special blood, atoning blood—the only blood which could cleanse sins.

When the soldier pierced the deceased Jesus' side with his sword, both "blood and water came out" (John 19:34 NKJV). This offered proof that He who died on the center cross was not only the Son of God but also the Son of Man—that His death was a real death, and thus His resurrection would be a real resurrection.

Not only does Jesus' baptism and crucifixion bear witness that He is the Son of God, but the Holy Spirit also confirms this truth with His testimony. The Holy Spirit is behind all of the declarations of Scripture regarding the sonship of Christ, beginning with Moses and all the prophets as well as the writers of the New Testament. The Holy Spirit supported the witness of the apostles, as seen in Acts 5:32: "We are witnesses of these things and so is the Holy Spirit, who is given by God to those who obey him" (NLT). In addition to His witness through the Word, the Holy Spirit also witnesses to the heart of individual believers as well as to the community of believers that Jesus is the Christ.

---

1. What is the testimony of Jesus' blood, His baptism, and the Holy Spirit concerning Jesus Christ?
2. Why should we believe their testimony?

"Mary's virginity protected a great deal more than her own moral character, reputation, and the legitimacy of Jesus' birth. It protected the nature of the divine Son of God. . . . Jesus had to have one human parent or He could not have been human, and thereby a partaker of our flesh. But He also had to have divine parentage of He could not have made a sinless and perfect sacrifice on our behalf."—John MacArthur

---

B. Belief in the Son of God (vv. 9-11)

⁹ If we receive the witness of men, the witness of God is greater: for this is the witness of God which he hath testified of his Son. ¹⁰ He that believeth on the Son of God hath the witness in himself: he that believeth not God hath made him a liar; because he believeth not the record that God gave of his Son. ¹¹ And this is the record, that God hath given to us eternal life, and this life is in his Son.

In numerous ways, we accept the witness of other people. Juries listen to various witnesses and then decide who is telling the truth based on these testimonies. If we act on the basis of human witnesses, how much more should we rely on the witness of God? People can deceive us, but God will not. He is the personification of truth; His testimony is always trustworthy (v. 9).

Those who do not believe that Jesus is the Son of God make the Father out to be a liar (v. 10). Nothing shows more disdain toward "God, who does not lie" (Titus 1:2 NIV). Paul wrote to the Romans, "For what if some did not believe? Will their unbelief make the faithfulness of God without effect? Certainly not! Indeed, let God be true but every man a liar" (3:3-4 NKJV).

The sum and substance of God's testimony is that He has given believers life in the Son, even eternal life (1 John 5:11). This life which we have received by the grace of God was purchased by the Son, resides in the Son, and is ours as we believe in the Son and walk in obedience to Him. This never-ending life begins now and will come to its fullest realization in the future. Knowing Christ means enjoying a little bit of heaven while we are still on earth. Think of what life will be like when we are free from all sorrow and sadness, and when all imperfections have been removed. John alluded to this glorious state earlier when he said: "Beloved, now we are children of God; and it has not yet been revealed what we shall be, but we know that when He is revealed, we shall be like Him, for we shall see Him as He is" (3:2 NKJV). The apostle Paul drew a contrast between this present life and our future life in these words: "I consider that the sufferings of this present time are not worthy to be compared with the glory which shall be revealed in us" (Rom. 8:18 NKJV).

---

1. What inward witness do believers have (vv. 9-10)?
2. What is the "record" mentioned here (v. 11)?

"I became a Christian because the evidence was so compelling that Jesus really is the one-and-only Son of God who proved His divinity by rising from the dead. That meant following Him was the most rational and logical step I could possibly take."—Lee Strobel

---

C. Eternal Life in God's Son (vv. 12-13)

12 He that hath the Son hath life; and he that hath not the Son of God hath not life. 13 These things have I written unto you that believe on the name of the Son of God; that ye may know that ye have eternal life, and that ye may believe on the name of the Son of God.

In the clearest possible language, John draws a distinction between those who have received Christ into their heart and those who have not. It is the difference between being spiritually alive and spiritually dead. Make no mistake about it, only those who have Christ have life. By faith, Christ lives and reigns within those who have accepted Him as Savior and Lord. The moment we are redeemed by the blood of the Lamb, we experience life in a way those who reject Christ can never know. We enter into a foretaste of what we will enjoy on an exponentially larger scale for all eternity.

Since eternal life originates in Christ, it stands to reason that one cannot have this life apart from Him. The external appearance and good deeds of some individuals may suggest they deserve life based on their own merit. But God looks on the heart, and only the heart that is committed to Christ enters into everlasting life. When Jesus asked His disciples if they wanted to leave Him like many others had done, Peter responded, "Lord, to whom shall we go? You have the words of eternal life" (John 6:68 NKJV). Those who have not believed in Christ are dead in sin, alienated from God, and have nothing to look forward to but eternal death.

In 1 John 5:13, the apostle says he is writing to those who believe that Jesus is the Son of God so they may know they have eternal life. What wonderful news! The false teachers of John's day had vigorously denied the sonship of Christ and, lest some believer might have doubts about his or her standing with Christ, John offers these words of encouragement and affirmation. For those in his day and for all generations to follow, the apostle offers the assurance of eternal life to those who "believe on the name of the Son of God."

----

1. Why is there no life without the Son (v. 12)?
2. Why did John write this letter (v. 13)?

"Christ is an ever-flowing fountain; He is continually supplying His people, and the fountain is not spent. They who live upon Christ may have fresh supplies from Him for all eternity."—Jonathan Edwards

----

III. LIVE WITH CONFIDENCE IN GOD (1 John 5:14-21)

A. Ask According to His Will (vv. 14-15)

¹⁴ And this is the confidence that we have in him, that, if we ask any thing according to his will, he heareth us: ¹⁵ And if we know that he hear us, whatsoever we ask, we know that we have the petitions that we desired of him.

The idea of Christians being able to boldly approach God is found several times in this epistle and is supported by the writer of the Book of Hebrews: "Seeing then that we have a great High Priest who has passed through the heavens, Jesus the Son of God, let us hold fast our confession. For we do not have a High Priest who cannot sympathize with our weaknesses, but was in all points tempted as we are, yet without sin. Let us therefore come boldly to the throne of grace, that we may obtain mercy and find grace to help in time of need" (4:14-16 NKJV).

We can approach the throne of grace with confidence when our prayers are in accordance with God's will. When we pray in the name of Jesus—that is, when we pray as Jesus would pray in a given situation—we can offer that prayer boldly, knowing that God hears us and will answer our petition. Jesus said, "Whatever you ask in My name, that I will do, that the Father may be glorified in the Son. If you ask anything in My name, I will do it" (John 14:13-14 NKJV). The Lord favorably regards any prayer we offer in His name. When we humbly submit to His will, God will grant our petition because what we are asking is for His glory and our good.

• How do we know if we are praying according to God's will?

"Do we approach God from a beggar's perspective or as His cherished child? If we have any difficulty seeing Him as our loving Father, we need to ask Him to help us develop a healthy Father/child relationship."—David Jeremiah

B. Pray for a Faltering Brother (vv.16-17)

¹⁶ If any man see his brother sin a sin which is not unto death, he shall ask, and he shall give him life for them that sin not unto death. There is a sin unto death: I do not say that he shall pray for it. ¹⁷ All unrighteousness is sin: and there is a sin not unto death.

John follows his strong statement related to answered prayer with a few specific instructions. He calls on Christians to pray for fellow believers who get caught up in sinful activity. When, by an impulse of the Holy Spirit, a Christian realizes that another believer has fallen into sin, the Christian is to go to God in prayer on behalf of the faltering believer. The assurance is that God will answer his or her prayer and bring renewed life to the one who has succumbed to temptation. Jesus set us an example in the case of the apostle Peter. Foreseeing that Peter would fall, Jesus interceded for him. He said to Peter, "I have prayed for you, that your faith should not fail; and when you have returned to Me, strengthen your brethren" (Luke 22:32 NKJV).

However, there is "a sin unto death" (1 John 5:16). The apostle does not advise believers to pray for those guilty of such sin, nor will the Holy Spirit prompt the Christian to pray for them. In the Old Testament, there were sins punishable by death. In the New Testament, Ananias and Sapphira were guilty of lying to the Holy Spirit and met instant death. There is also a form of apostasy from which there is no recovery. When a person rejects Jesus Christ as the way of salvation, "there no longer remains a sacrifice for sins" (Heb. 10:26 NKJV), for Jesus is the only Savior (see 6:4-6; 10:26-29). Then there is "blasphemy against the Spirit," which "shall not be forgiven" (see Matt. 12:22-32)—intentionally and knowingly attributing the miraculous works of Christ to the devil.

John tells us "all wrongdoing is sin" (1 John 5:17 Amp.) and needs to be repented of.

• How should we reach out to a believer who falls into sin?

"It is important that when we are engaged in admonition or exhortation or confrontation with a brother who is overcome in sin, we call attention to the truth in an extraordinarily compassionate and tender and loving spirit."—R. C. Sproul

---

C. Do Not Practice Sinning (vv. 18-21)

¹⁸ We know that whosoever is born of God sinneth not; but he that is begotten of God keepeth himself, and that wicked one toucheth him not. ¹⁹ And we know that we are of God, and the whole world lieth in wickedness. ²⁰ And we know that the Son of God is come, and hath given us an understanding, that we may know him that is true, and we are in him that is true, even in his Son Jesus Christ. This is the true God, and eternal life. ²¹ Little children, keep yourselves from idols. Amen.

John gives a summary of the message he has related throughout his first epistle. He reminds believers that because we are born of God, we do not practice

Principles of an Overcoming Life

sin; and because our life is under the blood of Jesus, Satan cannot touch us (v. 18). We are safe in the hands of God. However, those who have not put their trust in the Lord have reason to fear the Evil One.

Salvation is not guesswork. Repeatedly John used the words "we know." As partakers of the divine nature, we have a certainty about our relationship with God. While we have absolute assurance about our life in Christ, the godless world around us is in the grip of Satan (v. 19). While we enjoy the life we have with Christ now and forever, they have nothing to look forward to but spiritual death, physical death, and even the second death.

John spent much of his time in this epistle defending the faith and refuting the false teachers who denied that the Son of God has come. Once again, he affirms that we know Jesus is the Son of God, He has given us eternal life, and He purchased that life for us with His own blood (v. 20).

The apostle closes this book with a warning to guard against idolatry, keeping away from anything that would take God's place in our heart. We are to avoid the worship of false gods and inward idols that would take us away from our love for God. We are to trust God to defend us against Satan and his minions, and find our fulfillment in God alone.

---

1. How do verses 18 and 19 compare the status of the world with the condition of Christians?
2. Why must God give us "an understanding" (v. 20)?
3. Why do you suppose John ended his letter by writing, "Keep yourselves from idols" (v. 21)?

"Anyone can carry his burden, however heavy, until nightfall. Anyone can do his work, however hard, for one day. Anyone can live sweetly, patiently, lovingly, purely till the sun goes down."—Robert Louis Stevenson

---

CONCLUSION

The key to victorious living is confidence in God. Have you found that confidence? Do you believe Him to be an all-sufficient One who will see you through every situation life may bring your way? Are you practicing the principles of victorious Christian living set forth by John in this epistle? It begins when you place your faith in Jesus Christ and continues as you walk daily with Him.

GOLDEN TEXT CHALLENGE

"WHO IS HE THAT OVERCOMETH THE WORLD, BUT HE THAT BELIEVETH THAT JESUS IS THE SON OF GOD?" (1 John 5:5).

John declared that victory is promised to those who love God. He emphasized that all who are born of God have victory over the world. That means that no system of error, regardless of how subtle or highly organized, will be able to overthrow the child of God. It also means that faith must be everything to us if it is to be victorious.

Believing in Jesus Christ is a powerful act on the part of a human being. It is the victory that overcomes the world.

Daily Devotions:

M. Living in Covenant With God
   Genesis 17:1-9
T. Confidence in God
   Psalm 20:1-9
W. Trust in the Lord
   Jeremiah 17:5-8
T. Overcoming Evil
   Matthew 5:38-48
F. Power to Overcome
   Luke 10:17-20
S. Overcome With Good
   Romans 12:17-21

Introduction to Summer Quarter

The first unit (lessons 1, 3-8), "The Exodus," details events from the life of ɔses and the establishment of the Israelite nation.

The writer of these lessons is the Reverend Rodney Hodge (A.B.), an or- ɪined minister who has served as minister of music for more than thirty years at ɔrthwood Temple Pentecostal Holiness Church in Fayetteville, North Carolina. ɘ holds degrees from Emmanuel College and the University of Georgia and ɪ graduate studies in history at the University of Georgia.

The Pentecost lesson (2) was compiled by Lance Colkmire (see biographical ɪormation on page 16).

"The Doctrine of Salvation" (lessons 9-14) reveals God's plan of redemption ɔugh topical Old and New Testament studies.

The studies were written by Dale Coulter, associate professor of Historical ɪeology at Regent University School of Divinity. He holds a D.Phil. from Oxford ɪiversity, an M.Div. from Reformed Theological Seminary (Orlando, FL), and ɜ.A. from Lee College. Prior to joining the faculty at Regent in 2007, he taught ' eight years at Lee University. He is the author of two books, including a work holiness, and numerous articles with various academic journals. Desiring to ɪintain a connection between the church and the academy, he holds the rank ordained bishop with the Church of God and continues to teach at his local ɪurch in Virginia Beach as well as speaking engagements in other churches.

God Raises Up a Deliverer (Moses)

Exodus 2:1 through 4:17

Unit Theme:
The Exodus

Central Truth:
God hears those who call upon Him in times of trouble.

Focus:
Observe how God responded to Israel's cry for help and be confident that He hears our prayers.

Context:
Events taking place between 1560 and 1440 BC in Goshen, Midian, and Mount Horeb

Golden Text:
"I love the Lord, because he hath heard my voice and my supplications" (Ps. 116:1).

Study Outline:
I. God Prepares a Deliverer
(Ex. 2:1-25)
II. God Calls the Deliverer
(Ex. 3:1-22)
III. God Assures the Deliverer
(Ex. 4:1-17)

INTRODUCTION

The narrative of the Old Testament is characterized by key personalities—Adam, Noah, Abraham, Jacob, Joseph, Moses, Joshua, David, and a host of other less-prominent characters. Moses stands out as one of the greatest. The call of God on his life demanded tremendous faith and determination to carry it out. Moses was commissioned to deliver an enslaved people from their masters, lead them to a covenant with God himself, and then forge a nation out of them. He hand-delivered a complete set of religious and civil laws by which Israel became organized, including the Ten Commandments, which have been the basis for moral behavior in civilized cultures everywhere. Moses is known as deliverer, leader, lawgiver, judge, and prophet of Israel.

Moses was born around 1520 BC. According to the historian Josephus, his birth was foretold to Pharaoh by magicians, and to his father by a dream, though this is not verified in Scripture. Pharaoh was paranoid that the Hebrews might join any rebellion against the Egyptians, so this is a valid possibility. Exodus 2:2 tells us Moses' mother saw something special in her infant, so much so that she went to great lengths to protect his life. This is supported by the writer of Hebrews, who said, "By faith Moses, when he was born, was hid three months of his parents, because they saw he was a proper child; and they were not afraid of the king's commandment" (11:23). Moses' parents probably recognized a prophetic hand on him. Placing the infant in a basket on the Nile might have been a strategic measure—believing that Pharaoh's daughter would find him.

Just who were Moses' parents? Exodus 2:1 says, "There went a man of the house of Levi, and took to wife a daughter of Levi." In 6:20 we are told, "Amram married his father's sister Jochebed, who bore him Aaron and Moses" (NIV). We see this again in Numbers 26:57-59, and 1 Chronicles 6:1-3. According to these texts, Moses was the son of Amram, who was the son of Kohath, who was the son of Levi. Thus, Moses would have been the great-grandson of Levi. This is impossible because four hundred years had elapsed since Jacob and his sons moved to Egypt. In Numbers 3:27-28, we see that the family of Kohath included 8,600 males. To grow to such a size would have taken approximately twelve generations. Most likely, then, Amram and Jochebed were well-known ancestors in Moses' lineage, and the exact names of his parents are not known.

Though adopted and raised as an Egyptian, the Lord still determined that the child would hold to his Hebrew roots. With his own mother as a nurse, he was likely taught the faith of his fathers and the history of his people. The years spent in the court of Pharaoh are not covered in the Old Testament, but Acts 7:22 tells us he "was educated in all the wisdom of the Egyptians and was powerful in speech and action" (NIV).

I. GOD PREPARES A DELIVERER (Ex. 2:1-25)

A. Moses' Parents (v. 1)

¹ And there went a man of the house of Levi, and took to wife a daughter of Levi.

Moses was likely born during the reign of Thutmose I, the great empire build-er of Egypt. By this time the Israelite population had mushroomed, and any sense of goodwill between them and the Egyptian rulers had eroded. Pharaoh's paranoid concern that these foreigners might rise up as an enemy led him to take severe measures. He enslaved the Hebrews and ordered the midwives to kill newborn Hebrew boys. "The future generation of men would be dead, and the girls would eventually be married to Egyptian slaves and absorbed into the Egyptian race" (*Bible Exposition Commentary*).

When this failed, Pharaoh directed male babies to be thrown into the Nile to drown. Israel's plight became desperate. Moses' parents, both of which were of the house of Levi and are unnamed here, likely already feared for the life of their other son, Aaron, who was three years old when Moses was born.

B. A Striking Child (vv. 2-3)

² And the woman conceived, and bare a son: and when she saw him that he was a goodly child, she hid him three months. ³ And when she could not longer hide him, she took for him an ark of bulrushes, and daubed it with slime and with pitch, and put the child therein; and she laid it in the flags by the river's brink.

God is always at work behind the scenes preparing the way for His people. Although Canaan was the inheritance of Abraham's descendants, during the four hundred years they were in Egypt it was a constant battlefield. Invaders from the north frequently fought here with the Egyptians from the south, and the land and inhabitants faced regular devastation. Even though slavery was a terrible ordeal, the "Jewish people could hardly have multiplied or have developed national strength in such a land [as Canaan]" (*Teacher's Commentary*).

Because the Hebrews knew their heritage, they also knew there would rise a deliverer. This had been promised to Abraham. Thus, every mother longed to bear the male child of that promise. As soon as Moses was born, something about the infant was seen as special by his parents, and they determined not to let him be killed. "They took the robust, handsome appearance of the baby as evidence that God had given him for a great purpose" (*Wycliffe Bible Commentary*). Keeping the birth of the boy a secret was very difficult, since all Egyptians were now spies against the Hebrews.

After three months, it became clear that the family could no longer hide the infant from spying eyes. The mother placed the boy in a boat-like basket of papyrus, tar, and pitch, and set the basket in the Nile near a place where Egyptians came to bathe. Moses' sister, Miriam, was left to watch to see what would happen. This was a planned strategy and, at the same time, a form of compliance to the law that male infants be thrown into the Nile.

Was the basket actually left to float in the water? The term *flags* was a general term for river weeds that grow on the edge of a river. Most likely the basket "laid on the bank, where it would naturally appear to have drifted by the current and arrested by the reedy thicket" (*Jamieson, Fausset and Brown Commentary*).

---

1. What was special about baby Moses?
2. How did Moses' mother show her faith in God?

"As parents, you may confidently rear your children according to God's Word. While bringing up your children, you are to remember that your children are not your 'possessions' but instead are the Lord's gift to you. You are to exercise faithful stewardship in their lives."—John C. Broger

---

C. Providential Discovery (vv. 4-6)

[4] **And his sister stood afar off, to wit what would be done to him.** [5] **And the daughter of Pharaoh came down to wash herself at the river; and her maidens walked along by the river's side; and when she saw the ark among the flags, she sent her maid to fetch it.** [6] **And when she had opened it, she saw the child: and, behold, the babe wept. And she had compassion on him, and said, This is one of the Hebrews' children.**

The fact that Miriam stood by to watch what would happen to the baby in the basket indicates that the mother believed he would be retrieved from the water. This was not an ill-planned maneuver, but a preconceived one where she trusted the providence of God to intervene. Still, there was a measure of desperation in her action. To keep the baby at home was an even greater danger to his survival.

The Egyptians held a great reverence for the river as a source of life. From a practical perspective, this was true. Without the river, life in Egypt would have been nearly impossible. The "spiritual" implications added by superstition and idolatry made the river sacred. "It was considered an act of special devotion to plunge at certain seasons into the waters of the sacred stream" (*Jamieson, Fausset, and Brown Commentary*). The area where Moses was placed was probably fenced off, thus protected from crocodiles. The princess would certainly have risked her safety in infested waters.

This princess daughter of Pharaoh was possibly Hatshepsut, who later herself assumed the throne in Egypt and ruled adeptly for twenty-two years, all the while giving Moses a brilliant education.

• How did Pharaoh's daughter respond to her discovery?

"What a mercy was it to us to have parents that prayed for us before they had us, as well as in our infancy when we could not pray for ourselves!"—John Flavel

---

D. A Nurse and a Princess (vv. 7-10)

(Exodus 2:7-9 is not included in the printed text.)

¹⁰ And the child grew, and she brought him unto Pharaoh's daughter, and he became her son. And she called his name Moses: and she said, Because I drew him out of the water.

The fact that Moses' own mother became his nurse and was readily available indicates several things: (1) The family lived in close proximity to the royal properties. (2) The parents may have been domestic servants on the royal grounds. (3) The princess was emotionally detached to the plight of the Hebrew people as a whole while still compassionate when she had personal contact with the infant.

Providence placed Moses in the palace of the Pharaoh where he could learn the wisdom of Egypt. God never calls the qualified, but rather qualifies those whom He calls. He puts them in places where they will learn the wisdom and knowledge needed to carry out His plan. The princess took the infant as her own son, totally ignorant that she was a pawn of God's plan. She indeed had a noble heart, adopting him as her own. The Egyptian word *Moses* means "son" or "born," but sounds like a word in Hebrew that means "to draw out of the water."

The deliverer of the Israelites needed to know the ways of the Egyptians. He needed to be recognized by his own people as one having influence. "If he was to hate and to war against idolatry, and to rescue an unwilling people from it, he must know the rottenness of the system, and must have lived close enough to it to know what went on behind the scenes, and how foully it smelled when near" (*Bible Illustrator*).

---

1. How did Moses' sister serve him (vv. 7-8)?
2. Explain the irony in verse 9.
3. Why did Pharaoh's daughter name the child "Moses" (v. 10)?

"A providence is shaping our ends; a plan is developing in our lives; a supreme and loving Being is making all things work together for good."—F. B. Meyer

---

E. Moses Flees to Midian (vv. 11-15)

(Exodus 2:11-15 is not included in the printed text.)

When he was forty years old, Moses realized just how fully he was committed to his birth roots. He killed an Egyptian who was beating an Israelite. The next day he tried to play peacemaker between two other Israelites, believing this would be an act of endearment to them. However, he discovered that his killing of the Egyptian the day prior had been seen and word had gotten out. We might infer here that Moses knew the volatility of his position in the Egyptian court. His Hebrew heritage had probably already raised some eyebrows as to where his loyalties lay. The fact that the Pharaoh immediately sought him out to kill him affirms this. Moses quickly fled from Egypt, leaving behind all the wealth and status he had achieved.

Just how did Moses come to feel such loyalty to his birth roots? There are several possible answers. First, because he was nursed by his own mother (and probably maintained contact with his family), he was emotionally tied to his own people. Second, even though he was an insider in the Egyptian royal household, he was also privy to its ill-doings. The unnecessary cruelty toward the Israelites likely was a constant cause for his tender conscience to be tested. Third, God's hand was on his life, forming Moses into a servant-leader who would later be known as the meekest man on earth (see Num. 12:3).

---

1. What did Moses do, and why (vv. 11-12)?
2. Why did Moses flee from Egypt (vv. 13-15)?

F. New Life in Midian (vv. 16-22)

(Exodus 2:16-20 is not included in the printed text.)

²¹ And Moses was content to dwell with the man: and he gave Moses Zipporah his daughter. ²² And she bare him a son, and he called his name Gershom: for he said, I have been a stranger in a strange land.

The founder of the Midianites was Midian, son of Keturah, the wife of Abraham's later years. This desert land was a far different place from where Moses had grown up. At age forty, this was very much a "midlife crisis" point. Here he met the seven daughters of Reuel, who was later known as Jethro (although this may have simply been his priestly title). Moses' natural bent to help the underdog caused him to intervene in these girls' conflict with local shepherds. His heroic act brought the favor of their father, and thus a marriage to one of them. For the next forty years, Moses took on the role of a quiet sheepherder in the Sinai Desert. The knowledge gained here would later be immensely helpful as he governed the Israelites for forty years in the same terrain.

Did Moses give up on the dream and calling he had felt throughout his life? We don't know, but God used this time to mature him and wait for perfect timing

---

for the difficult tasks ahead. Also, even though Reuel was "the priest of Midian" (v. 16), it is uncertain as to whether he knew Jehovah or was pagan.

---

1. What do Moses' actions in verses 16 and 17 say about him?
2. How did the sisters describe Moses (v. 19)?
3. What did Moses name his son, and why (v. 22)?

"God's providence is His constant care for and His absolute rule over all His creation for His own glory and the good of His people."—Jerry Bridges

---

G. A New Pharaoh in Egypt (vv. 23-25)

(Exodus 2:24-25 is not included in the printed text.)

23 And it came to pass in process of time, that the king of Egypt died: and the children of Israel sighed by reason of the bondage, and they cried, and their cry came up unto God by reason of the bondage.

We are not told here how long the "process of time" was, but Acts 7:30 says it was forty years, or one generation. God had not forgotten the cries of His people, and now the *kairos* (set time) for deliverance was at hand. Moses was now to the natural eye nothing but the shepherd of stubborn sheep, but "this was just the kind of preparation he needed for leading a nation of stubborn people" (*Bible Exposition Commentary*).

It is not certain why the death of one Pharaoh and the rise of another is important to the story. The deceased king was possibly Thutmose III, who had greatly oppressed the Israelites. He would be followed by Amenhotep II. This new Pharaoh likely knew only *about* Moses, and had not known him personally. Certainly during the intervening forty years, the oppression of the Israelites had continued.

---

1. Describe the status of the children of Israel (v. 23).
2. What is encouraging about verses 24 and 25?

God's Amazing Ways

Why was the deliverance of Israel so long in the making? In Genesis 15:16, God told Abraham that his descendants would be in slavery for four hundred years, and this was for an odd reason: ". . . the iniquity of the Amorites is not yet full." The Amorites were the race living in Canaan. They were a very depraved people. For those four hundred years, God would hold back—in His grace—judgment on them until their sin was irreversible. Thus, for centuries His own people suffered.

Sometimes we have to go through problems, not because of any wrongdoing on our part, but so that His mercy might be extended to our enemies. Thus, the admonition from Jesus to "love your enemies, and pray for those who persecute you" (see Matt. 5:44). God's ways are not our ways. It is His will that we pray for our enemies, and yet those prayers ultimately bring blessing to us. Not to do so only prolongs our own problems.

II. GOD CALLS THE DELIVERER (Ex. 3:1-22)

A. God Appears to Moses (vv. 1-9)

(Exodus 3:1, 5-9 is not included in the printed text.)

² And the angel of the Lord appeared unto him in a flame of fire out of the midst of a bush: and he looked, and, behold, the bush burned with fire, and the bush was not consumed. ³ And Moses said, I will now turn aside, and see this great sight, why the bush is not burnt. ⁴ And when the Lord saw that he turned aside to see, God called unto him out of the midst of the bush, and said, Moses, Moses. And he said, Here am I.

It is obvious that Moses' life can be divided into three equal forty-year periods. It is equally obvious how different these three periods were. The first period consisted of training and education in Pharaoh's court, while at the same time watching the oppression of his relatives. The second was a quiet time when Moses could pray for and reflect on the plight of his people back in Egypt. The present text comes at the end of this period. The third period was the actual deliverance of Israel and the forming of a nation.

Moses led his flock to "the mountain of God" (v. 1). This title was likely given by Moses in retrospect later as he wrote about his experiences there. He is credited with writing the Pentateuch (first five books of the Old Testament). Possibly *Horeb* refers to the mountain range, and *Sinai* to the particular peak. Was there some anticipation on Moses' part that he was about to have a meeting with God? We don't know, but the call to be a deliverer had never left him.

Burning bushes were not uncommon in the desert, where the heat could cause spontaneous combustion. Moses could have moved on, but the fact that the bush was not consumed triggered something in him. Perhaps he saw the bush as the fire of God, an empowering force that could not be stopped.

---

1. What was unusual about what Moses saw (vv. 2-3)?
2. What instructions did God give Moses (v. 5)?
3. Explain Moses' initial response to God (v. 6).
4. What had God "seen" and "heard" (vv. 7, 9)?
5. What was God's plan (v. 8)?

"When you become consumed by God's call on your life, everything will take on new meaning and significance. You will begin to see every facet of your life—including your pain—as a means through which God can work to bring others to Himself."—Charles Stanley

---

B. The Call (vv. 10-12)

¹⁰ Come now therefore, and I will send thee unto Pharaoh, that thou mayest bring forth my people the children of Israel out of Egypt. ¹¹ And Moses said unto God, Who am I, that I should go unto Pharaoh, and that I should bring forth the children of Israel out of Egypt? ¹² And he said, Certainly I will be with thee; and this shall be a token unto thee, that I have sent thee:

When thou hast brought forth the people out of Egypt, ye shall serve God upon this mountain.

If God was finally about to deliver His people, why was Moses so reticent to step into his role as leader? Instead of immediately submitting to the call, he made excuses. His earlier impetuousness had turned into stubbornness. Probably he was afraid of failure, for having lived forty years in obscurity certainly did not make him the prime candidate to march into Pharaoh's court. Also, his advanced age might have left him insecure in his abilities. Still, we know that he was healthy, having led his flocks up a mountain range. Whatever the reasoning and self-image, God would not take "no" for an answer. The question "Who am I?" is irrelevant when the Almighty says, "I will be with you."

That God was now ready to bring the people into "a land flowing with milk and honey" (v. 8), promised to Abraham centuries earlier, should have excited Moses. Interestingly, while *honey* might be figuratively used to denote bountiful food and provision, it also literally refers to bees' honey, which has always abounded in Canaan. God was making ready a rich land for His people.

---

1. How did Moses question God, and why (vv. 10-11)?
2. What sign did God give to Moses (v. 12)?

C. God Identifies Himself (vv. 13-20)

(Exodus 3:15-20 is not included in the printed text.)
¹³ And Moses said unto God, Behold, when I come unto the children of Israel, and shall say unto them, The God of your fathers hath sent me unto you; and they shall say to me, What is his name? what shall I say unto them? ¹⁴ And God said unto Moses, I AM THAT I AM: and he said, Thus shalt thou say unto the children of Israel, I AM hath sent me unto you.

Moses was confused as to how to identify to His own people the One who was sending him. Moses knew he had to present himself adequately. In asking for the name of God, he wanted to know the character of God. In other words, he was asking God, "What does Your name mean?"

The answer from the Lord was clear: "I am the self-existent One who always was, always will be, and is totally dependable and faithful." This is the same type answer Jesus gave when He said, "I am the bread of life" (John 6:35); "I am the light of the world" (8:12); "I am the way, the truth, and the life" (14:6); and many more.

The Lord assured Moses that the Israelites would follow his leadership (Ex. 3:18). In fact, He told him everything that would happen when he returned to Egypt. Egypt would resist him and face terrible judgments (vv. 19-20). The phrase "God of the Hebrews" (v. 18) was not an admission that there are multiple deities, but simply a term that the polytheistic Pharaoh would understand.

The request to leave Egypt for a three-day journey to worship their God seems odd to us, especially since the real motive was to leave permanently. It was in God's plan, however, to completely display the tyrannical nature of Pharaoh. Also, Hebrew worship included the sacrifice of animals, some of which were sacred to the Egyptians. It would seem on the surface to be a respectful notion for the Hebrews to carry out their worship in a means not offensive to the Egyptians.

1. What question did Moses ask (v. 13)?
2. What did God call Himself, and why is that name significant (vv. 14-15)?
3. What was Moses to tell his people (vv. 16-17)?
4. How would the Hebrew people respond to Moses (v. 18)?
5. How would Pharaoh respond to Moses (v. 19)?

"The character of God is today, and always will be, exactly what it was in Bible times. God is forever what at that moment, three thousand years ago, He told Moses that He was."—J. I. Packer

---

D. The Promise of Favor (vv. 21-22)

21 And I will give this people favour in the sight of the Egyptians: and it shall come to pass, that, when ye go, ye shall not go empty: 22 But every woman shall borrow of her neighbour, and of her that sojourneth in her house, jewels of silver, and jewels of gold, and raiment: and ye shall put them upon your sons, and upon your daughters; and ye shall spoil the Egyptians.

It is not clear whether the long struggle with Pharaoh would cause favor in the eyes of the Egyptians as a whole toward the Hebrews, or whether they would be simply so worn down as to want to give them anything they wanted just to be free from plagues. In either case, the slaves would walk away with the wealth of their masters in their pockets. The gold and silver booty would later be used in the construction of the Tabernacle. In other words, it became an offering of worship unto God. Proverbs 13:22 says, "A sinner's wealth is stored up for the righteous" (NIV).

• How would the children of Israel "spoil the Egyptians" (v. 22)?

III. GOD ASSURES THE DELIVERER (Ex. 4:1-17)

A. Moses Balks, God Demonstrates (vv. 1-9)

(Exodus 4:6-9 is not included in the printed text.)

1 And Moses answered and said, But, behold, they will not believe me, nor hearken unto my voice: for they will say, The Lord hath not appeared unto thee. 2 And the Lord said unto him, What is that in thine hand? And he said, A rod. 3 And he said, Cast it on the ground. And he cast it on the ground, and it became a serpent; and Moses fled from before it. 4 And the Lord said unto Moses, Put forth thine hand, and take it by the tail. And he put forth his hand, and caught it, and it became a rod in his hand: 5 That they may believe that the Lord God of their fathers, the God of Abraham, the God of Isaac, and the God of Jacob, hath appeared unto thee.

Despite everything that God himself had just laid out, Moses still balked at obeying for fear that the Israelites would not believe he had been sent to them. His complaints came from personal inadequacy. All the elaborate details and instructions seemed to have intensified his fear of failure. The man who had once been too self-confident was now bent completely in the other direction. We may criticize his reticence, but everyone wants to know for certain that it is God leading us, and not our own imaginations and personal ambitions. And there was no written Word of God to direct Moses.

Moses was given two frightening demonstrations of the miraculous—the turning of his staff into a snake and the appearance of leprosy on his hand (vv. 3-8). Having to grab the snake by the tail was extremely dangerous, and doing as he was commanded required faith. Snakes symbolized power and life in the Egyptian mind-set. God was proving that He had control over such, and He was conferring this power to Moses' use. The leprous hand was equally frightening. There was no cure for it, and it was considered to be a death sentence. When his hand was suddenly cured, Moses surely was awed, and by the two signs he should now have the confidence that he was certainly commissioned by God for the job ahead.

The Lord then gave Moses the promise of a third sign—the ability to turn water from the Nile into blood (v. 9). All these he later used to convince the people to follow him (vv. 29-31).

- List the three ways God would enable Moses to show his people God was with him.

"God has a course mapped out for your life, and all the inadequacies in the world will not change His mind. He will be with you every step of the way. And though it may take time, He has a celebration planned for when you cross over the Red Seas of your life."—Charles Stanley

---

B. Lack of Eloquence (vv. 10-17)

¹⁰ And Moses said unto the Lord, O my Lord, I am not eloquent, neither heretofore, nor since thou hast spoken unto thy servant: but I am slow of speech, and of a slow tongue. ¹¹ And the Lord said unto him, Who hath made man's mouth? or who maketh the dumb, or deaf, or the seeing, or the blind? have not I the Lord? ¹² Now therefore go, and I will be with thy mouth, and teach thee what thou shalt say. ¹³ And he said, O my Lord, send, I pray thee, by the hand of him whom thou wilt send. ¹⁴ And the anger of the Lord was kindled against Moses, and he said, Is not Aaron the Levite thy brother? I know that he can speak well. And also, behold, he cometh forth to meet thee: and when he seeth thee, he will be glad in his heart. ¹⁵ And thou shalt speak unto him, and put words in his mouth: and I will be with thy mouth, and with his mouth, and will teach you what ye shall do. ¹⁶ And he shall be thy spokesman unto the people: and he shall be, even he shall be to thee instead of a mouth, and thou shalt be to him instead of God. ¹⁷ And thou shalt take this rod in thine hand, wherewith thou shalt do signs.

Moses still had one complaint left—that he was not eloquent in speech. He had been tending sheep in Midian for forty years, and now God wanted to give speeches in Hebrew to a vast number of enslaved people. However, if God could perform the miraculous acts that had just been displayed, He could certainly anoint the man's lips to speak proper words. This was not humility, but negative pride.

Moses addressed God here as "Lord," but his attitude was still not one of submission. The Lord agreed to let Aaron come along as a spokesperson, but this would later prove to be a problem. It was Aaron who went along with the people to build the golden calf. Moses should have trusted the Lord completely here. It was a mistake he would pay for later. There is a lesson here for every believer. When God lets us have what we selfishly want, it usually turns out to be anything but a blessing to us.

Moses would prove to be eloquent in his own right, as his later speeches and the writing of the Pentateuch prove. The Book of Deuteronomy is a powerful farewell address. Centuries later, Stephen said Moses was "mighty in words and in deeds" (Acts 7:22).

---

1. What did God ask Moses in verse 11, and why (vv. 10, 12)?
2. Whom did Moses' "whomever" (v. 13 NASB) not include, and why not?
3. How would God work through Moses' brother (vv. 14-16)?
4. What role would Moses' rod play (v. 17)?

"God put each of us here to be a power. There is not one of us but is an essential wheel of the machinery and can accomplish all that God calls us to."—A. B. Simpson

---

CONCLUSION

Henry Wadsworth Longfellow said, "Though the mills of God grind slowly,/Yet they grind exceeding small;/Though with patience He stands waiting,/With exactness grinds He all." At times our plight in life seems miserable, without end or remedy, yet we must realize that God does act in our behalf. He is never too late or too early. Ours is only to trust Him.

Paul said of the various trials of the Israelites, "Now these things were our examples, to the intent we should not lust after evil things, as they also lusted" (1 Cor. 10:6). In other words, the testimony of what others have faced, and how God did intervene, should build our faith.

GOLDEN TEXT CHALLENGE

"I LOVE THE LORD, BECAUSE HE HATH HEARD MY VOICE AND MY SUPPLICATIONS" (Ps. 116:1).

Some Bible scholars associate Psalm 116 with the serious sickness of King Hezekiah. But this is based on tradition. However, we can safely say the writer of this psalm had passed through a similar sickness as Hezekiah that had brought him near to death. He felt and sang as one who had just received a new lease on life. Having been restored to life, he deeply felt what God had done for him. He experienced a new personal affection for God that gave him a new joy. It is the basis of new love. His restored life was a direct answer to prayer. It reminded him of God's interest in him. God loved him; and love begets love.

For this psalmist, the fact that God hears him is a basis of love. "He hath heard my voice and my supplications"—this tells him that God is responsive to His children. We can only love living persons. We use the term *love* in a very inappropriate way when we apply it to things. God *hearing* is God *living*; and the living God can be the object of human love.

Daily Devotions:

M. A Prophet Like Moses
    Deuteronomy 18:15-19
T. The Leadership of Moses
    Psalm 77:13-20
W. Remember the Days of Moses
    Isaiah 63:8-14
T. The Appearance of Moses
    Luke 9:28-35
F. The Testimony of Moses
    Acts 7:30-36
S. The Faith of Moses
    Hebrews 11:23-29

Be Filled With the Spirit (Pentecost)

Numbers 11:10-29; Acts 2:1-17, 41-47; 4:31-35;
2 Corinthians 3:1-8; Galatians 5:22-26; Ephesians 5:18-21

Unit Theme:
Pentecost

Central Truth:
Scripture commands Christians to be filled with the Holy Spirit.

Focus:
Acknowledge that it is God's will for every Christian to be filled with the Holy Spirit, and live a Spirit-filled life.

Context:
Various passages on being filled with God's Spirit

Golden Text:
"Be filled with the Spirit; speaking to yourselves in psalms and hymns and spiritual songs, singing and making melody in your heart to the Lord" (Eph. 5:18-19).

Study Outline:
  I. Filled With the Spirit
     (Num. 11:24-29; Acts 2:1-4, 16-17)
 II. Spirit-Filled Living
     (Acts 2:41-47; Eph. 5:18-21; Gal. 5:22-25)
III. Spirit-Filled Unity and Service
     (Acts 4:31-35; 2 Cor. 3:5-6)

INTRODUCTION

Frequently, when speaking of God's will, we tend to think of specific actions such as vocations, marriage, even purchases. Rarely do individuals think about God's will in terms of spiritual growth and experiences. Today's lesson directs our attention to God's will for us in terms of the Holy Spirit's active work in our lives. The specific objective is to acknowledge it is God's will for every Christian to be filled with the Holy Spirit and live a Spirit-filled life.

The breadth of this lesson takes us to both sides of the outpouring of the Holy Spirit. We will begin with the work of the Spirit in the Old Testament and end with ministry in a New Testament congregation. This reminds us of the ongoing ministry of the Holy Spirit, which precedes the Day of Pentecost in Jerusalem and continues to this present day.

Since this is Pentecost Sunday, it would be good for us to understand the background of Pentecost with its origin in Judaism. Pentecost is a feast observed fifty days after the Passover. Devout Jews believe this day marks the anniversary of God's giving the Law. They carefully review the Torah (Pentateuch) and may stay up all night in order to do so.

In the New Testament era of the early church, Pentecost stands as that important day when the promised Comforter descends on the gathered disciples. Obediently they have been waiting for ten days. During this time, prayer and unity prevails. Then they experience the baptism of the Holy Spirit with the initial evidence of speaking in tongues. Immediately the church grows as three thousand come to faith in Christ.

This entire lesson points to the Spirit-filled life in both the Old Testament and the New Testament. However, it doesn't stop there. The Spirit-filled life isn't to be just a historical item of the past. God's will is for each of us to daily live the Spirit-filled life. This enables us to live with confidence as we face some of the difficulties that are common to life. It also empowers us to be witnesses of the saving and keeping power of the Lord Jesus Christ.

While studying this lesson, be sure to pay special attention to the diverse areas in which the Spirit-filled life can make a difference. It ranges from skills to community to worship. No dimension of our lives is to be separated from the impact of the Holy Spirit's ministry.

I. FILLED WITH THE SPIRIT (Num. 11:24-29; Acts 2:1-4, 16-17)

A. The Elders (Num. 11:24-29)

24 And Moses went out, and told the people the words of the Lord, and gathered the seventy men of the elders of the people, and set them round about the tabernacle. 25 And the Lord came down in a cloud, and spake unto him, and took of the spirit that was upon him, and gave it unto the seventy elders: and it came to pass, that, when the spirit rested upon them, they prophesied, and did not cease. 26 But there remained two of the men in the camp, the name of the one was Eldad, and the name of the other Medad: and the spirit rested upon them; and they were of them that were written, but went not out unto the tabernacle: and they prophesied in the camp. 27 And there ran a young man, and told Moses, and said, Eldad and Medad do prophesy in the camp. 28 And Joshua the son of Nun, the servant of Moses, one of his young men, answered and said, My lord Moses, forbid them. 29 And Moses said unto him, Enviest thou for my sake? would God that all the Lord's people were prophets, and that the Lord would put his spirit upon them!

It is difficult to realize the heavy load of leadership which Moses bears as Israel progresses toward the Promised Land. Regardless of God's miraculous provisions, the people repeatedly lapse into complaining. Often they direct it as a personal attack against Moses. The people's griping over their continuous diet of manna finally becomes too much for him, and Moses pours out his frustration to God (vv. 4-10).

Moses feels God has placed too great a burden on him. He didn't choose this position for himself. The people's attitudes and actions make it similar to a father needing to carry a nursing child. There isn't meat available to satisfy their appetites. Moses says he is unable to carry this burden alone. In fact, death appears to be more desirable than to continue in this path (vv. 11-15).

God doesn't deal specifically with Moses in terms of what he feels or states. Instead, He gives Moses the plan of action to alleviate the distress. First, he is to gather the leaders of Israel and have them stand at the Tabernacle. Second, the Lord will take some of the spiritual anointing which covers Moses and put it on the elders. Third, the Spirit upon the elders will enable them to share in the burden of leadership. Fourth, the people are to sanctify themselves in preparation for divine provision. Fifth, God will provide meat which will last a whole month (vv. 16-20).

In his frustrated mind-set, Moses questions the provision of so much meat. Even killing all their livestock wouldn't provide enough. God gently reminds him of His ability (vv. 21-23). Isn't it interesting how this man who experienced the power of God in the ten plagues on Egypt and the crossing of the Red Sea must now deal with doubt? This reminds us of the need to keep our faith strong, even in the time of crisis.

When the elders of Israel gather with Moses at the Tabernacle, they are given the Holy Spirit just as was upon their leader. Notice there is a verbal sign of this covering—they prophesy. It is an initial evidence which does not continue. The latter portion of verse 25 is most accurately translated "but they did not do so again" (NIV).

Two of the men listed as elders, Eldad and Medad, do not join the others at the Tabernacle. For some reason not stated, they are still in the camp when the Holy Spirit is given. However, that doesn't matter. They receive Him where they are and begin to prophesy. A messenger runs to Moses with this information. Joshua, the right-hand man of Moses, misunderstands or misinterprets what is taking place. He sees it as being "out of order" or possibly insubordination to Moses' leadership. In any case, he asks Moses to stop them.

Moses' reply indicates his mature grasp of what is taking place. He isn't threatened by these elders prophesying, even if it is in the camp away from the main group. This is a mighty blessing for individuals and for the whole nation. Moses desires for everyone to have this experience and empowerment.

How blessed we are to know that the fullness of the Holy Spirit is now available to all! We just need to be open to receiving and seek this blessing for service.

---

of them that were written (v. 26)—"listed among the elders" (NIV)

---

1. Why do you suppose "the Lord came down in a cloud" (v. 25)?
2. What did God do for the elders, and why (vv. 25-26)?
3. Explain Moses' desire expressed in verse 29.

"We do not use the Holy Spirit; He uses us."—Warren Wiersbe

B. The Obedient (Acts 2:1-4)

¹ And when the day of Pentecost was fully come, they were all with one accord in one place. ² And suddenly there came a sound from heaven as of a rushing mighty wind, and it filled all the house where they were sitting. ³ And there appeared unto them cloven tongues like as of fire, and it

sat upon each of them. **⁴ And they were all filled with the Holy Ghost, and began to speak with other tongues, as the Spirit gave them utterance.** When studying this passage, there is a tendency to emphasize the phenomena described in verses 2 and 3. It is hard to imagine what it would have been like to be in that room, more than likely rather crowded, and seen and heard what took place.

For today's lesson, let's focus on the people. Just prior to His ascension, Jesus directs His followers to go to Jerusalem and wait for the promised gift of the Holy Spirit (Luke 24:49; Acts 1:4-5). There is a definite place for this to take place, but no specific timetable other than "in a few days" (Acts 1:5 NIV). Obedient to His word, 120 of them gather in Jerusalem. Instead of scattering throughout the city, they wait as a unified body.

Acts 1:12-26 describes some of their activities. Foremost is their continued emphasis and commitment to prayer (v. 14). They also did some business by filling Judas' vacant position in the Twelve. There's no hint of their spending time in aimless waiting or casual visiting. They aren't complaining about how much longer it will take.

In 2:1-4 the Holy Spirit comes upon this gathered group with audible and visual phenomena. More important is the evidence of their being filled with the Holy Spirit. The Holy Spirit enables them to speak languages they had never learned but could be understood by the various nationalities gathered in Jerusalem for the Feast of Pentecost.

---

cloven (v. 3)—"divided" (NKJV)

---

1. What were the two sounds heard that testified to the Holy Spirit's coming (vv. 2, 4)?
2. What happened to "each of them" (v. 3), and why?

C. The Fulfillment (vv. 16-17)

¹⁶ But this is that which was spoken by the prophet Joel. ¹⁷ And it shall come to pass in the last days, saith God, I will pour out of my Spirit upon all flesh: and your sons and your daughters shall prophesy, and your young men shall see visions, and your old men shall dream dreams.

The events within the location where the believers were waiting for the promise apparently spills out into the streets. Knowing how narrow the streets are and how closely houses are packed together, it quickly becomes evident to people in the area that a phenomenon is occurring. They respond with amazement, since they know these Galileans could not possibly be fluent in all the languages of their native areas (vv. 7-10). Notice there isn't the thought of each one simply speaking a few words or phrases which may be easily learned. Instead, there is the sense of speaking fluently.

Besides the amazement of the multitude witnessing this mighty outpouring, they also are perplexed. What is the significance or meaning? In response to the people's questioning, the Twelve address the group. Beginning at verse 14, Peter stands out as the primary spokesperson. Notice how he addresses them. He recognizes some as visiting during the feast time and others as residents of Jerusalem.

It's interesting how Peter orders his presentation. First, he addresses those who have discarded these actions as the result of drunkenness. It's only 9:00 in the morning. No group would begin partying so early, enabling them to be intoxicated at this hour. Though Peter didn't, he could have pointed to wine causing slurred speech. Its influence never enables anyone to speak precisely and in a language never learned.

Having eliminated the scoffers' suggestion, Peter points to the Scriptures. He announces with clarity their seeing the fulfillment of the prophecy of Joel 2:28-29. Though given centuries earlier, they now are privileged to witness its taking place. Through the outpouring of the Holy Spirit, all can experience His ministry through them in what was previously limited to a select few. Neither gender nor age are qualifications for this blessing.

• What is the significance of the term "all flesh" (v. 17)?

"The Holy Spirit gives power for Christian service, the evidence of which [in Joel 2:28-29] is prophecy, dreams, and visions."—French Arrington

---

II. SPIRIT-FILLED LIVING (Acts 2:41-47; Eph. 5:18-21; Gal. 5:22-25)

A. A Fellowship Community (Acts 2:41-47)

41 Then they that gladly received his word were baptized: and the same day there were added unto them about three thousand souls. 42 And they continued stedfastly in the apostles' doctrine and fellowship, and in breaking of bread, and in prayers. 43 And fear came upon every soul: and many wonders and signs were done by the apostles. 44 And all that believed were together, and had all things common; 45 And sold their possessions and goods, and parted them to all men, as every man had need. 46 And they, continuing daily with one accord in the temple, and breaking bread from house to house, did eat their meat with gladness and singleness of heart, 47 Praising God, and having favour with all the people. And the Lord added to the church daily such as should be saved.

After the Day of Pentecost the fledgling church numbers over three thousand. There is no structured government other than the informal leadership of the Twelve. They have no church buildings, but they do have a bond of community. Verse 42 shows they follow a set of doctrinal beliefs. This centers on the life and teachings of Jesus as well as the Old Testament Scriptures. From this we see the importance of doctrine rather than personal experience being the foundation of the church. First Timothy 4:16 speaks clearly of this: "Watch your life and doctrine closely. Persevere in them, because if you do, you will save both yourself and your hearers" (NIV).

The early church's fellowship is seen in their praying and eating together. Sharing food around a table provides an intimate approach which enables conversation to flow. It quickly becomes an opportunity to know others on a deeper level beyond the usual topics of the weather and various current events. Verse 46 of the text indicates this to be a regular, daily practice. Being in the same city and sharing the special relationship in Christ causes them to seek out each other. This verse also points to the attitude. These were joyous actions arising from sincere hearts.

This fellowship community then experiences marvelous spiritual results. The miraculous occurs within their community and those who are interested in what is being said and done. Also, more individuals are accepting Christ and becoming a part of the church. Note the response of those observing this body of believers. They are positive toward them. Positive behavior, coupled with the joy of the Lord, impacts those with whom we come in contact.

---

1. Who "gladly received" Peter's message, and what was the evidence (v. 41)?
2. To what were the believers devoted (v. 42)?
3. Describe the relationships of the early Christians (vv. 44-46).
4. How was the world influenced by the church (v. 47)?

What Impact?

When asked how she knew she was a Christian, one lady who worked as a maid responded, "Now I sweep the dirt into a dust pan instead of under the carpet." This raises a further consideration. Having received the baptism in the Holy Spirit, what impact has it made in my lifestyle?

B. A Worshiping Community (Eph. 5:18-21)

18 And be not drunk with wine, wherein is excess; but be filled with the Spirit; 19 Speaking to yourselves in psalms and hymns and spiritual songs, singing and making melody in your heart to the Lord; 20 Giving thanks always for all things unto God and the Father in the name of our Lord Jesus Christ; 21 Submitting yourselves one to another in the fear of God.

Spirit-filled living must include the dimension of worship. To adore and offer our thanksgiving to the Sovereign Lord is to be an ongoing response of believers who are filled with the Holy Spirit and continuing to walk in His influence.

Verse 18 begins with a concept contrast. The apostle Paul points to those individuals who submit to the gratification of wine. They recklessly pursue the taste and short-lived excitement of heavy indulgence with significant negative results. In marked contrast to such a behavior, believers are encouraged to allow the continuance of the Holy Spirit's guiding and fulfilling of their lives. We are to open ourselves daily to the divine impact of the Spirit.

"Speaking to one another" (v. 19 NKJV) through godly songs should be an ongoing part of the Spirit-filled life whenever and wherever believers are in the company of each other. Music is a universal language of cultures to express joy and sorrow. It is only logical for the melodies of the heart to be released into audible song.

The apostle Paul points to a variety of musical literature which is to fulfill our need and desire for expression. This should be a reminder to the worship leader in local congregations to use different types of music. The *psalms* mentioned here most likely refer to the Old Testament Psalms, which were a part of Jewish worship. *Hymns* very likely were the new songs written by believers in the early church to express doctrinal concepts. *Spiritual songs* refer to those that are testimonial, expressing an experience with God.

A worshiping community is also to be a thankful group of believers (v. 20). Thankfulness should include the "small things" of life as well as the larger, seemingly more important aspects. Listening to a small child's simple prayer of thanks can expand our horizon of thankfulness.

Verse 21 teaches that submission to one another plays a part in a Spirit-filled community as we worship together. No one is exempt from being in submission to others. Being filled with the Spirit and operating in the gifts doesn't release anyone from ecclesiastical authority or even parental authority when it applies. Divine order includes both leadership and submission "out of reverence for Christ" (NIV).

---

to yourselves (v. 19)—"to one another"

---

1. What does it mean to be "filled with the Spirit" (v. 18)?
2. What does verse 19 teach about worship?
3. What should "the fear of God" cause us to do (v. 21)?

"A Christian man is the most free lord of all, and subject to none; a Christian man is the most dutiful servant of all, and subject to everyone."—Martin Luther

---

C. A Fruitful Community (Gal. 5:22-25)

22 But the fruit of the Spirit is love, joy, peace, longsuffering, gentleness, goodness, faith, 23 Meekness, temperance: against such there is no law. 24 And they that are Christ's have crucified the flesh with the affections and lusts. 25 If we live in the Spirit, let us also walk in the Spirit.

Here we reach the final evidence or test of Spirit-filled living. The claim is to be backed by genuine, visible evidence. The expression "The proof is in the pudding" also applies to Spirit-filled living. We must demonstrate our testimony.

Before considering the initial two verses, it is vital to understand our position in Christ. Verse 24 reminds us that Christ's children have experienced a crucifixion of their sinful nature with its passions and desires. Since the Spirit has quickened us who were dead in our sins, it becomes our responsibility to practice the new life empowered by the Divine working in our being. We can't mature in Christ and fulfill His purpose if we sit by passively.

Galatians 5:22-23 is a familiar passage. However, familiarity doesn't guarantee either a good understanding or fulfillment of it. First, consider the unity indicated here. The "fruit" is singular, not plural. All the nine virtues listed here are part of a single whole. The implication is that no one can claim to be evidencing the fruit of the Spirit without working to cultivate each of the individual virtues.

Following is a brief statement of what each of these virtues demonstrates:

Love—the distinctive mark of the Christian, which is an act of the will God accomplishes through us

Joy—a cheerful gladness that flows from our salvation, regardless of our circumstances

Peace—the reconciliation with God that enables us to be free from tension, even when in conflict situations

Longsuffering (patience)—being forbearing and non-retaliatory, even when individuals deliberately attempt to provoke us

Gentleness—kindness and politeness that treats others with utmost respect

Goodness—inner character development expressed by moral and ethical values

Faith—faithfulness seen in loyalty and trustworthiness

Meekness (gentleness)—submissiveness and humility before God and others

Temperance (self-control)—self-mastery enabling one to control his or her thoughts and actions

Here we see how the Holy Spirit longs to work in our lives as individuals and as a corporate body of believers. Our claim of the Spirit's fullness in our lives must be reflected in words and actions.

• How do these verses describe the Spirit-filled life?

"There never will exist anything permanently noble and excellent in the character which is a stranger to resolute self-denial."—Sir Walter Scott

---

III. SPIRIT-FILLED UNITY AND SERVICE (Acts 4:31-35; 2 Cor. 3:5-6)

A. Unity and Generosity (Acts 4:31-35)

31 And when they had prayed, the place was shaken where they were assembled together; and they were all filled with the Holy Ghost, and they spake the word of God with boldness. 32 And the multitude of them that believed were of one heart and of one soul: neither said any of them that ought of the things which he possessed was his own; but they had all things common. 33 And with great power gave the apostles witness of the resurrection of the Lord Jesus: and great grace was upon them all. 34 Neither was there any among them that lacked: for as many as were possessors of lands or houses sold them, and brought the prices of the things that were sold, 35 And laid them down at the apostles' feet: and distribution was made unto every man according as he had need.

After the disciples had praised and glorified God (see vv. 24-28), they presented to Him a single and a simple petition. They did not ask for deliverance from the threatenings of the Sanhedrin, or for protection from violence. They knew He would do this if it were His will for them. Their one petition was that He grant them boldness to preach His Word (vv. 29-30).

Unexpectedly the prayer was followed by a tremendous spiritual outpouring upon them. The place where they were gathered was shaken, and the disciples were filled anew with the Holy Spirit. This does not indicate that there had been any diminution of the Spirit in their lives since the Day of Pentecost; there was nothing lacking in spiritual fullness. But this powerful repetition of the infilling further emboldened the disciples to speak His Word in the face of danger.

The common sharing of goods which the Christians had begun earlier (2:44-45) was greatly increased in the face of danger. The Christians sold their houses and lands, pooled their resources, and lived together in unity. Because they were fully united in faith, purpose, and service, the common sharing of material goods was both desirable and spontaneous. No brother of the church desired to have more than any other.

Despite the danger they faced, the disciples of Christ enjoyed a glorious period of power and growth (4:33). The unity of the church was not a pretense, for the people worshiped, worked, believed, and shared together. Growth and grace were the consequence of this unity and fellowship. The emphasis of their ministry was the resurrection of Jesus. This was the great hope and confidence of the church then, and it still is today.

In verses 34 and 35, we read about the common sharing of goods that was practiced at this point in the early church history. God did not command the people to sell their houses and pool their money; it was an ideal of the people themselves. Love made them desire to share, and share alike. Moreover, the disciples were fully expecting the Lord to return momentarily, at which time they would have no need of houses and lands. The practice of community sharing began as a generous gesture of brotherly love; there was no duress or pressure about it. Each person acted voluntarily. It is good when Christians can be thus concerned and feel such responsibility for one another. While there was no commandment from God regarding this practice, He does call on His people to give and to assist when a fellow Christian is in need (1 John 3:17).

---

1. How and why was "the place . . . shaken" (v. 31)?
2. Explain the significance of "great grace" (v. 33).
3. Why were there "no needy persons among them" (v. 34 NIV)?

"The church exists to train its members through the practice of the presence of God to be servants of others, to the end that Christlikeness may become common property."—William Adams Brown

---

B. Able Ministers (2 Cor. 3:5-6)

5 Not that we are sufficient of ourselves to think any thing as of ourselves; but our sufficiency is of God; 6 Who also hath made us able ministers of the new testament; not of the letter, but of the spirit: for the letter killeth, but the spirit giveth life.

In verses 1-3, the apostle Paul said he did not need "letters of recommendation" to prove the legitimacy of his ministry. Instead, he said the Corinthian converts themselves were "our letter, written on our hearts, known and read by everybody" (NIV).

In verse 5 he makes it clear that he could not boast of his success in ministry, for his "sufficiency"—competence, capability, qualification—"is of God." He had no competence in himself to claim anything for himself. When we as Christians realize that our ability to minister to others comes from Christ and we are willing to glorify Christ for what He accomplishes through us, we will find success in our service.

Paul said that God "has made us competent as ministers of a new covenant" (v. 6 NIV). This "new covenant" is the gospel of Jesus Christ—the message that "giveth life" by the Holy Spirit.

We as members of the church of Christ have been entrusted with the gospel of Christ. It is written on our hearts, transforming us into messengers of the good news who can eternally influence other people through the competence Christ gives us.

• Explain the sufficiency or competence of believers.

"Lord, grant that I may always desire more than I can accomplish."—Michelangelo

---

CONCLUSION

When considering the work of the Holy Spirit, it is important to see His work evidenced in both Testaments. Since the Day of Pentecost and up to the present, we are blessed to experience the fullness of both Spirit baptism and daily empowerment. Those of us who have been so privileged to be part of a Spirit-filled community understand the blessings of His ministry in our lives.

GOLDEN TEXT CHALLENGE

"BE FILLED WITH THE SPIRIT; SPEAKING TO YOURSELVES IN PSALMS AND HYMNS AND SPIRITUAL SONGS, SINGING AND MAKING MELODY IN YOUR HEART TO THE LORD" (Eph. 5:18-19).

The service of song is a part of worship in which the Holy Spirit must be vitally involved. How often would barren and cold services be transformed into warm, lively, victorious events if the Holy Spirit were allowed to direct and anoint for the occasion? However much a song is perfect in practice and however fine in technique and performance, unless it is anointed by the Spirit, it will fail to accomplish the purpose of glorifying Christ.

Paul said singing and praise proceed from the heart and is unto the Lord. If singing is only from the lips, it will not bless the singer and surely will not touch others. All songs should be spiritual. Spirit-anointed singing will glorify Jesus, touch hardened hearts, and bless others.

Daily Devotions:

M. God's Spirit in a Ruler
   Genesis 41:37-43
T. Artisans Enabled by the Spirit
   Exodus 31:1-6
W. Spirit-Anointed King
   2 Samuel 23:1-5
T. Filled Again With the Spirit
   Acts 4:23-33
F. Gentiles Receive the Spirit
   Acts 10:44-48
S. Living in the Spirit
   Galatians 5:16-25

Moses and Aaron Confront Pharaoh

Exodus 5:1 through 6:13; 7:1-7

Unit Theme:
The Exodus

Central Truth:
God Enables us to accomplish difficult tasks.

Focus:
Highlight Moses and Aaron's confrontation with Pharaoh and trust God to empower us for difficult tasks.

Context:
Around 1442-1440 BC in Egypt

Golden Text:
"Moses and Aaron went in, and told Pharaoh, Thus saith the Lord God of Israel, Let my people go" (Ex. 5:1).

Study Outline:
I. God's Word Rejected
    (Ex. 5:1-21)
II. God Affirms His Promise
    (Ex. 5:22—6:13)
III. God Reveals His Plan
    (Ex. 7:1-7)

INTRODUCTION

Before Moses could return to Egypt, a number of preparations were required. First, he made a visit to his father-in-law, Jethro. He apparently did not tell Jethro the real reason for leaving, but only that he wanted to check on his relatives (Ex. 4:18). Moses probably felt the full story would have been seen as preposterous.

Moses took his wife, Zipporah, with him, as well as his two sons—Gershom and Eliezer (v. 20). Eliezer was probably still an infant at this time, born while Moses was away with the flocks. At any rate, this second boy had not been circumcised, which represents disobedience on Moses' part. How could he lead the people if he himself had not obeyed the symbol of the covenant God had with His people? Moses apparently became deathly ill because of his disobedience, so Zipporah circumcised her son (vv. 24-25). Possibly she had been resistant to this earlier, and only now was willing to allow it because her husband's life was in danger.

We do not hear about Zipporah again until after the Exodus from Egypt (18:1-5). She and the two children likely returned to Jethro rather than continue on with Moses.

The Lord had already told Moses that Pharaoh would be resistant, and his heart would be hardened. Thus, Moses was well aware that his return to Egypt would not be easy. Throughout the Book of Exodus, we are told that God hardened the heart of the Pharaoh. Did this preclude Pharaoh's right to self-will? No, for there are a number of references to Pharaoh hardening his own heart by his refusals. The apostle Paul commented on this in Romans 9:17-18: "For the Scripture says to Pharaoh: 'I raised you up for this very purpose, that I might display my power in you and that my name might be proclaimed in all the earth.' Therefore God has mercy on whom he wants to have mercy, and he hardens whom he wants to harden" (NIV). God sometimes uses rebellious hearts to forward His purposes. Nevertheless, it is not the Lord himself who hardens them. It is a result of their own decisions.

God told Aaron to meet with Moses—a sure additional sign of His work in progress (Ex. 4:27). They met at Mount Horeb, where God had appeared to Moses in the burning bush. The two brothers were joined in union to accomplish a monumental task. Together they returned to Egypt and immediately spoke with the Israelites, convincing them that God was now prepared to deliver them (vv. 29-31). Thus, our present lesson picks up with the brothers facing Pharaoh for the first time.

I. GOD'S WORD REJECTED (Ex. 5:1-21)

A. Thus Saith the Lord (vv. 1-2)

¹ And afterward Moses and Aaron went in, and told Pharaoh, Thus saith the Lord God of Israel, Let my people go, that they may hold a feast unto me in the wilderness. ² And Pharaoh said, Who is the Lord, that I should obey his voice to let Israel go? I know not the Lord, neither will I let Israel go.

This initial call to let the people go was not necessarily an unreasonable request of Pharaoh. To observe a religious ceremony by any people of the ancient world was common. There was no threat in this initial request. The phrase "Let my people go" has universal appeal for all humanity since the fall in the Garden of Eden. It is the picture of the entire story of redemption. Several observations can be made here: (1) People belong to God, not to the devil. He claims us all as His own. Still, we have to respond to ultimately be included as His. (2) All of humanity is in bondage to sin. Every human is born with a fallen nature that must be redeemed if he or she is to return to God. (3) Bondage brings a slavery to sin. No good works can overcome its grip. Humans are helpless on their own to free themselves.

Pharaoh's reaction was threefold: (1) He repudiated the idea that there might be a deity having any authority over him. In Egypt he was considered to be a god in his own right. Thus, his pride would not allow him to acknowledge one greater than himself. (2) He saw the Israelites as mere slaves, and thus not worthy of having a god to hear them. (3) His only concern was for productivity. Slaves were a commodity having no value, except for the work they could produce. From this we can say that the Egyptian mind-set and view of things divine had already hardened this man's heart.

---

1. What did Moses and Aaron request?
2. Why did Pharaoh say no?

"When you are arguing against Him, you are arguing against the very power that makes you able to argue at all."—C. S. Lewis

B. Necessity of a Sacrifice (v. 3)

³ And they said, The God of the Hebrews hath met with us: let us go, we pray thee, three days' journey into the desert, and sacrifice unto the Lord our God; lest he fall upon us with pestilence, or with the sword.

Moses made the point that the Israelites might be in danger of retribution from their God if they did not make this pilgrimage. Why would he say this if God was about to rescue the Jews from bondage? Probably for the same reason that Moses had put himself in danger by not circumcising his younger son. This would also be the same reason that Moses would later miss going into the Promised Land. The living God demands total obedience. The closer one walks with the Lord, the more narrow the path must become. Moses was making clear to the Pharaoh that they were not dealing with a whimsical, contrived deity. The true God was all-powerful and not to be taken lightly. At the same time, by not fully revealing that total deliverance from Egypt was the ultimate plan, Moses and Aaron were testing Pharaoh's initial reaction.

---

* What reason did Moses give in asking Pharaoh to reconsider his request?

"The Israelites could not sacrifice in the land of Egypt, because the animals they were to offer to God were held sacred by the Egyptians; and they could not omit this duty, because it was essential to religion even before the giving of the Law."—Adam Clarke

---

C. Pharaoh's Hardened Response (vv. 4-9)

⁴ And the king of Egypt said unto them, Wherefore do ye, Moses and Aaron, let the people from their works? get you unto your burdens. ⁵ And Pharaoh said, Behold, the people of the land now are many, and ye make them rest from their burdens. ⁶ And Pharaoh commanded the same day the taskmasters of the people, and their officers, saying, ⁷ Ye shall no more give the people straw to make brick, as heretofore: let them go and gather straw for themselves. ⁸ And the tale of the bricks, which they did make heretofore, ye shall lay upon them; ye shall not diminish ought thereof: for they be idle; therefore they cry, saying, Let us go and sacrifice to our God. ⁹ Let there more work be laid upon the men, that they may labour therein; and let them not regard vain words.

The key phrase in this passage is "the same day" (v. 6). Pharaoh's hardened reaction was both tough and immediate. He had no sympathy for the plight of the enslaved Hebrews. He apparently felt that they had too much free time on their hands—time spent pondering rebellion and freedom. Thus, to remedy the situation, he made their workload even harder.

The old Pharaoh who had been Moses' enemy was now dead. There does not seem to be a consensus among scholars as to which Pharaoh this was, but possibly Thutmose III. If so, then the new monarch was Amenhotep II, and he was probably a young man in his twenties. Generational gaps are nothing new.

Contrast the eighty-year-old Moses facing a proud monarch only a quarter his age. Moses had spent forty years in the desert learning humility so that he could become somebody, while the Egyptian ruler had been led from birth to believe that he himself was a god. The sheer self-deception inbred into him would not let him conceive of a foreign deity greater than himself.

Although Pharaoh was on the way toward a hardened heart, his reaction here was more one of facing a shift in paradigms. The Egyptian mind-set and view of life was so ingrained into him that his reactions here were to be expected. Anytime what we believe is challenged, it is difficult to see the error of our own thinking. For the believer, this is why the presence of the Holy Spirit is so important. Jesus said "the Spirit . . . will guide you into all truth" (John 16:13). Without the Spirit, we are just as capable of being totally deceived in our thinking as Pharaoh was.

---

1. Of what did Pharaoh accuse Moses (vv. 4-5)?
2. What additional work were the Hebrews given (v. 7), and how did this affect the "tale" ("quota," NKJV) of bricks demanded (v. 8)?
3. What was the motive behind the king's instructions (v. 9)?

"Better a shattered heart than a hardened heart."—Woodrow Kroll

---

D. The Burdens Increased (vv. 10-21)

(Exodus 5:10-21 is not included in the printed text.)

Pharaoh was not about to let go of his cheap source of labor. Instead of giving in, he made the work demands far greater. Up until now, the Egyptians had provided the straw used for binding the clay and making the bricks far more durable. Now the Hebrews had to gather the straw for themselves, as well as maintain the same quotas of finished product. This was nearly impossible, and the Israelite foremen were beaten by the Egyptian overseers. These Israelite foremen were able to get an audience with Pharaoh to plead their case, but it was to no avail. He still saw the people as lazy.

Just as Pharaoh apparently hoped, the Israelites turned their frustrations against Moses and Aaron. However, they should never have gone to Pharaoh in the first place. They should have talked first with Moses, who already knew that this would be a battle to the death. Foolishly, they called out to God to judge Moses for causing them a problem. It is interesting how people assume God's view on a matter to be the same as their own. "They call upon God to judge whilst by their very complaining they show that they have no confidence in God and His power to save" (*Wycliffe Bible Commentary*).

---

1. How were the Hebrew foremen treated, and why (vv. 10-14)?
2. What did the Hebrew foremen wish upon Moses and Aaron, and why (vv. 20-21)?

"It has become a settled principle that nothing which is good and true can be destroyed by persecution, but that the effect ultimately is to establish more firmly, and to spread more widely, that which it was designed to overthrow."—Albert Barnes

---

II. GOD AFFIRMS HIS PROMISE (Ex. 5:22—6:13)

A. Moses' Lament (5:22-23)

22 And Moses returned unto the Lord, and said, Lord, wherefore hast thou so evil entreated this people? why is it that thou hast sent me? 23 For since I came to Pharaoh to speak in thy name, he hath done evil to this people; neither hast thou delivered thy people at all.

Moses' feelings here are no different from anyone else who has set out to obey the call of God on his or her life. "There come times to every earnest labourer in God's service, when his efforts seem fruitless, and he gets downcast" (*The Bible Illustrator*). To Moses it appeared that all his hopes were in ruins, but appearances are like clouds in the sky—they pass. Here Pharaoh can be seen as typical of the Enemy that arises against every believer. God's chosen leaders all have to expect opposition from the Enemy and misunderstanding from among those they lead. This comes with the job description.

Even though Moses had to endure the criticisms of the Israelite foremen, he agreed with their accusations. His visit to Pharaoh had increased the plight of his people. Thus, his complaint to the Lord here was motivated by feelings of personal guilt and anguish. The fact that he took his problem to the Lord tells us he was not ready to forsake his call—he was simply discouraged. The worst thing we can do is turn our backs on God. If we have a problem, He can handle anything we have to say. "Spiritual leaders must be bold before people but broken before God and must claim God's promises and do His will even when everything seems to be against them" (*Bible Exposition Commentary*).

• Describe the emotion and content of Moses' prayer.

"There is no man in this world without some manner of tribulation or anguish, though he be king or pope."—Thomas à Kempis

---

B. God Jehovah Revealed (6:1-4)

1 Then the Lord said unto Moses, Now shalt thou see what I will do to Pharaoh: for with a strong hand shall he let them go, and with a strong hand shall he drive them out of his land. 2 And God spake unto Moses, and said unto him, I am the Lord: 3 And I appeared unto Abraham, unto Isaac, and unto Jacob, by the name of God Almighty, but by my name JEHOVAH was I not known to them. 4 And I have also established my covenant with them, to give them the land of Canaan, the land of their pilgrimage, wherein they were strangers.

To relieve Moses' anxiety, the Lord speaks to him twice with the purpose of encouraging him. It was natural that Moses would be discouraged after the first visit to Pharaoh. In verse 1 the Lord assures him that Pharaoh will be forced to let the Israelites go. This is an emphatic repetition of what was promised in 3:20. In 6:2 the Lord begins to speak again, this time reviewing the promises that have been made to His people (vv. 2-8), but now shows Moses His character revealed by the name *Jehovah,* or *Yahweh.* As such, He is always faithful and true to His people. He shows Himself "not only as Sustainer and Provider, but also as the Promise-Keeper, the One who was personally related to His people and would redeem them" (*Bible Knowledge Commentary*).

Why did God say His people had prior to now not known Him as *Jehovah*? Didn't the earlier patriarchs know Him as such? Yes, but in the past they had seen Him more in character (*El Shaddai*) as One who imparts life, increases goods, provides for, and so on. They did not see His raw power to deliver, to fulfill promises. "The fullness of time had come when God was to be known in the capacity and character of His name Yahweh, as He fulfilled what He had promised and did what He had decreed" (*Zondervan NIV Bible Commentary*).

---

1. What would God's "strong hand" accomplish (v. 1)?
2. In verse 4, what is Moses reminded of?

"Discouraged not by difficulties without, or the anguish of ages within, the heart listens to a secret voice that whispers: 'Be not dismayed; in the future lies the Promised Land.'"—Hellen Keller

---

C. God Takes a People for His Own (vv. 5-8)

⁵ And I have also heard the groaning of the children of Israel, whom the Egyptians keep in bondage; and I have remembered my covenant. ⁶ Wherefore say unto the children of Israel, I am the Lord, and I will bring you out from under the burdens of the Egyptians, and I will rid you out of their bondage, and I will redeem you with a stretched out arm, and with great judgments: ⁷ And I will take you to me for a people, and I will be to you a God: and ye shall know that I am the Lord your God, which bringeth you out from under the burdens of the Egyptians. ⁸ And I will bring you in unto the land, concerning the which I did swear to give it to Abraham, to Isaac, and to Jacob; and I will give it you for an heritage: I am the Lord.

The reiteration of promises by the Lord shows that very soon the Israelites would come to understand the meaning of "I am the Lord." God was taking this people to be His own, and would go to unlimited means to vindicate and free them. The promises made to Abraham many generations earlier were not forgotten. In verses 6-8 the phrase "I will" is used, indicating that He is faithful to His promises. Everything He says centers on three distinct promises: (1) deliverance from Egypt, (2) taking the people as His own, and (3) the gift of the Land of Promise. The "stretched out arm" (v. 6) is a gesture indicating the making of an oath. Moses was getting the divine word he needed for carrying out his mission.

---

1. What had the Lord "heard" (v. 5)?
2. What was Moses commanded to tell his people about the Egyptians (vv. 6-7)?

God's Watch Care

Even though Israel had suffered many years of slavery, God was still lovingly watching over His people. His concern is expressed by the prophet Hosea: "When Israel was a child, I loved him, and out of Egypt I called My son. . . . I drew them with gentle cords, with bands of love, and I was to them as those who take the yoke from their neck. I stooped and fed them" (11:1, 4 NKJV). Despite the appearances of abandonment, God was at work through the years preparing a people for Himself. He was never forgetful of their distress.

D. Moses' Loss of Confidence (vv. 9-13)

(Exodus 6:10-13 is not included in the printed text.)
⁹ And Moses spake so unto the children of Israel: but they hearkened not unto Moses for anguish of spirit, and for cruel bondage.

With a fresh sense of God's call upon him, Moses returned to the Israelite leaders with the divine message, "but they did not listen to Moses on account of their despondency" (v. 9 NASB). They were not impressed. "It was the inward pressure caused by deep anguish that prevented proper breathing—like children sobbing and gasping for their breath" (*Zondervan NIV Bible Commentary*). The horror of their situation caused them to refuse to even hear the possibility of their deliverance. They were so vexed that they were incapable of seeing beyond their immediate circumstance.

The response of the Israelites caused Moses to have another pendulum swing of the confidence meter. How could he face Pharaoh if his own people did not believe him? In verses 10-11, God speaks to him again, telling him to go to Pharaoh. Again Moses brought up his poor oratorical ability. The phrase "uncircumcised lips" (v. 12) indicates he felt morally incapable and unclean. Old insecurities are not easily dismissed. His excuses were answered by a firm charge for him and Aaron to go and do as they had been commanded.

---

1. How did the Israelites respond to Moses' message from God, and why (v. 9)?
2. Why did Moses hesitate to follow God's command concerning Pharaoh (vv. 10-12)?

"The ultimate ground of faith and knowledge is confidence in God."—Charles Hodge

---

III. GOD REVEALS HIS PLAN (Ex. 7:1-7)

A. Moses Like a God (vv. 1-5)

¹ And the Lord said unto Moses, See, I have made thee a god to Pharaoh: and Aaron thy brother shall be thy prophet. ² Thou shalt speak all that I command thee: and Aaron thy brother shall speak unto Pharaoh, that he send the children of Israel out of his land. ³ And I will harden Pharaoh's

heart, and multiply my signs and my wonders in the land of Egypt. **⁴ But Pharaoh shall not hearken unto you, that I may lay my hand upon Egypt, and bring forth mine armies, and my people the children of Israel, out of the land of Egypt by great judgments. ⁵ And the Egyptians shall know that I am the Lord, when I stretch forth mine hand upon Egypt, and bring out the children of Israel from among them.**

The Lord promised Moses that he would wield such power that he would appear as a god to Pharaoh. This exalted position was not for Moses' self-indulgence, but rather for the benefit of others. In the same sense, Jesus said, "He that believeth on me, the works that I do shall he do also; and greater works than these shall he do; because I go unto my Father" (John 14:12). As Abraham Lincoln said, "Nearly all men can stand the test of adversity, but if you really want to test a man's character, give him power." The Lord knew He could trust Moses with power, even though Moses was unsure of himself as a leader.

The Lord also gave Moses an outline of what was about to transpire. In spite of any spoken eloquence by Aaron or demonstration of power by Moses, Pharaoh would not yield, but rather dig his heels in against them. This would result in mighty acts of judgment, after which the Egyptians (if not Pharaoh himself) would certainly acknowledge that God is the Lord of all.

The power struggle between Moses and Pharaoh would be a gradual one. The question naturally arises as to why God didn't overthrow the Egyptians with one fatal blow. The answer is that God is gracious. It was not His will to force Pharaoh into submission, just as it is not His will to have to bring each of us to our knees before we surrender our lives to Him. No, He would rather lead us to Himself. Pharaoh was still one of His creatures, and opportunity to change his mind was amply given.

---

1. Explain the Lord's statement, "I have made you as God to Pharaoh" (v. 1 NKJV).
2. Describe the forewarning God gave to Moses (vv. 3-4).
3. What would the Egyptians discover, and how (v. 5)?

"Just as water ever seeks and fills the lowest place, so the moment God finds you abased and empty, His glory and power flow in."—Andrew Murray

---

B. Moses and Aaron Obey (vv. 6-7)

⁶ And Moses and Aaron did as the Lord commanded them, so did they. ⁷ And Moses was fourscore years old, and Aaron fourscore and three years old, when they spake unto Pharaoh.

The time had come for Moses to be completely compliant to the commands given him. Thus, he and Aaron went to Pharaoh. Their ages are given here, typical of how the Old Testament was written. When a major event was about to occur, the ages of prominent figures were given. Thus, after eighty years of preparation, Moses was ready to begin his true life's work. This should be an encouragement for anyone getting older. Often the greatest work we can do is when we have garnered the wisdom and experience necessary to trust God when times are tough.

_____

• Describe the obedience of Moses and Aaron.

_____

CONCLUSION

In his refusal to listen to Moses, Pharaoh was following two of the most fatal of natural human characteristics: First was his sense of self-sufficiency. He had been raised to think he was invincible—that he himself was a god. In a similar sense, young people think they will never grow old . . . that they can do anything they want . . . that they can test fate and win. The difficulties of life eventually prove otherwise. Second, Pharaoh had magicians and, in fact, an entire court of people, who flattered him constantly. It is far better to have someone tell you the truth than one who tells you what you want to hear. Paul asked in Galatians 4:16, "Am I therefore become your enemy, because I tell you the truth?"

GOLDEN TEXT CHALLENGE

"MOSES AND AARON WENT IN, AND TOLD PHARAOH, THUS SAITH THE LORD GOD OF ISRAEL, LET MY PEOPLE GO" (Ex. 5:1).

This is the first time God is called the "God of Israel" in the Scriptures. They were God's people, and as such they owed no allegiance to Pharaoh. As God's people, their right and obligation to worship Him was undeniable. To go three days' journey into the wilderness for that purpose was not unreasonable. God delivers people from sin that they may worship and serve Him.

Daily Devotions:
M. God's Presence Promised
  Joshua 1:5-9
T. Protection Promised
  Psalm 3:1-8
W. Victory Promised
  Jeremiah 1:17-19
T. Peace Promised
  John 16:28-33
F. Power Promised
  Acts 1:4-8
S. Way Out of Temptation Promised
  1 Corinthians 10:11-13

God's Awesome Power Displayed

Exodus 7:8 through 11:10

Unit Theme:
The Exodus

Central Truth:
God is just and will not allow evil to go unpunished.

Focus:
Review God's judgment against Egypt and praise Him for His powerful justice.

Context:
Rameses in Egypt, 1441-1439 BC

Golden Text:
"I [the Lord] will stretch out my hand, and smite Egypt with all my wonders which I will do in the midst thereof: and after that he [Pharaoh] will let you go" (Ex. 3:20).

Study Outline:
 I. Pharaoh Resists God's Power
    (Ex. 7:8-25)
 II. God Judges Egypt With Plagues
    (Ex. 8:5-7, 16-19, 22-24; 9:6-7, 10-11, 23-26; 10:13-15, 22-23)
III. God Prepares Israel for Deliverance
    (Ex. 11:1-10)

INTRODUCTION

Once Moses finally established in his heart that he was to confront Pharaoh until victory was achieved, there was no more wavering, no more insecurity in himself, no more lack of confidence in the Lord. This is the position we as Christians desire in our callings. We want to reach a point where the possibility of turning back or turning aside is not an option. We want to move confidently in our calling. Sadly, many of us drift through life knowing God has a distinct work for us, but never fully committing ourselves to it. Those who do, however, are the ones whose lives and ministry live beyond their years.

It was now fully obvious that the breaking of Pharaoh would be a gradual process. Through a succession of frightening judgments, Pharaoh would come to know that God is the only God and his unwinnable struggle was with the ultimate power of the universe. At first, Pharaoh was unyielding. Picture a man with an ax splitting a block of hard wood. The first blow seems to have no effect, but gradually the block has to respond to the constant strikes. Under the continual jolts of the supernatural, Pharaoh promised to yield, but then his inbred pride stopped him each time the plague was removed. Finally, the death of every firstborn in Egypt caused him to yield and let the Israelites go, but again pride overpowered him. In a fruitless attempt to stop the Israelites, he sent an army after them.

In this lesson we will study the confrontations between the two men, which represent the universal battle between God's will for humanity and the stubborn will of fallen people in their self-exalting pride. Just before the final plague (death of the firstborn), Moses again confronted Pharaoh. One statement he made tells us the reason for the plagues: "that you may know that the Lord makes a distinction between the Egyptians and Israel" (Ex. 11:7 Amp.).

From a natural perspective, there was already an obvious difference. The Egyptians were overlords; they had the achievements in science, culture, and power to prove it, and were immensely proud. The Israelites were slaves and saw themselves as such. They were incapable of discerning their own potential. In their eyes, they were "mere tools to be used by the master race, then tossed aside when they had served their purpose. Worthless. Poor. Subhuman" (*Teacher's Commentary*). Yet, God saw Israel for its potential, as well as for the promise He had made to Abraham. These were His people.

This is the ultimate message to each of us. We are His children, made in His image, each with worth and potential. We must come to this revelation. God can use the least likely—the weakest, the poorest, the least educated—to achieve great things for His kingdom.

I. PHARAOH RESISTS GOD'S POWER (Ex. 7:8-25)

A. Aaron's Rod Becomes a Snake (vv. 8-10)

8 And the Lord spake unto Moses and unto Aaron, saying, 9 When Pharaoh shall speak unto you, saying, Shew a miracle for you: then thou shalt say unto Aaron, Take thy rod, and cast it before Pharaoh, and it shall become a serpent. 10 And Moses and Aaron went in unto Pharaoh, and they did so as the Lord had commanded: and Aaron cast down his rod before Pharaoh, and before his servants, and it became a serpent.

The Lord knew that Pharaoh would require Moses and Aaron to validate themselves by more than words and threats. If they truly were sent as messengers from Israel's God, then they had to demonstrate it. God never expects His people to move and operate on His behalf without His power validating them. The apostle Paul reminded the Corinthians, "My message and my preaching were not with wise and persuasive words, but with a demonstration of the Spirit's power, so that your faith might not rest on men's wisdom, but on God's power" (1 Cor. 2:4-5 NIV).

God instructed Moses as to exactly what he and Aaron should do. Since he still felt incompetent in speech, Aaron was to throw the staff down before Pharaoh, and it would become a snake. This was the same staff Moses had seen turn to a snake back in the wilderness. Whether in the hands of Moses or Aaron, it was now to be considered as the rod of God.

• Where did Moses' rod come from? What made it special?

"Only one thing validates a message or a messenger: the whole counsel of the word of God."—Kay Arthur

B. Pharaoh's Sorcerers Respond (vv. 11-13)

¹¹ Then Pharaoh also called the wise men and the sorcerers: now the magicians of Egypt, they also did in like manner with their enchantments. ¹² For they cast down every man his rod, and they became serpents: but Aaron's rod swallowed up their rods. ¹³ And he hardened Pharaoh's heart, that he hearkened not unto them; as the Lord had said.

Snakes (in this situation, likely the cobra) represented immortality in Egyptian religion. All religion outside of worship of the Lord is ultimately satanically inspired, for the devil's aim is to keep people from knowing God. Thus, Moses and Aaron could not get away with a demonstration of God's power without it being imitated. "Satan opposes God's work by imitating it, and in this way he minimizes the power and glory of God" (*Bible Exposition Commentary*).

The sorcerers' action was not likely some sleight-of-hand trickery, but rather a real act inspired by Satan. Not everything supernatural is of God, but even the inferior imitations by the devil should convince anyone that the spiritual realm is just as real as the physical. Miracles of themselves are not a valid proof that one is inspired by God. Jesus said, "False Christs and false prophets will appear and perform great signs and miracles to deceive even the elect—if that were possible" (Matt. 24:24 NIV). Paul spoke of the Antichrist as performing all types of miracles (2 Thess. 2:9-10), and John saw the same (Rev. 13:13).

How do we reconcile this with what Paul said about demonstrating the gospel in power (1 Cor. 2:4)? The answer is simple. God's miracles are for the good of people and to draw them to Himself. Look at the miracles Jesus did—they were all done to help people. Jesus said, "Believe me when I say that I am in the Father and the Father is in me; or at least believe on the evidence of the miracles themselves" (John 14:11 NIV). The truly miraculous is never frivolous nor man-centered, but rather focused on good and the glory of the Lord.

Even though the magicians (whom Paul later possibly identified as *Jannes* and *Jambres* in 2 Tim. 3:8) could perform a magical feat, still Aaron's rod consumed theirs and proved that God is superior. The sorcerers did not give up trying, however. As God predicted, Pharaoh's heart was not softened, but hardened as he watched the proceedings.

---

1. How was God's work shown to be superior to the magicians' tricks?
2. How did Pharaoh respond?

"It is wonderful what miracles God works in wills that are utterly surrendered to Him. He turns hard things into easy, and bitter things into sweet."—Hannah Whitall Smith

---

C. The First Plague—Water Turned to Blood (vv. 14-25)

(Exodus 7:14-19, 24-25 is not included in the printed text.)

²⁰ And Moses and Aaron did so, as the Lord commanded; and he lifted up the rod, and smote the waters that were in the river, in the sight of Pharaoh, and in the sight of his servants; and all the waters that were in the

river were turned to blood. ²¹ And the fish that was in the river died; and the river stank, and the Egyptians could not drink of the water of the river; and there was blood throughout all the land of Egypt. ²² And the magicians of Egypt did so with their enchantments: and Pharaoh's heart was hardened, neither did he hearken unto them; as the Lord had said. ²³ And Pharaoh turned and went into his house, neither did he set his heart to this also.

The audience with Pharaoh ended with the sorcerers losing their staffs. Still, Pharaoh would not yield, so Aaron and Moses left. God then commanded them to meet the monarch the next morning as he went down to the Nile. It is unknown why Pharaoh went to the river daily, but it was possibly to carry out some religious ritual, recognizing the Nile River god, Hapi.

When Aaron struck the water, it was transformed. The *Wycliffe Bible Commentary* states: "Each year, toward the end of June, when the waters of the Nile begin to rise, they are colored a dark red by the silt carried down from the headwaters. This continues for three months, until the waters begin to abate, but the water, meanwhile, is wholesome and drinkable. The miracle [here] involved three elements by which it differed from the accustomed phenomenon: the water was changed by the smiting of Moses' rod; the water became undrinkable; and the condition lasted just seven days." God was in charge, and the breaking of Pharaoh's will had begun, despite the fact that he merely returned unmoved to his palace.

This was the beginning of woes for Egypt. The Nile was the source of water for both people and crops. Even though the people dug wells in order to get clean water, the fish in the river died, producing an even worse stench. Also, even though the magicians could duplicate the miracle, they didn't even try to reverse what had happened.

---

1. What was the first plague sent against Egypt, and what was its purpose (vv. 14-18)?
2. How invasive was this plague (vv. 19-21)?
3. How did Pharaoh respond (vv. 22-23)?

"There are many seasons in a man's life—and the more exalted and responsible his position, the more frequently do these seasons recur—when the voice of duty and the dictates of feeling are opposed to each other; and it is only the weak and the wicked who yield that obedience to the selfish impulses of the heart which is due to reason and honor."—James H. Aughey

---

II. GOD JUDGES EGYPT WITH PLAGUES (Ex. 8:5-7, 16-19, 22-24; 9:6-7, 10-11, 23-26; 10:13-15, 22-23)

A. The Plague of the Frogs (8:5-7)

⁵ And the Lord spake unto Moses, Say unto Aaron, Stretch forth thine hand with thy rod over the streams, over the rivers, and over the ponds, and cause frogs to come up upon the land of Egypt. ⁶ And Aaron stretched out his hand over the waters of Egypt; and the frogs came up, and covered

the land of Egypt. ⁷ And the magicians did so with their enchantments, and brought up frogs upon the land of Egypt.

The word *plague* (which appears first in Ex. 9:14) means "a blow, a strike" brought on by the hand of the Lord. The first plague was nasty and inconvenient, and now each successive one would become more severe. The first three (blood, frogs, gnats) could be classified as distressful and frustrating; the second (flies, death of livestock, boils) as painful and debilitating; and the last four (hail, locusts, darkness, death of firstborn) as destructive and fully life-threatening.

Just as before, Moses and Aaron commanded Pharaoh, "Let my people go" (8:1), and then warned him of an impending second plague. The frog represented fertility in Egypt, and the goddess (Heqet) of fertility, resurrection, and childbirth had the head of a frog. Pharaoh was warned that this plague would get into every nook and cranny of their homes, his own included. Psalm 105:30 says, "Their land brought forth frogs in abundance, in the chambers of their kings."

The sorcerers could duplicate what had been done, which only complicated the problem—more frogs (Ex. 8:7). They could not, however, stop the plague. Because the situation was so bad, Pharaoh summoned Moses and Aaron and entreated them to pray to God to stop the infestation. For the first time he promised to let the Israelites go to the wilderness to offer sacrifices. Moses was gracious to let Pharaoh name the time the plague would end—"tomorrow" (vv. 9-10). The Lord did lift the plague, but Pharaoh hardened his heart again and broke his promise (v. 15).

- Concerning the second plague, what were the magicians able to do (vv. 5-7), and what were they not able to do (v. 9)?

"The makers of false miracles are haughty, ambitious, suspicious to people, cruel, though they may speak about love for humanity."— *Troitsky Blagovestnik*

B. Plagues of Lice and Flies (vv. 16-19, 22-24)

(Exodus 8:22-23 is not included in the printed text.)

¹⁶ And the Lord said unto Moses, Say unto Aaron, Stretch out thy rod, and smite the dust of the land, that it may become lice throughout all the land of Egypt. ¹⁷ And they did so; for Aaron stretched out his hand with his rod, and smote the dust of the earth, and it became lice in man, and in beast; all the dust of the land became lice throughout all the land of Egypt. ¹⁸ And the magicians did so with their enchantments to bring forth lice, but they could not: so there were lice upon man, and upon beast. ¹⁹ Then the magicians said unto Pharaoh, This is the finger of God: and Pharaoh's heart was hardened, and he hearkened not unto them; as the Lord had said.

²⁴ And the Lord did so; and there came a grievous swarm of flies into the house of Pharaoh, and into his servants' houses, and into all the land of Egypt: the land was corrupted by reason of the swarm of flies.

It was becoming clear by now that no matter what plague came, Pharaoh would throw a fist back at God. He was willing to see his own kingdom and people destroyed because of pride in his heart. This time the judgment came without warning. When Aaron struck the earth with his rod, the dust turned into tiny insects. The King James calls them "lice." The Hebrew word used here is *kinnim,* which can mean "gnats" or "mosquitoes." Either way, it seemed to have been a judgment against the Egyptian god of the desert, Set. The insects were seen as filthy and unclean by the Egyptians, who were very conscious about hygiene. Priests even shaved their bodies so as to be acceptable before their gods. The infestation made any sense of cleanliness impossible.

In the earlier plague, the Nile had become a plague. Now the ground itself did so. The sorcerers tried to bring forth insects but could not. Recognizing the futility of the situation, they tried to convince Pharaoh that this was the "finger of God" (v. 19). By this they meant that it was supernatural, though they did not attribute it to Jehovah. "The fact that they had duplicated somewhat the earlier plagues makes their capitulation more striking" (*Wycliffe Bible Commentary*).

The next plague began the second cycle of judgments. The Israelites were not affected because verse 22 tells us such. We are not told if the earlier plagues touched them; it is likely they were completely protected. The flies here were probably what have become known as dog flies, which have a painful sting. The land was now becoming "corrupted" (v. 24), indicating the plagues were no longer a terrible nuisance, but a real danger to people's lives.

---

1. What caused the magicians to finally acknowledge God, and why (vv. 16-19)?
2. What "division" ("distinction" NIV) did God promise to make (vv. 22-23)?

"There is nothing into which the heart of man so easily falls as pride, and yet there is no more vice which is more frequently, more emphatically, and more eloquently condemned in Scripture."—Charles Spurgeon

---

C. Two More Plagues (9:6-11)

(Exodus 9:8-9, 11 is not included in the printed text.)
⁶ And the Lord did that thing on the morrow, and all the cattle of Egypt died: but of the cattle of the children of Israel died not one. ⁷ And Pharaoh sent, and, behold, there was not one of the cattle of the Israelites dead. And the heart of Pharaoh was hardened, and he did not let the people go.

¹⁰ And they took ashes of the furnace, and stood before Pharaoh; and Moses sprinkled it up toward heaven; and it became a boil breaking forth with blains upon man, and upon beast.

With "a very severe pestilence" (v. 3 NKJV) striking the nation's domesticated animals, it had to be evident that life would soon be unsustainable for anyone. Prior to this plague, Moses had again gone to Pharaoh demanding the people's release, but to no avail. With dead frogs rotting everywhere and swarms of insects spreading germs, animal diseases were a natural result. Possibly the destruction was caused by anthrax. Some animals were sacred to the Egyptians,

---

such as the bull and the cow, both of which represented deities. Meanwhile, the flocks belonging to the Israelites were all spared, and life in Goshen went on as normal. Pharaoh recognized this but hardened his heart even more.

In verse 10, animals are mentioned after the plague. Did they not all die? Possibly the plague killed all but those that were sheltered, or only a large percentage of the flocks had died.

Like the third plague (lice), the next plague (boils) came without warning. It was also the first to endanger human life. When Moses threw the ashes into the wind, this was a symbolic act, like those of Aaron with the rod earlier. The Egyptians worshiped "Skehmet, a lion-headed goddess with alleged power over disease; Sunu, the pestilence god; and Isis, the goddess of healing" (*Bible Knowledge Commentary*). The boils were a direct affront to Egyptians' faith in the powers of their gods. The magicians were again helpless, for they were also struck with boils.

---

1. What did Pharaoh's investigation discover, and how did he respond (vv. 6-7)?
2. How did the plague in verse 10 differ from the previous ones?
3. How were the magicians affected, and how did Pharaoh respond (vv. 11-12)?

"Deliver us from everything that may entangle our affections and harden our hearts."—William Tiptaft

---

D. The Plague of Hail (vv. 23-26)

(Exodus 9:23, 25-26 is not included in the printed text.)
24 So there was hail, and fire mingled with the hail, very grievous, such as there was none like it in all the land of Egypt since it became a nation.

Now began the third cycle of more severe plagues. The seventh plague of hail and lightning came in the form of a terrible storm. Pharaoh had refused to acknowledge the superiority of the Lord, and instead dug in his heels. Up until now, God had been gracious in not throwing His full fury at the Egyptians, because they would likely have already surrendered. How many times throughout history have peoples been victimized by the self-will of their leaders! The war was truly between Pharaoh and God. In grace and mercy, the Lord sent Moses to warn Pharaoh of the impending storm, allowing time for livestock and people to get to safety. The question arises as to how the people themselves were informed. It is doubtful that Pharaoh himself did so by decree, even though Moses told him to do so. Verse 20 indicates that those around Pharaoh who "feared the word of the Lord" moved as quickly as possible to protect the populace.

As predicted, the storm was horrendous, killing people and animals, and destroying everything else in its path. The flax and barley crops were destroyed (v. 31). These blossomed in January and were harvested in March or April. Wheat and spelt weren't harvested until June or July. It is thus speculated that this plague occurred in February.

• Describe the destructiveness of the plague of hail.

E. The Plague of Locusts (10:13-15)

¹³ And Moses stretched forth his rod over the land of Egypt, and the Lord brought an east wind upon the land all that day, and all that night; and when it was morning, the east wind brought the locusts. ¹⁴ And the locusts went up over all the land of Egypt, and rested in all the coasts of Egypt: very grievous were they; before them there were no such locusts as they, neither after them shall be such. ¹⁵ For they covered the face of the whole earth, so that the land was darkened; and they did eat every herb of the land, and all the fruit of the trees which the hail had left: and there remained not any green thing in the trees, or in the herbs of the field, through all the land of Egypt.

Quite a bit of detail is spent on the plague of locusts. First, there was the instructions to Moses (vv. 1-2), then the confrontation with Pharaoh (vv. 3-11). By now everybody in Egypt wanted to let the Israelites leave, and they were willing to beg Pharaoh to do so. We see some giving in on his part in saying he would let the men go, but not the women and children. Unwilling to deal with compromise, Moses and Aaron were driven out of Pharaoh's presence. It is easy to picture a fit of anger on Pharaoh's face—"Nobody tells me what to do!" This is the bottom line for rebellion against God throughout the ages.

When Moses extended his staff, an east wind began to blow (v. 13). This was unusual because normally the winds in Egypt come from the south. In verse 19, after Moses entreated the Lord for the plague to stop, a west wind blew the locusts into the Red Sea. The devastation left by the plague was so terrible that the ground was left black. This also served to destroy Egyptian trust in Nut, their sky goddess, and Osiris, the god of crop fertility. When the gods are helpless, all faith in them naturally wanes. As before, Pharaoh again begged for relief and promised to free the Israelites, but his heart was not penitent.

---

* Describe the impact of the locust invasion.

F. The Plague of Darkness (vv. 22-23)

²² And Moses stretched forth his hand toward heaven; and there was a thick darkness in all the land of Egypt three days: ²³ They saw not one another, neither rose any from his place for three days: but all the children of Israel had light in their dwellings.

Like the third (lice) and sixth (boils), this plague also came without warning. By now Pharaoh had to be asking himself, "What's next? Can I stand it?" When Moses extended his hand, a sudden darkness overtook the land (except for Goshen). This was likely not an eclipse of the sun (since Goshen still had light), but possibly a severe sandstorm, forcing everyone to stay indoors. This plague was possibly directed at the sun god, Re, which was seen as providing sunlight, warmth, and productivity in life. It is also of note that this god is usually seen in Egyptian art as a man with a pharaoh's crown on his head and a sun disk above it.

Pharaoh was now beginning to break, and was willing to let the people go, but not their flocks and herds. This is no wonder, since the Egyptian herds had been decimated.

- How do you suppose this three-day plague affected the mind-set of the Egyptians?

"The most tremendous judgment of God in this world is the hardening of the hearts of men."—John Owen

III. GOD PREPARES ISRAEL FOR DELIVERANCE (Ex. 11:1-10)
A. Announcement of the Last Plague (vv. 1-3)

¹ And the Lord said unto Moses, Yet will I bring one plague more upon Pharaoh, and upon Egypt; afterwards he will let you go hence: when he shall let you go, he shall surely thrust you out hence altogether. ² Speak now in the ears of the people, and let every man borrow of his neighbour, and every woman of her neighbour, jewels of silver, and jewels of gold. ³ And the Lord gave the people favour in the sight of the Egyptians. Moreover the man Moses was very great in the land of Egypt, in the sight of Pharaoh's servants, and in the sight of the people.

Although the Egyptian populace was by now clearly in the corner of Moses, they would have to suffer one more terrible plague because of Pharaoh's stubbornness. God had destroyed in their eyes any validity their own gods had. Along the way, the nation had been devastated economically. The only thing left to hit was the people themselves (though they had already felt the pain of boils.)

Up to this time, Moses had not been told how many plagues there would be. This is the way God usually leads. He only shows us the goal and then one step toward the goal at a time. Rarely are we given a complete roadmap to our destination. The time had come for the final deliverance, and the Lord told Moses this would be the last, and hardest, plague. In preparation for it, the Israelites were to request gold and silver from their slave masters, which they freely gave. The Egyptians had become oddly kind toward their slaves.

1. What did God promise Moses (v. 1)?
2. What were God's people instructed to do (v. 2)?
3. How did the Egyptians view the Israelites and Moses, and why (v. 3)?

"Now is our chance to choose the right side. God is holding back to give us that chance. It won't last forever. We must take it or leave it."—C. S. Lewis

B. Death of the Firstborn (vv. 4-10)
(Exodus 11:9-10 is not included in the printed text.)

⁴ And Moses said, Thus saith the Lord, About midnight will I go out into the midst of Egypt: ⁵ And all the firstborn in the land of Egypt shall die, from the firstborn of Pharaoh that sitteth upon his throne, even unto the firstborn of the maidservant that is behind the mill; and all the firstborn of beasts. ⁶ And there shall be a great cry throughout all the land of Egypt, such as there was none like it, nor shall be like it any more. ⁷ But against any of the children of Israel shall not a dog move his tongue, against man or beast: that ye may know how that the Lord doth put a difference between the Egyptians and Israel. ⁸ And all these thy servants shall come down unto me, and bow down themselves unto me, saying, Get thee out, and all the people that follow thee: and after that I will go out. And he went out from Pharaoh in a great anger.

With the final plague, there would be no opportunity to repent. This was also the last confrontation Moses had with Pharaoh. He simply laid out what was about to occur. This was like a last-second warning of an approaching tsunami. There was no time or means to get out of its way. The death angel was about to hit Egypt and hit hard. In every Egyptian household the firstborn son would die at midnight. In ancient cultures (and, to some degree, even today) the firstborn son in a family had special rights. Pharaoh's firstborn son was heir to the throne, and was considered to be a god.

Was God fair in this situation, especially since the Egyptian population now favored the Israelites and were generous to them? God is holy. He created all and has the right to do as He pleases. Remember, too, that the Egyptians had many gods, had refused to worship the Lord, and only recognized Him when brought to their knees. Also, their goddess Isis supposedly protected children. Any semblance of validity to the Egyptian pantheon of gods was now about to be destroyed.

Sowing and reaping are a fundamental law of life on Planet Earth. It is as concrete as gravity. Pharaoh had drowned Jewish babies, and now his army would drown. The Egyptians had robbed the Israelites of human dignity, and now they would suffer the same. Galatians 6:7 says, "Be not deceived; God is not mocked; for whatsoever a man soweth, that shall he also reap."

After delivering the message to Pharaoh, Moses left seething. His anger was surely at the recalcitrant spirit of a man who simply would not relent in his stubborn rebellion against God.

---

1. Why would the final plague occur "about midnight" (v. 4)?
2. Who would be affected by this plague (v. 5)?
3. How would the Israelites be affected (v. 7)?
4. Why do you suppose Pharaoh was given all the details of what would happen?
5. How did the Lord summarize the purpose of the plagues to Moses (v. 9)?

"They sow the wind, and reap the whirlwind" (Hos. 8:7 NKJV).

CONCLUSION

As we see in the story of the deliverance of Israel, God often chooses the most unlikely and imperfect of people to reveal His powerful justice. Paul spoke this clearly to the Corinthians: "Not many [of you were considered to be] wise according to human estimates and standards, not many influential and powerful, not many of high and noble birth. [No] for God selected (deliberately chose) what in the world is foolish to put the wise to shame, and what the world calls weak to put the strong to shame" (1 Cor. 1:26-27 Amp.). None can boast in themselves, but only in God who chooses to display His awesome power through them.

GOLDEN TEXT CHALLENGE

"I [THE LORD] WILL STRETCH OUT MY HAND, AND SMITE EGYPT WITH ALL MY WONDERS WHICH I WILL DO IN THE MIDST THEREOF: AND AFTER THAT HE [PHARAOH] WILL LET YOU GO" (Ex. 3:20).

The Lord God lays out a mission statement for the final forty years of Moses' life. Moses will appear before Pharaoh . . . God will perform incredible signs . . . and Pharaoh will let Moses lead the estimated two million Hebrews out of Egypt into the Promised Land.

However, the Lord did not tell Moses this would be a forty-year process, with most of that being spent wandering in the desert. Yet, at the end of this incredible trek, Moses would declare, "Oh, praise the greatness of our God! He is the Rock, his works are perfect, and all his ways are just" (Deut. 32:3-4 NIV).

Daily Devotions:
M. Remember God's Mighty Salvation
   Deuteronomy 4:32-40
T. God Rescues Israel
   Psalm 105:37-45
W. Wait for God's Salvation
   Lamentations 3:18-26
T. Power of Christ Displayed
   Matthew 4:23-25
F. Empowered for Victory
   Revelation 3:7-13
S. Song of Victory
   Revelation 15:1-4

The Passover Instituted

Exodus 12:1 through 13:10

Unit Theme:
The Exodus

Central Truth:
The Passover commemorates God's deliverance of His people.

Focus:
Discuss and value the meaning of the Passover.

Context:
Egypt, 1441-1439 BC

Golden Text:
"The blood shall be to you for a token upon the houses where ye are: and when I see the blood, I will pass over you, and the plague shall not be upon you to destroy you, when I smite the land of Egypt" (Ex. 12:13).

Study Outline:
 I. The Passover Event
    (Ex. 12:21-30)
 II. The Exodus
    (Ex. 12:31-42)
 III. The Passover Remembered
    (Ex. 13:1-10)

INTRODUCTION

At the end of the last lesson, Moses and Aaron were forced from the presence of Pharaoh, having told him that the worst for him and his people was about to occur. Chapter 12 shifts the focus to Moses giving instructions to the Israelites as to how they would celebrate the Passover (vv. 1-20). Our lesson will pick up with the actual observance (vv. 21ff.), but let's first set the stage.

God explained to Moses and Aaron the timing of the Passover and what it was to represent. No longer were the people simply the twelve tribes or descendants of the sons of Jacob, but now they were to be an identifiable nation. The feast of Passover would mark the beginning of a new age. This was also to be the first month of the religious year, and would be called *Abib*. The word means "fresh young ears" of barley, which was harvested in March-April. Centuries later the name would be changed to *Nisan*, meaning "early," while the people were in Babylonian captivity.

On the tenth day of this month, every family was to select a perfect one-year-old lamb or goat to be eaten in the Passover meal. On the fourteenth of the month, that animal was to be killed at dusk. Elaborate instructions for the preparation were given. Every family (or small families joined together) was to celebrate the meal, representing a joint worship by all the people. The blood of the animal had to be placed on the door frames of their homes, the meat roasted, and then eaten with bitter herbs and unleavened bread.

From a Christian perspective, we can see that this sprinkling of blood was a foretaste of the death of Jesus on the cross. Jesus is our perfect "Passover Lamb." His sacrifice brought our deliverance from the captivity of sin. Leviticus 17:11 says, ". . . for it is the blood that maketh an atonement for the soul," and Hebrews 9:22 says, ". . . without the shedding of blood there is no remission."

The blood on the doorpost was an absolute necessity. Without it, the death angel would have struck an Israelite household as surely as he did the Egyptian. The slaying of the animals was a substitute for the death of the Israelites' first-born sons. For us today, the blood of Jesus has to be applied to the doorposts of our hearts. How do we appropriate that sacrifice? By believing on Christ personally. Jesus said, "For God so loved the world, that he gave his only begotten Son, that whosoever believeth in him . . ." (John 3:16). When Thomas finally recognized Jesus on the night after His crucifixion, he declared, "My Lord and my God" (20:28).

On Israel's final night of slavery in Egypt, every firstborn son and animal of the Egyptian households was slain, while those of Israel were spared. This was the final judgment against all the gods of Egypt (Num. 33:4). The Passover was to be observed annually for generations to come as a lasting ordinance and remembrance of how God had delivered His people.

I. THE PASSOVER EVENT (Ex. 12:21-30)

A. Moses Gives Instructions (vv. 21-23)

²¹ Then Moses called for all the elders of Israel, and said unto them, Draw out and take you a lamb according to your families, and kill the passover. ²² And ye shall take a bunch of hyssop, and dip it in the blood that is in the bason, and strike the lintel and the two side posts with the blood that is in the bason; and none of you shall go out at the door of his house until the morning. ²³ For the Lord will pass through to smite the Egyptians; and when he seeth the blood upon the lintel, and on the two side posts, the Lord will pass over the door, and will not suffer the destroyer to come in unto your houses to smite you.

Just as the Lord had given the instructions for carrying out the Passover to Moses, Moses now gave them to the elders. They would then disseminate them to the people. A bunch of hyssop, a common bushy plant, was to be used to smear the blood on the doorposts. "The *Lord*" who would "smite" the Egyptians (v. 23) perhaps was the preincarnate Christ. The word *theophany* describes such manifestations by Christ in the Old Testament. This would be the same as when the Lord appeared to Abraham to tell him of the impending destruction of Sodom and Gomorrah (see Gen. 18:1).

Part of the instructions was that the lamb had to be roasted whole. Had it been boiled, the bones would have had to be broken—likely because families would not have had pots of sufficient size to contain it. It was important that the wholeness of lamb be preserved and observed. The unbroken body speaks clearly of the ultimate Lamb of God. John 19:31-37 gives detail of how Jesus' bones were not broken at His crucifixion. The psalmist prophesied this: "He keepeth all his bones: not one of them is broken" (34:20).

There is an interesting note to make concerning the firstborn. It apparently meant the firstborn son who was not yet grown, that is, not yet a father himself. Otherwise, Pharaoh would also have been slain, since he was the firstborn son of his father.

---

1. What was the chosen lamb called, and why (v. 21)?
2. List the specific instructions given to every Israelite family (vv. 22-23).

"We overcome the accuser of our brothers and sisters, we overcome our consciences, we overcome our bad tempers, we overcome our defeats, we overcome our lusts, we overcome our fears, we overcome our pettiness on the basis of the blood of the Lamb."—D. A. Carson

---

B. A Permanent Ordinance (vv. 24-27)

(Exodus 12:25-27 is not included in the printed text.)

24 And ye shall observe this thing for an ordinance to thee and to thy sons for ever.

The Passover was not to be a onetime event, but an annual memorial perpetually observed (until the true Lamb of God came). Its celebration every year would keep alive the story of deliverance. Every Hebrew child needed to understand its significance. Future generations needed to know how God had saved the people and made them into a nation He called His own. Passover was the people's link with the past, the glue that would help hold them together.

We know that the people did take this to heart, and even today, Passover is an extremely sacred time to Jews around the world. Interestingly, however, we as Christians have not been as diligent in teaching the meaning of the Lord's Supper to our children. Many church bodies are sporadic at best in observance, and even less faithful to explain its meaning.

• What did the Lord want the Israelites to do "forever," and why?

"God wants to see prayers that are filled with genuine praise and thanksgiving for what He has done in the past. He wants our hearts to be filled with awe and gratitude for His blessings. He wants us to set up memorials in our hearts testifying to the provisions He has given us."—Michael Youssef

---

C. The Israelites Obey (v. 28)

28 And the children of Israel went away, and did as the Lord had commanded Moses and Aaron, so did they.

This verse represents one of those rare times in Israel's history when they corporately did exactly as they had been commanded. After having watched all the plagues prior to now strike the Egyptians, while they were themselves sheltered, they moved in faith. Still, this faith was weak, in that very quickly they would doubt Moses' leadership and the benevolence of the Lord. In their present obedience, however, they used a flimsy bundle of hyssop plant to smear the blood on the doorposts of their houses. "Our faith may be as weak as the hyssop, but it's not faith in our faith that saves us, but faith in the blood of the Savior" (*Bible Exposition Commentary*).

• Why is complete obedience to God necessary?

D. The Midnight Horror (vv. 29-30)

²⁹ And it came to pass, that at midnight the Lord smote all the firstborn in the land of Egypt, from the firstborn of Pharaoh that sat on his throne unto the firstborn of the captive that was in the dungeon; and all the firstborn of cattle. ³⁰ And Pharaoh rose up in the night, he, and all his servants, and all the Egyptians; and there was a great cry in Egypt; for there was not a house where there was not one dead.

Just as predicted, at midnight the Lord struck all the households of the Egyptians. His judgment brought all of Egyptian society to one level. Pharaoh, with all his bodyguards and trained army, were helpless against this disaster.

While the previous nine plagues can be somehow explained as "natural" occurrences, this one was purely an act of God. "There are circumstances in the account of this plague which distinguish it from any known or specific form of disease" (*Biblical Illustrator*). Here we see a vivid reminder of God's hatred of sin. Every family in Egypt, from the least to the greatest, was struck.

• How widespread was the final plague?

False Gods Judged

The plagues God sent on Egypt were a judgment on the false gods of Egypt. Numbers 33:4 says, "Upon their gods also the Lord executed judgments." With the death of the firstborn, the Egyptian god of reproduction, Min, and the goddess of reproduction, Isis, were shown to be just what they were—idols without power that people worship. God dismantled every idol to show His people that He is the only God. Paul said, "We know that an idol is nothing in the world, and that there is none other God but one" (1 Cor. 8:4).

II. THE EXODUS (Ex. 12:31-42)

A. Pharaoh Summons Moses and Aaron (v. 31)

³¹ And he called for Moses and Aaron by night, and said, Rise up, and get you forth from among my people, both ye and the children of Israel; and go, serve the Lord, as ye have said.

The question arises as to just how the firstborn of Egypt were slain. Was it a painful death? Or, did they simply die in their sleep? If they had passed peacefully, likely most families would not have even known until the next morning. However, since the people by now respected Moses, who in any household could have gone to bed and slept calmly? Also, it would only take a few individuals discovering what had happened to quickly spread the grief to their neighbors—only to find that the plague had hit them all.

Pharaoh was certainly awake, for he did not even wait until the next morning to summon Moses. Back in 10:28-29, when Pharaoh had demanded he leave his presence, Moses had responded by saying that would be the last time Pharaoh saw his face. Yet, God did tell Moses to go and give the warning of this final plague (11:4). Now, once more Moses went to Pharaoh. The monarch was broken with grief (but not with remorse) and released the people without restriction.

• When were Moses and Aaron summoned, and what were they told?

B. The Command to Leave (vv. 32-36)

(Exodus 12:32-35 is not included in the printed text.)

³⁶ And the Lord gave the people favour in the sight of the Egyptians, so that they lent unto them such things as they required. And they spoiled the Egyptians.

Pharaoh demanded that the Israelites leave, and even entreated Moses to pray for the stricken people. His asking Moses to "bless me" (v. 32) is pathetic. He who had fought against God's will was now asking for a blessing, though he still was not remorseful for how he had treated the Israelites. We can contrast Pharaoh with David in his prayer for forgiveness after the murder of Uriah and his adultery with Bathsheba. David prayed, "The sacrifices of God are a broken spirit; a broken and contrite heart, O God, you will not despise" (Ps. 51:17 NIV).

The spirit in the Egyptians as a whole, however, was possibly different. Yes, they urged the Israelites to leave for fear that they *all* would die—not just their firstborn (v. 33)—but still they seemed to admire them as well. They lavished their former slaves with gold and silver (v. 35). This fulfilled the promise to Abraham that they would leave slavery "with great substance" (Gen. 15:14). The Egyptians also respected Moses (Ex. 11:3). There is no better witness to the world than a life that demonstrates the Lord's presence.

---

1. What did Pharaoh request about himself (v. 32)?
2. What did the Egyptians fear (v. 33)?
3. Describe the scene in verse 34.
4. Describe the despoiling that took place (vv. 35-36).

"The destruction of Egypt was by a pestilence walking in darkness (see Ps. 91:6). Shortly there will be an alarming cry at midnight, 'Behold, the bridegroom cometh.'"—Matthew Henry

C. The Journey out of Egypt (vv. 37-39)

37 And the children of Israel journeyed from Rameses to Succoth, about six hundred thousand on foot that were men, beside children. 38 And a mixed multitude went up also with them; and flocks, and herds, even very much cattle. 39 And they baked unleavened cakes of the dough which they brought forth out of Egypt, for it was not leavened; because they were thrust out of Egypt, and could not tarry, neither had they prepared for themselves any victual.

The Egyptians were now anxious for the Israelites to get out before their entire population was wiped out. The Israelites' quick departure is indicated by the unleavened lumps of dough. It is apparent that some organization had been taking part in preparation for this day. They moved like an army set in divisions. There was no chaos, but rather an orderly march with flocks and herds. Psalm 105:37 tells us that no one was too feeble to march. This was a miracle in itself, for all were healthy.

Since there were six hundred thousand men, then the total number of Jews numbered about two million, while the "mixed multitude" (Ex. 12:38) was of an indeterminate number. Who were these people? Some likely were Egyptians who had married Jews, while others were "slaves in the lowest grades of society, partly natives and captives obtained by recent judgments of the supremacy of Yahweh, and all availing themselves of the opportunity to escape in the crowd" (*Jamieson, Fausset, and Brown Commentary*). Whoever they were, they represent "those in this world who outwardly identify with God's people but inwardly are not truly the children of God" (*Bible Exposition Commentary*). This quickly became apparent when these rose up to complain against Moses (see Num. 11:4).

The entire body of those leaving had gathered at Rameses, and from there they journeyed to Succoth. Somewhere along the route they baked their unleavened bread. From Succoth, the march out of Egypt took place.

---

1. Describe the "parade" out of Egypt (see vv. 37-38).
2. Why had the Israelites "not . . . prepared any provisions for themselves" (v. 39 NASB)?

"Each of us may be sure that if God sends us on stony paths He will provide us with strong shoes, and He will not send us out on any journey for which He does not equip us well."—Alexander MacLaren

---

D. Four Hundred Thirty Years (vv. 40-42)

40 Now the sojourning of the children of Israel, who dwelt in Egypt, was four hundred and thirty years. 41 And it came to pass at the end of the four hundred and thirty years, even the selfsame day it came to pass, that all the hosts of the Lord went out from the land of Egypt. 42 It is a night to be much observed unto the Lord for bringing them out from the land of Egypt: this is that night of the Lord to be observed of all the children of Israel in their generations.

The length of time the Israelites spent in Egypt was four hundred thirty years. Acts 7:6 gives the round number of four hundred years, just as had been prophesied to Abraham (Gen. 15:13). God remembered His people and His commitment to Abraham. He is always faithful to His covenants. Dates for this time period are speculative, but was possibly from 1876 BC to 1446 BC.

Exodus 12 ends with rules for observance of the Passover. These were necessary because of the mixed multitude. If a man did not identify himself with the covenant by circumcision, then he could not celebrate Passover.

---

1. What had changed over 430 years (cf. Ex. 1:1-5 with 12:37)?
2. Recall "a night to be much observed" (v. 42) in your experience with the Lord.

"Soar back through all your own experiences. Think of how the Lord has led you in the wilderness and has fed and clothed you every day. How God has borne with your ill manners, and put up with all your murmurings and all your longings after the 'sensual pleasures of Egypt!' Think of how the Lord's grace has been sufficient for you in all your troubles."—Charles Spurgeon

---

III. THE PASSOVER REMEMBERED (Ex. 13:1-10)

A. Sanctify the Firstborn (vv. 1-2)

¹ And the Lord spake unto Moses, saying, ² Sanctify unto me all the firstborn, whatsoever openeth the womb among the children of Israel, both of man and of beast: it is mine.

Because they had been spared from the last plague, the Lord called for the firstborn of every Israelite family to be dedicated to Him. This also included the firstborn of livestock. This ordinance would not take effect, however, until the Jews reached the Promised Land. How sons and firstborn beasts were to be redeemed is explained in Leviticus 12 and Numbers 18:14-19. God adopted Israel as His "firstborn" nation. "From that time onward, that spared nation would dedicate the firstborn of its people and animals in commemoration of God's acts of love and his deeds that night" (*Zondervan NIV Bible Commentary*).

There was an interesting side benefit to this ordinance. Every time a firstborn son or animal was redeemed, adults could explain to their children how God had rescued them. This also solidified the concept of the importance of a firstborn son. The child had no control of his birth order, but he was still considered special to both his parents and particularly blessed by the Lord.

- What did the Lord command His people to do, and why?

"We need to realize that in all things our first duty and responsibility is to God himself."—Harry Ironside

B. Feast of Unleavened Bread Established (vv. 3-7)

(Exodus 13:5, 7 is not included in the printed text.)

³ And Moses said unto the people, Remember this day, in which ye came out from Egypt, out of the house of bondage; for by strength of hand the Lord brought you out from this place: there shall no leavened bread be eaten. ⁴ This day came ye out in the month Abib.

⁶ Seven days thou shalt eat unleavened bread, and in the seventh day shall be a feast to the Lord.

Here was established the Feast of Unleavened Bread, a seven-day festival following Passover. Like the Passover, it would have great teaching value in the home. For seven days, the people would eat bread without yeast as a reminder of the unleavened bread they brought with them out of Egypt. Then a feast would be held, celebrating their deliverance.

It would be a continual reminder of God's faithfulness in delivering the people from Egypt. In verse 16 the pronoun changes to "us," indicating that every generation would identify themselves as part of this great people. The Jews have retained their identify for nearly four thousand years, and much is due to their continual observance of their deliverance. No other people on earth can claim such.

- Contrast what the Lord delivered the Israelites "from" (v. 3) and where He was bringing them "to" (v. 5).

C. A Sign (vv. 8-10)

⁸ And thou shalt shew thy son in that day, saying, This is done because of that which the Lord did unto me when I came forth out of Egypt. ⁹ And it shall be for a sign unto thee upon thine hand, and for a memorial between thine eyes, that the Lord's law may be in thy mouth: for with a strong hand hath the Lord brought thee out of Egypt. ¹⁰ Thou shalt therefore keep this ordinance in his season from year to year.

Other peoples wore signs to remind them of their deities, but for Israel the Feast of Unleavened Bread was in itself to be a sign. Verse 9, along with Deuteronomy 6:8 and 11:18, was taken literally by many Jews and is the basis for *phylacteries*, which are small pouches containing passages of the Law. Phylacteries are worn on the arms and foreheads as a constant reminder of the deliverance and as a visual display of their faith in God.

- What responsibility were parents given?

"When the Word dwells as a familiar friend in the heart to direct, counsel, and comfort us, then it is a sign it abides there."—Richard Sibbes

---

CONCLUSION

The blood of the perfect Lamb saves us from sin, just as the blood on the doorposts of the Passover lambs saved the Israelites. Still, it was necessary for them to eat the flesh of the lamb. We must, in turn, feed on Jesus to have strength to face the challenges of daily life. Jesus turned many away when He said, "Except ye eat the flesh of the Son of man, and drink his blood, ye have no life in you" (John 6:53). Obviously He was speaking symbolically. We "eat" of Him by reading, studying, and believing His Word. Jesus said, "The words that I speak unto you, they are spirit, and they are life" (v. 63). Jesus' words have life in them, and by taking them into our hearts and minds, we appropriate spiritual nourishment.

GOLDEN TEXT CHALLENGE

"THE BLOOD SHALL BE TO YOU FOR A TOKEN UPON THE HOUSES WHERE YE ARE: AND WHEN I SEE THE BLOOD, I WILL PASS OVER YOU, AND THE PLAGUE SHALL NOT BE UPON YOU TO DESTROY YOU, WHEN I SMITE THE LAND OF EGYPT" (Ex. 12:13).

In giving the instructions to Moses concerning the Passover, God, for the first time in Jewish history, called His people "the congregation of Israel" (v. 3). There was to be one lamb for each home.

If there were not enough members of a household to consume a lamb, they were to merge with another family. Later, Jewish tradition stated that the number around the table for the Passover feast should be at least ten.

It is significant that the first ordinance of the Jewish religion was a domestic service. This arrangement was divinely wise. No nation has ever been really prosperous or permanently strong that did not cherish the importance of the home.

Ancient Rome failed to resist the enemy, not because her discipline had degenerated, but because evil habits in the home had ruined her population. We cannot overlook the simple and obvious fact that God has built His nation upon families.

Daily Devotions:
M. Passover Regulations
   Exodus 12:43-51
T. Passover Song
   Psalm 81:1-10
W. Promise of Passover
   Zechariah 9:9-11
T. The Lord's Supper Instituted
   Matthew 26:26-30
F. The Power of Christ's Blood
   Romans 3:21-26
S. Redeemed by Christ's Blood
   1 Peter 1:17-21

Miracle at the Red Sea

Exodus 14:1-31

Unit Theme:
The Exodus

Central Truth:
Christians can be assured that God works miracles.

Focus:
Consider the Red Sea event and appreciate the miraculous intervention of God.

Context:
The wilderness of Shur, Marah, Elim, and Rephidim

Golden Text:
"The children of Israel walked upon dry land in the midst of the sea; and the waters were a wall unto them on their right hand, and on their left" (Ex. 14:29).

Study Outline:
  I. God's People Fear Destruction
     (Ex. 14:1-12)
 II. God Assures His People
     (Ex. 14:13-18)
III. God Miraculously Delivers His People
     (Ex. 14:19-31)

INTRODUCTION

During all the plagues that had affected Egypt, the Israelites had only been observers, watching as God was working on their behalf but not having to do anything themselves to secure their release. Now the situation would be different. An entire people who had been slaves for hundreds of years were about to be forced to learn to be a unified nation. This was a daunting task.

At the end of our last lesson the people had traveled as far as Succoth, where they camped out temporarily. They desired to move quickly to the Promised Land, though their first destination was Mount Sinai. The most direct route was along the coast, but this would throw Israel into contact with powerful enemy nations. Also, Egyptian outposts were along this route, and soldiers stationed there would certainly challenge them. Taking a more circuitous route through Sinai was very difficult with such a large group of people, especially since they had no food or water supplies. Yet this is exactly what the Lord commanded.

There had to be many unanswered questions in Moses' mind, but by this time, he knew the track record of the Lord to be faithful. The nation would be provided with whatever they needed. The message is the same for us today. God knows what He is doing in our lives, so it is best to trust Him, regardless of plans, dreams, callings, and hopes that have not yet materialized. Proverbs 3:5 tells us, "Trust in the Lord with all thine heart; and lean not unto thine own understanding."

Nearly four hundred years prior to the Exodus, Joseph had made the Israelites promise that his bones would go with them when they left Egypt. Joseph knew the prophecy that had been given to his grandfather, Abraham, of a long enslavement. The fact that the Israelites now were carrying out his wishes (Ex. 13:19) was a sign to the people of God's faithfulness. However, they did not know it would still be many more years before Joseph's bones would be permanently buried (see Josh. 24:32).

An even greater sign of God's providence was the column (or pillar) of cloud by day which turned into a pillar of fire by night. The circumference base of this was large enough to provide cover for all of Israel (as well as the mixed multitude who tagged along). This was a visible symbol of God's presence among them.

I. GOD'S PEOPLE FEAR DESTRUCTION (Ex. 14:1-12)

A. The Lord's Strategy (vv. 1-5)

(Exodus 14:1-5 is not included in the printed text.)

Figuring out the exact route Moses and the Israelites took is nearly impossible. Commentators disagree over the details, and the places mentioned are difficult to establish on a map. We will suffice it to say that the Lord led Moses on what looked like a confused journey. There was, however, a method to the madness. "This apparent uncertainty in their line of march must have encouraged Pharaoh to believe that the Israelites could find no way across the water barrier and were thus trapped, wandering aimlessly" (*Wycliffe Bible Commentary*).

Probably the Israelites were confused themselves as to why Moses was leading them so zigzaggedly, but this would be typical of the next forty years. Psalm 103:7 says, "He made known his ways to Moses, his deeds to the people of Israel" (NIV).

Only Moses had the close relationship with the Lord to understand why certain actions were taken. As much as things are different for us under the new covenant, there is still a truth for us to follow. God shares secrets with His leaders that He doesn't reveal to those under their care. This is one more reason for us to pray for those in authority over us.

After the mass exodus, Pharaoh began to have second thoughts about what he had done. Even with the devastation of land and assets, as well as the loss of all the firstborn, it was obvious that the cheap labor force the nation had long enjoyed was now gone. Reports came to him from spies that the Israelites were confused, wandering around the desert aimlessly in their efforts to find a way out. This made them look like an easy target for recapture.

The phrase "the people *fled*" (v. 5) is revealing. Remember that Moses had sought permission for the people to go to the wilderness to worship the Lord, though it was obvious that they did not plan to return. Still, it was now certain that this was no temporary departure, but rather a plan of total permanent escape.

---

1. Where did the Lord tell Moses to set up camp, and why (vv. 1-4)?
2. Explain Pharaoh's change of mind (v. 5).

"Nothing whatever, whether great or small, can happen to a believer, without God's ordering and permission. There is no such thing as 'chance,' 'luck' or 'accident' in the Christian's journey through this world. All is arranged and appointed by God. And all things are 'working together' for the believer's good."—J. C. Ryle

B. The Decision to Chase (vv. 6-9)

⁶ And he made ready his chariot, and took his people with him: ⁷ And he took six hundred chosen chariots, and all the chariots of Egypt, and captains over every one of them. ⁸ And the Lord hardened the heart of Pharaoh king of Egypt, and he pursued after the children of Israel: and the children of Israel went out with an high hand. ⁹ But the Egyptians pursued after them, all the horses and chariots of Pharaoh, and his horsemen, and his army, and overtook them encamping by the sea, beside Pi-hahiroth, before Baal-zephon.

Forgetting all they had already suffered because of the Israelites, Pharaoh made a hasty decision to chase them. By now several days had passed. Likely the reaction would have been even sooner, except for the fact that the Egyptians were too busy burying their dead. Their grief apparently turned quickly to anger, and then to madness. Their fury was equally directed at themselves for having made the decision to release the Israelites.

Although the Israelite men numbered over six hundred thousand, they were unarmed militarily. Pharaoh set out with six hundred chariots—virtually everything he could muster—and went in pursuit.

1. Describe the Egyptian forces that rushed to the Red Sea (vv. 6-7, 9).
2. How does verse 8 describe the Israelites' attitude to this point?

"Everything we do proceeds from a decision of will, involves our intelligence and perception, leads to emotional reactions or experiences, is approved or disapproved by the conscience, and is registered in the memory in complete perspective."—Gordon Olson

C. Fear Strikes the Israelites (vv. 10-12)

¹⁰ And when Pharaoh drew nigh, the children of Israel lifted up their eyes, and, behold, the Egyptians marched after them; and they were sore afraid: and the children of Israel cried out unto the Lord. ¹¹ And they said unto Moses, Because there were no graves in Egypt, hast thou taken us away to die in the wilderness? wherefore hast thou dealt thus with us, to carry us forth out of Egypt? ¹² Is not this the word that we did tell thee in Egypt, saying, Let us alone, that we may serve the Egyptians? For it had been better for us to serve the Egyptians, than that we should die in the wilderness.

Unarmed, undisciplined, and helpless in their own eyes, the Israelites turned to see the Egyptians coming after them. The six hundred chariots apparently created a cloud of dust in the desert sand. The Israelites felt trapped, and were probably as angered at themselves for having followed Moses as they were at Pharaoh. Even as they cried to the Lord, they had no confidence in Him—despite all the miraculous intervention that had already occurred. Though their greatest moment of deliverance was about to materialize before their eyes, they were full of distrust and fear. They turned their bitter rage against Moses for deceiving them.

From a human perspective their prospects were certainly dim, and that is always the case when God is absent from the equation. That is why faith in divine intervention is necessary to life. Still, if one's god is only an idol, all the faith in the world is of no avail. What the Israelites forgot in their sudden fear was the record of all that God had already recently done for them.

The statement about "graves in Egypt" is one of sarcasm. Could much of their slavery have possibly been spent in building elaborate pyramid tombs for Egyptian royalty? Interestingly, the pyramids are not mentioned in the Bible specifically, but nevertheless go back to 2600 BC. "They mocked in the most satirical tone possible (since Egypt specialized in graves and had about three-fourths of its land area available for grave sites)" (*Zondervan NIV Bible Commentary, Old Testament*).

The Israelites were preferring the hardship of slavery over the unknown of where Moses was leading them. The unknown is always hard to choose, no matter how tough one's past circumstance. It takes faith to step into a new path, something that was sadly lacking among the Israelites.

---

1. What caused the Israelites' attitude to change suddenly (v. 10)?
2. Summarize the people's questions (vv. 11-12) with three adjectives.

"Never be afraid to trust an unknown future to a known God."—Corrie ten Boom

---

II. GOD ASSURES HIS PEOPLE (Ex. 14:13-18)

A. Stand Still (vv. 13-14)

13 And Moses said unto the people, Fear ye not, stand still, and see the salvation of the Lord, which he will shew to you to day: for the Egyptians whom ye have seen to day, ye shall see them again no more for ever. 14 The Lord shall fight for you, and ye shall hold your peace.

If we read these verses only, without those which follow, we see a noble Moses reassuring the people that God was on their side. Their faith was blocked by fear of the approaching Egyptian army. We also see that Moses' quick temper of earlier years was gone. Later the Israelites would try his patience to the limit, but not now. His command to the people indicates that he assumed God would simply come down on the scene and deliver them miraculously—without any action on their part. As said earlier, during all the ten plagues the Israelites had done nothing but sit by and watch. Also, if the Lord did give a fresh order for action, they had to be calmed down from hysteria in order to listen and carry it out.

Everything in Moses' words seems correct, trusting of God, and fully committed. His words are similar to those the psalmist would later say: "Be still, and know that I am God" (46:10).

---

1. When should a Christian "stand still" (v. 13)?
2. How does God "fight" for His people today (v. 14)?

"God never said that the journey would be easy, but He did say that the arrival would be worthwhile."—Max Lucado

---

B. Moses Corrected (v. 15)

¹⁵ And the Lord said unto Moses, Wherefore criest thou unto me? speak unto the children of Israel, that they go forward.

The Lord's rebuke here changes the perspective of the entire scene. Although not recorded, Moses apparently turned from facing the people and cried out to the Lord with the same attitude that they had just given him—fear and doubt. Because of the rebuke, we see duplicity on Moses' part. Standing still was not what God had in mind at all. Proverbs 11:3 says, "The integrity of the upright guides them, but the unfaithful are destroyed by their duplicity" (NIV). Moses acted strong in front of the people, but was as frightened as they were.

At first glance it would seem that the Lord was being harsh, but He was simply saying that this was not a time for praying, standing still, or waiting for a word. As He told Gideon, "Have I not sent you?" (Judg. 6:14 NKJV). When God commissions, He provides the way to do what He has sent us to do. The Hebrew word for "go forward" is *nasa*—a verb that indicates pulling up tent stakes or setting out on a journey. It requires action, not standing or waiting. Orders have already been given.

The rudder on a ship is of no value unless there is movement. God cannot direct someone who is not moving. Once movement begins, the rudder of God's provision opens the way.

Lest we be too hard on Moses, we must remember the trust in the Lord he had exhibited until now. Momentary panic can occur with the most faithful people. In stressful times, we must stop, take control of our emotions, and not let ourselves be paralyzed.

• What did the Lord command Moses to do?

C. Action Commanded (v. 16)

¹⁶ But lift thou up thy rod, and stretch out thine hand over the sea, and divide it: and the children of Israel shall go on dry ground through the midst of the sea.

At their first meeting with the burning bush, the Lord had given Moses authority to act by using his rod. Exodus 4:17 says, "And thou shalt take this rod in thine hand, wherewith thou shalt do signs." Three verses later, the same staff is called the "rod of God" (v. 20). This is reiterated in 17:9. Moses had far more authority in his hand than he yet realized. He needed to become aware of what he had and then be bold enough to use.

In the same sense, Jesus would later send the Twelve out with "power" (Matt. 10:1; Mark 3:15; 6:7; Luke 9:1), and also the Seventy (Luke 10:19). In John 1:12, we see that all who believe on Jesus are given the "power to become the sons of God, even to them that believe on his name." We might be amazed at what was given to Moses to wield, but we have been given something just as great, if not greater. Besides the name of Jesus (14:13-14), we have the promise of Acts 1:8: "But ye shall receive power, after that the Holy Ghost is come upon you."

• Describe God's miraculous promise.

"Press forward. Do not stop, do not linger in your journey, but strive for the mark set before you."—George Whitefield

---

D. The Final Trap for Pharaoh (vv. 17-18)

¹⁷ And I, behold, I will harden the hearts of the Egyptians, and they shall follow them: and I will get me honour upon Pharaoh, and upon all his host, upon his chariots, and upon his horsemen. ¹⁸ And the Egyptians shall know that I am the Lord, when I have gotten me honour upon Pharaoh, upon his chariots, and upon his horsemen.

The "final solution" regarding Pharaoh was now about to come to pass. God would not only deliver His people through the Red Sea, He would also eliminate any other problem or threat by the Egyptians. The entire military machine of Pharaoh would be destroyed in one fatal sweep. This would also be a burning of bridges for the Israelites. "In the years that followed, each time the Jews expressed a desire to return to Egypt, they should have remembered that God closed the waters and locked the door" (*The Bible Exposition Commentary*).

In the previous verses, the emphasis was on the implied pronoun *you*. Now it switches to *I*. In other words, "*You*, Moses, use your staff to part the waters. *I* [God] will harden one final time the heart of Pharaoh and bring them into My trap." We are to do what God tells us to do, and He will do His part . . . always.

---

1. How did Pharaoh's soldiers become like him (v. 17)?
2. What would all the Egyptians "know" (v. 18)?

"A leader who doesn't hesitate before he sends his nation into battle is not fit to be a leader."—Golda Meir

III. GOD MIRACULOUSLY DELIVERS HIS PEOPLE (Ex. 14:19-31)

A. The Cloud and the Wind (vv. 19-22)

¹⁹ And the angel of God, which went before the camp of Israel, removed and went behind them; and the pillar of the cloud went from before their face, and stood behind them: ²⁰ And it came between the camp of the Egyptians and the camp of Israel; and it was a cloud and darkness to them, but it gave light by night to these: so that the one came not near the other all the night. ²¹ And Moses stretched out his hand over the sea; and the Lord caused the sea to go back by a strong east wind all that night, and made the sea dry land, and the waters were divided. ²² And the children of Israel went into the midst of the sea upon the dry ground: and the waters were a wall unto them on their right hand, and on their left.

The "angel of God" was possibly a *theophany*—a pre-incarnate appearance of Christ. He moved from in front of the Israelites to also become a rear guard, thus protecting the people from the oncoming Egyptian army. Manifesting as a pillar of cloud behind them, which possibly was a very thick fog, the angel caused such darkness that the Egyptians were stopped in their tracks. Even though the text says *removed* in verse 19, the angel still provided a light in front of the Israelites to show them the way across the seabed. "What was light for Israel became darkness for the Egyptians" (*Zondervan NIV Bible Commentary*). Judgment and salvation are both demonstrated here as part of the character of the Lord.

While the angel was busy confusing the Egyptians and providing light for the Israelites, the Lord was also providing another miracle—the splitting of the sea. A strong east wind divided the water and dried the seabed to the point that the Israelites walked across on dry land. This had to be a very wide passageway, since there were two million people along with the herds, flocks, and personal belongings. The exact location of this miracle has been debated, but it was wide and deep enough that the Egyptian army would shortly be drowned therein when the waters collapsed from the wall the Lord had formed.

---

1. How did the Lord protect the Israelites (v. 19)?
2. Describe the miracle of verse 20.
3. When have you seen God transform an obstacle into a pathway (vv. 21-22)?

Led by God

The Israelites were led in three ways: a great leader in Moses, a pillar of fire by night, and a cloud by day. We do not have this same combination today, although God does provide anointed leaders. Instead of fire and a cloud, we have the Word of God and the Holy Spirit. The light of the Word (Ps. 119:105) and the guidance of the Holy Spirit (John 16:13) are a combination enabling us to follow the Lord at all times.

B. The Egyptian Army Destroyed (vv. 23-25)

²³ And the Egyptians pursued, and went in after them to the midst of the sea, even all Pharaoh's horses, his chariots, and his horsemen. ²⁴ And it

came to pass, that in the morning watch the Lord looked unto the host of the Egyptians through the pillar of fire and of the cloud, and troubled the host of the Egyptians, ²⁵ And took off their chariot wheels, that they drave them heavily: so that the Egyptians said, Let us flee from the face of Israel; for the Lord fighteth for them against the Egyptians.

At some point during the night, the Egyptians resumed their pursuit, despite the thick darkness. It is possible they did not know they were marching into the seabed, since it was now dry ground. This is illustrative of the way the devil works. Even when he knows defeat is coming, he continues his efforts. Verse 24 says "the Lord looked" at the Egyptian army and threw them into confusion. This might have been because some realized the dangerous position they were now in (with water walled up on either side of this canyon). Psalm 77:16-20 implies that a severe rainstorm came, thus causing the seabed to start becoming as mud. Chariot wheels began to bog down and come off, causing even more confusion. Pharaoh's heart may have been hardened to the point of no return, but the soldiers in his army were ready to give up the futile pursuit. "The Egyptians had enough and were willing to forget about Israel altogether, but it was too late" (*Zondervan NIV Bible Commentary*). Revenge of the Lord against them would now be final and complete.

- When did the Egyptians change their minds about pursuing the Israelites, and why?

"When by the malice of enemies God's people are brought to greatest straits, there is deliverance near to be sent from God unto them."— David Dickson

---

C. The Waters Close (vv. 26-30)

²⁶ And the Lord said unto Moses, Stretch out thine hand over the sea, that the waters may come again upon the Egyptians, upon their chariots, and upon their horsemen. ²⁷ And Moses stretched forth his hand over the sea, and the sea returned to his strength when the morning appeared; and the Egyptians fled against it; and the Lord overthrew the Egyptians in the midst of the sea. ²⁸ And the waters returned, and covered the chariots, and the horsemen, and all the host of Pharaoh that came into the sea after them; there remained not so much as one of them. ²⁹ But the children of Israel walked upon dry land in the midst of the sea; and the waters were a wall unto them on their right hand, and on their left. ³⁰ Thus the Lord saved Israel that day out of the hand of the Egyptians; and Israel saw the Egyptians dead upon the sea shore.

While it was obviously the Lord performing the great miracle, Moses was still empowered to finish the work. It was only as he stretched his hand (rod) over the sea that the waters returned, thus destroying the Egyptians. Even if they could swim, the crushing waters were so devastating that no one survived. The grim sight of dead bodies on the seashore certainly told the Israelites of the awesome power of the God who had rescued them. For generations to come, even today, pious Jews would recognize this as the ultimate display of God's power. This was the fulfillment of verse 18, where God said, "And the Egyptians shall know that I am the Lord."

---

1. How thoroughly were Pharaoh and his soldiers defeated (vv. 26-28)?
2. What unforgettable sights did the Israelites witness (vv. 29-30)?

"Finishing well brings more glory to God than beginning well."— Woodrow Kroll

---

D. Fear of the Lord (v. 31)

³¹ And Israel saw that great work which the Lord did upon the Egyptians: and the people feared the Lord, and believed the Lord, and his servant Moses.

The people were instilled with a fear of the Lord that day, but sadly it did not instill lasting faith. Old paradigms of doubt and despair are hard to break, even with a miraculous display. This was similar to the situation described in Mark 4:35-41. Jesus told His disciples, "Let us cross over to the other side." While in route across the Sea of Galilee, a windstorm arose, causing the disciples to fear for their lives. When they awakened Jesus (who was napping peacefully in the boat) and accused Him of being callous to their predicament, He calmed the waters. He then asked, "Why are you so fearful? How is it that you have no faith?" (v. 40 NKJV).

• How did the Red Sea experience shape the Israelites?

CONCLUSION

The Lord led the Israelites on a winding route in the Exodus from Egypt because He knew they were not ready to handle the Promised Land He had waiting for them. They were slaves who had to be transformed into sons. They needed the wilderness as a training school.

The shortest path is usually one that leads to a dead end. The paths of our lives seldom, if ever, run in a straight line. Yet, it is along the detours that we learn patience, learn to hear God's voice, and learn to serve even while we are waiting. Key leaders of the Bible had long times of waiting before they came to their destinations. We can expect no different. God never gets in a hurry, and as long as we follow Him, we are still headed toward our destination.

GOLDEN TEXT CHALLENGE

"THE CHILDREN OF ISRAEL WALKED UPON DRY LAND IN THE MIDST OF THE SEA; AND THE WATERS WERE A WALL UNTO THEM ON THEIR RIGHT HAND, AND ON THEIR LEFT" (Ex. 14:29).

Although God could have divided the Red Sea without any motion of the air, He chose to raise a strong east wind. Thus, He demonstrated that nature was obedient to Him and was governed by His will. Also, remember that the sea could not have been dried by any wind, however strong, unless it had been affected by the power of the Spirit, beyond the ordinary operation of nature.

It is probable that Moses and Aaron ventured first into this untrodden path, and then all Israel followed after them. This march through the paths of the great waters would have made their march afterward, through the wilderness, less formidable. Those who had followed God through the sea did not need to fear following Him wherever He would lead them.

Daily Devotions:

M. Song of Moses and Miriam
    Exodus 15:1-6
T. Song of Exodus
    Psalm 114:1-8
W. Song of Salvation
    Isaiah 12:1-6
T. Jesus Interrupts a Funeral
    Luke 7:11-17
F. Peter Surprises a Lame Man
    Acts 3:1-8
S. Israel's Experience as Our Example
    1 Corinthians 10:1-4

God's Great Commandments

Exodus 20:1-17; 24:3-8

Unit Theme:
The Exodus

Central Truth:
Obedience to God's commandments brings blessings.

Focus:
Learn and obey God's Word by the grace of Christ and the power of the Holy Spirit.

Context:
On Mount Sinai around 1438 BC.

Golden Text:
"He [Moses] took the book of the covenant, and read in the audience of the people: and they said, All that the Lord hath said will we do, and be obedient" (Ex. 24:7).

Study Outline:
 I. Israel Commanded to Love God
    (Ex. 20:1-11)
 II. Israel Commanded to Love Others
    (Ex. 20:12-17)
 III. Israel Promises Obedience to God
    (Ex. 24:3-8)

INTRODUCTION

After witnessing the greatest miracle imaginable, the Israelites broke out into song, led by Moses (Ex. 15:1-18). Throughout the lyrics, the Lord is exalted as above all others, and the song describes His "lovingkindness" for His people (v. 13 NASB). The Israelites were finally capturing that God truly did love them!

The song then speaks prophetically of how the Lord would lead them to conquer the nations and help them possess the Promised Land, which is called "thy holy habitation" (v. 13). This culminates in the following: "You will bring them in and plant them on the mountain of your inheritance—the place, O Lord, you made for your dwelling, the sanctuary, O Lord, your hands established" (v. 17 NIV). Based on what God had already done, they could boast in what would take place in the future. In their minds they knew they would never distrust Him again.

There is nothing like a song of victory after a battle is over. However, the Israelites faced many tough challenges ahead, and the excitement would quickly dissipate. They needed training, and the march to Mount Sinai was part of that training. Moses led the assembly for three days into the wilderness. By then all the water they had carried with them was gone, even though the march was only for about fifteen miles. When they came to Marah, the water they found was undrinkable, and all the joy of three days earlier was forgotten. Thus, the murmuring began afresh. It took another miracle of the Lord to turn the waters sweet for drinking (vv. 22-25).

Chapter 16 tells how God provided daily food, called *manna,* to keep the people fed. In chapter 17, we see the people again without water, yet God provides for them miraculously. Then they come to their first conflict with an enemy—the Amalekites. Here we meet faithful Joshua, who became Moses' protégé. He led the troops to their first military victory. Chapter 18 tells the story of the visit of Jethro, Moses' father-in-law.

At chapter 19, the people arrive at Mount Sinai, exactly three months after having left Egypt. They would remain here for one year, a time in which two things were accomplished: (1) They were given the Law of God and instructed in His ways. (2) They were unified into the semblance of a nation. This brings us to chapter 20, the text for today's lesson.

I. ISRAEL COMMANDED TO LOVE GOD (Ex. 20:1-11)
A. The Reason for the Law (v. 1)
¹ **And God spake all these words, saying.**
The Law (the foundation of the Mosaic covenant) was essentially a set of rules for helping the Israelites learn to live in freedom with each other. They had existed for generations in slavery, and were thus not prepared to make their own decisions. Therefore, much of the Law has to do with basic civil responsibilities. In the earlier Abrahamic covenant, God had given the Promised Land to them, but their ability to possess this inheritance would be dependent on following a unified code of ethics.

Beyond the legalisms, however, God was more interested in helping the Israelites grow in character. After all, they were His chosen people. Also, the Law was not given for them to use to achieve righteousness. Galatians 3:11 says, "But that no man is justified by the law in the sight of God, it is evident: for, The just shall live by faith." Right standing with God has always been by faith alone. The Law was given to reveal humanity's sinfulness—to demonstrate the vast chasm between God's holiness and our depravity. "The Law reveals God's righteousness and demands righteousness, but it cannot give righteousness" (*Bible Exposition Commentary*). The only way to righteousness is through faith in Christ. Paul said, "For he hath made him to be sin for us, who knew no sin; that we might be made the righteousness of God in him" (2 Cor. 5:21).

B. God's Relationship With His People (v. 2)
² **I am the Lord thy God, which have brought thee out of the land of Egypt, out of the house of bondage.**
The first four of the Ten Commandments deal with the Israelites' vertical relationship with the Lord, while the other six deal with their horizontal relationships with each other. Before giving the Commandments, however, the Lord made clear His bond with the people. Just as He had led Abraham out of Ur and made great promises to him, He now had led Abraham's descendants out of Egypt. He was their God, and fully expected them to recognize and obey Him.

The simple statement "I am the Lord" summarizes all that He intended to be for this people. It was as if He said, "Whatever you need, I am!"

---

1. How is Egypt described?
2. How does the Lord depict Himself?

"So often we try to develop Christian character and conduct without taking the time to develop God-centered devotion. We try to please God without taking the time to walk with Him and develop a relationship with Him. This is impossible to do."—Jerry Bridges

---

C. The First Commandment (v. 3)

³ **Thou shalt have no other gods before me.**

The first commandment should have made complete sense to the Israelites. The plagues God had sent upon Egypt made a sham of all the idol gods there. The ancient world was full of superstition and idolatry. God was revealing the truth to this people (that there is only one God) who, in turn, were supposed to show the rest of the world. Sadly, Israel did not perceive the obvious, for they soon fell into idolatry.

An idol is only a substitute for the real God. This eliminates any sense of pluralism. Judaism and Christianity recognize there is only one Creator. Any other deities people worship are false. The Jewish confession of faith is called the *Shema.* It is recited every morning: "Hear, O Israel: The Lord our God is one Lord" (Deut. 6:4).

• What forms of idolatry are most prevalent in our society?

"As long as you want anything very much, especially more than you want God, it is an idol."—A. B. Simpson

---

D. No Graven Images (vv. 4-6)

⁴ **Thou shalt not make unto thee any graven image, or any likeness of any thing that is in heaven above, or that is in the earth beneath, or that is in the water under the earth: ⁵ Thou shalt not bow down thyself to them, nor serve them: for I the Lord thy God am a jealous God, visiting the iniquity of the fathers upon the children unto the third and fourth generation of them that hate me; ⁶ And shewing mercy unto thousands of them that love me, and keep my commandments.**

These verses are not a redundancy of the first commandment. They speak of the mode of worship rather than the object. Images made of stone, wood, metal, gold, or silver—any representation that could be made with the intention to worship it—were forbidden. The Lord was not thwarting artistic expression, but simply telling the people to avoid substitutes for Himself in their hearts.

The word *jealous* (v. 5) does not mean "envious," for idols have no power, and the false deities they represent are not real. The Lord here expresses His desire for His people to have only what is best, what is real, and what will enhance their lives. This comes by worshiping God exclusively. This is not because God is insecure or envious, but rather because He knows what is best. He also knows that people create false realities based on their surroundings—what "seems to be." Thus, ancestral sins could be passed from one generation to the next because paradigms are established by what people see, hear, and experience in their familial settings. With several generations living together in extended families, it was likely for idols of one to be adopted by others. But, if the Lord were served exclusively, then blessings would be passed on. The faith of men like Abraham and David are great examples. Their lives positively influenced many generations after them.

---

1. What does God call Himself in verse 5, and why?
2. How can our lives affect the generations after us (vv. 5-6)?

"There is nothing so abominable in the eyes of God and of men as idolatry, whereby men render to the creature that honor which is due only to the Creator."—Blaise Pascal

---

E. Honor God's Name (v. 7)

⁷ Thou shalt not take the name of the Lord thy God in vain; for the Lord will not hold him guiltless that taketh his name in vain.

God demands that His name be honored and revered. Proverbs 22:1 says, "A good name is rather to be chosen than great riches, and loving favour rather than silver and gold." A person's character and reputation are represented by his or her name. To speak the Lord's name in vain is to dishonor it, to deny His character and goodness, and to criticize the Creator of the universe. Obviously, cursing and vile language that uses His name is included here, but even casual remarks when surprised or overwhelmed—in a phrase such as "Oh, my God!"—degrade His greatness. These should be totally avoided; they are abhorrent to any true worshiper. This commandment does not include legitimate oaths, which appear frequently in Scripture, but it does cover frivolous ones by people who have no intention of keeping them.

• List ways this command is commonly violated.

"God has never, in the history of mankind, allowed His name to go long offended."—David Wilkerson

---

F. Hallowedness of the Sabbath (vv. 8-11)

⁸ Remember the sabbath day, to keep it holy. ⁹ Six days shalt thou labour, and do all thy work: ¹⁰ But the seventh day is the sabbath of the Lord thy God: in it thou shalt not do any work, thou, nor thy son, nor thy daughter, thy manservant, nor thy maidservant, nor thy cattle, nor thy stranger that is within thy gates: ¹¹ For in six days the Lord made heaven and earth, the sea, and all that in them is, and rested the seventh day: wherefore the Lord blessed the sabbath day, and hallowed it.

For all the years they were in Egypt, the Israelites presumably had no day of rest. The fourth commandment (explained in four verses) invokes a day to cease from work. Even the Lord worked for six days in creating the universe, but rested on the seventh. "The command to remember the Sabbath is *moral* insofar as it requires of a person a due portion of his or her time dedicated to the worship and service of God, but it is *ceremonial* in that it prescribes the seventh day" (*Zondervan NIV Bible Commentary*). In the New Testament, or the church age, the day of worship for most believers is the first day, giving honor to the resurrection of Jesus from the grave.

The Lord was very serious about this command with the Israelites. To violate it intentionally meant the penalty of death (see Ex. 31:15; Num. 15:32-36). Also, the Sabbath had already been established with the appearance of manna. They were to gather enough manna on the sixth day to last through the seventh, for none would appear on that day (Ex. 16:23-25).

---

1. Why did the Lord establish "the sabbath day" (vv. 8-10)?
2. What example did the Lord set (v. 11)?
3. How should we observe the Lord's Day?

"O what a blessing is Sunday, interposed between the waves of worldly business like the divine path of the Israelites through the sea! There is nothing in which I would advise you to be more strictly conscientious than in keeping the Sabbath day holy. I can truly declare that to me the Sabbath has been invaluable."—William Wilberforce

---

II. ISRAEL COMMANDED TO LOVE OTHERS (Ex. 20:12-17)

A. Honoring Parents (v. 12)

¹² Honour thy father and thy mother: that thy days may be long upon the land which the Lord thy God giveth thee.

With the fifth commandment, the focus changes from our relationship with God to our relationship with other people. As opposed to present-day culture which puts such a premium on youth, God commanded that His people honor their parents, and especially the elderly. Leviticus 19:32 says, "Rise in the presence of the aged, show respect for the elderly and revere your God. I am the Lord" (NIV).

In modern culture almost everyone hates the idea of getting old, but equally hates the alternative. Interestingly, this commandment brings with it a promised blessing if obeyed.

Personal longevity is the fruit of honoring and obeying one's parents (as well as honoring other elderly people). Paul reiterates this as a "commandment with promise" (Eph. 6:2-3). Primarily, however, the Lord was speaking in Exodus of duration as a nation rather than individual lifespan. In other words, how a nation treats its elderly has much to do with the health and longevity of the nation itself.

---

1. List ways to honor one's parents.
2. What is promised to those who obey this command?

"'Children, obey your parents' (Eph. 6:1). Why does the apostle use the word *obey* instead of *honor*, which has a greater extent of meaning?

It is because obedience is the evidence of that honor which children owe to their parents, and is therefore more earnestly enforced."—John Calvin

---

B. Respect for Human Life (v. 13)

13 Thou shalt not kill.

Because man is made in God's image (Gen. 1:26-27), murder is a great offense to Him. The first case of murder was Cain killing Abel (4:8). When Noah stepped out of the ark after the Flood, one of the first things God told him and his sons was, "Whoever sheds the blood of man, by man shall his blood be shed; for in the image of God has God made man" (9:6 NIV). The Hebrew word used here (*ratsach*) signifies premeditated intentional murder. It does not apply to animals (v. 3), to defending one's home from robbers (Ex. 22:2), to accidental killing of another human (Deut. 19:5), or to the execution of murderers by the government (see Gen. 9:6).

Self-murder, or suicide, is not spoken of here, and the Bible never uses the word. However, there are examples, such as Saul and his armorbearer (1 Sam. 31:4-5). The larger point is that human life is sacred. There are difficult situations today where individuals take their lives, but are under the influence of medication or a mental condition that alters rational thinking. We have to trust the grace and mercy of the Lord to judge these situations.

- Do you agree or disagree that our society has embraced a "culture of death," as some claim?

"The Bible says that all people, not just believers, possess part of the image of God; that is why murder and abortion are wrong."—Rick Warren

---

C. Marital Faithfulness (v. 14)

14 Thou shalt not commit adultery.

Adultery involves married people, while *fornication* involves those who are unmarried. Both are sexual relationships outside of the bond of marriage and are forbidden by the Lord. Under the Mosaic Law, when a couple was caught in the act of adultery, both parties were to be executed (see Deut. 22:22). Adultery plays havoc with relationships and leaves a trail of problems behind it. David's affair with Bathsheba stands as a solemn example. Even though a son of this relationship (Solomon) would later become king, the costs in David's family were enormous. Violence—including, rape, murder, and revolt—were all consequences of his sin.

In the New Testament, Jesus expanded the meaning of adultery to include lust. He said, "Whosoever looketh on a woman to lust after her hath committed adultery with her already in his heart" (Matt. 5:28). When the woman caught in adultery was brought to Jesus in John 8, He told her to "go, and sin no more" (v. 11). He didn't excuse her sin, but forgave her and warned her against further adultery.

- How is adultery treated in contemporary TV sitcoms and movies?

"No sin that a person commits has more built-in pitfalls, problems, and destructiveness than sexual sin. It has broken more marriages, shattered more homes, caused more heartache and disease, and destroyed more lives than alcohol and drugs combined. It causes lying, stealing, cheating, and killing, as well as bitterness, hatred, slander, gossip, and unforgiveness."—John MacArthur

D. Against Stealing and Lying (vv. 15-16)

15 Thou shalt not steal. 16 Thou shalt not bear false witness against thy neighbour.

Respect for the property of others is a key element of any stable society. Since every good thing comes from the Lord, stealing is the same as taking from Him. In the New Testament, Paul exhorts, "Let him that stole steal no more: but rather let him labour, working with his hands the thing which is good, that he may have to give to him that needeth" (Eph. 4:28).

Just as the Lord insisted that His name be honored (Ex. 20:7), lying against someone hurts their name. Telling lies about another person causes unjustified injury to them. It endangers their character and wounds their feelings.

• How is lying a form of stealing?

"When we forget God, we lose the only true basis for morality and ethics, and we are cast upon the shifting sands of moral relativism in which anything goes, including lying, cheating, and stealing."—Judge Roy Moore

E. Against Covetousness (v. 17)

17 Thou shalt not covet thy neighbour's house, thou shalt not covet thy neighbour's wife, nor his manservant, nor his maidservant, nor his ox, nor his ass, nor any thing that is thy neighbour's.

To *covet* is to have an unhealthy desire for what belongs to someone else. It is closely associated with the eighth commandment (stealing). *Covetousness* can also be translated as "greed." Hebrews 13:5 tells us, "Let your conduct be without covetousness; be content with such things as you have. For He Himself has said, 'I will never leave you nor forsake you'" (NKJV). We should be content with the Lord, for He supplies all our needs. Jesus warned, "Take heed, and beware of covetousness: for a man's life consisteth not in the abundance of the things which he possesseth" (Luke 12:15).

• Why is it so easy to covet, and how can we guard against it?

"God's love is the most awesome thing about Him. It is not His justice, nor His majesty, nor even His blazing holiness, but the fact that He has made and keeps a covenant of personal commitment and love to His people."—Sinclair B. Ferguson

F. The Law of Love

The tenth commandment tells us not to covet what belongs to someone else. However, Paul gives *one* situation where it is good to covet: "But covet earnestly the best gifts: and yet shew I unto you a more excellent way" (1 Cor. 12:31). This is the lead-in for the great love chapter of the Bible—1 Corinthians 13. In Matthew 22:37-40, Jesus sums up all the Law in two commandments—love God and love people. If we do these, we will fulfill the Ten Commandments.

III. ISRAEL PROMISES OBEDIENCE TO GOD (Ex. 24:3-8)

A. Moses Gives the People the Lord's Commands (v. 3)

³ And Moses came and told the people all the words of the Lord, and all the judgments: and all the people answered with one voice, and said, All the words which the Lord hath said will we do.

Chapters 21-23 basically elaborate what was commanded in chapter 20. After the laws had been given, God summoned Moses to come before Him with Aaron, Aaron's two oldest sons, and seventy leaders of the people—a total of seventy-three men (24:1-2). All except Moses were to stay at a distance. After this meeting, Moses came back down Mount Sinai prepared to lay everything out before the people. It is not clear as to whether he first presented all that God had given him to the other seventy-two men. What is obvious is that God would use leaders under Moses with rank and authority.

_____

• How did the people respond to Moses' presentation of the Lord's commands?

_____

B. The Mosaic Covenant Confirmed (vv. 4-8)

⁴ And Moses wrote all the words of the Lord, and rose up early in the morning, and builded an altar under the hill, and twelve pillars, according to the twelve tribes of Israel. ⁵ And he sent young men of the children of Israel, which offered burnt offerings, and sacrificed peace offerings of oxen unto the Lord. ⁶ And Moses took half of the blood, and put it in basons; and half of the blood he sprinkled on the altar. ⁷ And he took the book of the covenant, and read in the audience of the people: and they said, All that the Lord hath said will we do, and be obedient. ⁸ And Moses took the blood, and sprinkled it on the people, and said, Behold the blood of the covenant, which the Lord hath made with you concerning all these words.

Before presenting the Law to the people, Moses wrote down everything God had given him, and then made sacrifices to the Lord. The burnt offerings and peace offerings were purely for worship and sealing of the covenant. They were not sin offerings. "These were redeemed people, who now, by these sacrifices of dedication and fellowship, were committing themselves and entering into a close and binding communion with their Redeemer" (*Wycliffe Bible Commentary*).

Moses then read the entire Book of the Covenant aloud to the people. After listening intently, the people affirmed their willingness to obey. The covenant was then ratified with the sprinkling of blood. They promised to obey God, and He would hold them to their promise.

This was something like a marriage ceremony. God had redeemed this people (Ex. 1—18) and had taken them as His own. Now He was about to come and dwell among them.

---

1. How many pillars did the altar have, and why (vv. 4, 7)?
2. What was the purpose of the sprinkling of the blood (vv. 5-6, 8)?

CONCLUSION

One purpose of the Law was to prepare a nation through which the Redeemer would come. To make the way for Jesus, God had to have a man (Abraham), and then a people (the Israelites), through whom His Son could be born as a man to redeem humanity from sin. Through his obedience to the covenant, Abraham was a blessing to Israel. Through Israel, the Redeemer was given to the world. Through Christ's obedience to the Father, the blessings of salvation are available to everyone who believes on Him.

GOLDEN TEXT CHALLENGE

"HE [MOSES] TOOK THE BOOK OF THE COVENANT, AND READ IN THE AUDIENCE OF THE PEOPLE: AND THEY SAID, ALL THAT THE LORD HATH SAID WILL WE DO, AND BE OBEDIENT" (Ex. 24:7).

The Israelites came together, heard the Word of the Lord, understood it, and promised to obey it. This is the pattern Christians should follow. We should regularly come together to hear the preaching and teaching of the Scriptures, apply ourselves to understand what we hear, and then commit ourselves to obey the Lord.

Daily Devotions:
M. Summary of the Law
    Deuteronomy 6:1-4
T. Promise of the Law
    Psalm 19:7-11
W. God's Law Will Bring Peace
    Micah 4:1-5
T. Christ Fulfills the Law
    Matthew 5:17-20
F. Obedience Evidences Love
    John 14:15-24
S. Be Doers of the Word
    James 1:22-25

The Priesthood Established

Exodus 28:1 through 29:46; 1 Peter 2:4-10

Unit Theme:
The Exodus

Central Truth:
The Levitical priesthood foreshadowed the priesthood of all believers in Christ.

Focus:
Consider God's establishment of the Levitical priesthood and realize that He has made believers in Christ Jesus a kingdom of priests.

Context:
Mount Sinai around 1438 BC

Golden Text:
"Ye also, as lively stones, are built up a spiritual house, a holy priesthood, to offer up spiritual sacrifices, acceptable to God by Jesus Christ" (1 Peter 2:5).

Study Outline:
I. Set Apart for God's Service
   (Ex. 28:1-4; 29:44-46)
II. A Heavy Responsibility
   (Ex. 28:26-30, 36-38)
III. The Priesthood of Believers
   (1 Peter 2:4-10)

INTRODUCTION

Exodus 25—27 describes the instructions God gave to Moses for collecting the building materials to assemble the Tabernacle and the pieces of furniture inside it. Elaborate details are given for how each important piece was to be made, and the fine metals and materials that were to be used. These included gold, silver, bronze, acacia wood, fine linen, wool, goat's hair, ram's skin, and hides of sea cows. Also required were olive oil, spices, and precious stones. Several articles of furniture are described before the Tabernacle itself, no doubt because of their greater importance. The Tabernacle simply provided shelter for the furniture inside.

The first piece of furniture described was the *ark of the covenant*—a rectangular chest made of wood and covered in gold. In the chest, Moses was to place *two stone tablets* with the Ten Commandments. These he would receive on the mountain. Also to be added was a *pot of manna* (see Heb. 9:4-5; Ex. 16:33) and *Aaron's rod* (see Num. 17:10). The lid for the ark was called the *mercy seat*. On this were to be two solid gold cherubim-winged angels facing each other as though shadowing the mercy seat. Other cherubim were woven into the curtains that covered the Tabernacle itself, and also on the veil (a thick curtain) that separated the Holy Place and the Most Holy Place (Ex. 26:31-33). Of most importance, however, was the space between the two cherubim's wings on the ark's covering. Here on the Day of Atonement, the high priest would sprinkle blood on the lid to make atonement for Israel's sin.

Next came instructions for building the *table of showbread* and the *lampstand*. After these, chapter 26 deals with the Tabernacle structure itself that would house the important pieces of furniture. Great detail is spent on the rich fabrics and skins that would be used to create the covering over it and the veil separating the Most Holy Place from the Holy Place.

Chapter 27 starts by describing the altar in the courtyard. God started from the inside and worked to the outside in giving Moses the plans. After the altar comes the outer courtyard with the curtained fence surrounding it. Finally, to supply light to the tent structure inside the court, directions were given as to how the lampstand was to function.

Next, the Lord gave instructions for the priesthood—the ministry group that was to preside over the spiritual life of the nation. This will be the subject of our lesson. The priests' duties included burning incense on the golden altar two times each day, maintaining the golden lampstand and the table of showbread (the bread of the Presence). They also offered sacrifices on the altar of burnt offering.

I. SET APART FOR GOD'S SERVICE (Ex. 28:1-4; 29:44-46)

A. Selection of Priests (28:1)

¹ And take thou unto thee Aaron thy brother, and his sons with him, from among the children of Israel, that he may minister unto me in the priest's office, even Aaron, Nadab and Abihu, Eleazar and Ithamar, Aaron's sons.

In Exodus 19:6, the Lord had said that He wanted Israel to be "a kingdom of priests" who would reveal His glory to the surrounding nations of the world. In order for this to happen, the Israelites had to be a holy people, and thus a means for them to accomplish this was established. The priests served in the Tabernacle to represent the people and mediate their sins before the Lord. They also represented the Lord to the people by teaching them the Law and helping them understand how to obey it.

Leviticus 10:8-11 records the only time God ever spoke directly to Aaron. This was just after his two sons, Nadab and Abihu, ignorantly or presumptuously offered unauthorized fire before the Lord and were slain. Their deaths demonstrated how serious the role of the priesthood was. After this, the Lord told Aaron to teach the people the rules revealed through Moses to the people. They must understand the seriousness of their relationship with a holy God.

To further grasp the weight of the priesthood, it would be wise to study Leviticus 8 and 9, which records the ordination process of Aaron and his four sons. At the conclusion of this weeklong ceremony, a visible manifestation of the glory of the Lord appeared, including supernatural fire that consumed the sacrifices on the altar. All of this indicated His approval. Sadly, however, on the first day of priestly duties after the ordination, Aaron had to face the death of his two eldest sons. Apparently they were not taking their roles seriously, and it cost them their lives. This left even greater responsibility and workload for the two remaining sons, Eleazar and Ithamar. After Aaron's death, Eleazar became his successor (Num.

20:22-29), and Ithamar's descendants carried out priestly duties even after the Captivity (see Ezra 8:1-2).

Why were Aaron and his sons chosen to be the priests? It was simply the Lord's decision, for they were certainly no more holy than anyone else. It was just as Jesus would later say to all of us, "You did not choose Me, but I chose you" (John 15:16 NKJV).

"The doctrine of election . . . is one of the sweetest and most blessed truths in the whole of revelation, and those who are afraid of it are so because they do not understand it. If they could but know that the Lord had chosen them, it would make their hearts dance for joy."—Charles Spurgeon

---

B. Priestly Garments (vv. 2-4)

² And thou shalt make holy garments for Aaron thy brother for glory and for beauty. ³ And thou shalt speak unto all that are wise hearted, whom I have filled with the spirit of wisdom, that they may make Aaron's garments to consecrate him, that he may minister unto me in the priest's office. ⁴ And these are the garments which they shall make; a breastplate, and an ephod, and a robe, and a broidered coat, a mitre, and a girdle: and they shall make holy garments for Aaron thy brother, and his sons, that he may minister unto me in the priest's office.

Elaborate garments were established for the priests to wear. There were three reasons for these: (1) They gave dignity and honor, just as a military uniform gives such to a soldier. (2) The various parts of the garments symbolized spiritual truths relating to their ministry. (3) God designed the garments, and if they didn't wear them accordingly, they would die.

The garments were to "exalt the office and function of the high priest as well as beautify the worship of God" (*Zondervan NIV Bible Commentary*). This speaks something to contemporary times and how we approach the worship of the Lord. Casual attire can be too casual if it leads to an attitude that is less than reverent. The "wise hearted" (v. 3) indicated anointed craftsmen would do the work of making the garments.

The special garments worn by the high priest were worn only when he served in the Tabernacle, and were of the same fine yarn and linen as used in the curtains of the Tabernacle. Eight actual parts of the costume are mentioned. Four were inner garments and were worn by all priests—*tunics, linen undergarments, girdles* (sashes), and *headbands* (see vv. 39-42). The other four were special overgarments to be worn by Aaron as the high priest—*breastplate, ephod* (waistcoat), *robe,* and *turban* (miter).

The ephod was the most distinctive piece of clothing. It was an embroidered apron made of two pieces, front and back, joined at the shoulder by straps, and bound around the waist by a belt. On each of the two shoulder straps was an onyx stone, upon which was engraved the names of the twelve tribes, six on each stone (see vv. 7-12). Thus, "the priest bore upon his shoulders the burden of all Israel as he represented them before God" (*Wycliffe Bible Commentary*). This was the heart of intercessory ministry—bringing the burdens of others before the Lord.

---

1. Why did Aaron and his sons need "holy garments" (v. 2)?
2. What had God gifted certain individuals to do (vv. 3-4)?

"If a commission by an earthly king is considered an honor, how can a commission by a heavenly King be considered a sacrifice?"—David Livingstone

---

C. Sanctifying of the Tabernacle and Its Ministers (29:44-46)

⁴⁴ And I will sanctify the tabernacle of the congregation, and the altar: I will sanctify also both Aaron and his sons, to minister to me in the priest's office. ⁴⁵ And I will dwell among the children of Israel, and will be their God. ⁴⁶ And they shall know that I am the Lord their God, that brought them forth out of the land of Egypt, that I may dwell among them: I am the Lord their God.

This chapter of Exodus is all about the details God instructed for the ordination of Aaron and his sons as priests, culminating in the verses of our text. During the week prior to the actual ceremony, the priests were required to remain in the Tabernacle area, and after the ceremony their work would begin. "They had to follow a daily, weekly, monthly, and yearly schedule, all of which was outlined in the Law that God gave Moses on Mount Sinai" (*Bible Exposition Commentary*).

It would be a grueling schedule which, it turns out, was even more difficult for Aaron and his two younger sons after the two oldest were killed. Twice each day—morning and evening—they were to offer a lamb, along with meat and drink offerings. Thus, every day the dedication of the people was renewed. More importantly, God would dwell in this Tabernacle and bless His people.

---

1. What does "sanctify" mean, and what is its purpose (v. 44)?
2. How does God describe His relationship with Israel (vv. 45-46)?

"No horse gets anywhere until he is harnessed. No stream or gas drives anything until it is confined. No Niagara is ever turned into light and power until it is tunneled. No life ever grows great until it is focused, dedicated, disciplined."—Harry Emerson Fosdick

---

II. A HEAVY RESPONSIBILITY (Ex. 28:26-30, 36-38)

A. Description of the Breastplate (vv. 26-29)

²⁶ And thou shalt make two rings of gold, and thou shalt put them upon the two ends of the breastplate in the border thereof, which is in the side of the ephod inward. ²⁷ And two other rings of gold thou shalt make, and shalt put them on the two sides of the ephod underneath, toward the forepart thereof, over against the other coupling thereof, above the curious girdle

of the ephod. **28 And they shall bind the breastplate by the rings thereof unto the rings of the ephod with a lace of blue, that it may be above the curious girdle of the ephod, and that the breastplate be not loosed from the ephod. 29 And Aaron shall bear the names of the children of Israel in the breastplate of judgment upon his heart, when he goeth in unto the holy place, for a memorial before the Lord continually.**

Neither the high priest nor his sons attending with him could dress in anything but prescribed garments, from underwear up. God himself was the designer. Verses 26-28 deal with the breastplate. It had twelve stones inset in rows of four, each stone representing a tribe of Israel. Thus the high priest carried the twelve tribes both in his heart and on his shoulders. Thus, he was responsible for all the people.

Detailed instructions were given by the Lord even for how to attach the breastplate over the ephod. Four gold chains were used (vv. 24-25). Two were slipped through gold rings on the upper corners of the breastplate and attached to rings on the shoulder pieces. The other two chains were attached to gold rings on the lower two corners of the breastplate and then hooked at the other ends to the side seams of the ephod, using blue lacing (v. 28).

Just as the twelve stones were all different, so were the different tribes within Israel, and so are people in general. Although races and cultures differ, they still all are part of humanity and are in the heart of God. They are all jewels to Him.

• What was written on the high priest's breastplate, and why (v. 29)?

"Only as we accept our responsibility and appropriate God's provisions will we make any progress in our pursuit of holiness."—Jerry Bridges

---

B. The Urim and Thummim (v. 30)

30 And thou shalt put in the breastplate of judgment the Urim and the Thummim; and they shall be upon Aaron's heart, when he goeth in before the Lord: and Aaron shall bear the judgment of the children of Israel upon his heart before the Lord continually.

The Urim and Thummim were some type of gemstones carried by the high priest and possibly used like dice to determine God's will in certain issues. Some think one was black and one was white, and that they were carried inside the breastplace (like in a pouch or an envelope). Perhaps they shined or emitted light in some way as to indicate what the Lord desired. It is impossible for us to determine just how they were used, yet they were seen as totally accurate.

We do not have such devices today for determining God's will in a matter; instead, we have the Word of God in our hand and the Holy Spirit in our heart. God leads through relationship with Him. If someone tried to follow the Word but had no relationship with the Lord, he or she could still fall into error. The Word reveals God's character and His purposes and shows what sin is and what displeases Him, while the Holy Spirit guides "into all truth" (John 16:13). The balance of the Word and the Holy Spirit's guidance make it possible for us to have divine direction, no matter the circumstance.

"We may not say that we have the answers. Questions of how to conduct oneself as a Christian, or how to serve as a Christian, must be answered by life itself—the life of the individual in his direct responsible relationship to God."—Elisabeth Elliot

---

C. The High Priest's Turban (vv. 36-38)

36 And thou shalt make a plate of pure gold, and grave upon it, like the engravings of a signet, HOLINESS TO THE LORD. 37 And thou shalt put it on a blue lace, that it may be upon the mitre; upon the forefront of the mitre it shall be. 38 And it shall be upon Aaron's forehead, that Aaron may bear the iniquity of the holy things, which the children of Israel shall hallow in all their holy gifts; and it shall be always upon his forehead, that they may be accepted before the Lord.

The high priest wore a turban, while other priests wore something more like a bonnet. On the front of the turban was a plate (or large badge) of pure gold, upon which was engraved the words "Holiness to the Lord." The gold signified the purity that God demanded of His people. In wearing the turban with this signet, the high priest identified himself with the sins of the people as they brought their offerings before the Lord. The high priest dared not enter the presence of the Lord in behalf of the people without this crucial element of his clothing. Twice in this section (vv. 35, 43), warnings were given that he might die without the proper apparel. As Christians, we make sacrifices, but ours are through the priesthood of Jesus Christ. The office of the high priest was a mediator until the true and perfect One came. Hebrews 7:27 speaks of our High Priest as One "who does not need daily, as those high priests, to offer up sacrifices, first for His own sins and then for the people's, for this He did once for all when He offered up Himself" (NKJV).

III. THE PRIESTHOOD OF BELIEVERS (1 Peter 2:4-10)

A. The Living Stone (v. 4)

4 To whom coming, as unto a living stone, disallowed indeed of men, but chosen of God, and precious.

Peter here describes Jesus as the stone upon which the Church is built. Though seen as worthless by secular people, this stone is living and gives life to others. He is living because He was raised from the dead. At the time of writing, believers were scorned and seen as foolish for following One who had died. Yet, Christ's followers are members of a glorious body designated as holy by God himself. In fact, they are the elect of God! Because the stone is living, people may enter into relationship with Him.

- Contrast some people's views of Jesus Christ with God the Father's view of Him. Why the difference?

"When old companions, old lusts, and sins crowd in upon you, and when you feel that you are ready to sink, what can save you, sinking sinner? This alone: I have a high priest in heaven, and He can support in the hour of affliction."—Robert McCheyne

---

B. Living Stones (vv. 5-10)

⁵ Ye also, as lively stones, are built up a spiritual house, an holy priesthood, to offer up spiritual sacrifices, acceptable to God by Jesus Christ. ⁶ Wherefore also it is contained in the scripture, Behold, I lay in Sion a chief corner stone, elect, precious: and he that believeth on him shall not be confounded. ⁷ Unto you therefore which believe he is precious: but unto them which be disobedient, the stone which the builders disallowed, the same is made the head of the corner, ⁸ And a stone of stumbling, and a rock of offence, even to them which stumble at the word, being disobedient: whereunto also they were appointed. ⁹ But ye are a chosen generation, a royal priesthood, an holy nation, a peculiar people; that ye should shew forth the praises of him who hath called you out of darkness into his marvellous light: ¹⁰ Which in time past were not a people, but are now the people of God: which had not obtained mercy, but now have obtained mercy.

Ephesians 2:20 describes Jesus as the "chief corner stone" of the Church. The Church is the spiritual building. All believers are stones He is using in the construction of this building. The word *lively* (1 Peter 2:5) means "living." In Matthew 16:18, Jesus said to Peter, "You are Peter [Greek, *Petros*—a large piece of rock], and on this rock [Greek, *petra*—a huge rock like Gibraltar] I will build My church" (Amp.). Peter was not *the* rock, but just *one* rock (though large, as his later life proved) among many used to build the spiritual house. Peter did not see himself as superseding anyone else.

Those who follow Peter's example by building their lives on Christ "will by no means be put to shame" (1 Peter 2:6 NKJV). They accept Christ as the "precious" chief cornerstone (v. 7), while those who reject Christ trip and fall over Him, and are thereby ruined (v. 8).

In every stone (believer) in the building of God's house is part of a "holy priesthood" (v. 5). When we grasp what the priesthood represented under the Mosaic covenant, we are sobered at the responsibility that is laid upon us in the new covenant. We are ministering here on earth as holy priests, just as Jesus ministers in heaven as our High Priest.

Looking back at the horror Aaron experienced at the death of his two sons, we must take very seriously our role as priests in the Kingdom. This is a "royal" and "holy" calling to live as "God's own possession" (v. 9 NASB). "The closer we draw to the Lord, the less we can take with us." In other words, as we "draw near to God" and He draws near to us (James 4:8 NKJV), then the parameters of life narrow greatly. Equally important, Aaron and his sons did not choose the priesthood for themselves. No, God chose them. God chooses us as His ministers (and many other paths we cannot take if we expect to fulfill the call He places on our lives). We are called "out of darkness into [God's] marvellous light" (1 Peter 2:9).

While we live under a new covenant of mercy (v. 10), we should never downplay the serious responsibility we carry in the Kingdom. It is a lifetime calling. Aaron served as high priest until God chose the time of his death. Numbers

20:23-29 tells us when Moses removed the priestly garments from him and placed them on his son Eleazar, Aaron died immediately.

---

1. Who shall not be "confounded" ("put to shame" NKJV), and why not (vv. 5-6)?
2. How is Christ both the "chief cornerstone" and a "rock of offence" (vv. 7-8)?
3. What are Christ's followers called to be (v. 9)?
4. How does someone change after receiving Christ (v. 10)?

Christ's Jewels

The Lord went to great pains in giving instruction for the creation of the breastplate the high priest was to wear. Also, detail is given for how it was to be secured to the rest of the costume. Obviously, great pains were made to keep it from ever being lost, or separated from the priest's body. Isn't this the way God feels about His people? They are not only close to His heart—they are attached. Even greater, Jesus Christ is the eternal High Priest, and the names of His people are in His heart. They are His jewels, given to Him by His Father.

CONCLUSION

The priesthood is a serious matter, as shown by the deaths of Nadab and Abihu on the first day of their service. That Aaron and his other sons could not even grieve for them further drives the point. This is not just a Bible story from history for us to read, either. As God's people, our first obligation is to please the Lord and serve Him faithfully. If we focus on pleasing the Lord, He will use us to accomplish His work, and also reward us as faithful servants. This is exemplified by the way Jesus restored Peter after his denial. Jesus repeatedly asked him, "Do you love me?" (John 21:17). The qualification for ministry is not if we are talented, if we love people, or even if we love to minister, but if we love God. If we love Him, He qualifies us for the work.

GOLDEN TEXT CHALLENGE

"YE ALSO, AS LIVELY STONES, ARE BUILT UP A SPIRITUAL HOUSE, A HOLY PRIESTHOOD, TO OFFER UP SPIRITUAL SACRIFICES, ACCEPTABLE TO GOD BY JESUS CHRIST" (1 Peter 2:5).

Holiness, in addition to being a call and a growth, is a function in the temple of God. Since God chose in Old Testament times to establish fellowship with His people in a local, concrete way by means of the Tabernacle and then the Temple, it was fitting that Jesus (Matt. 16:18), Paul (1 Cor. 3:10-17; Eph. 2:19-22), and Peter (1 Peter 2:5) should use the figure of a building for the congregation of believers. Actually, the early Christians did not have church buildings at first. They usually met in someone's house. But they were conscious of being part of a great spiritual temple which God was erecting.

In the early days of Christianity, some people thought they could achieve greater holiness by solitary effort. So they moved to deserts and caves. Later, Monasteries were established as places for retreat from a sinful world. But Peter rebuked hermit asceticism. He told people to take their proper place in the life of the church. Christianity is a social faith. Fellowship with the Lord is more real when it is experienced in the group. In such a context it is also easier to give the Lord the praise which is due Him. In fact, all of the functions of worship and service have their divinely appointed center in the assembly of the saints.

Daily Devotions:

M. Phinehas: Zealous for the Lord
   Numbers 25:6-13
T. Hilkiah: Restores the Holy Book
   2 Kings 22:8-10
W. Joshua: Rebuilds the Altar
   Ezra 3:1-7
T. Access Made Possible
   Romans 5:1-5
F. Jesus Our High Priest
   Hebrews 4:14-16
S. The New and Living Way
   Hebrews 10:19-23

The Need for Salvation

Genesis 3:1-14, 16-19; Romans 1:28-32; 3:9-20; Ephesians 2:1-3

Unit Theme:
The Doctrine of Salvation

Central Truth:
All have sinned, and need God's provision of salvation through Jesus Christ.

Focus:
Realize all are born under the curse of sin and receive the salvation from sin provided through Christ.

Context:
Old and New Testament passages regarding the curse of sin

Golden Text:
"For all have sinned, and come short of the glory of God" (Rom. 3:23).

Study Outline:
   I. Humans Have Fallen Into Sin
      (Gen. 3:1-14, 16-19)
  II. Humans Declared Guilty of Sin
      (Rom. 3:9-20)
 III. Humans Are Trapped in Sin
      (Eph. 2:1-3; Rom. 1:28-32)

INTRODUCTION

Before we begin to explore the nature of salvation, we must first address the problem. The term *salvation* implies deliverance or redemption, and the natural question is, "From what?" Without a basic understanding of the problem of human existence, we cannot even begin to address the question of the solution to the problem. This is what this first lesson attempts to do.

The Christian message describes the problem of human existence by utilizing the term *sin*. When asking others what this term means, one will probably get a variety of responses that attest to a broad range of meaning. One person might say "missing the mark," while another might refer to an internal compulsion, and still another might talk about bad habits.

What connects these answers are two ways the Bible talks about sin. The first is to refer to sin in terms of deeds or actions that one either has committed or would have committed. To say "I have sinned before God" is to refer to an act of disobedience, and to confess one's sins is to focus on thoughts and behaviors contrary to God's law. One can commit a sin before God by thinking about an act of disobedience and deciding that he or she would do it if it were possible. As Jesus indicates, even the person who commits adultery in his heart is guilty whether the action is carried out or not (Matt. 5:28).

A second way the Bible talks about sin is in terms of a power within. Paul describes this power as a "law" waging war against his mind so that he cannot do the good he wants to do (Rom. 7:21-25). Sin is not so much an action as a condition. Theologians have described this condition in terms of a disease and a defect. The metaphor of *disease* points toward a loss of health through a foreign invader like a virus, while a *defect* suggests a lack of wholeness because some part of the body is not functioning as it should, like a physical deformity.

Christians claim that the problem of sin is really a problem about the human condition. Humans are born diseased and defective. This condition results from a breakdown in relationship with God and it leads to a breakdown in relationships with oneself, one's neighbor, and all of creation. Today's lesson tells the story of that breakdown.

I. HUMANS HAVE FALLEN INTO SIN (Gen. 3:1-14, 16-19)

A. The Nature of Temptation (vv. 1-6)

¹ Now the serpent was more subtil than any beast of the field which the Lord God had made. And he said unto the woman, Yea, hath God said, Ye shall not eat of every tree of the garden? ² And the woman said unto the serpent, We may eat of the fruit of the trees of the garden: ³ But of the fruit of the tree which is in the midst of the garden, God hath said, Ye shall not eat of it, neither shall ye touch it, lest ye die. ⁴ And the serpent said unto the woman, Ye shall not surely die: ⁵ For God doth know that in the day ye eat thereof, then your eyes shall be opened, and ye shall be as gods, knowing good and evil. ⁶ And when the woman saw that the tree was good for food, and that it was pleasant to the eyes, and a tree to be desired to make one wise, she took of the fruit thereof, and did eat, and gave also unto her husband with her; and he did eat.

The third chapter of Genesis presents the story of a primeval fall into sin. It is part of a larger narrative unity in Genesis 1—11 that concerns creation from chaos, reversal of creation back into chaos, and re-creation. Sin is a reversal of God's designs for creation. The third chapter presents this reversal in terms of a fracturing and undoing of the relational wholeness of creation.

The third chapter opens with the idea of the serpent as possessing a kind of "street smarts" among the other beasts (v. 1), which sets the tone for the role of the serpent as primary deceiver (v. 12). Used in its negative sense, *craftiness* is the reverse of prudence because it conveys the use of wisdom to manipulate the situation rather than resolve it (cf. Job 5:12; 15:5). The Book of Revelation echoes Genesis by identifying Satan as "the ancient serpent, who is called the devil . . . the deceiver of the whole world" (12:9 ESV).

The serpent's manipulation becomes immediately apparent at the first question of whether God said that Adam and Eve could not eat *any* of the fruit. While the focus is on every fruit-bearing tree in the Garden, the rationale behind the question is to get Eve to identify the forbidden tree and why it was off limits (vv. 1-3). It also reveals the serpent's strategy of manipulating the truth by subtle distortion.

The serpent turns around Eve's answer—that she will die—by saying eating the fruit will result in death to ignorance. The entry point for the deception was to re-describe eating the fruit as an attractive option. In doing so, the seeds of mistrust in the Creator are sown.

Eve's attraction to the fruit began with the serpent's redefining death from a negative experience to a positive one (death to ignorance). By doing so, he focused Eve on the immediate benefits so she would not weigh the long-term costs of eating the fruit. What makes the fruit tempting for Eve is its attraction to her. Temptation always begins with an inner attraction, which stems from a perception that engaging in an action will be good for us. The serpent had begun to convince Eve that the fruit was good for her. From this point in the story, the theme of attraction becomes dominant. Eve eats the fruit and offers it to her husband because it looked delicious and it seemed to have positive benefits (v. 6).

At the end of the day, when we are unsure of the right course of action, we must fall back on what we are sure about. Adam and Eve could have no doubt about the command itself, even if the serpent sowed seeds of doubt as to its meaning. The final act of disobedience was a failure to trust the wisdom of the Creator in giving the command.

---

1. Why did the serpent begin this conversation with a question (v. 1)?
2. How did the woman explain God's command about the tree (vv. 2-3)?
3. What made the serpent's proposal tempting (vv. 4-5)?
4. Why do you suppose the man joined in his wife's disobedience (v. 6)?

"Ability to resist temptation is directly proportionate to your submission to God."—Ed Cole

---

B. The Confrontation by God (vv. 7-13)

⁷ And the eyes of them both were opened, and they knew that they were naked; and they sewed fig leaves together, and made themselves aprons. ⁸ And they heard the voice of the Lord God walking in the garden in the cool of the day: and Adam and his wife hid themselves from the presence of the Lord God amongst the trees of the garden. ⁹ And the Lord God called unto Adam, and said unto him, Where art thou? ¹⁰ And he said, I heard thy voice in the garden, and I was afraid, because I was naked; and I hid myself. ¹¹ And he said, Who told thee that thou wast naked? Hast thou eaten of the tree, whereof I commanded thee that thou shouldest not eat? ¹² And the man said, The woman whom thou gavest to be with me, she gave me of the tree, and I did eat. ¹³ And the Lord God said unto the woman, What is this that thou hast done? And the woman said, The serpent beguiled me, and I did eat.

The effects of eating the fruit occur immediately and they point toward what God really meant by "death." Death was not about the loss of physical life, but the fracturing of the relational wholeness of creation. The first two chapters of Genesis describe this relational wholeness in terms of God bringing order out of chaos and causing everything to live in harmony. It is a picture of *shalom* (peace). Sowing fig leaves to make clothes immediately began to sever the relational connection between Adam and Eve (v. 7). This breaking of human

       The Need for Salvation

fellowship was followed by a breaking of fellowship with God (vv. 8-9). The relational wholeness is beginning to unravel.

As Jeremiah would later put it, sin involves the return to the formlessness and emptiness of chaos; death is a reversal of creation. It involves breaking apart the fundamental harmony and balance of God's design. In the same way that physical death is a breakdown in the body as a whole organism, spiritual death is a fracturing of the wholeness of creation.

What follows is a confrontation between God and the first humans (vv. 9-11). The result of this confrontation is a further fracturing as Adam blames Eve (v. 12) and Eve blames the serpent (v. 13). The subtle manipulation of the truth by the serpent had succeeded. What Eve had initially falsely perceived as good had turned out to be highly destructive.

---

1. Why had the man and woman not realized their nakedness before now (vv. 7-10)?
2. What did God ask Adam, and how did he respond (vv. 11-12)?
3. How was the woman's response like Adam's (v. 13)?

"There is in the heart of every man or woman, under the conviction of the Holy Spirit, a sense of guilt and condemnation. . . . When we realize how guilty sin is, and how condemned is the sinner, we begin to feel the weight of that load."—A. C. Dixon

---

C. The Consequences of Sin (vv. 14, 16-19)

(Genesis 3:18-19 is not included in the printed text.)

14 And the Lord God said unto the serpent, Because thou hast done this, thou art cursed above all cattle, and above every beast of the field; upon thy belly shalt thou go, and dust shalt thou eat all the days of thy life.

16 Unto the woman he said, I will greatly multiply thy sorrow and thy conception; in sorrow thou shalt bring forth children; and thy desire shall be to thy husband, and he shall rule over thee. 17 And unto Adam he said, Because thou hast hearkened unto the voice of thy wife, and hast eaten of the tree, of which I commanded thee, saying, Thou shalt not eat of it: cursed is the ground for thy sake; in sorrow shalt thou eat of it all the days of thy life.

The divine judgment asserts what has already become reality. When God pronounces that the serpent will crawl on its belly, it is a precursor to enmity between the serpent and Eve (vv. 14-15), which is a reflection of a divide that already existed. God's pronouncement to Eve that her husband will now "rule" over her is also significant and may have sexual connotations, given the focus on childbearing and nakedness (vv. 7, 16). The point is that sexuality now becomes a power struggle for dominance instead of a means to facilitate relational union according to the one-flesh design of marriage (2:24). For Adam, creation itself will fight against him in the form of "thorns" and "thistles," so growing food will be demanding work (3:17-19). God's judgment highlights the relational brokenness that had already occurred because of the act of disobedience. Each sinful action carries with it the seeds of destruction, which is God's judgment.

1. Describe the curse placed on the serpent (v. 14).
2. Describe the curse placed on the woman (v. 16)?
3. How would Adam's life become difficult (vv. 17-19)?

A Broken World

Ecosystems and weather patterns remind us of the relational dimension of life. Animals within an ecosystem need one another to survive. Carnivores at the top of the food chain require herbivores which themselves require plant life. Ecosystems are fragile, and any disturbance will throw the entire system into a chaotic state. When God created the world, it was harmonious. This divine ecosystem was broken at the first sin, and it has propelled humans down a path of division and disintegration that leads to death.

II. HUMANS DECLARED GUILTY OF SIN (Rom. 3:9-20)

A. Under Sin (vv. 9-18)

(Romans 3:9-17 is not included in the printed text.)
[18] There is no fear of God before their eyes.

Paul concludes an argument he had begun in the first chapter of Romans with a litany of phrases from the Psalms and Isaiah. His point is to show that all humans, Jews and Gentiles, stand "under sin" (Rom. 3:9). This is not only about the guilt of sinful deeds before God, but it also concerns sin as a power at work within humanity. "There is none righteous . . ." (v. 10). It is a condition that humans have inherited, which prevents them from functioning as God had designed them. As in the Genesis text, this power works within human desire and emotion to form attractions to what humans falsely perceive as good for them.

God has given humans over to their own desires (Rom. 1:24) in the same way that His judgment of Adam and Eve was a reflection of the consequences flowing from their own actions. The result is that the power of sin now dominates human behavior through distorted desire and emotion. "All have turned aside, together they have become useless" (3:12 NASB). It is a condition of brokenness because human desire and emotion no longer function as they should.

In verses 15-17, Paul borrows from Isaiah a picture of sin as exile (59:7-8), which underscores separation from God and one another. Humans no longer live according to *shalom*—the relational wholeness of the original creation. Drawing from the Psalms (5:9; 14:1-3; 53:1-3; 140:3), he layers a picture of exile with images of death, destruction, and the loss of meaning (Rom. 3:12-14). The conclusion is that not even the fear of God serves as a motivator to pursue wisdom any longer (v. 18).

---

1. How are all people alike (vv. 9-12)?
2. Describe the vocabulary of sinful people (vv. 13-14).
3. How do sinners affect their environment (vv. 15-17)?
4. Is verse 18 an accurate description of our society in general? Why or why not?

"Sin comes when we take a perfectly natural desire or longing or ambition and try desperately to fulfill it without God. Not only is it sin, it is a perverse distortion of the image of the Creator in us."—Augustine

---

B. The Law Cannot Justify (vv. 19-20)

¹⁹ Now we know that what things soever the law saith, it saith to them who are under the law: that every mouth may be stopped, and all the world may become guilty before God. ²⁰ Therefore by the deeds of the law there shall no flesh be justified in his sight: for by the law is the knowledge of sin.

Since this is a letter addressed to Christians in Rome, Paul returns to the use of "we" as a way of underscoring his solidarity with them. In particular, Paul is speaking as a Jesus-believing Jew to other Jesus-believing Jews. The term "law" (v. 19) is probably a more generic description of the Old Testament as a whole rather than a specific reference to the Pentateuch (Genesis through Deuteronomy), which was the Torah. This is because Paul has just employed passages from Isaiah and the Psalms to show how all stand "under sin."

The phrase "deeds of the law" (v. 20) probably refers to observance of Torah. Paul adds this phrase to a paraphrase of Psalm 143:2 ("in thy sight shall no man living be justified"). The point is that observance of Torah cannot put any human being in right relationship with God because all humans are under the power of sin. While the Law (Torah) can identify sinful behavior, it lacks the capacity to right human desire and emotion and thus bring reconciliation to God. Humans require a cure for their disease.

---

1. What purpose does the law of God serve?
2. What can the law of God not accomplish?

"No man taketh away sins (which the Law, though holy, just and good, could not take away), but He in whom there is no sin."—Venerable Bede

---

III. HUMANS ARE TRAPPED IN SIN (Eph. 2:1-3; Rom. 1:28-32)

A. Dead in Sin (Eph. 2:1-3)

¹ And you hath he quickened, who were dead in trespasses and sins; ² Wherein in time past ye walked according to the course of this world, according to the prince of the power of the air, the spirit that now worketh in the children of disobedience: ³ Among whom also we all had our conversation in times past in the lusts of our flesh, fulfilling the desires of the flesh and of the mind; and were by nature the children of wrath, even as others.

The image of death found in Genesis surfaces again in Paul's writings (Eph. 2:1). In this passage, Paul connects death to a course of behavior or a walk in which the individual follows the "prince of the power of the air" (v. 2). The ruler is later connected to the devil (4:27; 6:11). Paul is drawing on the Jewish idea of *halakah*, which refers to a way of walking in the world or how one carries oneself. It is more closely connected to the English term *lifestyle* because it points toward a pattern of behavior rather than a single act. The King James Version employs the older English term *conversation* (2:3) because of its connection to the Latin term *conversatio*, which refers to how we order our life.

Death, then, becomes a metaphor for a way of life that is alienated from God, which is another way of describing the breakdown in relations between God and humanity. Whether they consciously realize it or not, humans who live outside of God's purposes succumb to the death, disobedience, and destruction embodied in the reign of the devil.

Through a string of phrases, Paul connects a life in the grip of death with sinful passion and desire—"gratifying the cravings of our sinful nature and following its desires and thoughts" (v. 3 NIV). Through disordered desire and emotion, sin carries out its reign in human lives (Rom. 6:12). This diseased condition encompasses a loss of harmony in the inner life of the person. Alienation from God ultimately leads to alienation from oneself. Life outside of God involves an unsustainable way of living in which the individual slowly disintegrates through destructive behavior. It is akin to the loss of physical health in the body because the cells in the body begin to break apart and cannot function as a whole organism any longer. To live this way is to be under God's wrath (Eph. 2:3).

---

1. Describe the existence of those who are spiritually dead (vv. 1-2).
2. Explain the term "children of wrath" (v. 3).

"There are only two kinds of persons: those dead in sin and those dead to sin."—Leonard Ravenhill

---

B. Given Over to Sin (Rom. 1:28-32)

28 And even as they did not like to retain God in their knowledge, God gave them over to a reprobate mind, to do those things which are not convenient; 29 Being filled with all unrighteousness, fornication, wickedness, covetousness, maliciousness; full of envy, murder, debate, deceit, malignity; whisperers, 30 Backbiters, haters of God, despiteful, proud, boasters, inventors of evil things, disobedient to parents, 31 Without understanding, covenantbreakers, without natural affection, implacable, unmerciful: 32 Who knowing the judgment of God, that they which commit such things are worthy of death, not only do the same, but have pleasure in them that do them.

The argument has now come full circle. Paul describes a cascading effect of sin that moves from failure to acknowledge God and ends with enslavement. Paul notes there is a relationship between failure to acknowledge God as God, which is really the essence of idolatry, and possessing a warped way of thinking (v. 28). Paul describes various kinds of behaviors that such a way of thinking can produce from an insatiable desire to consume (covetousness) to a merciless passion to destroy (vv. 29-30). Paul lists self-destructive vices and vices that destroy others, all of which flow from a failure to be in right relationship with God.

Idolatry is an important subtext in this passage. For much of Israel's existence, idolatry was a constant problem. It involves treating a part of creation as though it were divine in some way. It is not always as obvious as constructing a shrine or an altar in the image of another human or of an animal, as verse 23 describes. Many times it is simply placing too much value on something. It may be better to think of idolatry as placing something or someone before God. Humans come to value things through their own emotion and desire to the point where some are willing to pay large sums of cash for collector's items that may have originally cost only a few dollars. The difference between one person's trash and another's treasure is the degree of value. Idolatry is about valuing any part of creation to the extent that one begins to treat it as though it alone brings meaning to life.

Connected to idolatry is the way in which disordered desire and emotion can cloud one's judgment. The term *reprobate* (v. 28) means "not standing the test, rejected" (W. E. Vine). The mind cannot make appropriate judgments as to the right course of action. Such a person is "without understanding, untrustworthy, unloving, unmerciful" (v. 31 NASB).

Depraved thinking is a manifestation of out-of-control desires and emotions that prompt humans to engage in actions they know will destroy themselves and others (v. 32). Those who know God's law and its condemnation of these behaviors may still give in to and even come to approve of destructive desires. One example is a person inflicting physical or emotional harm on someone else in a fit of rage—intense anger has clouded his or her judgment. A second example is an appetite for food, leading someone to overeat or to eat unhealthily. In these two examples, judgment becomes overwhelmed by emotion and desire.

These examples reinforce the connection between Romans and Genesis. For Eve, the temptation began with an attraction toward a fruit that she began to think of as good for her. Why did she perceive the fruit as good? The serpent had distorted the truth just enough to get her to focus only on the fruit and its short-term benefit. It is not terribly different from someone buying a new car for the immediate pleasure of driving a nice vehicle without due consideration to the costs involved in doing so. Temptation stems from the attractions to other illicit actions and objects that stem from disordered desire and emotion.

---

1. Why do some people "not see fit to acknowledge God any longer" (v. 28 NASB)?
2. List the inward traits of those who have completely forsaken God (vv. 29-31).
3. What is astonishing about these people's behavior (v. 32)?

"No man living in any known sin is ever comforted of God. The Holy Ghost never yet spake one word of all His abounding consolations to any man so long as he lived in any actual sin, or in any neglect of known duty."—Alexander Whyte

---

CONCLUSION

When we examine the impact of sin on the human race, it underscores the truth of Romans 3:12: "There is none who does good, there is not even one"

(NASB). Sin is the problem of human existence because it is a condition from which no human can escape without divine aid. We easily see both the relational design of creation and how fractured these relations are.

For example, marriage should support God's relational design for humanity, and yet it can become a place of abuse and betrayal. Also, God's intention that humans care for creation by consuming what they need and preserving what they do not has devolved into a destructive approach to the environment. These are merely two external manifestations of the alienation humans experience both from God and within their own hearts. The original sin of Adam and Eve resulted in a fracture within the relational wholeness of creation that has now become a great canyon.

GOLDEN TEXT CHALLENGE

"FOR ALL HAVE SINNED, AND COME SHORT OF THE GLORY OF GOD" (Rom. 3:23).
1. The sinful state of man is a universal condition.
2. Man's sinful state is an inward condition.
3. The sinful state of man is a visible condition.
4. The sinful state of man is a radical condition.
5. Man's sinful state is a tragic condition.
       —Lewis Drummond, *What the Bible Says*

Daily Devotions:
M. The Wickedness of Humanity
    Genesis 6:5-8
T. The Depravity of the Heathen
    Leviticus 18:24-30
W. The Weight of Sin
    Psalm 51:3-11
T. The Religious Called to Repent
    Matthew 3:7-12
F. Brought Near by Christ's Blood
    Ephesians 2:11-18
S. Spiritual Destitution
    Revelation 3:14-22

God's Plan of Salvation

Genesis 3:15, 21; Isaiah 51:4-11; 55:1-7;
Jeremiah 31:31-34; Ephesians 2:4-7; Titus 3:3-7

Unit Theme:
The Doctrine of Salvation

Central Truth:
God offers deliverance from sin and death through Jesus Christ.

Focus:
Discover and experience the deliverance from sin God has provided through Jesus Christ.

Context:
Selected Scripture passages highlighting God's eternal plan for saving lost humanity

Golden Text:
"God, who is rich in mercy, . . . even when we were dead in sins, hath quickened us together with Christ, (by grace ye are saved)" (Eph. 2:4-5).

Study Outline:
 I. Salvation Promised
    (Gen. 3:15, 21; Isa. 51:4-11)
 II. Salvation Foretold
    (Isa. 55:1-7; Jer. 31:31-34)
 III. Salvation Provided
    (Eph. 2:4-7; Titus 3:3-7)

INTRODUCTION

For Christians, salvation brings to mind the word *grace*. *Grace* refers not simply to divine favor at work *for* us, but to divine power at work *within* us. When we use *grace* to refer to God's favor, we employ phrases like "unmerited favor" or we talk about God's mercy for us as sinners. The Bible describes this favor in a variety of ways that ultimately ground it in God's own character. Mercy and favor flow from the love that is intrinsic to God's own life. "God is love," as 1 John 4:16 makes clear. This love manifests itself in a God who never gives up, but relentlessly pursues His people even when they betray Him and bring about their own exile. We might say that grace as favor concerns God's deep generosity that never depends on human action or inaction, but always initiates salvation.

As important as the favor of God is, it only identifies one aspect of God's grace. Favor remains external to us—the manifestation of God's love for us. The problem of human existence, however, requires more than an act of love for us. It requires the power of love within to cure us from the disease of sin and bring us back to life. This is why Scripture talks about God writing His law on human hearts and employs terms like "regeneration," "new creation," "renewal," and "quickened/made alive" (see 2 Cor. 5:17; Eph. 2:5; Titus 3:5). God's salvation begins with divine actions *for* us and concludes with divine actions *within* us.

The grace of God reaches out to us while we are exiled from God. The New Testament writers employ the literal exile of Israel and her slavery both in Egypt and in Babylon as windows on the human condition. Like ancient Israel, humans are enslaved to sin and living a life alienated from God. Salvation always requires an act of deliverance that humans cannot perform themselves. Humans cannot cure the disease of sin nor bring themselves back to life. Exiled people need a Deliverer whose relentless love can set them free.

I. SALVATION PROMISED (Gen. 3:15, 21; Isa. 51:4-11)

A. Grace Initiates the Promise (Gen. 3:15, 21)

¹⁵ And I will put enmity between thee and the woman, and between thy seed and her seed; it shall bruise thy head, and thou shalt bruise his heel.
²¹ Unto Adam also and to his wife did the Lord God make coats of skins, and clothed them.

The story of temptation and failure in the Garden of Eden does not end with the judgment of God. Divine acts of grace surround the fall of the first humans. The first acts of grace come in the second chapter of Genesis, which portrays the first couple as children encountering a new world for the first time. They learn to name their world through the use of language (vv. 19-20). They exhibit childlike wonder at God's handiwork as reflected in the poetic rhyme Adam offers in response to Eve's creation: "She shall be called Woman [*isha*], because she was taken out of Man [*ish*] (v. 23). Like any good parent, God provides for His children by placing them in a nurturing environment, providing them with the necessary resources, and establishing boundaries to guide in the right way.

When Adam and Eve fail to trust the God who has provided for them, the idyllic scene of the garden turns into a courtroom. There is no doubt of their guilt, and the divine pronouncement of judgment merely reinforces the consequences of their actions. The enmity between the serpent and the woman reflects a division that was already present when the serpent presented himself as tempter (3:1-5, 15). The pain of childbearing and the domination of the woman by her husband points back to the loss of intimacy at the realization of their nakedness (vv. 7, 16). The curse on the ground from not obeying God recalls the alienation from God as the first humans hid from His sight (vv. 8-10, 17-19). The divine pronouncement of judgment parallels a judgment built into the fabric of creation.

The second acts of grace fall within the pronouncement of judgment. God makes garments of skin for Adam and Eve to clothe their nakedness (v. 21). As biblical commentators have pointed out, God clothing them with garments points toward the priestly garments that Aaron and his sons were to wear so they could minister in the presence of God (Ex. 39:1, 41). The purpose of the priestly garments was to cover Aaron's nakedness and his guilt as he entered the Holy of Holies (28:42-43).

The act of clothing Adam and Eve's nakedness also points toward the New Testament. Paul describes water baptism in terms of being clothed with Christ (Gal. 3:27). The practice of early Christians was to baptize believers and then clothe them with a white robe to symbolize the new life in Christ. Paul also applies the idea of clothing to the resurrection when believers will "put on" incorruption and immortality (1 Cor. 15:53-54). God's provision of grace in the Garden points toward a deeper provision of clothing fallen humans with Christ's crucified and resurrected humanity.

From at least Irenaeus of Lyon (ca. AD 180), Christian tradition has interpreted the reference to the seed of the woman bruising the serpent's head (Gen. 3:15) as pointing toward Christ. Mary, the mother of Jesus, becomes the new Eve because her child Jesus triumphs over the principalities and powers in His death on the cross (Col. 2:15). Although the Genesis story does not make the connection, Christians like Irenaeus interpreted the bruising of the serpent as a symbol that pointed toward the victory over sin and death on the cross.

---

1. What did God forecast for Satan (v. 15)?
2. What did God do for Adam and Eve, and why (v. 21)?

"Grace grows from the heart of a gracious God who wants to stun you and overwhelm you with a gift you don't deserve—salvation, adoption, . . . His presence, His wisdom, His guidance, His love."—Bill Hybels

---

B. Grace Sustains the Promise (Isa. 51:4-11)

4 Hearken unto me, my people; and give ear unto me, O my nation: for a law shall proceed from me, and I will make my judgment to rest for a light of the people. 5 My righteousness is near; my salvation is gone forth, and mine arms shall judge the people; the isles shall wait upon me, and on mine arm shall they trust. 6 Lift up your eyes to the heavens, and look upon the earth beneath: for the heavens shall vanish away like smoke, and the earth shall wax old like a garment, and they that dwell therein shall die in like manner: but my salvation shall be for ever, and my righteousness shall not be abolished. 7 Hearken unto me, ye that know righteousness, the people in whose heart is my law; fear ye not the reproach of men, neither be ye afraid of their revilings. 8 For the moth shall eat them up like a garment, and the worm shall eat them like wool: but my righteousness shall be for ever, and my salvation from generation to generation. 9 Awake, awake, put on strength, O arm of the Lord; awake, as in the ancient days, in the generations of old. Art thou not it that hath cut Rahab, and wounded the dragon? 10 Art thou not it which hath dried the sea, the waters of the great deep; that hath made the depths of the sea a way for the ransomed to pass over? 11 Therefore the redeemed of the Lord shall return, and come with singing unto Zion; and everlasting joy shall be upon their head: they shall obtain gladness and joy; and sorrow and mourning shall flee away.

Over a twenty-year period (600-580 BC), the king of Babylon initiated three attacks on Judah that led to three waves of deportation to Babylon. Nebuchadnezzar's forces were brutal in their assault, and they carried off the majority of Israelites in hooks and chains. This is how the exile of the southern kingdom of Judah began. While the first part of the Book of Isaiah (chs. 1-39) warned against exile, the second part of the book (chs. 40-66) offer God's promises in the midst of exile.

The opening eight verses of Isaiah 51 resound with three cries of "hearken unto me" (vv. 1, 4, 7). There is a call going forth that reminds Israel of her identity as God's chosen people. The first markers of Israel's identity are the "rock" and "quarry" from which she was forged (v. 1 NIV). This is none other than Abraham and Sarah, who had received God's initial promise (v. 2). The purpose is to remind Israel that God had once called Abraham out of a desert place to a promised land (v. 3). The image of wasteland points toward the calling from Egypt, while the Promised Land is symbolized as a new Eden. Even in exile, God will fulfill His promises.

The second and third cries rehearse the same themes as the first. As God's people, Israel is reminded that God's law (Torah) will establish divine justice over against the injustice of the Exile (v. 4). The terms *righteousness* and *salvation* may also be rendered as "faithfulness" and "deliverance" because God's righteousness is His faithfulness to deliver Israel (v. 5). Because faithfulness is an extension of God's own character, it will endure (vv. 6, 8). The people of Israel no longer need to fear, despite the terrors of exile and the human leaders who threaten them. Even in the "valley of the shadow of death" they can rely on God to bring them through (Ps. 23:4).

In light of the sheer extravagance of God's promises, the text turns from a call to Israel as the people of God to a call from Israel to God. Israel cries out, "Awake . . . O arm of the Lord" (Isa. 51:9). Having been reminded of God's deeds in the past, Israel reminds God of those same deeds. The references to cutting "Rahab" (a poetical name for Egypt) and wounding the "dragon" most likely have in view the exodus from Egypt (v. 9). Pharaoh is the "dragon" whom God pierced by causing the Red Sea to crash down on him and his army even as the children of Israel crossed on dry ground (v. 10). Just like the song Moses and Israel sang after the destruction of Pharaoh, so the "redeemed" of the Lord will sing another new song at the return from exile (v. 11).

Isaiah 51 reminds Israel of God's promises in order to bring hope to their situation. These promises will endure because they remain grounded in the faithfulness of God's own character. Salvation is couched in the language of deliverance and redemption as a result of the connection to Abraham and the Exodus. This connection also points toward God forging an identity for the nation of Israel as His people. These promises will come to fulfillment when Jesus' own faithfulness forges a new people of God, made from Jews and Gentiles, by delivering all those who follow Him from spiritual slavery.

---

1. What blessings did God promise to send to the nations (vv. 4-5)?
2. What did God say about His righteousness (vv. 6, 8) and about those who receive it (v. 7)?
3. How had the Lord displayed His strength in the past (vv. 9-10)?
4. Why should the people of God live in anticipation (v. 11)?

"One way to get comfort is to plead the promise of God in prayer, show Him His handwriting; God is tender of His Word."—Thomas Manton

II. SALVATION FORETOLD (Isa. 55:1-7; Jer. 31:31-34)

A. A Call to New Life (Isa. 55:1-7)

¹ **Ho, every one that thirsteth, come ye to the waters, and he that hath no money; come ye, buy, and eat; yea, come, buy wine and milk without money and without price.** ² **Wherefore do ye spend money for that which is not bread? and your labour for that which satisfieth not? hearken diligently unto me, and eat ye that which is good, and let your soul delight itself in fatness.** ³ **Incline your ear, and come unto me: hear, and your soul shall live; and I will make an everlasting covenant with you, even the sure mercies of David.** ⁴ **Behold, I have given him for a witness to the people, a leader and commander to the people.** ⁵ **Behold, thou shalt call a nation that thou knowest not, and nations that knew not thee shall run unto thee because of the Lord thy God, and for the Holy One of Israel; for he hath glorified thee.** ⁶ **Seek ye the Lord while he may be found, call ye upon him while he is near:** ⁷ **Let the wicked forsake his way, and the unrighteous man his thoughts: and let him return unto the Lord, and he will have mercy upon him; and to our God, for he will abundantly pardon.**

The first seven verses of Isaiah 55 establish a contrast between two ways of life. One way is life in exile where the food costs too much and the labor is too hard (v. 2). Those who choose exile from God are enslaved by the powers of the world. In contrast, God offers life with Him. Recalling the imagery of the Promised Land flowing with milk and honey, God's life provides nourishment without exacting a price (v. 1). It foreshadows Jesus' call to "seek first the kingdom of God and His righteousness, and all these things shall be added to you" (Matt. 6:33 NKJV). There is an extravagant generosity embedded in the symbolism of eating rich food (Isa. 55:2). This is what life with God offers.

As the reader begins the third verse, the tone becomes more intimate. Like a close friend, God says, "Come over here and let Me whisper in your ear the words of life" (v. 3 paraphrased). The future of Israel is secured by the divine promise of "an everlasting covenant." Stemming from God's own steadfast love (*hesed*), the promise comes through a Davidic figure who will lead the people in such a manner that every nation will run to Israel (vv. 4-5). The intimacy carries over the theme from previous chapters where God described Himself as a husband in search of His unfaithful wife (54:5-6). God is the lover and friend who will deliver His people through His suffering Servant, who bears the sorrows and pain of exile to bring deliverance (53:4-5).

Such generosity calls for an immediate response to seek the Lord (55:6). The call for a renewal of the covenant is not unlike the call issued at Solomon's dedication of the Temple (2 Chron. 7:14). The difference is that God has initiated this renewal in Isaiah rather than wait for His people to call on Him. The call to seek the Lord is in the form of a response to God's prior gracious initiative. To renew the covenant also means to take seriously the way of life called for by the covenant. Israel must abandon the unrighteous thoughts and deeds that caused the exile in the first place (Isa. 55:7). God's new life is free, but it also recognizes there are relational boundaries that cannot be crossed.

---

1. Describe the Lord's amazing offer (vv. 1-2).
2. What was God's desire for His people (v. 3)?

3. To where would people run, and why (vv. 4-5)?
4. How does a person sincerely seek the Lord, and what will the result be (vv. 6-7)?

"Repentance is more than just sorrow for the past; repentance is a change of mind and heart, a new life of denying self and serving the Savior as king in self's place."—J. I. Packer

---

B. A Call to a New Covenant (Jer. 31:31-34)

31 Behold, the days come, saith the Lord, that I will make a new covenant with the house of Israel, and with the house of Judah: 32 Not according to the covenant that I made with their fathers in the day that I took them by the hand to bring them out of the land of Egypt; which my covenant they brake, although I was an husband unto them, saith the Lord: 33 But this shall be the covenant that I will make with the house of Israel; After those days, saith the Lord, I will put my law in their inward parts, and write it in their hearts; and will be their God, and they shall be my people. 34 And they shall teach no more every man his neighbour, and every man his brother, saying, Know the Lord: for they shall all know me, from the least of them unto the greatest of them, saith the Lord: for I will forgive their iniquity, and I will remember their sin no more.

Jeremiah recognizes that even with God's graciousness in desiring to reestablish His relationship with Israel, the problem of Israel's unsteady faithfulness remains. What is to prevent exile from happening again? The former covenant with God's law as establishing the relational boundaries was insufficient to keep Israel from engaging in idolatry and wickedness. Israel requires more than an external Torah to maintain her loyalty.

What Jeremiah announces is a "new covenant" in which God's law will no longer function as a set of external boundary markers for the nation of Israel (vv. 31-32). Instead, God will "write" His law on the hearts of His people (v. 33). The contrast is between an external command taught by others and an internal norm inscribed on the human heart (vv. 33-34). This is how God proposes to solve the problem of Israel's unfaithfulness. God's solution begins with forgiveness and concludes with empowerment to live.

---

1. Why was a "new covenant" needed (vv. 31-32)?
2. How is the new covenant superior to the old one (vv. 33-34)?

"The new covenant is the bond between God and man, established by the sacrificial death of Jesus Christ, under which all who have been effectively called to God in all ages have been formed into the one body of Christ in New Testament times, in order to come under His law during this age and to remain under His authority forever."—Tom Wells

---

God's Plan of Salvation

III. SALVATION PROVIDED (Eph. 2:4-7; Titus 3:3-7)

A. God's Rich Mercy (Eph. 2:4-7)

⁴ But God, who is rich in mercy, for his great love wherewith he loved us, ⁵ Even when we were dead in sins, hath quickened us together with Christ, (by grace ye are saved;) ⁶ And hath raised us up together, and made us sit together in heavenly places in Christ Jesus: ⁷ That in the ages to come he might shew the exceeding riches of his grace in his kindness toward us through Christ Jesus.

After providing a summary of their prior life outside of God, Paul reminds his Ephesian readers what God has done for them. The lavishness of God's promises in Genesis, Isaiah, and Jeremiah are now brought to fulfillment in Christ.

The appeal to the abundance of divine mercy and the depth of divine love echoes Isaiah's portrait of God as a lover who goes in search of his unfaithful spouse (Eph. 2:4). Paul reinforces the depth of God's commitment by repeating to the Ephesians that all of this occurred when they were still dead in sin (v. 5).

As a reminder from the previous lesson, *death* is a metaphor for a life that has become diseased and defective by virtue of alienation from God. It is diseased because the internal life of emotion and desire no longer functions as it should. Individuals are now led about by passions and bodily desires (v. 3). Although no longer in exile under Babylonian rule, the exile continues through the law of sin and death that permeates human existence. To be dead in sin, then, is to be caught up in a kind of slavery that culminates in the destruction and disintegration of the person.

Paul attempts to describe God's answer to a life in death by stringing together a sequence of verbs all with a prefix that implies a union or strong connection. Translators attempt to communicate the idea by supplying the additional English term *together*. Believers are made "alive *together*" (v. 5 NKJV), "raised . . . up *together*," and "sit *together*" (v. 6), all with Christ. By employing this language, Paul is conveying that the riches of God only come in and through union with Christ. It is another way of saying, "For all the promises of God find their Yes in him" (2 Cor. 1:20 ESV). In union with Christ, believers are liberated from the death of their previous existence and now fully participate in the benefits of the new age that Christ has inaugurated.

---

1. How did God best express His "great love" for us (v. 4)?
2. How is God now expressing His love to us (vv. 5-6)?
3. What does God promise to do in "the ages to come" (v. 7)?

Rescue From Final Death

When a person has a heart attack, the heart can go into a point of cardiac arrest where it no longer beats. The heart monitor registers a flatline. When the heart stops beating, there is no blood flow to the brain and brain death is imminent. In this situation the doctor normally performs CPR and injects epinephrine (adrenaline) into the body. Between pumping the chest and igniting the body through adrenaline, the hope is that the heart will begin to beat again before final death occurs.

Even though we humans are "dead" in our sins, the final death has not yet occurred. Instead, we are in a state of "cardiac arrest." Through the Son, God beats on the door of our heart. Through the Spirit, God "ignites" our love for Him so our heart can begin to beat again before we reach the final death.

B. God's Extravagant Love (Titus 3:3-7)

³ For we ourselves also were sometimes foolish, disobedient, deceived, serving divers lusts and pleasures, living in malice and envy, hateful, and hating one another. ⁴ But after that the kindness and love of God our Saviour toward man appeared, ⁵ Not by works of righteousness which we have done, but according to his mercy he saved us, by the washing of regeneration, and renewing of the Holy Ghost; ⁶ Which he shed on us abundantly through Jesus Christ our Saviour; ⁷ That being justified by his grace, we should be made heirs according to the hope of eternal life.

The passage in Titus picks up where the second chapter of Ephesians concludes. It begins with a description of the believer's former life. While the dominant metaphor is *slavery*, notice that it is still passions, emotions, and desires that create the chains (v. 3). The slavery carries out a war, both internally and externally, in which desires and passions become weapons that destroy the self and others. Sin, ultimately, *dehumanizes* human beings so they lose their humanity. What results is to treat themselves and others inhumanely.

The extravagance of God's love *humanizes* individuals again. The text communicates this powerfully with the Greek term *philanthropia*, which is translated as "love" or "loving-kindness," but means "love of humanity" (v. 4). In the Latin Vulgate, it is translated by the term *humanitas*, from which "humanism" comes. A genuine humanism comes from the rich love and kindness of God, who delivers individuals and puts them in touch with their own humanity once again.

According to Titus, God humanizes individuals through regeneration and internal renewal by the power of the Spirit (v. 5). There is no *human* action that can cure the disease of *human* inhumanity. This is why works are inadequate. Instead, humans require an internal transformation that involves simultaneously an inner renewal and a justification. Humans must be *put* right and declared to *be* right. Only God's extravagant love for humanity can accomplish this work.

---

1. List the characteristics of Paul's former lifestyle (v. 3)
2. Describe the "washing" and "renewing" only God can do (vv. 5-6).
3. What inheritance is promised in verse 7, who can receive it, and how?

"Saving us is the greatest and most concrete demonstration of God's love, the definitive display of His grace throughout time and eternity."—David Jeremiah

CONCLUSION

The message of Scripture is that humans are in exile, alienated from God by virtue of their slavery to sin. Life in exile is hard. It is not simply that individuals do not possess the economic means to buy the food they need to survive. Because the slavery of exile is an internal slavery stemming from disordered emotions and desires that give rise to behavior that destroys the self and others, humans must somehow be liberated from themselves. No human being has the capacity to bring about such deliverance.

It is into this situation of death that God reveals how deep and wide His love is. God is the lover who pursues people even before they realize they need His help. His love regenerates and revives, because the love of God the Father takes shape in God the Son and flows in human hearts through God the Spirit. God's love is nothing less than God's giving His life to bring life. This is the message of salvation. The dry bones will live because of God's faithfulness (Ezek. 37).

GOLDEN TEXT CHALLENGE

"GOD, WHO IS RICH IN MERCY, . . . EVEN WHEN WE WERE DEAD IN SINS, HATH QUICKENED US TOGETHER WITH CHRIST, (BY GRACE YE ARE SAVED)" (Eph. 2:4-5).

Grace is the fountainhead of our salvation. Because God is gracious, sinful people are forgiven, converted, purified, and saved. It is not because of anything that is or will ever be in us that we are saved, but because of the boundless love, goodness, pity, compassion, mercy, and grace of God.

Charles Spurgeon writes: "What an abyss is the grace of God! Who can measure its breadth? Who can fathom its depth? Like all the rest of the divine attributes, it is infinite. God is full of love, for 'God is love.' God is full of goodness; the very name 'God' is short for 'good.' Unbounded goodness and love enter into the very essence of the Godhead. It is because His mercy endureth forever that men are not destroyed; because His compassions fail not that sinners are brought to Him and forgiven" (*All of Grace*).

Daily Devotions:

M. The Rock of Our Salvation
   Psalm 62:5-8
T. Song of Salvation
   Psalm 98:1-6
W. Mercy and Redemption of God
   Psalm 130:1-8
T. Salvation Comes to Zacchaeus' House
   Luke 19:1-10
F. The Samaritan Woman Encounters Jesus
   John 4:19-29
S. Jesus Arrests Saul
   Acts 9:1-6

Jesus Christ Is the Savior

Isaiah 53:1-12; John 3:14-17, 36; 14:6; Acts 4:12;
Romans 5:12-21; Hebrews 10:5-18

Unit Theme:
The Doctrine of Salvation

Central Truth:
Jesus Christ is God's only means for salvation from sin.

Focus:
Affirm and believe that salvation from sin comes only through Jesus Christ.

Context:
Various passages exalting the uniqueness of Jesus Christ

Golden Text:
"For God so loved the world, that he gave his only begotten Son, that whosoever believeth in him should not perish, but have everlasting life" (John 3:16).

Study Outline:
I. The Only Savior
   (John 3:14-17, 36; 14:6; Acts 4:12)
II. The Perfect Sacrifice
   (Isa. 53:1-12; Heb. 10:8-10, 18)
III. The Great Life-Giver
   (Rom. 5:12-21)

INTRODUCTION

What sometimes is missing from the debates over the truth that only Jesus can save is the basis on which Christians make this claim. It has nothing to do with the question of whether God should accept a person's effort to live a morally upright life. Instead, it has to do with how finite human beings can come to share the life of an infinite God. This is the heart of the Christian message of salvation. Those lost in death can receive eternal life, which is the shared life of the Father, Son, and the Holy Spirit.

Once we consider how humans can receive the life of an infinite God, then all questions related to human effort recede. There is no possibility of any human being ever bridging the gulf between finitude and infinity. Moreover, this gulf is made even wider by the fact that humans are now diseased with sin and live in death. The gulf cannot be crossed from the human side of the equation. If God does not build the bridge, it cannot be built.

For Christians, this is precisely what happens in the Incarnation. God becomes flesh and tabernacles among us (John 1:14). In the joining together of Divinity and humanity in the Incarnation, the first bricks of this bridge are laid. This is the beginning of new creation.

Jesus must now become the suffering Servant whose life forms the medicine that destroys death. By the power of the Spirit, Jesus heals the sick, casts out demons, and establishes His new reign of life. Moreover, the course of His earthly confrontation with sin and death leads to His own death. Through Jesus' woundedness as the suffering Servant, the Spirit unleashes a river that brings life everywhere it flows. The guilt of past sin is removed, the pain of exile destroyed, and the promise of new creation made sure. All that humans need to do now is embrace this bridge by faith.

When we proclaim that Jesus alone can save, this means so much more than access to heaven. Salvation is the way into the life of the triune God now and forever.

I. THE ONLY SAVIOR (John 3:14-17, 36; 14:6; Acts 4:12)

A. The Only Way to the Father (John 3:14-17)

14 And as Moses lifted up the serpent in the wilderness, even so must the Son of man be lifted up: 15 That whosoever believeth in him should not perish, but have eternal life. 16 For God so loved the world, that he gave his only begotten Son, that whosoever believeth in him should not perish, but have everlasting life. 17 For God sent not his Son into the world to condemn the world; but that the world through him might be saved.

The overarching context of the Gospel of John is one of trial. In a trial, an attorney presents evidence to make his or her case through testimony, documentary material, and physical objects to exhibit. For the Gospel of John, Jesus presents Himself as an advocate (an attorney) and says that He will send the Spirit as another advocate to take His place (14:16). Witnesses like John the Baptist are brought forward to offer eyewitness testimony to Jesus' identity as the Son (1:19, 34). Finally, miracles are signs that serve as the documentary material for Jesus' claims to be from the Father (2:11, 23). As a trial, the Gospel of John seeks to establish that Jesus is "the Word . . . made flesh . . . (the only begotten of the Father), full of grace and truth" (1:14).

In his conversation with Nicodemus in chapter 3, Jesus mentions the story of Moses lifting up the serpent in the wilderness (vv. 14-15). The story concerns a time when Israel grumbled against God for being in the wilderness (Num. 21:4-9). As a result of their complaints, God sent poisonous serpents whose bite killed. When the Israelites repented, God had Moses make a bronze serpent and connect it to a pole that could be lifted up so the entire Israelite camp could see it. By looking at the bronze serpent, Israelites were immediately healed whenever they were bitten. The comparison Jesus makes is between His death on the cross and the bronze serpent. When He is lifted up on the cross, those who look on Him in faith will receive the life of God.

The salvation that comes through Jesus is an outworking of God's deep love for the world (John 3:16). God's purpose is not to condemn anyone, but to save everyone (v. 17). It is a universal call that extends to every human being without exception. While the offer is universal, the acceptance is particular to each person. The condemnation that comes to unbelief is self-condemnation because it is an extension of a love for the darkness and the world, a way of life that is perishing. It is like remaining on a sinking ship because you don't want to lose your valuable possessions when the lifeboat is ten feet away. The gold and diamonds on the ship are already condemned to sink into the sea. Those who love their possessions enough to remain on the ship have condemned themselves.

---

1. Compare the two "lifting ups" depicted in verses 14 and 15.
2. Why is John 3:16 such an important scripture?
3. What did Jesus Christ not come to do, and why not (v. 17)?

"When you take the Bible literally, for what it says, you have to come back to the fact that there is only one way of salvation; there's only one Savior."—Tim LaHaye

---

B. The Only Way to Eternal Life (3:36; 14:6)

3:36 **He that believeth on the Son hath everlasting life: and he that believeth not the Son shall not see life; but the wrath of God abideth on him.**

14:6 **Jesus saith unto him, I am the way, the truth, and the life: no man cometh unto the Father, but by me.**

By claiming to be "the way, the truth, and the life" and the only path to the Father (14:6), Jesus focuses on what it means for a finite creature to traverse the distance to eternity. Strictly speaking, *eternity* is not a place "out there" like Florida is a place. It is not located *anywhere* because it is *everywhere*, since God is eternal and God is everywhere. Put simply, *eternity* is a kind of existence rather than a place. To say "God lives in eternity," as though eternity were a place where God resides, is closer to the truth, but still focuses on location. Instead, it is better to say "God is eternal," because eternity has to do with the kind of life God possesses. God has no beginning or end; He is infinite, whereas human beings are finite.

The question is how human beings who are finite can come to possess a kind of existence like the one God possesses. How can human beings possess eternal life? The Gospel of John offers only one answer: "No one has seen God at any time; the only begotten God who is in the bosom of the Father, He has explained Him" (1:18 NASB). This is why John constantly focuses on union with the Son. It is only in union with the Son that humans come to share in the life of the Father.

If humans cannot possess eternal life apart from the Son who has fellowship with the Father and shares this fellowship with others, then the next question is how does one abide in the Son. The central answer is to believe on the Son (3:36). One must come to believe the biblical record about Jesus Christ. John said His Gospel was "written that you may believe that Jesus is the Christ, the Son of God, and that believing you may have life in His name" (20:31 NKJV). It is by faith alone (*sola fide*) that Christians are united to the Son and so receive all of His benefits. This faith emerges from the power and presence of the Spirit, who advocates for the Father and the Son by convicting the world of sin and guiding believers into the truth (16:7-15).

Jesus Christ Is the Savior

1. Upon whom does God's wrath remain, and why (3:36)?
2. How is Jesus Christ unique (14:6)?

"Jesus was the Savior who would deliver them not only from the bondage of sin but also from meaningless wandering through life."—Anne Graham Lotz

---

C. The Only Name That Saves (Acts 4:12)

¹² Neither is there salvation in any other: for there is none other name under heaven given among men, whereby we must be saved.

The emphasis on the "name of Jesus" in Acts highlights the resurrected Jesus as the center of the people of God. In Peter's sermon on the Day of Pentecost, he declares "whosoever shall call on the *name* of the Lord shall be saved," and then appeals to his listeners to "repent, and be baptized every one of you in the *name* of Jesus Christ" (2:21, 38).

Peter's declaration to the lame beggar, "In the name of Jesus Christ of Nazareth rise up and walk," becomes a flashpoint in the gospel proclamation to the Jews that Judaism must be reconceived around Jesus (3:6,16). When Peter and John are brought to the Sanhedrin to explain their behavior, the first question is "By what power, or by what name, have ye done this?" (4:7). Peter seizes the opportunity to say before the high court of Jewish life that the lame beggar was made whole in Jesus' name and that the name of Jesus has become the only way to salvation for the nation (vv. 10, 12). The *church* is Israel restored and gathered around the name of Jesus (see also Matt. 18:20).

• Besides Jesus Christ, what other names do people turn to for salvation, and why does this not work?

"Any man that is saved and sanctified can feel the fire burning in his heart, when he calls on the name of Jesus."—William J. Seymour

---

II. THE PERFECT SACRIFICE (Isa. 53:1-12; Heb. 10:8-10, 18)

A. The Stricken Savior (Isa. 53:1-12)

¹ Who hath believed our report? and to whom is the arm of the Lord revealed? ² For he shall grow up before him as a tender plant, and as a root out of a dry ground: he hath no form nor comeliness; and when we shall see him, there is no beauty that we should desire him. ³ He is despised and rejected of men; a man of sorrows, and acquainted with grief: and we hid as it were our faces from him; he was despised, and we esteemed him not. ⁴ Surely he hath borne our griefs, and carried our sorrows: yet we did esteem him stricken, smitten of God, and afflicted. ⁵ But he was wounded for our transgressions, he was bruised for our iniquities: the chastisement

of our peace was upon him; and with his stripes we are healed. ⁶ All we like sheep have gone astray; we have turned every one to his own way; and the Lord hath laid on him the iniquity of us all. ⁷ He was oppressed, and he was afflicted, yet he opened not his mouth: he is brought as a lamb to the slaughter, and as a sheep before her shearers is dumb, so he openeth not his mouth. ⁸ He was taken from prison and from judgment: and who shall declare his generation? for he was cut off out of the land of the living: for the transgression of my people was he stricken. ⁹ And he made his grave with the wicked, and with the rich in his death; because he had done no violence, neither was any deceit in his mouth. ¹⁰ Yet it pleased the Lord to bruise him; he hath put him to grief: when thou shalt make his soul an offering for sin, he shall see his seed, he shall prolong his days, and the pleasure of the Lord shall prosper in his hand. ¹¹ He shall see of the travail of his soul, and shall be satisfied: by his knowledge shall my righteous servant justify many; for he shall bear their iniquities. ¹² Therefore will I divide him a portion with the great, and he shall divide the spoil with the strong; because he hath poured out his soul unto death: and he was numbered with the transgressors; and he bare the sin of many, and made intercession for the transgressors.

The chapter begins with two questions; the first asks about faith and the second asks about revelation (v. 1). The phrase "arm of the Lord" is an ancient Near Eastern way of describing divine power at work. In 50:2, God asks, "Is my hand shortened at all, that it cannot redeem? or have I no power to deliver?" The connection between God's hand and God's power is clear. Isaiah 53 reflects back on the previous chapters to ask whether Israel will believe that God will deliver, and then points forward by asking how the power of God to deliver will make itself known. The shocking answer is that this power will manifest itself in the humility of the suffering Servant who conquers by being conquered (vv. 2-12).

The poem about the suffering Servant of the Lord begins with a biographical account. The Servant's personal history testifies to His humility. There is nothing about the origins or appearance of the Servant to distinguish Him from others (v. 2). Instead, His life is one of sorrow and rejection by those around Him (v. 3). These descriptions fit the lowly beginnings of Jesus in the backwater town of Bethlehem. The Gospel of Luke makes much of these humble beginnings by emphasizing that the people coming to visit the baby Jesus and singing about Him are themselves of no account. They are shepherds and women—people at the bottom of the social and economic ladder (1:46-56; 2:15-16).

While Isaiah 53 sets forth the suffering Servant as the means by which God's power will deliver Israel from exile, the previous chapters provide the context for the nature of this deliverance (chs. 49-52). These chapters suggest that God's deliverance concerns more than removal of guilt. This deliverance requires a full restoration from exile, which may best be summarized in the term *shalom*. It is a restoration of the kind of well-being and flourishing that *shalom* embodies. Such a restoration will come through the wounds and chastisement of the Servant (53:4-5). The language of sacrifice could not be clearer—"brought as a lamb to the slaughter" (v. 7). The Servant's innocence does not remove His being cut off from His people for their sin (vv. 8-9).

Moreover, if restoration includes Israel's recovery of the prosperity of the Promised Land, then the phrase "with his stripes we are healed" cannot simply refer to the healing of the soul (v. 5). The restoration of *shalom* includes a wholeness of body and soul in and through the deliverance of the suffering Servant. The liberating death and resurrection of Jesus heals human bodies and souls.

The poem turns at verse 10 with the expression "yet . . . the Lord." The connection with "the arm of the Lord" (v. 1) becomes clear at this point. God willed that the Servant become the conduit of divine power through intense suffering and sacrifice. The language of deliverance from Exodus gives way to the Levitical language of sacrifice. Israel will be made righteous by the sacrifice of the Servant who becomes a guilt offering (vv. 10-12). The Servant's faithfulness to the point of death (v. 12) brings an exaltation and prosperity to Him as He completes the work of the "arm of the Lord."

---

1. How was Jesus Christ a typical person (v. 2)?
2. Describe emotions Jesus experienced, and why (vv. 3-4).
3. What did most people think of Jesus (vv. 3-4)?
4. How was Jesus Christ like no one else who has ever lived (v. 5)?
5. List ways Jesus was like a lamb (vv. 6-7).
6. What brought pleasure (v. 10) and satisfaction (v. 11) to the Lord?

"You never hear Jesus say in Pilate's judgment hall one word that would let you imagine that He was sorry that He had undertaken so costly a sacrifice for us. . . . You never hear a groan or a shriek that looks like Jesus is going back on His commitment."—Charles Spurgeon

---

B. The Final Sacrifice (Heb. 10:8-10, 18)
⁸ Above when he said, Sacrifice and offering and burnt offerings and offering for sin thou wouldest not, neither hadst pleasure therein; which are offered by the law; ⁹ Then said he, Lo, I come to do thy will, O God. He taketh away the first, that he may establish the second. ¹⁰ By the which will we are sanctified through the offering of the body of Jesus Christ once for all.

¹⁸ Now where remission of these is, there is no more offering for sin.

In verses 5-7, the writer pictures Christ quoting Psalm 40:6-8 in order to argue that the sacrificial system did not actually cleanse the conscience. The superiority of Christ comes in His faithfulness to the will of God (Heb. 10:7, 9)—a faithfulness carried out amid groans and sufferings (5:7).

What Jesus combines as both priest and sacrifice is Someone who carries out the will of God in righteousness and who offers Himself for the guilt of the world. In other words, He combines both dimensions of sanctification—the ritual cleansing and setting apart through sacrifice, and the moral purity that should accompany such ritual cleansing. Since Christ is morally pure, His sacrifice can purify the conscience once and for all, which is why no more sacrifice is necessary (9:14; 10:17-18). The Old Testament system and priesthood could never bring about the internal moral purity that Christ's sacrifice can (vv. 11-13).

The remaining part of Hebrews 10 clarifies the connection between sacrifice and internal moral purity. In our previous lesson, we discussed Jeremiah's dilemma that the Law (Torah) provided the boundaries of covenant, but it could not make Israel faithful. The Law must be written on the heart to bring about the faithfulness covenant demands. According to Hebrews 10, this is what the sacrifice of Christ accomplishes (v. 16). It is not simply a removal of guilt through a ritual cleansing, but a perfecting of those who are being sanctified (vv. 10, 14).

1. Explain the phrase, "He takes away the first in order to establish the second" (v. 9 NASB).
2. What did Christ do "once for all" (vv. 10, 18)?

"Don't ever think that there are many ways to the Divine. Jesus is the one qualified mediator, the only qualified sacrifice, and the only qualified savior."—Erwin Lutzer

III. THE GREAT LIFE-GIVER (Rom. 5:12-21)

A. The Reign of Death (vv. 12-14)

(Romans 5:12-14 is not included in the printed text.)
Paul opens the final section of chapter 5 with a summary statement. He describes sin as a power that entered the world through one man (v. 12). When sin entered the world, it produced death, which then carried out a reign of terror from Adam to Moses (v. 14). The reign of sin and death were unfolding long before the Law identified sinful actions (v. 13). By referring to Adam and the existence of sin prior to the Law, Paul is attempting to show how all of humanity now lives with the realities of sin and death.

Death is not simply a physical reality resulting from the disintegration of the body, but it is also a psychological reality that emerges from the disintegration of the soul through disordered desire and emotion. Whenever humans experience a loss of psychological integrity through depression, anger, covetousness, or any other uncontrollable desire or emotion, they are caught in the grip of death.

1. What "passed upon all men," and how (v. 12)?
2. Who was "a type of Him who was to come," and how (v. 14 NKJV)?

"Death to the wicked is the king of terrors. Death to the saint is the end of terrors, the commencement of glory."—Charles Spurgeon

B. The Reign of Life (vv. 15-21)

(Romans 5:15, 17 is not included in the printed text.)
¹⁶ And not as it was by one that sinned, so is the gift: for the judgment was by one to condemnation, but the free gift is of many offences unto justification.

¹⁸ **Therefore as by the offence of one judgment came upon all men to condemnation; even so by the righteousness of one the free gift came upon all men unto justification of life. ¹⁹ For as by one man's disobedience many were made sinners, so by the obedience of one shall many be made righteous. ²⁰ Moreover the law entered, that the offence might abound. But where sin abounded, grace did much more abound: ²¹ That as sin hath reigned unto death, even so might grace reign through righteousness unto eternal life by Jesus Christ our Lord.**

Paul enters into a series of contrasts between a reign of life and a reign of sin and death (vv. 17, 21). To make sure the reader does not think these contrasts are equivalent, Paul provides a "much more" quality to the work of grace and the free gift that ensues (v. 15). This sets the tone for the contrast between Adam's disobedient trespass and Christ's obedient act of righteousness (vv. 15, 19). Christ was completely faithful to the plan of God, which itself is a reflection of God's own covenant faithfulness. Through Christ's faithfulness, humans now receive "the gift of righteousness" that comes with being made part of the family of God (v. 17).

Righteousness is a gift that Paul links to the term *justification* (vv. 16, 18). There is a declaratory sense involved in justification whereby the individual's sins are not attributed to him or her any longer on account of Christ. Yet, this declaratory dimension never occurs through the application of Christ's righteousness as it exists outside of the believer. The believer is united to Christ in the power and presence of the Holy Spirit (5:5), liberating him or her from the reign of sin and death. Justification then rests upon the faithfulness of Christ and the transmission of His righteousness through union with Him in faith. It is because of this life that grace can "much more abound" in the face of sin's concerted effort to use the Law to further enslave (5:20-21).

---

1. What is "justification," and how does it occur (vv. 16-18)?
2. Describe the power of God's grace (vv. 19-20).

United With Christ

Marriage is about two human beings intertwining their lives. They share their possessions and cultivate deep emotional bonds through friendship. More than this, however, they become "one flesh" in sexual union with one another, which results in the procreation of children. Through the power of the Spirit, Christians are united to Christ. His life becomes their life, and all that is His becomes theirs. As part of this union, Christ bestows charismatic gifts upon believers so they can become His hands and feet—His body at work in the world.

CONCLUSION

The heart of the Christian message of salvation resides in union with Christ. It is the name of Jesus that brings salvation and constitutes the new people of God. The union occurs through the Holy Spirit, who ignites faith in the hearts of believers. Paul describes it elsewhere as a marriage between Christ and the Church (Eph. 5:25-33). By virtue of their marriage to Christ, the way to eternity opens up as the life of the triune God flows into the lives of believers. The flow of this river of life brings righteousness, deliverance, and justification. It is a flow that leads a wholeness of relations between God and people. To open up this flow, the Servant had to be crushed, absorbing in His own body the disease of sin that His life might overcome death. Apart from receiving this life, there is no path to eternal life.

GOLDEN TEXT CHALLENGE

"FOR GOD SO LOVED THE WORLD, THAT HE GAVE HIS ONLY BE-GOTTEN SON, THAT WHOSOEVER BELIEVETH IN HIM SHOULD NOT PERISH, BUT HAVE EVERLASTING LIFE" (John 3:16).

Christ is the supreme demonstration of God's love. Such love proceeds from the loving heart of the heavenly Father and is poured out in our hearts by the Holy Spirit (Rom. 5:5). It has no limits; it is wide enough to embrace all people.

In His own life and ministry, Christ constantly made transparent the love of God. He embodied God's forgiveness, mercy, and compassion for the bruised and the broken, and for the wretched and lost. While He was in the throes of death, He turned to a thief, dying on a cross beside Him. As we observe His caring for people—people like us, facing life's disappointments, hardships, sorrows, and sins—we hear Him say, "Come unto me, all ye that labour and are heavy laden, and I will give you rest" (Matt. 11:28).

Amid all the uncertainties and changes that mark earthly life, there remains something that is fixed and absolutely constant—Christ's love for us. This unchanging truth owes its existence to the mercy of God and to the death of Christ.

Daily Devotions:
M. The Provision of God
   Genesis 22:9-14
T. God Preserves Israel
   Genesis 45:1-8
W. The Kinsman-Redeemer
   Ruth 4:1-10
T. No Other Foundation
   1 Corinthians 3:9-11
F. No Other Gospel
   Galatians 1:6-9
S. No Other Doctrine
   1 Timothy 1:3-11

Receiving God's Provision of Salvation

Acts 2:36-41; Romans 10:5-13; Galatians 2:16; 3:21-26; Ephesians 2:8-10

Unit Theme:
The Doctrine of Salvation

Central Truth:
All who repent from sin and confess Jesus Christ as Savior will be saved.

Focus:
Acknowledge and accept Jesus Christ as Savior and Lord of our lives.

Context:
New Testament passages about receiving the gift of salvation

Golden Text:
"If thou shalt confess with thy mouth the Lord Jesus, and shalt believe in thine heart that God hath raised him from the dead, thou shalt be saved" (Rom. 10:9).

Study Outline:
 I. Repentance From Sin
    (Acts 2:36-41)
 II. Confess Jesus as Lord
    (Rom. 10:5-13)
III. Receive Salvation by Faith
    (Gal. 2:16; 3:21-26; Eph. 2:8-10)

INTRODUCTION

In the previous three lessons, the focus was on the problem of human existence and its solution in Jesus Christ. The current lesson examines how individuals receive the gift of salvation.

God's plan of salvation simultaneously involves the personal and social dimensions of life. Conversion at the personal level always corresponds to God's formation of a people for His glory. Our personal declaration that Jesus is Lord adds another voice to a "choir"—Christ's church—that has been singing this song since the Holy Spirit's outpouring on Pentecost. By keeping in view both dimensions of conversion, we see why it involves public pronouncement as well as personal confession.

The Spirit initiates conversion in a person's heart by revealing the truth. This revelation communicates knowledge about Jesus and sparks a love for Him. Augustine of Hippo said the Holy Spirit gives rise to an inward delight for truth in which humans come to rejoice in and cling to what has been revealed.

When humans perceive the truth about Christ, they also come to understand the truth about themselves. We might call this the second stage of conversion in which the conscience becomes "pricked" by the truth. At this moment, the Spirit's revelation enables the person to choose to accept or deny Christ's truth.

Faith becomes possible as a result of this Spirit-inspired event. To complete the movement of faith the Spirit initiates, the person must now move toward Christ. Recognizing his or her own sinfulness and Christ's graciousness, the person confesses that Jesus is Lord. The sting of conscience prompts the internal act of faith that, in turn, finds its fulfillment in the public confession of Christ.

The process of conversion would be incomplete, however, if it ended at this point. The complete change of direction that repentance requires means the new believer must learn to move in and with the new community Christ has established. Water baptism should follow the personal dimension of conversion because this communal rite commits the new believer to the family of God. Conversion, then, is an internal movement with public practices that show one has joined Christ and His church.

I. REPENTANCE FROM SIN (Acts 2:36-41)

A. Entrance Into the New Israel (vv. 36, 39)

36 Therefore let all the house of Israel know assuredly, that God hath made the same Jesus, whom ye have crucified, both Lord and Christ.

39 For the promise is unto you, and to your children, and to all that are afar off, even as many as the Lord our God shall call.

Luke records the coming of the Spirit on the Day of Pentecost. Peter's sermon seems to confirm the purpose of Pentecost to form a new people of God who would become a light for the nations. Peter directs his sermon to "the house of Israel" and calls upon them to recognize Jesus as "both Lord and Christ" (Acts 2:36). Peter grounds this call on several quotations from the Psalms, including 110:1 ("The Lord said unto my Lord, Sit them at my right hand . . ."; see Acts 2:34-35). In light of Jesus' resurrection, the text suggests that the Messiah is the Lord now seated at the right hand of the Lord (the Father). From His exalted position, Jesus, the Messiah, sends the Holy Spirit as the promise to Israel and to "as many as the Lord our God will call to Himself" (v. 39 NASB). By extending the promise to "all who are far off," Peter's sermon also includes the Gentiles in the people of God, which anticipates the mission to the Gentiles that Luke describes in the second half of Acts.

Salvation is not an individual enterprise. It is admission to the new people God has called into existence. The giving of the Spirit at Pentecost renews the covenant and constitutes Jews and Gentiles as the new people of God. The Spirit will now lead this new community in mission to "the ends of the earth" (13:47). Part of God's provision of salvation is His church—this new community of believers to which all Christians belong.

---

1. Explain the meaning of Jesus being "made . . . both Lord and Christ" (v. 36).
2. How does God "call" individuals (v. 39)?

"When the great promise of the Spirit was fulfilled on the Day of Pentecost, it was fulfilled not in reference to the apostles only."—Charles Hodge

---

B. Initiation Into the Faith (vv. 37-38, 40-41)

³⁷ Now when they heard this, they were pricked in their heart, and said unto Peter and to the rest of the apostles, Men and brethren, what shall we do? ³⁸ Then Peter said unto them, Repent, and be baptized every one of you in the name of Jesus Christ for the remission of sins, and ye shall receive the gift of the Holy Ghost.

⁴⁰ And with many other words did he testify and exhort, saying, Save yourselves from this untoward generation. ⁴¹ Then they that gladly received his word were baptized: and the same day there were added unto them about three thousand souls.

As Peter concluded his sermon, the audience was "pricked in their heart" (v. 37). The verb *pricked* means to "pierce" or "stab," which is why some translations render it "cut to the heart" (NIV). It implies the initial stirs of the heart through conviction. It is a convicting realization that what has been said is the truth. This initial recognition of the truth indicts the heart and calls forth a response: "What shall we do?" (v. 37).

Peter's answer involves a twofold process: "Repent, and be baptized" (v. 38). The term for *repentance* (*metanoia*) involves a change of mind or direction in one's life. This change of direction corresponds to the internal recognition of the truth. The person's desires are redirected by being emotionally caught up in the truth. The change of mind follows from a change of heart.

When Peter makes his final appeal, "Be saved from this perverse generation!" (v. 40 NASB), around three thousand people respond to his call to undergo baptism in Jesus' name (v. 41). As an initiatory rite, baptism marks the decision to become part of the people of God. It is a public witness to an internal dynamic and therefore is part of conversion. Some people do not understand that conversion to Christ is both internal and external, because they fail to see two connections: (1) one cannot embrace Christ in the heart without publicly testifying to this change, and (2) one cannot embrace Christ without becoming part of His people.

Conversion is a powerful encounter with the risen Christ through the Spirit. It begins with an internal conviction about the truth, which reorients emotion and desire. This internal prompting leads to a change of direction in which the individual chooses to live in the truth of the gospel. It culminates in the public declaration of that internal change and full admission into the new people of God.

---

1. When was your heart first "pricked" by the Holy Spirit (v. 37), and how did you respond?
2. Why is water baptism necessary (vv. 38, 41)?
3. How can you and I be "saved from this perverse generation" (v. 40 NASB) in which we live?

"We need a quickening of faith; faith in the power of the God of Pentecost to convict and convert three thousand in a day. Faith, not in a process of culture by which we hope to train children into a state of salvation, but faith in the mighty God who can quicken a dead soul into life in a moment; faith in moral and spiritual revolution rather than evolution."—A. C. Dixon

II. CONFESS JESUS AS LORD (Rom. 10:5-13)

A. Confession as Covenant Renewal (vv. 5-8)

⁵ For Moses describeth the righteousness which is of the law, That the man whlch doeth those things shall live by them. ⁶ But the righteousness which is of faith speaketh on this wise, Say not in thine heart, Who shall ascend into heaven? (that is, to bring Christ down from above:) ⁷ Or, Who shall descend into the deep? (that is, to bring up Christ again from the dead.) ⁸ But what saith it? The word is nigh thee, even in thy mouth, and in thy heart: that is, the word of faith, which we preach.

What Paul says in Romans 10 is part of a longer section (chs. 9-11) in which he attempts to deal with the question of the status of Judaism after the coming of Christ. As a Jew, Paul is deeply concerned about his fellow Jews, especially since many of them have rejected Jesus. This is not simply a theological exercise for Paul. It is part of his prayer that his Jewish brothers and sisters be saved by seeing the truth of Christ (10:1-3).

The initial contrast between a righteousness grounded in the Law and a righteousness grounded in faith (vv. 5-6) serves to clarify the statement that "Christ is the end [goal] of the law for righteousness to everyone who believes" (v. 4 NKJV). Membership in the covenant God established with Israel can no longer be connected to the Law. In fact, Paul had already argued in Romans 4 that Israel's covenant membership had always been connected to the faith that Abraham exercised in response to the divine call on his life. Christ reveals that the Law's entire purpose—to maintain the identity of the people of God—has been fulfilled in Him. Membership in God's covenant people now revolves around faith in Christ.

Romans 10:6-9 offers an interpretation of the covenant renewal presented in Deuteronomy 30 to make its point. In Deuteronomy 30:11-14, "the word [that] is very near" (NKJV) is the commandment of God. God has now altered this formula, putting Christ in the place of the Law. While no one could bring Christ down from heaven or up from the Abyss (Rom. 10:6-7), this is unnecessary because Christ himself has come and God has raised Him from the dead. Everything has been accomplished in Christ, and all that remains is to embrace by faith the word that has come near (v. 8). Confession of Christ by faith is how God renews His covenant.

- How is "the righteousness . . . based on law" superior to "the righteousness based on faith" (vv. 5-6 NASB)?

"So what is the place of the Law in the life of the Christian? Simply this: We are no longer under the Law to be condemned by it, we are now 'in-lawed' to it because of our betrothal to Christ! He has written the Law, and love for it, into our hearts!"—Sinclair B. Ferguson

---

B. Confession as Personal Renewal (vv. 9-13)

⁹ That if thou shalt confess with thy mouth the Lord Jesus, and shalt believe in thine heart that God hath raised him from the dead, thou shalt

be saved. [10] For with the heart man believeth unto righteousness; and with the mouth confession is made unto salvation. [11] For the scripture saith, Whosoever believeth on him shall not be ashamed. [12] For there is no difference between the Jew and the Greek: for the same Lord over all is rich unto all that call upon him. [13] For whosoever shall call upon the name of the Lord shall be saved.

In the second part of Romans 10:5-13, Paul takes covenant renewal in the direction of personal renewal as he shows how God in Christ and by the Spirit had expanded the covenant to include everyone who believes. Although the Holy Spirit is not explicitly mentioned, Paul, in verse 13, implicitly refers to the Spirit by quoting Joel 2:32 that "everyone who calls on the name of the Lord will be saved" (NIV). The passage in Joel follows immediately after God's promise to pour out His Spirit in the last days. By utilizing Joel, Paul is recalling his earlier point that the Spirit is the One who sets free (Rom. 8:1-2).

Faith is an internal movement generated by the Spirit. As the love of God is poured into human hearts (5:5), it calls forth the voluntary public confession that "Jesus is Lord" (10:9-10 NIV). To proclaim Jesus as "Lord" is simultaneously to identify Him with one of the terms for God in the Old Testament and to elevate Him above all other claims to lordship, including the Roman emperor. It is Jesus whom the believer now trusts for his total well-being, not any political authority or any national identity.

Verses 11-13 give three promises to those who make Jesus their Lord: (1) they "will not be disappointed" (NASB); (2) they will become part of the one covenant people of God, whatever their ethnicity; (3) they will be saved.

---

1. What role does "confession" play in salvation (vv. 9-10)?
2. What do verses 11-13 teach about the "riches" of God?

"Believing and confessing go together; and you cannot be saved without you take them both. 'With the mouth confession is made unto salvation.' If you ever see the kingdom of heaven, you have to take this way."—D. L. Moody

---

III. RECEIVE SALVATION BY FAITH (Gal. 2:16; 3:21-26; Eph. 2:8-10)

A. Faith Alone Brings Justification (Gal. 2:16; 3:21-26)

[2:16] Knowing that a man is not justified by the works of the law, but by the faith of Jesus Christ, even we have believed in Jesus Christ, that we might be justified by the faith of Christ, and not by the works of the law: for by the works of the law shall no flesh be justified.

[3:21] Is the law then against the promises of God? God forbid: for if there had been a law given which could have given life, verily righteousness should have been by the law. [22] But the scripture hath concluded all under sin, that the promise by faith of Jesus Christ might be given to them that believe. [23] But before faith came, we were kept under the law, shut up unto the faith which should afterwards be revealed. [24] Wherefore the law was our schoolmaster to bring us unto Christ, that we might be justified by faith. ²⁵ But after that faith is come, we are no longer under a schoolmaster. ²⁶ For ye are all the children of God by faith in Christ Jesus.

Paul's reflections on justification by faith in Galatians are in part a response to a confrontation with Peter in Antioch. Paul recounts the confrontation as occurring over table fellowship (2:11-14). Peter had been eating with Jesus-believing Gentiles until a group arrived from the apostle James in Jerusalem. Paul refers to this group as the "circumcision" party (v. 12) because they were still following Jewish dietary laws that restricted what kind of food they should eat. To use Jewish dietary laws to justify not eating with Jesus-believing Gentiles was to continue to follow the Torah as the primary way of defining Jewish existence rather than Christ.

The point of the gospel of Jesus was not to turn Gentiles into Jews, but to turn both Jews and Gentiles into followers of Jesus. As Paul would later declare, "There is neither Jew nor Greek, there is neither slave nor free, there is neither male nor female; for you are all one in Christ Jesus" (3:28 NKJV). This is part of Paul's appeal to Peter in 2:15 when he begins with their common Jewish identity ("we who are Jews by birth," NIV). On the basis of this appeal, Paul says Peter should know that no one becomes justified by the "works of the law" (v. 16). The immediate context suggests that Paul has in mind the dietary laws Peter had suddenly "re-discovered" after the group for Jerusalem showed up.

This raises the question of *justification*. The term is a legal one and points toward right standing before God. *Justification* is the declaration that a person is a member of the new family of God. This declaration is grounded in the faithfulness of Jesus, who fulfilled all the demands of Torah and the Christian's union with Christ through faith. Faith in Christ alone produces right standing before God and membership in this new family.

In chapter 3, Paul clarifies the purpose of the Law as serving as a "schoolmaster" (vv. 24-25). The analogy he makes is between Torah and a slave whose job was to teach and train the children in a Greek and Roman household. Like the teacher-slave, the Law corrected Israel by pointing out her sin (v. 19). By employing a verb that means "enclosed" ("hath concluded," v. 22), Paul envisions the Law as putting Israel in a kind of prison of sin whereby it identifies sinful behavior but lacks the power to liberate from that behavior (vv. 21-23). Torah can only teach right and wrong; it cannot bring the life needed to live an upright life.

Verse 26 identifies how sinners achieve justification. It is by uniting with Christ Jesus that one becomes a son or daughter of God. This leads to the question of how that union occurs, to which "by faith" supplies the answer. The Law's role as teacher is no longer needed because Jews and Gentiles are united to one another in their union with Christ, which they achieve by faith.

---

1. What cannot justify us before God (2:16)?
2. How is faith in Christ like a key (3:21-23)?
3. Describe the believer's relationship with God (v. 26).

"Where the righteousness of Christ is imputed to an individual, a principle of holiness is imparted to him; the former can only be ascertained by the latter."—A. W. Pink

Receiving God's Provision of Salvation

B. Faith Alone Produces Good Works (Eph. 2:8-10)

⁸ For by grace are ye saved through faith; and that not of yourselves: it is the gift of God: ⁹ Not of works, lest any man should boast. ¹⁰ For we are his workmanship, created in Christ Jesus unto good works, which God hath before ordained that we should walk in them.

People need "grace" (v. 8) to free themselves from sin. As the divine Artist, God must reshape human lives which have become deformed through emotions and desires that are out of control and subject to the slavery of sin. Just as the Law cannot bring life, no human being can deliver themselves from this condition of slavery. Deliverance and healing cannot be "of works," which excludes any boasting that humans were the cause of their own cure (v. 9).

The term *workmanship* (*poiema*) combines the notion of a poet constructing a poem and a craftsman shaping a piece of material into something beautiful (v. 10). It stems from a verb that means to "make" or "manufacture," thus pointing to an act of creation. As a gift of God, salvation concerns God's act of re-creating human beings so they can begin to live new lives (v. 8). Humans must believe that the Creator God can and will re-create them in Christ (see also 2 Cor. 5:17). All righteous actions flow from God's creative handiwork in the human heart, in which God reshapes and reorients human emotion and desire so that believers now long to do what is right.

---

1. What is "the gift of God" (v. 8)?
2. How should we "walk" (v. 10)?

"God takes the broken material of our lives and re-fashions it into something beautiful. Salvation is God's gift to help us lead beautiful lives that show forth the glory of the Artist."—Dale Coulter

---

CONCLUSION

God's provision of salvation concerns entrance into a new community with a new way of life. Enlivened by the Spirit, Christians believe on Christ, which involves recognizing their own poverty and Christ's riches. In the midst of this act of faith, God is already reshaping human desire and emotion so that it comes to reflect the harmonious and loving relations between the Father, the Son, and the Holy Spirit. Believers are the artistic creation of the Divine Artist. This reshaping of human life, however, also occurs in the community to which God has called believers. Through the act of baptism, believers begin a lifelong journey of discipleship in which their lives will be reforged in the furnace of God's church. The provisions of salvation are personal and social because when God invites us to be united to Christ, He beckons us to become members of His bride.

GOLDEN TEXT CHALLENGE

"IF THOU SHALT CONFESS WITH THY MOUTH THE LORD JESUS, AND SHALT BELIEVE IN THINE HEART THAT GOD HATH RAISED HIM FROM THE DEAD, THOU SHALT BE SAVED (Rom. 10:9).

The Lord Jesus Christ was sent from God to be the Savior of the world. He accomplished all that was necessary for our salvation on the cross and by His resurrection. All we have to do to be saved is to exercise faith in Christ as our crucified and risen Savior.

To show that we have faith in Christ, we must publicly confess Him as Lord. No confession of man can add anything to the finished work of Christ; yet we are required to confess Him openly. This is because His glory and our good demand it. If we should conceal our faith in Him, who would be benefited? In what respect would He be glorified? Jesus required that all who would be benefited by Him should take up their cross daily and follow Him. And if we fail to do this, He will not acknowledge us as disciples.

Paul declared that whoever believes in Christ and confesses Him shall be saved. This statement is plain, positive, and unequivocal.

Daily Devotions:
M. The Ark of Safety
    Genesis 7:1-7
T. The Abrahamic Covenant Blessing
    Genesis 12:1-3
W. Calling Upon the Lord
    Psalm 18:1-3
T. Receive the Kingdom Like Children
    Mark 10:13-16
F. Humility Before the Lord
    Luke 7:36-48
S. Earnest Desire to Receive Salvation
    Acts 16:25-35

Benefits of Salvation

John 1:12-13; Romans 4:4-8; 8:14-17; 2 Corinthians 1:21-22; 5:17-21;
Ephesians 1:11-14; 1 Peter 2:9-10

Unit Theme:
The Doctrine of Salvation

Central Truth:
The Christian enjoys numerous benefits of salvation.

Focus:
Describe the benefits of our salvation and gratefully worship the Lord for so great a gift.

Context:
Five New Testament passages communicating the blessings of Christian living

Golden Text:
"Therefore if any man be in Christ, he is a new creature: old things are passed away; behold, all things are become new" (2 Cor. 5:17).

Study Outline:
 I. Made Children of God
    (John 1:12-13; Rom. 8:14-17; 1 Peter 2:9-10)
 II. Declared Righteous in Christ
    (Rom. 4:4-8; 2 Cor. 5:17-21)
 III. Sealed With the Holy Spirit
    (Eph. 1:11-14; 2 Cor. 1:21-22)

INTRODUCTION

While conversion entails a process that has personal and social dimensions, it is also a lifelong journey into the heart of God. The foundation on which this journey rests is the new identity the believer receives in Christ, which the New Testament variously describes as being a *new creation*, a *member of God's family*, a *disciple*, a *servant*, and a *follower of Christ*. Out of all of these descriptions, the name that the Roman world attached to the earlier followers of Jesus sums it up best: *Christian*.

Another way of describing this journey is by comparing it to physical growth and maturation. Scripture declares believers are "born of God" through the Spirit. The phrase "born again" refers to the new birth in which the Spirit regenerates the heart by redirecting thoughts, emotions, and desires back toward God. The Spirit becomes the indwelling source of action and power.

While *new birth* underscores a radical interior reorientation, *adoption* points toward a process of liberation and deliverance from the slave market of life. Just like the Israelites, God delivers believers from the slavery of "Egypt" (sin) and the alienation of exile (separation from God) so they can become His sons and daughters. As members of God's family, believers begin to cry out "Abba" because the Spirit gives them the right to use the language of family relations.

Upon entrance into His family, God declares believers to be righteous and initiates a process of growth. Believers grow into full citizens, functioning as priests who worship in God's presence and in whom the Spirit of God dwells. Believers are also sealed by the Spirit whose sanctifying and empowering presence serves as a down payment of their future inheritance with God. Filled with the Spirit, they become ambassadors in the world, calling all to join the family. The end of the journey is a fully transformed life, immersed into God's presence and rejoicing with the members of God's family. It is the jubilee of the Marriage Supper of the Lamb. By employing these metaphors, Scripture describes the benefits of salvation in terms of a deepening journey into the presence of God.

I. MADE CHILDREN OF GOD (John 1:12-13; Rom. 8:14-17; 1 Peter 2:9-10)

A. Born of God (John 1:12-13)

12 But as many as received him, to them gave he power to become the sons of God, even to them that believe on his name: 13 Which were born, not of blood, nor of the will of the flesh, nor of the will of man, but of God.

The Gospel and letters of John speak of individuals being made children of God. This theme takes root in the prologue to the Gospel as a response to an implicit question raised by the assertion that the world did not know the true Light nor did His own people even recognize Him (1:9-11). The question is whether anyone recognized the Light that God sent into the world. John's response is in the form of a second claim that this knowledge comes "to all who received him, [or] to those who believed in his name" (v. 12 NIV).

In these two claims, John combines *light* and *knowledge* with *faith* and *new birth*. Humans must be born of God—a birth distinct from biological birth and human sexuality. The birth of God occurs in and through the Spirit's activity (3:8). In 1 John, the idea that humans have God's own seed in them further emphasizes that they are the children of God (3:9). This is strong language and it suggests God calls humans to share His life. It is close to the idea that through God's promises believers may become "partakers of the divine nature" (2 Peter 1:4). Believers "become children of God" (John 1:12 NKJV) because God's seed remains in them through the Spirit's action within them (v. 13).

God gives those who believe on the name of Christ the "right" (*exousia*) to become the children of God (v. 12 NKJV). This authority stems from Jesus' relationship with the Father. As Jesus makes clear, His authority is an extension of "the Father who dwells in Me" (John 14:10 NKJV). On the basis of His authority, the incarnate Son can grant eternal life to whoever believes in Him (John 3:16; 17:2). The authority to become the children of God extends from the way the Son shares the life of the Father and bestows that life to believers. Authority is connected to relationship in a way analogous to how biological children have a "right" to their parents' possessions because of their relationship.

To believe on the Son is to receive Him as God's "light" or "knowledge" because He is the Word of God who has become flesh. By faith, believers come to have fellowship with the Father and the Son through the Spirit. This is because the Spirit gives birth to believers and breathes the life of God into them. Believers have become children of God, thereby possessing the "authority" or "right" to participate in God's own life—an eternal life.

1. Who becomes a child of God, and how?
2. Contrast spiritual birth with natural birth.

"In Jesus Christ there is neither male nor female, bond nor free; even you may be the children of God, if you believe in Jesus."—George Whitefield

---

B. Adopted by God (Rom. 8:14-17)

14 For as many as are led by the Spirit of God, they are the sons of God. 15 For ye have not received the spirit of bondage again to fear; but ye have received the Spirit of adoption, whereby we cry, Abba, Father. 16 The Spirit itself beareth witness with our spirit, that we are the children of God: 17 And if children, then heirs; heirs of God, and joint-heirs with Christ; if so be that we suffer with him, that we may be also glorified together.

Liberation from slavery is combined with the metaphor of *adoption* to draw a strong contrast between *fear* and *confidence* (v. 15). A parallel passage is 2 Timothy 1:7, where the contrast is between a "spirit of fear" and the spirit of "power . . . love, and . . . a sound mind." What gives confidence to the believer is the image of adoption into the family of God (Rom. 8:14-15). The contrast between slavery and adoption conveys the depth of God's love, which reaches out and brings the unwanted into His family. It also conveys the sense of a new name or new identity being given to the believer. As an adopted child of God, the believer receives all the rights and privileges that correspond to receiving a new name, which is why Paul speaks of sharing in the inheritance of God (v. 17).

While adoption conveys a new status and new identity, Paul underscores this identity by pointing to the Spirit's activity. First, the Spirit causes the language of family to arise within the believer. Paul is not concerned with merely speaking the words "Abba, Father" (v. 15); rather, the point is that no one can claim the privileges of family except the children of God. A clear witness of the believer's identity as God's child is that the believer changes the way he or she relates to God. God is now *Abba*, the Father who shares His life with them.

Second, the "Abba" cry is deeply experiential, emerging from the believer's heart and flowing to the Father. It is an internal testimony created by the intimacy that the Spirit generates between believers and God (v. 16). This testimony is the confidence that "I am loved" and "I am God's." One might liken it to the emotion that wells up within parents and children at spontaneous moments, even after the children have long left the home. This emotion reminds them of a deep relational connection—they are family. The knowledge of family is brought about by the Holy Spirit, who is the love of God poured into human hearts (5:5).

---

1. How do God's children live (v. 14)?
2. Describe the transformation in the life of someone whom God adopts (vv. 15-17).
3. What is the connection between the believer's suffering and glorification (v. 17)?

"Nobody is born into this world a child of the family of God. We are born as children of wrath. The only way we enter into the family of God is by adoption, and that adoption occurs when we are united to God's only begotten Son by faith. When by faith we are united with Christ, we are then adopted into that family of whom Christ is the firstborn."—R. C. Sproul

---

C. Citizens and Priests (1 Peter 2:9-10)

⁹ But ye are a chosen generation, a royal priesthood, an holy nation, a peculiar people; that ye should shew forth the praises of him who hath called you out of darkness into his marvellous light; ¹⁰ Which in time past were not a people, but are now the people of God: which had not obtained mercy, but now have obtained mercy.

The text from 1 Peter adds the language of citizenship and priesthood to familial language used by John and Paul. The terms "holy nation" and "royal priesthood" come from the giving of the Law at Mount Sinai when God declared, "You shall be to me a kingdom of priests and a holy nation" (Ex. 19:6 ESV). The Exodus tradition begins with God's deliverance of Israel from Egypt and concludes with God's making Israel a holy nation of priests. First Peter 2:9 makes this same point about Christians by claiming God has called them "out of darkness into His marvelous light" (NKJV). The ultimate purpose of God's act of liberation is to create a people who will worship Him in all their ways ("declare the praises," v. 9 NIV). By their acts of worship, this new nation will become a light to the world.

The image of an exodus from sin is only part of the benefits conveyed in this passage. The second image is one of return from exile. Centuries earlier, God had the prophet Hosea name two of his children "No Mercy" (*Lo-ruhama*) and "Not My People" (*Lo-ammi*) to convey the depth of Israel's alienation from God (Hos. 1:6, 9). At the same time, Hosea was to proclaim God's message of hope that Israel would once again be His people and receive His mercy (vv. 10-11). In 1 Peter, the theme of exile now applies both to Jews and Gentiles who had been separated from God by their sin (2:10). For believers, exile from God is over as they now take their place within the family of God.

Out of those who were alienated and enslaved, God has created a new people who are His temple and who serve in that temple as priests. These images build upon one another to convey the new people of God as the place of God's presence, the extension of God's power, and those who declare God's glory.

---

1. How should the believer's life "proclaim the excellencies" of God (v. 9 NASB)?
2. How does verse 10 describe the transformation of the believer?

"None can know their election but by their conformity to Christ; for all who are chosen are chosen to sanctification."—Matthew Henry

II. DECLARED RIGHTEOUS IN CHRIST (Rom. 4:4-8; 2 Cor. 5:17-21)

A. Counted as Righteous (Rom. 4:4-8)

4 Now to him that worketh is the reward not reckoned of grace, but of debt. 5 But to him that worketh not, but believeth on him that justifieth the ungodly, his faith is counted for righteousness. 6 Even as David also describeth the blessedness of the man, unto whom God imputeth righteousness without works, 7 Saying, Blessed are they whose iniquities are forgiven, and whose sins are covered. 8 Blessed is the man to whom the Lord will not impute sin.

Paul uses the examples of Abraham and David to drive home his point that the Law cannot justify. According to Genesis, Abraham was part of a nomadic family that went from Ur in southern Mesopotamia up to Haran and then down into Canaan (11:27-32; 12:5). His route most likely followed either the Tigris or Euphrates rivers. In other words, Abraham's family probably began somewhere in the southern part of modern Iraq (near Kuwait) and migrated to northern Syria near the border with Turkey, before finally turning back south to settle in Canaan (Israel). After reaching Canaan, God promises Abraham an heir in his old age because, through this heir, Abraham will become the father of many nations (Gen. 15). All of this happens to Abraham before he receives circumcision.

The story of Abraham's journey from Ur to Canaan and from a nomad to the father of Israel upholds the concept of justification by faith alone. It is Abraham's faith in God's promises that becomes the basis for divine acceptance, not circumcision and certainly not the Law. Paul draws a contrast between paying someone wages for their labor and reckoning someone righteous on the basis of their faith (Rom. 4:4-5). The former concerns recompense, while the latter is a pure gift. As Paul goes on to declare, Abraham's faith in the promise of God (v. 13) means God is not repaying him for some work, but giving him the gift of an heir. Abraham becomes the father of all believers because God's action toward him reveals how God will treat all those who believe in His promises.

To the example of David (v. 6), Paul adds a quotation from Psalm 32:1-2 to show how the blessing of God comes in the midst of sickness rather than as a payment for strength (Rom. 4:7-8). David was wasting away when he confessed his sins and the Lord forgave him (Ps. 32:3-5). From Romans 4, it is clear that David receives forgiveness, healing, and the blessing of God when he is at his weakest and most vulnerable state. God's counting David as righteous cannot be the result of any work on David's part.

The stories of Abraham and David reveal how God gives His promises and bestows divine blessings when humans are wandering through life as wounded sojourners. All God requires is that they trust that His gift is genuine and His promises are true. This faith is the basis on which God justifies individuals and counts them as upright in His sight.

---

1. Contrast faith with works (vv. 4-6).
2. How does God deal with the believer's sins (vv. 7-8)?

"The soul is the life of the body, faith is the life of the soul, and Christ is the life of faith. Justification by faith in Christ's righteousness is the golden chain which binds the Christian world in one body."—James H. Aughey

B. Reconciled and Created Anew (2 Cor. 5:17-21)

[17] Therefore if any man be in Christ, he is a new creature: old things are passed away; behold, all things are become new. [18] And all things are of God, who hath reconciled us to himself by Jesus Christ, and hath given to us the ministry of reconciliation; [19] To wit, that God was in Christ, reconciling the world unto himself, not imputing their trespasses unto them; and hath committed unto us the word of reconciliation. [20] Now then we are ambassadors for Christ, as though God did beseech you by us: we pray you in Christ's stead, be ye reconciled to God. [21] For he hath made him to be sin for us, who knew no sin; that we might be made the righteousness of God in him.

Paul describes salvation as *new creation* and *reconciliation*. By "new creation," he intends to forge a strong link between God's purposes in creation and in redemption (v. 17 NKJV). Salvation concerns God fulfilling His original purpose for creation. Scholars describe "new creation" in terms of the end of times breaking into the present earthly existence, which is simply to say that God's *final* purpose (the end) has now become realized in and through Christ. The plan of God has never changed, even if the sinfulness of creation has altered how God brings about that plan. One of the benefits of salvation is that Christians participate *now* in the wonders of the new heaven and earth.

As a metaphor for the restoration of God's original intention for humans created in His image, the idea of "new creation" naturally leads into a focus on reconciliation (vv. 18-19). Part of God's original purpose for humanity was to have an intimate relationship with Him, which Genesis 1—2 indicates through describing humans as the "image" and "likeness" of God and referring to God walking in the garden with Adam and Eve. While this relational intimacy was broken by the Fall, "in Christ" the relationship has been restored.

To expound on his point, Paul makes one of his strongest claims about Christ: God "made him to be sin" (2 Cor. 5:21). The Son of God took on the shape of human sinfulness in His death on the cross. While Hebrews asserts that Jesus committed no sinful action (4:15), Paul adds that He did enter into sinful existence. In His death, Christ experienced the full reality of sinfulness, since sin culminates in death (cf. Rom. 6:23). He took upon Himself the disease of sin so He might supply the cure. This is why verse 21 of our text ends with a reference to believers' becoming righteous in union with Christ. Christ took on the shape of sinful existence so humans might take on the shape of righteous existence.

It may be that Paul is drawing on his own experience of reconciliation on the road to Damascus (Acts 9:1-19). He was a persecutor of Christians when Christ appeared to him, yet his past was not counted against him. In his second letter to the Corinthians, Paul extends his own calling to challenge all believers to become "ambassadors for Christ" (5:20).

Verses 18-20 contain a rich set of terms to convey the missionary thrust that Christians should have with respect to reconciliation. Believers now participate in the "ministry of reconciliation" and so become "ambassadors" of the message of reconciliation. The term for *ministry* (*diakonia*) implies an act of service to others. In this sense, *ministry* is always modeled on the Incarnation, in which the Word became a human to serve other humans through His life, death, and resurrection. This service takes the shape of restoring broken relationships. As representatives of God, believers are sent out into the world to convey this message.

1. What does it mean to be "in Christ," and what is the result (v. 17)?
2. How are Christians to serve as Christ's ambassadors (vv. 18-20)?
3. How can we become "the righteousness of God" (v. 21)?

From Trash to Treasure

An old saying states that one person's trash is another person's treasure. Some individuals can see the worth of a dilapidated object and restore it to its original condition. We see this particularly with classic cars, which are restored and then put on display for others to enjoy.

God always sees His image in humans, who are His treasure. He can restore them when they have been discarded and placed on the junk pile of life. Once restored, believers become those who proclaim the message that anyone can be a "new creation" in the Master's hands.

III. SEALED WITH THE HOLY SPIRIT (Eph. 1:11-14; 2 Cor. 1:21-22)

A. The Spirit as Seal (Eph. 1:11-14)

[11] In whom also we have obtained an inheritance, being predestinated according to the purpose of him who worketh all things after the counsel of his own will: [12] That we should be to the praise of his glory, who first trusted in Christ. [13] In whom ye also trusted, after that ye heard the word of truth, the gospel of your salvation: in whom also after that ye believed, ye were sealed with that holy Spirit of promise, [14] Which is the earnest of our inheritance until the redemption of the purchased possession, unto the praise of his glory.

These verses form the conclusion to a *berakah*, which is a blessing directed to God for His great works. Within Judaism, these blessings usually concerned God's deliverance of His people. Here, the *berakah* concludes with a reference to redemption (v. 14). The use of *redemption* points back to verse 7 ("redemption through his blood"), and it calls to mind God's great act of delivering Israel from Egypt and giving to them the Promised Land as their inheritance. Paul utilizes a term for *inheritance* (*kleroun*) that means to "appoint" or "cast by lot" and, thus, calls to mind that division of the land according to lots (vv. 11, 14). The exact contents of this inheritance have already been spelled out to a certain extent: adoption, forgiveness of sins, blessings from the Spirit (vv. 3-4, 13). The "promised land" is now no longer physical Palestine, but the blessings in Christ.

The language of predestination in this passage should provide comfort for believers (v. 11). It does not point toward God electing some individuals for heaven and others for hell. Instead, it underscores that God's plan is not contingent on any other agents or events. Since the fulfillment of God's plan depends on God, believers can take confidence that His plan will come to pass. All of God's efforts are for His own glory and for the good of His creation (v. 12). This is comfort indeed.

The Spirit "seals" the believer as a mark of ownership (v. 13), like a rancher might brand his cattle. It is the Spirit who identifies God's children as His own.

The Spirit's indwelling presence is the believer's "guarantee" of everlasting redemption (v. 14 NKJV).

---

1. What has God predestined for His children (vv. 11-12)?
2. Explain the two names for Holy Scripture given in verse 13.
3. What is "the purchased possession" (v. 14)?

"Enter into the promises of God. It is your inheritance. You will do more in one year if you are really filled with the Holy Ghost than you could do in fifty years apart from Him."—Smith Wigglesworth

---

B. The Spirit as Down Payment (2 Cor. 1:21-22)

21 Now he which stablisheth us with you in Christ, and hath anointed us, is God; 22 Who hath also sealed us, and given the earnest of the Spirit in our hearts.

Paul's second letter to the Corinthians was written before the letter to the Ephesians. While directed to different local house churches with a diverse set of issues, Paul highlights many of the same themes to address these issues. In both letters, he describes the Spirit as a "down payment" or "pledge" (*arrabōn*) and a "seal" or "mark" (*sphragizō*) (see Eph. 1:13-14; 2 Cor. 1:22) from God, who also establishes believers together in Christ and "anoints" or consecrates them for His service (v. 21). The believer's experience of the Spirit's presence both marks the person and serves as a guarantee of God's final deliverance from sin at the end.

Paul's statement about the Spirit as a pledge of a future inheritance finds its counterpart in Hebrews 11:1, where faith is called the "substance of things hoped for." In that verse, the noun for *substance* can also refer to a title deed that serves as evidence connecting the owner to his property. As a vision of God's plan, faith lays claim to the heavenly land for which Christians long. The Holy Spirit's presence—giving rise to faith, uniting the believer to Christ, and marking the believer through the continual unfolding of blessings—serves as the guarantee of a future inheritance.

---

1. What does it mean to be "anointed" by God (v. 21)?
2. What does it mean to be "sealed" with the Holy Spirit (v. 22)?

"God knows what each one of us is dealing with. He knows our pressures. He knows our conflicts. And He has made a provision for each and every one of them. That provision is Himself in the person of the Holy Spirit, indwelling us and empowering us to respond rightly."—Kay Arthur

---

CONCLUSION

All the benefits of salvation flow from membership in God's family. Through adoption and new birth, the Spirit unites individuals to Christ and brings them into fellowship with the Father. Sealed with the Spirit's own presence, the believer embarks on a journey of growth and maturation. This journey can be described as a process of sanctification, but along the way there are sanctifying moments in which the Spirit breaks through in fresh ways causing the believer to burst forth again in the language of family. The "Abba" cry, the sighs too deep for words, and the spontaneity of tongues are different ways God reminds His children that they belong to Him. One day the journey in this life will end, as the door to the next life opens and the family celebration begins.

GOLDEN TEXT CHALLENGE

"THEREFORE IF ANY MAN BE IN CHRIST, HE IS A NEW CREATURE: OLD THINGS ARE PASSED AWAY; BEHOLD, ALL THINGS ARE BECOME NEW" (2 Cor. 5:17).

Anyone "in Christ" is a new creation. The expression "in Christ" occurs 165 times in Paul's writings. The expression reflects these aspects of the present work of Jesus: it indicates the presence of the Lord in practical and ethical areas of life; it refers to the reigning rule of the Lord in His Church as the victor over death; and it reflects the close relationship between the Christian and Christ.

Thus, to be "in Christ" is to be in a profoundly new experience—life at its fullest. Since the focus is primarily on the Lord, this new life is a reflection of the life brought about by His resurrection.

Paul precisely identifies this new creation as one in which the old has passed away. The Greek word for *old* means "former things." For Paul, "former things" included a life controlled by the flesh and by evil spirits. It also included a life dominated by the Law. Anything which once stood in the way of our open relationship with Christ is part of the "old things."

The verse concludes with this expression: "Behold, all things are become new." This is certainly a reminder of Revelation 21:5: "Behold, I make all things new." There is a newness in the redeemed life beyond human understanding. This newness is so radical that we seldom understand it in ourselves, much less in others. Nonetheless, it is a profound statement of the status we have in Christ Jesus.

Daily Devotions:
M. Righteousness Imputed to Abraham
   Genesis 15:1-6
T. The Blessings of Obedience
   Leviticus 26:3-13
W. Joy of God's People
   Zephaniah 3:14-17
T. A Glorious Hope
   Romans 8:18-21
F. Every Spiritual Blessing
   Ephesians 1:3-6
S. Complete in Christ Jesus
   Colossians 2:6-10

Our Ultimate Salvation

1 Corinthians 15:50-58; Philippians 3:20-21; 1 Thessalonians 4:13-18;
1 Peter 1:3-9; Revelation 19:1-9

Unit Theme:
The Doctrine of Salvation

Central Truth:
Faithful Christians can be confident and rejoice in their glorious future.

Focus:
Explore the Christian's glorious and eternal future, and remain faithful to Christ.

Context:
New Testament passages describing the eternal blessings of salvation

Golden Text:
"Let us be glad and rejoice, and give honor to him [Christ]: for the marriage of the Lamb is come, and his wife hath made herself ready" (Rev. 19:7).

Study Outline:
  I. The Great Transformation
     (Phil. 3:20-21; 1 Cor. 15:50-58)
 II. The Living Hope
     (1 Peter 1:3-9; 1 Thess. 4:13-18)
III. The Ultimate Worship Experience
     (Rev. 19:1-9)

INTRODUCTION

God's plan of salvation remains the same, whether it concerns the past, present, or future. When God created humans at the beginning of Creation, His desire was to extend divine fellowship to others. Endowed with God's image, the divine purpose for humanity was to welcome them into the intimate fellowship between Father, Son, and Holy Spirit. For this fellowship to reach completion, however, humans had to become more than their original creation. To share God's own life, humans must, in an important sense, take on the features of that life.

When we examine our ultimate salvation, we gain a glimpse of God's intention to endow humans with a form of existence that exceeds our original creation. Redemption from sin and death is part of this grand plan that Paul attempts to describe with phrases like "being clothed with incorruption and immortality" (see 1 Cor. 15:50-58). Human existence must be fully transformed. This transformation began with the Son becoming a human being in the Incarnation (John 1:1-18; Phil. 2:5-8). God took on the form of a servant by putting on human nature. Through His incarnation, death, and resurrection, the Son entered humanity, liberated it from sin and death, and bestowed upon it the gifts of incorruptibility and immortality. It is this new form of existence—a resurrected life—that becomes the basis for full participation in God's life.

The final union between the triune God and believers is a communion symbolized by the marriage between the Lamb and His bride (Rev. 19:7). To become members of the Bride, believers must be made like the Bridegroom. Heaven is less about a place and more about a presence. It is the fellowship of God and His people who have gained full admission into the Father's presence through conformity to the Son in the power of the Holy Spirit. One might even say that believers don't "go" to heaven as much as they become heavenly because they embody the glory of heaven—a glory that even now envelops them. This glory breaks through every time the kingdom of God manifests itself in the healing of the body, the deliverance from sin, and the gathering together of the church for worship. As Paul declares, believers are "being transformed into the same image from one degree of glory to another" (2 Cor. 3:18 ESV). At the coming of Christ, believers will simply walk through the door to another plane of existence with the triune God.

I. THE GREAT TRANSFORMATION (Phil. 3:20-21; 1 Cor. 15:50-58)
A. The Heavenly Commonwealth (Phil. 3:20-21)

20 For our conversation is in heaven; from whence also we look for the Saviour, the Lord Jesus Christ: 21 Who shall change our vile body, that it may be fashioned like unto his glorious body, according to the working whereby he is able even to subdue all things unto himself.

In this compact passage, Paul sets forth a basic framework through which he views the Christian life that the phrase "already/not yet" encapsulates. Christians already participate in heavenly life, which is why they are part of the heavenly commonwealth now. The KJV translates the Greek term *politeuma* (citizenship/ commonwealth) as "conversation" (v. 20) because, in Elizabethan English, it conveyed one's conduct or course of life and the society to which a person belonged. In this sense, it is closely connected to the modern English equivalents of *citizenship* and *commonwealth*, because the former implies conduct while the latter implies belonging to a society. As members of the heavenly commonwealth, believers live in light of God's reign and the new society His reign creates, even if the Kingdom has yet to be fully established.

Even though believers already participate in heavenly life, that life has not been fully consummated (the "not yet"). Believers await Jesus to descend from the heavenly commonwealth to claim His own. While verse 20 does not explicitly suggest a *descent*, the previous chapter's description of Jesus being exalted to God and given a name above every name suggests a prior *ascent* (2:9-11).

Verse 21 of our text continues the theme of "not yet" by focusing on what Jesus will do when He returns. The verbs Paul employs correspond to verbs he had used to describe Jesus in 2:6-11. Jesus, who was in the form (*morphē*) of God, was born in the likeness and "fashion" (*schēma*) of humanity (vv. 6-8). This same Jesus will change the form of human bodies (*meta-schēma-tisei*) so that they become like (*sum-morphē*) His own glorious body (3:21). Jesus descended to become like us so our human life could take on the shape of divinity. Moreover, Paul uses the same verb when he proclaims "that I may know him . . . becoming like him [*sum-morph-izomenos*] in his death" (v. 10 ESV). What awaits believers is the completion of a process of transformation that has already begun now as we participate in the heavenly commonwealth. Jesus initiated this process by becoming a human being and transforming human existence through His death and resurrection.

1. In what sense is the Christian already a citizen of heaven (v. 20)?
2. Describe the transformation believers anticipate (v. 21).

"Strange that I am not ever looking up, if I expect to see the door of heaven open, and the One I love coming out. Oh! what a scene, when He comes forth to change these vile bodies, fashioning them like to His own glorious body!"—G. V. Wigram

---

B. Resurrection of the Body (1 Cor. 15:50-58)

(1 Corinthians 15:50, 54-58 is not included in the printed text.)

51 Behold, I shew you a mystery; We shall not all sleep, but we shall all be changed, 52 In a moment, in the twinkling of an eye, at the last trump: for the trumpet shall sound, and the dead shall be raised incorruptible, and we shall be changed. 53 For this corruptible must put on incorruption, and this mortal must put on immortality.

This passage begins by contrasting a life in death, subject to decay, with a life that cannot perish (v. 50). The language underscores the continuity between the transformation that takes place through the new birth/sanctification and the transformation of the body. The latter represents the final defeat of sin and its offspring of death, portrayed as enemies that Christ defeats (vv. 55-56).

The terms *incorruptible* and *immortal* convey the kind of transformation the body must undergo (vv. 50, 52-54). The body must be outfitted for glory by becoming glorious. Paul uses the metaphor of *getting dressed* or *being clothed* ("put on") in order to describe what happens (vv. 53-54). The language suggests that heaven is just as much a state or condition as it is a place. Humans don't just *go* to glory, they are *made* glorious. The journey to heaven is less like traveling from one city to another and more like a transformational process in which believers become more like God, whose existence is eternal. It is comparable to the movement from a caterpillar to a butterfly. This movement is from a perishable body sown into the ground at death to a spiritual body that bursts forth at the resurrection (vv. 42-45).

The change that will bring about the transformation of the body will be instantaneous (v. 52). Two ideas convey the suddenness of the event—"in a moment, in the twinkling of an eye"—both referring to the smallest possible measure of time ("in a moment"). In addition, the sound of a trumpet will signal the change. Since Paul has already indicated that not everyone will "sleep" (v. 51), he may have in mind the way a trumpet sound awakens sleeping soldiers for battle. The trumpet is the alarm bell that signals a transformation that will be made complete in an instant.

The passage concludes with thanksgiving for this final victory, coupled with an exhortation to be "unmoveable" and "steadfast" in light of the future hope (vv. 57-58). The victory over death envisioned by the resurrection of the body is already at work in believers now, which supplies the power to work and live. The importance of the continuity between present and future realities for Christians cannot be overstated. Like the butterfly, the instantaneous nature of that final passage into glory is the culmination of the entire metamorphosis. As believers, we can rejoice knowing that even now God is conforming us to His Son through the power of the Spirit. This transformation concludes with full participation in the life of God precisely by becoming like Him, immortal and incorruptible.

1. What is impossible, and why (v. 50)?
2. Why do you suppose the Christian's transformation will happen so suddenly (vv. 51-52)?
3. What "must" happen, and why (v. 53)?
4. What will believers sing, and why (vv. 54-57)?
5. How should believers live, and why (v. 58)?

Christian Metamorphosis

The life of the caterpillar is a preparation for a new kind of existence. A caterpillar goes through life eating and consuming as much as it can. As the caterpillar eats, it sheds its skin in a process called "molting." When the caterpillar has reached its complete potential, it forms into a *chrysalis*, which looks like a sack. Inside the chrysalis, the caterpillar undergoes a process of rapid change called a *metamorphosis*. The caterpillar emerges from the chrysalis as a butterfly and pumps blood into its wings so that it can take flight.

In a similar way, God calls believers to shed their sinful selves so they can grow in Christ. For believers, death is a time of final preparation when the body will be fully transformed at the resurrection. Death has no sting of destruction because God has turned death itself into a "chrysalis" of life for believers. One day all believers will come forth with new bodies and meet Christ in the air.

II. THE LIVING HOPE (1 Peter 1:3-9; 1 Thess. 4:13-18)

A. Our Glorious Hope Amidst Life's Trials (1 Peter 1:3-9)

3 Blessed be the God and Father of our Lord Jesus Christ, which according to his abundant mercy hath begotten us again unto a lively hope by the resurrection of Jesus Christ from the dead, 4 To an inheritance incorruptible, and undefiled, and that fadeth not away, reserved in heaven for you, 5 Who are kept by the power of God through faith unto salvation ready to be revealed in the last time. 6 Wherein ye greatly rejoice, though now for a season, if need be, ye are in heaviness through manifold temptations: 7 That the trial of your faith, being much more precious than of gold that perisheth, though it be tried with fire, might be found unto praise and honour and glory at the appearing of Jesus Christ: 8 Whom having not seen, ye love; in whom, though now ye see him not, yet believing, ye rejoice with joy unspeakable and full of glory: 9 Receiving the end of your faith, even the salvation of your souls.

First Peter was written to a number of house churches scattered in various cities within Asia Minor (modern-day Turkey). These Christians were suffering immensely for their Christian commitments. They were being "tried with fire" (v. 7). Moreover, these were second- or third-generation Christians who had never seen Jesus, unlike the disciples and other first-generation followers. These believers trusted and were fully devoted to the risen Lord (v. 8).

The opening message of 1 Peter is that in the midst of their trials, these believers should recall God's plan as a way to help them endure to the end. This plan begins with the "foreknowledge" of the Father, which does not point so much to individual election as much as to the primacy of God in salvation (v. 2). His plan is to cleanse believers through the blood of Christ and sanctify them through the Holy Spirit.

In verse 3, Peter blesses God for the mercy revealed in His plan. "Mercy" refers to God's loving-kindness or covenant faithfulness. The concrete application of God's covenant faithfulness is found in the link between regeneration and the resurrection of Jesus. A hope that is alive brings the past and the future to bear on the present. As a past event, Jesus' resurrection marks a movement from death to life that occurs in the new birth of the believer and will occur in the final resurrection of believers.

Peter describes this inheritance with three terms that all point to its permanence—"incorruptible, . . . undefiled, and that fadeth not away" (v. 4). It is permanent because its ground is the triune God who is eternal. This is the "imperishable seed" with which the living word of God infuses believers (v. 23 NIV). It is not simply an unrealized future, but a present power that actively energizes believers and guards them during the time of trial (v. 5). Because God has not left believers alone in the midst of trial, they can rejoice even now (v. 6).

There is an important role for faith during the time of trial (vv. 5, 7). Trials test the faith of believers by causing them to return to the source of their existence and the One who can sustain them. If believers utilize the trials of life to fuel their faith in God, they will find themselves ready for the "appearing" (*apocalypsis*) of Christ, a term referring to the final revelation at the Second Coming.

The passage concludes with a description of the kind of rejoicing in which believers engage. Those who have not seen the earthly Jesus still rejoice because they have encountered the risen Lord of glory through their new birth into His kingdom. This joy is seemingly inexpressible because it contradicts the circumstances of the trial. How can one put into words the joy that emerges in the midst of pain and suffering because it is filled with the glory of the world to come? The incapacity to articulate fully the nature of Christian joy as it flows from heaven to the believer, regardless of the circumstances, does not negate the reality of this joy.

---

1. List the unique attributes of the inheritance described in verses 3-5.
2. How can a person's faith be "proved genuine" (vv. 6-7 NIV)?
3. How is salvation a process (vv. 8-9)?

"Jesus gives us hope because He keeps us company, has a vision, and knows the way we should go."—Max Lucado

---

B. The Coming of Christ (1 Thess. 4:13-18)

¹³ But I would not have you to be ignorant, brethren, concerning them which are asleep, that ye sorrow not, even as others which have no hope. ¹⁴ For if we believe that Jesus died and rose again, even so them also which sleep in Jesus will God bring with him. ¹⁵ For this we say unto you by the word of the Lord, that we which are alive and remain unto the coming of

Our Ultimate Salvation

the Lord shall not prevent them which are asleep. ¹⁶ For the Lord himself shall descend from heaven with a shout, with the voice of the archangel, and with the trump of God: and the dead in Christ shall rise first: ¹⁷ Then we which are alive and remain shall be caught up together with them in the clouds, to meet the Lord in the air: and so shall we ever be with the Lord. ¹⁸ Wherefore comfort one another with these words.

As an early letter, most likely written to a house church established during the first missionary journey (cf. Acts 17:1-9), 1 Thessalonians addresses issues that arose among the young Christians after Paul, Silas, and Timothy had departed. Based on reports from Timothy, Paul and his companions become aware of doubts about believers who had died.

The description of dead believers as merely being "asleep" (v. 13) echoes Jesus' statement that Jairus' daughter was not dead but asleep (Luke 8:52). Following Jesus, Paul adopts the use of *sleep* to point toward the resurrection (1 Thess. 4:13-15). Death is temporary and will give way to the dawn of the world to come when believers will rise at the return of the Lord. The letter does not dismiss grieving the loss of those who have died, but places this grieving in the context of the hope of resurrection, which points toward a temporary separation. Belief in Jesus' personal resurrection supplies the needed hope that all believers in Christ will one day rise in a grand reunion (v. 14).

To help the Thessalonians understand what happens to the dead in Christ, Paul declared what he had received "by the word of the Lord," which is most likely a reference to ongoing revelatory insight into Jesus' teaching on the Mount of Olives about His second coming (v. 15; Matt. 24:3-51). In his commentary on 1 Thessalonians, Ben Witherington identifies numerous parallels between Paul's words and Jesus' Olivet discourse. Following Jesus' words, Paul declares that the Lord will descend from heaven with angels at the sound of a trumpet (v. 16; cf. Matt. 24:30-31). Like theophanies in the Old Testament, Jesus' descent will be shrouded "in clouds," suggesting a reference to the glory of God (cf. Dan. 7:13). All of this will begin with a *shout*, a term that refers to military marching orders.

After describing how the Second Coming will begin, Paul offers a sequence of events that will unfold. The dead in Christ will rise first, followed by believers who are still alive (vv. 16-17). These two groups will "meet the Lord in the air" (v. 17). The term translated "meet" would have been familiar to the Thessalonians, since it was used to refer to a delegation going outside of the city to meet a Roman dignitary in order to escort him back into the city. The "coming" (*parousia*) of the dignitary required the pomp and circumstance of a full escort back into the city. Cicero, a Roman orator, used the term to describe the towns welcoming Julius Caesar on his tour in 49 BC (*Letter to Atticus*). At this Second Coming (*parousia*), all believers will be "caught up" to Christ in the clouds and become His entourage, escorting Him back to earth. Paul said this magnificent event of the return of their conquering Lord should give great comfort to believers (v. 18).

---

1. Who has "no hope" (13)?
2. Whom will Jesus "bring with him" when He returns (v. 14)?
3. List four promises from verses 15-17.
4. Whom can you "comfort" (v. 18) with the message of these verses?

"Jesus' coming is the final and unanswerable proof that God cares."—
William Barclay

III. THE ULTIMATE WORSHIP EXPERIENCE (Rev. 19:1-9)

A. The Judgment of God on the Forces of Evil (vv. 1-3)

¹ And after these things I heard a great voice of much people in heaven, saying, Alleluia; Salvation, and glory, and honour, and power, unto the Lord our God: ² For true and righteous are his judgments: for he hath judged the great whore, which did corrupt the earth with her fornication, and hath avenged the blood of his servants at her hand. ³ And again they said, Alleluia. And her smoke rose up for ever and ever.

The celebration of Revelation 19 comes in the middle of a section that deals with divine judgment on evil (chs. 17-20). What resides behind the forces of evil in the world, according to Revelation, is Satan, who is symbolized by the Dragon (12:3; 20:2). The Dragon has his earthly emissaries who carry out his work, including Babylon, or the "great harlot" (17:1 NKJV), representing the social, economic, and political structures that attempt to entice believers away from God. The image of a harlot, in particular, evokes the idea of religious adultery in which Israel worshiped the gods of the land instead of the Lord. The power structures of the day are alluring as well as destructive.

Revelation 18 concludes with the destruction of Babylon and all those associated with it. Merchants who collaborated with Babylon to produce wealth and opulence, as well as nations seduced by the great harlot, are thrown down with her (vv. 21-24). There is a call to rejoice because God has finally judged evil and vindicated His servants (v. 20), which sets the tone for chapter 19.

The multitude in heaven begins to shout and praise God for His deliverance from Babylon, or the great harlot (vv. 1-3). This praise is not primarily about vengeance, but about the restoration of justice and the defeat of evil. This is why John describes the judgments of God as "true and just" (v. 2 NIV). Divine judgment is an extension of God's justice, which is God setting right a world gone wrong. Justice is about the restoration of *shalom* (peace), harmony, and balance to the Creation. Such restoration involves the defeat and removal of all those forces that would seek to destroy *shalom*.

• Why are "Hallelujahs" resounding in this passage?

"Soon the battle will be over. It will not be long now before the day will come when Satan will no longer trouble us. There will be no more domination, temptation, accusation, or confrontation. Our warfare will be over and our commander, Jesus Christ, will call us away from the battlefield to receive the victor's crown."—Thomas Watson

B. The Victory of the Lamb (vv. 4-9)

⁴ And the four and twenty elders and the four beasts fell down and worshipped God that sat on the throne, saying, Amen; Alleluia. ⁵ And a voice

Our Ultimate Salvation

came out of the throne, saying, Praise our God, all ye his servants, and ye that fear him, both small and great. ⁶ And I heard as it were the voice of a great multitude, and as the voice of many waters, and as the voice of mighty thunderings, saying, Alleluia: for the Lord God omnipotent reigneth. ⁷ Let us be glad and rejoice, and give honour to him: for the marriage of the Lamb is come, and his wife hath made herself ready. ⁸ And to her was granted that she should be arrayed in fine linen, clean and white: for the fine linen is the righteousness of saints. ⁹ And he saith unto me, Write, Blessed are they which are called unto the marriage supper of the Lamb. And he saith unto me, These are the true sayings of God.

The worship in heaven emerges from the songs of triumph over the forces of evil and the full restoration of God's *shalom*. The work of the Lamb points to the One seated on the throne around whom the four living creatures fly with their cries of "Holy, holy, holy, [is the] Lord God Almighty" (4:8; 19:4-5). The sounds of worship overwhelm the reader as waves of praise crash down on the shores of heaven—thunderous explosions of "hallelujah" (v. 6 NIV). There is a kind of rhythm to the worship like the ocean's tides ebbing and flowing, crashing with explosive force, receding, and then coming again.

The focus of the worship turns away from victory over evil to the marriage of the Lamb and the Bride. The Revelation identifies the continuity between earthly existence and heavenly existence. The Bride must clothe herself with holiness as part of the preparation for the marriage (vv. 7-8). This preparation occurs now through maintaining the testimony of Jesus and being faithful witnesses even as Jesus was Himself "the faithful witness" (1:5; 19:10-11).

The passage concludes with an invitation to the Marriage Supper of the Lamb (v. 9). The challenge to be a faithful witness is really the challenge to conquer. Jesus promises new life to those who hear His message and conquer in His name (21:7). They will escape the second death and participate in the New Jerusalem, the city of God's final *shalom*.

---

1. How do the elders and four beasts worship God (v. 4)?
2. Who are genuine "servants" of God (v. 5)?
3. Close your eyes and imagine hearing the sounds of verse 6.
4. Describe the bride of Christ (vv. 7-9).

"Very soon the shadow will give way to Reality. The partial will pass into the Perfect. The foretaste will lead to the Banquet. The troubled path will end in Paradise. A hundred candle-lit evenings will come to their consummation in the marriage supper of the Lamb. And this momentary marriage will be swallowed up by Life. Christ will be all and in all."—John Piper

---

CONCLUSION

The great transformation of believers began when the Son took on the "form of a servant" (Phil. 2:7) and entered human existence so He might transform it into another kind of existence. What God is doing now, through the process of sanctification, will culminate in the final metamorphosis of the body as it takes flight into the heavenly realms. The trumpet of God will announce this final moment of change as the dead and the living in Christ are both snatched up to be with their Bridegroom who comes on the clouds of glory. The resurrection of the body will give them the wings necessary for this flight beyond the present realm of existence.

Even now, however, when believers speak with new tongues, they participate in heavenly existence. *Tongues* are the language of love. They symbolize the union between Bride and Bridegroom, and thus point believers to their future home. One day "when the perfect comes" (1 Cor. 13:9-10 NASB), the stuttering sounds of tongues will give way to the fluent language of the Kingdom as we see God's face in the faces of the transformed people of God, fully alive and fully whole. And so we say, "Even so, come, Lord Jesus" (Rev. 22:20).

GOLDEN TEXT CHALLENGE

"LET US BE GLAD AND REJOICE, AND GIVE HONOR TO HIM [CHRIST]; FOR THE MARRIAGE OF THE LAMB IS COME, AND HIS WIFE HATH MADE HERSELF READY" (Rev. 19:7).

The voice of the multitude gives another reason to rejoice: the wedding of the Lamb has come. This occasion, when Christ presents the Church to Himself, calls for rejoicing and gladness. It represents that time when ultimate victory is achieved. All that Christ has done for the Church and all that the Church has done to please Him come to their culmination at this point.

This occasion also calls for giving glory to the Lord. His work made the wedding possible. Only because He died on Calvary to pay the price for our sins can there be a wedding. Only because He called us to Himself and made us aware of our need can there be a wedding. Only because He received us to Himself when we responded to His call can there be a wedding. So, all the glory for the beautiful event referred to in this verse belongs to the Lord.

No details are given concerning the wedding of the Lamb. We are told that the Bride has made herself ready for the wedding. Paul referred to this in his letter to the Ephesians: "Husbands, love your wives, even as Christ also loved the church, and gave himself for it; that he might sanctify and cleanse it with the washing of water by the word, that he might present it to himself a glorious church, not having spot, or wrinkle, or any such thing; but that it should be holy and without blemish. . . . This is a great mystery; but I speak concerning Christ and the church" (5:25-27, 32).

Daily Devotions:
M. Abraham Gathered to His People
   Genesis 25:7-9
T. We Shall See Our Redeemer
   Job 19:25-27
W. Death of God's Saints
   Psalm 116:12-15
T. Present With the Lord
   2 Corinthians 5:1-8
F. The Crown of Righteousness
   2 Timothy 4:6-8
S. Universal Worship
   Revelation 5:11-14